Systems
Based
Independent
Audits

PRENTICE-HALL ACCOUNTING SERIES

H. A. Finney, Editor

Systems
Based
Independent
Audits

HOWARD F. STETTLER

Professor of Business Administration
University of Kansas

PRENTICE-HALL, INC., Englewood Cliffs, New Jersey

PRENTICE-HALL INTERNATIONAL, INC., London
PRENTICE-HALL OF AUSTRALIA, PTY. LTD., Sidney
PRENTICE-HALL OF CANADA, LTD., Toronto
PRENTICE-HALL OF INDIA PRIVATE LTD., New Delhi
PRENTICE-HALL OF JAPAN INC., Tokyo

Preface

Several developments in auditing education and practice have suggested that an appropriate time has arrived to undertake some major departures from tradition in the preparation of an auditing text. Of prime importance is the evolution that has occurred in the conduct of independent audit examinations. These examinations once consisted primarily of a mechanical verification of bookkeeping details. Then, there emerged the concept of direct verification of financial statement figures with heavy emphasis on supporting evidence that originates outside the accounting records, and finally today the trend is to what may be characterized as the "operating review" approach. The review approach stresses an evaluation of the accounting system and the related internal control as an indication of the probability that the financial statements produced from the system are accurate and reliable, and relies heavily on a "business" approach to the review of financial statements from the standpoint of the reasonableness of the figures and the variations, trends, and interrelationships that they set forth.

These changes in thinking and the approach to auditing mesh neatly with the emergence of the concept of "constructive auditing" and its compatriot, the burgeoning field of management advisory services. The influence of these factors on this text, as contrasted with its forerunner *Auditing Principles* (which will continue to be available), is evident in two important changes that are closely related. The first is the application of a "transaction" approach to auditing, thus departing from the customary balance sheet—income statement sequence. It substitutes an integrated discussion of the audit of the results of both halves of the common transactions, such as sales and receivables, cost of sales and inventories, and purchases and accounts payable. Among the reasons for moving in this direction is the close relationship and overlap that exists in the audit of accounts that have a common origin—as, for example, in the matter of "cut-offs." Similarly, the stress on the business approach to the reasonableness of figures in the financial statements leads naturally to a consideration of appropriate relationships of figures that share common origins.

Then too, in reality, transaction-related accounts tend to be dealt with as a unit in the review of internal control and the actual audit work, despite the separation suggested by the audit program and working papers. Of even more importance, the transaction approach makes more evident the careful attention the auditor gives to income statement figures. Such attention reflects the rising role played by the income statement, brought about by the present-day predominance of long-term financing (both bonds and equities) and the investor's interest in the income-producing ability of the enterprise.

Lastly, the transaction approach fits more closely the auditor's present-day emphasis on the accounting system as a key factor in the reliability of the statement figures that are produced. The fundamental duality of all transactions closely relates the accounting for debits and credits, whether they affect only one or both of the basic financial statements. The close relationship in the processing of the debit and credit aspects of transactions points to the desirability of reviewing the system from the standpoint of how various types of transactions are processed, rather than reviewing on an account basis, which involves both debits and credits, reflecting parts of two or more different types of transactions.

The second major change incorporated in this text, in contrast with its more traditional counterparts, is the expansion of the usual brief references to internal control considerations into a full scale discussion of the accounting system along with the aspect of internal control. Since the auditor must work so closely with the accounting system, and must understand how the final accounting figures are developed and what evidence exists in support of those figures, it is only natural that the auditor should be well acquainted with the matter of the system itself. Many accounting curricula have not been able to afford the "luxury" of including the study of this basic but somewhat technical aspect of accounting. In other instances, the glamour and fascination of electronic computers and other forms of high speed data processing have brought about a shift to the study of these important developments, to the neglect of the whole basic question of the accounting system, of which the electronic equipment is but one phase.

For these reasons, it seemed desirable to broaden the discussion of internal control to encompass the entire matter of the accounting system. Coincidentally, the transaction orientation which has been given to the study of auditing complements the inescapable relationship of the accounting system to the recording of transactions. At the same time, application of the concept of constructive auditing places greater importance on the study and evaluation of the accounting system and management advisory services that often result from such recommendations are closely tied to a knowledge of accounting systems.

Aside from the changes that have been described, every effort has been made to retain the features that have won acceptance for *Auditing Principles*: the stress on objectives and explanations of *why* things are done in a certain way, at the same time giving a detailed account with a strong practical flavor of *how* they are done; the use of a tightly knit organization plan that is consistent throughout the book, thus facilitating the reader's ability to grasp the material as it is presented; retention of the summaries at the conclusion of the discussion of each statement item covering internal control, standards of statement presentation, and audit objectives and procedures; frequent references to specific items in the illustrative working papers for the audit of Machine Products Co.; and continued use of an easy style that includes a "light" touch to aid the reader in making his way through the material and assimilating its content.

Since the Machine Products Co. illustrative working papers appear in *Practice Case for Auditing* by Sherwood W. Newton and Howard F. Stettler, which is designed to be used with this text, the working papers are not duplicated in this text. For those not using the practice case, the working papers for the audit of Machine Products Co. may be purchased separately under the title, *Audit Work Papers*.

In conclusion, the author gratefully acknowledges the cooperation of the following reviewers of the manuscript of *Systems Based Independent Audits:* Professor Roy E. Baker, Cornell University; Professor R. Gene Brown, Stanford University; Professor John C. Burton, Columbia University; Professor Emerson Henke, Baylor University; Professor Robert E. Seiler, The University of Houston, and Mr. Ronald C. Baldwin, CPA, *Haskins and Sells* (Boston Office).

Contents

tions and accounting. Segregation of duties between controller and treasurer. *Authorizing and Recording Transactions.* Machine proofs. Investigation of differences. Penny elimination. *Sound Practices of Administration. Quality of Personnel. Preserving and Strengthening Internal Control. Preventing and Detecting Embezzlement, Fraud, and Errors. Fidelity Bonds. Internal Control and the Independent Auditor. Recommendations to Management. Evaluation of Internal Control by the Independent Auditor. The Approach to Internal Control in a First Audit. The Internal Control Questionnaire. Timing the Review of Internal Control. No Substitute for Internal Control. Internal Control and the Small Business, Administrative Controls versus Financial Controls.*

Historical Development. Statement of Responsibilities. Verification. Evaluation. Compliance. Functional Approach to Internal Auditing. Operational Auditing. Internal Audit Reports. Selected Excerpts from Internal Audit Reports. Examples of Internal Audit Projects. The Place of the Internal Auditor in the Company Organization. Internal Auditing and the Small Business. The Independent Auditor and Internal Auditing. Internal Auditing and Independent Auditing Contrasted.

Achievement of Professional Status. INDEPENDENCE: KEYSTONE OF A PROFESSION. *The Difficulties of Remaining Independent. Independence and the C.P.A.'s Code of Professional Ethics. The Securities and Exchange Commission and Independence. Selection of the Auditor and Independence.* PROFESSIONAL ETHICS. LEGAL LIABILITY. *The Auditor's Liability to His Client. The Auditor's Liability to Third Parties. Liability Under the Federal Securities Acts. Accountants' Liability Insurance.* TESTING AND THE THEORY OF PROBABILITY. *Selecting the Items for the Sample. Testing and the Disclosure of Fraud. Size of the Audit Sample. Factors that Affect Sample Size. Materiality. Relative Risk. Competence of Evidence. Primary Evidence. Supporting Evidence.* Physical evidence. Documentary evidence. Externally created documents sent directly to the auditor. Externally created documents in the client's possession. Evidence originating within the client's organization. Internal evidence circulating outside the business. Internal evidence circulating only within the business. Verbal information and written certificates. Circumstantial evidence.

Examination (Inspection). Confirmation. Observation. Verification. Inquiry. Auditing in Evolution. Analytical Auditing. The Positive Approach. Terminology. Direct Versus Indirect Approach. Maintaining the Proper Perspective. Planning the Examination. Predominance of the Partnership Form of Organization. Line Organization for the Independent Auditing Function. Partner level. Manager or supervisor level. The senior accountant. Staff assistants. *Selection for Advancement. The Audit Program. Amount of Detail in the Program. Working Papers.* IDENTIFYING INFORMATION: PROPER HEADINGS. *The Trial Balance. Adjusting and Reversing Entries. Reclassification Entries. Alternative Forms of the Trial Balance. Indexing. Filing of Working Papers. Tick Marks. Confidential Treatment of Information Pertaining to the Client. Control of Working Papers. The Relationship of the Auditor and His Staff to Client Officers and Employees. Illustrative Audit Working Papers. The Approach of Succeeding Chapters. Internal Control and the Accounting System. Standards of Statement Presentation. Audit Objectives and Procedures.*

STANDARDS OF STATEMENT PRESENTATION. AUDIT OBJECTIVES AND PROCEDURES. *Establish Credibility of the Accounting Records.* Trace handling of representative transactions from origin to final account balances. *Ascertain Reasonableness of Account Balances. Review Cut-Off of Recorded Transactions.* Test cut-off shipments. Ascertain validity of recorded receivables. *Obtain Assurance that All Revenues Have Been Recorded.* Tuition fees. Rental income. Hotel room charges. Charity contributions. Church contributions. *Tie in Supporting Records with Statement Amount of Receivables.* Trial balance of subsidiary ledgers. *Establish Validity of the Recorded Receivables.* Confirmation procedures. Decisions relating to confirmation procedures. Alternative procedures. *Determine Collectibility of the Receivables.* Aging. Interpreting the aging results. Other procedures related to collectibility. *Timing of the Audit Work.* NOTES RECEIVABLE. *Inspection of Notes Receivable. Sight Drafts. Notes Receivable Discounted. Secured Notes. Interest.* SUMMARY.

Objectives of Internal Control. Purchasing Department. Receiving Department. Stores Department. Accounts Payable Department. Auditing invoices on a test basis. Accounts payable ledger. Month-end procedures. Audit implications of payables records. Alternative debit-distribution methods. Punched-card records. *Management Reports.* Purchasing activities. Accounts payable and receiving. Operating expenses. *Internal Auditing.*

Income Tax Considerations. STANDARDS OF STATEMENT PRESENTATION. AUDIT OBJECTIVES AND PROCEDURES. *Establish Credibility of the Accounting Records.* Trace handling of representative transactions from origin to final account balances. *Ascertain Reasonableness of Account Balances and Consistency in Application of Appropriate Expense Classifications.* Comparisons. Classification errors affecting factory overhead. Account analyses. *Ascertain that All Expenses of the Period Have Been Recorded by Searching for Unrecorded Liabilities.* Review of subsequent transactions. Materiality. *Tie in Supporting Records with the Statement Amount of Accounts Payable.* Test trial balance amounts against written confirmations or vendors' statements. *Ascertain that Expenses Have Been Properly Matched with the Revenues that They Have Produced. Determine that Proper Distinction Has Been Maintained between Operating Expenses and Nonoperating, Nonrecurring Losses and Expenses. Timing of the Examination of Income Accounts and Accounts Payable.* SUMMARY.

Objectives of Internal Control. Purchasing, Receiving, Stores. Shipping Department. Manufacturing Department. Stock Records. Selective inventory control. *Accounting Department. Physical Inventory Taking. Punched-Card Records.* Open-item system. Balance-forward system. Batch billing. General ledger accounting. Physical inventory taking. *Management Reports. Internal Auditing.*

STANDARDS OF STATEMENT PRESENTATION. AUDIT OBJECTIVES AND PROCEDURES. *Establish Credibility of the Accounting Records.* Trace handling of representative transactions from origin to final account balance. Entries under the retail inventory method. *Ascertain Reasonableness of Account Balances. Review Cut-off of Recorded Transactions.* Purchases cut-off. Adjustments to correct the cut-off of purchases. Cost of sales cut-off. Audit tests of the cost of sales cut-off. Cut-off tests and relative risk.

Objectives of Internal Control. Employment (Personnel) Department. Timekeeping Department. Payroll Department. Treasury Department. Cost Accounting. Alternative Payroll Records. Punched-Card Records. Management Reports. Internal Auditing. STANDARDS OF STATEMENT PRESENTATION. AUDIT OBJECTIVES AND PROCEDURES. *Establish Credibility of the Accounting Records.* Trace handling of representative transactions from origin to final account balances. Factory payroll. Office payroll. Officers' salaries. Observation of payoff. *Ascertain Reasonableness of Account Balances and Consistent Application of Appropriate Expense Classifications. Review Year-End Cut-Offs of Payroll Transactions.* Accrued payroll. Accrued vacation pay. Accrued pension payments. Accrued payroll taxes. Liability for amounts withheld from employees. SUMMARY.

Objectives of Internal Control. Authorization of Expenditures. Accounting for Expenditures. Plant Records. Alternative Records. Depreciation. Retirements. Maintenance Expenditures. Punched-Card Records. Management Reports. Internal Auditing. STANDARDS OF STATEMENT PRESENTATION. *Basis of Valuation. Liens. Depreciation Not to Be Netted Against Balances. Classification. Fully Depreciated Assets. Disclosure of Amount of Depreciation Charged Against Income.* AUDIT OBJECTIVES AND PROCEDURES. *Tie in Supporting Records with Statement Amounts for Plant Assets and Depreciation.* Trial balance of the plant ledger. Trial balance of construction work in process. *Ascertain that Additions to Plant Asset Accounts Have Been Correctly Recorded and that Capital and Revenue Charges Have Been Properly Distinguished.* Schedule major additions. Supporting data. Amounts properly capitalized. Maintenance and repairs. *Ascertain that Retirements of Plant Assets Have Been Correctly Recorded, with Proper Recognition of Any Gains or Losses.* Unrecorded retirements. *Establish Reasonableness of Depreciation Charges, Both Current and Accumulated Amounts.* Adequacy. Consistency. Accuracy. *Establish Existence of Plant Assets.* Current additions. Over-all review. Small tools. Remotely located equipment. Returnable containers. *Determine Ownership of Plant Assets and Existence of Liens.* Liens. *Making an Initial Audit.* Procedures when client maintains plant ledger. Procedures when no plant ledger is maintained. *Timing of the Examination of Plant Assets.* SUMMARY.

Objectives of Internal Control. Authorization of Purchases and Sales. Custody. Accounting Records. Bonding. Management Reports. Internal Auditing. STANDARDS

*Systems
Based
Independent
Audits*

Independent audits—
what and why

1

The opinion of an independent public accountant concerning the financial statements of a business is the best possible indication of whether persons who are not associated with the business may justifiably rely upon those statements in making important financial decisions. Such an opinion will ordinarily be based on a comprehensive examination of the statements and supporting data, and it will indicate whether or not the statements present fairly the financial position of the concern and the results of the firm's operations for the period specified.

Those who use financial statements are likely to insist that the statements have such an independent opinion, or "attestation," accompanying them. Any decisions to invest or extend credit can be only as sound as the information on which such decisions are based. Without the professional opinion of an independent public accountant, financial statements are open to question, because they will normally have been prepared by the same management officials who are responsible for the operation of the business.

Why Unaudited Statements Are Not Acceptable

Using financial statements prepared by management and submitted to third parties without the statements having been first subjected to an independent review would be comparable to having a judge hear a case in which he was a litigant, or to having a member of an opposing athletic team act as official referee and scorekeeper. In any of these situations, there is opportunity for the results to be affected by personal bias, self-interest, carelessness, or even outright dishonesty. In the case of financial statements, management understandably might be reluctant to admit that the receivable resulting from a sale that it had approved was doubtful of collection, or that depreciation charges were inadequate when salaries or bonuses are based on

1

reported net income. Furthermore, liabilities that have arisen but are not yet a matter of book record may easily be overlooked in the preparation of financial statements. In an extreme situation, figures might even be intentionally falsified to present an improved financial position or improved operating results. The possible effect of such eventualities on financial statements has prompted the observation that a balance sheet is sometimes not so much a "snapshot" of the financial status of a business as a "colored transparency."

Nevertheless, management is logically assigned to "keep the score" because it needs similar information for its own use in guiding the affairs of the business. The public accountant, acting independently and in a professional capacity, adds the necessary credibility to management's figures so that they may be freely relied upon by interested third parties.

Professional Qualifications to Perform Independent Audits

The need for independent audits to provide the added credibility that third parties seek is the principal reason for the development and growth of the public accounting profession. Under these circumstances, it is understandable that those who rely on accountants' opinions concerning financial statements would be quite concerned about the professional qualifications of the accountant making the examination.

A public accountant is an accountant who has chosen to serve the public rather than to become an employee of a business, and in many states anyone who wishes may designate himself as a public accountant. As a consequence, such a designation is no indication that a person is qualified to render competent service to the public. The public interest in this matter is the basis for legislation in all fifty states, the District of Columbia, and the two remaining territories of the United States, creating the designation "Certified Public Accountant" to indicate those persons who have proven their qualifications to render competent service to the public. The requirements for the C.P.A. certificate vary between jurisdictions, but each state requires the applicant to pass the Uniform Certified Public Accountant Examination prepared by the Board of Examiners of the American Institute of Certified Public Accountants.* This rigorous two-and-one-half-day examination lasting 19½ hours represents a thorough testing of the candidate's knowledge in the areas of auditing, accounting theory and practice, Federal income taxes, and commercial law.

---

* The A.I.C.P.A. is the national professional organization of Certified Public Accountants. The former name of the organization, "American Institute of Accountants," was changed in 1957 to indicate more clearly to the public that the organization represents only Certified Public Accountants, since membership is limited to C.P.A.'s. References to important pronouncements of the A.I.C.P.A. and its committees utilize the new name of the organization, even though in many cases the official name was American Institute of Accountants at the time of the original pronouncement.

Other requirements for the C.P.A. certificate normally include academic education and public accounting experience. The amount of required public accounting experience varies from one to five years, depending on state law and the applicant's educational qualifications. Generally speaking, applicants holding a college degree and meeting specified minimum requirements in the study of accounting, commercial law, and business are not required to have as much public accounting experience as are those with only a high school education or with a college degree in a field other than accounting.

The variations in state requirements for the C.P.A. certificate have led to two important studies in recent years. The first study, by the independent Commission on Standards of Education and Experience for Certified Public Accountants, recommended as a long-range goal that requirements for the C.P.A. certificate include a baccalaureate degree, an additional year of study under a postgraduate professional academic program, and a period of public accounting internship of approximately three months' duration. Subsequently, a Special Committee on the Report of the Commission on Standards of Education and Experience for C.P.A.'s was appointed by the American Institute of Certified Public Accountants. This committee concurred generally with the recommendations of the Commission, but agreed with a minority Commission opinion that public accounting experience should be retained as a requirement for the C.P.A. certificate. The Special Committee concluded, however, that some reduction in the experience requirement (which now averages about two years) would be warranted by the recommended increase in academic training. The recommendation to retain the experience requirement is based on the belief that the public interest is better served if the C.P.A. has worked in an environment in which third-party reliance concepts receive considerable attention, thereby better preparing him to perform independent audits after receiving his C.P.A. certificate, which is basically a license to practice.

In Canada, public accounting legislation corresponds generally with that in the United States, with the various provinces issuing the Chartered Accountant certificate that is the equivalent of the C.P.A. certificate in the United States. By contrast, the profession is administered quite differently in England, and, even though British accountants were much in evidence in the early days of the profession in America, the English system was not followed here. The government does not license in England; rather, the accountant gains public recognition of his attainments by achieving membership in one of the professional accounting associations, such as The Institute of Chartered Accountants in England and Wales, or The Association of Certified and Corporate Accountants. Membership requirements include passing the intermediate and final qualifying examinations and serving for three to five years as an articled clerk with an association member. College graduates are required to be articled for only three years, but the majority of the persons entering the profession still choose the alternative of five years of articled clerkship, which requires no collegiate education.

Importance of the Auditor's Independence

In addition to possessing adequate training and experience, the accountant who makes an examination for the purpose of attesting to the fairness of a client's financial statements must act in an independent capacity. Because the accountant is not an employee of the business, his actions are not subject to supervision by the management of the business, and this situation alone creates considerable independence. Independence is also an attitude of mind, and independent thought and action are equally as important as the independent relationship between the accountant and his client. Unless the accountant is independent, his opinion is no more reliable than the statements which have been prepared by management. The important concept of independence is more fully covered in Chapter 5.

Audits and Auditors

The examination upon which the opinion is based is known as an *audit examination,* and consequently, when the public accountant is doing such work, he is usually referred to as the "auditor." Because many businesses also have auditors in their own employ, the two types of auditors are usually distinguished by referring to the company auditors as "internal auditors," and using the term "independent auditors" to designate the public accountants who are engaged to examine the company's financial statements. In contrast to the independent auditor, the internal auditor is not concerned with the expression of an opinion on financial statements, and as an employee of his company he lacks the independence of the public accountant. As will be more fully explained later, the internal auditor is concerned primarily with assisting management in maintaining adequate control over company procedures and operations that cannot possibly be supervised by management on a personal basis.

The term "auditor" means literally "one who hears" and dates back to the days when public accounts were accepted and approved on the basis of hearing the accounts read. Thus, the original examinations of accounts merely involved hearing the accounts and transactions, and the person or persons who were responsible for examining and approving the accounts were known as *auditors.* A variation of this form of audit is still common in small, informal fraternal organizations, with the members "auditing" the revenues and expenses verbally reported by the treasurer. Audits of business enterprises performed for the benefit of the financial community are, however, far removed from a mere hearing of the accounts, as will become quite evident in later chapters. The audit activities involved are now often referred to as the performance of an "attest" function for the financial community.

The Auditor's Report

The auditor's opinion, based on his examination of a client's financial statements, is normally given in the form of a written report. The report may be quite lengthy, containing analytical comments about the financial position and operating results of the business, comments about the examination which was made, and various types of recommendations. The heart of the report, however, will normally be two paragraphs describing in general terms the scope of the examination which was made and giving the auditor's opinion based on such examination. In many cases, those two all-important paragraphs accompanying the client's financial statements may constitute the entire report, if it is felt that no additional comments are necessary.

Generally, the wording of the paragraphs will follow quite closely the sample report given below, which is based on the recommended wording of the Committee on Auditing Procedure of the American Institute of Certified Public Accountants.

To the Board of Directors,
ABC Company:

We have examined the balance sheet of ABC Company as of December 31, 19—, and the related statements of operations and retaind income for the year then ended. Our examination was made in accordance with generally accepted auditing standards, and accordingly included such tests of the accounting records and such other auditing procedures as we considered necessary in the circumstances.

In our opinion, the accompanying balance sheet and statements of operations and retained income present fairly the financial position of ABC Company at December 31, 19—, and the results of its operations for the year then ended, in conformity with generally accepted accounting principles applied on a basis consistent with that of the preceding year.

Martin, Noll, and Otis
Certified Public Accountants
January 28, 19—

Although the wording of the above report has been very carefully developed and studied, and has the endorsement of the American Institute of Certified Public Accountants, there is no compulsion upon the public accounting profession to render reports which are identical in form. In the wording of the report, as in the conduct of the underlying examination, the members of the profession are encouraged to exercise their individual judgment, subject only to the high standards which the profession seeks to maintain. Thus, whereas many accountants use the suggested form of report without change, others make modifications, but without departing from the fundamental points covered by the so-called "standard" form of report.

For instance, one firm of accountants has used the following interesting variation:

> In our opinion the accompanying financial statements present fairly the financial position of ABC Company at December 31, 19—, and the results of its operations for the year then ended, in conformity with generally accepted accounting principles applied on a basis consistent with that of the preceding year. This opinion is based on an examination of the statements which was made in accordance with generally accepted auditing standards, and included such tests of the accounting records and such other auditing procedures as we considered necessary in the circumstances.

Significance of the Report

The auditor's report is sometimes referred to as the auditor's "certificate." This term is a carry-over from the days when the auditor's report often stated, "We certify that in our opinion the accompanying financial statements are correct." Regardless of the name by which it is identified, the report is an extremely important document. It is the sole outward evidence of the major activity of the public accounting profession, and it is heavily relied upon whenever financial decisions are based upon financial statements. It is also the focal point of all independent auditing procedures. The auditor must never lose sight of the fact that all his auditing procedures are directed toward enabling him to formulate and report his opinion concerning a set of financial statements, thereby attesting to the fairness and reliability of the statements.

Thus, the logical place to begin the study of auditing is the auditor's report, even though in practice the report is the last step in the examination. In the following pages, each point in the report is carefully considered, and the reader should attempt to secure a complete understanding of the report and to determine exactly what the report says or does not say. Such an understanding, incidentally, has equal importance for the person who reads the report and relies on the auditor's opinion and for the auditor who is planning to report on the results of an audit examination.

Proper Addressing of the Report

The report is normally addressed to the person or group responsible for engaging the auditor. In the case of corporations, the auditor is most frequently selected by the board of directors or the stockholders, with the payment of the auditor's fees being made from corporate funds. The report will be used, however, by persons other than the ones to whom it is addressed and who pay the auditor's fees. This fact is responsible for the peculiar relationship between the auditor and his client. Even though the auditor receives his fee from the client, he must maintain complete independence in all matters and decisions relating to the audit examination. Only by maintaining such idependence and by competently performing the necessary work can the auditor look forward to achieving widespread acceptance of his reports. That C.P.A.'s have been generally successful in gaining such acceptance of their reports is indicated by the fact that the presence of the name of an individual or firm of C.P.A.'s on a report is commonly accepted much the same as is the "sterling" mark on silver.

Whose Statements Are They ?

Because the auditor's report on a client's financial statements is usually given on a separate sheet of paper rather than on the statements themselves, the report must carefully identify the statements which have been examined. This identification is made in the opening sentence, which gives the name of the business and the names and dates of the statements.

The question "Whose statements are they?" also refers to the matter of who is basically responsible for the representations in the statements. Because the statements accompanying the auditor's report are typed in the auditor's office, many persons reach the conclusion that the auditor is responsible for preparing the statements. Such a conclusion is incorrect, however, and will be avoided if the reader treats the word "of" in the phrase "We have examined the balance sheet of . . ." as not only identifying the company but also indicating that the statement belongs to the client and that the client is responsible for the figures and the manner in which they are presented. More specifically, of course, the responsibility rests with the management of the client concern, and the statements are a report by the management of its stewardship. The pamphlet *Auditing Standards and Procedures* prepared by the Committee on Auditing Procedure of the A.I.C.P.A. further stresses the responsibility of management:

> Management has the responsibility for adopting sound accounting policies, for maintaining an adequate and effective system of accounts, for the safeguarding of assets, and for devising a system of internal control that will, among other things, help assure the production of proper financial statements. . . . Accordingly, the fairness of the representations made through financial statements is an implicit and integral part of management's responsibility. . . . (The auditor's) responsibility for the statements he has examined is confined to the expression of his opinion on them. The financial statements remain the representation of the management.

In view of the primary responsibility which management must assume for the financial statements, the auditor has no right to make changes in those statements. For instance, if management has included in the inventory a substantial amount of obsolete parts valued at their original cost, the auditor has no right to change the treatment of this item in order to present more fairly the company's financial position and results of operations. His first course of action will normally be to attempt to convince management that its treatment of the item is wrong and that a more accurate and realistic treatment would be to reduce the carrying value of the obsolete parts to a realizable figure and to show the parts with this new valuation as a separate figure on the balance sheet. If management is not willing to follow the auditor's recommendations, the auditor will probably find it necessary to modify his opinion by pointing out that the statements do not present fairly the concern's financial position and results of operations to the extent that obsolete parts costing X dollars, but having a current realizable value of Y dollars, are carried at their original cost as a part of the regular inventory. Thus, although management has the final say as to what shall be in the financial statements and how various items are to be displayed, the auditor always has recourse to his report to point out anything which might be important to a third party reading the statements. Qualifications, exceptions, and other modifications of the auditor's report are more fully discussed in a later chapter.

The Examination

The report states that the financial statements, which have been carefully identified as discussed above, have been examined by the auditor. The meaning of the phrase "We have examined" may perhaps best be explained by pointing out that the auditor must determine whether he is satisfied with the statements, just as a prospective used car purchaser determines whether he is satisfied with a given automobile. In the latter case, the buyer's examination is directed toward such things as the mechanical condition of the motor and other parts, the appearance of the car, and the condition of the tires. If he is satisfied on these and other points, he will accept the car. In making the audit examination, the auditor determines whether the indicated amount of cash was actually on hand or in the bank, whether the receivables were all valid and collectible and had not been pledged, sold, or discounted, and whether they represented amounts due from sales made on or before the balance sheet date. He continues to examine the remaining items in the balance sheet and income statement in a similar manner, and if satisfied he will proceed to show his acceptance of the statements by expressing a favorable opinion on them.

Standards and Procedures

To inform the reader of the adequacy of the examination on which the auditor based his opinion, the report states whether the examination was made in accordance with generally accepted auditing standards and included all procedures which the auditor considered necessary in the circumstances. The term "standards" refers to an acceptable level of quality which must be maintained in ten basically different areas. These areas, as set forth by the A.I.C.P.A. Committee on Auditing Procedure, are as follows:

GENERAL STANDARDS

1. The examination is to be performed by a person or persons having adequate technical training and proficiency as an auditor.
2. In all matters relating to the assignment an independence in mental attitude is to be maintained by the auditor or auditors.
3. Due professional care is to be exercised in the performance of the examination and the preparation of the report.

STANDARDS OF FIELD WORK

1. The work is to be adequately planned and assistants, if any, are to be properly supervised.
2. There is to be a proper study and evaluation of the existing internal central as a basis for reliance thereon and for the determination of the resultant extent of the tests to which auditing procedures are to be restricted.
3. Sufficient competent evidential matter is to be obtained through inspection, observation, inquiries and confirmations to afford a reasonable basis for an opinion regarding the financial statements under examination.

STANDARDS OF REPORTING

1. The report shall state whether the financial statements are presented in accordance with generally accepted principles of accounting.
2. The report shall state whether such principles have been consistently observed in the current period in relation to the preceding period.
3. Informative disclosures in the financial statements are to be regarded as reasonably adequate unless otherwise stated in the report.
4. The report shall either contain an expression of opinion regarding the financial statements, taken as a whole, or an assertion to the effect that an opinion cannot be expressed. When an over-all opinion cannot be expressed, reasons therefor should be stated. In all cases where an auditor's name is associated with financial statements the report should contain a clear-cut indication of the character of the auditor's examination, if any, and the degree of responsibility he is taking.*

These standards, it will be noted, involve primarily questions of degree, evaluation, or judgment: is the auditor's technical training *adequate;* has *due* professional care been exercised; has internal control been *properly* evaluated as a basis for determining the *extent* of the tests to be made; has *sufficient* competent evidential matter been obtained; are informative disclosures *adequate?*

General Acceptance

The term "standard," as it is being used here, involves primarily the concept of a basis for comparison, as in the specimen units of weight and measure maintained by the National Bureau of Standards of the United

* American Institute of Certified Public Accountants, *Auditing Standards and Procedures* (1963).

States Government. But auditing standards are subjective, and the standard of comparison cannot be so readily determined as with the objective standards of weight and measurement. The basis of comparison for auditing standards is what is generally accepted by the profession, and of course, the auditor making the examination is responsible for determining what should be done in each instance in order to conform with generally accepted auditing standards. The standard is what other competent auditors would conclude to be necessary, given the same facts and circumstances.

Information about audit practices that conform to generally accepted auditing standards is available from various sources. Some of the most important materials are, as would be expected, published by the American Institute of Certified Public Accountants, and every practitioner should be familiar with the items in the following list:

Auditing Standards and Procedures
Statements on Auditing Procedure (supplementary statements to *Auditing Standards and Procedures*)
Audits by Certified Public Accountants
Case Studies in Auditing Procedure (Fourteen studies published to date.)
A Case Study on the Extent of Audit Samples
Audits of Brokers or Dealers in Securities
Audits of Savings and Loan Associations
Auditing in the Construction Industry
C.P.A. Handbook
Case Studies in Internal Control (Two studies published to date.)
Case Studies in the Observation of Inventory
Case Study on Audit of a Union—Industry Welfare Fund
Accounting Research and Terminology Bulletins
Opinions of the Accounting Principles Board
Inventory of Generally Accepted Accounting Principles for Business Enterprises
Accounting Research Studies
The Journal of Accountancy

The following two publications of the Securities and Exchange Commission are also of considerable importance to the practitioner:

Regulation S-X
Accounting Series Releases

Additional sources of information about auditing standards and the conduct of independent audit examinations include standard textbooks on auditing (such as this one), technical addresses and discussions at professional meetings, and the professional development program of the A.I.C.P.A.

A broad basis for auditing standards is necessary because there is no single set of auditing procedures which can be applied in all situations. The resulting need to select and apply appropriate auditing procedures as required by particular circumstances is one of the principal factors which justify the classification of public accounting and auditing as a profession. If audits could be made "by the book," auditing would be little different from any of the regularly recognized trades.

The approach to auditing standards in the United States and Canada presents a marked contrast to the practice of auditing in England. In that country, the profession has taken a less active part in the development of standards and accepted practices, relying instead on an extensive body of court cases that have involved auditors and the performance of their work under the various Companies Acts that date back as far as 1862. As a consequence, the study of auditing in England is greatly concerned with the multitude of cases that delineate the auditor's responsibilities and in effect set the minimum standards for his work.

Standards and Procedures Differentiated

Most of the preceding discussion has centered on auditing standards, which must be kept clearly differentiated from auditing procedures. *Procedures* refer to what is done, whereas *standards* refer to the quality of performance, involving decisions about how much evidence is necessary and how and when the required evidence is to be obtained. For instance, official action by the membership of the A.I.C.P.A. requires that, whenever practicable and reasonable, accounts receivable should be confirmed by correspondence with the debtors.* The actual process of confirming the accounts is an auditing procedure, but the fact that this procedure should be employed if practicable and reasonable is a generally accepted auditing standard. Any audit examination in which the confirmation procedure had been omitted, but was practicable and reasonable, would be deemed not in accord with generally accepted auditing standards. The profession has concluded that only through confirmation procedures is it normally possible to obtain sufficient competent evidence to afford a reasonable basis for an opinion regarding the receivables in a client's balance sheet.

Generally accepted auditing standards also extend to the matter of *how* any necessary procedure is performed. The question of *sufficient* and *competent* evidence in relation to the confirmation procedure encompasses such questions as whether to confirm all the accounts or only a few on a test basis, which accounts to select if only part are to be confirmed, whether to confirm at the balance sheet date or some other date, what will constitute an adequate percentage of returns from such a request, how differences are to be investigated and disposed of, and many other points. Each of these problems or questions must be resolved in terms of what a majority of auditors would do if faced with the identical situation.

* *Auditing Standards and Procedures*, p. 38.

No Listing of Procedures in the Report

Finally, with respect to the matter of procedures, it should be noted that no effort is made to list in the report the individual procedures which the auditor has applied. Instead, the report states that all procedures were used which the auditor considered necessary in the circumstances. The auditor's independence is asserted here, for he states, in effect, that the decisions concerning the choice of procedures were his own and were not influenced by the preferences of the client. The auditor thus declares that he assumes full professional responsibility for the procedures which he selected. The absence of any detailed listing of procedures and the full assumption of responsibility by the auditor for the procedures which were applied might be likened to the typical arrangement involved when a physician is requested to make a complete physical check-up. The doctor chooses the tests to be made, makes the tests, and evaluates the results. If the tests are all satisfactory, the patient is so informed without being given a detailed recitation of each test and its results. If a test should show an unsatisfactory condition, then the physician would make a report of the findings on that test, as would the auditor if his tests should show that the financial statements do not present fairly the financial position and results of operations of a business.

The Opinion Paragraph

The first paragraph of the report deals primarily with the scope of the auditor's examination and is therefore commonly referred to as the *scope paragraph*. The second paragraph, which contains the report of the auditor's findings, is usually referred to as the *opinion paragraph*. The selection and use of the word *opinion* is extremely significant. The auditor does not certify, guarantee, or give any other such positive indication that the statements are absolutely correct. Any expression stronger than an opinion would be illogical, for several reasons.

In the first place, the statements themselves are partly opinion, as in the case of the provision for depreciation and similar estimated items, so it would be illogical to expect the auditor's conclusion concerning the fairness of the statements to be more positive than an expression of opinion. Second, the auditor's findings are not based on a complete examination of all transactions, because practical and economic considerations make a complete examination unwarranted. With the typical examination comprised almost entirely of test-checks, the auditor's findings cannot possibly reflect absolute certainty. True, the tests will have been carefully selected, and the resulting opinion can be expected to be highly reliable, but there is always the possibility that discrepancies exist in some of the figures not covered by the tests, with the consequence that an expression of opinion is as far as the auditor should go.

Fairness

Perhaps the single most important element of the auditor's opinion relates to the question of whether the financial statements present *fairly* the client's financial position and results of operations. Fairness is a pervasive concept which extends to every phase of the financial statements. Thus, the auditor's assertion as to the fairness of the statements covers such matters as the adequacy of the provisions made therein for depreciation, bad debts, and income taxes; the propriety with which items have been classified within the financial statements; and the appropriateness of the descriptions of the various amounts shown in the statements. Stated in more general terms, in order for statements to present fairly the financial position and results of operations of a business, the statements must be factual, they must fully disclose all essential information, and they must not be misleading to the average reader.

Although the auditor's report is customarily addressed to a specific individual or group, who may often have independent knowledge of certain facts, such knowledge does not justify omitting the facts from the statements. Similarly, even though certain matters may be clear to the person or group addressed because of supplementary knowledge of the situation, if the matters would not be clear to other persons not possessing such knowledge, the manner in which the material is presented should be changed to clarify the situation. The auditor has no control over the use of audited statements on which he has expressed an opinion, and consequently the statements and the auditor's report may reach the hands of persons other than those to whom the report is addressed. Unless the statements present fairly all pertinent information which is known about the financial position and operating results of the business, such third persons who may come to rely on the statements and the auditor's opinion may be misled, and as a result incur serious financial losses. Such a situation may not only be detrimental to an auditor's reputation, but as stated in Chapter 5, may also result in recovery of the losses from the auditor.

For instance, assume that an auditor's examination reveals that substantial amounts of obsolete parts and unusable materials are carried in a client's inventory at their original cost. The board of directors has engaged the auditor and is known to be fully aware of the situation, so there might seem to be no need to comment on the situation in the statements or the auditor's report. Yet those statements might later be used as a basis for obtaining a bank loan, and if the bank suffered a loss on the loan because the bank was not fully aware of the condition of the inventory, the auditor would undoubtedly be liable to the bank for the loss. Even more important, however, would be the damaging effect on the auditor's reputation.

Generally Accepted Accounting Principles

In contrast to the general agreement that has been reached as to the composition of *generally accepted auditing standards,* a term which was incorporated in the standard form of audit report in 1941, there is but little agreement in the matter of *generally accepted accounting principles,* a much older term. For instance, in 1939 Stephen Gilman accused accountants of "...having committed themselves in their certificates as to the existence of generally accepted accounting principles while between themselves they are quarreling as to whether there are any accounting principles, and if there are, how many of them should be recognized and accepted."*

Gilman also suggested (p. 169) that perhaps much of the problem stems from the fact that each accountant, although never preparing a list of principles himself, has been comfortably certain that someone else must have done so. The A.I.C.P.A. has not, to this date, issued an official, comprehensive statement of accounting principles, and although the American Accounting Association issued a "Tentative Statement of Accounting Principles Affecting Corporate Reports," which was followed by three revisions, the latest in 1957, these statements have not achieved general acceptance.

Most accountants use the term *accounting principles* as the equivalent of *rules of accounting procedure,* and in this sense of the term there has been considerable agreement on what procedures are acceptable. For instance, it is generally agreed that Lifo, Fifo, and average inventory costing are acceptable while the base stock method is not. Similarly, standard costs, if they are current and realistic, may be used in valuing inventories for statement purposes, but the direct costing approach to inventory valuation is not acceptable.

Many conflicts that have arisen in the area of accounting principles have been resolved by the pronouncements of the A.I.C.P.A. Committee on Accounting Procedure through its *Accounting Research Bulletins.* The bulletins cover a broad range of topics and in general are sufficiently authoritative to place the burden of proof upon the accountant if he chooses to accept a procedure that is in conflict with a position taken by the Committee in one of its bulletins. This situation holds true on such diverse matters as the proper method of determining inventory valuation under the approach of cost or market, whichever is lower, the treatment of past service costs

---

* From Stephen Gilman, *Accounting Concepts of Profit.* Copyright, 1939, The Ronald Press Company, New York, p. 171.

arising out of pension plan agreements, and the allocation of income taxes to accounting periods other than the one in which the liability becomes payable.

The Problem of Alternative Principles

The work of the Committee on Accounting Procedure, though important, has nevertheless been largely of a stopgap nature. With no agreement on the underlying principles on which accounting is based, many conflicts have continued unresolved, to the detriment of the usefulness of reported financial information. The extensive use of financial information for comparative purposes is fully recognized, and yet such comparisons become almost meaningless if one company has costed inventory on the Lifo basis and another on a Fifo basis, or if one company has capitalized the intangible costs of drilling oil wells while another has expensed such costs as they are incurred, or if one company has used straight-line depreciation while another has used the sum-of-digits method. Each of these procedures is generally accepted, and yet reported financial results may vary widely, depending on the choice of procedure.

By permitting such conflicting procedures to remain equally acceptable, the accounting profession has assumed an untenable position that could easily cause a loss of public confidence in audited financial statements. The American Institute of Certified Public Accountants made no real attempt to attack the underlying problem until 1959, when it created the Accounting Principles Board. The Board, assisted by an accounting research staff, is charged with making a study of the basic postulates underlying accounting principles and of accounting principles themselves. Research staff studies in these two areas have been completed and published some time ago (*The Basic Postulates of Accounting,* by Maurice Moonitz, 1961, and *A Tentative Set of Broad Accounting Principles for Business Enterprises,* by Robert T. Sprouse and Maurice Moonitz, 1962), but the Accounting Principles Board has stated (April 13, 1962) that "...while these studies are a valuable contribution to accounting thinking, they are too radically different from present generally accepted accounting principles for acceptance at this time." Thus, the anticipated procedure that such studies would be adopted by the Board and then become the foundation for all subsequent pronouncements by the Board has not been realized.

In the interim, the Board is having its research staff conduct studies on specific problems, publishing the reports as *Accounting Research Studies.* The Board is also issuing numbered Opinions on certain controversial questions pointed up by these studies or developing from accounting practice, as in the case of accounting for the investment credit against Federal income taxes. Such Opinions have thus far been issued on much the same basis as the *Accounting Research Bulletins* of the predecessor Committee on Accounting Procedure, and therefore are not based on any unifying theory or accepted body of accounting postulates and principles.

Two important steps have, however, been taken in delimiting the area of generally accepted accounting principles. During the period that Paul Grady served as the Director of Research for the A.P.B., he was commissioned to prepare an *Inventory of Generally Accepted Accounting Principles for Business Enterprises,* which was published in 1965 and constitutes the first authoritative compilation of such principles. The second step has been the adoption by the governing Council of the A.I.C.P.A. of a recommendation that principles set forth in Bulletins of the Committee on Accounting Procedure that have not been withdrawn by the A.P.B., as well as all Opinions of the A.P.B., be deemed to have "substantial authoritative support" and are therefore properly considered to be "generally accepted accounting principles." The Council further recommended that when A.I.C.P.A. members express opinions on financial statements for fiscal years beginning after December 31, 1965, any departures in the statements from Bulletins not withdrawn by the A.P.B. or from Opinions of the A.P.B. should be disclosed either in a footnote to the financial statements or in a separate paragraph of the auditor's report. A departure from the Bulletins or Opinions should be acceptable to the auditor only if the departure has "substantial authoritative support and is an acceptable practice." The effect on the financial statements of the departure from principles espoused by Bulletins or Opinions is also to be set forth in the disclosure footnote or in the special paragraph in the auditor's report. It is hoped that this recommendation will cause some companies to alter accounting methods that have differed from the Bulletins and Opinions, but for those companies that continue to follow alternative principles that differ from the Bulletins and Opinions, readers of their statements will at least be able to determine the effect of following the alternative principles and to make adjustments to the statements to make them more comparable to the statements of other firms.

In terms of the auditor's over-all problem of satisfying himself that a client's statements have been prepared in conformity with generally accepted accounting principles, an important guide is Grady's *Inventory of Generally Accepted Accounting Principles for Business Enterprises,* which incorporates all of the Bulletins and Opinions, as well as references to many other authoritative sources such as the Securities and Exchange Commission. Further assistance can be obtained by consulting the annual A.I.C.P.A. publication, *Accounting Trends and Techniques,* which surveys the accounting practices and techniques reflected in the annual reports of 600 leading corporations.

Consistency

Any deviation from the consistent application of accounting principles must be disclosed to ensure that the reader of a financial statement will not be misled. For instance, either the accrual method or the installment method may be used in reporting profits on installment sales. As a consequence, a furniture store might decide to switch from the installment method to the accrual method (making allowance for anticipated losses and subsequent expenses), and the effect of the change would be to "double up" income in the year of change, substantially increasing the reported income for the year. Unless a person using the store's financial statements were informed of the change in accounting method, he might assume that the store had experienced an unusually good year, whereas in fact it may have been a poor year and consistent reporting would have shown a decrease in net income.

Qualifications and Exceptions

If the client places no limitations on the scope of the examination which the auditor is to perform, and if the auditor finds everything in order so that the financial statements do, in fact, present fairly the financial position and results of operations of the client in conformity with generally accepted accounting principles applied on a basis consistent with that of the preceding year, then, and only then, can the auditor's report take the form that has been previously suggested. On the other hand, if the client limits the scope of the auditor's examination so that the auditor is not able to satisfy himself that certain figures are fairly stated, or if generally accepted accounting principles have not been followed, or if they have not been consistently applied, then the auditor, in his position of trust and independence, must point out these shortcomings or deficiencies in his report. Comments on such deviations from the normal situation are referred to as "exceptions," and represent "qualifications" of the opinion which the auditor expresses. The matter of qualifications and exceptions is discussed at greater length in Chapter 23.

Auditing in Evolution

The present status of the auditor's report and independent auditing represents the culmination of a century of development. Initially, audits were performed primarily at the request of business owners who wished assurance that their bookkeeping had been accurately handled and that all cash was properly accounted for. With the development of partnerships, audits also became useful in determining the amount of profits to be distributed to the partners. The industrial revolution brought with it large-scale enterprises that needed outside financing to supplement owners' capital in order to permit the acquisition of machinery being developed. It was at this point, of course, that the independent audit came to the fore, and that third parties displaced business owners as the principal beneficiaries of auditing services.

In England, the requirement of the 1862 British Registered Companies

Act that the financial statements of stock companies be audited by a person independent of management greatly enhanced the status of professional auditors. On the other hand, the inevitable accompanying influence of government, through regulation and court interpretation of the adequacy of audits in relation to statutory requirements, has been repressive to technical advances and to expansion of audit services to meet new needs. Minimum requirements specified by statute or developed through court decisions tend also to become practical maximums, and experimentation or further development are generally discouraged.

By contrast, the profession developed in the United States with relative freedom in an atmosphere in which the auditor's services were sought voluntarily. For instance, *Dicksee's Auditing,* which was heavily documented with references to statutes and court decisions, was a leading authority in England and for a time in the United States. But in 1912, Robert H. Montgomery, a key figure in the development of the public accounting profession in the United States during much of the first half of the twentieth century, felt it necessary to prepare an American treatise on auditing. He had observed in professional practices in the United States a growing departure from the principles and procedures expounded by Dicksee. In the United States, more was being expected of the auditor, and a broader extension of the services of practitioners over the entire field of business activity had resulted. The auditor, in turn, had assumed responsibility for a more descriptive balance sheet intended to convey a picture of the status of the business as a whole, as contrasted with the type of balance sheet that was largely a representation of the debits and credits copied from the ledger.

In 1933, however, the accounting profession in the United States found itself in much the same position that the profession in England had occupied since 1862. The financial difficulties experienced during the Great Depression had highlighted the importance of complete and reliable financial information, and to assure the adequacy of such disclosures, the Securities Act of 1933 and the Securities Exchange Act of 1934 were enacted by Congress. Under these acts, companies making a public distribution of their securities or listing their securities on a national securities exchange are required to register with the Securities and Exchange Commission. Inasmuch as a concomitant of such registration is the submission of financial statements audited by an independent public accountant, the SEC is in the position of being able to exercise substantial regulation and control over the accounting profession. Fortunately, however, although the SEC has taken steps in this direction, the basic initiative still rests with the profession, as was evidenced most recently by the creation of the Accounting Principles Board and in the past by the profession's own development and presentation of the auditing standards underlying independent audit examinations. It is greatly to be hoped that the profession will continue this tradition of solving its problems from within.

Equally interesting changes have occurred in auditing practices. Initially, auditors concerned themselves with verification of clients' records, utilizing internal evidence available within the confines of the business. This was the period of re-adding long columns of figures and tracing postings from journal to ledger, often by way of the "holler and tick" method. With the subsequent growth of demand for reliable financial information by third parties supplying credit or capital to expanding enterprises, auditors turned to the examination of financial statements, and external evidence to corroborate company figures increased in importance. Now, the pendulum seems to be returning. Although external evidence is still important, auditors recognize that the accounting system that produces the financial and operating information to be reported is a key factor in the accuracy and reliability of the end results. As a consequence, auditors are increasingly redirecting their attention inward, although, in contrast to earlier practices, the attention is concentrated on the functioning of the accounting system, rather than the mechanical accuracy of the records, as in years past.

The Independent Auditor in Today's Business World

Although people well acquainted with business and financial circles recognize the public accountants who perform independent audits as highly skilled, competent, professional workers, many others have failed to recognize that the auditor of today is a far cry from his counterpart at the turn of the century. The uninformed are still quite likely to picture the auditor as a wizened individual wearing the traditional green eyeshade and sleeve garters. They would expect to find him perched atop a high stool, counting money or meticulously adding long columns of figures, and gaining his sole pleasure in life from the apprehension of luckless persons whose books failed to balance or whose cash account proved to be short.

It is hoped that the discussion of the work of the auditor as presented in the pages of this book will help to convey a more accurate impression of the present-day auditor.* Typically, he is a respected member of the business community and frequently holds important civic posts. His counsel is sought by businessmen, and, indeed, many members of the profession have transferred to business and occupy important management positions. In addition to rendering reports on financial statements for use by third parties, auditors are frequently called upon to assist in compiling information for use in collective bargaining, assembling figures to support claims for casualty losses, detecting and preventing fraud by employees, ascertaining sales or income figures to be used in bonus or percentage rental computations, assisting in the valuation of a business in connection with the purchase or sale of the

---

* For further information about auditors today, see "The Auditors Have Arrived," in the November and December, 1960, issues of *Fortune*.

business, and determining amounts due under patent royalty agreements or in connection with infringement proceedings. In addition to these extensive activities of an auditing nature, important services are also rendered in the areas of taxation and management controls. These services are a natural adjunct and outgrowth of the auditing function.

The great value of the services of the independent auditor in furthering the public interest and in assuring proper accounting for public money has been recognized by various actions of the Federal government. The Rural Electrification Administration requires local REA cooperatives that have borrowed Federal funds to submit financial statements audited by independent Certified Public Accountants, and a similar requirement exists for audited statements to be submitted to the Small Business Administration by small business investment companies licensed by the SBA. The Pension and Welfare Funds Disclosure Act requires the administrators of funds covered by the act to submit financial statements sworn to by the administrator or certified by an independent certified or licensed accountant. The SEC, as mentioned previously, also relies on independent audit examinations, and Congress has considered bills to require the submission of annual financial reports, supported by independent audits in some instances, by labor unions, public housing authorities, Federal credit unions, the Great Lakes Compact Commission, and some branches of the TVA. There has also been discussion of whether the Federal Deposit Insurance Corporation should require independent audits of all insured banks.

REVIEW QUESTIONS

1. Why are users of financial statements likely to insist that the statements be accompanied by the opinion of an independent public accountant?
2. What advantage accrues to the public through having certain persons designated as Certified Public Accountants?
3. Contrast the process of attaining recognized professional status as a public accountant in the United States and in England.
4. Give the usual short-form audit report that would normally be presented on satisfactory completion of an examination of a client's financial statements.
5. For what reasons might the auditor find it necessary to qualify his report?
6. Since the audit report is written at the completion of the examination of a client's financial statements, why is the report covered in this chapter rather than in a chapter near the end of the book?
7. Who is primarily responsible for the financial statements that are accompanied by an auditor's report?
8. Distinguish between auditing standards and auditing procedures.
9. Why should the auditor's findings based on his examination of a client's financial statements be in the form of an expression of opinion rather than a statement of fact?
10. Why is it important that financial statements be based on generally accepted accounting principles?

11. Does the selection of the term "generally accepted accounting principles" mean that the accounting principles in use today are not sound? Explain.
12. What relation do the A.I.C.P.A.'s *Accounting Research Bulletins* and *Opinions of the Accounting Principles Board* bear to generally accepted accounting principles?
13. Are the financial statements of two companies necessarily comparable, even though both sets of statements have been prepared in conformity with generally accepted accounting principles? Explain.
14. Has the requirement of independent audits under the British Registered Companies Acts been an unmixed blessing in England? Explain.

QUESTIONS ON APPLICATION OF AUDITING STANDARDS

15. "The only statement of fact in the auditor's certificate is his statement that his examination was made in accordance with generally accepted auditing standards." Do you agree? Explain.
16. The following booklets have been published by A.I.C.P.A., and are listed in the chronological order in which they were published:
    "Approved Methods for the Preparation of Balance Sheet Statements"
    "Verification of Financial Statements"
    "Examination of Financial Statements"
    Indicate some of the developments in auditing that are apparent from these titles.
17. Why has consistency displaced conservatism as a primary consideration in the preparation of financial statements?
18. Indicate some of the pros and cons of requiring that all experience for the C.P.A. certificate must be obtained in the employ of a C.P.A. in public accounting practice.
19. Why do you think that so many people hold an incorrect or obsolete picture of what an auditor is like and what he does?
20. When are the affairs of a business likely to necessitate securing an independent public accountant's opinion on the financial statements of the business?
21. In the typical situation, the public accountant is selected by the board of directors of a corporation and paid out of funds administered under the direction of the board, but his report on the financial statements is of primary interest and value to the stockholders and creditors of the corporation. Is the public accountant in such a situation failing to heed the Biblical admonition that he not attempt to serve two masters? Explain.
22. How would you explain to a friend of yours who has had no accounting training the meaning and significance of the term "generally accepted auditing standards," which appears in the short-form report?
23. The suggestion has been made that the standard two-paragraph report on the auditor's examination be shortened to read as follows: "In our opinion the accompanying balance sheet and statements of income and surplus present fairly the financial position of X company at December 13, 19—, and the results of operations for the year then ended." Would you approve of such a change? Explain.
24. If the auditor does not approve of a certain accounting treatment employed by the client, why does he not simply change the statements to reflect an acceptable treatment, rather than qualify his opinion by stating that generally accepted accounting principles have not been followed?

25. Most oil companies in the past capitalized all drilling costs on productive wells, but many companies are now capitalizing only the tangible drilling costs and are charging intangible costs, such as labor and depreciation on equipment, directly to expense. Of what interest would this information be to an auditor with several oil companies as clients?

26. Appended to the current financial statements of the Glimmer Manufacturing Co. is a typical short-form audit report, with no indication of any qualifications. Based on this report, could you properly conclude that the company is applying generally accepted accounting principles on the same basis that it did five years ago? Explain.

27. Would the owner of a business be likely to want an independent audit examination if he also managed the business? Explain.

28. In what ways does society as a whole benefit from the services of independent auditors, as contrasted with the benefits received by individual third parties?

The accounting system; its importance to independent audits

2

Although the independent auditor's examination focuses upon the financial statements on which he is requested to express his opinion, he must go to the source of those figures in order to determine whether they present fairly the client's financial position and results of operations in conformity with generally accepted accounting principles that have been applied on a consistent basis. It is for this reason that this text, which is primarily concerned with auditing, contains extensive reference to the accounting system: the means by which a business develops the information presented in financial statements or other reports for management and third parties. The auditor must be sufficiently aware of the objectives, methods, and end results of the accounting system to permit him to explore the system, evaluate its effectiveness, and make full use in his examination of the factual data that the system contains.

To introduce the discussion of accounting systems, the time-honored custom of defining the topic is here observed. The accounting system is the forms, records, procedures, and devices used to process data concerning the operations of an economic entity to produce the feedback in the form of statements and reports necessary for management to control those operations, and for such interested groups as stockholders, creditors, and government agencies to judge the effectiveness of the operations.

Output of the Accounting System

Financial statements and supporting detailed reports constitute the tangible output of an accounting system. An important intangible product of an accounting system is the internal control it affords over day-to-day operations. Discussion of this aspect of an accounting system is, however, deferred until the following chapter, for the importance of internal control to both management and the auditor is such that an entire chapter is justifiably devoted to that topic.

As to the tangible output of the system, the reports and statements produced must be so designed and arranged as best to satisfy the needs of the recipient for feedback concerning the operations that are under his direction and control. The concept of "responsibility reporting" for management reports is especially important in this regard. Under this concept, each management official receives reports that fully cover controllable expenses of all operations for which he is responsible; a manager who is responsible for the activities of other managers receives a report that summarizes the results achieved by each of the managers who are under his direction. The organization of the reports presented may thus be seen to be closely related to the flow of responsibility apparent in a formal organization chart. Further discussion of responsibility reporting is contained in Chapter 9, along with an indication of how such reports would be organized.

All reports should offer some means of evaluating reported results, such as a comparison with budgeted or standard amounts or with similar figures for the preceding month or the same month a year ago. Also, the reports should be timely, that is, available as soon after the close of the period being reported upon as is possible. Stale information is of little interest or value because it is received too late to institute any form of corrective action. Often stale information induces the development of "bootleg records" as an informal, unauthorized attempt to obtain needed information more promptly, but with the penalty of added cost for the duplicate records.

Classification of Accounts

Underlying any scheme of accounting reports is the set of detailed accounts in which all transactions and events affecting the business entity are recorded for summarization. A "classification of accounts" is simply a listing of all the accounts created within the accounting system, classified relative to the position of each account within the financial statement to which it is related.

Included with the classification of accounts or supplementary to it should be a description of those items that are properly charged or credited to each account. This information makes the classification document particularly useful in determining to what account a given transaction should be charged or credited. The accounts are generally numbered, so that the numbers may be used instead of account titles for machine processing and as a time-saving measure in recording transactions and otherwise referring to the various accounts. Numbers are usually assigned on a "block" basis, so that the number indicates the section of the balance sheet or income statement to which an account applies. For example, the following plan is commonly followed for many small businesses:

100's	Assets
200's	Liabilities
300's	Owners' equity
400's	Revenues
500's	Cost of sales and manufacturing expenses
600's	Selling expenses
700's	Administrative expenses

Subdivisions within the above groupings would also be numbered on a block basis:

110's	Cash
120's	Receivables
130's	Inventories
131	Raw materials
132	Work in process
133	Finished goods
134	Supplies

If further subdisions are required, the system can be expanded on a decimal basis:

132	Work in process
132.1	Material in process
132.2	Labor in process
132.3	Overhead in process

In the operating account groupings, revenues may be classified by territory and by product within each territory:

410	Territory I
411	Product A
412	Product B
420	Territory II
421	Product A
422	Product B

Under such a plan, the total sales of a given product can be obtained by totaling all "400" accounts ending with the related digit—411, 421, 431, and so on, for product A, or 412, 422, 432, and so on, for product B.

Expenses should be classified on a responsibility basis in order to obtain the control that is possible only through responsibility reporting. Thus, in the following example related to overhead expenses, the second digit refers to department and the third digit to the "nature" of the expense or the "object" of the expenditure that resulted in the expense:

550	Machine department
551	Supervision
552	Other indirect labor
553	Idle time
554	Factory supplies
555	Power and light
556	Depreciation
557	Taxes
558	Insurance
560	Assembly department
561	Supervision
562	Other indirect labor
etc.	

Although expenses are often reported solely on an object basis, the reader should recognize the shortcomings of such an approach from a control standpoint. If all factory supplies used are charged to a single account, such supplies in effect become a "free good" with no control over excessive use and waste. On the other hand, if supplies used are charged to a departmental account, the department head can be held responsible for efficient use of the supplies and elimination of waste.

Journals and Ledgers

Journals and ledgers constitute the formal records maintained in an accounting system. The journals may range from a combined cash and general journal for a small business, through the specialized columnar journals maintained by many larger businesses, to bound volumes of loose-leaf documents, such as sales invoices under a bookless form of journal, or to machine listings of transactions under mechanized systems. Journals represent a vital link in the "audit trail," making it possible to identify individual transactions and documents that become combined in the totals that are posted to ledger accounts.

Both general and subsidiary ledger records are customarily in the debit-credit-balance form, posted either by hand or by machine. It is becoming increasingly common, however, to utilize the bookless approach for subsidiary receivables and payables ledgers, in the form of files of unpaid invoices and vouchers. Under punched-card procedures, even the general ledger accounts are in bookless form until the end of the month, when the applicable transaction cards are totaled and added to the balances from the previous month contained in the balance forward cards. The ledger is then simply a binder of the monthly machine listings of transactions prepared when the account balances are updated.

Internal Forms

Printed forms and the variable data recorded on them constitute the life-blood of an accounting system. Many of the forms also serve an operating function, transmitting information or instructions that initiate action, as in the case of invoices, which state the amount of a sale and tell the customer when payment is to be made, or material requisitions, which authorize stockroom attendants to release specified materials in stated quantities.

Almost invariably, multiple copies of a form are prepared, involving the use of carbon paper, of chemically treated paper that reproduces without carbon paper, of hectograph or litho masters, or of photocopy or electrostatic reproduction to obtain additional copies. Carbon-paper reproduction is still the most widely used of the various alternatives, and numerous developments have facilitated such use. Among these are thin, inexpensive, one-time carbon paper that is discarded after use. One-time carbon can be inserted between copies of the forms mechanically by the printer, thus eliminating the higher clerical cost of inserting the carbon paper manually just prior to use. Carbon-inserted forms are supplied in pads, in unit snap-out sets, or in continuous form. The latter arrangement is most effective when repetitive preparation is involved; removing one completed set of forms automatically brings the next set into typing position.

Important collateral considerations with respect to forms are efficient design of the forms to minimize waste spacing motions on the typewriter and to facilitate reference to important data, prenumbering of the forms to make it possible to account for all forms written and to provide a convenient identification of each form, and a retention schedule that meets all operating and legal requirements and yet clears out valuable filing space at the earliest possible moment.

Data-Processing Equipment

The concern of the auditor with the accounting system as the source of the financial figures that he is auditing necessitates that he understand how the records are prepared. Figures may have to be traced through the audit trail from trial balance or a statement through the various processing steps back to original source documents in order to verify the final figures. Also, the controls exercised over the performance of the recording process will have a direct bearing on the amount of reliance that the auditor may be justified in placing on the figures resulting from the recording process.

Although recording in a very small business may be largely by manual methods, in larger businesses there will invariably be a variety of mechanical devices utilized in recording and summarizing data in the accounting records. As a consequence, for the auditor to understand the process by which the accounting records have been prepared and the controls incorporated in the processing system, he must know something about the various machines utilized in the system and how they operate. The remaining pages of this chapter are intended to provide such acquaintance and understanding with respect to the great variety of machines most frequently encountered in business today. There is no reference to computers, because they are sufficiently complicated in their programming and operation as to require an entire separate course of study, although there is a discussion of the auditing of computerized systems in Chapter 22.

Accounting Machines

Among the many advantages that are realized through the use of accounting, or "bookkeeping," machines are:

1. Increased accuracy, obtained by the use of various forms of machine "proofs."
2. Reduced accounting cost, the result of the rapid writing speed of the machines and the ability of the machines to perform several functions from a single keyboard input—for example, to write a figure on an accounting record and at the same time add and cross-add the figure into separate totals.
3. Increased control over accounting procedures, achieved through the existence of fixed machine sequences and routines that must be adhered to by the operator.
4. Decreased opportunity for fraudulent manipulation of records by persons other than the bookkeeper, because making false entries requires a knowledge of machine operation.
5. Improved appearance and legibility of records—particularly important for documents or records, such as invoices and statements that reach the hands of outsiders, whose opinion or image of the business is directly influenced by the appearance of documents that circulate outside the business.

In most accounting-machine operations, several records are created in a single writing: customer statement, accounts receivable ledger sheet, and sales journal; or paycheck, earnings statement, earnings summary, and payroll register. In such operations, the chronological record, such as a journal, remains around the platen of the machine, receiving entries by carbon impression from the original record being created. The journal is then advanced to a new writing line after each entry is completed. The individual records, as, for example, customers' statements and ledger sheets, are inserted, held in position during printing, and removed through what is known as a "front feed" device.

Accounting machines vary in cost up to several thousands of dollars, depending on the number of registers (individual adding devices that develop separate totals), whether or not a typewriter keyboard is incorporated for descriptive writing, and the number of automatic operations that can be controlled by means of program bars or panels. Automatically controlled operations generally available include carriage return and opening of the front feed device at the completion of a related set of entries, selection of registers into which a figure is added or subtracted according to the instructions set up on the program panel, transfer of totals between registers, printing of subtotals or totals upon completion of one or more entries, dating and numbering of forms, and counting the number of entries made.

Electronic machines, developed primarily for bank work, encode certain information magnetically on magnetic stripes on the reverse side of a ledger sheet as the information is printed on the face of the form. In this manner, the account number can be picked up automatically by the machine and compared with the account number indexed on the keyboard by the operator from the posting media. The machine rejects the ledger sheet if the two numbers do not agree. Other stripes can be used to automatically stop a form at the next writing line as the form is being inserted, and to introduce the most recent account balance and count of items posted into the appropriate registers of the machine. The ability of the machine to pick up the account balance directly from the ledger sheet can be coupled with a device that automatically inserts ledger sheets from a file and returns them to the file, one at a time. In this manner, a trial balance of a file of ledger sheets can be obtained without assistance by an operator, other than to insert the cards in the feeding device, wheel the device up to the accounting machine, and start the automatic operation. Even posting can be fully automated by using, along with the feeding device, a tape-reading unit that reads account number, transaction code, and amount from a punched paper tape into which this information has been encoded automatically by a document-reading machine.

In other types of applications, punched paper tape can be used in reverse fashion: a punching unit can be coupled to the accounting machine, thereby capturing on paper tape the information recorded by the accounting machine. The tape can then be used as input for other machines, and further processing of the originally recorded data performed automatically by those machines.

Punched-Card Machines

Although the traditional form of accounting machine discussed in the preceding section has many advantages over hand methods of recording, it is subject to the limitations of keyboard input. These limitations include the time required for the operator to index input on the keyboard, one figure at a time, and the chance of error in transferring data from a written source document to the keyboard. Also, of course, if the source documents must be sorted into a new sequence to facilitate machine handling, hand sorting must be employed.

Input to data-processing machines in the form of punched cards was the answer to these problems. The original punched-card data-processing machines were developed by Dr. Herman Hollerith for use by the United States Census Bureau to facilitate compilation of the 1890 census. The basic idea of controlling machines by punched card, however, goes back to the Jacquard loom of 1801.

The punched card is the heart of machine data processing, and in the United States it appears generally in one of two forms: the IBM 80-column card with rectangular punches, designed primarily for electrical sensing of the punched holes as the card passes under a series of wire brushes, and the Remington Rand 90-column card with round punches, designed originally for mechanical sensing of the punched information by pins that are lowered onto the card. The machines that handle the two types of cards are quite different in appearance, but the functions performed are practically identical. The various machines and the functions they perform are briefly described in the following sections. The cards that constitute the input and output of the machines are customarily identified by the functions they perform: *detail cards* contain the basic data to be processed; *header cards* contain information such as name and address, or account title, that pertain to a following group of detail cards; *master cards* are used to reproduce or gang-punch the fixed information they contain into blank detail cards; *summary cards* are punched automatically by machine with identifying information and totals obtained from a group of related detail cards; *mark-sensed cards* are marked by pencil for information in coded form, the pencil marks being translated into punched-hole form by a special machine.

Key punch. The translation of information from written to punched-hole form is accomplished by the key punch, which receives input information through a keyboard that is similar to the familiar typewriter keyboard. Most key punches print the corresponding number or character at the top of each column as the appropriate holes are punched into the card. The Remington Rand 90-column card is actually divided into an upper and a lower half, each consisting of 45 columns with six vertical punching positions. Through combinations of one, two or three punches in these six punching positions, it is possible to represent the ten numerical digits and twenty-six alphabetic characters, plus several special characters as well.

Through programming, the punch can be automatically controlled to skip designated columns or to duplicate fixed information, such as the current date. A self-checking number device is available for IBM key punches. Important identifying numbers, such as an account number or an item code, are developed with a final digit that is called a "check digit." As the number is punched, the self-checking device makes a calculation that will agree with the check digit only if the entire number, including the check digit, is correctly punched; incorrect punching is signaled by a red light and locking of the machine keyboard.

Verifier. Because figures developed from subsequent processing of key-punched cards can be only as accurate as the original punching, the key verifier is often used to determine whether cards have been punched correctly. Cards that have been punched are inserted in the machine; the operator reads from the source document and "keys" the information on the keyboard in the same manner as when the card was originally punched. The verifier, however, instead of punching a hole, determines whether the hole originally punched agrees with the key being depressed on the verifier. Whenever the two disagree, a red light signals an error. The operator rechecks the punching, and if the card is in error, a notch is punched in the card at the top of the column that is in error.

Reproducing punch. In reproducing, information punched in a group of cards is duplicated, card for card, into blank cards. By means of appropriate control-panel wiring, information that appears in the original cards can be omitted from the duplicate cards or punched in a different group of columns. Fixed information, such as a date, can also be generated by the machine and punched into all of the new cards as other information is being reproduced into the cards. The reproducing punch is also used in "gang punching," which involves repeated duplication of information punched in a master card into a group of blank cards. The IBM reproducing punch can also be connected to the tabulator in order to perform summary punching.

Sorter. One of the basic operations in accounting is to group like items together in order to obtain a total for the classification. In punched-card processing, the grouping of like items is accomplished by the sorter, through the simple process of arranging the cards in numerical sequence. Sorting may also be done alphabetically.

Cards are sorted one column at a time, beginning with the low-order column of the field that contains the classification coding, and proceeding by additional passes of the cards through the sorter to the column that represents the high-order position in the field. Sorting speed varies with the particular model, ranging up to 2,000 cards per minute.

Collator. The collator is basically another sorting device, but it is designed to handle certain special sorting operations. This machine, which has two feeding hoppers and four stacking hoppers, is able to:

1. Check a deck of cards to determine whether any cards are out of sequence.
2. Interfile two decks of cards that have first been placed in numerical sequence.

3. Match-merge two decks of cards—an operation similar to (2) except that only cards from the two decks bearing the same identifying numeric or alphabetic characters are interfiled. Unmatched cards from either feed hopper move to separate stacking hoppers.
4. Select cards from the two feed hoppers that do not match, placing these cards in separate stacking hoppers. The matching cards are also placed in separate stacking hoppers, rather than being interfiled as under (3).
5. Select any cards from a deck of cards that are punched with specified information. In this operation, the deck of cards being searched need not be in numeric or alphabetic sequence.

Tabulator. Also referred to as an "accounting machine," the tabulator summarizes and prints the data that have been transcribed and arranged in proper sequence on the various machines discussed previously. The tabulator is programmed by means of external wiring on interchangeable control panels. Card-to-card comparisons are programmed to detect the end of each group of cards coded with the same information, and upon sensing the changed coding, the tabulator is directed to print out totals that have been developed as the cards have been processed through the reading stations of the machine. Three "classes" of totals may be obtained: minor, intermediate, and major. For example, if cards are coded and arranged in order by state, by county within each state, and by city within each county, a minor total can be obtained at the end of the group of cards for each city, an intermediate total for the county, representing all the cities within the county, and a major total for the state, representing all the cities (and counties) within the state. Similarly, expenses can be totaled to give a major total for each class of expense (material, direct labor, overhead), an intermediate total for each department under each class of expense, and a minor total for each job-order number under each department in which material or labor has been expended.

In preparing reports or tabulations of various data, the data on each card may be "listed" or "detail printed." Alternatively, details can be omitted and only totals printed, in which case the information is referred to as having been "tabulated," or "group printed." Spacing of the continuous forms on which printing occurs is also subject to automatic control, so that, for example, with proper coding and arrangement of header and detail cards, a series of sales invoices, voucher checks, or similar documents can be prepared.

The tabulator can be connected by cable to a reproducing punch and controlled to "summary punch" any or all totals into summary cards. Summary punching would be used to obtain cards for monthly expense totals, these cards in turn being combined with summary cards for previous months to obtain year-to-date expense totals, which can also be summary punched if desired. Another use of summary punching is to obtain a "balance forward card," as when customer receivables statements are prepared from previous balance forward cards and current cards for sales and cash receipts.

Calculator. All four basic arithmetic computations are performed by the punched-card calculator, and, through programming, a variety of computations can be performed on the input factors contained in a single card, thus permitting the solution of relatively extensive equations. Calculation of overtime premium and Social Security and withholding taxes are but a few of the variety of business calculations that are readily handled by the calculator.

Other Accounting and Office Equipment

In addition to the machines and devices that have already been mentioned in this chapter, there is a wide variety of other office equipment that may be utilized in the operation of the accounting system, including such relatively common items as typewriters and adding and calculating machines. Most such equipment is available in manual or electric models, and with a variety of automatic features designed to increase output and improve accuracy.

Duplicating equipment. The need for multiple copies of documents in today's complicated business world is self-evident. Existing documents can be reproduced or "copied" photographically on light-sensitive paper, by heat transfer on heat-sensitive paper, or electrostatically on plain paper which has been given an electrostatic charge that duplicates the original document and attracts carbon particles which are then thermo-set to make the copy permanent.

When it is known in advance that multiple copies are needed, the opportunity for duplication extends from the use of carbon paper or chemically treated paper that reproduces from surface to surface by the pressure of writing, to direct or offset-ink transfer from hectograph masters, ink flow through the cuts in mimeograph stencils, or ink transfer from offset masters by the multilith process.

Addressing machines represent a specialized form of duplicating equipment. Information such as name and address is recorded on metal plates or stencil cards. A file of these plates or cards is then fed through the addressing machine, printing on envelopes, form letters, or a continuous sheet of paper.

Billing machines. Sales invoices may be prepared by typewriter or by a line of descendents of the typewriter family known as billing machines. Simple machines do little more than accumulate a total of all invoices written, but more advanced models can be programmed to make various calculations as the invoices are being written, including extensions and footings, and tax, discount, or freight calculations, which are then automatically reflected in invoice totals. The latter type of machine, of which the Computyper is an example, is actually a small computer, and may also be used for applications other than billing.

Cash registers; window-posting machines. The cash register is familiar to anyone in contact with a modern business conducted on a cash basis. The basic principle of a controlled-access cash drawer and a locked-in total that can be cleared only by a special authorizing key, can be supplemented on various models by a receipt printer and document-validating device and multiple totals to permit classification of various types of transactions (cash sales, credit sales, collections on receivables, and paid-outs), as well as classification of sales transactions by salesclerk, by department, and by such taxes as sales or excise taxes added to the merchandise price.

Descended from the cash register and based on the principle of locked-in totals is the window-posting machine. The machine is located at a teller's or cashier's window, and the operator performs regular accounting operations on the machine, such as posting sales or cash collections to customers' accounts receivable, but handles the transactions directly with the customer, including the receipt of cash. Each transaction is posted simultaneously to a customer receipt book and to a ledger card, thus permitting the customer to "audit" the recording of each transaction added to the locked-in totals.

Bank proof machines. Developed as a special-purpose machine for banks, the proof machine has also found application in commercial accounts receivable processing. Document amounts are indexed on the keyboard of the machine. The operator then depresses an appropriate classification key, which causes the amount to be listed on a master tape as well as on a tape for the classification selected; the document is automatically sorted into the appropriate pocket for all items of that classification. Totals are developed by the machine for all documents listed on the master tape, as well as for each of the classification tapes.

Accounting boards. Based on the principle of recording common information on two or more different records through a single hand written entry, the accounting board is intended primarily for accounting in the small business that cannot justify mechanization of its system. The most popular application of the accounting board is payroll preparation. Holes or notches punched in the pay check-earnings statement form and the employee's historical earnings record make it possible to collate these forms with the payroll journal, so that through carbon impression a single writing of the payroll information creates an entry on all of the related payroll records. Similarly, sales can be entered on a statement form, the customer's ledger sheet, and the sales journal with one writing. Comparable combinations can be used in recording cash receipts, liabilities, and cash disbursements.

Shortcomings of accounting boards include the fact that records are handwritten and that entry and calculation are separate operations, in contrast to the combination of these operations by accounting machines.

Needle-sort cards. The needle-sort principle is another low-cost data-processing application. Information is recorded on the cards, usually in handwritten form. Holes are punched in the margins of the cards as a part of the original printing process. The classification of information recorded on each card is then coded by notching the appropriate holes with a hand punch. The notched cards can be quickly sorted into any grouping desired simply by inserting a sorting needle through the appropriate marginal hole position. The notched cards drop off the needle, thus bringing together all cards of a like classification.

Cards, or documents such as checks, can be notched during printing to correspond with serial numbering, and the cards or documents can then be placed rapidly in numerical sequence at any later time simply by sorting with the needle through the various positions in which the serial-number information has been coded.

A tabulating punch has been developed which can punch a limited amount of quantitative data into the cards. Then, after the cards have been needle-sorted into the proper classifications, the cards in each group can be inserted in the tabulating punch, which will read the coded quantitative information and list and total the amounts on a paper tape.

SUMMARY

Although many different types of data-processing equipment have been referred to in the preceding pages, all of the equipment is related to the basic accounting operations of recording, classifying, and summarizing. The equipment merely represents a more efficient means of performing operations that have been performed manually in the past.

REVIEW QUESTIONS

1. Why should an auditor be well acquainted with the objectives, methods, and end results of accounting systems in order to make effective audits?
2. What are the elements that make up an accounting system?
3. What is meant by responsibility reporting? Why is it so important to the effective functioning of an accounting system?
4. How can a report be designed to assist the reader in evaluating the reported results?
5. Explain the purpose of a classification of accounts.
6. Journals are stated to be an important part of the "audit trail." Explain how they function in this regard.

7. What advantages are gained through the use of accounting machines?

8. Distinguish between detail cards, header cards, and master cards as used in punched card data processing.

9. What is the purpose of a "check digit" included in a number that is to be transcribed by key punch into a punched card?

10. Distinguish between gang punching and reproducing.

11. How are various classes of totals developed by the tabulator?

12. What is the difference between group printing and detail printing on the tabulator?

13. What functions are performed by an advanced model of a billing machine?

14. What is meant by the "customer audit" of transactions recorded on a window-posting machine?

QUESTIONS ON SYSTEMS APPLICATIONS

15. Compare and contrast the uses and accounting procedures related to responsibility reporting and those related to product costing.

16. Assume that you are preparing a chart of accounts for an appliance repair service. Customers bring small appliances to the shop for repair, but larger appliances are repaired in customers' houses. What reasons would lead you to recommend setting up separate revenue and expense accounts for outside service and in-shop service?

17. If responsibility accounting and reporting is to be followed for the item of factory supplies, what procedures and records must be utilized?

18. A construction company maintains a pool of heavy equipment that is used on construction jobs as needed, with the attendant depreciation expense charged to the job for which the equipment is used. What justification can you suggest for charging such depreciation on:
    (a) A straight-line basis. (time assigned to the job)
    (b) A units of use basis. (actual operating time on the job)

19. Explain why the accounting system should be able to provide the sales department with information on both average and marginal costs for all products.

20. Does responsibility reporting require that depreciation expense be reported as an expense of the department operating the equipment? Why? What other reasons can be given for accounting for depreciation expense in relation to the department in which the depreciable assets are used?

21. In a quarterly report to stockholders, the president of a company points out that profits are being held down by higher depreciation charges resulting from sizeable additions to plant and equipment. He goes on to quote the Treasurer of the company who said in explaining the increased depreciation, "...it is to the interest of our stockholders that we recover our invested capital by the fastest depreciation possible. ..." Do you agree with the Treasurer's statement? Explain.

Internal control

3

The concept of internal control has evolved gradually over the years, with the greatest period of development occurring during the decade beginning about 1940. Impetus for such development came from both management and auditors. Management has recognized internal control as a valuable tool in effectively carrying out its responsibilities, and auditors have pressed for improvement in internal control in their efforts to be of assistance to their clients, as well as to permit reductions in audit work made possible by the concomitant increase in the credibility of the accounting records. The effect on auditing has thus been to reduce the need for routine, mechanical verification of bookkeeping accuracy, permitting substitution of a less time-consuming approach that involves reasoning and judgment and stresses such activities as review, analysis, evaluation, and statistical sampling.

The importance of internal control in auditing is evidenced by the second standard of field work, which states:

> There is to be a proper study and evaluation of the existing internal control as a basis for reliance thereon and for the determination of the resultant extent of the tests to which auditing procedures are to be restricted.

Internal Control Defined

The Committee on Auditing Procedure of the American Institute of Certified Public Accountants has defined internal control in these words:

> Internal control comprises the plan of organization and all of the co-ordinate methods and measures adopted within a business to safeguard its assets, check the accuracy and reliability of its accounting data, promote operational efficiency, and encourage adherence to prescribed managerial policies. This definition pos-

sibly is broader than the meaning sometimes attributed to the term. It recognizes that a "system" of internal control extends beyond those matters which relate directly to the functions of the accounting and financial departments.*

This broad definition may be conveniently summarized by stating that internal control is the means by which management obtains the information, protection, and control that are vital to the successful operation of a business enterprise.

Information, Protection, and Control as Vital Aids to Management

Most information needed by management in order to keep informed about finances and the progress of operations comes from the accounting records. The information, to be of maximum value, must be reliable, complete, and available as quickly as possible.

As mentioned in the preceding chapter, the classification of accounts and all aspects of the accounting system must be designed with management's needs for information in mind. Information may be needed to answer such diverse questions as: "Do we have enough of part 1234 on hand to meet the anticipated customer demand for repair parts, or should more units be produced before we re-tool to produce successor part 1234a?" "How many men reported on the second shift last night and how much overtime was incurred?" "How much postage expense was incurred by the advertising department last month?"

Protection of the resources of the business is important against a multitude of possible losses ranging from embezzlement to such causes as careless use of supplies or productive materials, unwarranted extension of credit, failure to purchase from the lowest-cost supplier, inefficient workers, and outright theft.

Control is necessary to assure that management policies and directives are properly adhered to. Management is far removed from the scene of operations in the typical large business, and personal supervision of employees is an impossibility. As a substitute, management must rely on various control techniques to implement its decisions and goals. Control is necessary over a wide range of activities, such as the maintenance of adequate but not excessive inventory quantities, the consumption of supplies in the factory and office, and the payment of bills within allowed discount periods.

These brief comments should suggest that good internal control is a key factor in the effective management of a business enterprise. Internal control is also the means by which management can best discharge its primary responsibility, mentioned earlier, for the reporting of adequate and accurate

* *Auditing Standards and Procedures*, p. 27.

financial and operating information to such interested parties as stockholders and creditors.

Achieving Good Internal Control

There are various methods and techniques of achieving good internal control, but in the previously mentioned *Auditing Standards and Procedures,* the Committee on Auditing Procedure states that good internal control ordinarily includes at least these characteristics:

A plan of organization which provides appropriate segregation of functional responsibilities;
A system of authorization and record procedures adequate to provide reasonable accounting control over assets, liabilities, revenues, and expenses;
Sound practices to be followed in performance of duties and functions of each of the organizational departments; and
Personnel of a quality commensurate with responsibilities.

Plan of Organization

Proper allocation of responsibilities to key departments and the organizational independence of those departments are essential to a good plan of organization. In general, no one department should be responsible for handling all phases of a transaction, and if possible, the division of responsibility should keep operations and custodianship separate from accounting. Such division of responsibility provides for the efficiencies derived from specialization and makes possible a cross-check that promotes accuracy and yet entails no duplication or wasted effort. For example, the inventory records maintained by the accounting department of a wholesaler establish accountability over the goods stored in the warehouse. Periodic physical inventory counts reveal shortages that may occur in the warehouse or errors that may creep into the records, and knowledge that the results of their activities will be compared gives both the warehouseman and the inventory clerk an incentive to carry out their work with care. The warehouseman, in turn, will watch the accuracy of receiving room counts as goods are released for warehousing, for the receiving records of that department will be the basis for charging the inventory records for the goods for which the warehouseman must account.

Similar separation of duties would prevail in other phases of the wholesale operation. Goods would be reordered as needed by the merchandiser, the liability recorded by accounting, and the liability liquidated by a check signed by the treasurer after he has reviewed the supporting documents. Customers' orders would be processed by the sales order department and released to the warehouseman for filling after the treasurer's approval of the customer's credit. Both the shipping department and the customer would serve as controls over the accuracy of the order-filling by the warehouseman. An accounts receivable clerk would record the resulting receivable, which would be closed out only upon the treasurer's deposit of the customer's remittance.

Segregation of operations and accounting. Of maximum importance from an internal control standpoint in the suggested division of duties is the rule that no department should control the accounting records relating to its own operation. Division on this basis tends to result quite naturally where the usual operating departments are concerned, because the operating personnel will ordinarily have neither the training nor the inclination to assume the responsibility for maintaining the necessary records relating to the transactions which they initiate. Receiving cash, disbursing cash, granting credit, and collecting receivables are similarly foreign to the basic operating responsibilities of a business. As a consequence, operating personnel are likely to be equally as willing to delegate these responsibilities to others as to delegate the responsibility for recordkeeping. A frequent result of these circumstances is that both the accounting and the financial responsibilities are delegated to the same person. In a small business the bookkeeper is often given the responsibility for handling cash and accounts receivable. In larger businesses, the treasurer is likely to be made responsible for accounting as well as for cash and receivables.

The fact that both accounting and finance are concerned primarily with dollars and cents is probably the reason that "logical" thinking tends to place both responsibilities under one person. Enlightened businessmen, however, aware of the importance of good internal control and anxious to secure its benefits, have recognized that handling the financial matters of a business is just as much an operating responsibility as handling manufacturing or sales. Their recognition of this fact has shown the need for the segregation of accounting and finance. The resulting independent accountability established over financial operations is even more important than in the case of other operating functions. The universal usefulness of cash suggests a maximum need for separate accountability to assure that it is properly handled and used.

Segregation of duties between controller and treasurer. Accountability for the financial operations of a business should be established at the highest possible organizational level. A common approach is to delegate to a controller the accounting and other responsibilities important to achieving a good system of internal control. Typically, the controller is a top management official functioning on an equal plane with other officers directly under the president. The organization chart, Figure 3-1, illustrates such an arrangement.

The reader should note from the chart the many activities in addition to accounting for which the controller is responsible. In a small business the controller is likely to handle these other activities himself, but in a large concern the duties are ordinarily delegated to staff assistants or department heads.

The treasurer's responsibilities relate primarily to the finances of the business. He arranges to hold or obtain the funds necessary to finance the cost of expanded operations or to meet obligations as they come due, and is charged with securing any needed funds under the best terms commensurate with the needs of the business. In addition, the treasurer is responsible for the custody and handling of the liquid assets of the business —cash, receivables, and investments. Records establishing accountability over these assets are of course maintained under the controller in order to obtain the desired segregation of accounting and operations. For example, under the treasurer is the credit manager, charged with complete responsibility for credit and collections, but the original charge to accounts receivable and the accounting for receivables are both handled by the accounting department. Cash collections on these receivables are placed in the custody of the cashier, who is also responsible to the treasurer. Accountability over the cashier is established through the accounts receivable records and the

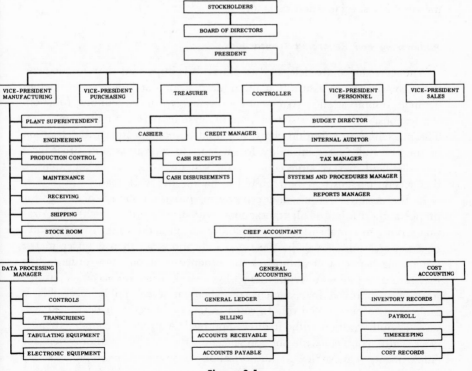

Figure 3-1

general ledger record of cash. The credit to receivables which relieves the credit manager of responsibility when cash is received on an account is offset by the debit to cash which charges the cashier with the collected funds.

It is interesting to note similar separation of responsibilities in everyday situations. In a department store, the accountability for cash collected is established by a cash register which is later "read" by the accounting department. The salesclerk and eventually the cashier are held accountable for the cash called for by the register reading. The ticket seller at a motion picture theater is charged for serially numbered tickets and must return either tickets or cash at the end of the day. Control over admission to the theater is through the ticket taker, who is usually charged with responsibility for mutilating the admission ticket so it cannot be resold or reused. In many large restaurants, a food checker stationed at the door leading from the kitchen to the dining room records on a guest check the menu price of food leaving the kitchen. A registering machine records these amounts, which then become the basis for determining the amount of cash to be turned in at the end of the day by the cashier.

It should be noted that in most instances the internal control gained through segregation of duties does not involve added expense, because no extra work is involved. In fact, some efficiency may be gained through the resulting specialization of labor.

Authorizing and Recording Transactions

Whenever duties are delegated to others, it is important that an adequate system be devised to assure that the duties will be handled in a satisfactory manner. Insofar as such systems touch or involve the accounting function, the responsibility for the system rests at least in part with the controller. The preceding organization chart, it should be noted, shows the delegation of the controller's responsibility for systems to a systems and procedures specialist, and in very large concerns the systems work may be so extensive that several persons may be required to handle the work load.

In the design of forms and procedures, provision should be made for proper authorization of all transactions, with the record of such authorization serving to establish full accountability for all actions taken. A signature or a person's initials will be the usual indication, as when a buyer in the purchasing department authorizes the issuance of a purchase order, when materials or supplies are requisitioned from stock, when an accounts payable invoice is approved for payment, or when an uncollectible receivable is authorized to be charged off. In some instances, however, a document will serve as authorization without direct approval. A properly completed time-clock card, coupled with the presence of the related authorization for employment, may suffice as authorization to prepare an employee's pay check, but in many instances additional control is provided by requiring the employee's supervisor to approve the time card before the employee's check can be prepared.

A carefully devised chart of accounts is also essential to good internal control. The accounts provided become the basis for the important summarization process of accounting, and explicit instructions setting forth the nature of the items to be entered in each account are important to the proper classification of the transactions to be recorded. Because the chart of accounts is the basis for the various reports prepared from the accounting records, the principles of responsibility reporting should be fully reflected in the development of the chart.

It is also desirable to have proof of accuracy, whenever feasible, of the figures being recorded in the accounts. The double-entry system itself is an example of this practice, but there are many additional ways of proving accuracy. For instance, the preceding organization chart shows a controls section in the data-processing department. Dollar control totals are developed for all data submitted for processing, and are recorded by this section. Then, after cards have been punched or magnetic tapes prepared, machine totals are obtained which must be balanced with the control figures maintained by the controls section before a report is released or before further processing is undertaken.

Other examples of proof of accuracy would include the preparation of monthly bank reconciliations, cross-footing columnar journal totals, balancing subsidiary ledgers and control accounts, and use of automatic accounting-machine proofs.

Machine proofs. Figure 3–2 illustrates an accounting-machine proof in the combined preparation of accounts receivable records and sales journal, including a distribution of sales by department. The proof is based on two recordings of each figure and the assumption that if an error is made, it is not likely to be repeated when the original amount is recorded a second time. The machine is programmed to compare both recordings, and at the completion of a posting line it will lock if the two recordings of each figure do not agree. This form of proof is known as a "line-lock proof."

The proof in the illustration that has been presented would be made by the machine register known as a "crossfooter." Other registers would develop vertical totals of all entries in the column for charges and the three sales distribution columns. The totals become the basis for monthly general ledger entries. In addition, the daily total of charges posted should be compared with the billing total of the invoices prepared in the billing operation, thus providing a further indication of the accuracy of the records.

Other proofs that will prove the accuracy of recorded entries and the pick up of the old balance are "old and new balance proof" and "direct proof." The former is adaptable to hand posting, because it involves offsetting accounts that have been posted, and then using an adding machine to list from each such account the previous balance as a negative figure and the current balance as a positive figure. The total thus obtained from all accounts with posting activity should equal the billing total for the day's invoices, less the cashier's total for cash received on account.

Direct proof is somewhat similar to line-lock proof, and may be illustrated as shown following.

Pick-up of Old Balance	Debit	Credit	New Balance	2nd Pick-up of Old Balance	Proof
			100.00		
100.00		40.00(-)	60.00(s)	100.00(-)	40.00 (T Cr)

The proof figure is compared with the amount on the source document, and if the accounting machine has a second register, the proof amounts can be accumulated and compared with a control total of the items posted.

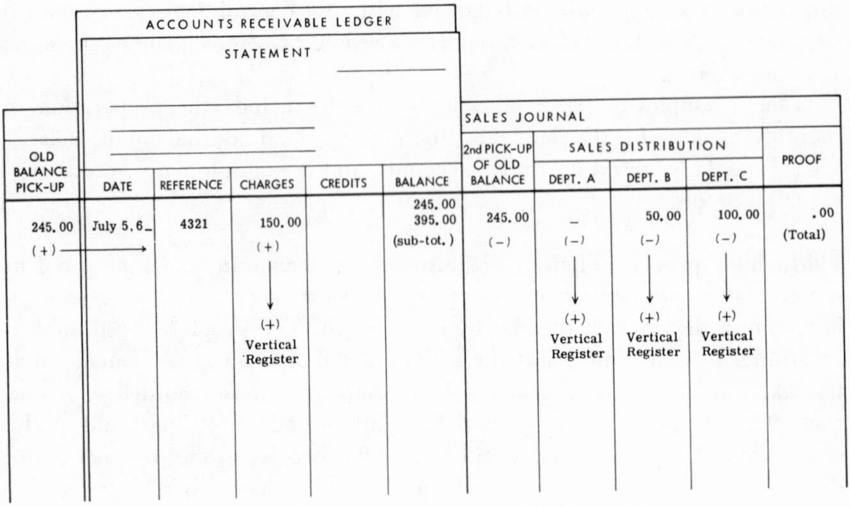

Figure 3-2

It should be noted that none of the above proofs indicates whether postings were made to the correct accounts. The following variation of the line-lock proof involves the use of account numbers (which must be shown on the posting media) and a "hash" total that makes it possible to prove all elements of the posting process, including selection of the correct account. The actuation of the various registers is controlled automatically by the machine's program device.

Accounting Machine Registers				Operations
No. 1	No. 2	No. 3	No. 4	
234.56	—	—	—	Previous proof balance picked up from ledger sheet
−100.00	100.00	100.00	—	Previous account balance picked up from ledger sheet
−134.56		134.56		Account number picked up from source document
.00				Proof of account selection and previous balance pick-up
	25.00	25.00	25.00	Posting of debit
	125.00			New account balance
		259.56		New proof balance
			25.00	Accumulation of debits posted for proof against control total

The most recent development in machine proofs involves the use of electronics and stripes of carbon coated on the reverse side of the ledger sheet. The electronic accounting machine records information on these carbon stripes in the form of magnetized spots simultaneously with the printing of information on the face of the ledger sheet. The machine automatically picks up account number and balance from the magnetized spots when a ledger sheet is inserted. No proof of such pick-up is necessary because there is no chance for human error. The account number is then read from the source document and indexed on the keyboard. If this number does not agree with the number picked up by the machine from the ledger sheet, the machine signals an error; the operator then compares the name on the ledger sheet and on the source document and verifies the indexing of account number on the keyboard to determine the error that has been made.

Investigation of differences. The preceding comments should be interpreted realistically. When proofs and controls reveal a difference, the decision on how to proceed should be made in the light of all factors bearing on the situation. For example, an error disclosed by a line-lock proof will obviously be corrected immediately. Similarly, if the machine total of items posted does not agree with a predetermined total of the items, the difference should be located and corrected. With all of the data conveniently available, the investigation should not require much time, and the cost involved is usually justified by the benefit that accurate records bring to the business image and good customer relations—plus the fact that the correction may cause additional funds to be collected.

On the other hand, a difference between the balances of individual customer accounts and the general ledger control account revealed by a month-end trial balance is a highly different situation. The time (and expense) necessary to locate and correct such a difference may be substantial. Factors to be considered in deciding whether to investigate would include the dollar amount of the difference, whether the detail balances are greater or less than the control balance, possible customer reaction if the error is in the detailed records, and the effect on the attitude and work of employees with recordkeeping responsibilities if it becomes apparent that inaccurate work is tolerated.

Penny elimination. The conclusion that should follow from what has been said about accuracy is that it is a relative rather than an absolute matter. Closely related to this point is a recent development known as "penny elimination," or "centsless accounting," as some wags outside the accounting department are prone to call it. The technique is based on the assumption that amounts of less than $1.00 with respect to internal accounting data are relatively meaningless for management control purposes. Consequently, figures can be rounded to the nearest dollar with little loss in meaning but with a considerable saving in clerical expense as a result of a clerk's having to handle and record fewer digits in each figure.

Note, however, that penny elimination has been referred to only in terms of internal accounting. Outsiders dealing with a business are unlikely to look with favor upon such an approach to records of their relationship to the business, and hence full penny recording is ordinarily followed in entries to such records. A result of this disparate treatment is that many accounting entries will fail to balance. For example, debits to accounts receivable should be made in the exact amount but the credits to sales accounts, in rounded amounts. The amount necessary to balance such an entry should be recorded as a debit or credit to an account in which all such adjustments are accumulated. The law of averages should bring the adjustments into approximate balance. Any remaining amount is simply treated as a miscellaneous income or expense.

Sound Practices of Administration

To avoid questions, attempts to shift responsibility for unsatisfactory performance, and inconsistent treatment of similar items, delegation of responsibility, procedures, and policies should all be reduced to writing. An organization chart is the usual means of formalizing a company's organization and showing lines of responsibility. Written job descriptions should, in turn, support the organization chart, setting forth the duties and responsibilities of each company officer and employee. Finally, the procedures manual should show the steps necessary to carry out the duties connected with each job.

Policies should also be set down in writing, to assure consistent treatment and conformance with management planning. The written statement of policies would be likely to cover such diverse matters as the basis for

calculating accrued vacation pay when an employee leaves of his own voli-
tion, the minimum cost of capital items that will be recorded as additions
to plant rather than as expenses, the minimum purchase order requiring
competitive bids, and the period of time various records are to be retained
before they are destroyed.

Operating reports, as already noted, are the means of indicating how well
responsibilities have been discharged, but further interpretation of the
accounting figures is usually desirable. Standard costs and budgets are
important techniques for giving such interpretation, for the standards or
budget amounts offer a basis for comparison. In addition, unfavorable
variations can be highlighted in accordance with the principle of management by exception, and the standard or budget figures challenge management and employees to their best performance by setting goals to be met.

Quality of Personnel

Obviously, no system can be better than the people who operate it; the
accountant who lacks adequate training and ability would be unlikely to
develop a good set of accounting records or produce reliable accounting
statements. Prospective employees should be carefully screened to assure
that only qualified people are employed, and talents should be utilized to
the maximum by advancing employees to more responsible positions as
quickly as their performance merits such advancement. Training programs
are an effective means of accelerating employee development and of increasing the number of persons who are available to assume greater responsibility.

There is also an important negative aspect to the matter of personnel in
relation to internal control. Job applicants should be asked to list all previous
jobs and the period of employment. Such employment should be verified
and the former employer asked to state whether the employee left without
prejudice; employees who have left previous employment under a cloud
are poor risks at best. A blank period in an applicant's employment record
may represent an attempt to conceal the fact that the person was discharged
with cause from a job during that period. Worse yet, the blank period
might represent a term of imprisonment resulting from a misdeed against
the public or another employer! Frequently, of course, a person who has
been convicted and served a prison sentence merits another chance, but it
is important that the second chance be tendered with all the facts at hand,
and that the person be placed in a job offering minimum temptation to
him and minimum risk to the employer.

Preserving and Strengthening Internal Control

The basic essentials of a good system of internal control may all be present
—a plan of organization, a system for accomplishing the work, good
administrative practices, and qualified personnel—but unless internal control

receives constant attention, it tends to disintegrate. "Short cuts" appear as quickly as weeds in a garden, employees become careless and slipshod in carrying out their duties, and conditions change, causing some procedures to become unnecessary and others to become inadequate. The amusing cartoon, Figure 3–3, suggests what easily happens when management becomes complacent about internal control!

One obvious and useful way of preserving internal control is for the members of management to remain alert to the problem and make regular tests and investigations of those phases of the system that relate to their immediate operating area. The weakness of this approach is, of course, that there is usually a multitude of more pressing problems, and unless there is knowledge of actual difficulty, the necessary review is likely to be bypassed or neglected entirely—just like those regular visits to the dentist.

In the retail field, agencies that specialize in providing a "shopping" service are engaged to determine whether salesclerks are following established procedures. The shoppers make purchases and observe whether the sale is properly rung up on the cash register, whether the clerk follows the required procedure in handling the customer's copy of the sales check or cash register receipt, and whether proper methods of making change are followed. In

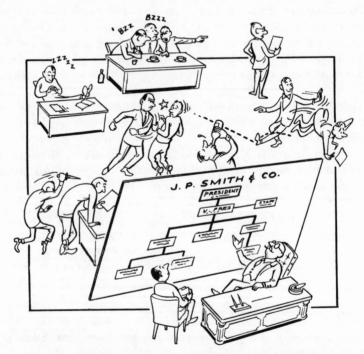

Figure 3-3. (FROM *Systemation*, JANUARY 15, 1959, PUBLISHED BY SYSTEMATION, INC., COLORADO SPRINGS, COLO.)

addition, each clerk's good and bad points in handling customers are noted and reported to the store management.

Of course, the best approach to maintaining and improving internal control is to designate a person trained in accounting, systems, and auditing to assume that function as a major responsibility. This is the typical solution to the problem in most medium or large businesses, with the title "internal auditor" used to identify the person or persons engaged in such activity. Because internal auditing is such an important function and is closely related to independent auditing in many ways, the entire following chapter is devoted to that subject.

As will be noted shortly, the independent auditor can also be of assistance in preserving and strengthening internal control, but the limitations of his examination and the fact that he is present only periodically make it unwise to rely on him as the principal factor in the maintenance of good internal control.

Preventing and Detecting Embezzlement, Fraud, and Errors

Embezzlement involves converting to a person's own use and benefit property that has been entrusted to his care. Fraud involves trickery or deceit, and is the frequent handmaiden of embezzlement, because the embezzler usually seeks some means of concealing his misappropriation. Fraud may also be practiced in an effort to conceal otherwise honest errors, or to create an appearance of good performance when such is not the case— as for instance by inflating the reported profits of a branch or omitting certain expenses incurred within a department.

The business enterprise should obviously be kept free of such practices if at all possible, but if they should occur, then early detection is highly desirable. Regular audits were originally the accepted way to cope with the problem, but today internal control is recognized as being a better solution because it is less costly and its continuous action permits earlier disclosure if fraud, embezzlement, or errors have occurred.

The principal means by which internal control provides the desired protection is the previously mentioned technique of dividing the responsibilities for handling the various phases of business transactions. Whenever possible, the following responsibilities should be handled by different persons:

1. Authorization of the transaction
2. Recording of the transaction
3. Custody of the assets involved in the transaction

The cross-check of results that follows from such a segregation of duties should produce early detection of errors, or losses from embezzlement, fraud, or carelessness, and in turn should effectively discourage any improper actions. An exception must be recognized, however, to the extent that two or more dishonest persons working in collusion can often overcome the efficacy of the best possible control.

Fidelity Bonds

The possibility of collusion, or that someone may devise a means of circumventing the established controls, suggests that fidelity insurance is an important second line of defense. Other advantages of bonding employees who are entrusted with the handling of company assets are the psychological deterrent that bonding seems to carry with it, and the careful investigation that bonding companies make of employees who are to be covered by their insurance. It is not uncommon for a job applicant to lose interest upon learning that he will be bonded if he accepts employment!

In many cases, dishonesty is given a second chance that is entirely unjustified. For instance, in one case a woman stole in excess of $30,000 from an employer, spent a year in prison, and then obtained a new job and relieved the new employer of more than $40,000! The second employer was doubly foolish, however, for the previous woman in the job had also stolen some $40,000! Many times, too, there may be outside indications that should not be ignored. The three "B's" (booze, babes, and bookies) are common in the lives of embezzlers, and it has been observed that the two major factors leading to embezzlement are slow horses and fast women.

But all too frequently the embezzler is a "trusted" employee of many years' service who had a good record prior to employment and has been circumspect in his behavior away from the business. In such cases a severe personal financial crisis, such as a major illness, is often revealed to be the cause that "triggered" the defalcation, and in most instances there is a sincere intent to pay the money back when things improve—evidenced by a careful record of the amounts stolen. Another source of danger is the disgruntled employee who knows that his employer's business is prospering and feels that he has not been fairly compensated for his part in his employer's success. Such an employee commonly convinces himself that he is not stealing but merely taking what rightfully belongs to him anyway. In view of such relatively uncontrollable risks, it should be obvious that fidelity insurance is indispensable and is actually a part of a program of good internal control.

Internal Control and the Independent Auditor

The discussion of internal control up to this point has stressed the important benefits to be derived by management from proper planning in this regard. Two aspects of internal control are, however, of major importance to the independent auditor as well. The first of these is the increased reliability of the accounting records when they are maintained under good conditions of internal control, and the second is the minimization of the likelihood that any form of shortage or defalcation of assets may have occurred without being detected. When the independent auditor is satisfied that these assurances are indeed present, he may understandably make a partial substitution of such assurance for the assurance normally gained through independent auditing procedures. The degree of internal control in the client's system will affect the auditor's examination in terms of

1. His selection of audit procedures to be utilized in the particular engagement.
2. The timing of the application of the procedures, that is, whether they are applied on a preliminary basis before the date of the financial statements or are applied after the statement date.
3. The amount of testing that is necessary to support the auditor's opinion on the financial statements.

It is important to note that there is no implication that the auditor is to include any expression of opinion in his audit report concerning the adequacy of the client's internal control. Although it might be argued that some outsiders, particularly investors, would be interested in the auditor's evaluation of the internal control, the matter represents merely one of the many aspects of good management. Labor policies, standard costs, budgets, insurance coverage, and capital replacement policies are all equally important with internal control in relation to good management, and as with all such considerations, the real test is the over-all operating result achieved in the form of net profit.

Recommendations to Management

The importance to *management* of the independent auditor's evaluation of internal control is, however, a different matter entirely. As has already been brought out, internal control is of primary concern to management, and yet at the same time management is somewhat removed from the day-to-day operation of internal control. Consequently, breakdowns or weaknesses in internal control noted by the independent auditor in the course of his examination will be of considerable interest to management, and even more important will be the auditor's recommendations for remedying the conditions that were observed.

Such recommendations offer a major opportunity for the auditor to be of service directly to his client, in contrast to the rendering of his report on the financial statements, which is of primary value to third parties. The recommendations can be readily prepared as a result of the intimate acquaintance the auditor gains with his client's operations and accounting system, and the value of these constructive suggestions can hardly be over-estimated from the standpoint of fostering good client relationships. Re-engagement of the auditor and recommendation of his services to friends and business acquaintances are the natural outgrowth of such "extra" services.

On occasion, the auditor may experience difficulty in encouraging the client to give adequate consideration to existing weaknesses in internal control and the possibilities for remedying them. If the appeal of the direct benefits the client should derive is insufficient ("After all, nothing suspicious has occurred so far, and our profits are good."), the auditor should not overlook the appeal of a potential reduction in the audit fee if the auditor can reduce the scope of his examination once the changes are made. That public accountants actually make such recommendations in the face of a potential fee reduction is eloquent evidence that they do, indeed, place service before personal gain!

In addition to the positive benefits of recommendations to management concerning internal control, there is also a negative aspect that should not be overlooked. Legal liability to his client may result from failure by the auditor to uncover the existence of employee defalcations. The auditor may gain additional protection against such liability through his recommenda-tions for the improvement of internal control insofar as such recommenda-tions would tend to increase the protection against a defalcation. If a defalcation should occur after the auditor had submitted suggestions that would have afforded protection against the defalcation, the auditor would have the added defense of contributory negligence by the client to offset any claim that the client might make of negligence by the auditor for failing to detect the defalcation more promptly.

Evaluation of Internal Control by the Independent Auditor

If the auditor is to proceed on the basis that the client's system of internal control directly affects the fundamental reliability of the client's accounting records, and if he is to limit the scope of his own examination in view of such reliability, then obviously the auditor must have a sound basis for formulating an opinion on the efficacy of the system. The answers to three closely related questions will ordinarily provide the basis for the auditor's conclusions.

1. What procedures are purportedly in use to accomplish effective internal control?
2. Are those procedures actually being followed?
3. How satisfactory are those procedures as a means of creating good internal control?

The Approach to Internal Control in a First Audit

Because the auditor will delve into almost every phase of a client's business in the course of his examination, it is important that he obtain a comprehensive over-all picture of the concern, as well as detailed familiarity with the various phases of operations and the corresponding elements of the accounting system. The most satisfactory approach to obtaining the desired familiarity and information is usually to start at the top and work down.

Discussion with major executives, some carefully propounded questions, and constant reference to an organization chart should yield a fairly complete picture of the scope of the company's operations, the nature of its products or serviecs, the alignment of principal responsibilities, and the composition of the basic management philosophy and policy that has developed. Next, a tour of the plant will likely be helpful in order to provide a picture of the physical relationship and arrangement of major departments, an idea of the manufacturing processes, the materials used and the manner in which they are handled and stored, and the general condition of the physical facilities.

With this background, the auditor is then in a position to investigate more detailed aspects of the company's procedures concerning such matters as material procurement, payroll methods, customers' order handling, shipping and billing, credit and accounts receivable, and cash receipts and disbursements. Further inquiry and discussion, observation, and reference to a chart of accounts, job descriptions, and procedures manuals will be helpful in this respect.

Preferably, the information obtained should be recorded in some manner to aid the auditor in refreshing his memory on subsequent engagements and in assisting new members of the auditor's staff to become oriented as they are assigned to the engagement. As is suggested in a succeeding chapter, the logical repository for such information is the "permanent audit file" maintained in conjunction with each client. The information may be recorded in the form of organization charts, giving names and brief descriptions of the duties of the persons involved, and narrative comments describing important procedures, supported by flow charts and sample copies of forms.

With such information at hand, the auditor should have a fairly clear picture of the procedures related to internal control. In a return engagement, the auditor need only inquire about changes that have occurred to bring himself up to date. He can then proceed to answer the remaining questions about internal control: "Are the prescribed procedures actually in effect?" and "How satisfactory is the internal control created by those procedures?" Both questions are readily approached through the aid of a single device that is widely used in auditing practice: the internal control questionnaire.

The Internal Control Questionnaire

For each segment of a concern's operations and accounting procedures, the questionnaire lists various points that have a bearing on the related internal control. For instance, the following portion of such a questionnaire illustrates the approach in conjunction with the operation of any petty cash funds that are maintained by the client.

EXAMPLE OF INTERNAL CONTROL QUESTIONNAIRE*
Petty Cash Funds

	Answer Yes No	Auditor's Verification Name and Date	Obser- vations	Tests
1. Is imprest fund system in use?				
2. Is the responsibility for each fund vested in one person only?				
3. Is the custodian independent of the cashier or other employees handling remittances from customers and other cash receipts?				
4. Is the amount of the fund restricted so as to require reimbursement at relatively short intervals?				
5. (a) Has a maximum figure for individual payments from the fund been established?				
(b) If so, state maximum figure. $...				
6. Are payees required to sign vouchers for all disbursements?				
7. Are advances made to employees and I.O.U.'s properly approved?				
8. (a) Is the cashing of personal checks prohibited?				
(b) If not, are such checks recashed at bank or included as vouchers supporting request for reimbursement? State procedure.				
9. (a) Are vouchers and supporting documents checked at the time of reimbursement by a responsible employee?				

* American Institute of Certified Public Accountants, *Case Studies in Internal Control—The Textile Company.*

(b) Does that employee verify the un-
     expended balance of the fund?

10. Are the amounts of the vouchers spelled
    out in words as well as written in num-
    erals?

11. Are vouchers marked so as to preclude
    their re-use?

12. (a) Is any part of the fund represented
      by cash in bank?

    (b) Are checks drawn on this account
      signed by the custodian only?

13. Are checks for reimbursement made out
    to the order of the custodian?

14. Is the fund checked by surprise counts
    made by an internal auditor or other
    employee independent of the custodian?

15. Describe the operation of the fund if
    the same is in part represented by bank
    account. (e.g., If an imprest fund, are
    all reimbursements deposited in the
    bank and a small working cash balance
    replenished therefrom, or does the cus-
    todian transfer amounts from cash to
    bank and vice versa in his discretion?)

	Name	Date	Comment
Originally prepared by:			
Reviewed in subsequent			
examination by: {			

Generally, the questionnaire is so worded that a "No" answer suggests an undesirable practice relative to achieving good internal control. The manner of verifying each answer is indicated by placing a check mark under either "Observations" or "Tests." The term "observation" includes not only visual determination—as for instance that there is a petty cash fund—but also the conclusions reached by inquiry and discussion. For instance, that responsibility is vested in one person only can be ascertained from the answers received to such questions as: "Is the petty cash box locked at all times?" "What persons have keys?" "What arrangements are made for the custodian's absence during the lunch period and at other times?" By contrast, the answer to item 6 in the questionnaire, "Are payees required to sign vouchers for all disbursements?" would usually be obtained by a test covering the review of several groups of vouchers for such signatures.

When a section of the questionnaire has been completed, a memorandum should be prepared giving the auditor's general conclusions about the internal control based on his review, listing recommendations that might be made to the client to effect improvement, and suggesting any changes that should be considered in the auditing procedures to be performed in light of the existing internal control.

Timing the Review of Internal Control

The preceding discussion has been based on the presumption that the auditor makes his review of internal control prior to embarking on any of his regular verification activities—a logical sequence inasmuch as his conclusions about internal control should directly affect the scope of his examination. Actually, however, tests of internal control cannot always be clearly distinguished from other tests that the auditor may conduct.

For instance, the review of internal control may require that the supporting details of several petty cash reimbursement vouchers be examined, and such examination would similarly be important in the verification of the general cash account balance and transactions. Or, along somewhat different lines, the review of internal control over accounts receivable will have a direct bearing on the number of accounts to be selected for confirmation by correspondence with debtors, but replies to the confirmation requests may reveal differences that suggest that the system of internal control is not actually working properly.

Because such a close relationship exists, some auditors do not attempt to review internal control as a separate phase of their examination. Instead, they seek the answers to questions about internal control in the course of the regular verification work, and then as weaknesses in internal control may appear, the scope of the related verification work is adjusted immediately to compensate.

No Substitute for Internal Control

The foregoing discussion contains the suggestion that the independent auditor can compensate for weaknesses in the client's system of internal control by increasing the scope of his verification work. Such a substitution can indeed be made, but only to a certain extent. It is possible that controls may be so deficient that the auditor can place no real reliance on the results produced by the client's accounting system. Complete verification of the record of every transaction, in addition to being prohibitive in cost, might still give the auditor insufficient basis for an opinion on the financial statements. Verification on an after-the-fact basis cannot give assurance equivalent to that obtained by proper controls exercised at the time transactions occur. There is no foolproof means of determining at the end of a year that every sale has been recorded, that every asset has been properly accounted for, and that every recorded expense produced the expected benefits to the business.

Under such circumstances, the auditor may have to conclude that it is impossible to marshal sufficient evidence to support a favorable opinion on the fairness of the financial statements. He will then be required to state in his report that he is unable to express an opinion and to give the reasons for his conclusion.

Internal Control and the Small Business

Quite obviously, most of the methods of achieving good internal control discussed in the preceding pages are readily adaptable only to businesses that are large enough to permit extensive division of responsibility. On the other hand, small businesses have less need to rely on a system of internal control for adequate information and control. The limited scope of operations and number of employees ordinarily make it possible for the manager to have personal contact with every phase of the business. For instance, retail store sales volume can be judged from the amount of customer traffic in the store and confirmed when the cash registers are cleared at the end of the day. Expense control is direct, because the manager will usually authorize all expenses, approve the bills, and sign the checks that have been prepared. In the small manufacturing plant, a standard cost system is hardly necessary to judge productivity of the workers; the number of workers relative to daily output of product affords a direct indication of efficiency and production problems, and personal observation of employees' work methods and habits is available to supplement over-all performance. Control also presents little problem, because most decisions will be made by the manager or with his advice, and routine procedures will normally involve the manager at some point, so that he can readily evaluate the procedures and determine that they are being followed.

Protection against losses from embezzlement is another matter, however, and considerable thought and care are warranted in developing a system and delegating responsibility in such a way as to maintain the maximum possible internal control. Unfortunately, many small businessmen seem unaware of the risks that are present and do not realize that there are some important measures that can be taken to achieve surprisingly good internal control and protection against losses at little additional cost.

Particularly important to the matter of adequate protection, especially in view of the inherent risks involved, is the bonding of all employees who handle money or other assets that have a ready market or use. The surety companies may also be relied upon to suggest certain minimum steps to be taken to reduce the risk of losses.

An internal control questionnaire specifically designed for use in audits of small businesses is presented below, to suggest the steps that are feasible in a small business to gain satisfactory internal control. The questionnaire is from an article on the evaluation of internal control in small audits by

Herbert J. Stelzer and appeared in *The Journal of Accountancy* for November, 1964. Note the many points at which it is desirable for the owner of the business to have direct contact with records and activities of the business.

THE SMALLTIME COMPANY
Internal Control Questionnaire

	Yes	No

1. *General*
   a. Are accounting records kept up to date and balanced monthly? ____ ____
   b. Is a chart of accounts used? ____ ____
   c. Does the owner use a budget system for watching income and expenses? ____ ____
   d. Are cash projections made? ____ ____
   e. Are adequate monthly financial reports available to the owner? ____ ____
   f. Does the owner appear to take a direct and active interest in the financial affairs and reports which should be or are available? ____ ____
   g. Are the personal funds of the owner and his personal income and expenses completely segregated from the business? ____ ____
   h. Is the owner satisfied that all employees are honest? ____ ____
   i. Is the bookkeeper required to take annual vacations? ____ ____

2. *Cash Receipts*
   a. Does the owner open the mail? ____ ____
   b. Does the owner list mail receipts before turning them over to the bookkeeper? ____ ____
   c. Is the listing of the receipts subsequently traced to the cash receipts journal? ____ ____
   d. Are over-the-counter receipts controlled by cash register tapes, counter receipts, etc,? ____ ____
   e. Are receipts deposited intact daily? ____ ____
   f. Are employees who handle funds bonded? ____ ____

3. *Cash Disbursements*
   a. Are all disbursements made by check? ____ ____
   b. Are prenumbered checks used? ____ ____
   c. Is a controlled, mechanical check protector used? ____ ____
   d. Is the owner's signature required on checks? ____ ____
   e. Does the owner sign checks only after they are properly completed? (Checks should not be signed in blank.) ____ ____
   f. Does the owner approve and cancel the documentation in support of all disbursements? ____ ____
   g. Are all voided checks retained and accounted for? ____ ____
   h. Does the owner review the bank reconciliation? ____ ____
   i. Is an imprest petty cash fund used? ____ ____

4. *Accounts Receivable and Sales*
   a. Are work order and/or sales invoices prenumbered and controlled? ____ ____

	Yes	No
b. Are customers' ledgers balanced regularly?	___	___
c. Are monthly statements sent to all customers?	___	___
d. Does the owner review statements before mailing them himself?	___	___
e. Are account write-offs and discounts approved only by the owner?	___	___
f. Is credit granted only by the owner?	___	___

5. *Notes Receivable and Investments*
   a. Does the owner have sole access to notes and investment certificates? _____

6. *Inventories*
   a. Is the person responsible for inventory someone other than the bookkeeper? _____
   b. Are periodic physical inventories taken? _____
   c. Is there physical control over inventory stock? _____
   d. Are perpetual inventory records maintained? _____

7. *Property Assets*
   a. Are there detailed records available of property assets and allowances for depreciation? _____
   b. Is the owner acquainted with property assets owned by the company? _____
   c. Are retirements approved by the owner? _____

8. *Accounts Payable and Purchases*
   a. Are purchase orders used? _____
   b. Does someone other than the bookkeeper always do the purchasing? _____
   c. Are suppliers' monthly statements compared with recorded liabilities regularly? _____
   d. Are suppliers' monthly statements checked by the owner periodically if disbursements are made from invoice only? _____

9. *Payroll*
   a. Are the employees hired by the owner? _____
   b. Would the owner be aware of the absence of any employee? _____
   c. Does the owner approve, sign, and distribute payroll checks? _____

Administrative Controls versus Financial Controls

The term "internal control" has been used in an unrestricted sense throughout this chapter, but the reader should recognize that in its broadest sense the term covers matters that are quite unrelated to accounting and the financial statements. The term "administrative controls" has been applied to those controls unrelated to the accounting or financial aspects of a business. Examples of such controls would include the establishment of product quality standards and the inspection of product for conformance with the standards, the operation of a training program for factory employees, and reports of absenteeism and lost-time accidents.

Such administrative controls are an important aspect of management's program of internal control, but inasmuch as administrative controls have no direct bearing on the accounting system and the financial and operating figures derived from the accounts, the auditor need not concern himself with such controls. There may be occasions, however, when some aspect of administrative control may prove useful to the auditor in establishing the reliability of the financial records, and in such instances the auditor should, of course, make an evaluation. For example, a company's shipping department might maintain tonnage statistics as a guide for staffing the department and in controlling the productivity of its workers. The auditor might find those statistics useful as further support of the company's sales and outgoing transportation expense figures, and in that case he should review the manner in which the tonnage statistics are accumulated in order to form an opinion as to their reliability.

Although administrative controls may have little bearing on the auditor's examination, the auditor will nevertheless come in contact with many of these controls in the course of his examination. If in the course of such contacts he recognizes an opportunity for strengthening and improving the controls, he should, of course, transmit his recommendations to the client. Such extra services provide an excellent opportunity to strengthen client relationships, and the practitioner who makes the most of such opportunities will usually find his clients enthusiastically recommending his services to others. Chapter 5 of *Auditing Standards and Procedures,* issued by the Committee on Auditing Procedure of the A.I.C.P.A., contains additional discussion of the distinction between administrative and financial controls and the importance of this distinction in relation to the independent auditor's examination.

REVIEW QUESTIONS

1. What benefits should good internal control within the accounting system provide for management?
2. How should responsibilities be divided to assure maximum internal control?
3. What are the principal characteristics of a good system of internal control?
4. Is it desirable that the treasurer of a business be responsible for the accounting function? Explain.
5. For what activities in addition to accounting should the controller normally be responsible?
6. In what way does a concern's chart of accounts become an important factor in internal control?
7. Indicate various techniques for obtaining proof of accuracy of the accounting records.

8. What is the principal element of sound practices of administration in achieving good internal control?

9. Why is it important that a prospective employee be requested to list all previous employers, the period of employment, and to account for all time since completing his education?

10. Of the three principal benefits of good internal control: information, protection, and control, which is likely to be most difficult to achieve in a small business? Why?

11. Does the report of the independent auditor ordinarily include any indication of the auditor's conclusions based on his review of internal control? Why?

12. What three questions should the independent auditor expect to obtain answers to in evaluating a client's system of internal control?

13. Distinguish between administrative controls and financial controls.

14. How can management assure itself that the various phases of its plan of internal control are fully operative?

15. What means are at the auditor's disposal in determining whether prescribed procedures designed to produce good internal control are actually being followed?

16. Why do most auditors make their review of internal control before beginning to apply any audit procedures? At what other time is the review sometimes made?

17. Why is the internal control questionnaire widely used in reviewing internal control?

QUESTIONS ON APPLICATION OF AUDITING STANDARDS

18. Which of the following proofs would you expect to be used with an electronic bookkeeping machine that "reads" magnetic stripes placed on the reverse side of the ledger page?
    a) Account selection proof with "hash" total.
    b) Batch total proof.
    c) Old and new balance proof.
    Justify your answer in each case.

19. a) What is the principal advantage of direct posting proof as compared with the old and new balance proof?
    b) How is the direct proof improved if handled on a two-register machine rather than a single-register machine?

20. Forms may be serially numbered for reference purposes or for control purposes.
    a) Name two forms that should be numbered for control purposes and for each indicate how a loss to the company might occur if the forms are not accounted for.
    b) Name two forms that should be serially numbered primarily for reference purposes.

21. Justify the inclusion of the following questions in an internal control questionnaire:
    Are accounts receivable aged regularly?
    Is the aging reviewed by a major official?

22. What information and reports should be available to the management of a retail organization about their accounts receivable and credit activity in order to exercise effective control?

23. A company prepares sales invoices in quadruplicate as soon as a customer's purchase order has been approved, with one copy being sent immediately to the accounting department. When the accounting department subsequently receives the shipping department copy showing that the goods have been shipped, the copy held in its files is sent to the customer to show the amount charged, and the shipping copy becomes the source document for the accounting entries.

    (a) Why would internal control be strengthened if the invoice forms were pre-numbered?

    (b) When should such numbers be accounted for? Why?

24. The typical examination of financial statements is not undertaken for the purpose of disclosing fraud or embezzlement that has caused a loss to the client, and the Committee on Auditing Procedure of the A.I.C.P.A. has stated that such an examination "...is not designed and cannot be relied upon to disclose defalcations and other similar irregularities...." Yet, it is generally understood that, when internal control is weak, the auditor should compensate for such weakness by expanding the scope of his examination. How can the stated position with respect to discovering defalcations be reconciled with the proper course of action when internal control is weak?

25. Why would the following question be included on an internal control questionnaire: "Is an expense manual in use setting forth the types of expenditures that are to be charged to the various expense accounts?"

26. The use of standard costs gives the independent auditor added assurance that manufacturing costs are properly stated. Does the absence of standard costs in a small business necessarily require that the auditor extend his examination to compensate for this deficiency in internal control? Explain.

27. State the reasons for the following procedure requirements, all of which help to strengthen internal control.

    (a) The ticket-taker of a motion picture theatre is required to tear each ticket presented for admission in two and present the stub to the patron.

    (b) The clerks of a department store are instructed to give the customer his cash register receipt along with the proper change.

    (c) The waitresses of the Elite Restaurant prepare the customer's check, which the customer then pays to the cashier. The waitresses are instructed not to make corrections on the check, but if an error is made to void the check and issue a new check. All voided checks are to be given to the manager at the end of the day.

    (d) The Larson Manufacturing Co. prepares six copies of each purchase order. The third copy is sent to the receiving department to be used as a receiving report but the form is so designed that the quantity ordered does not print on this copy.

    (e) After the treasurer of the Ardent Co. signs disbursement checks, the supporting data are returned to the accounting department, but the checks are given to his secretary for mailing.

28. All the following operations are performed by one person in connection with accounting for credit sales of the Johnson Department Store.

    (a) Credit sales for the day are totaled and reported to the general bookkeeper.

    (b) Cash collections on accounts receivable for the day are totaled and the cash and an adding machine tape of the cash receipts issued are turned over to the cashier.

    (c) Sales and cash collections are posted daily to the accounts receivable ledger.

(d) A trial balance of the receivable ledger is prepared monthly and the total compared with the total shown by the general control account.

(e) Statements are prepared and mailed on each account monthly. Accounts not paid by the tenth of the month are followed up with a series of collection notices and letters.

(f) Accounts determined to the uncollectible are reported to the general bookkeeper for write-off of the amount included in the control account.

If one or more of the above duties were to be assigned to other persons to secure better internal control, list the duties you would delegate in the order of their relative importance—that is, in order from the duty that it is most important to delegate to the duty that is least important to delegate.

Each of the duties delegated to another person would preclude some form of manipulation in which the accounts receivable clerk could engage. Select any three of the above duties and for each of those duties suggest some form of manipulation that could be prevented by delegating the duties.

29. State and justify your choice as to which of the three ways in which internal control meets the needs of management is involved in the following procedure, which is part of an effective plan of internal control: The purchasing department places a copy of every purchase order in an "Unfilled Orders" file, and the copy remains there until an invoice is received. The file is reviewed three times a week.

Internal auditing

4

The growing recognition by management of the benefits of good internal control and the complexities of an adequate system of internal control in a large business have led to the development of internal auditing as a form of control over all other internal controls. The emergence of the internal auditor as a specialist in internal control is the result of an evolutionary process that is similar in some ways to the evolution of independent auditing.

Historical Development

Internal auditing appeared on the business scene much later than auditing by public accountants. The principal factor in its emergence was the extended span of control faced by management in concerns employing thousands of people and conducting operations from widespread locations. Defalcations and improperly maintained accounting records were obvious problems under these circumstances, and the growth in the volume of transactions presaged a substantial bill for public accounting services for the business that endeavored to solve the problem by continuing the traditional form of audit by the public accountant.

The solution was, of course, to provide the needed auditing service on an internal basis, particularly as the magnitude of the problem made it possible for one or more persons to specialize in such auditing services and devote their full time to the needs of a single company. Other advantages also resulted from an internal approach to the problem: internal auditors tended to become better acquainted with the procedures and problems of the company, and the auditing activity could be carried on continuously, rather than once a year when outside auditing services were utilized. As a further inducement to the development of internal auditing, public accountants were at about this same time finding an increasing demand for independent audits leading to the expression of an opinion on financial statements, and they recognized that they could seldom perform the older type of detailed verification as effectively or efficiently as could the company's own specialist.

Railroads were one of the first groups to employ internal auditors, although the title customarily used was "traveling auditors." The traveling auditor's main function was to visit the railroad's ticket agents and determine that all tickets and cash had been properly accounted for. The scope of internal auditing services that developed from this elementary beginning is set forth in succeeding sections of this chapter.

Statement of Responsibilities

Suggestive of the relatively recent origin and development of internal auditing is the fact that the first extensive treatise on the subject was published in 1941, and that year also marked the formation of a national organization of internal auditors—the Institute of Internal Auditors. The Institute, understandably, holds a relatively advanced concept of the internal auditor's function in business and the responsibilities associated with that function, and the 1957 statement of the Institute in this connection represents a useful starting point for a discussion of internal auditing:

NATURE OF INTERNAL AUDITING

Internal auditing is an independent appraisal activity within an organization for the review of accounting, financial, and other operations as a basis for service to management. It is a managerial control, which functions by measuring and evaluating the effectiveness of other controls.

OBJECTIVE AND SCOPE OF INTERNAL AUDITING

The over-all objective of internal auditing is to assist all members of management in the effective discharge of their responsibilities by furnishing them with objective analyses, appraisals, recommendations, and pertinent comments concerning the activities reviewed. The internal auditor therefore should be concerned with any phase of business activity wherein he can be of service to management. The attainment of this over-all objective of service to management should involve such activities as:

Reviewing and appraising the soundness, adequacy, and application of accounting, financial, and operating controls.

Ascertaining the extent of compliance with established policies, plans, and procedures.

Ascertaining the extent to which company assets are accounted for, and safeguarded from losses of all kinds.

Ascertaining the reliability of accounting and other data developed within the organization.

Appraising the quality of performance in carrying out assigned responsibilities.*

As a convenient summary of these objectives, it might be stated that the internal auditor is primarily concerned with evaluation, compliance, and verification. The full scope of the internal auditor's responsibilities is discussed more fully under these three headings in the following sections. Verification is taken up first, inasmuch as activities related to this objective have been most important historically in the development of internal auditing.

Verification

The internal auditor's activities related to verification involve two areas: the accounting records and reports, and the underlying assets, equities, and operating results. Concern for these matters is implied in the work of the railroads' traveling auditors already mentioned, and on a more extensive scale, in the work of traveling auditors of large retail chain store organizations. The geographic separation of such branch operations from the home office and top management officials makes some form of verification of branch records and assets highly essential. Branch operations are seldom large enough to afford much opportunity for instituting satisfactory internal control, and home office management must have some way of ascertaining whether the responsibility for records and company assets delegated to local managers has been properly carried out.

Typical internal audit activities in the area of verification of assets would include counts of cash funds and undeposited receipts, proof of bank reconciliations, confirmation of accounts receivable by correspondence with customers, comparison of inventory quantities as shown by detailed inventory records with actual inventory quantities on hand as determined by physical count, examination of insurance policies in support of insurance coverage and prepaid insurance expense, and comparisons of plant asset records with the machinery, equipment, or other items actually in use. Such steps would be especially applicable in the conduct of branch examinations, but they are also appropriate in the examination of home office operations. Even when operations are centralized at a single location, the company officers who are charged with the responsibility for the concern's assets may be so far removed from day-to-day operations that asset verification can provide them with valuable assurance that assets under their jurisdiction are fully accounted for.

The matter of verification also extends to company records, and par-

---

* Institute of Internal Auditors, *Statement of Responsibilities of the Internal Auditor,* New York, 1957.

ticularly the reports prepared from those records. The management officials of large businesses are heavily dependent on accounting records and reports for feedback of the results of operations, and their operating decisions and control activities will of necessity be based largely on information generated by the accounting process. Obviously, management decisions can be no better than the information on which they are based.

Examples of verification activities designed to ascertain the reliability of company records and reports would include comparison of report figures with source information; proof of entries in source records, footing of those records, and proof of posting accuracy from such records to the ledger; tests of the accuracy of expense distribution coding on vendors' invoices; accounting for all copies of serially numbered forms such as checks, customers' invoices, purchase orders, and credit memos for sales returns and allowances; and proving the agreement of detailed accounts receivable ledgers with the accounts receivable control account. Particularly warranting such supplementary verification would be various types of statistical reports which are not based directly on general ledger information. An example of this type of report would be an aging of customers' accounts receivable balances, which would be useful in evaluating the activities of the credit and collection departments, estimating the provision to be made for bad debt losses, and determining any changes to be made in company policies in this area. Occasional verification of the aging of the accounts in such reports by the internal auditor would add substantially to management's assurance that it is basing its decisions and evaluations on accurate information. Other statistical reports that might be verified by the internal auditor would cover such matters as unfilled customers' orders, open purchase commitments, number of orders billed, number of shipments received and tonnage handled, production orders behind schedule, and employee absence and accident reports.

The verification activities of the internal auditor are closely related to the work of the independent auditor, and it should be apparent that this form of internal control activity would add directly to the credibility of a client's accounting records, thus justifying a reduction in the scope of the auditing work performed by the independent auditor. Also, in view of the similarity of such internal verification activity to the work of the independent auditor, it is not surprising that many internal auditors have been recruited from public accounting firms.

Evaluation

The second internal audit objective to be discussed is that of evaluation. This is perhaps the broadest of the three objectives, and the major developments and changes in the concept of internal auditing in recent years have occurred in relation to this objective. Entry of the internal auditor into the area of evaluation followed logically from the verification activities that once occupied the major portion of the time of the typical internal auditor. After-the-fact verification of accounting records and reports suggested that an even more useful activity would be to uncover and seek to remedy any weaknesses in the manner in which records and reports were prepared in the first place. Thus the evaluation of accounting procedures became the earliest type of activity pertaining to this objective.

The successful performance of such evaluation activities and the realization by management of the benefits to be derived led to gradual expansion so that now the evaluation objective commonly includes all or most of the following activities by internal auditors in companies that have taken a progressive and forward-looking approach to internal auditing:

Evaluation of internal control from the standpoint of how well the accounting system provides for—
  Information that is adequate and accurate
  Protection of resources of the business from losses due to theft, embezzlement, or carelessness
  Control over all phases of operations
Evaluation of clerical and accounting efficiency from the standpoint of such matters as—
  Effectiveness of procedures
  Use of mechanical and electronic equipment
  Utilization of space
  Adequacy of personnel
  Program of records retention and destruction
Evaluation of over-all performance of various operating departments from the standpoint of—
  Plan of organization
  Policies in effect
  Procedures being followed
  Individual performance

The "service to management" concept of internal auditing, plus the analytical skill developed by any capable auditor, accounts for the extension of the internal auditor's activities to all phases of a company's operations. In some instances, of course, technical matters will be encountered that are outside the internal auditor's area of competence, but if he senses a problem, technical assistance can usually be obtained from other departments or even from outside the company. For instance, the internal auditor might not be competent to evaluate the safety measures employed in the operation of a stamping machine, the illumination in a factory area where close-tolerance work is performed, or the techniques being used in time and motion studies, but if he senses that prevailing practices or conditions in any such situation may be susceptible to improvement, he should seek competent assistance in evaluating the technical problems involved.

Such a broad-scale concept of the internal auditor's responsibilities obviously carries him beyond the area of financial controls to which the independent auditor limits his attention and into the extensive and complex area of administrative controls as well. Under such circumstances, it is obvious that the internal auditor must be broadly trained, imaginative, and capable of comprehending a broad cross section of a company's operations and problems.

Compliance

Superior policies, procedures, or controls are of no value unless they are carefully followed in practice. Thus, once the internal auditor has evaluated a given plan of organization and operation, he will endeavor to ascertain whether the planned program is actually being carried out in practice. The techniques range from inquiry and observation to examination of the records and reports prepared and proof of completed work to establish that the work has been properly performed.

The compliance activities of the internal auditor are particularly important in companies with extensive branch operations. The procedures to be used in each branch will usually be carefully designed in the home office, and the internal auditor will thus concentrate on compliance and of course, verification, in making his examination of branch operations.

Functional Approach to Internal Auditing

Because in the early stages of its development internal auditing represented primarily a displacement of certain activities that had been performed by independent auditors, the typical internal auditing approach was statement-oriented. The internal auditor would thus direct his attention to such matters as the recording of sales, the handling of accounts receivable or accounts payable, the entries for inventories and cost of sales, and so on. Today, however, internal auditors who subscribe to the broadened concept of internal auditing and have been permitted to increase the scope of their services to management have generally found that a "functional" approach to their responsibilities is more logical and effective.

Thus, whereas at one time the internal auditor might have concerned himself with the examination of inventories and the related records, today he would probably direct his attention in separate projects to the activities of such departments as purchasing, receiving, inspection, stock records, stockkeeping, plant transportation, production control, and materials verification (physical inventory counts). The company organization chart, rather than the chart of accounts, has become the basis for delineating the projects to be undertaken, and the performance of individuals is thus highlighted. For example, in the examination of activities relating to customer credit, the credit manager becomes the focus of the internal auditor's attention. The success of the credit operation will depend on the procedures that the credit manager has instituted covering the investigation of new credit applications, the approval or rejection of credit, and the collection of delinquent accounts. The effectiveness of the planned procedures will, in turn, depend on the selection and training of the clerks handling the credit and collection activities and measures instituted to assure that prescribed procedures are carefully followed. Verification of various reports prepared for the use of the credit manager as well as his superiors will round out the internal auditor's review of the credit function, and as a final result of the examination the internal auditor will have gathered ample evidence for a meaningful appraisal of the credit manager's operations.

Operational Auditing

A natural outgrowth of the functional approach to internal auditing has been to expand the internal auditing horizon beyond the traditional accounting and financial activities. Many internal auditors have sought successfully to extend evaluations such as were suggested in the preceding section with respect to the credit function to all of the operating functions within the business, including sales, engineering, and production. The term "operational auditing" appropriately has been adopted to describe such activities. The operational audit concentrates on seeking out aspects of operations in which waste, inefficiency, and excessive costs would be subject to reduction by the introduction or improvement of operating controls. The General Accounting Office arm of the United States Congress in its operational audits has established a notable record of pointing out areas where corrective action has been needed in the multifarious activities in which the United States government and its departments and agencies have been engaged.

In operational auditing, the auditor becomes a part of the management team, taking a management approach in choosing operating areas to be reviewed and in evaluating the method of operation and the controls that he finds. The selected excerpts from a series of internal audit reports presented below reflect the possibilities inherent in operational auditing, the breadth of coverage involved, and the ability the internal auditor must possess to take a management approach to his work.

Internal Audit Reports

Any benefits to be derived from the internal auditor's activities will ordinarily be accomplished through the medium of reports on his findings and recommendations. Consequently, such reports must be carefully prepared, well written, and designed to catch and hold the attention of the person to whom directed. The reader's self-interest will, of course, be an important attention-getting device, but the report must set forth conclusions and recommendations quickly and succinctly, or the reader may lose interest before completing the reading of the most vital portion of the report. Supporting details should always be included to complete the picture, but they are best relegated to a less important position near the end of the report.

Because the internal auditor should not exercise direct authority over other persons whose work he reviews, his report is in effect delivered to his immediate superior, who in turn transmits the report to the person responsible for the operations that have been reviewed. It is desirable, however, that the internal auditor review his report informally in rough-draft form with the persons directly involved before the report is typed and released through the regular channels. Through this informal procedure the auditor can emphasize the point that a major purpose of his examination is to help the persons involved do a better job, and that he is not merely an "informer" on other persons' shortcomings. In addition, the persons directly involved will usually appreciate learning about the internal auditor's findings directly rather than after their superior has read the report. There is also an important safety factor in such an informal review, for if there should be errors in the internal auditor's findings, or if there are unconsidered factors that might make his recommendations unworkable, these will ordinarily be revealed and can be corrected before the report is officially released. Then, too, such employees may have detected short-comings or may have devised possible improvements that the internal auditor may have overlooked, and they may derive considerable personal satisfaction in discussing these ideas with the auditor and having them considered for action. The internal auditor also benefits from such a discussion if his own report can thereby be improved.

Some form of follow-up is desirable to insure action on the internal auditor's findings and recommendations. Frequently, the individual to whom the report is addressed is requested to prepare a written report within a certain number of days setting forth the action he intends to take to correct deficiencies that may have arisen. If such deficiencies are very serious, the internal auditor may make a follow-up review to ascertain that corrective action has actually been taken, but in most instances no further steps are taken by the internal auditor until the time of his next regular examination of the operations that are involved. At that time he should watch particularly for a recurrence or continuation of any problems on which he has previously reported. If he then finds that corrective action has not been taken as a result of his previous recommendations, his report should be proportionally stronger in pointing out such continuing situations.

Selected Excerpts from Internal Audit Reports

The internal audit reports from which the following passages have been selected were prepared by internal auditors of Lockheed Aircraft Corporation. The company's extensive internal auditing department has been granted freedom to operate under the most advanced concepts of the internal auditor's functions and responsibilities, and the selections are intended to suggest how far afield from the area of accounting the internal auditor can profitably proceed in seeking to fulfill his responsibility for service to management, and to illustrate the manner in which the examination focuses on the objectives of verification, evaluation, and compliance.

The first report deals with the activities of two sections of the company's inspection department.

PURPOSE AND SCOPE

We have made a review of the activities of the "A" and "B" Fabrication Inspection organizations in order to determine whether the functions and responsibilities assigned to those organizations were being performed in a satisfactory manner.

Our review was made to determine specifically:

1. Whether the Company had provided procedures, in conformance with military requirements, which should ensure, if followed, satisfactory quality control over the parts and assemblies produced by the "A" and "B" Fabrication organizations;
2. Whether inspection personnel had an adequate and consistent understanding of those procedures;
3. Whether inspectors had been provided with adequate criteria for the acceptance of parts of assemblies;
4. Whether inspections were adequate both as to timeliness and as to quality;
5. Whether generally adequate corrective action had been taken to prevent the recurrence of defects discovered; and
6. Whether the records of inspections maintained by the "A" and "B" Fabrication Inspection organizations were generally accurate and complete.

During the course of our examination, we (1) reviewed military specifications relating to quality control, (2) reviewed Company procedures relating to quality control, (3) interviewed and observed inspection personnel as to their understanding of those procedures, and (4) made tests of inspection records. Our review did not cover the use of sampling techniques by Inspection. We intend to examine this activity in connection with our review of the activities of the Inspection Technical Services Department.

OPINIONS, FINDINGS, AND SUGGESTIONS

We were very much impressed with the progressive attitude displayed by Inspection management in such matters as the adoption of a new approach to fabrication inspection which involves the inspection of parts in process rather than only after completion (on its face, a definite improvement over the old method), the adoption and increasing emphasis on sampling techniques in parts inspection, and the practice of encouraging Production to assume a greater responsibility in the discovery of defective parts.

In our opinion, the functions and responsibilities assigned to the "A" and "B" Fabrication Inspection organizations were being performed in a generally satisfactory manner.

Among the comments on specific findings are those relating to the examination of inspection tags prepared by the first of the two inspection groups:

We found that Inspection Tags prepared and processed by "A" Fabrication Inspection were reasonably complete and accurate with the following exceptions:

1. We noted a number of instances in which Inspection Tags bore manually written Inspection stamp numbers rather than the impression of the originating inspector's stamp. Since the purpose of issuing stamps to inspectors is to ensure that only authorized personnel accept or withhold parts, we believe that Inspection should not process any Inspection Tags which do not carry the originating inspector's stamp. The applicable Inspection directive clearly requires the use of the stamp.

We discussed this matter with the "A" Materials Review Coordinator and the Manager of the "A" Machined Parts and Sheet Metal Inspection Department and were informed that "A" Fabrication inspectors would be instructed to conform to the directive.

2. A comparison of 43 Inspection Tags with the Shop Orders against which the rejections had been made disclosed seven instances in which the Inspection Tag showed an incorrect Lot number and nine instances in which the Inspection Tag showed incorrect or incomplete Work Order charges. While errors in Lot numbers shown on Inspection Tags may not be overly significant, errors in Work Order charges shown on the Inspection Tags may result in incorrect accounting for rework and, possibly, replacement charges. Most of the Work Order inaccuracies which we noted involved instances in which not all of the Work Orders shown on the applicable Shop Order against which the rejection was made were noted on the Inspection Tag as required by the applicable Authorizing Directive.

We discussed this matter with responsible supervision and were informed that inspectors would be cautioned to improve the accuracy and completeness of Lot numbers and Work Orders shown on Inspection Tags.

The following report deals with an examination of certain controls maintained by the company's engineering department.

PURPOSE AND SCOPE

We have made an examination to determine whether it appears: (1) that the Engineering Branch management has provided adequate controls, which if operated effectively, would ensure, insofar as practicable, that production drawings, including Purchased Equipment drawings, Special Standards drawings, and related change documents will be accurate at the time of release to the Manufacturing organization; (2) that *certain* of these controls which we felt qualified to test were operating in a satisfactory manner; and (3) that the Engineering Branch management and the Project Engineering organization have provided an effective program designed to reduce engineering errors.

Specifically our review of certain of the controls was directed toward determining: (1) whether engineering approval signatures as required by Engineering Management Memo 2030 and other applicable engineering procedures were being obtained on all production drawings and changes released by the Project Engineering organization; (2) whether all production drawings and change documents were being checked by the Project Checking Groups or other authorized personnel before being released by the Project Engineering organization; and (3) whether all significant errors noted and recorded by engineering checkers on check prints which they reviewed were being corrected prior to the release of the applicable production drawing or change document.

Our examination of the controls which have been provided was limited because we did not feel qualified to make tests of production drawings to determine whether the reviews made by project supervision and design specialists were adequate or whether the checking activity was being performed in a satisfactory manner.

During our examination, we:

1. Reviewed the policies and procedures which pertained to the controls over the quality of engineering drawings and related change documents;
2. Carried on discussions with personnel engaged in those control activities;
3. Reviewed the error study programs of the Project Engineering organization;
4. Made such observations and tests as we deemed necessary.

OPINIONS, FINDINGS, AND SUGGESTIONS

Conclusion

We have discussed in the preceding paragraphs the direct measures which the Engineering Branch was taking at the time of our review in their program to reduce engineering errors. Previously we outlined other action taken which we classified as indirect.

We think that all of the error-reduction measures which we have discussed are very good but believe that the error-reduction program should go further. In that connection, it seems to us that the action taken thus far is directed more toward improving the means of detecting errors than on means for reducing the original commission of errors. We believe that if the original work performed by the design groups contained fewer errors this would tend to improve the quality of the checking work and, as a result, the drawings when released would contain fewer errors. We do not mean to imply that no effort has been taken to improve the quality of the original work for we have previously mentioned certain indirect action taken for that purpose. In addition, group engineers in each project informed us that drawings requiring correction as a result of the checking activity are reviewed in the design groups, and the persons responsible for the errors are required to make the necessary corrections. Such reviews serve a useful purpose of apprising design group personnel of the errors in drawings which they have released to the checking groups. Although this practice is commendable, we do not believe that such action alone is sufficient to bring about a strong and steady improvement in the quality of original work performed by the design groups. We feel that there is a need for a program of continuous accumulation and reporting of statistical information by design group relating to the number of errors found as a result of the checking activity. It seems to us that this would bring about a greater emphasis on the quality of the work performed by individual design groups and also provide a factual, numerical basis for the Project Engineers to use in evaluating the performance of the Design Group Engineers. We discussed this with cognizant personnel and were informed that such a program was being formulated. In view of this action, we have nothing further to suggest.

Examples of Internal Audit Projects

To suggest the possible breadth of a comprehensive program of internal audit, a number of internal audit projects have been selected from the three-year schedule of projects of the internal auditing department of Lockheed Aircraft Corporation. The complete schedule lists well over one hundred projects, which are grouped according to major departmental responsibilities: manufacturing, engineering, finance and accounting, marketing, and industrial relations. For example, under the Manufacturing Manager are grouped projects relating to manufacturing control, manufacturing engineering, material purchasing and handling, quality control, and production management. Nineteen separate projects concern manufacturing engineering, classified under the headings of tool engineering, process control, plant engineering, and project planning. The individual projects pertaining to tool engineering are:

> Tool Inspection Department
> Project Tool Control Department
> Perishable Tools and Small Tool Repair Parts
> Standard Tool Cribs
> Tool Shop Load Forecasting
> Project Tool Design
> Manufacturing Standards

The Place of the Internal Auditor in the Company Organization

In the previously quoted *Statement of Responsibilities of the Internal Auditor* prepared by the Institute of Internal Auditors, the ideal position of the internal auditor in the company's plan of organization is clearly set forth:

AUTHORITY AND RESPONSIBILITY

Internal auditing is a staff function rather than a line function. Therefore the internal auditor does not exercise direct authority over other persons in the organization, whose work he reviews.

The internal auditor should be free to review and appraise policies, plans, procedures, and records; but his review and appraisal does not in any way relieve other persons in the organization of the responsibilities assigned to them.

INDEPENDENCE

Independence is essential to the effectiveness of the internal auditing program. This independence has two major aspects:

(1) The organizational status of the internal auditor and the support accorded

to him by management are major determinants of the range and value of the services which management will obtain from the internal auditing function. The head of the internal auditing department, therefore, should be responsible to an officer of sufficient rank in the organization as will assure a broad scope of activities, and adequate consideration of and effective action on the findings or recommendations made by him.

(2) Since complete objectivity is essential to the audit function, internal auditors should not develop and install procedures, prepare records, or engage in any other activity which they normally would be expected to review and appraise.

The staff position of the internal auditor should be noted in the illustrative organization chart presented on page 41, as should the fact that in reporting to the controller in this instance, the internal auditor is reporting to a top executive who is immediately under the president of the company, and who is charged with the basic responsibility for the entire control function within the business. Such an arrangement should ordinarily be adequate to assure the internal auditor the freedom of action and attention to his recommendations essential to the conduct of an effective internal auditing program.

It should also be noted that in reporting to the controller in a staff capacity, the internal auditor should find it possible to remain free of any basic operating responsibilities. The value of an independent review is lost if the internal auditor designs accounting procedures, prepares bank reconciliations, or makes physical counts of inventory items for the purpose of adjusting perpetual inventory records—responsibilities that are sometimes assigned to the internal auditor "because he should be able to do a good job."

Maximum independence can be assured the internal auditor by having him report to the president, or even the board of directors, but the possible increase in independence would be more than offset by the inability of the president or board to effectively supervise his work and their preoccupation with matters of more general concern. On the other hand, it would be completely unsatisfactory to have the internal auditor operate under the jurisdiction of the treasurer or chief accountant. The internal auditor would then be placed in the position of having to review line functions under the control of his immediate superior, and would consequently feel under pressure to soften his findings should they be critical.

The performance of the audit function within the United States government presents an interesting example of independence. The Congress created the General Accounting Office in 1921 to oversee the government's accounting activities, and the G.A.O.'s auditing section makes regular examinations of all the government departments and agencies. The staff of some 3,000 accountants and auditors includes over 300 C.P.A.'s, and the results of its auditing activities are summarized by the Comptroller

General in his annual report to the Congress. The Comptroller General, who heads the General Accounting Office, is appointed for a term of fifteen years, subject to removal only by action of Congress, and is completely independent of the executive branch of the government.

Internal Auditing and the Small Business

Any attempt by business management to exercise some form of control over the operations for which it is responsible implies a need to follow up the controls to ascertain their continued effectiveness. For example, to reduce the risk of loss from theft or burglary, customers' checks should be endorsed "For Deposit Only" as soon as they are received, but this simple procedure is easily forgotten. Hence, the checks in the cash drawer should be examined from time to time to be certain that they have been properly endorsed.

A similar situation exists in the case of accounts receivable. The basic control would be that every invoice must be accounted for and charged to accounts receivable, with credits to accounts receivable to be made only from the cash receipts record, except as the manager may approve allowances, returns, or the write-off of uncollectible accounts. To satisfy himself that the controls are operative and all cash receipts have been properly accounted for, the manager should, from time to time, thumb through the posted invoices to ascertain that there are no missing numbers, test the accuracy of the listing of the invoices for the daily sales record, foot the record, and trace the posting to the accounts receivable control. Control account postings for cash receipts should be balanced with bank deposits, and the control account reviewed for any credit entries that have not been approved. Also, periodically the manager should balance customers' statements with the receivables control, place the statements in the mail himself, and then scrutinize the incoming mail for any correspondence from customers who have taken exception to the statements they have received.

In each of the above examples, the suggested follow-up of control measures is essentially an internal auditing function. In the very small business, the function may be carried out by the manager, or perhaps an independent auditor. In larger businesses, the treasurer, controller, or chief accountant may perform the necessary steps, and of course, if there is enough of this type of review work that should be done, it will be assigned to a specialist who will spend a portion of his time, or perhaps all of it, at such activities. In the latter situation, the individual will undoubtedly carry the title of internal auditor, but the function of internal auditing should be carried out regardless of the size of the business or the presence of an employee who is designated as the internal auditor. There is, however, a major advantage in having a regularly designated internal auditor: he can devote his undivided attention to the problems of verification, evaluation, and compliance and the internal auditing function is less likely to be pushed aside than if it is but one of several responsibilities of a single person. It is particularly easy for such a person to postpone or discontinue the review procedures because the business can continue to run without them—hence the advantage of having a full-time internal auditor if the position can be justified.

The matter of internal auditing and the small business is perhaps best summarized by stating that it is not a question of whether internal auditing should be done, but rather a question of who shall do it. If the internal auditing activities require only a portion of one individual's time, it is preferable that his other duties be staff functions rather than line responsibilities, and the individual should not regularly handle functions on which he will be expected subsequently to render impartial judgment in his capacity as internal auditor. As a very rough generalization, it might be stated that ordinarily a business with less than 500 employees is unlikely to be able to justify a full-time position for an internal auditor.

The Independent Auditor and Internal Auditing

There are several reasons for having included a chapter on internal auditing in this volume. First of all, internal auditing constitutes an important segment of all auditing activity, and a discussion of this aspect of the broader subject is therefore pertinent. A single chapter may appear to be inadequate attention to the problem, but there is further reference to the work of the internal auditor in subsequent chapters, and in addition, there is a close similarity between much of the work of the internal auditor and that of the independent auditor. Consequently, although subsequent chapters present auditing from the point of view of the independent auditor, much of the material is equally applicable to the work of the internal auditor.

The principal reason for the discussion of internal auditing, however, is the fact that it is part of the general problem of internal control, and hence is of vital concern from the standpoint of management and control over the accounting system. It should be readily apparent from the preceding description of the objectives and work of the internal auditor that when internal auditing is superimposed on all of the other forms of internal control, the resulting accounting figures must have a very high degree of accuracy and reliability. Under such circumstances the independent auditor can, of course, establish a sound basis for the expression of his opinion on the company's financial statements with an independent examination that involves a minimum amount of direct verification work.

Of course, reliance can be placed on the internal auditor's work only after the scope and thoroughness of the work have been carefully reviewed by the independent auditor. All of the following points should be covered in the review. First of all, the independent auditor should ascertain the general competence of the internal auditor and his staff, based on their training and experience and on the general impressions that he forms in his discussions with them. Also important is the position of the internal auditor in the company organization—his independence and freedom from operating responsibilities. The adequacy and extent of the internal audit work should be apparent from a review of completed projects and those scheduled for the future, and the independent auditor should ascertain that no important areas have been overlooked or covered with insufficient frequency.

Finally, the working papers and reports for a representative number of internal audit projects should be reviewed. The working papers should show that the work has been properly planned and that all necessary procedures have been included and properly executed. The reports, in addition to evidencing the work that has been done, should give the independent auditor a general picture of the adequacy of the procedures and internal controls that have been instituted, as well as of the accuracy of the accounting results that have been produced.

Internal Auditing and Independent Auditing Contrasted

Although there is considerable similarity between internal auditing and independent auditing, it is the differences between the two activities that are most important. The following summary of the principal differences should be helpful in maintaining a clear distinction between the two types of activity.

INTERNAL AUDITING	INDEPENDENT AUDITING
Audit is performed by a company employee.	Audit is performed by a professional practitioner who is engaged as an independent contractor.
Primary concern is in serving the needs of management.	Primary concern is in fulfilling the needs of third parties for reliable financial data.
Review of operations and internal control is made primarily to develop improvements and induce compliance with established policies and procedures; not limited to financial matters.	Review of operations and internal control is made primarily to determine scope of examination and reliability of financial data.
Work is subdivided primarily according to operating functions and lines of management responsibility.	Work is subdivided primarily in relation to principal balance sheet and income statement accounts.
Auditor is directly concerned with the detection and prevention of fraud.	Auditor is incidentally concerned with the detection and prevention of fraud, except as financial statements may be materially affected.

Auditor should be independent of treasurer and chief accountant, but subservient to needs and desires of other elements of management.	Auditor should be independent of management both in fact and in mental attitude.
Review of company activities is continuous.	Examination of supporting data to financial statements is periodic—usually once a year.

REVIEW QUESTIONS

1. Why, if a company is large enough to warrant having internal auditors, will it usually be desirable to have an internal audit program rather than rely on the independent auditor for the necessary work?
2. What are the three major objectives of the internal auditor?
3. Why is internal auditing likely to be especially necessary when extensive branch operations are conducted?
4. "Internal auditors need not be concerned about the accuracy of company records if the company has an independent audit, since the independent auditors will make the necessary verification." Do you agree? Explain.
5. Why may it be said that the internal auditor's evaluation activities are more useful than his verification activities?
6. Give some examples of evaluation activities of the internal auditor that are not directly concerned with internal control.
7. Distinguish between the functional approach to internal auditing and the financial statement approach.
8. What are the two major aspects of the internal auditor's independence?
9. What may the internal auditor gain through reviewing a draft of his report with the person responsible for the operation he has been auditing?
10. Suggest some of the internal audit steps that should be performed from time to time by the manager of a small business that does not have an internal auditor.
11. What steps should be taken by the independent auditor in his review of a client's internal audit activities?
12. Any one of several management officials may be selected to be responsible for the work of the internal auditor. List each official by title and explain why it would be good or bad to have the auditor report to him.
13. What difference exists in the ultimate purpose of the internal auditor and the independent auditor in reviewing internal control?
14. How do operational audits differ from the more traditional internal auditing?

QUESTIONS ON APPLICATION OF AUDITING STANDARDS

15. (a) Is it desirable to have a concern's internal auditor do all of the systems work for the concern? Explain.
    (b) Is it customary and appropriate for a concern's internal auditor to make recommendations for changes in the concern's accounting system? Explain.
16. How should the concern of the internal auditor and the independent auditor differ with respect to a company's internal control in the areas of financial controls and administrative controls?

17. If the internal auditor is satisfied that there is sufficient internal control to assure that all proceeds from the sale of scrap are accounted for, can he be satisfied that scrap is being properly handled? Explain.

18. In your internal audit review of general and administrative expense you ascertain that long-distance telephone toll expense has been increasing at an excessive rate. The company's procedures require that all long-distance calls be placed through the company switchboard operator, who ascertains from an approved list whether the caller is authorized to place long-distance calls. What additional action might be recommended as a means of attempting to control this item of expense?

19. What steps should the internal auditor take in auditing charges to the account "Freight and Express"? How would your answer differ if the company had a traffic department?

20. Suggest steps that the internal auditor should take in auditing insurance expense.

21. Since the internal auditor's main function is to be of service and assistance to management, can the independent auditor, who is checking on management, place any reliance on the internal auditor's work? Explain.

22. How would you reply to the head of an internal audit staff who made this statement: "We have a very efficient system of auditing disbursements. One man spends full time reviewing every voucher before it is paid. Thus we not only catch any discrepancies before payment is made, but the time of the person in the accounting department who formerly made the review has been saved."

23. As the internal auditor of Hustler's Department Store, you are discussing with the controller, to whom you are responsible, your plans for an examination of the credit department. The controller questions the need and propriety of the following procedures included in your program: (1) Review all credit applications, both accepted and rejected, for one month; (2) Review the complete files on all bad debts charged off in a selected month. How would you answer the controller?

24. Three principal objectives have been suggested, showing how internal audit activities can be of assistance to management. For each objective suggest some form of exception or recommendation that might arise from the internal auditor's examination of a company's voucher system for handling disbursements.

25. Suggest several procedures the internal auditor might employ relative to an examination of accounts receivable. Indicate to which of the three objectives underlying the internal auditor's work each procedure relates, showing at least one procedure for each objective.

Some professional and technical
auditing considerations

5

Earlier comments have suggested the importance of independent audits in financial dealings and the nature of the responsibilities that independent public accountants assume in making such examinations. Public acceptance of independent audit services, which are provided primarily by Certified Public Accountants, can be attributed to two major factors: general recognition that public accounting is a professional calling, and the zeal with which C.P.A.'s have guarded their independence in activities related to expressions of opinion on financial statements.

Achievement of Professional Status

A body of practitioners providing one or more related services does not become a profession merely by attaching that label to itself. Rather, professional standing is achieved as a matter of public acceptance in the case of those groups that have demonstrated that they are worthy of such recognition. Although there is no single list of qualifications guaranteed to produce recognition as a profession, the following attributes seem to be common to groups that are generally recognized as having achieved professional standing:

1. Provision of a service in a field in which the public is untrained and hence unable to evaluate the quality of the service performed.
2. Evidence of the public interest in the provision of qualified service in the form of laws restricting admission to practice to those who are properly qualified.
3. Provision of a service that is essentially intellectual and that requires mastery of a substantial body of specialized knowledge by means of a formal educational process.

4. Presence of an underlying service motive that transcends the desire for monetary gain.

5. Recognition by practitioners that financial return is not the accepted measure of success.

6. Existence of a strong voluntary organization dedicated to the advancement of the social obligations of its members.

7. Freedom from uninhibited competition so that practice may be carried on in an atmosphere of dignity and self-respect, with adequate opportunity for concentration on the improvement of services.

8. Active support of a code of ethical conduct through which the public may judge the professional stature of those in practice.

In general, Certified Public Accountants measure up to these qualifications quite well. To the extent that there is limited public recognition that the C.P.A.'s calling is truly professional, it would appear to be the result of the limited public contact with C.P.A.'s and their work, as contrasted with the situation concerning attorneys and physicians. Nevertheless, the complexity of the C.P.A.'s work, the rigorous qualifications for the C.P.A. certificate, and the high ethical standards that C.P.A.'s have set for themselves are bringing growing recognition of the C.P.A.'s professional standing.

Equally growing in recognition is the C.P.A.'s reputation for independence. The choice of a C.P.A. firm to tabulate votes and present the names of Hollywood's Academy Award winners offers an interesting illustration of the importance of this reputation, and although the actual services performed in this instance are not highly technical, it would seem that an important aspect of the engagement is the way it helps to fix in the mind of the public the C.P.A.'s uncompromising independence.

INDEPENDENCE : KEYSTONE OF A PROFESSION

The auditor's report on his client's financial statements indirectly refers to the auditor's independence when the auditor states that his examination has been made in accordance with generally accepted auditing standards. These standards (see p. 9) require that "In all matters relating to the assignment an independence in mental attitude is to be maintained by the auditor or auditors." The concern for independence is a unique aspect of the public accounting profession, and even then pertains only to the auditing phase of the profession's services. Normally, a member of a profession is expected to be concerned solely with the interests of his client, and deference to the interests of another party would be cause for breach of contract action by the client. But in performing independent auditing services, the public accountant must rise above the interests of his client and concern himself with the interests of third parties, often unknown to him, who will be relying on the financial statements in question. Only so long as the public accountant maintains his independence will his reports continue to be accepted by businesses, financial institutions, and investors. Should the practitioner lose his reputation for independence in his auditing work, his opinion would become no more acceptable than the representations by management in statements which it has prepared.

There is also a "collective" aspect of independence that is important to the public accounting profession as a whole. The public accountant is not, as a rule, personally known to third parties, such as stockholders, who rely on his professional opinion, and such groups accept auditors' opinions principally on faith in the entire public accounting profession. Under these circumstances, public knowledge of one individual's failure to maintain his independence tends to produce suspicion and a lessening of faith in the independent audits of *all* public accountants. Although occasional lapses in independence have occurred, the over-all record of the public accounting profession in maintaining its independence in auditing matters is suggested by the fact that audited statements are being used and demanded on an ever-widening basis.

Not all services provided by public accountants require them to act independently. Services which do not require independence include designing and installing accounting systems, assistance in matters of budgeting and budgetary control, preparation of tax returns, tax consultation and tax planning, consultation on business problems, and preparation of records and statements for small businesses. In providing such services, the accountant is *expected* to place the interests of his client foremost.

The Difficulties of Remaining Independent

The extensive consideration given here to the subject of independence in audit engagements is necessitated by the fact that independence is so difficult to maintain. The auditor must remain independent of the business whose statements he is examining, and yet that business will normally have engaged the auditor and will pay his fee! In such a situation, the auditor must of necessity watch every step he takes as carefully as if he were on a tightrope.

Should the auditor become carried away by his zeal for independence, he may find his client cooperating to the extent of making him *completely* independent, and looking for a new auditor. On the other hand, there is always a natural desire to want to please a client, but moving too far in this direction may easily result in giving approval to statements which are actually misleading. Such a misstep is almost certain to be followed by a loss of reputation and eventually by a loss of clients. Thus, it may readily be seen that the auditor finds his independence much more difficult to maintain than does the internal revenue agent or the bank examiner, for neither of these need ever be fearful of losing a client.

That maintaining the proper degree of independence is worth the effort is illustrated by the story of the newcomer to the profession who obtained his first big engagement as a result of losing out on another engagement when he refused to sacrifice his independence. The lost engagement resulted when a leading member of a financial institution in the city, who had an interest in the business the young auditor was examining, insisted that the statements be shown in a certain way. When the auditor refused to approve the statements in the desired form and could not induce the financier to change his mind, there was little choice but to terminate the engagement.

The auditor was certain this disagreement had succeeded in creating a powerful enemy, and he was understandably surprised when the financier contacted him not long afterward and asked him to examine another enterprise in which he had an interest. It developed that this time the circumstances were different, and to protect best his interests the financier was seeking an accountant who he was certain could be relied upon to maintain his independence.

The above incident is related by John L. Carey, Executive Director of the American Institute of Certified Public Accountants, in an article appearing in *The Accounting Review*.* In the same article, Mr. Carey goes on to point out, however, that in the interest of preserving and expanding his practice the auditor will naturally wish to do anything within the limits of reason and propriety to please his client and that therefore a delicate balance must be maintained. He says:

> No young man should enter public accounting practice without having a clear idea of just how far he is willing to go in satisfying each client, to just what extent he may subordinate his personal preference, just how much he can compromise, and exactly at what point he is determined to refuse to go further with a polite statement of the reasons. This kind of attitude can be developed only from a thorough understanding of the ethical concepts of public accounting, reinforced by why it is in the ultimate self-interest of the individual practitioner to observe them.

In a sense, it appears that the independent auditor's difficulties arise from an attempt to serve two masters. The auditor must please his client, and at the same time he must be certain that his report can be relied upon with complete confidence by third parties who are interested in his client's statements. Needless to say, concern for these third parties must always be foremost. Should this group lose confidence in the auditor's reports,

* Vol. XXII, No. 2, April, 1947, p. 121.

the auditor is certain to begin losing clients, for the client engages the independent auditor primarily to satisfy these third parties.

Independence and the C.P.A.'s Code of Professional Ethics

Inasmuch as a loss of faith in one member of the profession reflects also on the profession as a whole, the profession has taken steps to induce practitioners to remain independent and to strengthen public confidence in the auditor's independence. The principal approach to the problem has been through the promulgation of a code of ethics by the American Institute of Certified Public Accountants. The resulting code is, of course, enforceable only against those C.P.A.'s who voluntarily hold membership in the Institute, but the code serves as a guide for the entire public accounting profession. The various state societies of Certified Public Accountants have generally patterned their codes after that of the Institute, and in . those states where the state board of accountancy is empowered to formulate and enforce rules of ethical conduct, the Institute rules have also been used as a guide.

These rules cannot, obviously, fully guarantee independence, because independence is primarily a state of mind. The rules do, however, compel the auditor to avoid situations in which he might be tempted to compromise his independence; in addition, they reassure the public that the auditor will avoid exposing himself to such temptation. The complete code is presented in the Appendix, to which the reader is referred for the following rules, which are directly concerned with fostering and preserving the auditor's independence:

Rule 1.01: Requires a member to be independent of a client if an opinion is expressed on the client's financial statements. Any direct financial interest or material indirect financial interest is prohibited, as is any relationship to the client, such as promoter, underwriter, voting trustee, director, officer, or key employee. This rule, which became effective January 1, 1964, represents an extension of a prior rule that referred only to the prohibition of a material financial interest, and brings the profession's position on independence closer to that of the SEC, as expressed in its rules.

Rule 1.04: Prohibits fee arrangements in which the fee is contingent upon the findings or results of the service. The rule specifically excepts matters involving taxes. The accountant may serve as his client's advocate in tax matters because the responsibility for the ultimate decision on tax matters rests with the taxing authority.

Rule 2.02: Holds a member to be guilty of an act discreditable to the profession if in expressing an opinion on financial statements he fails to disclose any known omission or misstatement of significant information in the statements, or fails to conduct an examination adequate to support his opinion. Such acts would carry a strong presumption that the individual was not acting independently.

Rule 4.04: Prohibits engagement in any business or occupation conjointly with public accounting that would be incompatible with public accounting. Thereby excluded on the basis of detracting from the diginity of the profession would be such activities as auctioneer or door-to-door solicitor, and excluded on the basis of jeopardizing the accountant's independence would be such occupations as stockbroker or investment counselor.

The Securities and Exchange Commission and Independence

The mistaken idea is quite widely held that the Securities Act of 1933 and Securities Exchange Act of 1934 were intended to protect investors from losses resulting from doubtful investments. Actually, there is no intent in these acts to protect investors from their own poor judgment, and any such attempt would be completely inconsistent with the operation of a free economic society. The primary purpose of the acts is to help assure investors that they have reliable information on which to base their investment decisions. This objective is accomplished by requiring companies planning to sell securities in interstate commerce to file registration statements with the SEC, and requiring companies listed on national securities exchanges, as well as certain other companies exceeding a specified size, to file annual reports with the Commission. The financial statements included in these filings must be accompanied by the report of an independent public accountant.

Although the Commission carefully reviews such statements for over-all adequacy and conformance with its rules and regulations, it relies on the opinion of the independent public accountant retained by the registered company for assurance of the validity and fairness of the statements. The responsibility for the adequacy of the examinations of such statements has wisely been allowed to remain with the individual accountants and their profession, but the SEC does insist firmly on the independence of the public accountant in each case. The pertinent paragraphs of Rule 2.01 of the Commission's *Regulation S-X* state:

(b) The Commission will not recognize any certified public accountant or public accountant as independent who is not in fact independent. For example, an accountant will be considered not independent with respect to any person or any of its parents or subsidiaries in whom he has, or had during the period of report, any direct financial interest or any material indirect financial interest; or with whom he is, or was during such period, connected as a promoter, underwriter, voting trustee, director, officer, or employee.

(c) In determining whether an accountant may in fact be not independent with respect to a particular person, the Commission will give appropriate consideration to all relevant circumstances, including evidence bearing on all relationships between the accountant and that person or any affiliate thereof, and will not confine itself to the relationships existing in connection with the filing of reports with the Commission.

Findings by the Commission of lack of independence in specific instances are summarized in its *Accounting Series Release No. 47* and *No. 81.* The concern of the Commission over the matter of independence may be judged from the fineness of the line drawn in holding the public accountant to be *not* independent in the following instances:

1. More than 1 per cent of the accountant's personal fortune was invested in the capital stock of his client.
2. The accountant was indemnified by his client against all losses, claims, and damages arising out of his certification of the client's statements.
3. Shares of the client's stock were pledged to guarantee payment of the accountant's fee, and the accountant was granted an option to purchase the pledged shares at the market price at the date of the option.
4. A partner of an accounting firm was serving on the board of directors of a registrant, but he did not participate in any way in the accounting firm's audit of the registrant.
5. The son of a partner of an accounting firm that certified the financial statements of a registrant was serving as assistant treasurer and chief accountant of the registrant.
6. A senior staff member of an accounting firm had supervised the audit of the registrant and was appointed as controller to serve while the regular controller was in the armed forces. The employee remained on the staff of the accounting firm but relinquished all responsibility for the audit of the registrant and did no work in connection with the audit.
7. An accountant took an option for shares of his client's common stock in settlement of his fee.
8. The wife of an accountant had a 47½ per cent interest in one of the three principal underwriters of a proposed issue by the registrant.

The SEC has held that an accountant cannot do bookkeeping work for a client filing reports with the commission if such work involves making decisions at a managerial level, but mere posting of transactions journalized by client employees will not disqualify the accountant for loss of independence.

Selection of the Auditor and Independence

The question of who should select and engage the independent auditor is also related to the matter of the auditor's independence. The responsibility for selection will normally rest with the client, but such a generalization is subject to exception. For instance, the small businessman seeking a bank loan may be requested to submit audited statements. If the businessman is unfamiliar with the public accounting firms serving the community, the banker is likely to suggest a firm which he prefers. Such a recommendation carries with it an additional incentive for the recommended firm to maintain its independence, because only by so doing can additional referrals be anticipated.

The prospective borrower, on the other hand, can rest assured that the accountant or firm to which he is referred is capable and of good reputation. The banker has no other basis for his recommendation, because Rule 3.04 of the Code of Professional Ethics prohibits the auditor from paying a commission to the banker for referring a client to him. Because there is no conflicting inducement, the banker's self-interest in obtaining a reliable report can be expected to rule.

There is a special problem concerning the method of selecting the auditor in the case of large corporations which regularly have an independent examination. At one time it was customary to have the president, treasurer, or some management group engage the auditor, but this arrangement placed the auditor somewhat in debt to the very persons whose work he would be reviewing in the course of his examination, and he would therefore be subject to pressure from them.

To strengthen the auditor's position and to assure stockholders and other third parties that the auditor is not likely to be subservient to management, many corporations have delegated the responsibility for engaging the auditor to the board of directors, as this group is further removed from the daily operations and management of the business. If a committee of the board of directors makes the selection, it will usually be specified that such committee not include any officers of the corporation who are serving on the board.

To give even greater protection to the stockholders, some corporations place final responsibility for the auditor's selection with the stockholders by having that group vote its approval or disapproval of the auditor nominated by the board of directors.

PROFESSIONAL ETHICS

The question of the self-imposed rules of ethical conduct of the accounting profession has already been introduced with reference to the vital question of independence in relation to services involving so-called third-party reliance. These rules pertaining to independence, as well as the balance of the twenty-one rules adopted by the A.I.C.P.A., serve the dual function of presenting a guide for the Certified Public Accountant in the conduct of his practice and holding up a standard by which the public can judge the stature of C.P.A.'s in general.

Broader acceptance of public accounting services is the ultimate result of the increased confidence engendered by public reaction to the manner in which members of the profession conduct themselves. There is also mutual advantage to both the public and the practitioner when the business-seeking practices of the commercial world are eliminated and the practitioner can concentrate on providing the best possible service to his clients without fear of encroachment on his practice by other accountants. Likewise eliminated is the distraction of having to seek new clients, when reputation rather than promotion serves as the key to a growing practice.

To accomplish these ends, other rules of conduct prohibit payment of referral commissions to persons who are not public accountants; require that examinations supporting a C.P.A.'s opinion on financial statements must be performed by the C.P.A., a partner or employee, or another C.P.A.; prohibit an accountant from permitting his name to be used in conjunction with any forecast contingent upon future transactions; restrict advertising and solicitation of clients; prohibit the practice of public accounting through a corporate organization; and restrict competitive bidding for engagements.

Still another group of rules deals with the public accountant's relations with his client and his fellow practitioners. These rules cover such points as the confidential relationship between the accountant and his client, the impropriety of accepting fees from persons who are not public accountants for work referred to them arising out of the accountant's services to his client, and the prohibition of direct offers of employment to employees of other public accountants.

The complete set of rules is given in the Appendix, and further discussion of many of these rules is presented at appropriate points throughout the text.

LEGAL LIABILITY

Although the usual fee relationship may, on occasion, result in the exertion of considerable pressure on the auditor to compromise his independence, the opposing pressures are even greater: protection of his reputation, responsibility to his profession, and legal liability in the event that a client or third parties incur losses as a result of relying on incorrect or misleading financial statements accompanied by his opinion. Legal liability may also result from factors other than loss of independence, and the entire matter of the auditor's legal liability is briefly presented here to provide adequate orientation.

In contracting to perform services for a client, the public accountant in effect represents that he is competent to provide any professional services he may agree to perform, and that he will perform them with due professional care and with honesty and forthrightness. The law expects the accountant to reinforce these representations by pledging his personal fortune as assurance against misrepresentation or wrongdoing. The A.I.C.P.A. Code of Professional Ethics furthers this concept of responsibility by providing, in Rule 4.06, that a member may not practice under corporate form, in this manner seeking to avoid full personal liability. State statutes may also bear on this point by prohibiting the chartering of a corporation to practice as a Certified Public Accountant.

The Auditor's Liability to His Client

In common with other professional practitioners, the accountant ordinarily acquires considerable information about his client, and this information should not be disclosed to others. The client's engagement of the accountant establishes a fiduciary relationship which would be breached by the disclosure of confidential information to another party, and the law imposes a liability on the practitioner for any loss or damage incurred by a client resulting from a breach of this fiduciary relationship. The auditor may also create a liability to his client if he is negligent in the performance of an engagement. The law requires that a practitioner must exercise due professional care in the performance of work for his client, but whether a practitioner has been negligent and thereby committed a breach of contract raises a difficult legal question in that negligence is often difficult to distinguish from an error in judgment. The problem is aptly set forth in *Cooley on Torts,* a leading authority on such matters:

> In all those employments where peculiar skill is requisite, if one offers his services, he is understood as holding himself out to the public as possessing the degree of skill commonly possessed by others in the same employment, and if his pretensions are unfounded, he commits a species of fraud upon every man who employs him in reliance on his public profession. But no man, whether skilled or unskilled, undertakes that the task he assumes shall be performed successfully, and without fault or error; he undertakes for good faith and integrity, but not for infallibility, and he is liable to his employer for negligence, bad faith or dishonesty, but not for losses consequent upon mere errors of judgment.*

Client charges of negligence against the accountant may arise in various ways in conjunction with the provision of auditing services, but will usually involve failure by the accountant to detect fraud or other misstatements in the accounts or financial statements. For instance, an employee may have embezzled funds and attempted to conceal the shortage by means of fraudulent ledger entries. A situation of this type raises two independent questions: first, when the accountant is engaged to examine a concern's financial statements and express his opinion on the statements, does he assume any responsibility for the detection of fraud in the accounts, and second, should the fraud have been detected by his examination if it was made in accordance with generally accepted auditing standards?

* Thomas M. Cooley, *Cooley on Torts,* 4th ed. revised by D. Avery Haggard. Chicago: Callaghan, 1932, III, 335.

As to the first point, the Committee on Auditing Procedure of the A.I.C.P.A. has stated:

> In making the ordinary examination, the independent auditor is aware of the possibility that fraud may exist. Financial statements may be misstated as the result of defalcations and other similar irregularities, or deliberate misrepresentation by management, or both. The auditor recognizes that fraud, if sufficiently material, may affect his opinion on the financial statements, and his examination, made in accordance with generally accepted auditing standards, gives consideration to this possibility. However, the ordinary examination directed to the expression of an opinion on financial statements is not primarily or specifically designed, and cannot be relied upon, to disclose defalcations and other similar irregularities, although their discovery may result. Similarly, although the discovery of deliberate misrepresentation by management is usually more closely associated with the objective of the ordinary examination, such examination cannot be relied upon to assure its discovery. The responsibility of the independent auditor for failure to detect fraud (which responsibility differs as to clients and others) arises only when such failure clearly results from failure to comply with generally accepted auditing standards.*

From these comments, it is apparent that the detection of fraud is incidental to the primary purpose of the usual audit examination, but on the other hand, failure to adhere to generally accepted auditing standards could cause fraud to be overlooked. If the client, through expert witnesses, could demonstrate that the fraud would have been found had generally accepted auditing standards been followed, then the auditor's negligence would constitute a breach of the "due professional care" obligation of the contract between the auditor and the client. Under these circumstances, the auditor would be liable for damages to the client for the amount of defalcation occurring *after* the auditor should first have discovered the manipulation. Recovery of such damages will ordinarily be limited, however, to the amount of the auditor's fee, on the assumption that the client would have been in no better position had no audit been made.

Another situation in which the contract with the client imposes upon the auditor a legal duty to his client to exercise due professional care arises when the auditor is engaged to examine the financial statements of a business which the client proposes to purchase. The purchase price would be based, at least in part, on the audited statements, and if the statements subsequently are proved to be misleading or incorrect, the client would have a right to recover his attendant losses—provided, of course, that he could establish negligence on the auditor's part by showing that the auditor's examination was not made in accordance with generally accepted auditing standards. Liability may also arise from the giving of faulty tax advice.

These questions of legal liability to the auditor's client for negligence suggest the following observations. The auditor's first duty is really to

* *Auditing Standards and Procedures,* p. 10.

himself, and if he is satisfied that his work has been performed in accordance with the highest standards of his profession, he should be able to remain free of legal entanglements. An interesting corollary to this concept of first duty to self is that if the auditor's work is of such high quality that legal hazards are effectively avoided, the auditor has provided his client with the best possible service!

The Auditor's Liability to Third Parties

Third parties who rely on the auditor's opinion have more limited right of action in recovering losses than does the client, because no contractual relationship exists between these third parties and the auditor. There is no contract binding the auditor to the careful performance of his duties. Consequently, third parties are not entitled to recovery of losses from the auditor if the cause of the loss was negligence on the part of the auditor in making his examination.

Fraud and gross negligence are the usual bases for action by third parties against an auditor. Obviously the auditor should be liable if in expressing his opinion fraud is present in the form of an intent to deceive others, and the courts have carried such liability one step further to include gross negligence as well. The basis of reasoning here is that if the auditor expresses an opinion when actually there is no basis for an opinion, or if the basis is so flimsy as to lead to the conclusion that the auditor had no real belief in his opinion, then the auditor's negligence has been gross enough to support an inference of fraud (constructive fraud), even though intent to deceive has not actually been proven. Under such circumstances, injured parties who relied on the auditor's opinion would be entitled to damages to the full extent of their losses.

One of the landmarks in the development of the auditor's liability for negligence is *Ultramares Corporation v. Touche* (255 N.Y. 170, 174 N.E. 441–1931). The accountants had supplied their client with thirty-two copies of their report, aware in a general way that these would be shown to banks and other creditors. In ruling that the accountants owed no duty to such third parties to perform their examination without negligence, the Court of Appeals stated in a decision written by Justice Cardozo:

> Our holding does not emancipate accountants from the consequences of fraud. It does not relieve them if their audit has been so negligent as to justify a finding that they had no genuine belief in its adequacy, for this again is fraud. It does no more than say that, if less than this is proved, if there has been neither reckless misstatement nor insincere profession of an opinion, but only honest blunder, the ensuing liability for negligence is one that is bounded by the contract, and is to be enforced between the parties by whom the contract has been made. We doubt whether the average business man receiving a certificate without paying for it, and receiving it merely as one among a multitude of possible investors would look for anything more.

The final sentence of the above quotation suggests that the accountant's position may be different if he has knowledge that his audit is being performed for the primary benefit of a third party. English courts have recognized such liability in *Hedley Byrne & Co. Ltd. v. Heller & Partners Ltd.* (1963), but in the United States such liability to third parties is a matter of dictum, for no case has been decided with that particular point at issue.

For further information on the legal liability of accountants and auditors, the reader is referred to Chapter 6 of *C.P.A. Handbook* or *Accountants' Legal Responsibility*, both by Saul Levy and published by the A.I.C.P.A.

Liability Under the Federal Securities Acts

The Securities Act of 1933 wrought, in the form of statutory law, amazing changes in the public accountant's liability in connection with statements certified for a registered company, as compared with his liability under the common law. The effect of these statutes is summarized by Saul Levy:[*]

1. Any person acquiring securities described in the Registration Statement may sue the accountant, regardless of the fact that he is not the client of the accountant.
2. His claim may be based upon an alleged false statement or misleading omission in the financial statements, which constitutes his prima facie case. The plaintiff does not have the further burden of proving that the accountants were negligent or fraudulent in certifying to the financial statements involved.
3. The plaintiff does not have to prove that he relied upon the statement or that the loss which he suffered was the proximate result of the falsity or misleading character of the financial statement.
4. The accountant has thrust upon him the burden of establishing his freedom from negligence and fraud by proving that he had, after reasonable investigation, reasonable ground to believe and did believe that the financial statements to which he certified, were true not only as of the date of the financial statements, but beyond that, as *of the time when the Registration Statement became effective.*
5. The accountant has the burden of establishing by way of defense or in reduction of alleged damages, that the loss of the plaintiff resulted in whole or in part from causes other than the false statements or the misleading omissions in the financial statements. Under the common law it would have been the plaintiff's affirmative case to prove that the damages which he claims he sustained were proximately caused by the negligence or fraud of the accountant.

The accountant's liability under the Securities Exchange Act of 1934, arising in connection with the filing of annual reports with the Commission, differs from liability under the Securities Act of 1933 in that

[*] *C.P.A. Handbook.* New York: American Institute of Certified Public Accountants, 1952, Chapter 6, p. 39.

there is no provision extending the accountant's liability to an "effective date." Also, the plaintiff must prove that he relied on the financial statements and that such reliance was the cause of his damages. The accountant, in turn, does not have to prove the absence of negligence; he may simply prove that he acted in good faith and had no knowledge that the statements were false or misleading.

It should be noted that these laws concern only purchasers or owners of securities issued by registered companies; other creditors of such companies and owners or purchasers of securities of nonregistered companies must seek satisfaction under the common law discussed in the prior section.

Accountants' Liability Insurance

As has already been suggested, the accountant's first line of defense against damage claims by clients or third parties is the quality of the services he renders. High personal standards, an independent approach to audit engagements, careful supervision and review of work delegated to employees, and alertness and imagination in the performance of services for the public are indispensable because they can prevent claims from ever arising. Nevertheless, the tendency is toward increased legal responsibility for public accountants, and actual or threatened legal actions, coupled with the tendency of uninformed persons to consider the accountant's opinion as a guarantee, are an ever-present source of concern for the practitioner.

To protect himself from unwarranted claims by others, as well as from the ever-present possibility of a slip or blunder or faulty decision on the part of himself or an employee, the public accountant is well-advised to secure the protection offered by accountants' liability insurance. Such insurance protects the accountant against direct monetary loss arising out of claims related to services he has provided, as well as the legal costs of defending himself against real or alleged deficiencies in his work.

TESTING AND THE THEORY OF PROBABILITY

Auditing procedures are seldom applied to all items of a given type or class. The audit of every transaction is not only impractical from an economic point of view, but quite unnecessary if management has properly assumed its primary responsibility for the accuracy of the accounting records. Under these circumstances, effective internal control should assure the desired accuracy, and the auditor can obtain adequate evidence to support his opinion by limiting his examination to tests of the system of internal control and of the basic evidence underlying the financial statements.

The justification for accepting the results of a test in lieu of verification of each item lies in the theory of probability. The theory states, in effect, that a sample selected from a series of items will tend to evidence the same characteristics present in the full series of items, which is commonly referred to as the "population" or "universe." This tendency of the sample to evidence the characteristics of the population increases as the size of the sample increases and is expressed numerically in various probability tables and computations, such as Poisson's Distribution.

There is much misunderstanding outside mathematical and statistical circles about the relationship of sample size to probability. The usual assumption is that the probable correspondence between the sample and the population varies primarily with the relationship of the sample size to the total population. For instance, if samples of 100 are selected from a population of 1,000 items with 2 per cent of the items in error, about 90 per cent of those samples will show no more than 3 per cent errors and no less than 1 per cent errors. Many persons would assume that to get similar results from samples drawn from a population of 5,000, the samples would have to consist of 500 items, or 10 per cent of the population (as in the preceding case). Actually, a sample of 100 drawn from the population of 5,000 will give almost as accurate a picture as a sample of 100 drawn from a population of 1,000. Conversely, samples of 500 drawn from the population of 5,000 will actually give a considerably more accurate picture than will the samples of 100 drawn from the population of 1,000.

The brief and relatively general comments that follow relative to testing and the theory of probability are intended only to introduce the subject and provide the reader with a minimum basis for working with the problem as it arises in the examination of the various segments of the financial statements. For a more extensive development of the problem of sampling, and the statistical considerations involved when sampling is conducted on a scientific basis, the reader is referred to Chapter 26.

Selecting the Items for the Sample

There are a variety of ways of selecting the items for inclusion in a sample, each of which has certain advantages and disadvantages. The block method of selection is a favorite of long standing with auditors because it is the simplest method to apply. When the population from which the sample is drawn is arranged chronologically, as is true of entries in a journal, the selection will merely cover all entries occurring within a specified period of time, such as a week or a month. If the population is arranged alphabetically (an accounts receivable ledger), or numerically (a file of work orders), then the selection may be specified as all accounts from H through K, or all work orders from 1,950 through 1,975. The disadvantage of a block sample is that it does not give all items an equal chance of being selected, and hence can give a meaningful answer only about the items in the selected block. The mere fact that the examination of all checks drawn in April revealed no discrepancies offers very little basis for concluding that the checks drawn in October are likewise free of discrepancy. Similiarly, the correctness of all accounts from H through K does not represent very strong proof that the accounts from T through Z are also correct, particularly if these accounts are posted by a different bookkeeper.

Statisticians insist that a sample can be properly used to estimate the characteristics of the population from which it was drawn only if the sample is representative of the entire population. Representativeness, they maintain, can be reasonably achieved only by random selection of items for the sample. To obtain a truly random sample, each item in the population must be numbered, and then a table of random numbers (statistically proven for randomness) used to select the items to be included in the test. For auditing purposes, however, random selection is likely to be cumbersome and time-consuming when compared with other methods of selection, particularly when the population is not arranged in numerical sequence.

A fairly good approximation of randomness can be obtained, however, by the use of systematic or interval selection of the items, and the method will ordinarily be much easier and quicker to apply than true random selection. The method involves the selection of every Nth item in a series, where the value of N is determined by dividing the total number of items in the population by the number of items to be included in the sample. Thus, in a sample of 100 to be selected from a population of 1,500 sales transactions, every fifteenth transaction would be selected.

Still another commonly used type of sample is the stratified sample. This type of sample is designed to give the auditor greater assurance that the material items in the population are correctly stated. The stratification is made by selecting a breaking point and verifying all amounts larger than the breaking point and testing those less than the breaking point. Thus, the auditor's instructions might be, "Examine all disbursements of $500 or more and examine every twentieth disbursement under $500."

Testing and the Disclosure of Fraud

The preceding discussion of the auditor's use of testing techniques should remind the reader of the statement made earlier that the auditor's examination of a client's financial statements cannot be relied upon to detect fraud in the accounts in all cases. When fraud is present, but the number of fraudulent items is so small that the statements are not materially affected, there can be no significant assurance that any of the fraudulent items will appear in the auditor's sample or be otherwise detected. However, as the percentage of incorrect or fraudulent items is increased, the probability that one such item will appear in the auditor's sample is likewise increased.

Samples should always be large enough and so chosen that in any situation in which the statements are materially affected there will be a good probability that at least one of the fraudulent transactions will appear in the sample.

As the auditor's examination may bring him in contact with only a single spurious item or transaction, even though several are present in the records, the need should be readily apparent for extreme care in examining or verifying each item. Carelessness in reviewing but a single item could well be the cause of failing to detect existing fraud. Subsequent disclosure of the fraud by other means would not only be embarrassing to the auditor but might also result in a legal liability.

The presence of just one error or questionable item should be cause for considerable further investigation. If such investigation shows that the error resulted from an honest mistake, and there is adequate assurance that such mistakes have not been frequent, the matter may be dropped. But any indication that fraud was involved or that errors may have materially distorted a final figure should be cause for an immediate discussion with the appropriate representative of the client before proceeding further. One of the major purposes for such a discussion should be to determine whether the auditor or the client is to ferret out the particular difficulty. If the auditor is to do the work, the client should understand that such work will increase the fee for the engagement.

Size of the Audit Sample

Yet to be discussed is perhaps the single most troublesome problem in the use of tests, or samples—how large the sample should be in order that the auditor may be satisfied that "*sufficient* competent evidential matter" has been obtained. As sample size is increased, the reliability of the conclusions drawn from the sample likewise increases; but so does the cost of securing the sample. The cost may seem unimportant to the auditor in that the client pays the bill, but auditing services will continue to be used only if it is economically feasible to do so, and furthermore, every client can be assumed to be extremely cost conscious. If the auditor's timidity induces him to select large, comforting samples, the resulting excessive cost of the examination is likely to become apparent to the client, and he will seek the services of other auditors who can perform a competent examination for less cost.

Traditionally, the size of audit samples has been determined solely on the basis of the auditor's judgment of how much testing is enough. In a sense, the determination of sample size has been one of the true arts of the profession. As with other arts, there are basic principles to be considered in designing the finished work, but no formal devices have been used to lessen in any way the judgmental process involved. The auditor would no more think of using any device that would lessen his prerogatives in his sampling work than would the landscape painter think of using a color chart as a guide in mixing his pigments!

In recent years, however, considerable attention has been devoted to the proposition that the art of sampling can actually be improved in many instances with the assistance of scientific techniques. Considerable experimentation has been conducted in the application of statistical measurement to the factors of confidence and precision and the relationship of these factors to sample size, but discussion of these developments is deferred until Chapter 26.

Factors That Affect Sample Size

There are three nonstatistical factors that the auditor considers in reaching his decision on sample size: materiality, relative risk, and the reliability of the evidence being sampled. The melding of these factors in sample size determination is truly a professional skill, developed through training, experience, and the interchange of ideas with other members of the profession. The following pages, and frequent references to the factors in subsequent chapters, are intended to provide a general understanding of the approach to the determination of sample size, but the best guide to the problem in a specific situation is the series of auditing case studies published by the American Institute of Certified Public Accountants. Each study describes what some accounting firm actually did in making an audit of a specific business. All the pertinent details about the business are given, including financial statements and a description of the accounting system and internal control. This material is followed by a detailed account of the audit procedures actually employed by the auditor, including the extent of any samples when tests were made.

Although the conditions presented in each case are not likely to be duplicated in even a similar business in the same field, the reader can determine what was done in a given case and what factors governed the auditor's decisions. Then, faced with the problem of preparing an audit of a similar business, the reader can take any variations into account and modify the procedures to fit the changed conditions.

Materiality

The greater the relative significance of an item in the financial statements, the greater is the auditor's concern that the item is fairly stated. Factory supplies, for instance, would tend to be fairly constant in terms of quantities used and quantities on hand, and even if the dollar figure for unused supplies at the end of the year were grossly misstated, the effect on the cost of goods sold, net income, and current and total assets would be negligible. Under these circumstances, the auditor's tests of the year-end inventory of supplies would tend to be relatively limited, but the tests of the production inventories would be much more extensive. A 10 per cent misstatement of the production inventories, in contrast to a similar percentage misstatement of the supplies inventories, would have a much more significant effect on the financial statements, and the auditor would therefore seek to obtain greater assurance of the accuracy of the final figure for production inventories by making more extensive tests. Although it might seem that the larger sample size for the tests of production inventories would be necessary because more items are involved, this possibility is refuted by the proposition already presented, that the reliability of a sample is primarily a question of the absolute size of the sample, rather than its size relative to the total population of items.

Materiality may also be affected by factors other than the relative size of the figures involved. An understatement of accounts payable would tend to be more material than an understatement of the liability for pension payments, even though the same amount of misstatement were involved. The reason, of course, would be that the accounts payable figure would enter into a determination of the concern's current position and current ratio, whereas the pension liability would be discharged over an extended period of time, with the major portion of the amount to be paid more than a year after the balance sheet date. The misstatement of the pension amount would thus have less bearing on the ability of the concern to remain solvent by discharging liabilities maturing in the near future.

Although each item is judged in terms of materiality on its own basis, there is also a cumulative effect when the auditor differs with the client over the amounts at which a number of items are to be stated. If, for instance, the auditor's tests reveal an overstatement of inventory in the amount of $1,530, an overstatement of prepaid insurance of $625, and an understatement of accrued taxes of $1,780, each of these differences might well be adjudged as immaterial in relation to a net income of $30,000. The cumulative effect of these differences on net income would be another matter, since correction of all three items would reduce the income figure by $3,935.

There is no simple test or standard which can be applied in determining materiality, nor can one ever be devised, because the variables are different in each situation. The decision in each situation must be based on the pertinent relationships as determined by the professional judgment of the auditor. An important consideration here would be whether the effect of the questionable treatment of an item would be sufficient to cause an investor to buy or sell, cause a banker to make a loan, or to call or extend an existing obligation, or cause a customer or vendor to establish, discontinue, or resume relations. The ability to judge soundly in such situations so that every decision corresponds with what other auditors would decide under the same circumstances can come only from adequate training and experience, coupled with full knowledge of current thinking in the profession and the business world as well.

Relative Risk

Another factor that should influence the size of the auditor's sample is the relative risk that a figure might be misstated. Cash, for example, is subject to considerable risk of misstatement through fraud or manipulation as compared with such an item as plant or equipment. As a consequence, tests of cash transactions are likely to be more extensive than those of plant and equipment transactions, and more time may be devoted to the examination of cash than to plant and equipment, even though the latter item may be more material in relation to total assets.

The factor of internal control is also closely related to the question of relative risk and sample size. When accounts receivable or other assets are accounted for under good conditions of internal control, there is less risk that the figures may be incorrect than if internal control is inadequate. Relative risk may also be affected by general circumstances lying entirely outside the accounting system. The desire of management to minimize income taxes often leads to efforts to understate the income of an enterprise, and the situation is particularly aggravated if a change in income tax rates is anticipated. Indication of a decrease in tax rates would make it advantageous for a company to defer income in order that it be taxed at the lower rate in the following year, and the auditor should accordingly increase his vigilance and the extent of his tests in connection with accounts that might readily be manipulated to effect a decrease in net income in the year prior to the tax change.

Other possibilities that may enter into the risk that figures may be misstated would include a very weak financial position, a net loss for the year, or excessive profits for a year. The risk would be even greater in the latter instance if the company's union contract were scheduled to expire in the following year and the union had an established policy of bargaining in relation to the principle of "ability to pay." A complete change of management may also have a bearing on relative risk. There is an understandable tendency under these circumstances for the new management to be excessively diligent in recognizing losses and writing down assets as much as possible in the first year of operation. The losses can be attributed to the failings of the predecessor management group, and the way is then eased for reporting higher profits in following years as a result of reduced expense charges on the assets that have been written down.

An examination of financial statements in connection with the sale of a business is likewise fraught with inherent risks. The seller, who has primary responsibility for the financial statements and has a personal interest in showing the best possible picture, may have engaged in practices ranging from deciding all questionable items in his favor to outright fraud in the preparation of the accounting records and statements. The auditor should always be alert to such possibilities.

Competence of Evidence

Another factor to be considered in terms of its effect on the auditor's sample and the significance of the conclusions derived from the sample is the reliability of the evidence to be tested. If the reliability is low, the auditor's sample can be expanded in partial compensation, or supplementary tests of other related forms of evidence may be instituted. The auditor must determine the competence of the evidence he consults in the course of his examination much as Mother must in determining whether or not Junior has followed her instructions to wash his hands and face. In the domestic situation, the best evidence is obviously the actual witnessing of the dire deed, whereas the least competent evidence is Junior's solemn assertion that he did so wash his hands and face. Evidence falling somewhere between these two extremes would probably include hearing the water splashing in the bathroom and inspecting Junior's towel for dirty smudges.

Evidence available to the auditor also varies in reliability, and the auditor must constantly be aware of the relative reliability of the evidence he consults in the process of arriving at a basis for the expression of his opinion on the client's financial statements. Various classifications of evidence are presented in the following pages, together with a discussion of the relative reliability of each type of evidence and the factors affecting the reliability. The classifications are intended to serve only as a guide to the question of reliability, however. In all situations, the circumstances surrounding any particular items of evidence must be considered in reaching a conclusion about the reliability of the evidence.

Primary Evidence

The source of the figures in a concern's financial statements is the general ledger, which in turn receives its figures from the various journals, and it is these books of record that constitute the primary evidence in support of the financial statements. The auditor must, therefore, be certain that the statements agree with the ledger, and he must, in turn, satisfy himself that the figures in the ledger originated from the various journals. Ascertaining the agreement of the statements and the ledger balances is a relatively simple matter in view of the small number of figures ordinarily involved, but the many postings to the ledger in each month of the year present a more difficult problem. Closely related to this problem is the addition of the figures listed in the ledger and journals to arrive at balances and monthly totals.

Clearly, the solution is not complete verification of all footings and postings made during the year—but if the work is to be tested, how extensive should the test be? The answer here lies in the matter of internal control. Good internal control should assure both the client and the auditor that the work has been performed properly and accurately. The double-entry system itself, the balancing of subsidiary ledgers and control accounts, the cross-footing of journals, the use of bookkeeping equipment with built-in error-sensing devices, the division of responsibility for various phases of the work, and the work of the internal auditor, all have a direct bearing on the reliability of the records. In the case of large clients having excellent systems of internal control that the auditor is satisfied are actually working as planned, the auditor may well conclude that it is unnecessary to make *any* tests of postings and footings *per se*. He will, however, make other tests of the significant ledger balances, such as confirmation of accounts receivable through correspondence with customers, to help satisfy himself that the figures are fairly stated.

By contrast, if the client's organization is small and internal control correspondingly weak, the auditor may verify the footings and postings for several months to satisfy himself that the work has been correctly performed. In either situation, once the auditor is satisfied as to the agreement of the statements with the primary evidence in the form of the ledger and journals, he is in a position to look to the propriety, validity, and accuracy of the ledger balances and the entries in the journals. The evidence pertaining to these matters is considered to be supporting evidence, of which there are many types, varying greatly in reliability.

Supporting Evidence

The amount of supporting evidence to be consulted by the auditor in corroboration of the books of record will be in inverse relation to the internal control that entered into the preparation of those records. The wide variation in the reliability of such supporting evidence makes it extremely important that each form of such evidence be carefully weighed to ascertain its true significance. The basic types of supporting evidence are discussed below in the approximate order of their reliability, commencing with the strongest forms.

Physical evidence. The physical evidence classification is somewhat limited in that such evidence exists only in support of the so-called tangible assets, such as inventory and plant and equipment. Cash on hand is also included in the tangible classification for purposes of this discussion, although in the realm of property taxation all forms of cash are usually treated as intangible assets.

Although it should be evident that actual examination of a given asset is the best possible evidence that the asset exists, all physical evidence is not equally reliable. Counting the cash on hand would appear to be adequate evidence of the correctness of the corresponding ledger balance, but the evidence is not fully conclusive if customers' checks are included in the total. Coin and currency may be quite safely accepted at their face, as counterfeiting is quite difficult and rather effectively discouraged. A check, on the other hand, is not only easily counterfeited, but even if authentic may prove to be backed by insufficient funds. Consequently, a check should be further supported by evidence that the check was deposited and that the bank was able to collect the full amount. Even coins and currency may be questionable evidence under certain circumstances, as for instance if there are several separate cash funds maintained in separate locations. If the auditor does not take proper precautions, he may be misled into believing that he has accounted for the full amount of cash called for by the ledger, when in fact he may have counted the same coins and currency several times at different locations!

The physical goods supporting an inventory figure may also prove to be less than perfect evidence. Flasks of "rare perfume" may actually be only toilet water, or even less, and a storage area containing the exact number of television sets called for by the records may prove to be only a half-truth if the sets are defective, although carried at their full cost in the inventory. In another vein, an independent diamond expert's written report on the weight and quality of a packet of stones may be better evidence than the auditor's own examination of the gems. By contrast, if a major portion of a client's inventory is stored in a public warehouse, the auditor may conclude that he should visit the warehouse and gain physical contact with the goods, even though a warehouse receipt for the goods is available for inspection and the auditor could also obtain a written statement from the warehouse confirming the quantity of goods in storage for the client.

Documentary evidence. The type of evidence most commonly referred to by the auditor is documentary evidence. Documents vary widely in terms of their reliability as evidence, however, and further classification of documentary evidence is necessary to provide a clue as to its reliability. One important basis of classification is whether the source of the document is internal or external; that is, whether it was prepared within the client's organization or by someone who is independent of the client. Internal evidence may be further classified in relation to the degree of protection incorporated in its preparation.

Externally created documents sent directly to the auditor. If documents prepared by third parties are sent directly to the auditor, they ordinarily constitute evidence of a degree of reliability approaching that of physical evidence, or even exceeding the reliability of physical evidence, as in the case of the diamonds mentioned above. Such externally prepared documents lose part of their reliability if they pass through the client's organization before the auditor inspects them, as there is always a possibility that the documents may have been altered or replaced by fictitious documents.

Extreme caution must be exercised whenever the auditor plans to rely on documentary evidence. This point may be illustrated by reference to the use of external evidence in the verification of accounts receivable. The best indication of the validity of an account is to have the debtor confirm in writing to the auditor the amount which the debtor owes to the auditor's client. In requesting such confirmation, the auditor not only asks that the reply be sent directly to him, but also he encloses a return envelope addressed to him to be used for the reply. In addition, the auditor should verify the address to which the confirmation request is to be mailed to guarantee the authenticity of the reply. The possibility is always present that a fictitious account might be carried under the name of a well-known and reputable firm, but with an incorrect address given. This address would be one to which the person responsible for creating the fictitious account would have access so that he could then respond to the auditor's request with a fraudulent reply indicating that the balance shown by the client's records was correct. The effect of this sequence of events would be that the auditor would fail to detect the overstatement of accounts receivable.

Externally created documents in the client's possession. The possibility that externally created documents which are in the client's possession may be fictitious or altered should not be taken to suggest that such documents are valueless as evidence. They are substantially more reliable than documents originating within the client's organization, and items such as bank statements and vendors' invoices constitute two of the most widely used forms of evidence.

Two considerations should always be kept in mind when the auditor makes use of such evidence. First, the document should be noted for an over-all appearance of authenticity, and any alterations should be carefully investigated. Although it is not good practice for a business to send out papers on which corrections have been made, corrections do occasionally appear. The auditor's responsibility is, of course, to determine whether an alteration is a correction made to rectify an unintentional error which occurred when the document was prepared, or whether the alteration was made at a later date for the purpose of misleading subsequent users of the document.

The second consideration in relying on evidence of the class under discussion is the relative ease with which a document may be counter-feited. A note receivable is likely to be extremely weak in this respect, because notes are commonly executed on forms available at any bank or stationery store, and the maker's signature is the only distinguishing feature. As the auditor is not a handwriting expert, nor expected to be one, a counterfeit note could be readily prepared and passed off to the auditor as being authentic. The need for further supplementary evidence under such circumstances is obvious, and confirmation of the validity of the note by correspondence with the debtor is in order.

In contrast to the note receivable, a bond or stock certificate is quite commonly accepted on its face. Only a specialist can accomplish the intricate engraving of the certificate, and such specialists are ordinarily quite careful to accept business only from sources known to be authentic. Furthermore, the asset being verified and the certificate evidencing the asset gain additional reliability through the regulation of the exchanges and brokers through which securities are traded, as well as the precautionary measures instituted by the exchanges themselves. About halfway between the note receivable and the engraved certificate in relative difficulty of counterfeiting and substitution is the vendor's invoice. Such a document would have to be specially printed, as against the note form which can be purchased already printed, but the average printer in a large city would not be likely to be as careful about investigating his customer as would the engraver.

Evidence originating within the client's organization. The auditor obtains a considerable proportion of the evidence he needs from sources within the client's organization. Such evidence may be verbal, as is likely in connection with the review of internal control, but preferably and more frequently it will be documentary. In either case the evidence is likely to be less reliable than the classes of evidence previously discussed, for two reasons. First, the employees giving the information or preparing the documents are under the direct control of management, and therefore the evidence may not be fully acceptable in attempting to corroborate the representations of management. Second, if a defalcation has occurred, information given by employees or documents prepared by them may be falsified in an effort to conceal any manipulations relating to the defalcation.

Internal evidence circulating outside the business. In spite of the limitations, however, in some instances evidence from internal sources may approach the reliability of externally created documents. For instance, a paid check bearing evidence of having passed through the bank is generally considered to be fairly conclusive evidence that a liability has been paid, that an expense has been incurred, or that the cost of a new asset has been properly shown in the records.

There are several reasons why a paid check may be considered as having a high degree of competence as evidence. Because cash is the most liquid of assets, there will normally be relatively good internal control in the handling of cash including its disbursement by check. The assurance of validity created by the presence of good internal control is further enhanced by the fact that a paid check has passed through the hands of persons outside the originating organization, presumably with no objection having been raised concerning the correctness of the check. Finally, the paid check gains in reliability through the opportunity of being tied in with the bank statement, which is externally created.

Only a few internally created documents are subject to any outside review, and none of them has as many protective features as does the paid check, particularly with respect to the limited availability of blank forms and the difficulty of making alterations. Other documents would include a copy of a purchase order returned with the vendor's acknowledgement, a copy of a bill of lading receipted by the carrier's agent, and a bank deposit slip showing a teller's stamp to indicate that the funds had been receive.

Internal evidence circulating only within the business. Many internal forms and records, even though not receiving the additional validation accruing to such documents which circulate outside the business, may still have a high degree of reliability, with internal control the determining factor. The internal control may be in the form of extensive review of the document by other employees after it is prepared, or segregation of duties so that the person preparing the document has no operating responsibility and therefore no reason for preparing a misleading document or giving misleading verbal information. A good illustration is a receiving report prepared in the receiving department. The report will be compared in the accounting department with the company copy of the purchase order for the material and with the vendor's invoice, and will be reviewed again when the invoice is paid by the treasurer's office. A work-order authorization created by a management committee, used by the accounting department to accumulate costs related to the order, and used as the directive to the maintenance department to do the work, is another illustration of a document receiving the benefit of good internal control measures.

On the other hand, an authorization created by the credit manager directing the bookkeeper to write off an uncollectible account is of limited value as evidence, because the bookkeeper would not be expected to make a critical review of the authorization. But the situation is greatly changed if the credit manager sends the authorization to a member of the controller's staff for approval, along with a copy of the customer's ledger sheet, a record of the collection action which has been taken, and any related correspondence. The controller's representative can act with full freedom because there is no direct line of responsibility between him and the credit manager. He is not likely to approve the authorization unless it is valid, as he would have no reason to do otherwise, having no access to any cash.

Verbal information and written certificates. When the purpose in obtaining verbal information or written certificates from employees is to corroborate data obtained from other sources, the evidence may well be quite satisfactory. A repair man, traveling outside the home office with a complete inventory of repair parts, may be requested to send the auditor a certificate listing the repair parts in his possession. Such a certificate is of little value as evidence that the repair man actually has the listed parts in his possession. On the other hand, if the information in the certificate is desired to verify home office records showing the amount of parts inventory charged out to the repair man, and the repair man is fully accountable for the value of those parts, the worth of the certificate as evidence would be considerably greater. To further illustrate the point, a verbal or written statement from the credit manager indicating the loss he anticipated from accounts receivable included in the balance sheet would hardly be a sound basis for determining the adequacy of the provision for bad debt losses. But if the auditor had already aged the accounts receivable and arrived at his own estimate of the possible loss, and the estimate of the credit manager was in line with the auditor's estimate, the auditor should be entitled to additional confidence in the credit manager's estimate, and his own as well.

To summarize briefly, the important factors affecting the reliability of internal evidence are (1) whether the documents have circulated through the hands of outside parties, (2) whether good internal control was involved in the preparation and use of documents, and (3) whether the evidence obtained must stand alone or serves to corroborate other information.

Circumstantial evidence. Those forms of evidence already presented represent direct evidence that may be consulted in the process of examining financial statements, but circumstantial evidence, which is a form of indirect evidence, is also quite important and useful. Circumstantial evidence involves circumstances from which a reasonable inference can be drawn of the occurrence of a given fact. More directly in the realm of auditing, it involves circumstances that support an inference as to the reasonableness or correctness of a given figure in a client's financial statements, or of the financial statements as a whole. Some of the forms of circumstantial evidence that the auditor commonly considers in the course of his examination include:

1. The system of internal control.
2. The general orderliness and neatness of the client's records, storage areas, and production areas.
3. The qualifications and ability of the persons responsible for supervising and maintaining the accounting records.
4. The absence of any known or apparent reason to misstate figures in the financial statements.
5. The reasonableness of the financial statement figures in relation to general economic conditions, industry trends, and known changes within the client's own organization and operation.
6. The outward consistency of the financial statement figures in relation to each other and to prior years, as in the case of the percentage of gross margin, the percentage of various expenses to sales, the number of days' sales outstanding, and the turnover of inventories.

Circumstantial evidence is perhaps most widely considered in the examination of the statements of our large, quasi-public, industrial organizations and public utilities. The mass of detailed evidence existing in such concerns is so great that it makes extensive examination of the evidence economically unsound, and the strong circumstantial evidence available makes extensive reference to such detailed evidence completely unnecessary. Perhaps the most important feature in an examination for these concerns is the careful review of the extensive internal controls that are almost certain to be present, plus sufficient tests to assure the auditor that the controls are operating effectively. Even the tests of supporting evidence to the statement figures tend to be as much for the purpose of proving the internal control as for proving the figures themselves.

For small businesses, however, the situation is completely reversed. The centralization of authority and responsibility in one or two individuals makes the very strongest case of circumstantial evidence practically meaningless, and the auditor has no alternative but to compensate by making extensive reference to all the available forms of supporting evidence. Whether the business be large or small, however, the auditor must select his evidence carefully, determine just how much evidence he should examine based on the circumstances, and evaluate the evidence judiciously in formulating his opinion concerning the financial statements in question.

REVIEW QUESTIONS

1. Do all services provided by public accountants require that the practitioner act independently? Explain.
2. Why does a public accountant find it more difficult to remain independent than does an internal revenue agent or a bank examiner?
3. Why is the public accounting profession as a whole desirous of inducing each member to maintain complete independence when examining financial statements for a client?

4. The Code of Professional Ethics of the American Institute of Certified Public Accountants (Rule 1.04) prohibits rendering professional service when the fee is contingent upon the findings or results of the service. Show how this rule relates to the independence of the public accountant.

5. Why is the Securities and Exchange Commission concerned with the independence of public accountants?

6. Show how the independent auditor's failure to act independently may affect not only certain individuals, but all members of society as well.

7. What is accomplished by the Code of Professional Ethics of the C.P.A. in addition to the matter of independence?

8. Explain how the auditor's failure to maintain his independence may result in legal liability.

9. Under what circumstances may an auditor incur legal liability for failure to detect fraud?

10. How is the auditor's liability likely to differ in the case of ordinary negligence as against gross negligence or fraud?

11. Has the Securities Act of 1933 served in general to increase or decrease the accountant's liability? Explain.

12. To what extent is a plaintiff's case easier to establish under the Securities Act of 1933 than under the common law, when bringing action against an auditor to recover losses incurred as a result of relying on misleading financial statements?

13. What protection does the public accountant gain from accountants' liability insurance?

14. How is the theory of probability useful to the auditor in his work?

15. What are the advantages and disadvantages of the block type of sample?

16. What type of sample should the auditor generally use when the population being tested includes both large and small amounts? Explain.

17. Under what circumstances can an independent audit examination be relied upon to disclose the existence of fraud in the accounts?

18. What nonstatistical factors are likely to have a bearing on the auditor's determination of the amount of evidence that should be examined?

19. Although the auditor must determine for himself whether or not an item is material, what is the main consideration which should enter into such a determination?

20. What classifications of evidence have been suggested as giving an indication of the reliability of evidence?

21. Why are externally created documents less reliable if they are in the client's possession?

22. What factors are most important in determining the usefulness of circumstantial evidence in the auditor's examination?

QUESTIONS ON APPLICATION OF AUDITING STANDARDS

23. Both public accountants and plumbers are engaged in providing services to the public that may be said to be important to the general welfare of society. Are both groups properly classed as professions? Explain.

24. Of what value are the rules of professional ethics relating to independence, when independence resolves itself into being essentially a state of mind and

hence might be lacking even though none of the rules relating to independence had been violated?

25. Physicians commonly charge for their services on the basis of the patient's ability to pay. Would you recommend that independent auditors follow the same practice, basing the fee on the net profits of the client's business? Explain.

26. As a practical matter, does nomination of a company's auditor by the board of directors with a formal vote of approval by the stockholders give the stockholders an effective voice in the matter? Why? Propose some other approach to the problem.

27. Compare the short-run and the long-run advantages or disadvantages of maintaining complete independence when making an examination of financial statements for a client.

28. How can an auditor claim to be independent when he subscribes fully to the right of his client to determine the form and content of the statements which he is to certify?

29. Justify the fact that Rule 1.04 of the Code of Professional Ethics permits the accountant to accept an engagement on a contingent fee basis if the engagement pertains to representing the client in tax matters before a taxing authority.

30. What is the apparent reason that the Securities and Exchange Commission would not recognize an accounting firm as independent for purposes of expressing an opinion on a client's financial statements, when members of the staff of the accounting firm had prepared the books of entry and the ledgers?

31. Would it be permissible for a C.P.A. to accept an audit engagement with the understanding that he will accept shares of stock in the client company in satisfaction of his fee? Explain.

32. Company A and Company B are similar in all respects and each have $1,000,000 in accounts receivable. The receivables for Company A, however, are represented by 980 accounts, whereas the receivables for Company B are represented by 150 accounts. Would an independent auditor testing the validity of the accounts receivable by corresponding with selected customers be likely to cover the same percentage of the dollar total of receivables in each instance? Explain.

33. A cash credit posted to an account receivable subsequent to the balance sheet date would represent evidence that an actual receivable existed and that no loss would be incurred on the amount of the receivable that was collected. Would the evidence be equally conclusive as to the validity of the account (that is, that the receivable was not fraudulent) and as to its collectibility? Explain.

34. Would circumstantial evidence in the form of a decrease in the percentage of purchase discounts to purchases be of more concern to the internal auditor or the independent auditor? Explain.

35. Suggest forms of evidence that might be available in support of each of the following items and classify each item of evidence in relation to the classification presented in this chapter:
    (a) The number of shares of capital stock authorized to be issued.
    (b) The fact that the client is the owner of the real estate carried in the balance sheet.
    (c) The fact that an account receivable has been paid.
    (d) The fact that a note payable has been paid.

36. With respect to accounts receivable, suggest various factors that would have a bearing on relative risk and hence affect the scope of the independent auditor's examination of accounts receivable.

37. Would an auditor have satisfactorily proven the accuracy and validity of all general ledger entries for the month of March if he traced each total or individual entry in the month of March in each book of original entry to the posting in the proper general ledger account? Explain.

38. Assume that securities that are readily marketable but owned as a measure of protection to assure a continued supply of materials from the company involved have been improperly classified as a current asset. Assume also that installment notes payable maturing in the following year have not been shown as a current liability. If equal amounts were involved in each case, would the effect of the misstatement on the company's financial position be equally material? Explain.

39. Your client, which owns and operates radio station WHY, reports a 200 per cent increase in net income over last year. Of what value would the following information be to you in determining the scope of your examination? "A nation-wide survey of radio stations showed that stations in cities of 100,000 population or greater averaged a 50 per cent decline in net income as compared to last year, whereas stations in cities under 100,000 population showed only a 10 per cent decline in net income."

40. The balance sheet of the Jay Co. lists accounts receivable totaling $100,000 and total assets of $1,000,000; the income statement shows a net income of $150,000. You estimate bad debt losses on the receivables to be $5,000. How much would you be willing to permit the company's provision for losses on bad debts to vary from your $5,000 estimate without considering the difference to be material, and assuming that losses have been provided for on the same basis as in prior years? Give reasons for your answer.

41. List, in order of reliability, the various items of evidence that might be examined in support of each of the following:

    (a) A credit posted to a past-due account after the balance sheet date, showing the account was paid in full.
    (b) The material costs shown on a job cost card.
    (c) An account receivable on which no reply was received to the auditor's request that the customer confirm the balance of the account to the auditor.

42. Of what significance would the following information be to an auditor examining a client's financial statements:

    (a) Sales prices of the client's product are declining.
    (b) The product guarantee has been increased to three years from one year.
    (c) The rate of gross profit increased substantially over last year as a result of discontinuing the manufacture and sale of one line of products.

43. The attribute of independence has been traditionally associated with the C.P.A.'s function of auditing and expressing opinions on financial statements.

    Required:
    (a) What is meant by "independence" as applied to the C.P.A.'s function of auditing and expressing opinions on financial statements? *Discuss.*
    (b) C.P.A.s have imposed upon themselves certain rules of professional conduct that induce their members to remain independent and to strengthen public confidence in their independence. Which of the rules of professional conduct are concerned with the C.P.A.'s independence? *Discuss.*
    (c) The Wallydrag Company is indebted to a C.P.A. for unpaid fees and has offered to issue to him unsecured interest-bearing notes. Would the C.P.A.'s acceptance of these notes have any bearing upon his independence in his relations with the Wallydrag Company? *Discuss.*

(d) The Rocky Hill Corporation was formed on October 1, 1964, and its fiscal year will end on September 30, 1965. You audited the Corporation's opening balance sheet and rendered an unqualified opinion on it.

A month after rendering your report you are offered the position of secretary of the Company because of the need for a complete set of officers and for convenience in signing various documents. You will have no financial interest in the Company through stock ownership or otherwise, will receive no salary, will not keep the books, and will not have any influence on its financial matters other than occasional advice on income tax matters and similar advice normally given a client by a C.P.A.

1. Assume that you accept the offer but plan to resign the position prior to conducting your annual audit with the intention of again assuming the office after rendering an opinion on the statements. Can you render an independent opinion on the financial statements? *Discuss.*

2. Assume that you accept the offer on a temporary basis until the Corporation has gotten under way and can employ a secretary. In any event you would permanently resign the position before conducting your annual audit. Can you render an independent opinion on the financial statements? *Discuss.*

(Uniform C.P.A. Examination)

The auditor's approach

6

The opinion that an independent auditor expresses on the fairness of a client's financial statements is reached by a process of evaluating the evidence gathered in the course of his examination. The examination should be so conducted that the auditor can assert in his short-form report on the examination that, "Our examination was made in accordance with generally accepted auditing standards, and accordingly included such tests of the accounting records and such other auditing procedures as we considered necessary in the circumstances." This statement, in turn, must be made in the light of the standard of field work that states,

> Sufficient competent evidential matter is to be obtained through inspection, observation, inquiries, and confirmations to afford a reasonable basis for an opinion regarding the financial statements under examination.

To this end, we deal first with the principal techniques used by the auditor to acquire the evidence on which the expression of opinion in his report is based.

Examination (inspection)

One of the auditor's principal problems is to substantiate the authenticity of various recorded figures and entries. Evidence of such authenticity is frequently gained by reference to documents pertaining to the transaction that occurred. For instance, the record in the voucher register of a liability for the purchase of materials can be substantiated by "examining," or "inspecting," the vendor's invoice setting forth the amount owed for the materials and the paid check through which settlement of the obligation was effected. The examination of these supporting documents should not, however, imply the type of scrutiny designed to detect a counterfeit hundred-dollar bill, but rather a comparison of the voucher register entry with the related dollar amount and other pertinent information revealed by the invoice and paid check. Other verbs often used to convey the same meaning as "examine" and "inspect" are "vouch," "compare," "sight," and "agree," as in the audit instruction, "Vouch the entry in the voucher register by reference to the supporting vendor's invoice," or "Compare the voucher register entry and the related invoice," or "Sight the vendor's invoice in support of the voucher register entry," or "Agree the amount recorded in the voucher register with the supporting vendor's invoice." When the existence of a physical asset is to be ascertained, the verb "inspect" is customarily used, as in the instruction, "Inspect all additions to plant costing in excess of $500." If the matter of existence of an asset involves a determination of the number of units present, the statement of the instruction may take the form, "Count the cash and marketable securities on hand."

Another term sometimes used to convey the same meaning as "examine" and "inspect" is "check," but the term is also used in other ways, as in "Check the footing of the accounts receivable trial balance." Although the layman thinks of the auditor's work as a checking process, the word "check" is best avoided in technical references. To instruct an assistant to "Check the invoices from vendors" might mean anything from determining that they were all the same color to placing a check mark on each invoice, whereas the presumed intent of the instruction could be conveyed with less equivocation by the instruction "Compare vendors' invoices with the related voucher register entries as to vendor's name and amount of the entry." Audit instructions should always be as clear and explicit as possible so as to avoid misunderstanding, and the student should begin immediately to avoid using such indefinite terms as "check" in his thinking and in the expression of his ideas whether in verbal or written form.

Confirmation

The process of confirmation is closely related to that of inspection, but is used in the situation where the supporting evidence is obtained by direct request rather than by reference to items of evidence that are readily available. The most common usage of the term is in connection with the verification of accounts receivable. A letter is written to the customer asking him to confirm the correctness of the balance of his account as stated in the letter.

Observation

In ascertaining compliance with a concern's prescribed procedures, the auditor will make frequent use of the technique of observation. The observation procedure would be used, for example, in connection with the client's physical inventory taking. In order to ascertain that the client's employees have made a physical count of all inventory items on hand, and have adhered to the instructions that were established to assure an adequate and complete count, the auditor would observe the inventory activity as it is taking place.

Verification

In a general sense, all of the auditor's activity related to the formulation of his opinion on a concern's financial statements is referred to as *verification,* although the term is also used in a more limited sense, as in the verification of footings, extensions, or postings. The latter processes are relatively mechanical, however, such as adding a column of figures to prove that the footing (total) derived by the client is correct, or tracing and verifying the posting of an item from a journal to the proper account in the ledger.

Inquiry

In the course of his examination, the auditor will find it necessary to obtain much of the information that he needs by direct inquiry of the persons who are likely to be able to supply the information. Through inquiry the auditor may seek to ascertain the duties performed by a given individual, or by carefully phrased questions to ascertain that the individual is properly carrying out the responsibilities that have been assigned to him. For instance, the treasurer of a concern will usually sign all checks, thus giving him control over the disbursement of all funds. Effective control would, however, require that the supporting documents be carefully reviewed before approving each disbursement. A "casual" inquiry may often be most revealing. A remark that "It must take a lot of time to sign so many checks each day" may elicit the reply that it takes only a few minutes. A likely implication of the reply would be, of course, that the treasurer does little more than sign the checks and no useful review of disbursements is being made.

Inquiry is also useful as a means of securing certain information that may be needed. If, for example, the cost of a major overhaul of a machine has been expensed, inquiry will probably be the only means by which the auditor can ascertain that the expenditure did not actually materially better the machine or extend its useful life.

Auditing in Evolution

The approach of the independent auditor in applying the above procedures in his examinations has in a sense moved through a complete evolutionary cycle while at the same time reaching a higher professional plane.

At one time the auditor was preoccupied with the client's records, primarily to establish bookkeeping accuracy and the absence of fraud. Next, the auditor directed his attention to the extensive examination of supporting evidence originating outside the client's organization in order to gain the necessary assurance for the expression of his opinion concerning the client's financial statements. Now, however, the extensive development of internal controls in large businesses has made it possible for the independent auditor to once again direct a substantial portion of his attention to the records themselves and other internal considerations. In contrast, however, to the earlier type of internally oriented examination, the present approach involves tests and a professional review rather than mechanical verification, and, of course, reference to physical and externally created evidence is necessary to add the credibility necessary to make the statements useful to third parties.

With the redirection of an important part of his attention to internal matters, the independent auditor has of necessity become quite expert in the matter of internal control, and this development has offered a vital opportunity to be of service beyond the expression of opinion on the concern's financial statements. The alert auditor has seized this opportunity by preparing a supplementary report setting forth his suggestions to the client for ways of strengthening management's control over operations, improving the internal reports that are prepared, reducing the cost of accounting, and increasing the protection against defalcations and similar losses. Such suggestions, which are essentially a by-product of the audit examination, often prove to be more important than the audit itself, with a gratifying effect on auditor-client relations.

Analytical Auditing

The redirection inward of part of the auditor's attention, stressing the client's accounting system and the manner in which it develops financial information about the concern, has been accompanied by a more intensive study of the resulting financial figures themselves. The figures should "make sense," by being consistent with each other and with known external changes that are taking place. Changes from the previous year, or even month-to-month changes in the financial figures as well as changes in ratios between various figures, should all be logical and reflect changes in operations or financial position that are known to have occurred. The rate of turnover of accounts receivable, for example, should be expected to drop if credit terms have been lengthened or economic conditions among a concern's customers are known to have worsened, producing slower collections. Likewise, a known oversupply of a major material used in the manufacture of a company product, and the resulting deterioration of the market for the material, should result in lower inventory cost for the material and an increased gross margin from sales—unless the price of the company's product has undergone similar pressure.

This type of analytical review of the figures on a client's financial statements is also sometimes referred to as the "business approach" to auditing.

The goal of such analyses is the auditor's satisfaction that the financial figures being examined properly reflect the events of the past year. Comparisons represent the heart of the analytical activity, because figures taken individually are relatively meaningless. The same figures take on greatly increased credibility if comparisons with previous figures, with related figures in the financial statements, with other companies' statements or with trade averages, and with known changes in general economic conditions, all point to the fact that the figures appear to be fairly stated.

On the one hand, if the analytical comparisons show changes that are not consistent with known or expected changes in the actual activities of the business, the questionable figures must be given closer attention in the detailed verification phase of the examination. For instance, the auditor might note that inventories have increased, but there would be no reason to question the figures if the increase was accompanied by a proportionate increase in sales. On the other hand, if during the same period the client was known to have instituted new mathematical inventory control techniques which were expected to reduce the amount of inventory carried, closer review and more extensive testing of the final inventory figures would be called for. As another example, substantial gains or losses on dispositions of plant assets that cannot be accounted for in any other way would point to incorrect depreciation rates that may also be in effect for assets still owned by the client.

The Positive Approach

Although the public usually thinks of auditing activities in terms of the detection of errors and the revelation of shrewdly concealed defalcations, the auditor's examination is not primarily oriented toward such matters. The approach is much more positive, along a line of reasoning that may be characterized as follows: *if* the client's accounting system is designed to achieve good internal control, and *if* the system is actually operating as planned, then the final results (the accounting statements) *should* be fully acceptable. The auditor's examination can thus be oriented toward determining the efficacy of the intended internal controls, ascertaining whether they are actually functioning as planned, and then testing the final accounting results to determine that they are in fact sufficiently reliable and accurate to merit the auditor's favorable opinion.

In proving to his satisfaction that a concern's financial position and results of operations are fairly presented by the concern's financial statements, the auditor is presumably satisfied that no major error or defalcation of assets has escaped his attention, but this is not the same as saying that he directs his activities primarily toward such possibilities. Although many auditing procedures are designed to test accuracy and to reveal manipulations undertaken to conceal the true financial situation, the customary expectation in applying the procedures is to prove that the client's figures are acceptable, rather than to disclose errors or defalcations. Nevertheless, the auditor must be aware of the types of errors that may arise and the methods of concealing embezzlement or theft, so that his investigation will be reasonably certain to disclose any material irregularities that have occurred. Likewise, a treatise on auditing must discuss these problems—often at great length in order to afford the reader a clear picture of how some of the more common types of fraud and manipulation are carried out, and how certain auditing procedures must be performed in order to assure the detection of manipulations in the rare cases that do occur. The reader is encouraged, however, not to lose his true sense of direction as the devious and tortuous pathways of embezzlement and fraud are explored, but to constantly remind himself that the basic purpose of the independent audit and the related audit procedures is to enable the auditor to reach an opinion as to the fairness of the client's financial statements.

Terminology

Certain descriptive terms used in auditing circles are sometimes confusing to persons not acquainted with the profession, and several of these terms are discussed briefly at this point for purposes of clarification. Two such terms are "balance sheet audit" and "balance sheet audit and review of operations." The confusion over these terms arises from the fact that even the audit which concentrates on the balance sheet must include some review of operations. For example, repair and maintenance expense accounts should be reviewed to ascertain whether any expenditures of a capital nature have been improperly expensed, and the profit and loss accounts as a whole should be reviewed inasmuch as the net profit derived from these accounts directly affects the retained earnings account on the balance sheet.

Fortunately, both "balance sheet audit" and its lengthier counterpart are disappearing from general usage. Most credit grantors now recognize that the balance sheet alone is not an adequate basis for making credit decisions, and therefore little demand exists today for the balance sheet audit.

Although most audits now cover both the balance sheet and the income statement, the cumbersome term "balance sheet audit and review of operations" is rapidly being replaced by the more accurate and descriptive term "examination of financial statements." In addition to its relative brevity, the newer term is more desirable because it avoids the implication of the older term that the income statement receives only a cursory review. The auditor's opinion covers both statements and must be equally well supported with respect to each statement. The following chapters of this book deal almost exclusively with the objectives, techniques, and problems associated with the performance of an audit examination designed to enable the auditor to express an opinion on both the balance sheet and the income statement.

Occasionally, however, circumstances may warrant auditing work which is more extensive than the examination of financial statements. Internal control may not be adequate to assure management that employees are performing their duties properly and accurately, and at the client's request or the auditor's insistence, certain phases of the examination may be expanded to include what is known as a "detailed audit." As the purpose of such auditing is to review employee performance, each step performed by an employee or a group of employees must be audited.

Direct versus Indirect Approach

The auditor's general approach is one of working "backward." Beginning with the end result of the client's accounting process, the financial statements, the auditor retraces the client's steps until he has reached a point where he is satisfied with the evidence he is examining. In the direct approach to auditing, the auditor works directly from the account balance supporting a figure in the financial statements to evidence through which he can satisfy himself that the account balance is properly stated. In the verification of cash balances, for example, the auditor can refer directly to cash on hand, and to the bank statement and the related reconciliation of the book and bank balances.

In some instances, however, the balance of an account may be verified more readily through an examination of the transactions affecting the account. The account for plant and equipment may represent the sum of the cost of many hundreds of pieces of equipment, but there will be relatively few transactions affecting the account during the year. Assuming that intially the auditor has satisfied himself that the account was fairly stated at some given date, in subsequent examinations the simplest approach to the verification of the account balance is to examine the intervening transactions that have affected the account since the previous balance sheet date. A slight variation of this indirect approach would be employed in the examination of an income statement account such as the sales account. The auditor would first prove that the balance of the account represented the sum of the twelve monthly postings from the sales journal. One or more monthly totals in the sales journal would be proved by footing the entries for the individual sales invoices, and these detail entries would in turn be proved by examining the supporting sales invoice copies, along with the related shipping department notices of shipment and the copies of the original orders received from customers. In completing these steps, the auditor forges a chain of evidence linking the statement figures and the basic documents evidencing the transactions that have occurred. The auditor is retracing the tracks left by the functioning of the client's accounting system. The resulting evidence is sometimes referred to as the "audit trail," which the client should take care to establish and preserve.

The review of internal control ordinarily involves the same type of retracing of the client's steps that occurs in the indirect approach to the verification of an account balance. In his review, the auditor seeks to satisfy himself that prescribed procedures are actually being followed, and in so doing he will make tests of the various figures and entries to gain assurance that they have actually been derived in the manner represented.

The resulting extensive contact that the auditor must have with the client's accounting system is the principal reason why accounting systems are covered in considerable detail in this text, supplementing the discussion of purely audit considerations.

Maintaining the Proper Perspective

Almost any type of auditing activity involves a considerable amount of detail, but the independent auditor should be constantly alert to the pitfall of becoming so absorbed in the detailed aspects of his examination that he loses sight of the "big picture." His opinion does not state that each figure in the financial statements is presented fairly, but rather that the statements as a whole present fairly the financial position and results of operation of the concern.

Under these circumstances, each figure in the financial statements is somewhat like a piece of a jigsaw puzzle that must bear the proper relationship to the other pieces that join it and to the picture as a whole. The auditor should be satisfied that the figures bear a reasonable relationship to the physical enterprise as he has come to know it, to other related figures in the statements, and to known external conditions. Thus the physical condition of the plant, the amount of inventory in storage, the rate of inventory turnover and the rate of gross margin, and sales and price trends for the industry, all hold as much importance for the auditor as the verification of individual figures. The implication of these considerations is that the auditor must look well beyond journals, ledgers, and supporting documentary evidence in the course of his examination. He should attempt to become as familiar with the business, the industry, and market conditions as are the company officials themselves.

The combination of familiarity with the operations and problems of a business, an independent viewpoint, and the broad knowledge gained through training and experience place the auditor in an excellent position to make valuable constructive suggestions to the management of the client.

The suggestions should, of course, be communicated in writing rather than verbally in order to provide an exact record of the recommendations that have been made. Chapter 25 contains illustrations of such recommendations.

Planning the Examination

In addition to the proper perspective, the auditor's approach requires an effective plan of action, and the standards of field work set forth by the A.I.C.P.A. point out that "The work is to be adequately planned and assistants, if any, are to be properly supervised." To assure conformance with the planning that he has undertaken, the auditor usually reduces his plan of action to a set of written instructions, referred to as the "audit program." The supervision of audit staff men engaged in the examination is a basic responsibility of those at each of the supervisory levels within the accounting firm. The organization of a typical public accounting firm is first considered in the following pages, and then further attention is directed to the matter of the audit program.

Predominance of the Partnership Form of Organization

Although there are many individual practitioners in the public accounting profession, most auditing is performed by accountants operating under a partnership arrangement. Such an arrangement makes possible convenient interchange of ideas in accord with the proposition that "two heads are better than one," provides the opportunity for specialization that makes it possible to provide more extensive services to clients with greater competence, and permits the development of an organization of sufficient size to handle audit engagements that would be beyond the capacity of the individual practitioner. The need to be able to provide the necessary services for such super corporations as American Telephone and Telegraph Company and General Motors has led to accounting firms that are national and international in scope, in contrast to other professions, in which organizations seldom extend beyond local partnerships.

Some large national public accounting firms have more than a hundred partners and thousands of employees serving their clients from scores of offices located throughout the world. Within these larger firms, individuals normally specialize in such fields as auditing, management services, income taxes, and estate and gift taxes. The auditing staff is usually the largest and may reflect further specialization in accordance with the business activities of the firm's clients. Thus there may be specialists in the auditing of manufacturing concerns, banks, department stores, oil companies, public utilities, and many other types of businesses. Management services encompass a broad range of activities which are ideally subject to specialization, for included are such diverse areas as work simplification, production control, operations research, accounting systems, and electronic computers.

The corporate form of organization has no place in the provision of such services as we have been considering, and Rule 4.06 of the Code of Professional Ethics of the A.I.C.P.A. provides:

> A member or associate shall not be an officer, director, stockholder, representative, or agent of any corporation engaged in the practice of public accounting in any state or territory of the United States or the District of Columbia.

Public accounting is a personal service which is not only ill-adapted to the impersonal corporate form of organization, but carries with it an obligation to clients and the public as a whole for integrity and high standards of performance. Full financial responsibility for malpractice or any other form of improper action is one of the best forms of assurance that this obligation to others will be effectively discharged, and it would be undesirable to permit such financial responsibility to be avoided through the limited liability which is enjoyed by corporate organizations.

Line Organization for the Independent Auditing Function

The organization within the typical public accounting firm follows the military form of line organization. Although the following discussion pertains only to the assignment of responsibilities within the area of auditing services, the same general plan is followed in the other service areas. There is, however, less routine work in the nonauditing activities, with the result that staff assistants are less commonly utilized and there is a higher proportion of partners and managers.

Partner level. The partner is at the highest level of authority, and the partners are individually and collectively responsible for all work performed by the firm. Each partner enjoys a share in the profits of the firm and is responsible for the contribution of a portion of the firm's capital. Newly admitted partners are frequently permitted to make their capital contribution on an installment basis out of their share of the profits. Each office of a firm will ordinarily have one partner who is responsible for the management of that office. The management of the entire firm may be in the hands of a single managing partner, or more frequently, there will be a partners' management committee.

An audit partner will generally (1) sign personally all reports or letters expressing the opinion of the firm, (2) pass judgment on any controversial issues concerning the scope of an examination or the application of generally accepted accounting principles, and (3) review the work of subordinates who are under his direction. How far the partner will go into details in his review of audit programs, working papers, and reports will generally depend on the policies of his firm, his faith in the quality of work done by his subordinates, and his individual temperament. In addition to these duties, the partner is responsible for obtaining new clients, and he will ordinarily be present at any important conferences with present or prospective clients.

Manager or supervisor level. A manager or supervisor assumes the lesser responsibilities of the partner and the more important ones of the senior accountant. Thus he takes over much of the work of planning and supervising audit engagements, reviewing work papers, making any necessary revisions of audit reports, and contacting the senior accountant or officials of the client as problems arise. He assumes full responsibility for making most decisions which may be necessary, but he must also recognize those problems of sufficient importance to warrant being referred to a partner for final disposition.

The senior accountant. The senior accountant will generally be responsible for all details of the audit engagement, including preparation of the audit program, direction of the work in the field, and writing the audit report. He schedules the work of any assistants working under him, assists them in performing the work, reviews the working papers which they have prepared, undertakes the more difficult phases of the work himself, determines modifications to be made in the audit program as circumstances may warrant, and conducts most of the discussions with the client which arise during the course of the work.

Staff assistants. Much of the actual verification work on an audit is carried out by staff assistants, or "junior accountants" as they are quite commonly called. Even though the beginning assistant must be carefully instructed and supervised, he will be allowed to work more and more on his own as he demonstrates his ability to understand and carry out directions contained in the audit program. Other factors affecting his rate of progress will be his ability to write clearly, and his proficiency in distinguishing between minor problems and questions that he should handle himself and matters which should be referred to the senior accountant for disposition.

There will be ample opportunity to judge the assistant's proficiency at putting his thoughts on paper, for he will have to describe in the working papers the work he has done and his findings and conclusions. The importance of clear, forceful exposition in such cases stems from the fact that often the senior will evaluate the work done by the assistant almost entirely on the basis of the written comments in the working papers. Writing ability must also be demonstrated before an assistant can become a senior accountant, because the senior is expected to write the reports which are presented to the client. These reports must be extremely well written, as they are likely to be the principal means by which the client judges the work of the accounting firm.

Learning to distinguish questions and problems which should be taken up with the senior accountant from those which the assistant himself should be expected to resolve is important for the following reasons. Petty questions are bothersome to the senior accountant and tend to make it more difficult to complete the examination within the time estimate for the job. At the same time, such questions show an undesirable lack of self-assurance and self-reliance. The opposite extreme is also to be avoided, however. The cocky assistant who overestimates his competence is too likely to make decisions which ought to be referred to the senior accountant; consequently the senior can never be sure when one of these decisions will turn out to be incorrect and result in negating all the careful work that has been done.

Selection for Advancement

Because the senior accountant is usually permitted to choose the staff assistants who will work with him, he will tend to select the men who have demonstrated their ability to grasp and follow instructions, work quickly and accurately, and ask only the necessary minimum of questions. With the assistance of such men he can expect to turn out a good audit well within the estimated time. The result of this arrangement is a natural process of selection which quickly brings to the fore men with the proper ability and other necessary characteristics, and no staff man should ever assume that he was not promoted to senior accountant because no one was aware of his talents.

Managers and partners in an accounting firm have equally close contact with the employees they supervise. Consequently, promotion on the basis of clearly indicated merit is the rule, and a staff man can expect to advance just as quickly as he has shown that he is ready for additional responsibility. That such advancement is likely to be rapid and limited only by the ability of the individual is indicated by the need for men that has resulted from the continuing rapid expansion of the profession and the steady flow of men out of the profession into responsible jobs in industry.

The Audit Program

In the audit program, accountants from the level of partner on down have an effective tool for planning audit work and supervising and controlling the performance of that work. The program is, of course, an outline of all procedures to be followed in order to arrive at an opinion concerning a client's financial statements. The basic responsibility for preparing the program will usually rest with the senior accountant, although any important questions about the program will be cleared with the manager, who may in turn refer some of the questions to the partner in charge of the engagement. The manager will then make a final review of the completed program, and the partner may make a spot review of certain major phases of the program, based on his knowledge of the client's affairs and any difficulties which are likely to develop.

Because each audit is a special situation, each audit program must be tailor-made to fit all the variables in the particular engagement. Among the factors which must be considered in preparing an audit program are internal control, the client's accounting procedures, the timing of the work in relation to the balance sheet date, any special instructions, and the size, nature, and extent of the client's operations. Some accounting firms use a preprinted "standard" program as a starting point and make whatever additions, deletions, or changes may be necessary to fit the requirements of the particular engagement. The standard program may be a maximum program that includes all possible procedures that might be used, or a minimum program incorporating only those procedures that are likely to be utilized in every engagement. If the first type of program is used, it is desirable that any listed procedure that is not to be performed carry a notation explaining why the procedure was eliminated. The value of such a notation can perhaps best be illustrated by considering the probable line of questioning of an attorney for the prosecution in a suit against the auditor for negligence in failing to unveil a defalcation or fraud in the accounts! The minimum standard program would seem to be a satisfactory solution to the problem, but it has its own shortcomings in that the user may easily become careless or succumb to a false sense of security and fail to recognize supplementary procedures that are required by a particular situation. Either type of standard program, however, if effectively used can save time and give added assurance that important procedures will not be overlooked in preparing the program.

Other accounting firms feel that either type of standard program, even though used primarily as a point of departure, tends to make audits stereotyped and mechanical, with a corresponding loss of alertness and imagination on the part of the auditor. These firms prefer to approach each engagement as a completely new situation and build the entire program around that situation. They feel that such an approach encourages a closer acquaintance with conditions which should affect the program and produces the best possible program, because each procedure will be specifically designed to meet the immediate need.

Amount of Detail in the Program

Under either of the above techniques for preparing the audit program, there is considerable latitude as to the extent to which the procedures are to be detailed. For instance, the program might simply state, "Count petty cash funds," or it might set forth each step to be carried out in counting the petty cash fund, as in the following highly detailed program:

1. Determine the location and balances in all funds before the examination is begun.
2. Count is to be made as of the beginning of business on January 2.
3. Cash receipts on hand are to be segregated and controlled during the count of petty cash and to be counted immediately on the conclusion of the petty cash count.
4. Cash and cash items are to be listed in detail in the working papers.
5. Rolled coins need not be opened, but packaged currency should be counted.
6. All I.O.U.'s included in the fund should be approved by the treasurer, and working papers should indicate the date on which they were made and the position of the maker.
7. All checks representing accommodation cashings should be listed, showing the position of the drawer and the date of the check. These checks should be prepared as a separate bank deposit and controlled to the bank by the auditor.
8. Paid bills or receipts evidencing disbursements should be listed in detail showing the payee, reason for the payment, and the date. Approval should be noted in the papers and reviewed to see that it conforms to company policy.
9. Disbursements should be reviewed to see that they conform to company policy concerning the type of items which should be paid from petty cash funds.
10. Be certain that the custodian of the petty cash fund is present during the count, and secure from him a receipt signed in ink for the return of the fund at the conclusion of the count.

As each step in the audit program is carried out, the initials of the person doing the work should be placed adjacent to the particular instruction. This requirement enables all affected persons to determine that no prescribed steps have been omitted and provides a permanent record of exactly what work was done and who did it. The assumption should not be made, however, that carrying out the instructions of the program is a simple, mechanical process once the program has been set. Each procedure should be subject to modification as the audit progresses if conditions prove not to be as anticipated or if excessive errors or the suspicion of fraud enter the picture.

Working Papers

The auditor's working papers are an important element of his examination. The need for skill and care in their preparation is evident in the various purposes which they serve: (1) they assist directly in the performance of the audit; (2) they provide an historical record showing all the work that has been done; (3) they contain the basis for the auditor's opinion; (4) they provide information to be used in the auditor's report; and (5) they aid partners, managers, and seniors in reviewing and evaluating the work of those under their supervision.

The working papers prepared by the auditor are his property, even though they have been prepared from the client's records. They should be carefully preserved, because they will have to be consulted if another audit is made for the following year. Often they may prove useful in providing information of assistance to the client on problems arising at a later date, and of course should a charge of negligence ever be brought against the auditor, the auditor's working papers will constitute the principal evidence in his defense. The auditor must, however, be careful that he leaves no "holes" in this defense. An interesting analysis of some of the legal traps that the auditor may thoughtlessly leave in his working papers is presented by Saul Levy in *The Journal of Accountancy* for May, 1956.

Identifying Information: Proper Headings

Each sheet of working paper should be complete in itself to preclude any question about what it is or where it belongs should it become separated from the remainder of the working paper file. Most important in this respect is the heading, which should always contain three items of information: (1) name of the client; (2) title of the particular schedule, for example, "Analysis of Changes in Provision for Doubtful Accounts"; and (3) the date of the statements being examined. If more than one sheet of paper is necessary to complete a given schedule or analysis, each sheet should not only contain the full three-part heading but should also carry a notation that other pages are a part of the same schedule. Thus, the notation "1 of 2" indicates that the schedule is continued on a second page carrying the notation "2 of 2."

Each sheet of working paper should also contain the name or initials of the person who prepared the paper and the date on which the work was done. This information aids in fixing the responsibility for each phase of the work and makes it possible to contact the proper person if at any time there is any question about the schedule or the work that was done.

Occasionally, members of the client's staff will assist the auditor by preparing certain schedules and analyses, which are then reviewed and tested by the auditor in the course of his examination. Such working papers should contain a notation that they have been prepared by the client (the initials "P.B.C." are often used for this purpose), as well as the initials of the auditor who performed the necessary verification. When working papers are reviewed by the senior accountant, manager, or partner, the reviewer should initial each sheet that has been reviewed to indicate that the review has been made and to fix responsibility for such review.

The Trial Balance

The key to any set of working papers is the trial balance, and the auditor will normally prepare his trial balance as soon as the client has made all year-end adjustments. The trial balance is prepared either directly from the ledger or from a trial balance that the client has prepared. In the latter case, as soon as the auditor's trial balance has been completed and the footings proved, each figure should be traced to the ledger for verification purposes, and the auditor should also ascertain that all ledger balances have been listed in the trial balance.

One of the advantages of working from the client's trial balance is in knowing that the ledger is in balance. Then, too, if the auditor's figures are not in balance, he can be certain the error is his own, and the error can be more readily located.

If in preparing his trial balance the auditor discovers that the ledger is out of balance, he should not attempt to locate the error unless the client specifically authorizes such action. Locating errors is a clerical job for which the client is not likely to be willing to pay professional fees. If the client does authorize the auditor to locate the error, the client should understand that such work will increase the audit fee beyond any estimate that may have been given previously.

Each trial balance page is likely to contain seven relatively standard column headings, as follows:

Account Title	Index	Final Balance Dec. 31, 19— (Last Year)	Balance per Books Dec. 31, 19— (This Year)	Adjustments and Reclassifications Dr. Cr.	Final Balance Dec. 31,19— (This Year)

The heading for the first column is self-explanatory, and the matter of indexing is discussed later in this chapter. The final figures from the previous audit are included for comparative and reference purposes, as well as to assure the proper starting figure when utilizing the indirect approach of verifying intervening transactions in order to establish the correctness of the closing balance of an account. The column for this year's balances should always include all income and expense balances, even if the balances of these accounts have already been closed to the retained earnings account. The working papers must contain the full detail of the income statement, assuming that the auditor's opinion is to cover that statement as well as the balance sheet.

The figure used for the balance of the retained earnings account should be the balance at the beginning of the year, with dividends and the current year's earnings shown below. The sum of these three figures will then be the year-end balance of the account needed to balance the statement, and in this way the balance sheet and income statement will be fully tied together. These points are illustrated in the sample working papers for the audit of Machine Products Co.

Adjusting and Reversing Entries

Unrecorded transactions or incorrect account balances may necessitate the recommendation of adjusting entries to the client and the incorporation in the working papers of those adjustments accepted by the client. The auditor may only recommend that the adjustments be made, in view of the client's primary responsibility for the accounting records and the financial statements. In the event of the client's refusal to make a recommended entry, the auditor's recourse is through a qualification of his opinion concerning the financial statements if a material item is involved.

Although some clients are quite willing to make any adjustments that are suggested, it is well to consider human nature and the client's point of view in deciding whether or not a given adjustment or group of adjustments should be presented to the client. First of all, most people take considerable pride in their work and are likely to resent having their mistakes and shortcomings pointed out to them. Furthermore, by the time the auditor is ready to present his recommended adjustments, the client will probably have closed the books for the year under examination and have begun entering transactions for the following year, thus making it difficult for the client to record the adjustments in the records. Additional resistance may stem from the fact that the client has already released preliminary financial figures to stockholders or creditors, making it awkward to have the audited statements show different figures. Lastly, minor adjustments that do not materially affect the financial statements are likely to raise a question as to the auditor's sense of proportion and true understanding and appreciation of the magnitude of the client's business—to say nothing of arousing a suspicion that the auditor's fee may be excessive as a result of the auditor's preoccupation with unimportant details. Under these circumstances, the auditor should give serious consideration to the question of presenting adjustments to the client unless their effect individually or in total is such that the auditor would be forced to qualify his opinion on the financial statements if the client refused to accept the adjustments.

In the case of a small client, who may not have an accountant qualified to handle the full accounting responsibility, it may be necessary to make numerous adjustments to correct such things as the balance of prepaid insurance or the provision for depreciation, and to record figures that the client was unable to determine, such as the accruals for property and income taxes. Generally, however, there is little basis for the widespread belief that an audit is likely to produce a long series of adjusting entries—particularly in the case of larger concerns that have competent employees in charge of the accounting function.

Any adjustments accepted by the client will, of course, be entered by the auditor in the proper columns on his work sheets. Most auditors also insist that the entries be recorded on the client's records to keep them in conformity with the financial statements, although if the books have been closed, entries affecting the nominal accounts can be posted to retained earnings. To facilitate the client's recording of the entries, the auditor usually furnishes a list of the entries, along with any reversing entries to be made. A reversing entry will be necessary if the client has already recorded in the next accounting period a transaction that actually affects the fiscal year that the auditor is examining. For example, customers may have returned merchandise prior to the end of the year, but if the receiving department records of the returns were slow in reaching the accounting department, the entry for the returns might inadvertently be dated and posted to the records for the succeeding year. An adjustment to record the returns in the year under examination would result in duplicating the actual book entries to sales and accounts receivable, but by means of a reversing entry the effect of the original entry by the client would be cancelled.

Reclassification Entries

Reclassification entries relate primarily to transfers of balances made within the auditor's working papers. For example, the client may debit sales returns and allowances directly to the sales account, but if the total of these debits is to be shown separately on the statements, the auditor will transfer them to a separate line on his work papers by means of a reclassification entry. Another illustration would be the handling of credit balances in accounts receivable. If the auditor believes these are important enough to be classified as a liability, he accomplishes the change by means of a reclassification entry.

The entries for adjustments and reclassifications will normally be recorded on separate pages in the working papers, because only the adjustments will be presented to the client for entry in the accounting records. To further identify each type, adjustments may be numbered 1, 2, 3, and so forth, and reclassifications may be numbered 101, 102, 103, and so on. In addition to an entry number, each adjustment or reclassification should carry a description setting forth the reason for the entry and an indication of the working paper schedule from which the information for the entry was obtained. When the entry is posted to the auditor's working trial balance or lead schedule, the index number of the sheet to which the entry was posted should be noted alongside the appropriate figure on the adjusting entry page. The notation of the posting reference in this manner not only shows that the entry has been posted to the working papers, but also facilitates location of the sheet to which the entry was posted by anyone reviewing the working papers.

The staffman should list all adjusting or reclassification entries that he believes should be made. When the working papers are subsequently reviewed, the reviewer may conclude that an entry is unnecessary because it is immaterial, incorrect, or improper for some reason, and in that case he should note the working papers accordingly, as for instance "Pass—not material," followed by his initials to show who made the decision.

Alternative Forms of the Trial Balance

In the sample headings for the trial balance given earlier, it should be noted that separate columns were not provided for debit and credit balances. The answer lies in the fact that separate sheets are used for assets, equities (liabilities and the owners' investments), and income statement items. If a credit belongs on the asset page, as, for instance, the balance of the provision for doubtful accounts, the amount will be shown in red, or encircled; and similar treatment will be accorded any debit balances on the liability page. Incomes and expenses can be distinguished on the third page of the trial balance by separate grouping and by the description of each item.

In one form of the trial balance, all accounts are listed on the appropriate trial balance page in the same sequence in which they appear in the ledger. The ledger sequence will, of course, usually correspond with the sequence in the statements. Remaining columns to the right of the "Final Balance" column can then be used to group similar items which will appear as one figure in the statements. Thus the balances of three separate bank accounts and the petty cash fund can be listed in one column and the total of this column shown in the balance sheet as "Cash." Combining related accounts on a statement greatly increases readability.

Under a second form of the trial balance, related account balances are first listed on separate "lead schedules," or "grouping sheets," and only the totals of the lead schedules are brought to the top trial balance pages. This method is sometimes referred to as the "working trial balance" method, or the "working balance sheet and profit and loss" method. Under this arrangement the top trial balance schedules, which summarize these totals, will be similar to the final form of the client's statements, and the statements to be presented in the auditor's report can be readily prepared from these schedules.

The advantage of the working trial balance arrangement is the ease with which the manager or principal in charge of the work can review the work papers. At the very front of the work paper file is a bird's-eye view of the statements with all obscuring details removed. Major problems are quickly spotted under such an arrangement. At the same time, all details are readily available in the lead schedules, which were the source of the figures on the top trial balance schedules.

The disadvantage of the working trial balance arrangement is the difficulty of transcribing ledger balances to the trial balance pages. Before a figure can be entered, the proper lead schedule must be located, and if the accounts in the ledger are not carefully arranged in statement order, considerable time can be lost turning from one lead schedule to another. And, of course, if the sheets do not balance, the process of locating the error by verifying each figure is equally cumbersome. Many auditors feel that the advantages of the working balance sheet form of trial balance far outweigh the disadvantages, and the arrangement is quite widely used. All illustrations of work papers accompanying this text are based on the use of the working trial balance.

Indexing

The auditor's trial balance should always show an index number for each figure to assist any person using the working paper file in locating the work sheet schedule which supports any given figure. Each accounting firm ordinarily has a uniform plan of indexing used on all working papers prepared by the staff. The advantage of a uniform plan is that any person connected with the firm can locate almost instantly any particular schedule in a file of work papers, regardless of who prepared the file.

Indexing systems vary greatly, and the system used in the illustrative working papers for this book is only one of many satisfactory systems. It was selected for use here largely because the author is familiar with this system, having worked with it for several years. The basic outline of the system is as follows:

Trial Balance	Index
Assets	B/S-A
Liabilities and owners' equity	B/S-L
Income and expense	P/L

Account	
Cash	A
Receivables and provisions for losses or discounts	B
Inventories	C
Prepaid Expenses	L
Investments	N
Intangible assets	P
Plant and equipment and accumulated depreciation	UV
Notes payable	AA
Accounts payable	BB
Accruals	CC
Accrued Federal income taxes	FF
Deferred income	GG
Contingent liabilities	KK
Long-term liabilities	NN
Capital stock	SS
Surplus	TT
Corporation minutes	XX
Sales and sales deductions	10
Cost of goods sold	20
Selling expense	30
General and administrative expense	40
Other income	50
Other expense	60

To illustrate the use of this plan, we might take the example of cash which was used earlier. On the working trial balance page bearing the reference B/S-A in the upper right-hand corner (usually in red to draw attention) would appear the item "Cash." In the index column on the line for "Cash" would appear the letter "A." This indicates that all the details concerning the cash figure are shown on a lead schedule indexed "A," which should appear in the working paper file in its proper alphabetical sequence.

The lead schedule would have the same column headings as the top trial balance sheet and would contain the following detail in the first four columns:

Account Title	Index	Final Balance Dec. 31, 19— (Last Year)	Balance per Books Dec. 31,19— (This Year)
First National—General A/c	A-1	$ 76,205.81	$ 81,201.27
First National—Payroll A/c	A-2	5,000.00	5,000.00
Last National—Special A/c	A-3	12,305.80	7,506.50
Petty cash	A-4	500.00	500.00
		$ 94,011.61	$ 94,207.77
			to B/S-A

Schedule A-1 would probably contain a reconciliation of the general account in the First National Bank as of the balance sheet date. Each figure in the reconciliation would be referenced to a supporting schedule, each with its own index. These supporting schedules might be indexed as follows:

List of outstanding checks	A-1 / 1
Deposit in transit and authenticated duplicate deposit ticket	A-1 / 2
Bank confirmation	A-1 / 3
Summary of detailed audit of receipts and disbursements for September	A-1 / 4
Checks listed for investigation during detailed audit	A-1 / 4a

Filing of Working Papers

Usually two types of working paper files are maintained: annual audit files and permanent files. The annual audit files contain the papers covering a specific engagement, for example, Wilson Company, Audit, October 31, 19—. The arrangement of the working papers in the annual audit file should be about as follows:

1. Point sheet or agenda of work to be done, listing questions that have arisen in the course of the examination or as a result of the review of the working

papers, and the comments giving the answers to the questions or the disposition of points that have been raised.

2. Audit program.
3. Internal control questionnaire.
4. List of adjusting and reclassification entries.
5. The auditor's trial balance, or working balance sheet and income statement.
6. Lead schedules, or grouping sheets.
7. The detailed working papers and supporting schedules pertaining to each lead schedule.

The permanent files contain information which will be of value to each successive audit that is made. Such information would include data concerning the corporate charter, long-term leases, bond indenture provisions, accounting procedures, and data showing bad debt experience or changes in the accounts for accumulated depreciation.

When a staffman goes to a client's office to begin an engagement, he should take with him the permanent file and the audit file for the previous year. The file for the previous year will serve as a guide in preparing work papers for the current year and carrying out many of the instructions in the audit program. The permanent file will provide much necessary information which has been secured in previous years.

Tick Marks

The auditor makes frequent use in his work papers of a variety of symbols to indicate the work that has been done. These symbols are commonly referred to as tick marks. One of the tick marks which is used almost universally by auditors is as follows: $\mathcal{H}$. Although there is almost a limitless variety, others likely to be used are $\smile$ $\curlyvee$ $\circ$ ϕ.

As these tick marks have no special or uniform meaning in themselves, no tick mark should ever be used without giving an explanation of its meaning. On a bank reconciliation schedule, the legend explaining the marks used might appear somewhat as follows:

$\mathcal{H}$ Traced to ledger balance.
$\checkmark$ Traced to bank statement.
ϕ Paid check inspected.
F Footed and cross-footed.

The appropriate tick mark would then be placed next to any figures which had been verified as indicated by the legend.

Confidential Treatment of Information Pertaining to the Client

In the course of making his examination the auditor will have almost unlimited access to information about the affairs of his client, and most of this information will find its way into the working papers. Much of the information will be of a type which the client would not ordinarily disclose to outsiders, including such matters as the amount of sales and gross margin by classes of products, changes in product design and production, and the salaries of various officers and employees. Failure to keep such information confidential could easily be harmful to the client, damaging to the reputation of the practitioner who violated his client's trust, and reflect unfavorably on the profession as a whole. Clients would hesitate to engage auditors if in so doing they would run the risk of losing control over information that has been closely guarded from outsiders, and conversely, auditors would be hindered in making their examinations if clients attempted to withhold information in order to keep it confidential.

The A.I.C.P.A. has recognized the importance to present and prospective users of public accounting services, as well as the profession itself, of treating all information confidentially, and to assure all who might be concerned that confidences will not be breached, has incorporated the following rule into its Code of Professional Ethics as Rule 1.03: "A member or associate shall not violate the confidential relationship between himself and his client." To illustrate the effect of this rule with respect to the accountant's working papers, the Institute's Committee on Ethics has stated that if an accountant sells his practice, he should not release his working papers to his successor without first obtaining the permission of the client.

Although the auditor is governed by the same professional considerations that apply to the attorney or the physician with respect to information he receives about the affairs of his client, communication between the auditor and his client is not privileged under the common law. Except in certain states where this privilege is given by statute, the auditor, unlike the attorney or physician, may be required in court to produce his working papers and to divulge any information which he may hold concerning his client.

Control of Working Papers

The auditor should never leave his working papers unattended while he is working in the client's office. The papers should be placed in a securely locked brief case or in a sealed file drawer at lunch time and overnight in order to keep any persons in the client's office from gaining unauthorized access to the papers. Such close control is necessary for two reasons. One reason is that persons in the client's employ might attempt to alter information recorded in the work papers for purposes of misleading the auditor or concealing some misdeed. Another reason lies in the fact that the papers are likely to contain information which should not be made available to members of the client's organization, such as information concerning the scope of the examination or the method to be used in selecting items to be test-checked. Also, some of the information in the working papers about the affairs of the client and salaries of various officers and employees will be restricted by the client to a limited number of employees, and the auditor would be violating his confidential relationship with the client if such information should become available to unauthorized personnel.

The Relationship of the Auditor and His Staff to Client Officers and Employees

The comments on preceding pages perhaps suggest that the typical auditor is cold, impassive, and likely to be aloof to those about him. Perhaps in the days when auditors were primarily concerned with the detection of fraud, the typical auditor might have fitted the above description. Today, however, the breadth of the auditor's work is reflected in a very different type of personality. Partners and managers should be able to meet client executives on their own ground and be able to enter actively into discussions ranging from operating problems of the business to business conditions in general, and from state, national, and foreign affairs to the lighter concerns of the day. Cordiality, an easy manner, interest in a client's problems, and the ability to grasp questions and return helpful answers are as important to client relations as is the "bedside manner" of the physician.

Although contacts with client executives may well be on a social basis as well as a business basis, restraint is advisable, because the auditor must sometimes say "No" to the client, and independence can be difficult to maintain in the face of close friendship or personal indebtedness. At the staff level, contact with employees of the client should be limited to the confines of the client's office as much as possible. Fraternization with employees, particularly when it is solely an outgrowth of contacts in the client's office, is almost certain to present problems in the client's office, and again independence may suffer as a result.

Cordiality is another matter, however, and everything should be done to make the auditor's intrusion upon the daily routine of the client's office as painless and as unobtrusive as possible. Consideration for employees should include recognition that they have their regular work to perform and may not be able to drop everything to assist the auditor. Also, the auditor's tone of voice and manner should be such as to dispel the notion that the auditor considers every employee a potential thief or embezzler and that he gains his principal satisfaction from crucifying any hapless employee whose inadvertent mistake he may have discovered. In part, the problem is merely one of courtesy, and minor aspects of the solution to the problem include having the auditor bring his own supplies, avoid the use of the client's telephones, particularly for personal calls, and seek permission to use the client's machines or accounting records only when they are not in use by the client's employees.

Illustrative Audit Working Papers

To assist the reader in visualizing the final appearance of a set of audit working papers, illustrative schedules are available in a supplement to this book. These working papers have been adapted from the audit of a medium-sized manufacturing firm employing about 500 persons. The manufacturing process consists primarily of machining rough castings or forgings and assembling these finished pieces, along with a large number of purchased parts, into subassemblies and final assemblies of the half-dozen major types of machines which the company sells. The illustrative working papers should be especially interesting and informative in view of the fact that the company's cost records are based on standard costs, and consequently yield much valuable information from both a management and an auditing point of view.

The Approach of Succeeding Chapters

The organization of most audit programs and working papers, as well as traditional auditing textbooks, is related to the items listed in the financial statements. Thus, the progression begins with cash and proceeds through the various assets, the liabilities and owners' equity, and revenues and expenses. But such an arrangement is somewhat arbitrary and artificial, besides presenting awkward problems of how matters with dual implications should be classified. For example, should the matter of depreciation be treated with expenses or with the discussion of property, plant, and equipment? Similarly, the problem of ascertaining whether sales have been recorded in the appropriate accounting period concerns both receivables and sales, and hence it could be treated under either statement item.

Another difficulty with the traditional arrangement is that it gives the impression that the examination of income statement accounts is of secondary importance. The balance sheet accounts are usually covered first, and the audit program and textbook space devoted to balance sheet accounts far exceeds that concerning the income statement accounts. This implied emphasis on the balance sheet is, of course, entirely out of step with enlightened thinking that recognizes the prime importance of income statement information to most users of financial statements.

These problems are resolved in the following chapters by the use of what may be referred to as a "transaction approach" to the subject matter, in which both aspects of a transaction, such as sales and receivables, are treated together. Further justification for this approach exists in the heavy emphasis of present-day audits on the client's operations, as contrasted with earlier-day preoccupation with the accounting records and the secondary evidence supporting such records. Another advantage of the transaction approach in the particular context of this book is that the extensive material on internal control and accounting systems is naturally oriented to the handling of transactions, rather than to individual accounts, each of which involves only half of a typical business transaction. The net result of orientation to transactions is a more cohesive approach to the audit and to the inter-relationships existing within the accounting records and financial statements. The reader is introduced to the subject matter through consideration of sales transactions and the related sales and receivables figures, purchase transactions and the related asset and expense figures, inventory transactions and the related asset and expense figures, cash transactions and the figures related to those transactions, and so on.

Internal Control and the Accounting System

In each area, consideration is first given to internal control and the accounting system of which it is a part. The importance of these topics to auditing is evident in the effect of internal control on the auditor's choice and timing of procedures and on the extent that supporting evidence is sampled. The constant reference to records and documentary supporting evidence, in turn, points to the importance of knowledge and understanding of the accounting system that produces such records and evidence under varying conditions of internal control.

Each section on internal control includes comments on the closely related matter of internal auditing. A word of explanation is in order, however, about this material. The only internal audit procedures referred to are those pertaining to the accounting system and the related financial controls. These are the aspects of the internal auditor's work that are of most concern to the independent auditor. There is no attempt to suggest a complete internal audit program, which would cover other management controls in addition to those related only to financial matters. Also, the reader should recall that most internal audits today are oriented to functional responsi-bilities, rather than to types of transactions or the chart of accounts.

Standards of Statement Presentation

Next, standards of statement presentation are introduced. These, too, have a bearing on the accounting system, and they must be carefully considered during the course of the auditor's examination. Although chronologically the financial statements and accompanying auditor's opinion are prepared for typing as a final audit step, the auditor must look toward the statements and his report throughout his examination. The question of compliance with generally accepted standards of statement presentation must frequently be resolved at the time that detailed audit procedures are being executed. It is only at such time that a change from Fifo to Lifo inventory valuation would be disclosed, or that the auditor would detect that advances to company officers are included in the accounts receivable control, whereas in the balance sheet they must be shown separately from amounts due from customers. Thus, standards of statement presentation must be kept in mind as the auditor carries out his audit procedures, and hence they are discussed prior to taking up the procedures that the auditor employs.

Audit Objectives and Procedures

The final topic considered under each transaction segment is that of audit objectives and procedures, and it is at this point that the discussion turns to the major auditing activity: the examination of underlying evidence to substantiate the financial statements and the related ledger balances. The term "substantiate" is used to describe this process rather than "verify" inasmuch as the latter term has connotations of positiveness that are inappropriate in relation to the general approach followed today in independent audit examinations.

In attempting to substantiate a statement figure the auditor will have certain objectives in mind, and these objectives will in turn guide his selection of audit procedures and their application in light of the particular circumstances. The pertinent objectives are set forth for each audit area, and because they represent the heart of the auditing problem, they merit the student's closest attention. If the objectives are thoroughly understood, audit procedures that will accomplish the desired objective become almost self-evident. By way of illustration, if the objective is to ascertain the collectibility of the client's accounts receivable, the importance of aging the accounts should immediately come to mind, along with the over-all possibility of relating the number of days' sales outstanding to the client's credit terms. For specific accounts that might concern the auditor, subsequent collection of an account provides one of the best indications of collectibility, but if the account is still unpaid at the time of the auditor's investigation, an alternative approach is to ascertain the customer's general credit standing and financial position.

The most common procedures for attaining the various audit objectives are set forth in the following chapters. The reader should recognize, however, that a compilation of these procedures would not constitute an audit program. Not all these procedures would be used in any given audit, as many alternative procedures are suggested. Furthermore, because practically every procedure is applied on a test basis, the extent to which each procedure would be applied would have to be determined on the basis of the facts in each case. Some guides to making the proper decisions are given, but actual experience is the final solution to the problem of learning to make sound decisions. Such experience can be approximated by consulting such material as the A.I.C.P.A.'s *Auditing Standards and Procedures* and its series entitled *Case Studies in Auditing Procedure.* The value of the case studies lies in the fact that they set forth what qualified auditors have considered necessary to meet generally accepted auditing standards in specific audit situations that are fully described.

REVIEW QUESTIONS

1. What matters requiring the exercise of judgment are suggested by the auditing standard pertaining to the auditor's field work?
2. What are the major steps in an independent audit examination that has a positive approach?
3. Enumerate the principal auditing procedures utilized by the independent auditor.
4. How has "analytical auditing" evolved from the redirection inward of the auditor's attention, focusing on the accounting system?
5. Contrast the direct and indirect approach to the auditor's verification of an account balance.
6. Distinguish between an examination of financial statements and a detailed audit.
7. What are the advantages of the partnership form of organization in public accounting as contrasted to the individual proprietorship?
8. Why do the Rules of the Code of Ethics prohibit the practice of public accounting under the corporate form of organization?
9. What are the main functions normally performed by the partner of a public accounting firm?
10. Discuss the relative importance of technical ability and sound judgment at the junior level and at the partner level in public accounting.
11. What factors should be considered in preparing an audit program?
12. What are the advantages and disadvantages of using a "standard" audit program?
13. What purposes are served by the auditor's working papers?
14. What information should be included in the heading of each working paper schedule?
15. Distinguish between adjusting and reclassification entries.
16. What type of information is likely to be found in the auditor's permanent files?
17. Why is it essential that the auditor keep careful control over his working papers?
18. What purpose is served by including Rule 1.03 pertaining to the confidential relationship between the auditor and his client in the Code of Professional Ethics?
19. Why would a compilation of the procedures discussed in succeeding chapters not constitute an audit program for a specific audit?

QUESTIONS ON APPLICATION OF AUDITING STANDARDS

20. The bookkeeper of Sizzles and Burns Company follows the practice of charging supplies to a prepaid expense account when purchased. At the end of the year an inventory of supplies is taken and the appropriate adjustment made to the prepaid expense account. This adjustment has already been made for the

fiscal year ended February 28. In the course of your audit review of the client's records you discover that during the year a $50 purchase of advertising supplies was incorrectly charged to "Office Supplies on Hand." What adjusting entry would you make in your working papers to correct this error?

21. Your client took a physical inventory at September 30, the close of the concern's fiscal year, and adjusted the perpetual inventory control account for the inventory shortage that was determined to have occurred. You discover in your audit that goods costing $567.80 and selling for $793.25 were shipped prior to the end of the fiscal year but the entries for the cost of sales and the corresponding sales entries were not made until the following month.
    (a) Assuming that the client has not yet closed its books, give the adjusting entries (if any) that the client should make.
    (b) Give the reversing entries (if any) that the client should make.

22. In the course of your examination of your client's records as of December 31, you discover the following items relating to inventory:
    Merchandise costing $1,200 was received on December 29, and counted in the physical inventory on December 31, but the invoice was not entered in the voucher register until January 5.
    An invoice for $500 was recorded in the voucher register on December 27, but the merchandise involved was not received until January 6.
    (a) Assuming that the inventory account (perpetual basis) has been adjusted to agree with the physical inventory taken on December 31 without consideration of the effect of the two items stated above and that the client's books have not been closed for the year, give the adjusting entries that should be made by the client.
    (b) Give the reversing entries, if any, that should be made next year.

23. Rule 4.06 of the A.I.C.P.A. Code of Professional Ethics prohibits a member from being associated in any way with a corporation engaged in the practice of public accounting. Could a member of the Institute accept a job with an automobile manufacturing concern that involves visiting the company's dealers, reviewing their accounting records, and suggesting changes to bring the records into conformity with the standard accounting system that the dealers are required to follow? Explain.

24. "Auditing is basically an analytical activity, but it can be made a constructive activity as well if the auditor has the proper viewpoint." Explain.

25. Why should the loss from doubtful accounts shown in the annual audit file also be recorded in the permanent file? What other related figures should also be posted to the permanent file from the annual audit file?

26. Suggest the objectives of an examination intended to permit you to satisfy yourself that the amount of trade receivables in your client's balance sheet has been fairly stated.

27. Large public accounting firms sometimes try to arrange the audit assignments of each staff man so he can become a specialist in handling audits for some particular type of business, such as retail stores, financial institutions, oil companies, or manufacturing concerns. What advantages and disadvantages may result from such specialization?

28. "While in general the independent auditor should not strive to assure himself that the items on the financial statements are accurate to the penny, cash would be an exception to that rule." Comment.

29. As the auditor for Kermit and Fox, a wholesaling concern, you note the very weak financial condition of the concern. Vendors selling to the organization have not been paid according to credit terms, and large amounts have been

borrowed from local banks. A number of these loans are past due, and the bankers are threatening to bring involuntary bankruptcy proceedings.

Shortly after completing the Kermit and Fox examination, you begin your examination of Smith Manufacturing Co., where you find a substantial receivable from Kermit and Fox. Although part of this account is already past due, you find the credit manager of Smith Manufacturing Co. believes that the account will be collectible in full, and no provision has been made for a possible loss on the account.

How would you proceed in your examination of Smith Manufacturing Co.?

30. To what extent should an accountant assigned to a repeat engagement make use of the working papers of the audit for last year, assuming another staff member made the examination?

31. In connection with the auditor's examination of the figure for inventory shown on the client's financial statements, suggest a specific audit procedure under each of the five types of audit procedures listed in this chapter.

PROBLEMS

32. Index the following related working paper schedules in accordance with the plan outlined in the text.

Inventory summary

Analysis of raw materials control account

Analysis of work in process control account

Test counts of raw materials

Summary of raw materials reduced to market

Pricing tests of raw materials

Number of days' supply on hand—major items of raw materials, current production

Number of days' supply on hand—major items of raw materials, replacement parts

33. From the following list of account balances supplied by your client, the Adams Co., prepare working balance sheet and profit and loss schedules, and any lead schedules that may be necessary. Do not head up money columns for other than the current year's balance.

Accounts payable	$ 45,328.14
Accounts receivable—trade	95,821.50
Accumulated depreciation on plant and equipment	4,871.30
Accrued property taxes payable	405.01
Accrued salaries payable	819.20
Common stock	80,000.00
Cost of goods sold	196,093.84
Current provision for doubtful accounts	1,005.90
Depreciation expense	1,421.15
Dividends declared and paid	12,000.00
Due from officers and employees	2,807.10
Estimated loss on doubtful accounts	2,190.18
First National Bank—Payroll account	1,000.00
First National Bank—Regular account	4,875.50
Income taxes payable	5,771.85
Income tax expense	5,771.85
Inventory—Main warehouse	85,914.20

Inventory—Branch warehouse.. 23,109.45
Inventory shortage 1,390.58
Last National Bank—Special account 2,019.80
Merchandise in transit... 6,990.05
Net sales... 287,194.52
Officers' salaries... 15,120.30
Office salaries.. 20,201.58
Office supplies expense 721.37
Petty cash fund 250.00
Plant and equipment 12,304.10
Prepaid expenses.. 470.50
Prepayments to suppliers 7,120.18
Reno Bank and Trust Co.—Branch collections 1,805.70
Retained earnings—beginning of year 86,208.26
Selling expenses 13,318.43
Social Security taxes payable 191.54
Taxes expense... 1,809.10
Withholding taxes payable... 362.18

34. You have been engaged to review the records and prepare corrected financial
statements for the Graber Corporation. The books of account are in agreement
with the following balance sheet:

GRABER CORPORATION
Balance Sheet
December 31, 1967

Assets		Liabilities and Capital	
Cash........................	$ 5,000	Accounts payable	$ 2,000
Accounts receivable..............	10,000	Notes payable	4,000
Notes receivable	3,000	Capital stock	10,000
Inventory	$ 25,000	Retained earnings	27,000
	$ 43,000		$ 43,000

A review of the books of the corporation indicates that the errors and omissions indicated below had not been corrected during the applicable years.

December 31	Inventory Over-valued	Inventory Under-valued	Prepaid Expense	Prepaid Income	Accrued Expense	Accrued Income
1964....	$....	$ 6,000	$ 900	$....	$ 200	$....
1965....	7,000	....	700	400	75	125
1966....	8,000	....	500	....	100	....
1967....	....	9,000	600	300	50	150

The profits per the books are: 1965, $7,500; 1966, $6,500; and 1967, $5,500.
No dividends were declared during these years and no adjustments were made
to retained earnings.

Required:
Prepare a worksheet to develop the correct profits for the years 1965, 1966,
and 1967 and the adjusted balance sheet accounts as of December 31, 1967.
(Ignore possible income tax effects.)   (Uniform C.P.A. Examination)

35. Comparison between the inter-office account of City Wholesale Hardware Co. with its suburban branch and the corresponding account carried on the latter's books shows the following discrepancies at the close of business, September 30, 1967.
    1. A charge of $870 (office furniture) on HO taken up by branch as $780.
    2. A credit by HO for $300 (merchandise allowance) taken up by the branch as $350.
    3. HO charged branch $325 for interest on open account which branch failed to take up in full; instead, branch sent to HO an incorrect adjusting memo, reducing the charge by $75 and set up a liability for the net amount.
    4. A charge for labor by HO, $433, was taken up twice by branch.
    5. A charge of $785 was made by HO for freight on merchandise, but entered by branch as $78.50.
    6. Branch incorrectly sent HO a debit note for $293, representing its proportion of bill for truck repairs; HO did not record it.
    7. HO received $475 from sale of truck which it erroneously credited to branch; the branch did not charge HO therewith.
    8. Branch accidentally received a copy of HO entry dated 10/10/67 correcting No. 7 and entered a credit in favor of HO as of September 30, 1967.

    The balance of the account with the branch on the head office books showed $131,690 receivable from the branch at September 30, 1967. The inter-office accounts were in balance at the beginning of the year.

    (a) Prepare a schedule showing your computation of the balance of the inter-office account on the branch books before adjustment on September 30, 1967.
    (b) Prepare journal entries to adjust the branch books.
    (c) Prepare a reconciliation of the balances of the branch and home office accounts at September 30, 1967, after making the adjustments in (b).
    (Uniform C.P.A. Examination)

36. You have been engaged to audit the Thomas Trading Company as of December 31, 1967. A summary of the general ledger accounts is presented below. Based on the transactions as stated and the supplementary information, you are to prepare working papers which show in detail "Ledger Balance 12/31/67," "Audit Adjustments," "Profit and Loss for Year," and "Balance-Sheet 12/31/67." Columns for "Surplus Changes" may be included or entries to "Surplus" may be shown in the other columns provided such entries are clearly identified as applicable to "Surplus."

    Key all audit adjustments and in journal form present the adjusting entry together with a brief explanation of the purpose of or reason for the entry. A worksheet for Balance-Sheet accounts and a separate worksheet for Profit and Loss accounts may be prepared. There are no posting errors or mathematical errors in the trial balances or in the transactions for the year.

Summary of Transactions Recorded During the Year

(a) Accounts receivable	$190,000	
Sales		$190,000
Sales on account.		
(b) Cash	181,000	
Accounts receivable		180,000
Recoveries of accounts charged off in prior years		1,000
Cash collections from accounts.		

(c) Purchases 140,000
    Accounts payable 12,000
        Cash 152,000
            Purchases for the year and payment of the opening
            balance of accounts payable.

(d) Prepaid expenses 2,000
    Expenses 2,000
            Net change in prepaid expenses during the year.

(e) Expenses 24,000
    Interest on bonds 6,000
    Life insurance-company president 1,000
        Cash 31,000
            Disbursement for operating expenses, bond interest
            (including interest deposited with trustee) and life
            insurance premium.

(f) Investment in B Co. 30,000
    U.S. tax notes. 2,000
    Marketable securities 10,000
        Cash. 42,000
            Disbursement on January 1, 1967 for stock of B
            Company, tax notes and marketable securities.

(g) Cash 205,000
    Bonds payable. 200,000
    Unamortized bond discount 5,000
            Issuance for cash on January 1, 1967 of $200,000
            of 3% twenty-year bonds at $102.50.

(h) Bonds payable. 100,000
    Unamortized bond discount 2,000
        Cash 102,000
            Redemption at $102 on January 1, 1967 of the outstanding
            issue of 5% bonds which were due January 1, 1972.

(i) Accounts receivable 5,000
    Cash 5,000
            Cash advance to the company president.

(j) Cash 40,000
    Common stock 10,000
    Surplus 30,000
            Issue for cash on June 30, 1967 of 10,000 shares of
            no-par common stock at $4 per share. (See comment
            under " Additional Information, Item 3.")

(k) Treasury stock. 7,000
    Cash. 7,000
            Purchase on July 31, 1967 of 2,000 shares of the com-
            pany's own common stock at $3.50 per share.

(l) Cash. 4,000
    Treasury stock. 4,000
            Sale at $4 per share on August 31, 1967 of 1,000
            shares of the stock reacquired on July 31, 1967.
            (See Item k above.)

(m) Reserve for 1966 income taxes 9,000
    Cash. 9,000
            Payment of 1966 income taxes in full.

(n) Machinery... 10,000
      Cash   10,000
          Payment for machinery purchased on January 2, 1967
          together with $299 freight and $800 installation cost.

(o) Depreciation expense................................... 15,000
      Accumulated depreciation—building   4,000
      Accumulated depreciation—machinery   11,000
          Depreciation expense for the year at the rate of 10%
          on machinery and 2% on buildings.

(p) Purchases 20,000
      Accounts payable   20,000
          Set up the unrecorded purchases and accounts payable
          at December 31, 1967.

(q) Inventory 30,000
      Purchases   30,000
          To adjust the inventory balance as of December 31,
          1966 to the correct balance as óf December 31, 1967.

(r) Cash 10,000
      Dividend and interest income..........................   10,000
          Interest and dividend collected. The dividend of $9,000
          was from B Company. It was declared on January 10,
          1967. The surplus accounts of B Company decreased
          $10,000 during the year 1967.

(s) Bad debt expense 475
      Reserve for bad accounts   475
          Provision for estimated loss on accounts receivable. The
          company bases its provision on $\frac{1}{4}$ of 1% of sales under
          the theory that the net uncollectible receivables (charge-
          offs less recoveries) arising in each year will approximate
          that amount.

(t) Accounts receivable.................................... 15,000
    Purchases 1,000
    Goodwill 14,000
      Cash   30,000
          On July 1, 1967 the company purchased the inventory
          and receivables of the Cole Sales Co. at a cost of
          $30,000. The purchase was made primarily to obtain an
          exclusive agency having seven years of remaining life.
          The inventory obtained in the purchase was valued at
          $1,000 and the receivables, all of which were collectible,
          amounted to $15,000. (Also see the following item.)

(u) Reserve for losses 14,000
      Goodwill   14,000
          The $14,000 set up as goodwill as a result of the
          business of the Cole Sales Co. was written off to reserve
          for losses "in order to avoid showing goodwill on the
          balance-sheet."

(v) Expenses 15,000
    Purchases 5,000
      Reserve for possible inventory price declines   5,000
      Reserve for losses   15,000
          The directors decided that, in view of the general
          business uncertainty, the reserve for losses and the reserve
          for possible inventory price decline should be increased.

These provisions were charged to expense of the year, the inventory provision being charged to purchases and the loss provision to expenses.

(w)	Reserve for losses	3,000	
	Cash		3,000
	Payment to B. Walter, an employee, in settlement of his claim for personal injury as a result of an accident on March 2, 1967. The charge was to reserve for losses.		
(x)	Surplus	4,000	
	Treasury stock	100	
	Common stock		4,000
	Dividend and interest income.........................		100
	A stock dividend of 10% was declared and paid on September 1, 1967. The stock was credited to capital stock accounts at $1 per share.		
(y)	Depreciation expense	5,500	
	Reserve for losses		5,500
	The board of directors approved the following action applicable to 1967 accounts: "In view of the 50% rise in machinery prices over average prices at which the company acquired its machinery now in use, it is suggested that depreciation on machinery should be increased 50%, with the credit made to reserve for losses rather than to the depreciation reserve in order to keep the latter account on a cost basis."		
(z)	Reserve for 1966 and 1967 income taxes	3,800	
	Reserve for losses		3,800
	The reserve for income taxes was debited $3,800 with a corresponding credit to reserve for losses in order to reduce the reserve for income taxes down to the estimated liability as of the close of 1967. (The amount of $2,200 liability may be assumed to be the correct liability for the purpose of this solution even though you may adjust net profit.)		

Additional information was developed during the course of your audit (which is the first audit that the company has ever had) as follows:

(1) The cash surrender value of life insurance was $2,000 on December 31, 1966 and $2,500 on December 31, 1967.

(2) On December 31, 1967, the "bid" price of the bonds included under marketable securities was $13,500 and the "ask" price was $14,000.

(3) Common stock has no par value. The original issue of 30,000 shares was at $2 per share. The company set up each share at $1 per share in the stock account in order to have the account show the number of shares outstanding. The board of directors approved this practice.

(4) The analysis of surplus shows the following summary of transactions since inception of the company.

Amount received from issuance of 30,000 shares of common stock at $2 per share above the amount credited to the capital stock account	$ 30,000
Net operating profits..	90,000
Total...	$120,000
Dividends paid..	25,000
Balance December 31, 1966	$ 95,000

Account	Ledger Balances 12/31/66 Debit	Credit	Summary of Transactions Debit	Credit	Ledger Balances 12/31/67 Debit	Credit
Cash	$ 8,000		(b) $181,000 (g) 205,000 (i) 40,000 (l) 4,000 (r) 10,000	(c) $152,000 (e) 31,000 (f) 42,000 (h) 102,000 (j) 5,000 (k) 7,000 (m) 9,000 (n) 10,000 (t) 30,000 (w) 3,000 (b) 180,000		
Accounts receivable	17,000		(a) 190,000 (i) 5,000 (t) 15,000		$ 57,000	
Inventory	20,000		(q) 30,000		47,000	
U. S. tax notes					50,000	
Marketable securities			(f) 2,000		2,000	
Life insurance-company president	3,000		(f) 10,000		13,000	
Investment in B Co. (90% owned)	7,000		(e) 1,000		8,000	
Land	10,000		(f) 30,000		30,000	
Buildings	200,000				10,000 200,000	
Accumulated depreciation-buildings		$ 50,000		(o) 4,000		$ 54,000
Machinery	100,000		(n) 10,000		110,000	
Accumulated depreciation-machinery		50,000		(o) 11,000		61,000
Goodwill				(u) 14,000		
Unamortized bond discount	3,000		(t) 14,000	(g) 5,000		
Prepaid expenses	1,000		(h) 2,000		3,000	
Accounts payable		12,000	(d) 2,000 (c) 12,000	(p) 20,000		20,000
Reserve for '66 & '67 income taxes		15,000	(m) 9,000 (z) 3,800			2,200

Account	Ledger Balances 12/31/66 Debit	Ledger Balances 12/31/66 Credit	Summary of Transactions Debit	Summary of Transactions Credit	Ledger Balances 12/31/67 Debit	Ledger Balances 12/31/67 Credit
Reserve for possible inventory price declines		5,000		(v) 5,000		10,000
Bonds payable		100,000	(h) 100,000	(g) 200,000		200,000
Reserve for losses		10,000	(u) 14,000	(v) 15,000		17,300
			(w) 3,000	(y) 5,500		
				(z) 3,800		
Reserve for bad accounts		2,000		(s) 475		2,475
Common stock		30,000		(j) 10,000		44,000
				(x) 4,000		
Surplus		95,000	(x) 4,000	(j) 30,000		121,000
Treasury stock			(k) 7,000	(l) 4,000	3,100	
			(x) 100			
Sales			(c) 140,000	(a) 190,000		190,000
Purchases			(p) 20,000	(q) 30,000	136,000	
			(v) 5,000			
			(t) 1,000			
Expenses			(e) 24,000		37,000	
			(v) 15,000			
Depreciation expense			(y) 5,500	(d) 2,000	20,500	
			(o) 15,000			
Bad debt expense			(s) 475		475	
Recoveries of accounts charged off in prior years				(b) 1,000		1,000
Dividend and interest income ...				(r) 10,000		10,100
				(x) 100		
Interest on bonds			(e) 6,000		6,000	
	$369,000	$369,000	$1,135,875	$1,135,875	$733,075	$733,075

Revenue and receivables
systems; internal control

7

The consummation of a sales transaction produces revenue for the seller and a corresponding inflow of assets—usually in the form of a receivable but sometimes directly in the form of cash. Typical procedures and records related to credit sales are covered in this chapter; cash sales are discussed in Chapter 14 along with other transactions resulting in the receipt of cash.

Objectives of Internal Control

Internal control over sales and receivables is generally expected to give assurance that:

1. All orders received are filled promptly.
2. Customers are correctly billed for all merchandise released by the shipping department.
3. All receivables resulting from completed sales transactions are correctly recorded.
4. Amounts receivable from customers are collected if at all possible.
5. Collections on receivables are fully accounted for.
6. Reports adequately summarize sales and credit activities and reveal the current status of uncollected receivables.

The manner in which such controls are effected and the related procedures and records involved in the handling of sales and receivables are portrayed in the flow charts, Figures 7–1 and 7–2. The division of responsibility apparent in the charts is an important factor in the achievement of satisfactory internal control. The various activities and the associated records are more fully discussed under the headings of the various departments and activities that are involved.

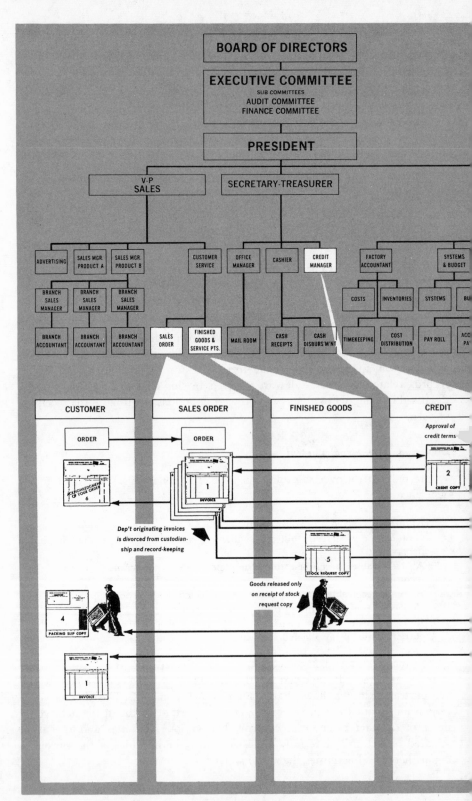

Figure 7-1   152

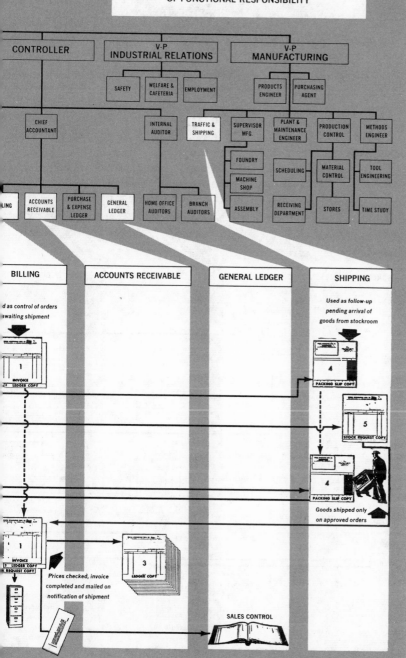

SALES

PROCEDURAL FLOW CHART SHOWN IN RELATION
TO ORGANIZATION CHART TO PORTRAY
THE CONTROL OBTAINED THROUGH SEGREGATION
OF FUNCTIONAL RESPONSIBILITY

CONTROLLER

V-P
INDUSTRIAL RELATIONS

V-P
MANUFACTURING

SAFETY | WELFARE & CAFETERIA | EMPLOYMENT

PRODUCTS ENGINEER | PURCHASING AGENT

CHIEF ACCOUNTANT

INTERNAL AUDITOR | TRAFFIC & SHIPPING

SUPERVISOR MFG. | PLANT & MAINTENANCE ENGINEER | PRODUCTION CONTROL | METHODS ENGINEER

FOUNDRY

SCHEDULING | MATERIAL CONTROL | TOOL ENGINEERING

MACHINE SHOP

...LING | ACCOUNTS RECEIVABLE | PURCHASE & EXPENSE LEDGER | GENERAL LEDGER | HOME OFFICE AUDITORS | BRANCH AUDITORS | ASSEMBLY | RECEIVING DEPARTMENT | STORES | TIME STUDY

BILLING

...d as control of orders
...awaiting shipment

1
INVOICE
...2] LEDGER COPY

1
INVOICE
...3 LEDGER COPY
...K REQUEST COPY

Prices checked, invoice
completed and mailed on
notification of shipment

ACCOUNTS RECEIVABLE

3
LEDGER COPY

GENERAL LEDGER

SALES CONTROL

SHIPPING

Used as follow-up
pending arrival of
goods from stockroom

4
PACKING SLIP COPY

5
STOCK REQUEST COPY

4
PACKING SLIP COPY

Goods shipped only
on approved orders

Figure 7-1 (Continued)   153

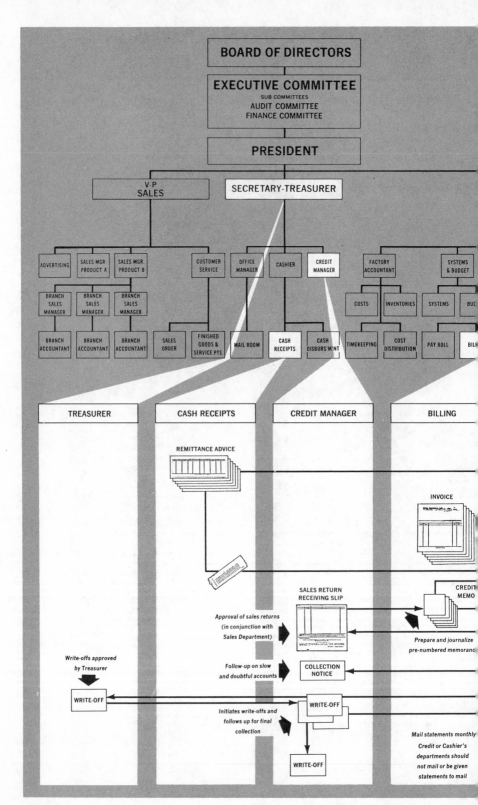

Figure 7-2

154

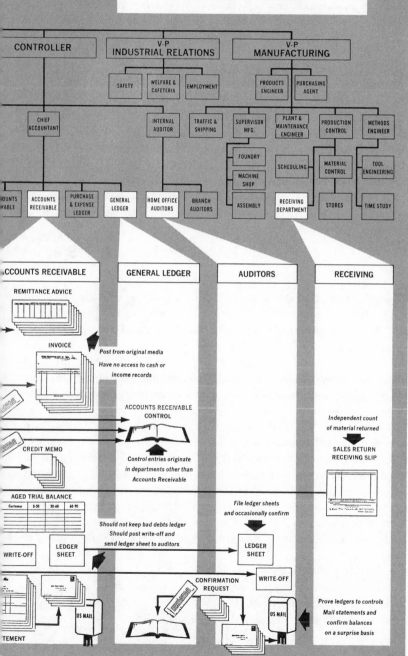

ACCOUNTS RECEIVABLE

PROCEDURAL FLOW CHART SHOWN IN RELATION
TO ORGANIZATION CHART TO PORTRAY
THE CONTROL OBTAINED THROUGH SEGREGATION
OF FUNCTIONAL RESPONSIBILITY

CONTROLLER

V-P INDUSTRIAL RELATIONS

V-P MANUFACTURING

SAFETY — WELFARE & CAFETERIA — EMPLOYMENT

PRODUCTS ENGINEER — PURCHASING AGENT

CHIEF ACCOUNTANT

INTERNAL AUDITOR — TRAFFIC & SHIPPING — SUPERVISOR MFG. — PLANT & MAINTENANCE ENGINEER — PRODUCTION CONTROL — METHODS ENGINEER

FOUNDRY — SCHEDULING — MATERIAL CONTROL — TOOL ENGINEERING

MACHINE SHOP

ACCOUNTS RECEIVABLE — PURCHASE & EXPENSE LEDGER — GENERAL LEDGER — HOME OFFICE AUDITORS — BRANCH AUDITORS — ASSEMBLY — RECEIVING DEPARTMENT — STORES — TIME STUDY

ACCOUNTS RECEIVABLE

REMITTANCE ADVICE

INVOICE

Post from original media
Have no access to cash or
income records

CREDIT MEMO

AGED TRIAL BALANCE

Customer	0-30	30-60	60-90

WRITE-OFF — LEDGER SHEET

STATEMENT

US MAIL

GENERAL LEDGER

ACCOUNTS RECEIVABLE CONTROL

Control entries originate
in departments other than
Accounts Receivable

Should not keep bad debts ledger
Should post write-off and
send ledger sheet to auditors

CONFIRMATION REQUEST

AUDITORS

File ledger sheets
and occasionally confirm

LEDGER SHEET

WRITE-OFF

US MAIL

RECEIVING

Independent count
of material returned

SALES RETURN
RECEIVING SLIP

Prove ledgers to controls
Mail statements and
confirm balances
on a surprise basis

Figure 7-2 (Continued)   155

Sales Department

Sales procedures and records are directly affected by various needs related to the successful operation of the sales department. The over-all sales function encompasses such activities as market research, product planning and development, price determination, budgeting of sales and selling expenses, advertising, and sales promotion. Accounting data are essential to the effective conduct of such activities: sales records are vital to market research; product planning and development require data on present and future product and packaging costs, and price determination and choice of methods of distribution require information on product, packaging, and distribution costs, analyzed by product, type of customer, and size of sale transaction. Such cost information is also important in avoiding violations of the Robinson-Patman Amendment to the Clayton Act, which prohibits price differences in interstate commerce that are not justified by cost differences.

The activities and records involved in executing the sales function are discussed under the various responsibility subdivisions of a typical business organization.

Sales Order Department

In large concerns, a separate department within the sales organization is ordinarily assigned the responsibility for processing and following up on customers' orders. Customarily referred to as the sales order department or customers' order department, the responsibilities of the department are likely to include establishing control over all orders received, screening and editing the orders, obtaining credit authorization, preparing shipping orders and back orders, and developing statistics to enable management to appraise sales trends and service to customers.

Control over orders received is important in assuring that all orders are filled. If orders are received on prenumbered forms prepared by salesmen, control may be achieved by accounting for the serial numbers on the forms submitted. If customers order directly, control may be established by serially numbering the orders as they are received, or by preparing a serially numbered company order form in the case of telephone orders. Records must be maintained of all open orders, the record on a particular order being closed when notice is received that the order has been shipped and billed.

Orders should first be screened to identify orders from new customers whose credit has not been established. Such orders are routed to the credit section for credit approval, establishment of credit limits, preparation of an address card or plate, and setting up of an accounts receivable record. Orders would then be "edited" to ascertain that the items ordered are actually handled by the company and are currently in stock, and that code numbers, descriptions, and prices are correct. "Back orders" may be written at this time for items temporarily out of stock, or they may be written later after notice from the shipping department that certain items ordered could not be shipped. A back order is merely a new order prepared to cover items that are not currently available. Back orders are held in a tickler file and released for processing as soon as the merchandise is available.

If customers submit their orders on a company form, the original order form can be used in filling the order, as there will be complete uniformity in the forms used, which is necessary to facilitate order filling and shipping. For protection against loss of such orders before shipping and billing are accomplished, a microfilm record is sometimes prepared of each order before it is released for further processing.

In most instances, the sales order department prepares a separate shipping order or production order from the customer's order form. When stock items are ordered, inventory records may be consulted to determine whether the items are on hand before the shipping order is prepared. Under such an arrangement, complete prebilling can be followed, thus permitting preparation of the customer's invoice as a sales order operation; one copy of the invoice form then serves as the shipping order. If a production order must be written, the expected completion date and shipping date are determined as a step in the editing process.

The shipping order is a major document in the processing of customers' orders, and it is important to recognize the uses of the various copies of the shipping order that may be prepared. These would include:

1. Shipping copy—authorizes order fillers to select items from stock and forward them to the shipping department, where the shipping copy constitutes authorization to release the goods for shipment to the customer. After a record of the shipment is made in the shipping department, the shipping copy is forwarded to the billing section, where the prenumbered shipping copies should be accounted for in order to assure that all goods shipped have been billed.
2. Credit copy—used to clear customer's credit standing, as discussed in a following section.
3. Acknowledgment copy—sent to the customer to tell him that the order has been received and when shipment is expected to be made.
4. Bill of lading copy—contains the same variable information as the shipping copy, but the printed information is that of a bill of lading. Three copies are desirable—two for the carrier and one to be signed by the carrier's agent as a receipt for the goods. The latter copy may then be retained and filed to constitute a shipping record.
5. Packing slip—packed with the goods to assist the customer's receiving department in identifying the shipment and its contents.
6. Sales order follow-up copy—filed in the sales order department on the basis of expected date of shipment and removed from the file upon receipt

of the completed shipping copy, which should be routed through the sales order department on the way to the billing department. Open orders in the follow-up file are the source of management report figures on order backlogs.

7. Cross-index file copy—filed alphabetically by customer name to facilitate answering inquiries from customers.

If products are produced on order from the customer rather than being shipped from inventory, a production order is prepared. Preparation of production orders is usually a function of the production scheduling and control department, but in simple situations the sales order section may prepare the production order. Adequate information would have to be available to the sales order department on such matters as specifications and production requirements.

Credit Department

Because most sales other than retail sales are likely to be on a credit basis, the approval of the credit department must be obtained sometime before an order is finally shipped. If credit rejections occur quite frequently, the credit check should probably be made before the order department processes the order. In other cases, shipping orders are routed from the order department to the credit department, and only those approved and released by the credit department are filled. One company which operated in an industry where competition necessitated that shipments be made as soon as possible found that orders were very seldom rejected for credit reasons. To speed up shipment, all shipping orders were sent directly to the shipping department without credit approval. A copy of the shipping order was, however, sent to the credit department, and in those rare instances when credit had to be denied, the shipping department was merely notified not to ship the goods. Although this arrangement placed some additional burden on the shipping department, considerable benefit was received in the form of faster handling of customer orders.

Shipping Department

A primary responsibility of the shipping department is to see that nothing leaves the company premises except under proper authorization. Such authorization might be a shipping order, an approved debit memo for return of goods to a vendor, or possibly a factory work order covering the removal of a piece of equipment to be sold or junked. The authorizations should, of course, be serially numbered so that the accounting department can subsequently ascertain that a proper accounting charge has been made for every item which left the plant. Preferably, the shipping department should be separate from and independent of the receiving department to prevent goods from being received and shipped without entering into the accounting processes designed to establish control over shipments.

Billing Department

Usually a part of the accounting department, the billing department is charged with the preparation of customer invoices. Receipt of the shipping copy of the shipping order is the usual basis for invoice preparation, and accounting for the prenumbered shipping copies generally takes place at this point to assure that all shipments are billed.

Information necessary for billing may include prices, credit terms, special discounts, freight to be charged to the customer, and sales or other taxes that are passed on to the customer. The information may be noted on the shipping order in advance or determined by the billing clerk in the course of preparing the customer's invoice. The invoice forms may be loose forms that are assembled by the billing clerk, but more efficient unit sets or continuous forms are customarily used. Writing equipment may be simply a typewriter; a billing machine that accumulates one or more totals as invoices are written; a combined billing and computing machine, such as the Friden Computyper that extends quantity and price and calculates discounts, taxes, and similar figures as well as developing various totals; or a punched-card tabulating machine.

A control total of all invoices written is an important by-product of the billing operation; if this total is not automatically developed as the invoices are written, an adding machine tape listing should be prepared. The control total is important to internal control over the accuracy of accounts receivable records which are prepared following the billing operation.

Also related to the billing operation is the possibility of integrated data processing through the simultaneous preparation of punched cards or punched paper tape which can then be used for completely automatic sales analysis and accounts receivable posting on data-processing equipment.

The number of invoice copies to be prepared varies widely from company to company and may even vary within a given company depending on the requirements of each customer. The Federal government, for example, may require that as many as eight or ten copies of an invoice be submitted. The variability of such requirements is a strong argument for the preparation of duplicate invoice copies by the hectographic process rather than by carbon impression, because greater flexibility is possible in the number of copies that are prepared. Copies may be designated and used as follows:

1. Customer copies—including the original of the invoice and as many additional copies as the customer may request.
2. Accounts receivable copy—may represent a posting medium, or, when placed

in a customer's receivable file, may constitute the actual accounts receivable record under bookless bookkeeping procedures. The control total of invoices written is important in the control of accounts receivable records.

3. Sales journal copy—under bookless bookkeeping procedures, a numerical file of these copies and adding machine tapes of daily totals would constitute the sales journal.

4. Analysis copy—used for sales analysis purposes, preparation of salesmen's commission records, and development of cost of sales figures credited to general ledger inventory accounts.

5. Salesman's copy—informs the salesman that the customer's order has been filled and permits the salesman to compute commissions that have been earned.

Punched-card billing. Cards may be key-punched from customers' orders with pricing information, extended on a punched-card calculator, and, with the addition of name and address header cards, used to prepare customer invoices on the tabulator. Automatic carriage controls make it possible to prepare the invoices consecutively on continuous forms.

Key punching is costly, however, and subject to errors, particularly with respect to pricing. Thus, a more satisfactory approach to punched-card billing is to use prepunched cards. One simple but effective method is based on tub-file, or open-item, inventory records. As inventory is received, gang punching is employed to prepare, from a master card, detail inventory cards equal to the number of items received. These cards then contain such data as item code number, description, cost, selling price, weight, and warehouse location, and are placed in the inventory file. Cards are removed from the inventory file on the basis of customers' orders—one card for each unit of merchandise ordered; hence, an order for ten units would require ten cards. The pulled cards, together with header cards, are then tabulated to prepare the invoices. The tabulator is programmed so that, for multiple cards for a given item, the quantity (one) and price punched in each card are accumulated and then printed when the tabulator senses that the next card is for a different item. In this manner, ten cards for an item selling for $2.50 would cause this printing to occur:

$$10 \text{ (description)} \qquad \$2.50 \qquad \$25.00$$

Another method of preparing billing cards without key punching is related to a plan known as "batch billing." This plan is discussed in the procedures chapter dealing with inventories.

Sales Analysis

The analysis of sales is primarily an accounting function, and in relatively simple situations involving a small number of separate product or department classifications, the sales analysis is likely to be accomplished on a columnar basis in the preparation of the sales journal. Various other analysis techniques may be utilized if the number of columns becomes too cumbersome or if cross-classifications are desired. Cost of sales may be analyzed on the same basis as sales in order to develop gross margin figures, and must also be analyzed by inventory class if multiple perpetual inventory accounts are maintained. In such cases, cost of sales figures must be added to the analysis copy of the sales invoice.

Other techniques for making sales analyses include columnar analyses on multiple work sheets, posted account distribution (each sales amount is posted to one or more separate accounts), register distribution utilizing a multiple-total accounting machine, hand-sort distribution involving sorting the invoices into designated classifications and then totaling the amounts by adding machine, and unit ticket methods involving hand, needle, or machine sorting of the unit tickets. Unit ticket methods are especially advantageous if sales invoices are mixed media (two or more classifications appearing on a single invoice) and if cross-classifications are to be made (for example, the same amount classified by product, by type of customer, and by salesman). Unit tickets may be hand sorted and added, or, when appropriate forms are used, needle sorted and added by hand or on the special tabulating punch, or machine sorted and tabulated on punched-card machines.

Peg-strip summarization is quite effective if a limited number of products is involved and invoices or sales tickets are prepared by route salesmen as the sales are made, as in dairy or bakery sales. Each product is printed on a separate line of the peg-strip sales invoice form. At the end of the day, the forms turned in by a salesman are "shingled" and the amounts recorded are added across to obtain the total sales of each product by the salesman. These totals are recorded on a salesman summary form, and the summaries are in turn shingled and added to obtain daily totals for each product classification. Monthly totals are obtained by shingling and adding the daily total forms.

Accounts Receivable Department

The records maintained by the accounts receivable department are designed primarily for the benefit of the credit department. Credit is extended only if the records show that a customer is not delinquent in paying for past purchases and if a new order does not cause the balance of the account to exceed the credit limit that has been established. A customer's payment history is also an important factor in deciding whether an established credit limit can be increased. The principal reason for maintaining accounts receivable records, however, is related to the collection of amounts owed. Preferably, the records should show the status of each charge to the customer's account, so that if payment has not been made by the date that it is due, follow-up effort can be initiated.

Customer statements. Trade practices with respect to credit terms—and whether monthly statements are mailed to customers—will ordinarily have a direct effect on the form of accounts receivable records. Most industrial concerns use terms that require payment of each invoice on its specific due date. Terms such as 2/10, n/30 or n/15 would be in this category, and it is becoming increasingly infrequent to prepare monthly statements when such terms are in use. Follow-up is initiated on the specific invoice involved if payment is not received shortly after the due date. Under these circumstances, bookless bookkeeping procedures may be advantageously employed. Invoices are placed in the accounts receivable ledger file in customer sequence and are removed from the file when they are paid. The paid invoices, filed by date of payment, then constitute the daily record of cash receipts. Partial payments, overpayments, and credit balances present somewhat of a problem but can be handled by preparing and filing cash credit forms. In punched-card accounting methods, which are referred to later in this chapter, credit terms requiring payment of each invoice on its due date are generally handled by the "open item" method.

Credit terms such as n/10, E.O.M., or 2/10, n/30 prox., that require payment on a given date for all purchases for the preceding month, generally function most effectively if the customer is furnished a statement detailing the purchases that have been made. The importance of such a statement is particularly evident in retail thirty-day charge account operations, because the customer does not, as a rule, keep a record of the purchases made and hence cannot readily determine the amount he is to pay unless he receives a statement of his account. As the statement includes a record of all transactions with the customer for the month, the seller's accounts receivable records are most efficiently prepared as simply a duplicate of the customer's statement. Some form of posted accounts receivable record is therefore commonly employed with monthly credit terms.

Ledger posting of sales. For the business that requires a distribution of sales into a limited number of classifications, the sales distribution and posting to customers' accounts and statements can be combined in a single operation by utilizing either an accounting board (if volume is limited) or an accounting machine. In either case, pick-up of the old balance of the account should be proved, sales distribution credits should be balanced against accounts receivable debits, and both figures should be proved against the predetermined total of the sales invoices provided by the billing department. The accounting-board approach should provide for a proof of the calculation of new balances, a step that is unnecessary in accounting-machine applications because the mechanical accuracy of the machines is very high. A line-lock and batch proof is most effective in accounting-machine applications to prove the pick-up of the old balance and the posting of the transaction amount.

If accounts receivable volume is sufficient to warrant sub-ledger controls, posting media must first be sorted into control groups and totals obtained for each group. When the volume of transactions is large, a bank proof machine is effective in performing the sorting and totaling operations. The totals derived through this step should be proven against predetermined totals of the posting media independently derived in the course of previous processing of the media.

Ledger posting of cash receipts. Cash receipts are posted in much the same way as sales; the posting media will normally be customers' remittance advices, often in the form of the voucher portion of a voucher-check, or the top half of the monthly statement that was sent to the customer. Posting of cash receipts to customers' records can readily be combined with the preparation of the cash receipts journal. A line-lock proof can be accomplished in the following manner if the posting is done by book-keeping machine and assuming that cash discounts are involved:

First pick-up of old balance	$500.00	
Credit for payment received	−100.00	
New balance	$400.00	
Second pick-up of old balance	−500.00	
Discount allowed	2.00	
Bank debit	98.00	
Proof	$ .00	Total

Accumulation of the bank debit amounts by the bookkeeping machine would also permit a batch proof of the cash amounts posted against the cashier's deposit total.

The use of accounts receivable records in collection follow-up of amounts owed by customers suggests the importance of clearly designating in the records which charges have been paid and which are unpaid. Bookless records automatically develop such information because only unpaid charges remain in the file. With posted records, the best approach is to "key" each cash credit to the charge or charges which it covers by identifying the credit entry with an alphabetic character which is also recorded adjacent to each charge that has been paid by the customer's remittance.

Noncash credits may arise from sales returns, allowances, or bad debt write-offs. From an internal control standpoint, it is important that such credits be originated or approved by a department or person having no responsibility for handling cash or posting accounts receivable records.

The credits may be posted in separate posting runs or combined with cash credits for posting.

Month-end procedures. Most concerns that send monthly statements to their customers do so at the end of the month, although occasionally statements are mailed on a cycle basis during the month. With cycle mailing, the statements for each group of accounts (one or more ledgers) are mailed each month on a stated day, such mailings occurring throughout the month for the various groups. Regardless of the mailing plan, ledgers should be balanced with the related control accounts before mailing occurs, as an added assurance that the statements are correct and that all are present. Internal control is strengthened if the monthly trial balances are prepared, occasionally at least, by someone other than the regular accounts receivable bookkeeper.

Other end-of-month procedures include aging of accounts receivable balances and carrying balances forward to new statement forms for the following month. The purpose of aging is to provide the credit manager and other interested persons with a picture of the current status of the accounts receivable, and hence of the effectiveness of credit and collection activities since the previous aging of accounts. Carrying balances forward to new statement forms is merely a mechanical procedure necessitated by the mailing of statements for the preceding month. The new forms are usually addressed by the use of address plates before balances are carried forward.

Given the proper forms and an accounting machine of sufficient capacity, all three of the month-end procedures just discussed can be performed in a single operation. Based on the month in which unpaid items were charged, the amounts are listed horizontally on the new statement in boxes designated "current charges," "charges one month old," "charges two months old," and so forth. The total balance of the account is then written in its appropriate box and, by proper programming of the accounting machine, proved against the aging detail. The total balances are accumulated for proof against the ledger control, and the amounts in the individual aging categories are accumulated to provide the over-all aging of the accounts. The aging analysis on each customer's statement is a valuable collection device, for it reminds the customer if amounts were past due at the beginning of the month, and there is usually printed on the statement form a request that the customer remit any past-due amounts that were not paid during the month covered by the statement.

Aging on a "specific invoice" basis gives the most accurate picture of the condition of the accounts and is readily accomplished if the receivables records consist of open invoices under the bookless-records approach or if charges and payments are keyed in a ledger posting plan. If charges are not keyed to payments, the simplest way to age the account is on a first-in, first-out basis, which assumes that the balance is composed entirely of the most recent charges.

Installment accounts. Conventional posting to statement and ledger sheets is readily adapted to installment accounts, but alternative approaches are also followed. Window posting is particularly applicable. Charges and credits are posted by machine to both the ledger record of the account and the customer's record book. Locked-in totals and "customer audit" of the record of each transaction that is made in the customer's record book assure proper accounting for all cash received, despite the apparent violation of internal control when the same person receives cash and posts the records.

If the charge to the installment account results from a single transaction, as in the case of a loan or the purchase of a major item, and there is a fixed schedule for repayment, the payments and remaining balance can be scheduled in advance on the ledger record. "Posting" of the payments received can then be reduced to stamping the date when payment is received in the space provided adjacent to the particular payment that has been made. When a partial payment of an installment is made, the unpaid balance of the installment can be recorded in a debit-credit-balance section of the ledger card, along with penalty fees for late payments and other miscellaneous debits and credits to the account. Subsequent payment of these charges is posted as a credit in this portion of the ledger card, and the new balance of these miscellaneous items is extended.

Installment accounts cannot be aged in the same manner as regular charge accounts. The status of an account is best indicated by aging the entire balance according to the period of delinquency involved. One interpretation of delinquency is the number of installments that remain unpaid relative to the schedule for such payments. Another approach is to age the balance according to the number of months that have elapsed since the last payment was received on the account. Thus, even though five payments have been missed, if a payment was made in August and the accounts are being aged as of August 31, the account balance would be aged in the "current" classification. Experience has convinced credit men that the period elapsing since the most recent payment was made on an account is the best indicator of the likelihood that the entire account balance will be collected.

Cycle billing. Public utilities introduced cycle billing as a means of spreading work peaks involved in meter reading, billing, and cash handling. The technique was later adapted to department store charge-account receivables, but substantial changes in accounting procedures were required, as contrasted with the simplicity in converting to cycle billing in a public utility.

Department store applications are based on a "credit history card" to which is posted for each cycle period the total sales to the customer, total cash received, total credits for returns and allowances, and the ending balance of the account. These cards are filed alphabetically but are divided into about twenty groups, or cycles, so that one cycle can be billed on each business day of the month. Throughout the month, posting media for each day are sorted according to the cycle to which they apply, totals are obtained, and the totals are posted to the applicable cycle control accounts. The cycle totals are also summarized and posted to an over-all receivables control. The posting media are then filed in front of the credit-history cards to which they apply. Credit inquiries concerning the present balance of an account or delinquency status are answered by reference to the most recent billing balance shown on the credit-history card, plus any posting media that have been filed with the history card since the last billing date.

Prior to the billing date for a cycle, statement forms are addressed for all customers in that cycle. On the billing date, by means of an accounting machine, the posting clerk enters the customer's previous account balance (from the credit-history card) on the statement form, then enters the charges, cash receipts and noncash creidts and causes the machine to total. Totals accumulated by the machine for the customer's charges, cash receipts, and noncash credits are printed on the credit-history card, and the new balance computed by the machine is printed on the history card and the statement. Other registers in the machine accumulate figures for the entire posting run for old balances, debits, the two types of credits, and new balances. At the end of the run, the total of the new balances is compared with the balance shown by the cycle control; if the figures agree, presumably all procedures for the cycle period have been correctly executed and the cycle is in balance. If the cycle is out of balance, the error can be localized by comparing the total of the old balances with the cycle control balance at the previous billing date, and the totals for the three types of media can be compared with corresponding totals developed from the cycle control. An adding-machine listing of the media can be run if one of the media totals does not agree, in order to determine whether those media were correctly posted. Any remaining differences will require further investigation by traditional methods.

The fact that the records are essentially bookless in form makes it quite difficult to locate and eliminate errors. As a result, most department stores establish a maximum tolerable difference and make no further investigation of differences less than that amount. Errors resulting in overcharging a customer are likely to be reported by the customer so that subsequent correction can be made. Undercharges are likely to go unreported, thus eliminating the possibility of correction unless an item was billed to the wrong customer and that customer reports the error. In that situation, the item can then be charged to the customer who was originally undercharged. When differences between the detail accounts in a cycle and the cycle control are not located and corrected, it is important that such differences be recorded and reported regularly on a comparative basis so that appropriate steps can be taken if the differences should reveal a strong trend or become excessive.

After the detail for a cycle has been balanced, each statement and the related posting media are microfilmed for record purposes, and then the statement and the posting media are mailed to the customer. Inclusion of the media with the statements tends to reduce the number of inquiries from customers about transactions appearing on their statements, and makes it possible to do "nondescriptive" billing, in which only the amount of each transaction is shown, eliminating the writing of date and description for each transaction.

The advantages of cycle billing may be summarized as:

1. Elimination of monthly activity peaks with respect to balancing and mailing statements, carrying balances forward, aging the accounts, and handling cash collections. (Note that there is little change insofar as posting peaks are concerned, because under conventional posting the work is handled on a daily basis.)
2. Posting economy as a result of nondescriptive billing and having only once a month to locate an account, insert the account in the carriage of the accounting machine, and pick up the old balance.
3. Elimination of the need to prove each entry to the account as it is made.
4. Preparation of a trial balance as a by-product of posting rather than as an added operation.

Disadvantages include:

1. The current status of an account at any time other than the billing date must be determined by reference to the unposted media filed with the credit-history card.
2. Weakened internal control resulting from the possibility of accidental loss or purposeful destruction of posting media prior to the time they are billed. The bookless approach also makes it difficult to identify and correct errors that may occur.
3. Some customers are likely to object to paying bills at a date other than the tenth of the month, and may simply defer making payment until that time, thus reducing the cash available for operating needs of the business.

Punched-card records. The punched cards for debits to receivables records may be summary-punched as by-product of punched-card billing, they may be prepared by tape-to-card converter from a punched paper tape that is simultaneously punched as invoices are written on a billing machine, or the cards may be key-punched from invoices. In processing, the cards are listed in invoice-number order to create the traditional sales journal, and then the cards are filed in customer-number sequence. The filing may be manual, or the cards may be machine-sorted and then merged with the existing file of accounts receivable debit cards through use of a collator.

The file of debit cards is maintained on either an "open item" or "balance forward" basis. Under the open-item approach, which is roughly comparable with manually processed bookless records and is used with comparable credit terms, debit cards may be manually removed from the current file on the basis of cash receipts information transmitted by the cashier. The extracted cards can then be listed to produce a cash receipts journal. Partial payments would require key-punching of two credit cards, one to be placed in the open-item file behind the debit to which it applies; the other for preparation of the cash receipts journal. Upon final payment of the invoice, both the debit and the partial-payment cards would be removed, the net of the two cards representing the amount of cash received. As an alternative approach to processing open-item punched-card receivables, cash receipts cards can be key-punched from the detail of cash received (usually the customers' remittance advices) and then sorted and used in the collator to select the matching debit cards from the open-item file.

Key punching can be eliminated if the customer is furnished with a prepunched card which he then returns with his remittance. This "turn-around" document then becomes the cash credit card.

At the end of the month, open-item statements are readily prepared, if desired, by sorting customer name-and-address header cards in with the open-item cards and, with the assistance of the automatic carriage on the tabulator, listing the cards on statement forms. An aged trial balance is also prepared from the cards as a relatively simple tabulating-machine operation. Through control-panel wiring, cards are selected according to the month of sale and listed in appropriate columns, with appropriate counters accumulating totals for those columns for print-out at the completion of the run.

Maintenance of the receivables file by the balance-forward method involves a different procedure for handling the recording of collections from customers. Cash credit cards are key-punched from customers' remittance advices, or turn-around prepunched cards returned by the customers are used. The cards are listed to create a cash receipts journal and are then filed by customer number behind other related cards in the accounts receivable file.

At the end of the month, header cards are interfiled and statements are prepared on the tabulator, showing all transactions in each customer's account for the month and the account balance at the end of the month. The balance of each account is summary-punched to create the basis for the start of next month's receivable file. If desired, a total of all the accounts receivable can also be obtained as the statements are being prepared, thus making it possible to determine whether the accounts are in balance with the accounts receivable control. The balances can be aged, but aging must be made on a first-in, first-out basis, utilizing relatively complicated control-panel wiring.

The choice between the open-item and balance-forward methods should be made primarily on the basis of the credit terms to customers. It is interesting to note, however, that only the balance-forward method produces a useful record of past transactions with each customer. If such a record is desired by the credit department as an aid in administering credit, the balance-forward method would have to be used.

Supplementary Controls Over Sales and Other Revenues

The recording of sales made by wholesale or retail branches is often controlled through memorandum perpetual inventory records maintained on a selling-price basis. For example, a retail store inventory record would be charged at retail for all merchandise shipped to the store, and such charges must subsequently be accounted for in the form of cash, charges to accounts receivable, or inventory still on hand, plus the effect of price changes and a reasonable allowance for shortages.

Incidental revenue of a business should be subject to as much control as is possible, although the infrequency of transactions makes adequate separation of duties rather impractical. Whenever feasible, such revenue should be determined by the accounting department or reported to it independently of any cash received. Thus investment income should be scheduled and recorded by the accounting department independently of the treasurer's department. The accounting entries for the income should not be based on an advice from the treasurer's department that the income has been received. Proceeds from sales of plant assets should be estimated or determined by contract in advance of the removal of the assets from the plant. If the accounting department is given advance notice of the estimated proceeds, then as soon as the work order for the removal of the assets comes through, the accounting department can check to see that the proper amount of proceeds is received shortly afterward. The accounting department should also receive advance notice of any sales or shipments of scrap.

Revenue from vending machines presents special problems of internal control. Under no circumstances should payment for merchandise be made in cash from coins in the machines. Coins should be collected at regular intervals, deposited intact, and credit made to a special account. Payments for merchandise should be by regular company check and charged against the special account to which the collections were credited. These figures should then be analyzed periodically to determine that the reported proceeds bear a reasonable relationship to payments made. If the margin between the proceeds and payments falls below the known difference between unit costs and unit selling prices, there is a strong presumption that revenue is not being reported or that part of the purchased merchandise is being diverted for personal gain.

Management Reports

Information developed by the accounting system and reported to management with respect to sales in accordance with the dictates of responsibility reporting should be presented under the headings that are set forth below:

Sales Order Handling.
Daily reports
  1. Volume of orders received.
  2. Number of orders not completely processed at the end of the day.
  3. Order backlog, representing unfilled manufacturing orders or back orders for regularly stocked merchandise—number and amount of orders received, filled, and on hand at the end of the day.
  4. Sales lost because out of stock and no back order issued—number of orders and amount.
Monthly reports
  1. Cost per order handled.
  2. Average number of orders not completely processed at the end of each day.
  3. Order backlog at end of month, net change since previous month and same month last year, and aging of the amount according to month shipment is expected to be made.
  4. Sales lost.

Shipping.
  1. Numbers of orders shipped and total weight.
  2. Cost per order and per hundredweight of goods shipped.

Billing.
  1. Number of invoices written and total number of line items.
  2. Cost per invoice and per line item.

Credit.
  1. Number and amount of requests for credit: approved, rejected.
  2. Delinquency—aging of accounts, turnover, number of days' sales outstanding.
  3. Schedule of uncollectible accounts to be charged-off, classified by reasons for noncollectibility.
  4. Amount of write-off for uncollectible accounts, current and past periods; percentage relationship to credit sales and accounts receivable.
  5. Ratio of credit sales to total sales.
  6. Collections on accounts receivable previously written off as uncollectible.
  7. Operating costs—amount and cost per unit of activity, such as credit applications received, sales orders, and delinquent accounts.

Accounts Receivable.
  1. Number of entries posted and cost per entry.
  2. Differences between general and sub-ledger controls and trial balance listings of detailed accounts receivable.

Sales Analysis.
1. Sales by department or major product lines.
2. Sales by territory, salesman, type of customer, and method of sale, further analyzed by department or product line.
3. Sales returns and allowances, classified by cause, if available.
4. Gross margin analysis of sales, in same classifications as for sales.
5. External comparisons in terms of total industry sales and market potential.

Internal Auditing

The examination of sales and sales activities conducted by the internal auditor should cover such areas as internal control, management reports, and customer relations. The internal auditor should determine that a satisfactory separation of duties is in effect covering handling of customers' orders, shipping, billing, receivables, and authorization of credits for returns and allowances. Branch sales activities should receive particularly careful review by the internal auditor.

The recording of sales transactions should be tested and detail figures should be traced to account postings and report summaries in order to establish the reliability and accuracy of the reports which go to management. The reports should also be reviewed to determine that they are presenting all necessary information in the most useful form.

Confirmation of accounts receivable balances by corresponding with customers is one of the more important internal auditing activities designed to verify accounts receivable figures. Fictitious accounts, collections which have been misappropriated, and bookkeeping errors can all be readily disclosed by effective confirmation procedures. As a supplement to confirmation of accounts receivable balances, the internal auditor should make direct verification of the entries to the accounts receivable records. Verification of the trial balance of accounts receivable and comparison of the trial balance total with the balance of the accounts receivable control is also important.

Because satisfied customers are vital to a successful business, the internal auditor may well devote part of his time to a study of customer relations. He should watch for courteous treatment of customers by all employees, salesmen's knowledge of the products they sell to permit maximum servicing of customers' needs, time required to fill and ship customers' orders, and accuracy of filling and billing orders, to mention only a few of the possibilities in the area of customer relations.

The internal auditor should also evaluate employee performance from the standpoint of how well the assets of the company have been protected and conserved. In the course of his examination, he should satisfy himself that sound judgment was exercised in extending credit to customers, that credits for returned goods are supported by records showing that the goods were actually returned, that allowances were granted only when fully warranted by the circumstances, and that accounts were written off as bad debts only after all reasonable steps were taken to collect the accounts.

Because delinquency reports and aging analyses are so vital in appraising credit operation, the internal auditor should ascertain that these reports have been correctly prepared. The reports should be traced to supporting work sheets, and the work sheets should in turn be reviewed to determine that they reflect the actual condition of the accounts receivable.

The above comments should suggest that the internal auditor's examination of sales and receivables should be on a broad, constructive basis. In addition to testing and appraising the work being done at the time, he should also step back from the details and take an over-all look at the situation, trying especially to determine whether there are things not being done which might aid management or improve operating results. The appraisal of reports going to management, as mentioned earlier, is an example of such constructive activity. Other things the internal auditor should be alert for would include such broad items as the effectiveness of the company's sales and advertising policies and the question of whether all potential revenue is being developed and recorded. Included in the latter category would be the question of whether scrap, waste, or industrial by-products which are being discarded as valueless may actually have some commercial value, whether all revenue from such items as scrap sales or vending machine proceeds is being reported and accounted for, and whether employee discount privileges are being abused by employees making purchases for persons outside the family. Similarly, credit policies should be reviewed and consideration given to whether appropriate promotional effort is being directed toward present and past customers.

REVIEW QUESTIONS

1. What are the more important functions of the sales order department?
2. What is the main responsibility of the shipping department from the standpoint of internal control?
3. How is incidental income of a business best controlled?
4. Why should the margin on vending machine sales be computed regularly?
5. What types of analyses can be given in internal reports on sales which will be of assistance to management?
6. What are some of the causes of excessive returns and allowances?
7. Why should the auditor determine which person in the client's organization is responsible for approving noncash credits to receivables?
8. What duties with respect to receivables should be handled separately under a good system of internal control?
9. "A comprehensive system of internal reporting is an important phase of good internal control." Explain.
10. List the assurances that a good system of internal control over sales and receivables should be able to provide for management.
11. Indicate the uses of the various copies of a typical shipping order.

12. Explain how maintaining tub-file or open-item inventory records can reduce the amount of clerical work in conjunction with punched-card billing procedures.
13. What are the various techniques that can be used in making sales analyses?
14. Why is it desirable to "key" the posting of cash credits to accounts receivable ledger records?
15. What are the functions of the credit history card used in cycle billing?
16. Distinguish between the open-item and balance-forward approach to punched-card receivables records.
17. State three principal areas that should be covered by the internal auditor in his examination of sales and sales activities.
18. What are some of the aspects of customer relations that should be reviewed by the internal auditor?

QUESTIONS ON SYSTEMS APPLICATIONS

19. Explain why it is desirable, from an internal control standpoint, to have invoices prepared and mailed by a separate billing department rather than by the clerks who handle the accounts receivable ledgers.
20. In a department store, no control is maintained over the issuance of sales-check books, but control is established as soon as the first sales check from a new book appears in the day's transactions. Explain the weakness in this arrangement by showing how an employee could readily defraud the store.
21. Why should sales clerks in a retail store not be permitted to have the keys which are used to "read" or clear the cash registers?
22. The writing of the shipping order and the customer's invoice can be combined in a plan known as "prebilling." Explain why it would be particularly important to have perpetual inventory records available for use by the sales order department when prebilling is used.
23. Contrast the differences in the amount of customer credit history information available under balance-forward punched-card records and open item punched-card records.
24. When sales and receivable accounting is by punched card, at what points in the system is summary punching necessary, and what are the functions of the cards that are summary punched?
25. A punched card should be used for more than one purpose in order to gain full advantage for the cost of preparing the punched card. List the various cards that would be used in a sales-accounts receivable system, and for each type of card indicate the multiple uses of the card.
26. "Cycle billing eliminates work-load peaks that would otherwise occur in posting accounts receivable transactions." Do you agree? Explain.
27. The provision for losses on uncollectible receivables may be based on past experience as either a percentage of sales or as a percentage of accounts receivable balances. Would the charge to expense show a greater year-to-year variation under the percentage of sales or the percentage of receivables approach? Why?

PROBLEMS

28. The customer billing and collection functions of the Robinson Company, a small paint manufacturer, are attended to by a receptionist, an accounts

receivable clerk and a cashier who also serves as a secretary. The Company's paint products are sold to wholesalers and retail stores.

The following describes *all* of the procedures performed by the employees of the Robinson Company pertaining to customer billings and collections:

1. The mail is opened by the receptionist who gives the customers' purchase orders to the accounts receivable clerk. Fifteen to twenty orders are received each day. Under instructions to expedite the shipment of orders, the accounts receivable clerk at once prepares a five-copy sales invoice form which is distributed as follows:

   (a) Copy #1 is the customer billing copy and is held by the accounts receivable clerk until notice of shipment is received.

   (b) Copy #2 is the accounts receivable department copy and is held for ultimate posting of the accounts receivable records.

   (c) Copies #3 and #4 are sent to the shipping department.

   (d) Copy #5 is sent to the storeroom as authority for release of the goods to the shipping department.

2. After the paint ordered has been moved from the storeroom to the shipping department, the shipping department prepares the bills of lading and labels the cartons. Sales invoice copy #4 is inserted in a carton as a packing slip. After the trucker has picked up the shipment the customer's copy of the bill of lading and copy #3, on which are noted any undershipments, are returned to the accounts receivable clerk. The Company does not "back order" in the event of undershipments; customers are expected to reorder the merchandise. The Robinson Company's copy of the bill of lading is filed by the shipping department.

3. When copy #3 and the customer's copy of the bill of lading are received by the accounts receivable clerk, copies #1 and #2 are completed by numbering them and inserting quantities shipped, unit prices, extensions, discounts and totals. The accounts receivable clerk then mails copy #1 and the copy of the bill of lading to the customer. Copies #2 and #3 are stapled together.

4. The individual accounts receivable ledger cards are posted by the accounts receivable clerk by a bookkeeping machine procedure whereby the sales register is prepared as a carbon copy of the postings. Postings are made from copy #2 which is then filed, along with staple-attached copy #3, in numerical order. Monthly the general ledger clerk summarizes the sales register for posting to the general ledger accounts.

5. Since the Robinson Company is short of cash, the deposit of receipts is also expedited. The receptionist turns over all mail receipts and related correspondence to the accounts receivable clerk who examines the checks and determines that the accompanying vouchers or correspondence contains enough detail to permit posting of the accounts. The accounts receivable clerk then endorses the checks and gives them to the cashier who prepares the daily deposit. No currency is received in the mail and no paint is sold over the counter at the factory.

6. The accounts receivable clerk uses the vouchers or correspondence that accompanied the checks to post the accounts receivable ledger cards. The bookkeeping machine prepares a cash receipts register as a carbon copy of the postings. Monthly the general ledger clerk summarizes the cash receipts register for posting to the general ledger accounts. The accounts receivable clerk also corresponds with customers about unauthorized deductions for

discounts, freight or advertising allowances, returns, etc. and prepares the appropriate credit memos. Disputed items of large amount are turned over to the sales manager for settlement. Each month the accounts receivable clerk prepares a trial balance of the open accounts receivable and compares the resultant total with the general ledger control account for accounts receivable.

Required:
Discuss the internal control weaknesses in the Robinson Company's procedures related to customer billings and remittances and the accounting for these transactions. In your discussion, in addition to identifying the weaknesses, explain what could happen as a result of each weakness.

(Uniform C.P.A. Examination)

29. The United Charities organization in your town has engaged you to examine its statement of receipts and disbursements. United Charities solicits contributions from local donors and then. apportions the contributions among local charitable organizations.

The officers and directors are local bankers, professional men and other leaders of the community. A cashier and a clerk are the only full-time salaried employees. The only records maintained by the organization are a cashbook and a checkbook. The directors prefer not to have a system of pledges.

Contributions are solicited by a number of volunteer workers. The workers are not restricted as to the area of their solicitation and may work among their friends, neighbors, co-workers, etc. as convenient for them. To assure blanket coverage of the town new volunteer workers are welcomed.

Contributions are in the form of cash or checks. They are received by United Charities from the solicitors, who personally deliver the contributions they have collected, or directly from the donors by mail or by personal delivery.

The solicitors complete official receipts which they give to the donors when they receive contributions. These official receipts have attached stubs which the solicitors fill in with the names of the donors and the amounts of the contributions. The solicitors turn in the stubs with the contributions to the cashier. No control is maintained over the number of blank receipts given to the solicitors or the number of receipt stubs turned in with the contributions.

Required:
Discuss the control procedures you would recommend for greater assurance that all contributions received by the solicitors are turned over to the organization. (Do not discuss the control of the funds in the organization's office.)

(Uniform C.P.A. Examination)

30. The Installment Jewelry Company has been in business for five years but has never had an audit made of its financial statements. Engaged to make an audit for 1967, you find that the company's balance sheet carries no allowance for bad accounts, bad accounts having been expensed as written off and recoveries credited to income as collected. The company's policy is to write off at December 31 of each year those accounts on which no collections have been received for three months. The installment contracts generally are for two years.

Upon your recommendation the company agrees to revise its accounts for 1967 to give effect to bad account treatment on the reserve basis. The reserve is to be based on a percentage of sales which is derived from the experience of prior years.

Statistics for the past five years are as follows:

	Charge Sales	Accounts Written Off and Year of Sale			Recoveries and Year of Sale
1963	$100,000	(1963) $550			
1964	250,000	(1963) 1,500	(1964) $1,000		(1963) $100
1965	300,000	(1963) 500	(1964) 4,000	(1965) $1,300	(1964) 400
1966	325,000	(1964) 1,200	(1965) 4,500	(1966) 1,500	(1965) 500
1967	275,000	(1965) 2,700	(1966) 5,000	(1967) 1,400	(1966) 600

Accounts receivable at December 31, 1967 were as follows:

1966 sales ....$ 15,000
1967 sales 135,000
　　　　　　　　　　　　　　　　　　　　　　　　　　　　$150,000

Required:

Prepare the adjusting journal entry or entries with appropriate explanations to set up the Allowance for Bad Accounts. (Support each item with organized computations; income tax implications should be ignored.)

(Uniform C.P.A. Examination)

31. Graystone Electronics Corporation's sole activity in 1967 was a federal government fixed-price incentive contract awarded in January 1967. The Corporation's prior government contracts were cost-plus-fixed-fee or firm fixed-price contracts which were completed by December 1966.

Provisions of the fixed-price incentive contract include the following:

1. Graystone is to construct 8 identical digital computers, deliveries to be made between July 1967 and June 1968.
2. The total contract target price is $780,000, which includes a target cost of $700,000. The total adjusted price cannot exceed a ceiling of $810,000.
3. The incentive clause states:

"The total adjusted price (final contract price) shall be established by adding to the total adjusted cost (final negotiated cost) an allowance for profit determined as follows:

When The Total Adjusted Cost Is:	The Allowance For Profit Is:
Equal to the total target cost	Total target profit.
Greater than the total target cost ..	Total target profit less 20% of the amount by which the total adjusted cost exceeds the total target cost.
Less than the total target cost	Total target profit plus 20% of the amount by which the total adjusted cost is less than the total target cost."

The following information is available at December 31, 1967:

1. Costs accumulated on the contract:

Direct materials	$170,000
Direct labor	192,000
Overhead	240,000
Total	$602,000

2. The estimated costs to complete the contract:

Direct materials	$ 30,000
Direct labor	48,000
Overhead	60,000
Total	$138,000

3. Past experience indicates that 1% of the gross amount of accumulated overhead charges will be disallowed by government auditors as contract costs. No provision has been made for this disallowance.
4. In addition to the estimated 1% disallowance in "3," the following 1967 costs will probably be disallowed:
   (a) Depreciation on excess equipment, $1,000. The equipment was sold in January 1968.
   (b) Special nonrecurring recruiting costs, $4,000.
5. The Corporation failed to take cash discounts totaling $2,000 in 1967. Lost discounts are credited to costs when found by government auditors. The Corporation treats cash discounts, when taken, as a reduction of costs.
6. All costs that will probably be disallowed have been treated consistently as period costs by the Corporation. Estimated allowable costs have been consistently allocated equally to identical units being manufactured under a contract.
7. Five computers were delivered in 1967 and billed at the target price. Progress payments of $75,000 were received for each computer delivered.

Required:
(a) Prepare a schedule computing the estimated total adjusted price (estimated final contract price) for the fixed-price incentive contract.
(b) Prepare a schedule computing the work-in-process inventory at estimated cost at December 31, 1967.
(c) Assume that the estimated total adjusted price determined in (a) was $800,000. Prepare a schedule computing the estimated total amount receivable from the federal government at December 31, 1967 for the computers that were delivered. (Uniform C.P.A. Examination)

Auditing revenues
and receivables

8

Although the consummation of a sale occurs near the end of the business operating cycle, the closely related areas of sales and receivables have been chosen to introduce the approach to systems and auditing. There is the advantage of being a relatively familiar territory in that the accounting procedures and forms already discussed are likely to be fairly well known to the average reader as a result of his participation as the second party in many sales transactions. Also, the audit objectives and procedures for this area are more clear-cut and obvious than for most other income statement and balance sheet items. Once the concept of audit objectives has been grasped from the study of this chapter, the reader should be able to develop objectives for other statement items and to test his own ideas against those presented in these pages. The reader will gain considerable benefit if he attempts to develop the audit procedures through which the objectives may be attained, and then compares them with the procedures that are set forth here in satisfaction of the related objectives.

The reader should recognize the importance of understanding the accounting system which produces the figures to be audited, as well as the significance of internal control in assuring that all transactions have been correctly recorded and that the resulting account balances are reasonable representations of the transactions and events that have occurred.

Equally important to the competent expression of an auditor's opinion on a client's financial statements is an understanding of accounting principles, particularly in relation to standards of statement presentation that derive from such accounting principles. The discussion of these standards precedes the material on audit objectives and procedures, because these standards must be kept in mind in the course of examining the detailed records supporting the financial statements. It is in the examination of the detailed records that the auditor obtains much of the evidence showing whether statement standards have been met in the operation of the client's accounting system.

Audit objectives are the key to audit procedures, and the procedures flow logically from the stated objectives. The reader should note this relationship carefully and give close attention to the manner in which the procedures are carried out, as well as to various factors that may have a bearing on the actual execution of the procedures. All of these matters are involved in conducting an examination that meets the requirements of generally accepted auditing standards.

The résumé at the close of the chapter of the key points of internal control, standards of statement presentation, and audit objectives and procedures is intended to assist the reader in reviewing and consolidating the key points of the discussion.

STANDARDS OF STATEMENT PRESENTATION

The following standards for the presentation of revenue from sales in the income statement are equally applicable to the traditional multiple-step form of income statement and to the single-step form.

1. Nonoperating, nonrecurring revenue should be segregated from the regular operating revenue of a business. *Material* nonrecurring items should be taken directly to retained earnings or reported as "special items" in the income statement below net income.
2. Sales should be reported in full and not shown net of cost of sales or other expenses of producing the revenue. (Some businesses prefer to have their published statements begin with the figure for gross margin in order to keep information on sales trends and margin percentages confidential.)
3. Sales may be shown net of returns and allowances unless the amount offset is material.
4. If there are several major classes of revenue, the amount of each class of revenue should be shown separately to give the reader maximum information. (An electric and gas utility might thus show separate revenue figures for gas sales and electricity sales, and a manufacturing company should preferably show as separate figures contract sales to government defense agencies and sales to regular customers.)

Of the foregoing standards, only the first item is of such importance that the treatment of a material item in violation of the standard would be likely to necessitate a qualification of the auditor's opinion. The basis for the qualification would, of course, be that the statements were not prepared in conformity with generally accepted accounting principles.

The standards for the presentation of receivables are predicated on the fact that trade receivables are generally described in terms such as "Accounts Receivable," "Accounts and Notes Receivable," or "Accounts Receivable less Allowance for Uncollectible Accounts." If no further information is given, the statement reader should be warranted in making the following assumptions:

1. That all the receivables resulted from arm's-length transactions with third parties, and not from transactions with officers, employees, or subsidiary companies.
2. That only receivables resulting from normal trade transactions with customers are included.
3. That any potential losses have been provided for, and that therefore the full amount shown is expected to be realized in cash. (Notation should be made if a provision for doubtful accounts has been deducted from the gross receivables, with only the net amount shown in the balance sheet.)
4. That the amount of cash to be realized will be received within one year, or within one complete operating cycle if the cycle is longer than a year.
5. That the business has full ownership of the receivables, with no liens outstanding against them and no contingent liability for discounted receivables.
6. That no liabilities have been offset against the receivables.

Because statement readers are entitled by custom and good accounting practice to make the above assumptions, the auditor must determine in the course of his examination that none of the assumptions has been violated. If his examination reveals that material amounts of receivables exist which cannot be properly classified with the trade accounts receivable, separate classification of those receivables in the balance sheet is essential. Some of the more common types of items which may have to be shown separately would include:

Installment receivables.
Receivables from officers or employees.
Receivables arising from sales or advances to nonconsolidated subsidiaries.
Receivables arising from transactions other than the sale of merchandise (for example, proceeds of the sale of plant assets, insurance claims, claims for tax refunds, or utility deposits).
Credit balances in accounts receivable (if material, these balances should be reclassified as current liabilities).

It is important that any receivables from officers of the client company be given full disclosure in view of the fiduciary relationship that exists between the officers and the company. Disclosure is, however, like all other matters, subject to considerations of materiality, although it should be recognized that, for any given company, the dollar figure at which an item would become material would vary according to the item involved. Assuming total receivables from customers of $100,000, a $2,000 receivable from an insurance claim would probably not be sufficiently material to warrant separate disclosure, but a $2,000 loan to the president of the company would be an entirely different matter.

There are few procedures specifically designed to reveal the existence of receivables from other than customers, and as a consequence the auditor should be alert in performing each procedure relating to receivables or other accounts, in order that any facts bearing on the classification or presentation of receivables will be noted and given adequate consideration. If accounts receivable have been sold with recourse for uncollectible accounts, or if the accounts have been pledged to secure an indebtedness, the auditor must be certain that the statements contain full disclosure of the facts.

AUDIT OBJECTIVES AND PROCEDURES

In substantiating the amount of sales or other revenues and receivables shown in the financial statements, the auditor must seek to attain a number of major objectives:

1. Establish credibility of the accounting records.
2. Ascertain reasonableness of account balances.
3. Review cut-off of recorded transactions.
4. Obtain assurance that all revenues have been recorded.
5. Tie in supporting records with statement amount of receivables.
6. Establish validity of the recorded receivables.
7. Determine collectibility of the receivables.

Each of these objectives is developed in considerable detail in the following sections of this chapter, and the audit procedures customarily employed in attaining the objectives are then fully discussed. The extent of the tests to be made in applying the procedures and the choice between alternative procedures are matters of professional judgment to be resolved in accordance with generally accepted auditing standards. Every effort has been made to set forth the factors that should be considered in reaching the necessary decisions that must be made.

An overriding consideration in the examination of sales and other revenues —and, indeed, all income statement amounts—is the fact that the net result of the revenues and expenses matched in the income statement is the vitally important figure of net income for the period. The net income figure is given further credibility through the balancing aspects of the double-entry system and the examination of all amounts included on opening and closing balance sheets, including the balancing item of retained earnings. Verification of all other entries effecting a change in the retained earnings figure for the year in turn supports the fairness of the remaining balancing figure: net income for the year. Thus, the examination of opening and closing balance sheets provides further substantiation of the revenues and expenses reported in the income statement.

Establish Credibility of the Accounting Records

Although the auditor also seeks independent corroboration of financial statement amounts, he places substantial reliance on the accounting records from which the figures are derived. The amount of reliance he may properly place on the records is, of course, directly affected by the conditions of internal control inherent in the preparation of the records. The following procedures constitute the methods by which the auditor arrives at his independent substantiation of the credibility of the accounting records.

Trace handling of representative transactions from origin to final account balances. To satisfy himself that account balances are the result of properly recording bona fide transactions under reasonable internal control, selected representative transactions are traced from their origin to the related account balances of which they become a part. For a typical credit sale in a manufacturing or wholesaling concern, reference would be made to the customer's order, tracing this information to the invoice form, verifying prices against authorized price lists and quantities against the completed shipping order or other shipping department records, tracing the transaction to the sales journal, proving the daily journal total by comparison with the billing control total or by footing the entries in the journal, proving the recap of daily figures in arriving at the total for the month, and tracing the total to the related entries in the sales and receivables accounts. Sales returns and allowances and collections on accounts receivable would be tested in a similar fashion. Tracing one or two entries of each type should be adequate if the client's plan of internal control is actually in operation and is sufficient to give reasonable assurance that all transactions have been properly recorded; but when internal control is weak, additional transactions should be tested by the auditor. The added tests should give the auditor the same assurance about the credibility of the records as would the internal control, had it been adequate.

In light of the above comments, the reader will recognize the importance of evaluating the internal controls in effect relative to each step in the procedures for handling the various types of sales transactions. Similarly, the intimate contact with the major types of transactions presents the ideal opportunity to ascertain that the transactions are being recorded in conformity with generally accepted accounting principles.

Ascertain Reasonableness of Account Balances

Supplementing the evidence of the credibility of the accounting records gained from the effectiveness of the system of internal control and tests of transactions is evidence in the form of the reasonableness of the resulting figures. Sales figures should follow seasonal patterns without undue variation, and year-to-year changes should follow industry trends and known cyclical influences. Deviations from such expectations require support in the form of explanation or justification as evidence that the deviations are not the result of intentional manipulation of the figures, honest errors, or changes in classification or method of recording repetitive transactions.

Illustrative working paper schedule 10 shows each of the major sales classifications analyzed by monthly totals in order to bring to light any unusual monthly variations in the sales figures. Improper crediting of a material amount of nonoperating, nonrecurring revenue to a sales account should, for example, be readily apparent from a review of monthly sales totals. On the other hand, variations may have been caused by actual operating events which, upon thorough investigation, fully account for the changes in operating results. Examples of such events would include strikes in the client's or suppliers' plants, vacations, delivery on a large contract, opening of a new branch, or introduction of a new product of new model.

Other comparisons evident on schedule 10 include the relationship of sales totals for the current year to the previous year, and reference to industry trends. Justification of the substantial increase in sales of automated machines is stated in terms of known events occurring within the company. Sales returns and allowances are related to sales on a percentage basis, showing no change relative to the preceding year that would warrant further investigation. Another important comparison is in terms of gross margin. Cost of sales amounts result from entirely different transactions and records, and are usually handled by persons who have no responsibility for sales transactions. Consequently, a consistent year-to-year relationship between sales and cost of sales reinforces the credibility of each of the figures.

Similarly with respect to accounts receivable, schedule B shows a comparable receivables turnover relative to sales for the current and preceding years, and schedule B-2 shows that the aging analysis of the accounts is consistent with the preceding year, as is the actual write-off of uncollectible accounts.

Yet another approach to the reasonableness of the accounting figures is the scanning of account entries for amounts that appear out of line with other entries in an account, and for irregular entries from other than the normal sources of entries to the account. Thus an entry to the sales or accounts receivable accounts from the cash disbursement record or the general journal would warrant careful investigation.

Concerning any revenues that are not derived from regularly recurring operations of the business, proper presentation in the income statement should be carefully considered. Minor amounts of regularly recurring revenue not related to the regular operations of a business should be reported in the income statement under a separate heading following the figure for income from operations. Examples would include income from investments, cash discounts earned, and incidental gains from the disposition of property.

Material amounts of nonoperating, nonrecurring gains should preferably be credited directly to retained earnings to avoid distorting net income, and any taxes relating to such items should similarly be taken to retained earnings. If the items are reported in the income statement, they should be shown net of taxes after the figure for net income for the year, and the final income statement figure should be clearly labeled as being the balance of net income after the special credit.

Review Cut-Off of Recorded Transactions

The cut-off in recording sales transactions at the year end should result in sales transactions being recorded in the accounting period in which they occurred. Ordinarily, occurrence of a sale generates objective evidence that a sale has been consummated in the form of the receipt of cash or the creation of a legally enforceable receivable for a stated amount. Rendering of a service or legal transfer of title to goods or other property generally governs. Release of goods from the seller's plant in fulfillment of a valid sales contract may be accepted as sufficient objective evidence of a sale, however, even though the actual terms of the sale may defer transfer of legal title until the goods are delivered to the customer's premises.

Proper cut-off in the recording of credit sales should result in the revenue being recorded in the period in which it was realized and in the receivable being recorded only if it represents a valid, legally enforceable claim against the purchaser. In most cases, revenue is "earned" as a result of consummating a sales transaction, but under certain conditions the revenue may not be earned until a later date. Proper cut-off necessitates deferring the amounts involved and reporting them as revenue only after goods have been delivered or services rendered. Magazine subscriptions paid in advance and sales amounts applicable to product service warranties are common examples of such deferred recognition of sales revenues. The credit portion of such a transaction represents a liability to the customer for goods or services, and should be presented in the balance sheet until the revenue has been earned.

The same considerations apply in relation to the cut-off of sales returns and allowances.

Test cut-off of shipments. The above discussion suggests that the auditor should satisfy himself that revenue is recorded in the same period in which the shipment of goods occurred. Such satisfaction is gained by testing shipments made prior to the close of the year according to shipping department records and determining that the sales have been entered in the sales journal in the same period. Conversely, sales entered in the sales journal near the close of the year should be tested against shipping department records to ascertain that the goods were shipped in the same period. Such tests can be made most readily if the shipping copies of shipping orders are attached to copies of the invoices. Under such circumstances, the last shipping-order number shipped prior to the close of the year can be noted from shipping department records, and each invoice reviewed to determine the relationship of the number of the attached shipping order to the last number for which shipment was completed.

Ascertain validity of recorded receivables. Because evidence of a valid receivable at the balance sheet date indicates that the corresponding sales revenue has been realized, the audit of receivables helps to establish the propriety of the recorded sales, as well as the cut-off of sales transactions. The relationship of the examination of the balance sheet receivables figure to the income statement figure for sales is particularly significant when the auditing of receivables is accomplished as of the balance sheet date. Confirmation of receivables balances by correspondence with debtors is especially meaningful, because the customer can be expected to take exception to amounts charged at the balance sheet date for sales that were not consummated until a later date. The significance of receivables confirmation work with respect to the sales cut-off is substantially lessened under present-day practices of performing much of the audit work at a date prior to the balance sheet date, although when the auditor notes unusual conditions at that time he should be alert for similar conditions at the balance sheet date. For example, receivables work is most helpful in revealing the practice of recording sales in instances where goods have been shipped on approval or on a consignment basis. Establishing the validity of the recorded receivables is discussed later in this chapter as a separate objective.

Obtain Assurance that All Revenues Have Been Recorded

Although the examination of a client's financial statements for the purpose of expressing an opinion on those statements ordinarily does not include responsibility for the detection of fraud, such as failing to record sales and appropriating the related remittances from customers, the auditor is nevertheless well advised to be on the alert for any indication that fraud may have occurred. Even though the prevention and detection of fraud are primarily the client's responsibility, it is always embarrassing to the auditor, at the very least, to have a shortage or defalcation come to light after the completion of an audit.

The question of whether all sales have been recorded is partially answered, at least so far as year-end sales are concerned, by procedures intended to establish that the sales cut-off was properly made. Other evidence of the recording of all sales is provided by a good system of internal control that is functioning as intended. One of the major objectives of internal control over sales is to give assurance that all sales are recorded. Similarly, the review of sales figures for over-all reasonableness provides an indication of whether all sales have been recorded—particularly with respect to the relationship between sales and cost of sales, or the resulting gross margin figures.

If internal control is weak, the auditor may conclude that his tests of transactions should be extended to compensate. Tests to determine whether all shipping orders were accounted for by number and whether they resulted in billings to customers are particularly important. Shipping department tonnage figures, and the relationship on a physical basis between purchase and sale quantities, after giving effect to changes in inventory quantities, are also helpful if such records are maintained. The number of gallons of gasoline purchased and sold through a filling station offers a good illustration of the opportunity to use this technique.

Any possible sources of miscellaneous revenue should be considered in relation to the objective of accounting for all revenue. If the auditor notes that scrap results from production, that vending machines are present, or that a catering concern is serving meals to employees, any revenue produced should be accounted for and traced to the records.

Purchase discounts should be reviewed for abnormal month-to-month variations and for changes in the relationship to total purchases. Discussed more fully in the chapter on the audit of cash transactions is the fact that a cash shortage can be concealed by overstating cash disbursements and understating purchase discounts. Also, invoices may be paid at the gross figure but within the discount period, and then refund checks may be requested from the vendor and misappropriated.

In certain special types of business there are often interesting indirect means of checking on whether all revenue has been recorded.

Tuition fees. The financial record of tuition fees received by a school or college can be verified against the registrar's records of students enrolled, thus making it possible to obtain the practical equivalent of independent verification of the records of revenue.

Rental income. Physical inspection should be made of rental properties to establish the number of rental units or the number of square feet of floor space. Then by reference to lease agreements the auditor can determine the amount of rental income which should have been realized during the year. If the recorded amount is less because vacancies occurred, the vacancy periods should be verified against dates on lease agreements and, if necessary, by written confirmation from the former tenant and the next tenant to occupy the space. Reported vacancies existing at the time of the audit can be verified by inspection of the property.

Hotel room charges. An excellent source of information for corroborating the recorded revenue from hotel room charges exists in the form of the work reports which the maids file with the head housekeeper. The rooms reported as having been made up can be tested against rate schedules and recorded revenue as a check on the recording of revenue by front office employees.

Charity contributions. The use of prenumbered contribution forms is the best method of establishing internal control over contributions made. The auditor should satisfy himself that the forms have been accounted for, and he should test the recap of the amounts shown on the individual cards. If lists of contributors are published, the auditor should make test comparisons between such lists and the recorded revenue, working from the lists to the records.

Church contributions. Members' pledges and careful accounting for contributions received against those pledges are the best form of internal control over regular contributions to churches. The auditor should consider the desirability of obtaining written confirmations covering unpaid pledge balances. Loose collections should always be kept under the joint custody and control of two church officials. The treasurer should be responsible for overseeing the counting of the funds and making the deposit, with the recording secretary bringing the deposit onto his records solely on the basis of the receipted bank deposit slip.

The auditor should review the amounts of weekly loose collections for any unusual variations, and the amounts should be related to the attendance records maintained by the head usher. If there is any indication of irregularity (even churches are not immune), there is no way in which the auditor can prove what has occurred, but he should certainly make strong recommendations concerning possible improvements in internal control, and he may also wish to suggest certain changes in personnel.

Tie in Supporting Records with Statement Amount of Receivables

At this point we shift our attention to the receivables that result from credit sales transactions. Because the auditor's examination is concerned primarily with the individual account records that underlie the balance sheet figure for receivables, the auditor must satisfy himself that the supporting records represent the amount of receivables stated in the balance sheet.

Trial balance of subsidiary ledgers. The client is also interested in the correspondence between detailed records and the controlling accounts that provide the amounts shown in the financial statements, and hence the preparation of subsidiary ledger trial balances is a customary accounting procedure.

When relatively few accounts are involved, the auditor often includes a complete trial balance in his working papers, as is illustrated in schedule B-1 of the illustrative working papers. Such a trial balance is usually prepared on a sheet of twelve- or fourteen-column paper because the same schedule can also be used for other purposes. If an employee of the client prepares the trial balance to reduce the audit time and expense, which is a frequent and desirable practice, the auditor should trace each name, address, and amount to its appropriate ledger page and should prove the footing of the trial balance in order to verify the accuracy of the schedule. Tick marks, explained by an accompanying legend, should be used to show what work has been performed, and of course the total of the receivables trial balance should be cross-referenced to the lead schedule to show that the amount is in agreement with the general ledger balance.

When a large number of accounts is involved, the auditor's trial balance of the receivables will usually take the form of an adding-machine tape, which should be attached to a sheet of working paper and properly identified. If internal control is extremely good, the auditor may limit his examination to a test of a trial balance tape prepared by the client. Such a test might be set up to include all the large accounts with balances in excess of a stated amount and a certain number of the accounts with smaller balances. The testing should be from the trial balance to the ledger sheets, because the purpose of the test is to prove that all amounts shown on the trial balance are represented by actual accounts in the ledger.

Another reason for making the test in this direction is that the relative risk of a possible misstatement of the receivables suggests that overstatement of the receivables is more likely than understatement. Manipulation to overstate the receivables could result from an attempt to better the apparent financial position of the concern, or the overstatement could result from the abstraction of cash received from customers. In the latter case, if the customer's account has been credited to avoid any implications that the account has become delinquent, the manipulator may have found it impossible to make a corresponding credit to the general ledger receivables control account. Under these circumstances there would be a likelihood that fictitious amounts would be inserted in the trial balance to present an appearance of balance between the detailed ledger and the control account. In order to detect such manipulations when the auditor is limiting his comparison of trial balance and detailed ledger to a test, it is essential that the auditor work from the trial balance to the ledger. The footing of the client's trial balance must also, of course, be proved in order to complete the verification process.

In very large businesses, particularly in the retail field, receivables may be so numerous that many subsidiary ledgers may be maintained, each with its own control. Under such circumstances, particularly because internal control is likely to be good, the auditor will usually limit his trial balance and other work to only a few selected ledgers, with different ledgers selected each year. In addition to proving trial balances of these ledgers against their respective controls, the auditor should balance the total of all individual controls with the master and general ledger control accounts.

Whenever the subsidiary ledger accounts fail to balance with the control account, the auditor should refer the matter to the client. Locating the difference is a clerical matter, and the auditor should not do the work unless he is specifically authorized to do so and the client understands that the audit fee will be increased accordingly. Should the receivables ledger be out of balance in a situation where internal control is weak, the auditor should be alert to the possibility that fraud may have occurred, particularly if the control account exceeds the total of the individual receivables.

It is important that the incidental aspects of trial balance procedures not be overlooked. The resulting intimate contact with the receivables is one of the principal means of disclosing the existence of accounts with officers or subsidiary companies, accounts arising from nontrade transactions, accounts payable beyond the period of one year or the operating cycle (if longer than one year), accounts with credit balances, accounts that are secured, and accounts that have been pledged. In the latter case, the lender will probably have stamped the applicable ledger sheets, "This account pledged to____under loan agreement dated____," in order to protect his interest in the accounts.

Establish Validity of the Recorded Receivables

The objectives and procedures relating to the substantiation of receivables and inventories underwent drastic change in the late 1930's. These changes and the events leading to these changes are discussed briefly at this point to give the reader a better understanding of generally accepted auditing standards, as they exist today, concerning receivables and inventories. Prior to 1939, independent examinations of financial statements seldom included procedures designed to enable the auditor to determine whether the receivables were valid obligations of existing concerns, and whether the inventories actually existed and were accurately counted as a basis for the final inventory figure. Although such procedures were occasionally carried out either at the suggestion of the auditor or at the request of the client, they were excluded from most examinations as being too costly and relatively unnecessary. Management usually certified the validity of the receivables and the accuracy of the inventory count as well as the existence of the inventory, and this arrangement was generally understood and accepted by those who used audited financial statements.

In 1939, however, disclosures concerning the gigantic $20,000,000 McKesson and Robbins fraud provided dramatic evidence of the need to strengthen auditing standards with respect to receivables and inventories. The American Institute of Certified Public Accountants responded promptly and in September, 1939, adopted a report known as "Extensions of Auditing

Procedure," which increased materially the auditor's responsibility concerning receivables and inventories. In spite of the problems involved and the added expense to clients desiring an unqualified opinion on their financial statements, this report stated that henceforth an examination designed to permit the expression of an unqualified opinion must include correspondence with debtors of the client to establish the validity of receivables and must include observation and tests of the client's inventory taking to establish the existence and accuracy of the inventory. These added requirements are now understood to be part of generally accepted auditing standards, and the resulting rise in the level of auditing standards has been highly beneficial. Financial statements and the accompanying auditors' opinions are now more meaningful and useful. There is substantially less likelihood that audited statements may at a later date prove to have been misstated, through no fault of the auditor, but with undesirable repercussions that result from a lack of understanding of the situation.

Confirmation procedures. The technique of ascertaining the validity of receivables through correspondence with the debtors is known as confirming, or circularizing, the accounts. Accounts may be confirmed on either a positive or a negative basis. For positive confirmation the customer is requested to reply stating whether or not the amount shown as owing to the client is correct. For negative confirmation a reply is requested only if the amount shown is not correct. In either case the actual request should come from the client, because no relationship exists between the auditor and the debtor.

The positive confirmation request is usually in the form of a letter such as the one shown in Figure 8-1. A possible answer to the letter is included.

A negative confirmation request may also be made in letter form, but frequently it will be made in the form of a sticker or rubber stamp placed on a copy of the monthly statement which is regularly sent to each customer. Such a request is usually made in the following form:

Please notify our auditors at the address given below if this statement is *not* correct.

Black and Decker, Certified Public Accountants
234 Baltimore
Kansas City, Missouri

Should a discrepancy exist, any information you can furnish concerning the discrepancy will be greatly appreciated. Please use the enclosed business reply envelope in replying.

When confirmation is being requested on installment receivables from retail customers, considerable care should be exercised in wording the request. Many customers are inclined to assume that any correspondence from the seller is likely to be a dun for a payment on their account, and it is surprisingly difficult to avoid having the auditor's confirmation request placed in the same category. If the customer has made all payments that are due and then receives a confirmation request which he mistakes for a dun, the resulting reaction by the customer is not likely to help the client's customer relations. In one instance, a woman came into a retail store credit office in tears after a confirmation request had been received. Shortly before,

---

Bus. Customers
Large Dollar Balances

MACHINE PRODUCTS CO.
WICHITA, KANSAS

December 12, 19__

Sampson and Co.
234 Erie Street
Chicago, Illinois

Gentlemen:

    In connection with the regular independent examination of our financial statements now being made by Black and Decker, Certified Public Accountants, please confirm to them the amount of your indebtedness to us at November 30, 19__. The amount of this indebtedness as shown by our records is indicated below in the space provided for your reply.

    Please indicate whether the stated amount is correct. If a difference is reported, please give our auditors any information which might aid them in reconciling the difference. *asking for a reply*

    Your reply should be made directly to Black and Decker, and a stamped, addressed envelope is enclosed for your convenience.

        Very truly yours,

        MACHINE PRODUCTS CO.

        H. A. Onsgard

        H. A. Onsgard,
        Treasurer

AP or customer - reluctant to tell.

Black and Decker:

    The amount of $1,864.32 representing our indebtedness as shown by the records of Machine Products Co. at November 30, 19__ is correct with the following exceptions (if any): *Our records show $1,265.29 The difference appears to be a payment which we made on November 28, 19—.*

              Signed *Sampson + Co.*

              By *D. A. Verbeck*

Figure 8-1

her husband had given her the money to pay the installment due, which she had done. But when the confirmation request arrived, the husband assumed that the wife had used the money for some other purpose and threatened violence for her assumed failure to use the money as she had been instructed! To further illustrate the problem of inducing the customer to read the request without misunderstanding, the letter used in the examination of a large luxury-class retail department store concluded with the sentence, "This is not a request for payment; please do not enclose a check or money with your reply." In spite of this directive, for several days after the requests had been mailed, one of the auditors had to spend one or two hours per day listing the checks enclosed with confirmation replies!

Confirmation requests should be mailed in envelopes bearing the auditor's return address, so that any which cannot be delivered will be returned to the auditor. The return envelope to be used by customers in replying should similarly bear the auditor's address.

The requests will usually be prepared by employees of the client, using a duplicated form and filling in name, address, and amount if the confirmation is in letter form. The customer's name, address, and amount due on each request should be verified against the appropriate ledger sheet by the auditor to avoid errors, whether or not intentional. In addition, each request should be compared with the verified trial balance in the auditor's work papers in order to determine that no accounts have been omitted. If the circularization is on a test basis, the work papers should show which accounts have been selected. After the confirmation requests have been verified, they must remain under the auditor's control until they are placed in a U.S. Mail depository. Failure to follow this precaution would give employees an opportunity to alter or remove confirmations pertaining to altered or fictitious accounts. For similar precautionary reasons, the requests should not be mailed through the client's mail department, but should be placed directly in the U.S. Mail.

The working papers should be noted to show all accounts on which replies have been received to positive confirmation requests. The letters should be kept in the audit file, and a summary of the confirmation results prepared as illustrated in schedule B-1. Replies which show differences should be carefully investigated and the explanation for any difference noted on the reply. The need for great care in investigating differences is indicated by the fact that each such difference is a potential clue to a defalcation or misstatement of the accounts until it is otherwise explained. Requests returned by the post office because they were undeliverable warrant particularly close attention.

Replies suggesting that a charge has been made but no goods purchased, that too much has been charged, or that credit has not been given for a payment which has been made are always dangerous, although investigation will usually show that an error was made in figuring an invoice, that a debit or credit was posted to the wrong account, or that the remittance was in transit. Any undue delay in entering the credit for a collection on account should always suggest the possibility of lapping, a form of manipulation in which a remittance from customer A is appropriated, and then a later remittance from customer B is used to credit the account of A, a remittance from C is used to credit B, and so on.

If a client's internal control is especially good and no material differences are reported, the differences may be turned over to one of the client's employees for investigation, with a report to be made back to the auditor. The selected employee should obviously have no responsibility for receivables or the handling of cash, and a member of the internal auditing staff will usually represent a good choice.

The preceding comments concerning the confirmation of receivables should suggest the great value of this procedure. In addition to providing additional information concerning the effectiveness of the client's internal control, confirmation may reveal fictitious receivables and related fraud, errors or manipulation of the sales cut-off, consignment shipments charged as receivables, amounts which are in dispute, and freight allowances to be granted customers paying the freight on sales made f.o.b. destination. Nevertheless, it should be recognized that a reply to a positive confirmation request (or the absence of a reply to a negative request) does not necessarily constitute infallible evidence of the validity of an account. The person signing the reply may not have ascertained all the facts before returning the request without exception, and there is always a possibility that an address has been used for a fictitious account at which a party to the fraud may obtain the letter and return it properly signed.

Decisions relating to confirmation procedures. There are many points in the confirmation process where decisions must be made. These decisions should be made at the senior level or higher, and must reflect generally accepted auditing standards. The first necessary decision will be whether to confirm all accounts or only part of the accounts on a test basis. If a test is considered adequate, the extent of the test must be determined, as well as the basis for selecting the accounts to be tested. In any case, of course, the auditor must determine whether positive confirmations, negative confirmations, or both will be used.

Factors suggesting the need for extensive circularization, usually on a positive basis, would be weak internal control, indication that many amounts are in dispute, suspicion that fraud or numerous bookkeeping errors exist, or the existence of accounts with balances which are large relative to total receivables. On the other hand, if internal control is good and there is a large number of uniformly small accounts, negative confirmation of only a small proportion of the accounts may be adequate. Large utilities, for example, are likely to have good internal control and a large number of uniformly small accounts in their receivables from residential customers. In such instances negative confirmation of only one or two per cent of the accounts may be adequate. The purpose of such a circularization is not to directly prove the validity of the accounts, but to prove the effectiveness of the internal control measures, which would in turn indicate the validity of the accounts.

If there are a few large accounts along with a great number of small accounts, both positive and negative confirmations may be employed. In such a case the audit program might contain the instruction, "Confirm on a positive basis all accounts with balances of $1,000 or more, and confirm on a negative basis an interval sample of 15 per cent of all accounts with balances under $1,000." The selection of larger accounts for confirmation gives the auditor a maximum of information with a minimum expenditure of time and gives relatively good assurance that the receivables are not materially misstated. The smaller accounts should not be ignored, however, for the auditor is also interested in the over-all accuracy of the accounting. It is also desirable that the selection of accounts to be confirmed include accounts that are seriously delinquent, that have been turned over to a collection agency for further collection effort, or that have been written off as uncollectible. Ordinarily a sampling of such accounts is adequate; but if internal control is weak, it should be recognized that these accounts are potential danger spots, and the circularization of the accounts should be relatively extensive.

On occasion, the client may request that certain accounts not be confirmed because of possible unfavorable customer reaction. The auditor should obtain a signed request listing the accounts that are not to be confirmed, and he should be certain that the signer is a person of top-ranking authority rather than an employee who may be attempting to conceal a defalcation. The auditor must then decide whether he can satisfy himself as to the validity and accuracy of these account balances by alternative procedures (see below), and in addition he must determine what effect, if any, honoring the request and substituting alternative procedures will have on his report on the financial statements. (See Chapter 23 for further discussion of exceptions and qualifications in the auditor's report.)

Confirmation results should be summarized for review by the manager or partner, in some fashion similar to the illustration on schedule B-1. When positive confirmation requests are used, the auditor must watch to see that replies are received covering an adequate percentage of the dollar amount of the accounts. Particular note should be made that replies are received on any accounts which are exceptionally large or otherwise unusual. If the response is not adequate, second requests carrying an appropriate notation to that effect should be mailed. In some instances third requests, telegrams, or registered letters may be warranted.

Alternative procedures. Occasionally no reply can be obtained on confirmation requests to certain major accounts. For instance, some companies and government agencies will not confirm balances as a matter of policy because their accounting records are so widespread that an undue amount of time would be required to answer the many requests which are received, and there would be no assurance that a reply would cover all open items. Sometimes, however, a reply can be secured from a company such as a retail chain maintaining a centralized accounts payable department for the payment of all branch accounts payable if the confirmation request details the open charges existing against each branch. Needless to say, if the auditor is fairly certain that a company will not respond to a regular confirmation request, he should not send a negative request and accept the absence of a reply as evidence of the validity of the account.

If no reply can be secured from a major confirmation request, or if confirmation is not practicable or reasonable for some other reason, alternative procedures may be employed to determine the validity of the accounts. Reference to evidence of subsequent payment of an account ordinarily constitutes the best indication of the validity of the account. The best form of evidence is the customer's remittance advice which accompanied the payment. This document will have originated outside of the client's organization, and in addition will specify the exact items being paid, so that there is no chance of accepting as evidence a remittance which actually pertains to a charge made after the confirmation date. Other forms of evidence relating to the payment of the account, arranged in descending order of reliability, would be the check sent in by the customer, an authenticated bank deposit ticket listing a deposited check for the amount in question, entry of the remittance in the cash receipts book, and a credit posted to the customer's account. In a few special cases, the auditor may control all incoming mail and inspect all remittances received after the balance sheet date as evidence of the validity of the receivables at the balance sheet date. English accountants place great reliance on the subsequent payment of accounts receivable, and written confirmation of receivables is not required by their generally accepted auditing standards. The occurrence of the McKesson and Robbins fraud in the United States is largely responsible for the variation between the standards in England and the United States.

Should the customer be slow in paying his account, the auditor may refer to other evidence indicating that a valid receivable exists. Such evidence would include the shipping department's notice of shipment, accompanied possibly by a receipted copy of the bill of lading, the customer's purchase order, and any correspondence referring to the shipment of the goods. It is also helpful to know that the customer indicated by the records is actually an existing business organization. Assurance of this fact can be obtained by reference to the *Dun and Bradstreet Reference Book,* a business or city directory, or a credit report if one is on file.

Determine Collectibility of the Receivables

The reader should be careful to recognize that the confirmation of a receivable does not give any proof that the account will be collected. The customer's acknowledgment of his indebtedness is no indication of ability to pay. Therefore the auditor must employ other procedures in order to determine the collectibility of the receivables. The problem of collectibility, of course, relates primarily to the adequacy of the provision for doubtful accounts, because this provision should be sufficient to reduce receivables to an amount not in excess of the expected collections.

Aging. The best indication of the collectibility of a client's receivables can usually be gained by aging the accounts. As a general rule the longer an account has been unpaid, the less likelihood there is that the account will be paid. Open balances may be aged either according to the month of sale or according to whether the balance is current or past due, with separate columns to show how long the amounts are past due.

A choice must also be made as to whether to age the accounts on a first-in, first-out basis or on a specific-invoice basis. The difference between these two bases and the results obtained may be illustrated readily by the following simple example. The account which is shown is to be aged as of December 31.

Date	Explanation	Debit	Credit	Balance
Sept. 4	Inv. # 2418	$864.15		$ 864.15
Sept. 7	Inv. # 2463	152.97		1,017.12
Sept. 10	Cash		$864.15	152.97
Nov. 26	Inv. # 2738	201.64		354.61
Dec. 2	Inv. # 2773	286.51		641.12
Dec. 6	Cash		201.64	439.48

Aging this account by month of sale on a first-in, first-out basis, $286.51 would of course be classified as a December sale, leaving the remainder of the balance of $439.48 to be classified in some other month. The remainder is $152.97, and as it does not exceed the November sale of $201.64, the entire $152.97 would be classified "November." However, when payments are matched with charges on a specific-invoice basis, the balance is shown to be made up of the December charge of $286.51 and the September charge of $152.97. The customer has for some reason failed to pay the

September invoice for $152.97, and the period of time which has elapsed since the transaction occurred suggests considerable doubt that the amount will be collected. Thus aging the amount as "September" on a specific-invoice basis is much more realistic and informative than aging the amount as "November" under the first-in, first-out basis.

Although the above illustration would suggest that the specific-invoice basis should always be used, the alternative method is actually used quite frequently, primarily because it is easier to apply. The illustration does not indicate any particular difficulty in applying the specific-invoice basis, but relatively few entries are involved. When numerous transactions occur each month, the matching of debits and credits becomes rather a lengthy process unless the client has keyed debits and credits as remittances have been received.

On the other hand, if the individual receivables are small and relatively homogeneous, the quicker first-in, first-out method, even though less accurate and reliable, will produce a sufficiently useful picture of the receivables to permit a reasonable determination of the adequacy of the provision for doubtful accounts. As a general rule, however, large accounts which might have a substantial effect on the over-all picture should be aged on a specific-invoice basis.

The entire balance of an installment account is usually aged according to the month in which the most recent installment payment was received. Alternatively, the balance may be aged according to the number of months that payments are in arrears.

There is obviously a possibility for a considerable saving in audit time if the accounts have already been aged by the client or if the client prepares an aging schedule for the auditor. If the client's internal control is good and a large number of accounts is involved, the auditor may accept the client's aging after making sufficient accuracy and reliability tests of the client's analysis. Although the tests should cover a few accounts which are shown as delinquent in order to determine that they have been properly aged, the major work should relate to accounts which are classified as current. The client has already confessed to the existence of those accounts which are shown as delinquent, so the auditor's main concern is whether the client has attempted to create an unduly good picture of the receivables by classifying delinquent accounts in the current column.

Interpreting the aging results. Once the auditor has the complete aging analysis before him, he must determine whether the provision for doubtful accounts appears adequate in the light of that analysis. In some instances, particularly for retail department stores, a schedule of estimated losses for each age group of an aging analysis may be developed from past experience. Such a schedule might appear as follows:

Age Group	Estimated Percentage of Loss
Current...................................	0
Past due	
1 month	10
2 months............................	20
3 months............................	30
4 months............................	40
5 months............................	50

Because differing conditions cause different results, no single schedule can be used for all clients, even if they are in the same field of business. Whenever a small number of accounts with large balances is present, individual consideration of each past-due amount is practically a necessity. Any useful information observed at the time the accounts are aged should be noted in a remarks column of the schedule. Notations of collections on past-due amounts received between the aging date and the date the work is done represent particularly useful information.

Later, the senior accountant will go over past-due accounts with the credit manager, and using the remarks on the aging schedule and information furnished by the credit manager (verified by reference to credit reports, correspondence, or other data when necessary), prepare an estimate of possible losses from doubtful accounts. If this estimate exceeds the provision made in the records, the auditor should request the client to increase the recorded provision. Should the client refuse to make the requested adjustment and the amount involved be material, the auditor should qualify his opinion to the effect that the recorded provision for doubtful accounts is inadequate. Needless to say, an excessive loss provision is just as undesirable as one that is insufficient.

As a rough check of the auditor's aging analysis, and to show any trends that may be developing, the turnover of accounts receivable or number of days' sales outstanding should be computed and compared with figures for previous years.

Other procedures related to collectibility. The auditor should analyze all changes in the account Provision for Losses on Doubtful Accounts, and the calculation of the current year's provision for losses should be reviewed. The dollar amount of the sales or receivables used as the base in this calculation should be verified, the percentage loss factor applied to the base should be unchanged from the previous year unless warranted by circumstances, and the product of the base times the rate should be verified. Past bad debt losses should be reviewed to determine whether the loss factor being used is adequate based on past experience. The permanent files should be brought up to date each year to show the annual losses and provision for losses. Schedule B-2 is an example of the working paper analysis of the provision for losses to be included in the current working paper file.

An intelligent appraisal of the adequacy of the current year's loss provision must be based in part on a knowledge of the client's credit and collection policies and any changes which have occurred in these policies. The lengthening of credit terms, the reduction of minimum credit standards for accepting new accounts or increasing high credit limits, a change in collection procedures, or laxness in following up on delinquent accounts may all have repercussions on the client's bad debt losses. Needless to say, the auditor should be aware of these possibilities and, if necessary, recommend changes in the percentage loss factor used in providing for losses. Discussion with the credit manager and follow-up clerks and a review of a limited sample of new account applications which have been approved are means of securing the desired internal information, and the auditor should always keep abreast of general economic conditions and developments.

Another important point that warrants careful attention is whether the posting of credits for returns or allowances may have been delayed either unintentionally or for the purpose of improving operating results and the current financial position. In addition to inquiry made of the proper persons about such a possibility, the auditor should review the returns and allowances posted in the period following the balance sheet date. An abnormal amount would indicate a possible carryover from the year under review, and supporting papers covering individual returns and allowances should be examined on a test basis to determine whether the cut-off at the end of the year was made cleanly.

Timing of the Audit Work

Ideally, the audit procedures discussed above would be carried out after the close of the client's fiscal period, as all of the records would then be complete and the final statement figures could be verified. In practice, however, the ideal is not satisfactory for two reasons. First, so many concerns have a December 31 fiscal year that the public accounting profession would be unable to perform all the required work within a reasonable period of time after December 31. Second, clients usually want their reports as soon after the close of the year as possible, thus further crowding the work if it were all to be done after December 31.

To meet this situation, public accountants have been doing an increasing amount of the necessary auditing work on a preliminary basis. In some instances involving large clients with excellent systems of internal control, more than 50 per cent of the audit time may be expended prior to the balance sheet date, and it is not unusual to begin working on the audit for the following year shortly after the completion of the audit for the current year.

One important phase of the examination that can be commenced prior to the end of the year is the review of internal control. A very brief supplementary review after the close of the year should then be adequate to reveal whether any significant changes in internal control have occurred following the preliminary review. Similarly, much of the work on sales can be partially performed on a preliminary basis, leaving only a review of the operating results recorded between the preliminary and balance sheet dates to be completed later. Tests of the cut-off of sales, returns, and allowances must, of course, be deferred until after the end of the year.

Similar opportunities for preliminary work exist in the case of receivables, particularly if internal control is good. If there are numerous accounts, all with relatively uniform balances, the examination can be started as much as six months before the end of the year. Weak internal control or the existence of relatively few accounts that have sizable balances would, however, ordinarily make it advisable to defer the examination until the end of the year, or no more than one or two months prior to that date.

Trial balance work, confirmation, and aging would all be appropriately performed on a preliminary basis. If the results of this work are favorable, good internal control should give adequate assurance that similar conditions will exist at the balance sheet date. It is, nevertheless, advisable to seek further confirmation of such conclusions by testing intervening transactions and carefully reviewing year-end balances for unwarranted changes. If the year-end trial balance reveals the existence of large individual receivables balances, the auditor should determine that the balances are current and have not increased materially since the preliminary work was done. When substantial increases are noted, or when large new receivables appear on the trial balance, confirmation should be requested as of the balance sheet date to establish the validity of the balances.

NOTES RECEIVABLE

Although most sales are completed on an open-account basis, in some fields trade acceptances are common, and installment sales of equipment are usually covered by notes. In addition, of course, financial institutions usually require notes to be signed on loans or advances. The objectives and procedures presented in connection with the examination of accounts receivable are generally applicable to notes receivable as well, but certain additional procedures are necessary when notes receivable are present.

Inspection of Notes Receivable

Because a note may be negotiated to a third party without notice to the maker, confirmation of the recorded receivable with the maker of the note is not conclusive evidence that the payee of the note still has a valid asset. To satisfy himself that notes receivable have not been sold, discounted, or pledged, the auditor should make a physical inspection of the notes. This inspection, or "count" of the notes as it is usually called, should include a comparison of the following information appearing on the notes with the client's note register, ledger sheets, or other record of the notes: name of payee, names of endorsers (if any), name of maker, principal amount of the note, date the note was made, maturity date, and interest rate (if any). The count should be made as of the close of business on the last day of the fiscal period, and control should be maintained over the notes until all other liquid assets, such as cash or securities, have been counted to preclude conversion of any of the notes into cash and use of such cash to cover up any shortage which might exist. The form of working paper for the count of notes receivable will be similar to schedule N.

Endorsements should be carefully investigated at the time of the count inasmuch as they may be a clue to a temporary conversion of a note. The note might have been pledged or discounted with the proceeds used to the personal advantage of some employee. Subsequent reacquisition of the note would, of course, be necessary to restore it to its proper place at the time of the auditor's count. Due dates should also be watched, because notes due more than one year after the balance sheet date may have to be placed in a noncurrent category.

Any notes owned by the client but not on hand at the time of the count should be confirmed with the present holders as well as with the maker. Notes not on hand should be out for a good reason, such as collection, or collateral for a loan. If for the latter reason, notation to that effect is required in the balance sheet.

To protect against unauthorized use or conversion of notes, the client should assign the responsibility for custody of notes receivable to a person who has no access to cash or to the accounting records.

Sight Drafts

If goods have been shipped subject to an order bill of lading with sight draft attached, there will be no evidence of the receivable in the client's possession, and the customer will not confirm the obligation. The auditor must look to the bank or other agency to which the order bill of lading and sight draft were sent for confirmation of the receivable. If the bank is able to confirm that it held the sight draft at the confirmation date, or received it shortly thereafter, and if the auditor can satisfy himself that the goods had actually been shipped on or before the confirmation date, this combination of facts is the equivalent of ordinary confirmation.

Notes Receivable Discounted

Notes receivable records should be reviewed to determine whether credits to the notes receivable account represent actual collections or the proceeds of discounting. If notes have been discounted with recourse, the resulting contingent liability must be noted in the balance sheet. Furthermore, the auditor should obtain a written confirmation from the party who discounted such notes (usually the client's bank) listing all unpaid notes still being held. In the case of banks, such a listing will be obtained in connection with the use of the standard bank confirmation form $\left(\text{see schedule } \dfrac{A\text{-}2}{1}\right)$ which requests the bank to provide complete information on any notes that it is holding that were discounted by the client. If any notes still held by the discounting party are past due, the resulting liability should be reflected in the client's financial statements. All notes not yet paid, whether or not they have matured, should also be confirmed directly with the maker, as there is always a possibility that the note that was discounted at the bank may be fictitious.

Secured Notes

If notes are secured by collateral, the debtor should be asked to confirm the description and amount of collateral which was pledged. The collateral should be examined to ascertain that it has been properly accounted for and not merged with the client's assets or otherwise converted. Lastly, the value of the collateral should be ascertained in order to determine whether the security is ample.

When the security given on a note is in the form of a mortgage, the mortgage should be examined or otherwise accounted for, and the auditor should ascertain that the mortgage has been recorded. In the case of savings and loan associations and commercial banks making regular real estate loans, there are many other documents that should be reviewed by the auditor, at least on a test basis. Such review will help to establish that the client's regular procedures and requirements are being followed, and will provide further evidence of the validity of the notes. The documents will include the loan application, appraiser's report and, photographs of the property, attorney's title-search opinion or a title insurance policy, receipted tax bills or other evidence that property taxes have been paid, and an insurance policy or other evidence that the property is insured.

Interest

If the client normally follows the accrual basis in accounting for interest on notes receivable, the auditor should satisfy himself that interest has been properly accrued at the balance sheet date. In addition, sufficient tests should be made to satisfy the auditor that all interest income earned during the year has been accounted for. The auditor's working papers relative to interest on notes receivable follow a form similar to schedule N.

SUMMARY

To assist the reader in "pulling together" the discussion in each of these chapters dealing with the audit examination, the principal points are summarized under the headings of internal control, statement presentation, and audit objectives and procedures. The condensation should also be useful as a "recall" device as the reader attempts to review the basic auditing process by retracing ground that he has previously covered.

Internal control

The summary under this heading is limited to the material pertaining to the organization of the accounting and custodianship functions and the segregation of the related duties.

Duties which ideally should be performed by different individuals—
Order processing.
Preparation of shipping order.
Credit authorization.
Shipping.
Billing.
Accounting for serially numbered forms.
Sales distribution.
Maintenance of perpetual inventory records to establish accountability for sales.
General ledger entries.
Subsidiary ledger entries.
Trial balance of subsidiary ledger.
Mailing of statements to customers.
Collection follow-up.
Cash handling.
Approval of noncash credits.
Accounting control over miscellaneous revenue.

Statement Presentation

Separate classification should be made of—
Major types of operating revenue.
Nonoperating revenue.
Receivables not arising from arm's-length transactions.
Receivables not arising from normal trade transactions.
Receivables maturing beyond one year or the period of the firm's operating cycle.
Credit balances.

Material, nonoperating, nonrecurring gains should be credited directly to retained earnings.

Revenues should not be reported net of cost of sales or expenses, but may be shown net of returns and allowances.

Estimated losses on receivables should be provided for and the existence of such a provision indicated.

Liens or any contingent liability for discounted receivables should be disclosed.

Audit objectives and procedures

(Most of these procedures are normally conducted on a test basis.)

Establish credibility of the accounting records.

Trace handling of representative transactions from origin to final account balances.

Ascertain reasonableness of account balances, relating amounts to other statement figures for current and past years, making year-to-year and month-to-month comparisons, and scanning accounts for unusual entries, such as for nonoperating, nonrecurring revenues.

Review cut-off of recorded transactions.

Test cut-off of shipments.

Ascertain validity of recorded receivables, watching for unearned revenue.

Obtain assurance that all revenues have been recorded.

Review effectiveness of internal control and extend tests of transactions if necessary.

Test cut-offs.

Review gross margin percentages for changes that cannot be accounted for.

Relate dollar sales to records of sales quantities and changes in inventory quantities, or other independent records.

Relate purchase discounts to total purchases.

Consider likely sources of miscellaneous revenue and ascertain that any such revenue appears to be fully accounted for.

Tie in supporting records with statement amount of receivables.

Prepare trial balance or prove client's trial balance by tracing amounts to subsidiary ledger and footing the listed amounts.

Establish validity of the recorded receivables.

Request positive or negative confirmation of receivable balances.

Alternatively, verify subsequent collection of accounts not confirmed, or examine evidence of shipment of goods and of the customer's existence.

Determine collectibility of the receivables.

Age the accounts or test the client's aging.

Review changes in the turnover of receivables.

Review the status of major delinquent accounts not paid by close of the audit period by discussion with the credit manager and reference to other available information.

Verify client's computation of current provision for estimated losses.

Examine supporting evidence for write-offs of uncollectible accounts.

Account for the evidence of indebtedness when notes are held.

Account for collateral or other security.

Account for interest earned and prove accrued interest receivable.

REVIEW QUESTIONS

1. List the points which should be considered in presenting revenue in the income statement.
2. Why can the auditor limit his examination of revenue to a review of internal control and comparison and scanning techniques, assuming that internal control proves to be satisfactory?
3. What are the auditor's objectives in substantiating revenue and receivables?
4. Describe the auditor's verification of the handling of sales transactions which he selects for his tests of credibility of the accounting records in the audit of a manufacturing concern.
5. What are some of the types of credits to revenue accounts which might involve unearned income?
6. What types of comparisons should the auditor make in satisfying himself that revenues have been appropriately and consistently classified?
7. In what ways can the auditor detect fraud involving the failure to record all sales?
8. How should the auditor go about determining that all rental income has been recorded?
9. If a balance sheet includes an amount classified under current assets, which is described simply as "Accounts Receivable," what assumptions should the reader of that statement be warranted in making about that amount?
10. How were generally accepted auditing standards strengthened as a result of the McKesson and Robbins investigation?
11. When the auditor makes a test comparison of the receivables trial balance and the subsidiary ledger, should selected accounts in the ledger be traced to the trial balance, or vice versa? Explain.
12. What is meant by verification of the sales "cut-off"? Explain the importance of such verification from both a balance sheet and an income point of view.
13. Distinguish between confirmation of accounts receivable balances on a "positive" basis and on a "negative" basis.
14. Under what circumstances is the auditor most likely to use a positive confirmation request? A negative confirmation request?
15. What summary information should always be included in the work papers concerning the confirmation of receivables?
16. If your client refuses to permit you to circularize accounts receivable, what other procedures might be used in lieu of confirmation in order to enable you to form an opinion on the amount of accounts receivable shown in the balance sheet?

17. Distinguish between aging of receivables on a first-in, first-out basis and a specific invoice basis. Which of the two methods will produce the most useful analysis for audit purposes? Explain.

18. How does the auditor satisfy himself as to the adequacy of the provision for doubtful accounts?

19. What phases of the examination of receivables can be carried out on a preliminary basis?

20. In what ways do auditing procedures for notes receivable differ from those for accounts receivable?

QUESTIONS ON APPLICATION OF AUDITING STANDARDS

21. Partner Adams, in reviewing an audit report prepared by Senior Baker, notes that the client has enjoyed a substantial increase in sales for the year but only a slight increase in net income. If Adams asks Baker about the reason why net income did not increase proportionately with sales, should Baker be expected to know the answer? Why?

22. Give the audit steps you would follow in verifying the amount of profit to be recognized for the current year on a partially completed fixed-price construction contract. What evidence would you expect to examine?

23. Suggest various ways in which a branch manager of a retail chain store, who receives a bonus based on the store's profit, might attempt to inflate that profit. All accounting for the store is done locally under the manager's supervision.

24. Your client, Fly-by-Night Airlines, Inc., has received a retroactive adjustment of its income for carrying U.S. mail for the past three years, involving an additional payment to the company of $3,000,000 allocated about equally to each of the years. Your client realizes that the entire amount cannot be reported as income of the past year because such treatment would materially distort the net income. On the other hand, the client does not want the additional income buried as a credit in the statement of retained income. Suggest another alternative.

25. How would you make tests to ascertain that all income had been recorded in an examination of a hotel bar serving liquor by the drink?

26. Your client uses a standard cost plan whereby all materials drawn from stock are charged to work in process. Of the materials charged, the amount resulting in good production, including a standard allowance for scrap and spoiled material, is transferred to finished goods. Any remainder is charged to a materials use variance account. Standards are revised annually.

    During the year under examination, your client developed some changes which resulted in more efficient use of material, and as a consequence the materials use variance account had developed a sizeable credit balance by the end of the year. The client looks upon this balance as a gain from increased efficiency and proposes treating the balance as an item of income on the income statement. Would you agree to the client's proposal? State your reasons. If you would not agree, what treatment would you recommend?

27. Review of the monthly sales figures for product Y produced by your client reveals that a greater than seasonal decrease in sales occurred in the last three months of the year. What steps would you take in view of this fact?

28. Discuss the propriety and desirability of showing "net sales" as the first figure on an income statement prepared for
    (a) Publication for use by third parties.

(b) Presentation to top management.

29. Does the independent auditor assume responsibility for anything more than the fairness of the net income figure on the income statement, in rendering an unqualified opinion on a client's financial statements? Justify your answer.

30. Since the independent auditor is concerned primarily with determining whether he may properly express an unqualified professional opinion on the fairness of a client's financial statements, rather than with detecting defalcations of the client's funds, why would he include procedures in his audit which will indicate whether lapping has occurred?

31. Assume that you are engaged in an examination of financial statements for the year ended December 31, 1967, and Congress has already legislated lower corporate income tax rates for 1968. If your cut-off tests are to be made by selecting shipments from the shipping records and tracing the items to the sales register to determine whether sales were shipped and billed in the same period, would relative risk suggest that most of the shipments should be selected from the last few days of December, 1967, or the first few days of January, 1968? Explain.

32. (a) In connection with your receivables confirmation work for the December 31, 1967 audit of Grey and Co., one request covering a balance of $629.51 is returned by the customer with the notation "We do not owe the above amount, since it was paid by our check dated December 30, 1967." What would you do with this exception?

    (b) How would your answer be different if the customer said that the date of the check was December 20, 1967?

33. As an alternative to confirming an account receivable balance, the validity of the account can be verified by examining evidence in support of subsequent payment of the account. Assuming that the account has been paid, describe the evidence you would examine and state how you would obtain the evidence of such payment if the receivable records are maintained by filing invoice copies under a ledgerless plan of recording.

34. As the independent auditor for the Jameson Co., you have had employees of the credit department prepare negative accounts receivable confirmation requests, which you compared as to customer name and balance with the trial balance in your working papers before mailing the confirmation requests. No exceptions were noted from these procedures, and your audit report is subsequently issued in due course. Later, the client discovers that several sizeable accounts receivable balances are entirely fictitious, apparently not discovered by you since a false address was typed on the related confirmation requests. The employee responsible for the fraud had merely collected the requests at this address and destroyed them, so you assumed that the accounts were correct. The loss on these accounts was sufficient to place Jameson Co. in bankruptcy, and you are being sued for damages by a creditor of Jameson who relied on your audit report in extending credit to the company.

    Is it likely that the creditor will be able to recover his damages from you? Why?

35. As you are selecting accounts receivable to be confirmed, the credit manager points out six accounts totalling $2,345.60 out of a total of $354,689.20 that he asks you not to confirm. He states that there has been a dispute in each case with voluminous correspondence as to whether the merchandise delivered met the customers' specifications, and that confirmation requests would not yield a useful reply and merely agitate the customers involved. How should such a request normally be handled, and how would you proceed in this instance?

36. One of your client's customers paid his account in cash to the bookkeeper, who appropriated the money. To conceal the defalcation the bookkeeper credited the account and debited a fictitious account established in the name of a company in St. Louis. The address given on the ledger card, however, was the address of a friend, who agreed to forward any mail received bearing the company's name to the bookkeeper in Springfield, Illinois. You sent a positive confirmation request on the account, and in due time received a reply acknowledging that the balance shown was correct. What possibilities would exist of detecting the fraud in the course of your regular examination of financial statements? Since internal control is known to be weak, your examination normally includes a number of additional tests of the client's records.

37. "Whether confirmation requests are sent on charged-off accounts would depend largely on the client's internal control." Explain.

38. How would you satisfy yourself that no notes receivable have been discounted (thus giving rise to a contingent liability)?

39. The junior accountant whom you have assigned to age the client's installment receivables presents you with a schedule in which each past due installment is aged according to the number of months it is past due, and the remaining balance of each account is aged as not yet due. What would you say to him?

40. The following procedure might appear in the audit program for either an independent or an internal audit, but would be undertaken with differing objectives in each case:

    Select ten new charge accounts opened during the year (assume that a department store is involved) and inspect credit reports in support of these accounts.

    State to what extent the objectives would be similar or different for the two types of audits.

41. No reply has been received on the second request for confirmation of the receivable balance from Sharp Cutlery Co., so you ask your assistant to use alternative procedures to establish the validity of the account and the collectibility of the balance. His working papers show that he verified the December 31 balance of $2,356.19 on the basis of the following cash credits which were posted to the account:

January 12	$1,057.25
17	623.41
20	849.20

    Explain why the verification is unsatisfactory, and what should have been done.

42. What steps should you take with respect to a confirmation request returned by the post office marked "No such person at this address"? Would you proceed differently if the envelope were marked "Moved—left no forwarding address"? Explain.

43. "Since the validity of a receivable evidenced by a note can be ascertained readily by confirmation, there is no reason to inspect the note itself." Do you agree? Explain.

44. As partner of a public accounting firm, would you be willing to sign an unqualified opinion on a report that contains the following two statements? Explain. "Cash on hand was counted on February 28." "Notes Receivable were counted on March 3, the day the treasurer returned from a week's absence. The treasurer alone possesses the combination to the safe in which the notes are kept."

PROBLEMS

45. The State Gas Company follows the practice of cycle billing in order to minimize peak work loads for its clerical employees. All customers are billed monthly on various dates, except in those cases when the meter readers are unable to enter the premises to obtain a reading.

The following information for the year ended September 30, 1967, is presented by the company:

Cycle	Billing Period	Customers Billed Number	Customers Billed Amount	Customers Not Billed
1	Aug. 7–Sept. 5 (inclusive)	2760	$13,800.00	324
2	Aug. 12–Sept. 10 (inclusive)	3426	13,704.00	411
3	Aug. 17–Sept. 15 (inclusive)	3265	14,692.50	335
4	Aug. 22–Sept. 20 (inclusive)	2630	12,492.50	370
5	Aug. 27–Sept. 25 (inclusive)	3132	13,311.00	468

You are further advised that all customers have been billed for prior periods and that the company's experience shows that charges for those customers whose meters were not read average the same amount as the charges for the customers billed in their cycle. In addition, the company assumes that the customers' usage will be uniform from month to month.

From the above information, compute the unbilled revenues of the company as of September 30, 1967 arising from cycles No. 1 and No. 3. (*Do not* compute revenues from cycles 2, 4, and 5.) (Uniform C.P.A. Examination)

46. The Professional Men's Association of Middleton is made up of men in the various professions, including C.P.A.'s. From the start it has been tax exempt from Federal income and excise taxes, other than payroll.

The dues for members are $40 a year, after an initiation fee of $100. The Association has had a consistent policy of operating on a cash basis. It does not deposit initiation fees received with applications and does not consider them as income until the membership committee has acted thereon. Then the successful applicants' fees are deposited and the unsuccessful applicants' checks are returned to them.

The fiscal year ends August 31. Each year the directors choose from the membership a C.P.A. to make a thorough audit; and no one is allowed to audit two consecutive years. This year you have been selected for the first time, but you are solemnly warned that the directors will not tolerate any suggestion of putting the accounts on an accrual basis. You accept. An adequate fee is provided.

The secretary furnishes you with the following information:

Membership at September 1, 1966		2,980
Elected during year		123
Dropped for nonpayment of dues 15		
Died... 37		
Expelled 1	53	
Net gain..		70

Your examination of records shows the following:

Notices that "dues are due" are sent out in August. Dues for a full year, not to be prorated, must be paid when elected to membership. Prior to the end of the preceding fiscal year 410 members had paid their dues and in the current fiscal year 457 members had paid their dues for the year beginning September 1, 1967. One of these had died very suddenly on August 30 and is included in the 37 above. No refunds are made for deaths taking place after the fiscal year begins; however, refunds of one-half the dues are made to expelled members. There were 36 applications pending at the end of the fiscal year. During the course of your audit, the committee met and approved of 34. You further find that at the *beginning* of the year there were 47 such applications and that 45 had been acted upon favorably and are included in the 123 above.

The directors are interested in learning if there is a substantial difference between the income from dues on a cash basis as compared to the accrual basis.

Required:
(a) Prepare a schedule of income from membership showing:
   1. Changes in members
   2. Income from initiation fees
   3. Income from dues for the year, accrual basis
   4. Income from dues for the year, cash basis
   5. Total income from membership
   6. Reconciliation of the income from dues cash basis to the accrual basis
(b) What other audit procedures would you use to verify the income from membership? Give reasons.   (Uniform C.P.A. Examination)

47. Your client, The Summer Comfort Corp., manufactures air conditioners in various sizes from ½ H.P. to 1½ H.P. The air conditioners are sold to distributors, who in turn sell to retail appliance dealers in their assigned areas. Distributors make the bulk of their purchases during the period from February through August. To induce distributors to buy in advance of the normal purchase period and thus reduce company inventories, which tend to build up under the company's policy of constant year-around production, discounts on list prices are given during certain months, as follows:

September	10%
October	8
November	6
December	4
January	2

The company's fiscal year closes on August 31. In discussions with company officials, you learn that the larger volume of sales this year reduced overhead expenses when figured on a per-unit basis; variable costs per unit changed very little. In view of last year's very favorable sales trend, distributors ordered very heavily during the pre-season period this year; but as the regular sales season progressed, it became evident that air conditioners were in over-supply, and sales by The Summer Comfort Corp. to its distributors dropped accordingly during that period. Sales of units by sizes and certain other information for the current year, as determined from analyses maintained by the company, were as follows:

	No. of Units Sold	Total Sales	Distributor List Price	Cost of Sales
½ H.P.	815	$ 80,096.53	$ 99.60	$ 54,533.28
¾ H.P.	1,521	239,166.24	159.50	170,020.44
1 H.P.	1,648	372,475.36	231.15	246,163.34
1½ H.P.	1,120	330,287.48	299.75	214,905.60

The sales account for the current year appears as follows in the general ledger:

Date	Description	Ref.	Dr.	Cr.	Balance
Sept.		SR		$ 18,718.42	$ 18,718.42
Oct.		SR		47,835.96	66,554.38
Nov.		SR		78,201.39	144,755.77
Dec.		SR		99,831.56	244,587.33
Jan.		SR		122,293.66	366,880.99
		CR		1,416.90	368,297.89
Feb.		SR		176,785.06	545,082.95
Mar.		CD		586.39	545,669.34
		SR		259,978.03	805,647.37
Apr.		SR		103,991.21	909,638.58
May		SR		41,596.48	951,235.06
June		SR		31,197.36	982,432.42
July		SR		20,909.24	1,003,341.66
Aug.		SR		20,687.24	1,024,028.90

The following information relating to your examination for the current year is also obtained:

Examination of the cash receipts record for January reveals that the amount of $1,416.90 was received from the sale of an automatic drill press. The general journal also carries the following entry relating to the sale of the drill press:

Accumulated depreciation	$3,153.02	
Loss on disposition of plant assets	$2,116.38	
Machinery		$5,269.40

Examination of the purchase discount account has revealed that there is no entry for discounts taken in March.

The following information is abstracted from the audit working papers covering the previous year's examination of sales:

	No. of Units Sold	Total Sales	Distributor List Price	Cost of Sales
$\frac{1}{2}$ H.P.	762	$ 74,361.80	$ 99.60	$ 52,503.05
$\frac{3}{4}$ H.P.	1,428	225,966.72	159.50	164,371.01
1 H.P.	1,560	293,539.60	191.75	239,940.11
1 $\frac{1}{2}$ H.P.	782	231,394.45	299.75	154,511.25

Net Sales by Months

Sept.	$ 15,042.24
Oct.	30,753.02
Nov.	39,276.96
Dec.	56,157.69
Jan.	65,517.31
Feb.	116,995.22
Mar.	183,849.65
Apr.	91,924.87
May	83,568.48
June	58,497.65
July	41,784.33
Aug.	41,895.15
	$825,262.57

Required:

Using the information presented above, prepare working papers covering your examination of sales and gross margin for the current year. (Assume that internal control has already been reviewed and showed no serious weaknesses.)

48. You are a senior accountant on the staff of Marin and Matthews, Certified Public Accountants. You are conducting the annual audit of the Never-Slip Corporation for the calendar year 1967.

    You are now working on the audit of the accounts receivable and related allowance for bad debts accounts. The study of the internal control has been completed, and the audit program has been completely carried out.

    All data and information for the setting up and completion of your working papers are summarized below.

GENERAL LEDGER

Accounts Receivable

1967		
Dec. 31	Balance	$184,092.42

Allowance for Bad Debts

1967			1967		
July 31	G.J.	$570.00	Jan. 1	Balance	$2,712.50
Oct. 31	G.J.	954.16	Dec. 31	G.J.	2,698.10

Bad Debts

1967			1967		
Dec. 31	G.J.	$2,698.10	Aug. 1	C.R.J.	$85.00

GENERAL JOURNAL

July 31

Allowance for bad debts	$570.00	
Accounts receivable		$570.00
To charge off bad accounts (detail omitted)		

October 31

Allowance for bad debts	954.16	
Account receivable		$954.16
Accounts charged off:		
Baker, J. A.	$110.00	
Dehner & Son	9.75	
Meek, Roger	350.00	
Wagner, James	494.41	
	$954.16 -964.16	

December 31

Bad debts..............................	$2,698.10	
Allowance for bad debts		$2,698.10
Annual charge based on 1/2 % of net credit sales		

CASH RECEIPTS JOURNAL

On August 1 the $85.00 account of Lester Griem, previously charged off as of July 31, was collected in full. Credit was to bad debts.

SUMMARY OF AGING SCHEDULE

The summary of the subsidiary ledger as of December 31, 1967 was totaled as follows:

Under one month	$ 92,715.60
One to three months..................................	58,070.15
Three to six months	29,126.89
Over six months.....................................	4,624.10
	$184,536.74

Credit balances:

Dabney Cleaners...................	$ 16.54—O.K.—Additional billing in January 1968
Britting Cafeteria	72.00—Should have been credited to Britt Motor Co.*
Wehby & Son.....................	384.00—Advance on a sales contract
	$472.54

* Account is in one to three months classification.

The customers' ledger is not in agreement with the accounts receivable control. The client instructs the auditor to adjust the control to the subsidiary ledger after any corrections are made.

ALLOWANCE FOR BAD DEBT REQUIREMENTS

It is agreed that ½% is adequate for accounts under one month. Accounts one to three months are expected to require a reserve of 1%. Accounts three to six months are expected to require a reserve of 2%. Accounts over six months are analyzed as follows:

Definitely bad	$ 416.52
Doubtful (estimated 50% collectible)	516.80
Apparently good but slow (estimated 90% collectible)	3,690.78
	$4,624.10

GENERAL NOTES

The general ledger has not been closed.

The allowance for bad debts account is to be adjusted to the required amount determined after all adjustments and corrections have been made.

Required:

(a) Prepare audit working papers in reasonable detail for the accounts receivable and allowance for bad debts accounts. Introduce any new accounts or more discriminating classifications if advisable. Make appropriate cross references by numbers in parentheses.

(b) Prepare correcting entries with adequate explanations *and* key to the working papers.   (Uniform C.P.A. Examination)

49. Your client is the Quaker Valley Shopping Center, Inc., a shopping center with 30 store tenants. All leases with the store tenants provide for a fixed rent plus a percentage of sales, net of sales taxes, in excess of a fixed dollar amount computed on an annual basis. Each lease also provides that the landlord may engage a C.P.A. to audit all records of the tenant for assurance that sales are being properly reported to the landlord.

You have been requested by your client to audit the records of the Bali Pearl Restaurant to determine that the sales totaling $390,000 for the year ended December 31, 1967 have been properly reported to the landlord. The Restaurant and the Shopping Center entered into a 5-year lease on January 1, 1967. The Bali Pearl Restaurant offers only table service. No liquor is served. During meal times there are four or five waitresses in attendance who prepare handwritten prenumbered restaurant checks for the customers. Payment is made at a cash register, manned by the proprietor, as the customer leaves. All sales are for cash. The proprietor also is the bookkeeper. Complete files are kept of restaurant checks and cash register tapes. A daily sales book and general ledger are also maintained.

Required:

(a) List the auditing procedures that you would employ to verify the total annual sales of the Bali Pearl Restaurant. (Disregard vending machine sales and counter sales of chewing gum, candy, etc.)

(b) Prepare the auditor's report that you would submit to the Quaker Valley Shopping Center, Inc. Assume that your examination of the records of the Bali Pearl Restaurant disclosed that sales were properly reported to the Shopping Center. (Uniform C.P.A. Examination)

50. You have examined the financial statements of the Heft Company for several years. The system of internal control for accounts receivable is very satisfactory. The Heft company is on a calendar year basis. An interim audit, which included confirmation of the accounts receivable, was performed at August 31 and indicated that the accounting for receivables was very reliable.

The Company's sales are principally to manufacturing concerns. There are about 1,500 active trade accounts receivable of which about 35% in number represent 65% of the total dollar amount. The accounts receivable are maintained alphabetically in five subledgers which are controlled by one general ledger account.

Sales are machine-posted in the subledgers by an operation that produces simultaneously the customer's ledger card, his monthly statement, and the sales journal. All cash receipts are in the form of customers' checks and are machine-posted simultaneously on the customer's ledger card, his monthly statement, and the cash receipts journal. Information for posting cash receipts is obtained from the remittance advice portions of the customers' checks. The bookkeeping machine operator compares the remittance advices with the list of checks that was prepared by another person when the mail was received.

Summary totals are produced monthly by the bookkeeping machine operations for posting to the appropriate general ledger accounts such as cash, sales, accounts receivable, etc. Aged trial balances by subledgers are prepared monthly.

Sales returns and allowances and bad debt write-offs are summarized periodically and recorded by standard journal entries. Supporting documents for these journal entries are available. The usual documents arising from billing, shipping and receiving are also available.

Required:

Prepare in detail the audit program for the Heft Company for the year-end examination of the trade accounts receivable. Do not give the program for the interim audit. (Uniform C.P.A. Examination)

51. In your audit of the Longmont Company you prepared a schedule of notes receivable. This company, a manufacturer, does not have many notes receivable and therefore does not keep a note register. All notes have resulted from sales to customers. The following schedule was prepared:

Column Number	Column Heading
1.	Name of maker
2.	Names of endorsers
3.	Date of note
4.	Due date
5.	Principal
6.	Interest rate
	Discounted (To the bank)
7.	Date
8.	Rate
9.	Amount of discount
	Interest
10.	Collected
11.	Accrued
12.	Prepaid
13.	Payment on principal
14.	Balance due
15.	Collateral held

Required:

Draw a line down the middle of a lined sheet(s) of paper.

(a) On the left of the line state the specific source(s) of information to be entered in each column and, where required, how data of previous columns are combined.

(b) On the right of the line state the principal way(s) that such information would be verified.   (Uniform C.P.A. Examination)

52. Following is the account of Creek and Brook, a customer of your client, whose financial statements you are examining as of November 30. In connection with this examination, you are asked on December 8 to do the following:

(a) Age the account on a first-in, first-out basis.

(b) Age the account on a specific invoice basis.

(c) Suggest possible explanations for past due amounts listed for (b).

Creek and Brook

Terms : 2/10, n/30

July	1	Balance forward			$3,829.01
	5	Inv. 813,	$1,406.18		5,235.19
	15	Cash		$1,406.18	3,829.01
	23	Inv. 841,	621.75		4,450.76
	31	Inv. 860,	416.01		4,866.77
		Cash		3,829.01	1,037.76
Aug.	13	Inv. 874,	534.51		1,572.27
	17	Inv. 880,	108.94		1,681.21
	20	D.M. 21—Correct Inv. 841	25.16		1,706.37
	23	Cash		1,029.44	676.93
	25	Inv. 892,	321.65		998.58
		Freight	27.62		1,026.20
	27	Cash		108.94	917.26
Sept.	3	Inv. 903,	251.18		1,168.44
	10	Cash		534.51	633.93
	18	Inv. 918,	634.15		1,268.08
	25	Cash		349.27	918.81
Oct.	4	Inv. 1,001,	65.82		984.63
	10	Cash		225.94	758.69

Creek and Brook (Cont'd)

Terms: 2/10, n/30

14	Inv. 1,012,	491.50		1,250.19
15	C.M. 14		25.24	1,224.95
18	Cash		592.05	632.90
26	Inv. 1,025,	161.35		794.25
Nov. 5	Inv. 1,042,	225.18		1,019.43
7	Inv. 1,049,	42.51		1,061.94
15	Cash		500.00	561.94
Dec. 4	Cash		200.00	361.94

53. The Bryant Department Store has arrangements for customers to pay for purchases over $10.00 on a time-payment plan. The plan calls for a 10 per cent down payment, a carrying charge of 10 per cent on the balance after the down payment, and payments of $5.00 per month on balances up to $100.

An examination of financial statements for the store should include some form of aging analysis of the installment accounts, for purposes of evaluating the store's provision for doubtful accounts.

(a) Suggest two different methods of aging such accounts.

(b) Apply each of these methods to the following accounts, in an examination of balances at January 31.

(c) Based on the results of your aging, which of the following two accounts would you judge to be the better risk from the standpoint of collectibility?

J. K. Baker

May	10	Clothing	63.81		
		Carrying charge	5.74		
		Down payment		6.38	63.17
June	13	Cash		5.00	58.17
July	19	Cash		5.00	53.17
Dec.	30	Cash		5.00	48.17
Jan.	20	Cash		5.00	43.17

A. S. Burton

June	20	Sporting goods	86.54		
		Carrying charge	7.79		
		Down payment		8.65	85.68
July	20	Cash		5.00	80.68
Aug.	20	Cash		5.00	75.68
Sept.	20	Cash		5.00	70.68
Oct.	20	Cash		5.00	65.68
Nov.	20	Cash		5.00	60.68

54. SENECA MEMORIAL HOSPITAL

Roy Sanders, a senior accountant on the staff of Young and Mitchell, a leading national public accounting firm, was employed in the Philadelphia office of the firm and had been a senior accountant for about a year and a half. He was currently in charge of the examination of the financial statements of the Seneca Memorial Hospital for the year ended June 30, 1968. The hospital served the people in Seneca and those from the rural areas within a radius of about 50 miles. The operating revenues of the hospital were derived primarily from charges to patients, but operations were further supported by income from endowment funds which had been established by various leading and public-spirited citizens of Seneca. Although the present hospital building and much of its equipment had resulted from fund raising campaigns and special gifts over the past 20 years, the hospital had a notable record of service to the Seneca area for over 60 years.

The affairs of the hospital were directed by a self-perpetuating board of 20 trustees, all of whom were leading figures in the Seneca area. Robert R. Samuelson was president of the board, having served in that capacity for 17 years and as a member of the board for 30 years. He was an attorney with a well-established practice in Seneca and was a very active member of the Pennsylvania Bar Association.

Director of the hospital was Leroy Johnson, who was assisted in the areas with which we are concerned by Andrew Wiley, Comptroller, and Frank Abbot, Credit Manager.

Roy Sanders felt that the present year's examination was progressing smoothly and that the work was well along. At the moment, he was reflecting on the examination of accounts receivable—the stickiest part of the entire examination. He recalled that in a supplementary report by his firm to the Board of Trustees made in connection with last year's examination, the following statement had been included:

"It is estimated that accounts receivable amounting to over $160,000 are more than one year old. This is the result of a failure to charge-off accounts and an apparent lack of a standard, routine follow-up as well as the many instances when patients are discharged without an effective attempt to realize a collection of the balance due.

"There are procedures and form letters in use for credit follow-up, but our observation was that they are applied on a selective, individual basis instead of a regular routine.

"The accounts have never been completely aged to determine the status and trend of collections. As a result, we found no person who could accurately evaluate the status of the accounts."

Sanders also remembered a public statement made by Mr. Samuelson following a recent Board of Trustees meeting. Mr. Samuelson had said, "An examination of the status of our accounts receivable indicates that there is need of more arduous efforts in collecting accounts from those who can afford to pay, should pay, but are willing to evade a just debt where possible. Those responsible for many of these accounts have ignored our request for payment, and your Board of Trustees is instituting for the next fiscal year a more stringent collection policy. In a charitable institution it is always difficult to know when the debtor should be considered a worthy recipient of beneficence and when the debtor should be made to pay through the medium of all legal collection forces available to the institution. While the trustees, if they err, would err in favor of benevolence where needed, yet it is only fair to remind those who owe the hospital and can afford to pay that they may expect payment to be enforced."

The problems implicit in the above statement were quite apparent to Sanders. The hospital's own figures for the year under examination showed that, including endowment fund income of $46,000, the excess of revenues over expenses was only $20,000 on total billed charges of $1,420,000 and that there was an accumulated deficit from past operations of $162,000. The continued operation of the hospital was thus dependent on the recovery of the major portion of the operating expenses from the hospital's patients, but a "hard" attitude on rates and collections would be inconsistent with the continued need for gifts which were secured largely on the strength of the beneficent activities of the hospital.

Frank Abbot, the credit manager, was in the middle of this conflict in objectives. In discussing the current year's results with Abbot, Sanders had learned that Abbot had requested permission to press for collections on a number of accounts of people in Seneca who were clearly able to pay, but Abbot had been dissuaded by the hospital director from proceeding. The director had stated that his desire to refrain from taking action was based on repercussions that might result from one group of board members. This incident had occurred about six months ago, and as a result Abbot had concluded that there was no point in pressing anyone for collection. Since then, his clerical assistants had practically discontinued the mailing of follow-up letters which had been used in an effort to obtain collection after two statements had been mailed to the responsible party.

These were some of the thoughts that came to Sanders' mind as he reviewed the working papers covering the work done by his assistants in the examination of accounts receivable. How should Sanders proceed in concluding the examination of receivables? Among the voluminous details in the working papers were the following data, to which Sanders would be expected to give particular attention:

Balance Sheet—Unaudited
June 30, 1968

Assets :		
Cash	$	14,000
Accounts receivable (net)		497,000
Inventories		112,000
Property and equipment (net)		677,000
Other assets		43,000
		$1,343,000
Current Liabilities		47,000
Net assets		$1,296,000
Fund Capital :		
Expendable principal		$1,458,000
Accumulated deficit		162,000
Net expendable principal		$1,296,000

Summary of Hospital Operations—Unaudited
Year Ended June 30, 1968

Earnings from patients—gross	$1,420,000
Less—Provision for uncollectible accounts, charity allowances, loss on state aid, etc.	121,000
Net earnings	$1,299,000
Operating expenses	1,325,000
Excess of expenses over net earnings	$ 26,000
Endowment income	46,000
Net income	$ 20,000

Selected Balance Sheet and Operating Figures

	Amount at June 30, or for Year Ended June 30		
	1966	1967	1968
Gross earnings from patients	$1,174,000	$1,254,000	$1,420,000
Allowance for :			
Free treatment (Note 1)	80,000	101,000	66,000
Uncollectible accounts (Note 2)	39,000	48,000	55,000
Accounts receivable	625,000	742,000	698,000
Uncollectible accounts charged off (Note 3)	106,000	68,000	274,000
Balance, reserve for bad debts	273,000	354,000	201,000

Analysis of Accounts Receivable at June 30, 1968
Together with Hospital Estimate of Reserve Necessary
to Provide for Uncollectible Accounts

	Amount Receivable	Estimated Loss
In-Patient Accounts, loss estimated by Mr. Abbot		
New Account cards (Note 4) :		
Free treatment balances	$104,000	$104,000
Regular accounts	322,000	20,000
Total new account cards (4,281 accounts)	$426,000	124,000
Employee free treatment balances	17,000	17,000
Old account cards (1,038 accounts):		
(Should be able to collect 50% if turned over to collection agency, less 30% fee—per Mr. Abbot)	91,000	59,000
Patients still in hospital or recently discharged	49,000	6,000
Due from Blue Cross or from state *	30,000	
Out-Patient accounts (9,266 accounts) :		
40% loss estimate used last year (deemed " not unrealistic " by Mr. Wiley)	97,000	39,000
Totals (Note 5)	$710,000	$245,000

Aging Test, New Ledger Cards for Patients A Through Cz

The ledger cards involved represented $97,000 of the total of $426,000 on new ledger cards. Young and Mitchell staff auditors aged all accounts selected for written confirmation from this block. These included 28 accounts with balances of $600 or more and totaling $31,000 (positive confirmation requests), and a block of 50 accounts totaling $4,200 (negative confirmation requests). (Additional accounts confirmed from other ledgers gave confirmation coverage of 16 per cent.) The remaining ledger cards in the A–Cz group were aged by a hospital employee. Balances were aged according to the date of discharge, and the results of the two aging analyses were combined. These showed the balances to be distributed as follows:

Discharged—June 1968	7.2%
May 1968	18.0
April 1968	10.7
March 1968	6.4
February 1968	5.4
January 1968	5.4
December 1967	5.4
November 1967	3.8
October 1967	4.3
September 1967	4.6
August 1967	5.8
July 1967	3.6
Prior to 7/1/67	19.4
	100.0%

NOTES

(1) An account receivable is established for every person treated by the hospital, and all services rendered are charged to the account at the regularly established rates. Free treatment represents the estimated loss on state aid cases, certain Blue Cross cases (low-income families), and services to hospital

employees (for whom all charges are waived). The estimated loss is based on the amounts charged, less collections from the state and Blue Cross. The state increased the state aid stipend to hospitals July 1, 1967, and as a result a total of $108,000 was received from the state during the current year, as against $87,000 in the preceding year.

(2) The hospital has regularly followed the policy of providing for uncollectible accounts on the basis of 4% of in-patient charges and 10% of out-patient charges (exclusive of charges on state aid or other welfare cases). Out-patient charges in the year ended June 30, 1968, amounted to $66,000.

(3) Mr. Abbot prepares each year a list of all accounts which he deems to be uncollectible (including remaining balances on state aid and other welfare cases), which Mr. Johnson presents to the Board of Trustees for their approval. For instance, the 1968 charge-off of uncollectible accounts included:

1,206 State aid account balances	$126,000
2,091 Other in-patient accounts	129,000
2,642 Out-patient accounts	19,000
Total	$274,000

Mr. Abbot was unable to write off all of the out-patient accounts that he believed to be uncollectible, because the hospital director had stated that the trustees did not want more than $20,000 charged off in any one year. (The balance of the out-patient accounts at 6/30/67 was $88,000.)

(4) A new bookkeeping machine was installed on July 1, 1967, and a new form of ledger card was used on all accounts receiving charges beginning on that date. Hence any account on a new card was no more than one year old, with the exception of accounts which had been billed prior to July 1, 1967, but on which collections were received after that date. In such instances the balance due was transferred to a new ledger card so that the cash collected could be posted on the new machine. Cash collections were received by the cashier department under Mr. Wiley, and postings were made by other employees to the ledger from copies of the receipt forms prepared by the cashiers.

(5) The hospital made no effort to balance the detailed accounts receivable cards against the general ledger control. The only listing of the ledger cards was made by the auditor as a part of his examination, and the total shown was derived from such a listing. The total of the ledger cards at June 30, 1967 was $751,000. No effort had been made to locate the difference.

(This case, prepared by the author, appeared in *The Journal of Accountancy,* November, 1959.)

Purchases, expenses, and
accounts payable systems;
internal control

9

The immediately preceding chapters have dealt with the accounting results of business outputs—sales and receivables. In this and the following chapter we turn our attention to the inputs that give rise to such outputs: materials purchased, services acquired (excluding labor and the attendant payroll records), and the recording of the liabilities that are thereby created. The discussion in this chapter pertains to internal control and the accounting system as they relate to these inputs; the next chapter is devoted to the independent audit of the transactions and accounts associated with these inputs.

Objectives of Internal Control

Internal control over purchases and the incurrence of liabilities should give assurance that:

1. Purchases or other commitments are initiated only by authorized personnel.
2. Purchase orders for goods and materials are placed as needed and for optimum quantities.
3. Follow-up is made on purchase orders if delivery has not been made by the scheduled delivery date.
4. Incoming shipments are accepted only if the receiving department has authorization in the form of a copy of the purchase order.
5. Quantity and quality of goods received are as specified before payment is authorized.
6. Terms, prices, and clerical accuracy of vendors' invoices are correct before payment is authorized.
7. Refund or credit is received for all purchase returns and allowances.
8. Payment of invoices is made in sufficient time to avoid lost discounts, and any discounts that are lost are reported as a separate figure.

9. Detailed liability records are in balance with control balances and with vendors' statements.

Some concerns achieve additional control, particularly with respect to avoiding fraudulent payments to fictitious vendors, by maintaining a list of approved vendors, against which all invoices must be screened before payment may be authorized.

The implementation of the internal control objectives listed above is suggested by Figure 9–1 presented on the following pages. Particularly important is the division of responsibilities shown in the chart. The activities and records associated with such responsibilities are described under each of the departmental headings in the following sections.

Purchasing Department

The purchasing cycle is initiated upon determination of a need for goods or services to be acquired. In some instances, such determination is made within the purchasing department on the basis of a review of quantities on hand and past usage as shown by perpetual inventory records. In other cases, storekeepers and shop foremen will prepare purchase requisitions and forward them to the purchasing department on the basis of observed needs. More commonly, however, purchase requisitions are prepared by the production control department on the basis of needs shown by perpetual inventory records maintained in that department, plus an analysis of the materials requirements for production scheduled on the basis of orders received or inventory requirements.

Regardless of where the initiating responsibility is lodged, there are three major problems associated with purchasing: (1) when to order, (2) how much to order, and (3) from whom to order. The question of when to order depends primarily on quantities on hand, rate of use, and the lead time from placement of the order to receipt of the goods. Other factors that are sometimes considered are the cost of owning and storing excess quantities held as a "cushion," and the contrasting factors of the risk and loss or cost of going "stock-out."

How much to order can be answered judgmentally or mathematically in arriving at the "economic order quantity" or "EOQ." Factors to be considered include expected rate of use, fixed costs of ordering, receiving, and paying for what has been purchased, set-up costs, storage costs, interest on investment, risk of obsolescence or deterioration, quantity discounts, and shipping cost.

In deciding from whom to order, the choice of vendors would depend on price (often determined from competitive bids), payment terms, quality, reliability, location, promised delivery dates, and possibly "reciprocity"— the practice of ordering from concerns who reciprocate by buying the purchaser's product or service. Credit standing may also be a factor, for an order placed with a financially weak concern might result in lost sales or costly production delays if financial failure of the concern should occur.

Once the above decisions are made, the order is placed by means of a purchase order form. This form serves many purposes, as indicated by the following typical distribution of the multiple copies prepared:

1. Vendor's copy—representing the formal order.

2. Vendor's acknowledgment copy—signed and returned by the vendor to indicate that the order has been received and accepted, and the date shipment can be expected.

3. Requisitioner's copy—to inform the person who submitted the initial purchase requisition that an order has been placed.

4. Purchasing department "tickler" copy—filed according to the date the goods are expected to be received, so that follow-up procedures can be instigated if the goods do not arrive on time.

5. Purchasing department cross-reference copy—filed alphabetically.

6. Receiving copy—authorizes the department to accept the goods when they arrive, thus avoiding the cost of handling and repacking misdirected shipments or incorrect items. Order quantities are generally blocked out on this copy in order to force receiving clerks to make an actual count of the goods received. This copy may also be used as a receiving report if date and quantity received are recorded on the copy, thus obviating considerable handwriting that would be necessary to prepare a separate receiving report.

7. Receiving file copy—filed chronologically by date of receipt of goods to provide a departmental record of all shipments received.

8. Accounts payable department copy—gives prices and terms to be used in auditing the vendor's invoice preparatory to payment. Alternatively, the invoice may be sent to the purchasing department for approval of prices and terms.

9. Stores and inspection department copies—used when these departments should be notified that materials will be arriving, in order that proper preparations may be made.

Purchase returns and allowances should be subject to equally tight control. The purchasing department should prepare an accounts payable debit memo to initiate the adjustment. One copy of the prenumbered form would be sent to the supplier, representing a request for adjustment, another would be sent to the shipping department to authorize shipment if materials are to be returned, and other copies would be held in the purchasing department. One of these copies should be held in a tickler file pending notification from the supplier setting forth the amount of adjustment granted. This information would then be noted on the tickler copy, which would

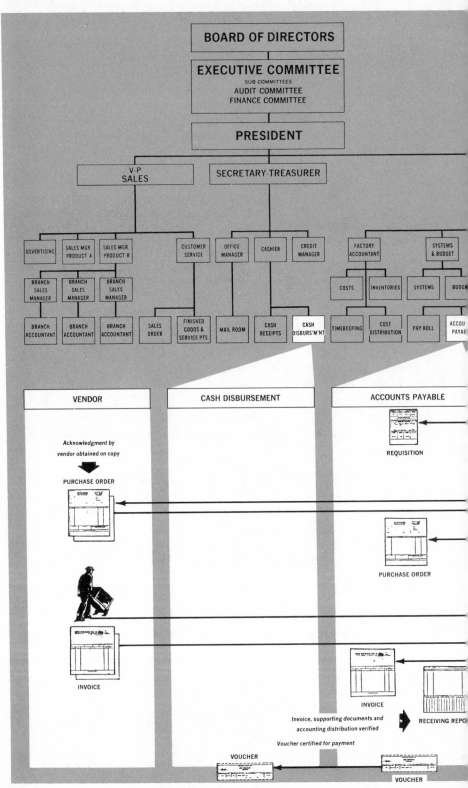

BOARD OF DIRECTORS

EXECUTIVE COMMITTEE
SUB COMMITTEES
AUDIT COMMITTEE
FINANCE COMMITTEE

PRESIDENT

V-P SALES

SECRETARY-TREASURER

| ADVERTISING | SALES MGR. PRODUCT A | SALES MGR. PRODUCT B | | CUSTOMER SERVICE | OFFICE MANAGER | CASHIER | CREDIT MANAGER | | FACTORY ACCOUNTANT | | SYSTEMS & BUDGET |

| BRANCH SALES MANAGER | BRANCH SALES MANAGER | BRANCH SALES MANAGER | | | | | | COSTS | INVENTORIES | SYSTEMS | BUDGE |

| BRANCH ACCOUNTANT | BRANCH ACCOUNTANT | BRANCH ACCOUNTANT | SALES ORDER | FINISHED GOODS & SERVICE PTS. | MAIL ROOM | CASH RECEIPTS | CASH DISBURS'M'NT | TIMEKEEPING | COST DISTRIBUTION | PAY ROLL | ACCOU PAYAE |

| VENDOR | CASH DISBURSEMENT | ACCOUNTS PAYABLE |

REQUISITION

Acknowledgment by
vendor obtained on copy

PURCHASE ORDER

PURCHASE ORDER

INVOICE

INVOICE

RECEIVING REPO

Invoice, supporting documents and
accounting distribution verified

Voucher certified for payment

VOUCHER

VOUCHER

Figure 9-1   224

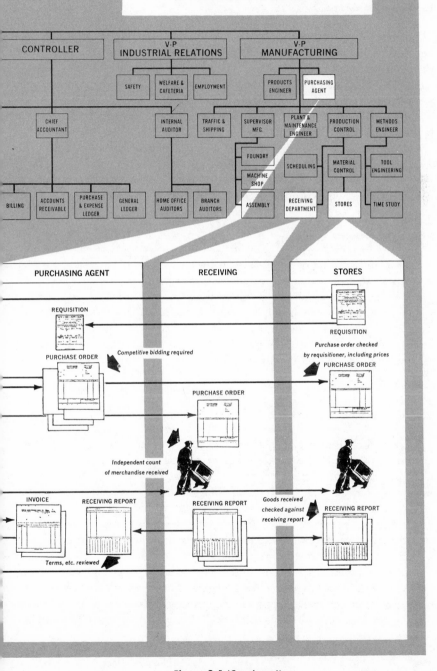

PURCHASES

PROCEDURAL FLOW CHART SHOWN IN RELATION
TO ORGANIZATION CHART TO PORTRAY
THE CONTROL OBTAINED THROUGH SEGREGATION
OF FUNCTIONAL RESPONSIBILITY

CONTROLLER | V-P INDUSTRIAL RELATIONS | V-P MANUFACTURING

SAFETY · WELFARE & CAFETERIA · EMPLOYMENT · PRODUCTS ENGINEER · PURCHASING AGENT

CHIEF ACCOUNTANT · INTERNAL AUDITOR · TRAFFIC & SHIPPING · SUPERVISOR MFG. · PLANT & MAINTENANCE ENGINEER · PRODUCTION CONTROL · METHODS ENGINEER

FOUNDRY · SCHEDULING · MATERIAL CONTROL · TOOL ENGINEERING

MACHINE SHOP

BILLING · ACCOUNTS RECEIVABLE · PURCHASE & EXPENSE LEDGER · GENERAL LEDGER · HOME OFFICE AUDITORS · BRANCH AUDITORS · ASSEMBLY · RECEIVING DEPARTMENT · STORES · TIME STUDY

PURCHASING AGENT

REQUISITION

PURCHASE ORDER

Competitive bidding required

RECEIVING

PURCHASE ORDER

STORES

REQUISITION

Purchase order checked
by requisitioner, including prices

PURCHASE ORDER

Independent count
of merchandise received

INVOICE · RECEIVING REPORT

RECEIVING REPORT

Goods received
checked against
receiving report

RECEIVING REPORT

Terms, etc. reviewed

Figure 9-1 (Continued)   225

be forwarded to the accounts payable department to authorize deduction of the adjustment from a subsequent payment to the supplier. Serial numbers of the prenumbered forms should be accounted for at that time.

Receiving Department

The receiving department should maintain a record of all shipments received. A copy of the purchase order properly noted to show receipt of the goods, or a copy of a receiving report prepared by the receiving department, filed chronologically by date shipment was received, often constitutes the record of receipts. A separate receiving report form would ordinarily be prepared when a series of shipments is to be made against a single purchase order, or if several copies of the receiving report are desired.

The quantity or weight received is customarily determined by the receiving department, but in some instances the count is made in conjunction with subsequent handling of the goods, such as by the inspection department, or by the price-marking department in a retail store.

Stores Department

In a manufacturing or wholesaling concern, custody of materials received is transferred to a stores or warehouse department; in a retail store, the goods received will usually be transferred directly to the selling department. In any event, the accounting records should establish accountability for the materials or goods in the department to which they have been transferred. When that is the case, the stores or other department that receives the materials should be certain that it receives everything for which it is to be charged.

Accounts Payable Department

As receiving reports and vendors' invoices are received by the accounts payable department, the two records are compared, and those that match are forwarded for further processing. Unmatched invoices or receiving reports should be held in separate files until the matching documents arrive. These files are particularly important at the end of a concern's fiscal year in order to reconcile physical inventory counts with book records, and to ascertain the amount of unrecorded liabilities which should be reflected in the financial statements.

The corresponding purchase order copy should next be placed with each matched invoice and receiving report. These records are then ready for auditing to determine approval for payment. To control the auditing steps, a voucher form or an "audit block" stamp may be used. The rubber-stamp impression, such as is illustrated below, would be placed directly on each invoice.

MATERIALS RECEIVED			
PRICES			
EXTENSIONS AND FOOTINGS			
ENTERED IN INVENTORY			
DISCOUNT —			
COMPUTED BY			
AMOUNT			
APPROVAL FOR PAYMENT			
CHECK NUMBER			
DISTRIBUTION —			
ACCOUNT	201		
	501		
	824		
	837		

Figure 9-2. AUDIT BLOCK

As each audit step is completed, the clerk should initial the appropriate item on the voucher or audit block, thereby fixing responsibility for performance. The steps include verification that the quantity received agrees with the quantity ordered and invoiced, that the price and terms on the invoice agree with those specified by the purchase order, and that extensions and footings on the invoice are correct.

Discounts should be calculated, and preferably deducted from the invoice amount, so that the invoice is recorded "net." Under such an arrangement, if an invoice is not paid within the discount period, the lost discount is recorded as an expense at time of payment, thereby clearly signalling an exception in the processing of invoices for payment. Finally, indication should be given of the general ledger account or accounts to which the invoice is to be charged. If standard costs are being used, purchases must be priced and extended at standard, with the difference between standard and invoice cost charged to a price variance account.

The final step is a review made to ascertain that all required steps have been completed. Then the invoice may be forwarded to the inventory control clerk for entry in the detailed perpetual inventory records.

Upon return from the inventory-recording operation, the invoice would be recorded in the general accounting records to reflect the liability and the corresponding debit to an asset or an expense. To establish control over the recording operation, invoices are usually batched and a prelist tape prepared for each batch. The recording process described at this point involves an accounting machine to post in duplicate to copies of a voucher-check form and to a columnar invoice (voucher) register with expense-distribution columns. The voucher portion accompanies the check to the vendor, serving as an advice to indicate what invoice or invoices are being paid. Information recorded on the voucher, and by carbon duplication on the voucher register, includes entry date, vendor name, invoice number, and amount. The amount is also printed a second time in the appropriate debit-distribution column of the voucher register.

If each invoice carries a specific due date, generally only one invoice is recorded on a voucher-check. But if a vendor specifies that all invoices are to be paid on the tenth of the following month, or the fifteenth or thirtieth that follows next, several invoices can be recorded on the voucher during the period prior to the payment date, and the voucher is then referred to as a "built-up" voucher.

A running total of invoices posted to the voucher can be maintained, and each entry proved under the following arrangement:

Pick up previous balance	$100.00
Enter new invoice on voucher	50.00
Subtotal of invoices listed	$150.00
Second pick-up of previous balance	−100.00
Debit distribution—a/c xxx	− 30.00
a/c yyy	− 20.00
Proof	$ .00

Vertical registers would develop a total of all invoices posted for proof against the prelist tape, and also develop totals for each of the debit-distribution columns for posting to the general ledger at the end of the month.

Filing of invoices and voucher-check forms by due date completes the accounts payable operations. On the due date, the forms are released for payment; these procedures are discussed in a later chapter.

Auditing invoices on a test basis. Experience has shown that most vendors' invoices are correctly prepared, and that such errors as do occur are about equally in favor of the customer and the vendor. Also, a substantial dollar proportion of all purchases is frequently represented by relatively few invoices. Often, study will show that the largest invoices constitute only about twenty per cent of the invoices but eighty per cent of the dollar purchases. In view of such circumstances, some companies make a complete audit only of invoices exceeding a stated dollar amount. Invoices for a lesser amount are test-audited, usually to the extent of about ten per cent of those invoices. Records should be kept of all errors found on the invoices of each vendor, so that in the event that errors become excessive for any given vendor, those invoices can be subjected to 100 per cent verification and correction of errors until the condition is corrected.

The premise that underlies such a test approach is that the cost of auditing smaller invoices is likely to exceed any net saving resulting from the correction of errors revealed by the audit. The actual conditions must, however, be examined in each situation prior to embarking on a test-audit program. Some auditing of smaller invoices should always take place to guard against a vendor whose billing or shipping procedures may go out of control, or an unscrupulous vendor who, learning of his customer's accounts payable audit practices, may seek to take advantage of the situation.

Accounts payable ledger. The reader will have recognized that the accounts payable system described utilizes a bookless record of accounts payable details. A traditional posted accounts payable ledger can, however, be readily incorporated in either a machine-posted or hand-posted system. An accounts payable ledger record is likely to be essential if advances are made to suppliers, to be liquidated by subsequent shipments; if installment purchases or partial payments are frequently made; or if the volume of business with each vendor must be known, to qualify for special rebates or volume discounts.

Month-end procedures. The detailed accounts payable records should be balanced with the control account at least once a month in order to prove the accuracy of the records, or to instigate a search for errors if the records are not in balance. A tape listing of accounts payable details would be prepared from the unpaid invoice file, or from the accounts payable ledger sheets if that form of record is maintained. Another important month-end procedure is the balancing of detailed payables records with vendors' statements in those instances when statements are furnished. Bookkeeping errors and unrecorded invoices may be detected as a result of such comparison.

Smaller businesses often record purchases on a cash basis; that is, when payment is made. The debit distribution is then handled through the cash disbursement record. In this way, the recording of each purchase in a voucher register is eliminated. The owner or manager of the business may, however, prefer statements prepared on an accrual basis as being more meaningful. If so, an adjusting entry for unpaid invoices at the end of the month can easily be developed if disbursements in the first few days of the following month are limited to invoices dated in the previous month. When all of such invoices have been entered and paid, a subtotal of cash disbursements and debit distribution to that date provides the information necessary for a work sheet adjustment to an accrual basis for purchases.

Whenever a physical inventory of materials or goods on hand is taken, the figure developed serves as a basis for adjusting general ledger perpetual inventory records. In making that adjustment, consideration should be given to inventory that has been received and included in the physical count but has not yet been charged to the inventory account. The necessary figure can be developed from the accounts payable department's file of unmatched receiving reports after all receiving reports issued prior to the inventory count have been processed.

Audit implications of payables records. A company's payables are the receivables on the books of its vendors, and, as was noted in the receivables chapter, confirmation of accounts receivable is an essential audit procedure. The manner in which most companies handle their payables often makes it difficult, if not practically impossible, to reply to receivables confirmation requests. In fact, as was noted in the receivables chapters, chain store organizations and railroads frequently rubber-stamp confirmation requests with the notation that their records do not make it possible for them to reply to such requests.

From the discussion in the immediately preceding sections, the reasons for such responses should be apparent. Most important among these are the difficulty of determining the exact amount owing to a given vendor when some of the invoices may be in unmatched invoice files awaiting notification of the receipt of materials, others may have been sent out to other departments for approval, and still others may be distributed throughout the tickler file, awaiting payment.

Often the only way to answer such requests is to wait a reasonable length of time and then base the reply on information gained from the file of paid invoices. These are usually filed alphabetically, and by referring to invoice dates and payment dates, those unpaid at the confirmation date can be determined. Even this may not be possible in a large chain organization, however, for the invoices are often retained in the individual branches or stores, the home office making payments based only on lists of items approved for payment by the various branches or stores. Payment to a vendor is then made by preparation of a single check covering all purchases by the various subunits.

Alternative debit-distribution methods. As an alternative to columnar distribution of debits in the voucher register, a "register" distribution can be made by the accounting machine. All debits are listed in a single column in the voucher register, along with the appropriate account-number designation. By depressing the proper register control key as each debit amount is listed, the machine operator is able to develop classification totals equal in number to the register capacity of the accounting machine.

"Unit ticket distribution" represents another approach to handling debit distribution and is particularly applicable if insufficient registers are available for register distribution. The unit ticket is placed over the proper voucher register columns, so that identifying information, account number, and amount of each entry are recorded on a unit ticket, the voucher register receiving the same information by carbon impression. The unit tickets are then filed until the end of the month, when they are sorted by account number and totaled to obtain the debit distribution for the amount of vouchers payable recorded during the month.

"Posted distribution" is largely a variation of the unit ticket method. The actual general ledger account sheet to which a debit applies is merely inserted in the accounting machine in place of the unit ticket. If a running balance of the accounts is desired, the previous balance must be picked up before the debit is posted. Advantages of the method include having up-to-date totals of the accounts affected by the debit distribution, along with complete detailed information of all account charges coming from the voucher register. Posting time and cost would be slightly higher than under other debit-distribution methods.

Punched-card records. Although certain purchasing department forms and records are sometimes handled in punched-card form, our attention will be limited to accounts payable applications. After invoices have been audited and approved for payment, they are batched and totaled and then released for key punching. For each invoice a payables card is punched showing vendor name and number, invoice date, due date, number, gross amount, discount (if any), and net amount. Immediately following the punching of the payables card, one or more distribution cards are punched, depending on the number of different accounts to which the invoice is to be charged. Common information is duplicated automatically from the payables card to the distribution card or cards.

When punching is completed, the entire file of cards punched is listed on the tabulator to prepare the daily invoice register. All details punched in the cards are listed on the register. In addition, the tabulator is programmed to compare the gross amount punched in each payables card with the amount punched in related distribution cards, in what is known as a "zero-balancing" operation. Such balancing proves the equality of the debits and credits punched in the two types of cards. Further proof of punching accuracy is gained by balancing the machine total of all payables cards against the batch control total prepared prior to punching.

Following proof of the day's work, the distribution cards are separated from the payables cards; the distribution cards are held until the end of the month, when they are sorted by account number and group-printed to obtain account totals for general ledger posting and analysis purposes. Each day's payables cards are sorted by due date and filed with cards bearing the same due date.

On or shortly before the due date, the payables cards due on that date are removed from the file and used to prepare checks and remittance advices.

As desired, payables cards in the unpaid file can be tabulated by due date to gain an indication of future cash needs. Also, of course, tabulation of the unpaid payables cards at the end of the month produces the total necessary to determine whether the detailed records are in balance with the general ledger control account for payables.

Management Reports

As would be expected, the type of management information needed varies with the departmental operation that is involved, and the following material is subdivided on that basis.

Purchasing activities. The purchasing department has need of both external and internal information. Market developments are of particular importance and should cover such matters as present and anticipated price and supply movements, changes in freight tariffs, and development of new materials and sources of supply. Internal information useful in purchasing is extremely diverse and would include such matters as:

1. Inventory position and estimated future demand to serve as a basis for decisions on volume of purchases.

2. Outstanding purchase commitments, possibly classified by inventory categories and scheduled delivery dates. In retail organizations, such information is commonly combined with inventory position and budgeted sales information to arrive at an "open-to-buy" figure for each department.

3. Standard cost price variances, with freight-in included in determining the variance or reported as a separate figure for control purposes.

4. Volume of orders placed with major suppliers.

5. Expense and activity reports, analyzing expenses incurred by the purchasing department and comparing the expense figures with budget amounts and previous-period expenses. The expenses should also be related to activity figures whenever possible to obtain unit costs, such unit costs being compared with standards, if available. Reports of activities may cover number of orders placed, number of shipments received, number of purchase returns and percentage relationship to purchases, average processing time for purchase requisitions, and percentage of orders received after scheduled delivery date.

Accounts payable and receiving. Accounts payable activity is particularly important from the standpoint of anticipating cash requirements. Useful for this purpose is a daily report showing the accounts payable balance at the beginning of the day, the dollar amount of invoices processed and added to outstanding payables for the day, the dollar amount of invoices paid for the day, and the balance at the close of the day. Further information for cash-planning purposes is sometimes provided by an analysis of the accounts payable balance according to scheduled dates of payment. An indication of the efficiency of the department in processing invoices on schedule may be gained from the monthly amount of purchase discounts lost. The usefulness of such a figure for control purposes points to the desirability of recording purchases at net and showing discounts lost, rather than recording purchases at the gross invoice amount and recording income from purchase discounts taken.

Operating data should be available in the form of the number of invoices processed, and operating expenses should be related to both budgeted amounts and the volume of work processed. Other useful operating statistics would include the number of unmatched invoices and receiving reports at the close of each week or month, and the number and types of errors disclosed by the invoice-auditing process.

Operating expenses. Reports of operating expenses are directly related to the coding and recording of charges that occur as part of accounts payable operations. Final expense reports are also dependent upon further allocation of many charges that are incurred. These allocations may be based on actual use or current activity, such as factory supplies or repair expenses; other expenses such as electricity, taxes, and insurance may be allocated on a fixed formula based on such factors as number of square feet, number of machines, and number of employees.

The income statement, usually prepared on a monthly basis, represents the summation of all operating results, and should be prepared in such a way as to be of maximum value to the president and board of directors. For the statement to achieve maximum utility, figures should cover both the month and the year to date and should be so reported as to permit ready comparison with budgeted amounts or standard costs and with figures for preceding periods.

Supporting the income statement should be a top-level report showing all expenditures classified on a responsibility basis. The following headings suggest the possible arrangement of such a report:*

Total expenditures:
    Departmental controllable expense—
        President's Office
        V.P. production
        V.P. sales
        V.P. finance
        V.P. personnel
    Noncontrollable expenses—
        Depreciation
        Taxes
        Insurance
    Productive payroll
    Material purchased

Disposition of total expenditures:
    Standard cost of sales
    Cost variation
    Inventory changes
    Selling expenses
    General and administrative expenses
    Costs capitalized

* This material is adapted from "Responsibility Accounting," by John A. Higgins, appearing in *The Arthur Andersen Chronicle*, April, 1952.

Each of the top executives listed above under "Departmental controllable expenses" should in turn receive a more detailed report showing a breakdown of the expenses for which he is responsible, classified in accordance with the responsibilities of those persons immediately under him. For instance, the vice-president in charge of production might receive the following report:

Productive labor	Tool room
Controllable expenses—	Inspection
Vice-president's office	Receiving
General superintendent's department	Shipping
ment	Stores
Production control	
Purchasing	
Maintenance	

A report showing a further breakdown of expenses would be prepared for each of the activities under the vice-president. Thus the general superintendent would receive a report summarizing the productive payroll and the controllable expenses in each department under him. The foreman of each of these departments would, in turn, receive a breakdown, such as the following, showing the expenditures for which he is responsible:

Productive labor	
Controllable expenses—	
Supervision	Supplies
Setup	Small tools
Repair and rework	Other
Overtime premium	

The preceding discussion obviously applies only to relatively large manufacturing concerns. On the other hand, the principles of reporting by functional activity apply to even the one-man business. The sole proprietor should have comparative figures to analyze the success of his business activities, and to be of maximum value these figures should be broken down to show such functional items as material costs, selling expenses, general expenses, noncontrollable expenses, and income taxes. Although budgets and standard costs will be beyond the realm of practicality in his case, the sole proprietor can, nevertheless, often obtain comparative data for his classes of costs and expenses in the form of percentages of net sales for similar businesses. By comparing these percentages with those for his own business, he can tell whether his costs and expenses are in line with those of similar businesses. The figures to be used in making such comparisons can usually be obtained from the Department of Commerce or from a trade association for the particular type of business.

Internal Auditing

The extension of internal auditing beyond the limits of financial records is well illustrated by the opportunities for effective work within an operating department such as purchasing. The examination of that department would ordinarily involve sufficient investigation to determine whether orders have been placed only after careful consideration of quantities on hand and future needs, whether adequate effort was made to obtain the best prices commensurate with quality, that competitive bids were obtained whenever warranted or required by established policies, and that adequate follow-up measures have been employed to assure that goods ordered were received according to schedule. Reported figures on outstanding purchase commitments and volume of purchasing activity should be tested or verified.

Receiving operations should be reviewed to ascertain that goods are accepted only under authorization of an existing purchase order, that sufficient care and thoroughness are exercised in counting or weighing goods prior to completion of related receiving reports, that adequate receiving records are maintained, and that goods are counted and forwarded to stores or operating departments promptly after they are received.

Accounts payable records should be reviewed to ascertain that timely follow-up is instituted on unmatched invoices and receiving reports, and paid invoices should be tested to ascertain that all required preaudit procedures were performed correctly and appropriate initials and approvals shown to evidence performance of the established steps. The internal auditor should also ascertain that adequate procedures are in effect to assure payment of invoices on the due date, and that valuable purchase discounts are not being lost through oversight or procedural breakdowns.

Review should be made to determine compliance with established procedures of all aspects of the handling of purchase returns and allowances—particularly with respect to accounting for the serial numbers of all debit memos and to determining that proper credit has been received for the amounts due. The accuracy of recording invoices and debit memos should also be tested. Other operations properly subjected to scrutiny by the internal auditor would be the month-end verification of detailed payables records against vendors' statements and general ledger controlling accounts.

With respect to expense accounts, an important internal audit step is the review of the accounts payable audit operations that precede the payment of invoices—particularly the coding of the debits resulting from the recording of such invoices. Expense allocations should be reviewed to ascertain that they are equitable and are in accordance with current conditions. The presentation of expenses in internal reports should be adequate to meet the diverse needs of management for information about operating results. Reports should contain neither too much nor too little detail, because either condition can destroy their effectiveness and usefulness. The classification and distribution of costs and expenses in the records should be tested and reviewed for propriety, and miscellaneous expense accounts should be analyzed in order to detect any items improperly charged to those accounts.

REVIEW QUESTIONS

1. What are the objectives of internal control over purchases and the incurrence of the resulting liabilities?
2. What different departments should be involved in the segregation of duties relative to purchases and the incurrence of the resulting liability?
3. What are the three major problems with respect to purchasing activities?
4. Show the various uses to which the various copies of a purchase order may be put, and name the recipient of each copy.
5. Under what circumstances is it not convenient to use a copy of the purchase order as a receiving report?
6. What use would be made of information from the files of unmatched receiving reports and unmatched invoices at the end of a concern's fiscal year when the physical inventory is taken?
7. Why is it preferable to deduct cash discounts from invoice amounts and to record the purchases at "net"?
8. What is a built-up voucher and when would it be used?
9. Why is it often feasible to audit vendors' invoices on a test basis?
10. Under what circumstances would it be desirable to maintain a posted accounts payable ledger rather than using a bookless record?
11. What procedures should a concern use at month end to determine whether its payable records are in balance and correct?
12. Explain what is meant by a "posted distribution" of debits arising from accounts payable.
13. In punched-card accounts payable records, what are the purposes of the payables and distribution cards that are prepared, and how many of each would be prepared?
14. Explain "zero balancing" and state when it is used in connection with punched-card accounts payable records.
15. What accounts payable reports can be prepared to assist in anticipating cash requirements?
16. What points should the internal auditor investigate in an internal audit of the purchasing department?

QUESTIONS ON SYSTEMS APPLICATIONS

17. Questions about the amount of business transacted with a vendor can be readily answered from a regular posted accounts payable ledger record, but how can the information be obtained if a) ledgerless records are maintained or b) the records are maintained by punched card?
18. Explain why there would not be a regular frequent comparison made between the file of unmatched receiving reports and unmatched invoices, but an

occasional comparison of the two files should be made. State how the purpose of comparing the two files could be accomplished in another way.

19. Would you consider it proper for a concern to "hold open" its voucher register in order to record invoices dated prior to the balance sheet date but received after the balance sheet date? Justify your answer.

20. What are the advantages of a ledgerless plan of accounts payable records? Under what circumstances is a posted ledger form of payables records more satisfactory than the ledgerless plan?

21. Your client has received a confirmation request from the auditor of a vendor concerning the balance of the receivable from your client as of April 30. It is now May 10, and your client asks you for detailed instructions on how to obtain the necessary information to ascertain whether the balance shown on the request is correct. Your client's accounts payable records consist of a file by due date of invoices that have been vouchered and entered in the voucher register but not yet paid. After payment, the invoices are placed in a paid file in alphabetical sequence by vendor, chronologically for each vendor. State the instructions that you would give the client; the instructions should be adequate to cover most likely possibilities.

22. With respect to cash discounts on purchases:

   (a) There are two different ways of handling such discounts in the accounting records. Give the wording of the column heading for such discounts in the cash disbursement record under each method of recording the discounts.

   (b) Which method, in the first year of a retailing concern's operations, will produce the highest amount of income? Why?

PROBLEMS

23. The normal procedure in Jones Wholesale Co. is for Mr. Jones to place orders for merchandise by telephone or by letter. When the merchandise arrives, the receiving clerk records the information in a book of receipts showing date received, shipper's name, description of merchandise, and quantity received. The bookkeeper matches vendor invoices against this record, marking the invoices OK if the quantity shown in the receiving record agrees with the invoice quantity. The bookkeeper then prepares a check for the purchase, enters the check in the cash disbursement record with a charge to inventory, and passes the check and invoice to Mr. Jones for approval of prices and other matters and for his signature on the check. Invoices are returned to the bookkeeper and placed by him in a numerical file by check number; the bookkeeper also places the checks in envelopes and mails them.

   State the changes that you would recommend in the above system to improve internal control, and explain how internal control would be improved by the changes.

24. Prepare a detailed set of instructions for a company employee whose responsibilities are to maintain files of outstanding purchase orders, unmatched receiving reports, and unmatched vendors' invoices, and to audit and approve invoices prior to their entry in the voucher register.

25. The accounting and internal control procedures relating to purchases of materials by the Branden Company, a medium-sized concern manufacturing special machinery to order, have been described by your junior accountant in the following terms:

"After approval by manufacturing department foremen, material purchase requisitions are forwarded to the purchasing department supervisor who distributes such requisitions to the several employees under his control. The latter employees prepare prenumbered purchase orders in triplicate, account for all numbers, and send the original purchase order to the vendor. One copy of the purchase order is sent to the receiving department where it is used as a receiving report. The other copy is filed in the purchasing department.

"When the materials are received, they are moved directly to the storeroom and issued to the foremen on informal requests. The receiving department sends a receiving report (with its copy of the purchase order attached) to the purchasing department and sends copies of the receiving report to the storeroom and to the accounting department.

"Vendors' invoices for material purchases, received in duplicate in the mail room, are sent to the purchasing department and directed to the employee who placed the related order. The employee then compares the invoice with the copy of the purchase order on file in the purchasing department for price and terms and compares the invoice quantity with the quantity received as reported by the shipping and receiving department on its copy of the purchase order. The purchasing department employee also checks discounts, footings, and extensions and initials the invoice to indicate approval for payment. The invoice is then sent to the voucher section of the accounting department where it is coded for account distribution, assigned a voucher number, entered in the voucher register and filed according to payment due date.

"On payment dates prenumbered checks are requisitioned by the voucher section from the cashier and prepared except for signature. After the checks are prepared they are returned to the cashier, who puts them through a check signing machine, accounts for the sequence of numbers and passes them to cash disbursements bookkeeper for entry in the cash disbursements book. The cash disbursements bookkeeper then returns the checks to the voucher section which then notes payment dates in the voucher register, places the checks in envelopes and sends them to the mail room. The vouchers are then filed in numerical sequence. At the end of each month one of the voucher clerks prepares an adding machine tape of unpaid items in the voucher register and compares the total thereof with the general ledger balance and investigates any difference disclosed by such comparison."

Required:
    Discuss the weaknesses, if any, in the internal control of Branden's purchasing and subsequent procedures and suggest supplementary or revised procedures for remedying each weakness with regard to
    (a) Requisition of materials.
    (b) Receipt and storage of materials.
    (c) Functions of the purchasing department.
    (d) Functions of the accounting department.
26. In connection with your examination of the financial statements of Jones and Smith as of June 30, you have sent requests to the company's major suppliers for copies of statements of their accounts with Jones and Smith. Such requests were sent even though Jones and Smith showed no balance owing to the supplier at June 30. The statement received from the Victory Supply Co. and your client's account payable record of transactions with that company are given below. Prepare a reconciliation of the balances of the two records, showing the apparent explanations for the various reconciling items, and state what further investigation you would want to make of the Victory Supply Co. account, and what action you would recommend to your client.

Jones and Smith

May	2	2/10, n/30	S	$1,891.20		$1,891.20
	12	2/10, n/30	S	341.52		2,232.72
	14		CR		$1,000.00	1,232.72
	20	n/30	S	418.21		1,650.93
	24		CR		341.52	1,309.41
June	1		CR		409.85	899.56
	12	2/10, n/30	S	634.86		1,534.42
	17		CR		870.79	663.63
	19	2/10, n/30	S	594.37		1,258.00
	24		CR		601.37	656.63
		C/M, invoice 6/12	J		33.49	623.14
	29	2/10, n/30	S	463.81		1,086.95

Victory Supply Co.

May	4	VR		$1,891.20	$1,891.20
	12	CD	$1,020.41		870.79
	14	VR		341.52	1,212.31
	22	VR		418.21	1,630.52
		CD	341.52		1,289.00
	30	CD	418.21		870.79
June	14	VR		634.86	1,505.65
	15	CD	870.79		634.86
	20	VR		594.37	1,229.23
	22	CD	601.37		627.86
	26	CD	33.49		594.37
	29	CD	594.37		—

27. In the course of your examination of the Student Book Store as of December 31, you make a search for unrecorded liabilities which includes a review of disbursements recorded subsequent to December 31. You find the following schedule in support of check No. 3429 for $948.60, which was charged to the perpetual inventory account:

	Quantity	Unit Cost	Total
Inventory of consigned kits, October 1	34	$6.84	$232.56
Kits received since last report	125	6.84	855.00
Inventory of consigned kits, December 31	14	6.84	95.76
Kits sold, October-December	145		991.80
Incoming express charges on kits received			43.20
Balance due remitted herewith			948.60

Further investigation discloses the following information:

(a) The kits on hand at December 31 were included in the physical inventory.

(b) The perpetual control account was credited $425.89 to reduce it to agree with the physical inventory.

(c) The express charges were charged to the transportation-in account when they were paid.

(d) Kit sales are included with regular sales, which are the basis for the cost of sales entry under the retail inventory method.

(e) The amount remitted is correct.

Prepare the adjusting journal entry for your working papers that you would recommend based on the above information.

Auditing purchases, expenses, and accounts payable

10

Under accrual accounting, the system used by most businesses, purchases do not directly affect the income statement but flow through the inventory account, eventually appearing as cost of goods sold. Although discussion of the auditor's examination of purchase transactions is included in this chapter, the expense item that eventually appears in the income statement is not taken up until the following chapters, which deal with inventory and cost of sales. Hence, the discussion of statement presentation in this chapter covers only expenses and accounts payable. Some general comments and observations with respect to the pervasive effect of income taxes are first presented to provide some essential background.

Income Tax Considerations

Federal income taxes have had a marked effect on accounting, and understandably the effect comes to a focus on net income and the income statement. The influence of income taxes has manifested itself in three different ways:

1. Although Congress has attempted to bring the tax laws into closer agreement with the accounting approach to the determination of income, many differences will continue to exist in view of the importance of revenue-raising requirements of the Federal government and the need to consider ease of administration and enforcement of the tax laws. In many instances where accounting and tax rules differ, concerns keep additional memorandum records in order to obtain the necessary information for tax purposes. On the other hand, other concerns, particularly the smaller ones, have merely adopted certain tax rules for accounting purposes in order to reduce the burden of recordkeeping. The latter approach is justifiable, however, only

to the extent that the differences involved are minor, but frequently accounting considerations have been sacrificed to tax expediency regardless of the effect on net income. Typical examples of problem areas include the treatment of losses on the trade-in of capital assets, the use of maximum depreciation or amortization rates permissible for tax purposes rather than rates that are sound from an accounting viewpoint, the tax advantages of sum-of-years digits or double declining balance depreciation methods as compared with straight-line depreciation, and the failure to accrue estimated future expenses which cannot be deducted for tax purposes until the expenses are actually paid.

2. When sound accounting considerations are not sacrificed to expediency, and material differences thereby arise between reported income and taxable income, the complicated and controversial problem presents itself of allocating income tax expense to periods other than the one in which the tax liability has occurred. Generally accepted accounting principles dictate that such allocation must be made in order to avoid misleading distortion of reported net income.

3. The understandable desire to minimize the burden of income taxes has had a subtle but pervasive effect on reported financial and operating results. Whereas it was once accepted that any attempt to misstate the financial results of a business would likely be in the direction of overstatement in order to show a better position than actually exists, today the reverse is often true. The opportunity to save tax dollars has led to practices ranging from deciding all questionable matters in favor of the alternative that will reduce taxes, to outright fraudulent understatement of income. The popularity of Lifo inventory costing and depreciation methods that produce decreasing depreciation charges is largely the result of the income tax advantages related to the use of such methods, and reported income has decreased accordingly. There are, of course, strong arguments for using Lifo and decreasing-charge depreciation methods for accounting purposes, but the point is that income tax advantages rather than accounting considerations are largely responsible for the current popularity of these methods.

The above points should be kept in mind by the auditor at all times, since at any point in his examination he may encounter an item that has been treated in a questionable manner to gain a desired tax effect, an item that is treated differently for accounting and for tax purposes, or a change in accounting treatment intended to produce a tax advantage.

STANDARDS OF STATEMENT PRESENTATION

The standards for the presentation of expenses in the income statement are based on the same considerations as the standards for the presentation of revenues.

1. Nonoperating, nonrecurring expenses and losses should be segregated from the regular operating expenses of a business. *Material* nonrecurring expenses or losses should be taken directly to retained earnings.

2. Significant expenses should be given as separate amounts in the interests of adequate disclosure. Cost of sales, depreciation and depletion, interest expense, and Federal income taxes are items which are normally shown separately.

3. The amount of Federal income taxes shown as an expense should be based on transactions reflected in the income statement, except for minor recurring differences resulting from differences between book and taxable income. If the amount shown for Federal income tax expense differs materially from the amount to be paid, as when income taxes are apportioned to expenses or incomes not appearing in the current income statement, or when there has been a carry forward or carry back of losses, the explanation for the difference should be given.

There are relatively few considerations in the presentation of accounts payable in the balance sheet:

1. Only amounts owed to regular trade creditors are properly included as accounts payable. Liabilities arising from other types of transactions and material amounts owed to nonconsolidated affiliated companies should be shown separately.

2. Assets and liabilities should not be offset; hence, material amounts of accounts payable debit balances should be reclassified to the asset side of the statement.

Standards of statement presentation should be kept in mind as the auditor proceeds with the corroboration of statement figures, for many departures from the standards can be detected only through the execution of the customary audit procedures—even though the basic purpose of many of the procedures may not be directly related to matters of statement presentation.

AUDIT OBJECTIVES AND PROCEDURES

The objectives in the examination of expenses bear a close relationship to the objectives in the examination of revenues. Expenses are but one type of purchase transaction, and all purchase transactions are closely related to accounts payable because they originate through the accounts payable auditing and recording process. The objectives in the examination of the amounts resulting from purchase and expense transactions are:

1. Establish credibility of the accounting records.

2. Ascertain reasonableness of and consistency in application of appropriate expense classifications.

3. Ascertain that all expenses of the period have been recorded by searching for unrecorded liabilities.

4. Tie in supporting records with the statement amount of accounts payable.

5. Ascertain that expenses have been properly matched with the revenues that they have produced.

6. Determine that proper distinction has been maintained between operating expenses and nonoperating, nonrecurring losses and expenses.

Establish Credibility of the Accounting Records

Tests of recorded transactions constitute the principal means of ascertaining whether internal control is adequate and of determining whether the financial statements developed from the accounting records are representative of the financial and operating activities that have taken place.

Trace handling of representative transactions from origin to final account balances. Under conditions of good internal control, an exhaustive review of relatively few purchase transactions should enable the auditor to reach a conclusion on the credibility of the accounting records in which such transactions have been reflected. If internal control is weak, thus minimizing the inherent credibility of the accounting figures, testing must be expanded sufficiently to support a direct inference concerning the credibility of the records based largely on the results of the auditor's sampling of the recorded transactions.

Because procedures are likely to vary according to the type of transaction involved, care should be exercised to see that each major type of purchase or expense transaction is represented in the sample that is chosen.

Purchases of both raw materials and finished parts should be selected for review, and if some purchases are made on the basis of competitive bids whereas others are not, each method of purchasing should be represented in the sample. Transactions related to various other expenses, such as utilities and taxes, should also be sampled, and a petty cash reimbursement transaction should be included.

The examination should confirm that required documents, such as purchase orders, invoices, and receiving reports, are present in support of the selected transactions, and that there is evidence that specified approvals have been given. Voucher register entries should reflect correctly the selected transactions, including the charge to the appropriate distribution account for the asset or expense involved. Voucher register footings should ordinarily be tested and totals traced to the related ledger accounts.

Various expenses, such as cost of sales, payroll, depreciation, and interest, that involve procedures other than the usual accounts payable procedures, are discussed individually in subsequent chapters.

Ascertain Reasonableness of Account Balances and Consistency in Application of Appropriate Expense Classifications

The auditor's tests of entries in the voucher register and payrolls should largely indicate to the auditor's satisfaction whether or not costs and expenses have been properly classified. To further indicate the reasonableness of the client's classifications and to establish that the classifications have been consistently followed, the auditor should make extensive use of comparisons. Lastly, certain accounts which are most susceptible to the improper classification of charges should be analyzed or scanned for possible errors.

Comparisons. Perhaps the most important comparisons which the auditor should make are between the various costs and expenses for the current year and those for the preceding year. It is largely for this reason that final figures for the preceding year are included in the auditor's working trial balance. Figures should be compared in terms of absolute amounts, unit costs, and percentage relationships to sales whenever possible. Note that schedule P/L in the illustrative working papers, the top trial balance of the income statement accounts, is set up to permit two of these types of comparisons. Any substantial variations disclosed by such comparisons should be investigated and the explanations noted in the auditor's working papers. Because variations may be the clue to classification errors or changes in classifications, it is important that the auditor's investigations be thorough and that explanations not be accepted merely because they sound logical.

Comparisons should also be made of the monthly amounts charged to some of the more active expense accounts, such as cost of sales and payroll accounts. Such a comparison is illustrated by schedule 20-1, which summarizes the monthly factory payroll distribution entries. Again, it is important that variations be investigated and explanations noted in the working papers.

When clients operate under a standard cost system, the system automatically compares material, labor, and overhead costs with standard amounts and reports the variations as separate figures. Schedule 20 illustrates the manner in which such variances are treated in the operating accounts and shows how the major classes of variances can be subdivided to give management additional information. As with other variances, the auditor should investigate any amounts which appear out of line.

If clients prepare budgets, the auditor should avail himself of the opportunity to compare actual and budgeted amounts. Such a comparison gives further evidence of the validity and consistency of the client's classification of expenses. Management officials should be thoroughly familiar with the causes for any budget variances, and the auditor should, therefore, discuss the variances with such officials. The auditor's general knowledge of the client's operations for the year should enable the auditor to ascertain whether the stated explanations of the budget variances are reasonable. The additional comprehension of operating figures which management gains through comparisons with budgeted amounts is a vital element of effective internal control. The auditor's examination of costs and expenses and his investigation of variations in those items may be reduced accordingly.

The various explanations which the auditor makes in his working papers concerning variations which he has noted may often be valuable apart from their significance in the substantiation of reported costs and expenses. If the auditor prepares a long-form report, the explanations will provide the necessary information for the auditor's analysis of the results of operations. The analysis of operating results is usually one of the most important sections of a long-form report.

Classification errors affecting factory overhead. In reviewing the various expense accounts and in comparing totals for the current and preceding years, the auditor should note that the accounts have been properly classified as either factory overhead, selling expenses, or general and administrative expenses. There need be only limited consideration of whether an account is more properly classified as selling expense or general and administrative expense, as the choice will not affect net income. The question of classification is more important, however, if it involves a choice between factory overhead and either of the other two operating expense classifications. The reason is that factory overhead amounts are partly deferred in the inventory accounts, whereas selling and general and administrative expenses are charged against income in their entirety as they are incurred. Thus any error or change in classification which would affect the factory overhead total would also affect the amount of net income. As a consequence, the error would be more material than an error or change which had an offsetting effect on totals within the income statement.

Account analyses. The second major procedure by which the auditor may satisfy himself that costs and expenses have been properly classified involves the analysis or scanning of selected accounts. The accounts chosen should be those likely to be charged with items which are unusual or which occur only infrequently. Such items are, of course, more susceptible to classification errors. Typical examples of accounts that usually warrant the auditor's special attention would include miscellaneous expense, corporate expense, entertainment expense, royalty expense, charitable contributions, and legal and other professional fees. Other accounts which would tend to fall in the same category, but which are usually verified in connection with the examination of related balance sheet accounts, would include repairs and maintenance, interest expense, and losses on sales of securities or plant assets.

As illustrated by schedules 40–2 and 40–3, major charges noted in analyzing or scanning the various accounts should be described, and the auditor's verification of the amounts should be noted. Typical verification procedures would include reference to authorization for the expenditures and examination of invoices or paid checks.

Manufacturing concerns are likely to find that factory overhead has been underapplied or overapplied to production, and if such a situation exists, the auditor should give it very close attention, especially if the amount is material. The occurrence of such a situation indicates that the overhead rate used during the year was not in line with the actual operating results. There may be some instances in which the auditor would feel justified in allowing the amount of underapplied or overapplied overhead to be treated as a profit and loss item, but more frequently he will find that such a treatment would actually distort net income. In such cases the auditor should request the client to adjust the amount of overhead applied to agree with the actual experience for the year. As illustrated by adjusting journal entry number 2 in the illustrative working papers, the adjustment will affect both inventory and cost of sales and will thus change the amount of net income for the year.

Ascertain that All Expenses of the Period Have Been Recorded by Searching for Unrecorded Liabilities

The problem of recording all expenses and liabilities pertaining to the period under examination is essentially a problem of proper cut-off. The auditor employs many procedures in his review of this cut-off, but past emphasis on the balance sheet examination has caused the cut-off test to be referred to as a search for unrecorded liabilities. Disclosure of an unrecorded liability, however, automatically brings to light an unrecorded debit to an asset or to an expense account—most frequently, the latter.

The more commonly used procedures in searching for unrecorded accounts payable are suggested here, but the procedures discussed should not be assumed to exhaust every possibility. Procedures related to the search for other unrecorded liabilities are discussed in Chapter 20. In a first audit, a search for unrecorded accounts payable should also be applied to the records at the close of the preceding year. The liability aspect of items disclosed by a search of the records for the preceding year is unimportant, but any material amounts of expenses recorded in the current year which are applicable to the preceding year should be removed from expenses and charged to retained earnings in order to obtain a proper statement of expenses for the current year.

Review of subsequent transactions. The most important procedure in the auditor's search for unrecorded liabilities will usually be his review of transactions recorded subsequent to the balance sheet date. The procedure is based on the assumption that all liabilities will eventually be reflected in the accounts, either through payment or by other means. Hindsight thus becomes a major element in the auditor's examination.

The principal records which should be subjected to such a review are the cash disbursements record, the voucher register, and the general journal. Because the first two records overlap to a considerable extent, care must be taken to avoid duplication in examining those records.

The typical approach is to begin with voucher register entries, selecting all major amounts and a few smaller amounts from entries recorded after the balance sheet date. The supporting vouchers and invoices should then be pulled to permit the auditor to determine whether any liability existed at the balance sheet date. Full information should be noted in the working papers concerning any liabilities disclosed in this manner, as was done on schedule BB-2.

Next, the cash disbursements record should be reviewed. All major disbursements should represent the payment of vouchers included in the year-end balance of accounts payable, or vouchers reviewed in connection with the examination of voucher register entries made after the balance sheet date. Investigation of any disbursements not previously covered in such examinations is likely to reveal an unrecorded liability.

The review of the general journal involves no special procedures, but each entry should be carefully studied for any hint that a year-end liability may be involved.

Materiality. Unrecorded liabilities revealed by the above procedures may vary in materiality even though amounts may be identical. The three items shown below illustrate this phenomenon:

Invoice Date	Date Goods or Services Received	Date Recorded in Records	Freight Terms	Description	Amount
12/29	12/31	1/3	F.O.B. Shipping Point	Materials	$500
12/28	1/3	1/3	F.O.B. Shipping Point	Materials	500
12/30	12/29	1/3	. . . .	Machinery repairs	500

All three items involve liabilities not recorded at December 31. Further investigation of the first item reveals that it was not included in the inventory cut-off reconciliation figure for unmatched receiving reports, so that it has the effect of understating either purchases or, under the perpetual inventory method, the inventory variation. These errors would in turn cause an overstatement of income. The machinery repair item also understates an expense and overstates income. The second item represents a purchase of materials for which title is presumed to have passed at the balance sheet date,* and there is hence an unrecorded asset for merchandise in transit, but the item would not affect the income statement.

---

* Based on the usually valid presumption that invoices are dated the day that materials are shipped. On occasion, however, as a favor to the customer, or as a means of inducing a customer to accept advanced delivery, an invoice may be dated forward. This possibility should be considered in the review of subsequent transactions, for an item may have been shipped and received by the client prior to the year end, and yet the invoice might be dated for the following year.

Differences in the materiality of each of the three items obviously are not related to the unrecorded liability, because all of the items are for the same amount and none of the amounts has been reflected in the records. Our attention must therefore be directed to the unrecorded debits for any indication that the items vary in materiality. The first and third items are more material for the following reasons:

1. They affect net income whereas the second item affects assets, and net income is usually the most important figure on the financial statements.

2. The effect on net income of each of these items will be proportionally greater than the effect on total assets by the second item, because invariably the net income figure will be smaller than the figure for total assets.

3. Because the unrecorded liability for the second item is offset by an unrecorded asset, items 1 and 3 will cause a greater distortion of the very important current ratio.

The matter of materiality might be further refined by considering an unrecorded liability for the purchase of plant equipment costing $500. This item, because it does not affect net income, would be less material than items 1 and 3, but it would be more material than item 2 because of the greater distortion of the current ratio.

In most cases when unrecorded liabilities are found, they will involve merchandise in transit, as the normal accounting routines do not provide for recognition of such liabilities. As suggested by the preceding discussion, such unrecorded liabilities will have only a nominal effect on the financial statements unless relatively large amounts are involved. The result is that adjustment of the statements to reflect such items is often waived as not materially affecting the statements. Many a junior accountant, on being assigned for the first time to the search for unrecorded liabilities, has discovered thousands of dollars of unrecorded liabilities for merchandise in transit. His sense of accomplishment in having detected a misstatement of such a large amount in the client's figures is often rudely dissipated by the senior accountant's decision to pass any adjustment of the amount on the grounds of immateriality! Nevertheless, the working papers should contain a record of all unrecorded liabilities noted in the examination. Individual items may be immaterial, but the cumulative effect of a number of such items may well be another matter, and all of the information should be present so that the final decision on materiality can be made by the senior accountant, or perhaps even by the manager or partner. One accountant has said that he likes to have the information available, even on immaterial amounts, because the information can sometimes be used for "bargaining" purposes. That is, if there is another, more important adjustment that the client is reluctant to make, he may be induced to make the one adjustment on the condition that the auditor will agree to waive the second adjustment.

If unrecorded liabilities affect net income, their relative materiality is partly offset by the effect of income taxes in the case of a corporation. A $10,000 understatement of expense would cause income to be overstated by only about $5,000. With corporate income tax rates at about 50 per cent, the decrease of $10,000 in income before taxes would be offset by about a $5,000 decrease in income taxes, leaving only a $5,000 decrease in net income after taxes. It might appear that the client would be anxious to make such an adjustment, and if so the auditor should certainly oblige. On the other hand, unless tax rates change, the adjustment will merely cause a shift in taxes between two years, and the client may prefer not to reopen his records for the adjustment if the auditor concludes that the effect is not material.

Tie in Supporting Records with the Statement Amount of Accounts Payable

Prove trial balance. A trial balance of the detailed accounts payable at the balance sheet date is essential to establish agreement between the detailed records and the general ledger control. Preferably, the trial balance should be prepared by the client, and the auditor can then limit his work to tests of the client's work, but occasionally the auditor may have to prepare the trial balance himself. If the auditor prepares the trial balance, the previously stated admonition is pertinent that audit time should not be spent in locating the cause of an out-of-balance condition.

The detailed records supporting the trial balance may be an accounts payable ledger, the "open" items on a voucher register, or a file of unpaid vouchers. In addition, if the client has posted an adjusting entry for unmatched receiving reports or invoices on hand but not yet entered in the voucher register, the receiving reports and invoices involved will represent part of the supporting details for the trial balance. Work sheet BB illustrates this point. In testing the client's trial balance against the source records, the extent of the test will, of course, vary with the degree of internal control that is present. As a minimum, the major amounts and a few of the smaller amounts should be traced to the supporting details, and the footing of the trial balance should be proved except under conditions of extremely good internal control. Under conditions of weak internal control, the accounts payable ledger figures or voucher register amounts should be tested by reference to supporting invoices. The invoices should be originals, made out to the client, bear a recent date, and give no indication of having been paid; receiving reports should evidence the receipt of the materials involved. Should receiving reports indicate that the materials were received after the balance sheet date, the dollar amounts involved should appear as reconciling items on the physical inventory reconciliation.

The testing of the trial balance can be performed subsequent to the balance sheet date with little difficulty if the source has been an accounts payable ledger or the open items on a voucher register. The auditor need only pay close attention to posting or payment dates in selecting the proper figures from the ledger or voucher register. The problem is complicated, however, if the trial balance is prepared from a file of unpaid vouchers and the auditor is unable to be present to test the trial balance as soon as it has been completed. The make-up of the unpaid voucher file will change from day to day, and it will be next to impossible to locate invoices removed from the file for payment unless sufficient identifying information is shown on the trial balance. Even then, the testing is slowed by the fact that many invoices to be tested will have to be located in the file of paid invoices. The client's employees should be utilized to locate the desired invoices, if at all possible, in order to facilitate the auditor's work. Another approach to the problem is to have the client enter initially in the cash disbursements record for the following month only the unpaid invoices which had been entered as vouchers payable before the close of the year. The auditor can then work from these items and their total in proving the accounts payable figure.

During the course of his review and tests of the trial balance of accounts payable, the auditor should be alert for any balances that should be considered for reclassification, including debit balances and amounts resulting from transactions other than regular trade purchases. Debit balances should be investigated to determine the reason for their existence and to ascertain their collectibility. If material amounts are involved, regular accounts receivable procedures should be applied, including confirmation. Another point to be noted in reviewing the accounts payable detail is the presence of any amounts that are past due. An analysis of such past-due amounts is often included in long-form reports that are to be used for credit purposes.

Test trial balance amounts against written confirmations or vendors' statements. Unlike the examination of accounts receivable, where some confirmation of balances is a required procedure, confirmation of accounts payable balances is not required. It is, however, highly desirable to confirm accounts payable balances on a full or test basis if internal control is weak or if vendors' statements at the balance sheet date are not available in the client's files. The additional assurance to be gained from confirmation procedures under these circumstances is highly desirable in view of the possible material effect on the financial statements of a misstatement of accounts payable.

There are perhaps three reasons for the fact that confirmation of accounts payable is not a standard procedure required in all cases. The first is that external evidence which is likely to be quite reliable is available in support of the accounts payable figure. That evidence consists of invoices and statements received from vendors. The reader should recall that in the case of receivables most supporting evidence is likely to be created by employees of the client. A second reason is that under normal operations all accounts payable existing at the balance sheet date can be expected to be paid within a short time thereafter. The entries for such payments and the resulting paid checks form further evidence in support of the balance sheet figure for accounts payable. For receivables, however, some accounts may be slow in paying, and confirmations are the only possible substitute in the absence of evidence concerning payment of an account.

A third reason for not confirming accounts payable is the fact that the greatest risk relates to unrecorded liabilities, and there is no indication of where a confirmation should be sent in such cases. In the case of receivables, the risk of overstatement is greatest, and the necessary recording of fictitious amounts can be readily detected by confirmation of the receivables balances.

If internal control is satisfactory, and if the client regularly receives statements from vendors and reconciles the statements with the detailed accounts payable records, the auditor should be able to satisfy himself that accounts payable are stated correctly by reviewing the statements. He should ascertain that the statements bear evidence that they have, in fact, been reconciled, and he should determine in a general way that the total amounts on the statements presented to him bear a reasonable relationship to the total recorded accounts payable. Any unusual reconciling items should be noted and traced through the records to determine that any necessary adjustments have been made.

If the client does not regularly receive statements from vendors, the auditor should consider the desirability of applying confirmation procedures to the accounts payable. Confirmation may be omitted if internal control is very good, but even then added assurance to be gained from confirmation of a few of the more active vendors' accounts is highly desirable. If internal control is weak, extensive confirmation should be employed, and even though vendors' statements may be available in the client's files, direct confirmation of a few key accounts is desirable as a further test of the client's records. It is especially important to request confirmation from any vendor from whom substantial purchases have been made but for whom there may be no liability shown in the year-end records.

Vendors will usually be quite prompt in responding to accounts payable confirmation requests. One factor is the desire to be of service to their customers, but there is also a direct benefit in the form of assurance that the customer's records will be corrected if any discrepancies have occurred. The most satisfactory manner of confirming accounts payable is to request the vendor to send directly to the auditor a statement of the customer's account, or an itemized statement of open charges at the specified date. The advantage of requesting a statement rather than verification of a single amount lies in the added information that is then available to reconcile the differences that are almost certain to exist between the client's and the vendor's records. The auditor should prepare a listing of any differences representing shipments in transit at the balance sheet date. The listing will be helpful in determining whether the amounts involved are sufficiently material to require that an adjusting entry be made.

In cases where substantial purchase commitments are known to exist, the auditor may wish to include in the confirmation letter a request that the vendor state the amount of unfilled purchase orders from the client held at the balance sheet date.

Ascertain that Expenses Have Been Properly Matched with the Revenues that They Have Produced

Tests of the accounts payable cut-off and the search for unrecorded liabilities, coupled with the operation of a double-entry system, largely dispose of the question of the proper matching of expenses with revenues. Other aspects of the problem are covered in connection with the auditor's examination of accrued liabilities and the write-offs of various asset accounts such as inventory, property, plant, and equipment, and patents, franchises, goodwill, or other intangibles. Nevertheless, the auditor will be well advised to take a broad look at his client's operations, to determine whether all types of expenses that would be expected in the light of the client's operations are represented on the income statement in reasonable amounts. Familiarity with the client's operations should disclose whether proper expense accounting has been applied for such items as royalties, commissions, interest, consignments, travel expense advances, and the myriad of taxes to which most businesses are subject.

Determine that Proper Distinction Has Been Maintained between Operating Expenses and Nonoperating, Nonrecurring Losses and Expenses

The segregation of operating expenses and losses of a nonoperating, nonrecurring nature is primarily a question of statement presentation. There is a possibility, however, that such items might have been buried in the operating expense accounts, and the auditor should be alert for that possibility as he makes his comparisons and analyses of the various expense accounts.

Timing of the Examination of Income Statement Accounts and Accounts Payable

The review of the client's system of internal control, which is one of the major aspects of the auditor's examination of the operating accounts, can readily be performed on a preliminary basis several months before the close of the year. At the year end the auditor should, however, make sufficient inquiries to satisfy himself that no material changes have been made in the system of internal control since the time of his preliminary examination. If changes have occurred, the new system should be reviewed and tested in the usual fashion. Weaknesses in the system would lessen the reliability of the accounting figures and necessitate an expansion in the scope of the auditor's examination.

Year-to-year and month-to-month comparisons can also be made at a preliminary date, but the transactions for the remainder of the year would require the same thorough review. Consequently, the reduction in year-end audit time would be relatively slight and the total audit time would be increased, with the result that this work is usually postponed until the close of the year.

When internal control is satisfactory, accounts payable can be verified on much the same basis as accounts receivable. That is, most of the work can be done a month or two before the balance sheet date, supplemented by a review of transactions occurring between the preliminary and balance sheet dates. However, because such transactions are so variable, and because financial position or operating results can be so readily altered through failure to record transactions creating a liability, many accountants prefer to do all work on liabilities after the balance sheet date. In all cases, of course, the vital review of subsequent transactions must be made after the balance sheet date.

SUMMARY

Internal control

Duties which ideally should be performed by different individuals—
  Purchasing
  Receiving
  Inspection
  Storing
  Auditing accounts payable
  General ledger entries
  Subsidiary ledger entries—
    Liabilities
    Debit distribution to expense or asset
  Trial balance of subsidiary ledger
  Reconciliation of vendors' statements with detailed records

Statement presentation

Nonoperating expenses should be reported separately from regular operating expenses.
Material, nonoperating, nonrecurring expenses and losses should be charged against retained earnings.

Major types of expenses, such as cost of sales, depreciation, interest, and income taxes, should be reported separately.

Income taxes should be allocated in order to keep reported income tax expense on a comparable basis with reported income.

Only amounts owed to regular trade creditors should be shown as accounts payable.

Assets and liabilities should not be offset.

Audit objectives and procedures

Establish credibility of the accounting records.

Trace handling of representative transactions from origin to final account balances.

Ascertain reasonableness of account balances and consistency of application of appropriate expense classifications.

Make month-to-month and year-to-year comparisons.

Compare expense-to-sales percentages and ratios relating balance sheet and income statement amounts.

Analyze or scan accounts likely to contain unusual items.

Ascertain that all expenses of the period have been recorded by searching for unrecorded liabilities.

Review transactions recorded subsequent to the balance sheet date.

Tie in supporting records with statement amount of accounts payable.

Prepare a trial balance or prove client's trial balance by tracing amounts to supporting records and footing the listed amounts.

Test trial balance amounts against written confirmations or vendors' statements.

Ascertain that expenses have been properly matched with revenues that they have produced.

Review cut-offs.

Search for unrecorded liabilities.

Review write-offs of assets.

Review operations to determine whether all normal expenses are represented.

Determine that proper distinction has been maintained between operating expenses and nonoperating, nonrecurring losses and expenses.

Be alert for such items when reviewing accounts and making comparisons.

REVIEW QUESTIONS

1. What are the independent auditor's objectives in the examination of purchases, expenses, and accounts payable?

2. Why is the confirmation of accounts payable not required procedure?

3. If receiving reports attached to invoices included in the accounts payable total show that the goods were received after the balance sheet date, what should the auditor do?

4. What procedure will usually be most important in the auditor's search for unrecorded liabilities? Why?

5. Why do unrecorded liabilities affecting income tend to be more material than those which are offset by an unrecorded current asset?

6. Should accounts payable confirmation requests be sent only to vendors to whom amounts are owing at the balance sheet date? Explain.

7. How might the review of the account "Professional fees and expenses" help to disclose possible unrecorded or contingent liabilities?

8. Why are budgets considered a form of internal control?

9. Manufacturing costs should be accounted for on two separate bases to assure adequate internal control. Explain.

10. What investigation should the internal auditor make of the various reports of expenses which are used by management?

11. List the standards for the presentation of costs and expenses in the income statement.

12. What procedures might the auditor follow in testing the records relating to the cost of merchandise mark-downs in a retail store?

13. What balance sheet procedures help to assure the auditor that revenues and expenses have been properly matched?

14. What procedures enable the auditor to determine whether costs and expenses have been appropriately classified on a consistent basis?

15. Of what value are the comments placed by the auditor in his working papers to explain variations in expenses which he has noted in his comparison studies of expenses?

QUESTIONS ON APPLICATION OF AUDITING STANDARDS

16. In what sequence would you assume that most companies file paid invoices? Why? In what sequence would the auditor ordinarily prefer that the paid invoices be filed? Why?

17. Why, in the audit of a savings and loan association, would it be desirable to obtain written confirmations on some of the depositors' accounts that were closed out during the year?

18. In connection with the internal auditor's objectives of evaluation, compliance, and verification, list exceptions that he might discover in pursuing each of these objectives in an examination of the accounts payable function.

19. Prepare a memorandum describing the steps you would have followed in your review of subsequent disbursements for possible unrecorded liabilities. All liabilities are first recorded in a voucher register.

20. What documents, approvals, or authorizations should the treasurer of a company review before signing a check which liquidates a liability for materials purchased, assuming that a good system of internal control is in effect?

21. The internal audit department of your client has one representative who spends all his time in the accounts payable department reviewing and approving vouchers and supporting data before they are paid. No other internal audit work is done in connection with accounts payable. Does this evidence good internal audit and control? Explain.

22. Liabilities are often disclosed through the review of other accounts. List six different accounts which might disclose unrecorded liabilities, and in each case state how the liability would be discovered.

23. Prepare a working paper memo describing the procedures and tests you conducted in order to satisfy yourself that the amount of sales discounts for November is correctly stated.

24. Your client's operations are completely decentralized, and the manager of one of the manufacturing and sales branches is suspected of manipulating accounting figures in order to overstate the net income figure on which his bonus computation is based. State four ways in which he might have accomplished an overstatement of net income and give the audit procedures you would employ in order to detect any of these manipulations that occurred.

25. Under what circumstances will the amount of depreciation reflected in the income statement vary from the amount credited to the accumulated depreciation account for the year? Which figure should be reported in an income statement footnote reporting the amount of depreciation for the year? Why?

26. Suggest several instances in which the results of confirmation procedures with respect to balance sheet accounts might affect figures on the income statement.

27. How would you verify the balance in the account "Unapplied factory overhead" at the end of the year?

28. How would you verify the balance of the material price variance account for a client who records all purchases at standard cost?

29. Should the following amounts be shown separately on a published income statement, or may they be combined with other accounts to increase readability of the audited statement? Give reasons for your answers.
    (a) Bad debt expense.
    (b) Depreciation expense.
    (c) Interest expense.

30. How will the organization of the working papers for expenses be affected if the income statement is to be of the single-step variety?

PROBLEMS

31. On January 11, 1968 at the beginning of your annual audit of The Grover Manufacturing Company's financial statements for the year ended December 31, 1967, the Company president confides in you that an employee is living on a scale in excess of that which his salary would support.

    The employee has been a buyer in the purchasing department for six years and has charge of purchasing all general materials and supplies. He is authorized to sign purchase orders for amounts up to $200. Purchase orders in excess of $200 require the countersignature of the general purchasing agent.

    The president understands that the usual examination of financial statements is not designed, and cannot be relied upon, to disclose fraud or conflicts of interest, although their discovery may result. The president authorizes you, however, to expand your regular audit procedures and to apply additional audit procedures to determine whether there is any evidence that the buyer has been misappropriating Company funds or has been engaged in activities that were a conflict of interests.

    Required:

    (a) List the audit procedures that you would apply to the Company records and documents in an attempt to

1. Discover evidence within the purchasing department of defalcations being committed by the buyer. Give the purpose of each audit procedure.

2. Provide leads as to possible collusion between the buyer and suppliers. Give the purpose of each audit procedure.

(b) Assume that your investigation disclosed that some suppliers have been charging The Grover Manufacturing Company in excess of their usual prices and apparently have been making "kick-backs" to the buyer. The excess charges are material in amount.

What effect, if any, would the defalcation have upon (1) the financial statements that were prepared before the defalcation was uncovered and (2) your auditor's report? *Discuss.* (Uniform C.P.A. Examination)

32. Compare the confirmation of accounts receivable with the confirmation of accounts payable under the following headings:

(a) Generally accepted auditing procedures. (Justify the differences revealed by your comparison.)

(b) Form of confirmation requests. (You need not supply examples.)

(c) Selection of accounts to be confirmed. (Uniform C.P.A. Examination)

33. The Moss Company manufactures household appliances that are sold through independent franchised retail dealers. The electric motors in the appliances are guarantied for five years from the date of sale of the appliances to the consumer. Under the guaranty defective motors are replaced by the dealers without charge.

Inventories of replacement motors are kept in the dealers' stores and are carried at cost in The Moss Company's records. When the dealer replaces a defective motor, he notifies the factory and returns the defective motor to the factory for reconditioning. After the defective motor is received by the factory, the dealer's account is credited with an agreed fee for the replacement service.

When the appliance is brought to the dealer after the guaranty period has elapsed, the dealer charges the owner for installing the new motor. The dealer notifies the factory of the installation and returns the replaced motor for reconditioning. The motor installed is then charged to the dealer's account at a price in excess of its inventory value. In this instance, to encourage the return of replaced motors, the dealer's account is credited with a nominal value for the returned motor.

Dealers submit quarterly inventory reports of the motors on hand. The reports are later verified by factory salesmen. Dealers are billed for inventory shortages determined by comparison of the dealers' inventory reports and the factory's perpetual records of the dealers' inventories. The dealers order additional motors as they need them. One motor is used for all appliances in a given year, but the motors are changed in basic design each model year.

The Moss Company has established an account, Estimated Liability for Product Guaranties, in connection with the guaranties. An amount representing the estimated guaranty cost prorated per sales unit is credited to the Estimated Liability account for each appliance sold and the debit is charged to a Provision account. The Estimated Liability account is debited for the service fees credited to the dealers' accounts and for the inventory cost of the motors installed under the guaranties.

The engineering department keeps statistical records of the number of units of each model sold in each year and the replacements that were made. The effect of improvements in design and construction is under continuous study by the engineering department, and the estimated guaranty cost per unit is adjusted annually on the basis of experience and improvements in design.

Experience shows that, for a given motor model, the number of guaranties made good varies widely from year to year during the guaranty period, but the total number of guaranties to be made good can be reliably predicted.

Required:
  (a) Prepare an audit program to satisfy yourself as to the propriety of the transactions recorded in the Estimated Liability for Product Guaranties account for the year ended December 31, 1967.
  (b) Prepare the worksheet format that would be used to test the adequacy of the balance in the Estimated Liability for Product Guaranties account. The worksheet column headings should describe clearly the data to be inserted in the columns.   (Uniform C.P.A. Examination)

34. You are examining the records of a moderate-sized manufacturing corporation in connection with the preparation of a balance sheet and operating statement to be submitted with your unqualified opinion. There is some internal control, but the office and bookkeeping staff comprises only three persons. You decide to audit two months' transactions in detail. The sales are $1,000,000 per year.

  Submit a detailed, explicit audit program setting forth the steps you believe are necessary in connection with the following expense accounts.

  The total of one year's charges in each account is set forth opposite each caption:

```
Advertising  ..............................................$60,000
Rent  ......................................................  8,000
Salesmen's commissions  ...................................  39,000
Insurance  ................................................   4,000
```

(Uniform C.P.A. Examination)

35. You have been making annual audits of the XYZ Sales Company. During the last few years the company's earnings have shown a slight but steady decline.

  At the beginning of this year's audit, you obtain company-prepared financial statements which show a significant increase in earnings for this year over the prior three years. The company is engaged in a wholesaling operation and resells to retailers the products purchased from various manufacturers. There have been no unit price changes in either purchases or sales. The method of operation remains the same, so that increased efficiency does not account for the increase in income. The company's other sources of revenue remain the same. In short, the business has been run on the same basis as in the past. In addition, you are aware that management is anxious to present a favorable statement of income, since it is facing a struggle for control with a group of stockholders who charge that income has declined owing to mismanagement. You conclude that net income may be overstated by understating expired costs and expenses or liabilities, or overstating assets.

  The company is on a Fifo inventory basis. A physical inventory was taken at the year-end. A tag system was used and all tags were accounted for.

Required:
  Draw a line down the middle of a lined sheet(s) of paper.
  (a) To the left of the line, state the ways that expired costs and expenses or liabilities may have been understated, or assets overstated.
  (b) To the right of the line, for each item mentioned in part (a), outline in a few words the audit steps that would reveal each understatement or overstatement.   (Uniform C.P.A. Examination)

36. Prepare a work sheet covering your examination of the account "Miscellaneous Administrative Expense," in connection with your year-end examination of Pratt Products Co. The general ledger account appears as follows:

Miscellaneous Administrative Expense

Date	Description	Reference	Dr.	Cr.	Balance
Jan. 31		VR	$1,000.00		$1,000.00
		J-3	7.86		1,007.86
Feb. 28		VR	20.00		1,027.86
		J-8	8.15		1,036.01
Mar. 31		VR	2,015.00		3,051.01
		J-15	7.29		3.058.30
Apr. 30		VR	1,636.28		4,694.58
		J-23	9.05		4,703.63
May 31		VR	250.00		4,953.63
		J-29	7.36		4,960.99
June 30		VR		$17.64	4,943.35
July 31		VR	1,020.00		5,963.35
		J-32	8.17		5,971.52
Aug. 31		VR	15.00		5,986.52
		J-36	7.63		5,994.15
Sept. 30		VR	20.00		6,014.15
		J-40	7.02		6,021.17
Oct. 31		VR	2,481.39		8,502.56
		J-43	7.82		8,510.38
Nov. 30		VR	318.81		8,824.19
		J-47	8.20		8,832.39
Dec. 31		VR	569.95		9,402.34
		J-50	8.92		9,411.26

Reference to journal voucher J-23 reveals that the amount of $9.05 represents bank service charges for the month of March. Other journal entries are presumed also to be for bank charges. Your year-end bank reconciliation shows that service charges for December were $9.45.

The voucher register contains a miscellaneous column which is analyzed at the end of the month and recapped to show the charges to the various accounts that are affected. Analysis of the individual entries reveals the following breakdown of the monthly charges to Miscellaneous Administrative Expense:

January
Barton and Barrister..	$1,000.00

February
R. B. Holden, Cashier	$ 20.00

March
American Red Cross..	$ 100.00
Bright & Early	1,900.00
R. B. Holden, Cashier	15.00
	$2,015.00

April
R. B. Holden, Cashier	$ 110.00
Barton and Barrister....`...................................	1,000.00
Proxy, Inc..	476.28
Damon Runyon Cancer Fund...............................	50.00
	$1,636.28

May
R. B. Holden, Cashier .... $ 250.00

June
R. B. Holden, Cashier .... $ 17.64 Cr.

July
R. B. Holden, Cashier.................................... $ 20.00
Barton and Barrister.....................................   1,000.00
                                                            $1,020.00

August
R. B. Holden, Cashier .... $ 15.00

September
R. B. Holden, Cashier .... $ 20.00

October
Barton and Barrister..................................... $2,456.39
R. B. Holden, Cashier 25.00
                                                            $2,481.39

November
United Fund Drive....................................... $ 250.00
R. B. Holden, Cashier 63.81
                                                            $ 313.81

December
R. B. Holden, Cashier .... $ 20.00
Bonn's Department Store 234.95
R. B. Holden, Cashier 315.00
                                                            $ 569.95

The following information is obtained by examination of supporting records and discussion with various company officials.

The custodian of the office petty cash fund, R. B. Holden, submits a voucher the first of every month claiming reimbursement for disbursements made during the preceding month. The voucher for December disbursements is always made before the end of the month, however, in order to reflect December transactions in the proper year.

All postage used in the general office is purchased with petty cash funds, and represents the only petty cash disbursement affecting Miscellaneous Administrative Expense, except as follows:

(a) The voucher for disbursements made in April included an advance of $225 to P. D. Holcomb, President, to cover expenses of a trip to visit the company's East Coast warehouse. The actual expenses were $187.36, and the balance of the advance was returned to Holden the following month.

(b) Several office employees worked overtime during October to prepare a special report, and were reimbursed from the petty cash fund for the cost of their suppers and cab fares to their homes, in the total amount of $43.81.

(c) P. D. Holcomb received an advance of $300 in December for expenses relating to a trip to attend a trade association meeting to be held from January 3 to January 6.

Minutes of the Board of Directors contain the following actions:

Meeting Date	Action
11/14	Re-appointed the firm of Bright & Early to make the annual examination of the company's financial statements.

Meeting Date	Action
12/15	Authorized retaining Barton and Barrister for legal services for another year, retainer fee of $4,000 to be paid quarterly, in advance, beginning in January.
1/15	Authorized contribution to American Red Cross, $100.00.
3/15	Authorized mailing to stockholders of annual report for previous year, together with notice of annual stockholders meeting and proxy form for stockholders unable to attend the meeting.
	Authorized engagement of Proxy, Inc., to solicit return of stockholders' proxies, for fee of $300 plus out-of-pocket expenses.
4/15	Authorized contribution to Damon Runyon Cancer Fund $50.
11/15	Authorized contribution to United Fund Drive, $250.

The statement from Bonn's Department Store contains the description "Purchases by A. C. Powers." On questioning Mr. Powers, the office manager, you learn that this is a bill covering the purchase of Christmas gifts for office employees.

The statement from Barton and Barrister attached to the voucher entered in October reads as follows:

Retainer Fee	$1,000.00
Legal and out-of-pocket expenses relating to defense of patent infringement suit	1,456.39
	$2,456.39

Your working papers should explain all unusual items, and should show any adjustments or reclassifications you would recommend. Show all possible adjustments, regardless of materiality. In addition, prepare a list of points concerning items about which you would want further information, or which you would want to bring to the attention of the senior accountant.

Cost of sales and inventory

systems; internal control

11

Accounting for production and inventory costs is a major problem in most manufacturing and merchandising concerns, and represents a substantial proportion of the total accounting activity. The number of transactions and dollars involved, plus the number of employees who handle the inventories from time of acquisition to time of disposition, all point to a need for good internal control over an important series of activities. Yet many businessmen tend to consider internal control over inventories to be less important than internal control over cash and receivables. When such an attitude exists, the cause can usually be traced to the fact that cash and receivables are both recognized as being highly susceptible to direct monetary losses resulting from fraud or carelessness. Inventories, on the other hand, are often assumed to be of limited usefulness to anyone except the business that owns them, or possibly its customers, and therefore subject to fewer losses.

Actually, however, inventory is subject to a multitude of losses and excessive costs, but most of them tend to remain hidden unless they are intentionally uncovered and presented for the consideration of management. The following list is intended merely to suggest the wide variety of losses and excessive costs which might occur in connection with inventories. The causes are classified according to the particular operating functions which would be responsible:

PURCHASING

Buying in uneconomical quantities.
Failing to obtain best prices commensurate with desired quality standards.
Failing to give proper consideration to transportation costs and the most economical mode of transportation. (A traffic department is often created to handle this very technical problem.)
Overbuying in relation to current needs, resulting in excessive financing and storage costs and possible losses due to obsolescence or deterioration.

Failing to order promptly and to follow up on orders, resulting in production delays and lost sales.

RECEIVING

Inaccurate counting, permitting shortages in goods received to go undetected. Accepting goods which are not as ordered, causing production problems, loss of customer goodwill, or added cost of packing and returning the goods.

INSPECTION

Failing to detect material or merchandise which is defective or otherwise fails to meet company standards.

STORING

Careless handling, resulting in breakage or deterioration.
Failing to provide adequate protection against access to inventories by outsiders or unauthorized employees, resulting in lost or unaccounted for materials.
Overlooking inventory items and improperly reporting them as being out of stock.

MANUFACTURING

Careless handling and processing, resulting in excessive scrap and rework costs.

SHIPPING

Careless checking of quantities, resulting in shipping more goods than are billed to the customer.

ACCOUNTING

Failing to provide adequate, current, and reliable data on which to base decisions.
Failing to maintain accounting records in such a way that losses will be disclosed and reported.
Failing to exercise proper care in approving disbursements.

The above examples should suggest to the reader that proper segregation of duties and precise recognition of responsibilities are at least as important to good internal control over inventories as they are to good internal control over other more liquid assets.

Objectives of Internal Control

Internal control over cost of sales and inventories should give assurance that:

1. The need to reorder is signalled as soon as the amount of inventory on hand reaches a minimum safety level.

2. Inventory quantities are adequately protected against losses from theft, spoilage, unauthorized withdrawals by employees, and the ravages of the elements.

3. There is separate-item accountability for both units and dollars for inventory quantities received, on hand, and issued or sold.

4. Differences between book and physical inventories are ascertained, differences adjusted, and the amount of overage or shortage properly accounted for.

5. Proper authorization exists for inventory quantities removed from stock.

6. All transactions pertaining to the issue or sale of inventory quantities are accounted for and entered in the controlling records.

7. Inventory issues are costed according to an acceptable method and the costs accounted for in a manner that provides adequate information for management.

Control over inventories is illustrated in the procedural flow charts illustrated in Chapter 9 on purchases and Chapter 7 on sales. The activities and records pertaining to inventories on those flow charts are described under the various departmental headings in the following sections.

Purchasing, Receiving, Stores

The activities associated with the purchase of inventories were discussed in Chapter 9 and covered the receipt and storage of purchased goods and materials, as well as the general ledger accounting charge to inventory accounts for related dollar amounts.

Shipping Department

Control over all outward movement of assets should be centered in the shipping department, which should operate under the general requirement that nothing is to be released from the department without written authorization. Such authorization would be in the form of a shipping order for sales of inventory or production items, a copy of a debit memo for purchased goods being returned to the vendor, or a work order for machinery or equipment being disposed of. The department will generally maintain a chronological record of all shipments that have been made.

Manufacturing Department

The requisition which relieves the storeroom of responsibility for inventory items transfers that responsibility to the manufacturing department. Responsibility accounting should relate material costs, and the labor and overhead expended to convert the materials to finished goods, to the foremen or other supervisors who are responsible for the various aspects of the manufacturing activities. Breakage, damage, scrap, and rework costs should all be reported on a responsibility basis, as a natural outgrowth of the responsibility for production materials. When manufacturing is completed, the manufacturing department is relieved of responsibility for the inventory when the product is either returned to the stockroom or transferred to the shipping department.

Stock Records

The key to effective inventory control is in the unit records that are the basis for determining when to reorder and how much to reorder, that establish accountability for the inventory quantities that have been received, and that develop unit costs for systems that are based on actual costs. In addition to showing the current inventory balance of each item, the records should show past usage, quantities reserved for scheduled future production, quantities on order from vendors, and possibly unit and total cost.

The records are often maintained by hand on cards or sheets with individual visible index filing (for example, on Kardex panels), by accounting machine or posted ledger cards, or by punched-card techniques, which are discussed later in the chapter. The stock records activity may be under general or cost accounting, purchasing, or, in a manufacturing concern, under the production planning and control unit.

Receipts of inventory may be posted from copies of receiving reports sent directly to the stock records unit from the receiving department, or from production order forms in the case of manufactured items. If actual costs (rather than standard or estimated costs) are used for accounting purposes, the entry for quantity received must be accompanied by an entry for the related cost. The cost of purchased items is obtained from the purchase invoice; hence posting cannot occur until after invoices have been matched with receiving reports and audited for errors. For manufactured items, the cost information is obtained from job order or process cost sheets or from standard cost records.

Issues are posted from shipping orders in the case of sales, or from materials requisitions when inventory is withdrawn to enter production. Serial numbers of the issue forms should be accounted for to assure that none have been lost or overlooked. Failure to post a withdrawal would result in an overstated inventory balance and possibly an out-of-stock condition as a result of not reordering because the inventory stock would appear to be adequate in terms of the balance shown on the stock records.

In systems based on actual costs, the form recording an issue must be costed and extended, so that both quantity and dollars can be posted to the records. Average costs are the easiest form of actual costs to apply when records are kept in a stock ledger. Once a new average has been calculated and recorded following receipt of an additional quantity, that average cost is used to cost all issues until a new receipt changes the figure. Fifo and Lifo costs are more difficult to account for, because each receipt of inventory must be kept as a separate lot on the records until the entire quantity involved in the lot has been issued.

Selective inventory control. In most instances, an analysis of inventory activity will reveal that the bulk of the dollar value of inventory transactions is concentrated in a small proportion of the inventory items. A common finding is that about twenty per cent of the items will account for as much as eighty per cent of the dollar value of the volume handled. Because comprehensive inventory controls are costly to maintain, there has been considerable success with efforts to reduce the control over the substantial proportion of inventory items that are of limited dollar importance. Stock records for these low-value items are dispensed with, and for factory materials and parts which enter into the production process, no material requisitions are prepared. The 'inventory items are merely stored in areas that are accessible to all workers and are withdrawn at will as they are needed for production.

The sacrifice of accountability and any attendant losses under such an arrangement should normally be less than the savings in recordkeeping, especially because pilferage can still be restricted through normal inspection controls at plant exits. Cost transfers for items withdrawn for production or sale can be made on the basis of a "standard" cost geared to current cost information, the transfers being made on the basis of quantities required by bills of material for completed production.

The problem of determining when to reorder items not accounted for by stock records may be resolved in either of two ways. Bins and storage areas can be inspected periodically and orders placed to restock quantities that are low in much the same manner as in a grocery supermarket. Another approach is to determine a minimum reorder quantity based on the usual considerations and set this amount aside in a separate bin or package. Then, whenever the regular supply is exhausted and the segregated quantity must be drawn upon, a travelling requisition stored with the reserve quantity is removed and sent to the purchasing department to initiate repurchase.

Accounting Department

Inventories should be controlled by both detailed unit records and general ledger perpetual inventory accounts. The general ledger records establish over-all dollar accountability and are the basis for developing inventory variation amounts when the results of a physical inventory are used to adjust the book records. The variation between book and physical inventory indicates how accurately both physical quantities and the related book records have been handled during the year. It is seldom feasible to attempt to prevent inventory differences from developing, so the main concern should be to keep the differences from becoming excessive.

General ledger perpetual inventory records are also essential for the preparation of interim financial statements. The operation of the records allocates the amount of goods available for sale into the amount remaining on hand for display in the balance sheet and the cost of goods sold figure for the income statement.

Debits to the general ledger inventory accounts originate in the voucher register, or in monthly journal entries that record the amount of materials, labor, and overhead utilized in production for the period. The accumulation of factory costs in inventory accounts should provide the necessary information for management on cost trends and the relative profitability of various products. The costs should also be accounted for on a responsibility basis as an aid in the controlling of the costs.

Credits to inventory originate in monthly journal entries, which represent a compilation of the amounts shown on material requisitions for the period, or in the totals obtained from costing the items listed on each sales invoice.

Physical Inventory Taking

The accuracy of the physical inventory will directly affect financial position and operating results; therefore, the need for precautionary measures to assure an accurate inventory should be evident. This need is further evidenced by the fact that the physical inventory determines how effective the various departments have been in carrying out their responsibility to account for all inventory items with which they have been charged.

The first step in securing good internal control over the taking of the physical inventory is to select for planning and supervising the work a person who has a sufficient grasp of all phases of company operations. Such a person should be able to anticipate the many contingencies and problems that are likely to arise and be able to handle them properly. This person, who will probably be the controller or some other responsible person of sufficient rank and stature, should outline the actual procedures to be followed in taking the inventory. Written instructions should be prepared covering each separate job to be assigned to other employees, and steps should be taken to be certain that these instructions are fully understood and that each individual is impressed with the importance of carefully following the instructions.

Counting of inventory items should normally not be done by the same employees who are responsible for custody of the inventory. If counting is done by teams of two employees, however, one member of each team may be an employee who is responsible for handling inventory items, as he will be better informed as to the exact description and location of the items to be counted. Other considerations in planning and completing the physical count are the following:

1. The receiving and shipping departments should be cleared of all merchandise before counting is begun, and receiving memos and shipping documents prepared near the date of the inventory count should clearly show the date goods were received or shipped. These dates are extremely important in obtaining a good cut-off of transactions in the accounting department.

2. If all plant activity cannot be stopped during the inventory counting, provision must be made for items which are transferred from one location to another. The same item must not be counted in both locations, and of course care must be taken to see that an item which has been moved has not been omitted entirely from the counting process.

3. Inventory items should be stacked in neat piles if at all possible to facilitate accurate counting.

4. Consignment goods, obsolete or defective parts, or any other items not to be included in the inventory should be clearly marked.

5. Supervisors should be on hand to observe the counting process and to be certain that instructions are being followed. Each department should be inspected and "cleared" by a supervisor before the counting is considered to have been completed.

6. A "blind" second count is always the best assurance that counting has been accurately performed. The two counts should be compared by a third person, and differences should be cleared by having a recount made immediately.

7. Count tags or tickets should be prenumbered and all numbers accounted for as soon as the tickets are turned in to ascertain that no tickets are omitted from the final inventory figures.

8. If detailed perpetual inventory records are maintained, the records should be adjusted to agree with the physical count. Major differences should be carefully investigated before the physical count is accepted as being correct. There is always a possibility that the inventory was stored in two locations, one of which was overlooked, that recent receipts or shipments have not been posted, or that items have not been properly identified.

9. After the inventory counts have been prepared and checked as suggested above, the individual items can be priced and extended and inventory totals ascertained for comparison with the general ledger control and adjustment of that account.

Inventory counts are often recorded originally on count tags. The example on page 270 illustrates the usual features of such a tag. The first counter or count team fills in the stock number, description, and location, completes the data for the first count, attaches the tag to the inventory, and removes the first-count stub. The second counter or team inserts the information for the second count, verifying descriptive information. The inventory is then inspected by the supervisor, who, if satisfied with the manner in which the work has been done, authorizes the second-count stubs to the "pulled." The "taken" stub stays with the inventory to evidence that the item has been counted and to aid in identification if a recount must be made. The first- and second-count stubs are matched according to the tag numbers, and the first and second counts are compared. If discrepancies appear, recounts are made.

Next the quantity figures should be compared with perpetual inventory records if such records are maintained. Following this step, the information on the inventory tags is usually transcribed onto inventory summary sheets, which facilitate pricing, extending, and totaling the inventory. An example of such a summary sheet is shown as Figure 11–1.

Punched-Card Records

There are two basically different punched-card systems for maintaining inventory records: the open-item or tub-file system, and the balance-forward system. The open-item system is relatively simple to operate, requires practically no key punching and only a minimum of equipment, and is readily adaptable to Fifo, Lifo, or standard costs but not to average costs.

Open-item system. For each item stocked in inventory, a stockkeeping unit must be established. The unit may be a case, a dozen, a gross, a hundred pounds, or any other quantity. The principle of the open-item inventory system is that there is a one-to-one correspondence, with one punched card in the tub file for each stockkeeping unit of an item on hand in the inventory.

A master card is maintained for each inventory item, showing description, the stockkeeping unit, warehouse location, selling price, and any other desired information. As purchase quantities of an inventory item are received, the master card plus a supplementary card showing unit cost for the purchase lot are used to gang-punch sufficient tub-file cards to equal the quantity received, in terms of the stockkeeping unit. These cards are then filed behind remaining cards in the tub file from previous purchases of the inventory item.

As orders are received from customers, or as stock requisitions are written, open-item cards are removed from the tub file equal to the number of units requisitioned or sold. If Fifo costs are being applied, the cards are removed from the front of the pack for the inventory item; if Lifo costs are being applied, the cards are simply withdrawn from the back of the pack. Also filed within the pack is a card to signal that the quantity on hand has reached the reorder point. This card is inserted in the pack whenever a new purchase has been received, its position from the end of the pack being determined by the reorder quantity established for the item. When this

No. 234

TAKEN

SECOND COUNT

No. 234

STOCK NO. ....

DESCRIPTION ....

LOCATION ....

ON HAND | QUANTITY | UNIT |

COUNTED BY ....

FIRST COUNT

No. 234

ON HAND | QUANTITY | UNIT |

COUNTED BY ....

PAGE NO. _____

INVENTORY DATE ....

DEPARTMENT ....   EXTENDED BY ....

ENTERED BY ....   FOOTED BY ....

PRICED BY ....   REVIEWED BY ....

TAG NO.	STOCK NO.	DESCRIPTION	QUANTITY	UNIT	PRICE	EXTENSION

Figure 11-1

card is pulled as an order is being filled, the card is sent to the purchasing department as notice that an additional quantity should be purchased.

If quantities withdrawn are being shipped to customers, the cards removed from the tub file are also used for billing. Name-and-address header cards are added to the cards pertaining to the customer's order, and the invoice is prepared on the tabulator. Programming through the control panel causes the tabulator to accumulate the unit quantity and the selling price from each card for an item, and to strike a total when the last card for the item has been read. The result printed on the invoice would then appear as follows:

Quantity	Unit	Description	Price	Total
7	cases	24-12 oz. Red Catsup	$3.00	$21.00

Balance-forward system. The balance-forward system requires a punched card for each receipt of a new quantity and for each issue from inventory. The receipt card may be the purchase distribution card punched in the accounts payable operation; the issue cards may be key-punched from customer orders or requisitions, or they may be partially prepunched cards, with the quantity introduced by key punching or mark sensing. Costing is generally at standard cost, unless a punched-card calculator is available to compute a new average cost after each receipt of additional items.

The heart of the system is the file of balance-forward cards. There should be a card for each type of item carried in the inventory, and the card should contain, as implied by the name, the current inventory balance, along with a variety of other descriptive and operating information. Each day, receipts and issues cards are match-merged with the file of balance-forward cards. From the resulting file, a daily transaction register is run on the tabulator, showing for each item the previous balance, receipts, issues, and the new balance. The new balance is also summary-punched into a new balance-forward card. In some systems, the balance-forward card also contains a minimum reorder quantity, which the tabulator can compare with the balance on hand to determine whether the difference is positive or negative. Negative cards are punched with an "X" and can be sorted out of the new balance-forward cards on the basis of the presence of the "X". A listing of these cards then informs the purchasing department that the inventory items are to be reordered. When orders are placed, an on-order card can be included in the transaction register run to calculate a balance "on hand and on order," which when compared with the reorder point will produce a positive availability so that the item will not again be listed on the reorder report to the purchasing department.

Information on past sales or use activity is ordinarily important in reordering and in controlling inventory quantities. To provide such information, past usage can be accumulated on the balance-forward cards, the figure being restored to zero at the beginning of each year, or oftener if seasonal factors have an important influence.

Batch billing. In a variation of the balance-forward method known as "batch billing" (the billing term stems from the fact that completed cards for accounts receivable billing are produced in the process), card pulling and key punching are greatly reduced or eliminated and average costs are calculated for the inventory balance. The major factor in this system is a calculating punch that must be capable of performing a number of related steps in sequence.

A card is punched for each item on a customer's order, showing only three items of information: customer number, inventory code number, and quantity ordered. When a batch of these cards is available, they are sorted by inventory code number and then match-merged, along with receipts cards, with the balance-forward cards. In a single pass through the calculator, the following steps are performed:

1. Goods received, in both units and dollars, are added to the previous balance obtained from the balance-forward card.

2. A new average cost is calculated by dividing the total dollars calculated in the preceding step by the total units calculated in that step.

3. The new average cost, and description of the item and selling price, are punched into each order card.

4. The quantity punched in each order card is extended by the average cost and the selling price, and the extensions are punched into the order card.

5. The quantity and average-cost amount for each order card are deducted from the totals obtained from the previous balance-forward and receipts cards, and when all cards pertaining to a given item have been processed, a new balance-forward card is punched to show the units and dollars remaining on hand, plus the other fixed information that appeared in the previous balance-forward card.

After all cards have been processed in the above manner, the order cards are sorted into sequence by customer number, name-and-address header cards are added, and invoice billing is accomplished. One copy of the invoice is used as the shipping order.

General ledger accounting. Debits to inventory accounts arising from purchases originate in accounts payable operations and the resulting voucher register. Debits for goods manufactured result from the cost accounting process. Customer order cards or stock issue cards are the source of inventory credits and cost of sales debits. Totals are developed from these cards for end-of-month posting. In this connection, it may be pointed out that two month-end sorts may be necessary: one according to the various inventory accounts to be credited, and another according to the cost of sales or manufacturing inventory accounts to be debited.

Physical inventory taking. Prepunched cards are frequently used in taking a physical inventory. Quantities may be recorded on the cards in writing and then key-punched. Alternatively, mark sensing may be used, or punching can take place along with the physical counting by means of special cards which are scored for the punching positions and then punched at the scene of operations, utilizing a small portable punching device that involves a stylus and a template. Blind second counts can be accomplished by recording an initial count on the prepunched card, inserting the card in a window envelope which permits only the item description to be viewed, and then recording the second count on the envelope itself, to be compared later with the first count recorded on the card.

Subsequent machine processing would include arranging the cards in order by prepunched inventory tag number to determine whether all cards are present, extending quantity and unit cost on a calculating punch to obtain total inventory cost for each item, sorting the cards according to inventory codes and classifications, and then listing the cards on the tabulator to obtain a complete inventory record and totals. Comparison with detailed perpetual inventory record balances and adjustment of those balances to correspond with the count figures can also be accomplished by machine processing.

Management Reports

Effective control and management of a large business will depend heavily on adequate reports covering all activities relating to inventories. First-hand information is obviously impossible to obtain, and reports must serve instead to convey the important facts concerning materials and material cost. Monthly operating statements serve as an over-all check on day-to-day decisions, and top management will rely heavily on these statements in evaluating the performance of individuals to whom inventory responsibilities have been delegated. To prepare such statements, the accounting department must keep its records in a manner which will permit determining the cost of sales. Using this key figure, and without the expense of a physical inventory, dollar inventory balances can be reported. These balances may be broken down by department, by type of inventory, or in any other manner which will add to the significance of the reported figures.

The cost of sales figure also makes possible the preparation of a monthly income statement, with its important net income figure. Gross margin, another important figure on the income statement, will ordinarily be broken down by departments to give further information.

Annually, when the physical inventory is taken, variances between book balances and the physical inventory should be reported. A small variance carries assurance that inventory materials have been properly handled and accounted for, that monthly accounting reports have not contained misleading figures, and that the physical inventory was accurately taken. A large variance indicates, of course, an unsatisfactory performance in one or more of these areas, and an effort must be made to determine at what point or points the difficulty occurred.

There are many other important figures which should be reported to facilitate effective control over inventories and the various functions related to inventories. Outstanding purchase commitments should be reported if they are an important factor in total inventory position. Large department stores, which usually have carefully developed merchandise budgets, report an "open-to-buy" figure for each department, based on a comparison of budgeted amounts and inventory on hand and on order. Other figures important to department store operation are inventory variances and mark-downs. Mark-downs are sometimes reported under as many as a dozen classifications to meet the demand for detailed information to be used in exercising effective control over merchandising policies and procedures.

In manufacturing concerns employing standard cost systems, material price variances can be developed to reveal market price trends and purchasing efficiency. Material use variances and scrap and rework figures will reveal at a glance the care and efficiency with which the manufacturing department is handling the materials for which it has been charged.

Inventory reports analyzing turnover for various classes of items, or showing an age breakdown for the items, are useful in reviewing inventories for slow-moving or obsolete items. When write-downs of such items are made, classification of the resulting losses according to cause helps to make the information more useful to management.

Responsibility reporting of the operating expenses of the various departments concerned with handling inventories and the related accounting records is essential for control of those expenses. Further useful interpretation of such expense figures can be made if activity figures are also reported, such as number of orders handled, tonnage moved, or number of transactions posted. Comparative costs per unit of activity present the best indication of operating efficiency.

Internal Auditing

Each department which shares in the responsibility for inventories should come under the scrutiny of the internal auditor. His examination should disclose whether procedures reflecting good internal control are being followed, whether operations have been conducted efficiently and without waste, and whether transactions have been accurately recorded and reported. The accounting department should come under particularly close scrutiny. Records showing the dollar value of goods on order should be verified. Paid invoices should be reviewed to ascertain the accuracy of the recording of these invoices in both the general records and the detailed perpetual inventory records.

The storage function should be audited from the standpoint of whether prescribed procedures for receiving and issuing materials are followed. Of perhaps even greater importance are the physical aspects of the storage function. Materials should be stored in an orderly fashion and properly protected against breakage, damage from the elements, and unauthorized withdrawals.

The internal auditor should have an important part in the taking and valuing of the physical inventory. He should review and approve the detailed plans and instructions for taking the inventory. He should observe the actual inventorying to ascertain whether the established procedures are being followed, and often he will have direct supervisory responsibility in connection with this work. He should satisfy himself that all materials have been counted, and that all count tickets or inventory sheets have been accounted for. He should make tests of inventory pricing, taking particular note that market values have been used when these are below cost and that damaged or obsolete items have been segregated and priced at their realizable value. Extensions and footings should also be tested by him, and of course the internal auditor should verify the inventory variances developed from the comparison of the book and physical inventory amounts.

REVIEW QUESTIONS

1. Why do business concerns frequently have less internal control over inventories than over cash and receivables?
2. What assurances can be obtained through good internal control over cost of sales and inventories?
3. What forms of authorization should the shipping department have in order to release items for shipment?
4. "A material requisition for inventory entering into production is a form of transfer of responsibility for the inventory items involved." Explain.
5. What functions of inventory control are provided by unit stock records?
6. Why is it important that the stock records department account for the serial numbers of shipping orders and material requisitions?
7. Explain "selective inventory control."
8. If a physical inventory is taken and the amount of inventory is determined to be less than that called for by the records, does the difference necessarily represent physical units that have disappeared? Explain.
9. Distinguish between the open item and balance forward methods of punched-card inventory control records.
10. What are the advantages of the "batch billing" method of maintaining inventory records by punched cards?
11. What machine operations would follow the recording of physical inventory quantities on prepunched cards?

12. State the objectives of the internal auditor in making an examination of the purchasing department.

QUESTIONS ON SYSTEMS APPLICATIONS

13. Your client maintains material inventories on a standard cost, perpetual inventory basis. The cost of materials used for the year is down substantially, both as a percentage of sales and as a percentage of total costs. What account balances should be closely analyzed for any indication that the cost of materials used for the year may be stated incorrectly?

14. Customers' orders are edited, approved for credit, and sent to the shipping department to be filled. Quantities shipped are noted on the form, and it is then forwarded to the accounting department for billing and recording in the perpetual inventory records.
    (a) Indicate the principal shortcomings of the system.
    (b) What recommendations would you make to the client to improve the system?

15. This (1967) is your first audit of the Zjax Company. In reviewing the company's accounting procedures for purchases, you learn that one person compares all receiving reports with vendor's invoices. Receiving reports for which no invoices have been received are placed in an unmatched receiving report file. Invoices for which no receiving reports have been received are placed in an unmatched invoice file. Matched receiving reports and invoices are sent on to be recorded in the voucher register and paid. The client gave no consideration to these files in adjusting the book inventory to agree with the physical either last year or this year. Given the following information, what adjusting entries would you recommend?

	12/31/66	12/31/67
Unmatched receiving reports	$1,405.76	$ 760.85
Unmatched invoices	$3,915.20	4,201.90

(All purchases are f.o.b. shipping point. The company follows the perpetual inventory method.)

16. When detailed perpetual inventory records are maintained under standard costs, receiving reports and inventory withdrawal requisitions can be sent directly to the stock records department for posting, immediately upon receipt or issuance of the goods. If average costs are used, what clerical steps would have to occur before the receiving reports and withdrawal requisitions can be posted? Why?

17. Explain the importance, from an internal control standpoint, of
    (a) Prenumbering and accounting for all material requisition forms.
    (b) Avoiding any delays in posting material requisitions to the detailed perpetual inventory records.

18. (a) Under what circumstances is it likely that a company's detailed perpetual inventory records will show dollars as well as quantities?
    (b) Under what circumstances would the records be likely to show quantities but not dollars?

19. The Ace Wholesale Co. keeps detailed perpetual inventory records showing quantities but no cost information. The periodic inventory method is used for general ledger accounting purposes, with a physical inventory taken only once a year, on December 31.

    (a) What are the probable reasons that the company maintains the detailed records on a perpetual basis?

    (b) How might the company, under these circumstances, go about preparing monthly financial statements?

20. Past history on rate of sale or use of inventory items is important for reordering purposes. How can such information be obtained when inventory records are maintained by punched card on (a) an open item basis or (b) a balance-forward basis?

21. Suggest various nonaccounting matters that the internal auditor should review and investigate in connection with his audit of inventories.

PROBLEMS

22. As part of a test of inventory control, you examined .the perpetual inventory records of stockroom M. A full set of records (subsidiary and control) is maintained in the factory while a controlling account is also kept in the accounting department.

    You are required to set up a summarizing schedule in money amounts which simultaneously reflects the flow of materials (starting with initial inventory and ending with final inventory), and reconciles the accounting department records with those of the factory in regard to opening inventory, receipts, and withdrawals of materials and ending inventory.

    The items to be considered in preparing this schedule are as follows:

    (1) Receipts of materials in stockroom M, entered properly on factory records but treated by the accounting department as stockroom N, $240.

    (2) Correction made by the accounting department of an error in a prior period. The error was the recording of an $800 withdrawal of materials as $500. The original item had been correctly entered by the factory record clerk.

    (3) A shortage of item M-143, amounting to $45 which was noted and entered during the period on the factory records, but information on which had not been transmitted to the accounting department.

    (4) An initial inventory according to factory records of $11,000 in stock room M. Receipts of $14,000 and withdrawals of $13,000 according to the records of the accounting department.

(Uniform C.P.A. Examination)

23. The Borow Corporation is an importer and wholesaler. Its merchandise is purchased from a number of suppliers and is warehoused by Borow Corporation until sold to consumers.

    In conducting his audit for the year ended June 30, 1967, the Company's C.P.A. determined that the system of internal control was good. Accordingly he observed the physical inventory at an interim date, May 31, 1967, instead of at year end.

    The following information was obtained from the general ledger:

Inventory, July 1, 1966	$ 87,500
Physical inventory, May 31, 1967	95,000
Sales for eleven months ended May 31, 1967	840,000
Sales for year ended June 30, 1967	960,000
Purchases for eleven months ended May 31, 1967 (before audit adjustments)	675,000
Purchases for year ended June 30, 1967 (before audit adjustments)	800,000

The C.P.A.'s audit disclosed the following information:

Shipments received in May and included in the physical inventory
but recorded as June purchases .... $ 7,500
Shipments received in unsalable condition and excluded from physi-
cal inventory. Credit memos had not been received nor had
chargebacks to vendors been recorded
   Total at May 31, 1967   1,000
   Total at June 30, 1967 (including the May unrecorded
   chargebacks)..   1,500
Deposit made with vendor and charged to purchases in April 1967.
Product was shipped in July 1967   2,000
Deposit made with vendor and charged to purchases in May 1967.
Product was shipped, F.O.B. destination, on May 29, 1967 and
was included in May 31, 1967 physical inventory as goods in
transit   5,500
Through the carelessness of the receiving department a June ship-
ment was damaged by rain. This shipment was later sold in June
at its cost of $10,000.

Required:
In audit engagements in which interim physical inventories are observed, a frequently used auditing procedure is to test the reasonableness of the year-end inventory by the application of gross profit ratios.

Prepare in good form the following schedules:

(a) Computation of the gross profit ratio for eleven months ended May 31, 1967.

(b) Computation by the gross profit ratio method of cost of goods sold during June 1967.

(c) Computation by the gross profit ratio method of June 30, 1967 inventory.

24. The Du-Rite Corporation was established in 1967 and manufactures a single product which passes through several departments. The Company has a standard cost system.

The Company's inventories at standard cost are as follows:

		December 31, 1967
Raw Material		—0—
Work-in-process:		
Material		$ 75,000
Labor		7,500
Overhead		15,000
Total		97,500
Finished goods :		
Material		60,000
Labor..		20,000
Overhead		40,000
Total..		120,000
Total inventories		$217,500

The Company's preliminary income statement for the year ended December 31, 1967, prior to any year-end inventory adjustments, follows:

Sales		$900,000
Cost of goods sold :		
Standard cost of goods sold :		
Material.......................................	$300,000	
Labor	100,000	
Overhead	200,000	
Total	600,000	
Variances :		
Material.......................................	25,400	
Labor	25,500	
Overabsorbed overhead	(16,500)	
Total	34,400	634,400
Gross profit		265,600
Selling expenses :		
Salaries.......................................	28,000	
Commissions	72,000	
Shipping expense	18,000	
Other...	7,000	
Total	125,000	
General and administrative expenses....................	50,000	175,000
Profit from operations		90,600
Other income :		
Purchases discount	8,000	
Scrap sales	9,000	17,000
Net income before taxes		$107,600

All purchase discounts were earned on the purchase of raw materials. The Company has included a scrap allowance in the cost standards; the scrap sold cannot be traced to any particular operation or department.

Required:
  (a) Prepare a schedule computing the actual cost of goods manufactured. The schedule should provide for a separation of costs into material, labor and overhead costs.
  (b) Prepare a schedule comparing the computation of ending inventories at standard cost and at actual cost. The schedule should provide for a separation of costs into material, labor and overhead costs.
  (c) Without prejudice to your solution to "b," assume that the finished goods inventory was composed of 1,000 units with a cost of $180 each. The current market price for the product is $250. The Company, however, has an old contract to sell 200 units at $175 each. The normal gross profit rate is $33^1/_3\%$ of cost. The shipping expense for the old contract will be $5 per unit; the sales commission is 8% of the sale.
  Prepare a schedule to adjust the finished goods inventory to the lower of cost or market. (Uniform C.P.A. Examination)
25. In an annual audit at December 31, 1967 you find the following transactions near the closing date:
  (1) Merchandise costing $1,822 was received on January 3, 1968 and the related purchase invoice recorded January 5. The invoice showed the shipment was made on December 29, 1967, *f.o.b. destination.*
  (2) Merchandise costing $625 was received on December 28, 1967 and the invoice was not recorded. You located it in the hands of the purchasing agent; it was marked *on consignment.*

(3) A packing case containing product costing $816 was standing in the shipping room when the physical inventory was taken. It was not included in the inventory because it was marked *hold for shipping instructions*. Your investigation revealed that the customer's order was dated December 18, 1967 but that the case was shipped and the customer billed on January 10, 1968. The product was a stock item of your client.

(4) Merchandise received on January 6, 1968 costing $720 was entered in the purchase register on January 7, 1968. The invoice showed shipment was made f.o.b. supplier's warehouse on December 31, 1967. Since it was not on hand at December 31, it was not included in inventory.

(5) A special machine, fabricated to order for a customer, was finished and in the shipping room on December 31, 1967. The customer was billed on that date and the machine excluded from inventory although it was shipped on January 4, 1968.

Assume that each of the amounts is material.

(a) State whether the merchandise should be included in the client's inventory.

(b) Give your reason for your decision on each item in (a) above.

(Uniform C.P.A. Examination)

Auditing cost of sales
and inventories
12

Even under perpetual inventory accounting systems, the expense element relative to goods purchased for resale is ultimately determined as a residual, based on the valuation of a physical count of inventory quantities remaining on hand at the end of the year and the subtraction of this figure from the balance remaining in the inventory account after cost of sales has been recorded. Hence, despite the general preference today for the income statement point of view rather than the balance sheet point of view, the reader will find that the discussion of auditing relative to cost of sales and inventories is heavily weighted with inventory considerations.

STANDARDS OF STATEMENT PRESENTATION

Although the public accounting profession has successfully solved the problem of accepting full responsibility for the fairness of inventory figures, including quantities and physical existence, other inventory problems have kept the over-all situation concerning inventories in a most chaotic state. In many ways the greatest single problem confronting the entire accounting profession today is to bring some semblance of order out of the muddled inventory situation. At the heart of the matter is the last-in, first-out method of apportioning material costs between items on hand and items sold. Changing price levels, high income tax rates, and changes in the income tax regulations have been the catalysts which have induced the acceptance of Lifo and created the present inventory problem.

The adoption of Lifo is commendable, of course, from the point of view of income determination, for Lifo produces a better matching of current costs with current revenues. But although it has gone far to solve one problem, it has created numerous others. It has resulted in a balance sheet figure for inventories which is inconsistent with the current basis on which other current assets are stated and is all but meaningless from the standpoint of credit analysis. Also, it has detracted from the value of historical comparisons of both balance sheets and income statements for those concerns which have changed to Lifo. Lastly, because the change to Lifo has not been universal, companies employing different inventory costing bases cannot be effectively compared for investment or credit purposes. To further compound the confusion, studies by the Research Department of the American Institute of Certified Public Accountants covering 600 published corporate annual reports have shown that about one-third of the reports do not reveal the cost method used in determining inventory figures! Ironically, these same studies show that most of the companies are not only faithfully following the generally accepted principle of valuing inventory at the lower of cost or market but are carefully disclosing their adherence to this method, which has almost universal acceptance.

Although it is difficult to say how these troublesome matters will eventually be resolved, it is the author's belief that the advantages of Lifo in determining income will eventually lead to its universal adoption. In many cases, however, book inventories will be carried on some other basis and converted to Lifo by means of price indexes. In the balance sheet, inventories will be stated at market value, with the difference between the market figure and the Lifo cost shown as an unrealized credit adjustment of the total owners' equity. Until this or some other millennium is reached, however, clients remain free to choose between Lifo and Fifo despite the divergent results produced, and to carry Lifo inventories on balance sheets at antiquated acquisition costs. Auditors, in turn, are indeed stultifying themselves in many instances when they report that their clients' statements present *fairly* the financial position and results of operations of the concern. The only saving factor is that it can truthfully be said that the statements have been prepared in conformity with generally accepted accounting principles.

For the present, acceptable standards of statement presentation should at least be raised to require full disclosure of (a) the method by which inventory costs have been determined, and (b) the current replacement cost of the inventories. Only with such information to aid them can analysts and investors make intelligent use of financial statements. The standards of statement presentation given below relative to inventories reflect the proposals just made and therefore deviate somewhat from certain practices still considered to be acceptable. The added requirements are not, however, unreasonable. Standards relative to the cost of sales figure in the income statement are given first.

1. Cost of sales should not be netted against sales; both figures should be shown "broad" in the income statement.

2. Although inventory shortages, mark-down expense, standard cost variances, and losses from reduction of inventory to market value may be com-

bined with the cost of sales figure in published statements (unless abnormal amounts are involved), all such figures should be reported separately for internal purposes.

3. The basis on which inventories have been valued should be stated. At present, this would usually be the generally accepted basis of the lower of cost or market, supplemented by an indication of the method of determining cost.

4. When inventories are stated at cost, market value should be given parenthetically, and if inventories have been reduced to market, cost should be given parenthetically.

5. The effect of any change in the method of valuing inventories should be set forth in the statements, and the lack of consistency in methods should be noted as an exception in the opinion paragraph of the auditor's certificate.

6. Full disclosure should be made if all or part of the inventories have been pledged to secure outstanding obligations.

7. Principal classes of inventory should be shown separately generally in order of their liquidity, if significant in amount. In addition to the traditional three-way separation between raw materials, work in process, and finished goods, other separations might include such items as goods out on consignment and merchandise in transit.

8. Purchase commitments should be disclosed if they are material or out of line with past practice, and losses should be provided for on firm purchase commitments.

9. Provisions for possible inventory price declines occurring after the balance sheet date should be made only by appropriations of retained income, and these reserves should not be deducted from inventory, but shown as a portion of retained income.

AUDIT OBJECTIVES AND PROCEDURES

The substantiation of the figures for inventory is likely to present the greatest single challenge to the auditor making an examination of the financial statements of a concern engaged in manufacturing or distribution. On the one hand, inventories are likely to be a major item on the balance sheet, with a crucial bearing on financial position and a direct influence on the determination of net income. At the same time, however, the client is likely to encounter maximum difficulty in arriving at a reasonable inventory figure, and the auditor will ordinarily have equal difficulty in satisfying himself that the client's figure is reasonable.

Previous to the McKesson and Robbins exposé, most auditors carefully avoided accepting any responsibility for determining the physical existence of inventories or the accuracy with which inventory quantities were determined. The typical auditor merely deferred to the ability and integrity of management in determining physical inventory quantities, and he effectively sidestepped any personal responsibility by stating that the existence of the inventory and the accuracy of the quantities had been certified to him by management. This condition was undoubtedly the result of the way auditing developed—that is, largely as a means of establishing the fact that cash had been properly accounted for and that no bookkeeping errors had occurred. The early auditor was a specialist in figures and recording; he was never expected to know enough about merchandise or manufacturing processes to be able to assume any responsibility for the determination of inventory quantities.

As the use by third parties of audited statements grew, some public accountants attempted to take a more realistic view of their responsibilities, which included satisfying themselves as to the existence of inventory and the accuracy of inventory quantities. Such progressive accountants met with little success, however. Bankers and other credit grantors were complacent and quite content with the status quo. Clients had little to gain from their point of view from any extension of the auditor's procedures to cover inventory quantities. Furthermore, they were naturally opposed to any change which would increase the cost of the annual audit. Even many public accounting practitioners were skeptical: how could an auditor know whether a barrel contained an expensive chemical or merely sand; whether all or only part of the machining operations on a casting had been performed; whether a bolt of cloth was low-count muslin or high-count percale? In addition, how could auditors possibly undertake to do any additional work at the time when most clients closed their books on December 31? Sufficient staff men could not be secured to perform the extra work, and it was already difficult enough to keep existing staff occupied after the close of the busy season, without adding more staff at the peak and compounding the problem.

Into this situation the McKesson and Robbins case injected itself with explosive force. In addition to overstated receivables and other incorrect figures, the audited balance sheet had shown $10,000,000 in inventory which was completely nonexistent! The responsibility of the public accounting profession quickly became apparent—the then-existing gaps in the typical audit examination must be filled. Any tendency to suggest that added procedures were impractical or beyond the capacity of the profession would result in a loss of confidence in the profession. The challenge was met when the American Institute of Certified Public Accountants issued the bulletin, *Extensions of Auditing Procedure.*

Although the additional responsibility recommended by this bulletin presented many problems to the profession, certain changes had occurred in business that somewhat simplified the problem of meeting peak manpower requirements. The natural business year was being adopted in a few instances, but even more important, the growth of internal control made it possible to do an increasing proportion of the audit work before the end of the year.

Furthermore, a gradual broadening of the scope of public accounting services provided some additional work for the increased staff during the off-peak periods.

Present-day objectives in the auditor's examination of the figures in the client's financial statements for cost of sales and inventories are:

1. Establish credibility of the accounting records.
2. Ascertain reasonableness of account balances.
3. Review cut-off of recorded transactions.
4. Establish the physical existence of the inventory and the reasonableness of inventory quantity figures determined by the client.
5. Determine that inventory items have been fairly valued in accordance with an acceptable method which has been consistently applied.
6. Determine that clerical operations (transcribing, extending, and footing) have been performed with sufficient accuracy.

A moment's reflection on the above objectives should suggest that each of the last three objectives relates to the client's physical inventory. The physical inventory is the means by which a client operating under the periodic inventory method determines the year-end inventory figure and calculates cost of sales. For the client operating under the perpetual inventory method, the physical inventory is the means of disclosing any adjustments which should be made to the perpetual inventory records in order that those records will clearly reflect the true inventory status for management and statement purposes. Because under either method the physical inventory has a direct bearing on the determination of financial position and results of operations, the reason for the auditor's preoccupation with the reliability of the physical inventory should be apparent.

In connection with the physical inventory, the A.I.C.P.A. bulletin *Extensions of Auditing Procedure** states:

> That hereafter, where the independent Certified Public Accountant intends to report over his signature on the financial statements of a concern in which inventories are a material factor, it should be generally accepted auditing procedure that, in addition to making auditing tests and checks of the inventory accounts and records, he shall, wherever practicable and reasonable, be present, either in person or by his representatives, at the inventory-taking and by suitable observation and inquiry satisfy himself as to the effectiveness of the methods of inventory-taking and as to the measure of reliance which may be placed upon the client's representations as to inventories and upon the records thereof. In this connection the independent Certified Public Accountant may require physical tests of inventories to be made under his observation.

The requirements of *Extensions* and the objectives that have been listed above apply with equal force to inventories at the beginning of the year

---

* Originally published as a separate pamphlet in 1939, *Extensions* is now incorporated in *Auditing Standards and Procedures*.

under examination. It should be recognized that a misstatement of the opening inventory will have just as much effect on the reported net income for the year as a misstatement of the closing inventory. In a repeat examination the auditor will, of course, have satisfied himself as to the reasonableness of the opening inventory in connection with his examination for the preceding year. But in a first examination he is expected to apply the same standards and objectives to both opening and closing inventories, except that, obviously, observation of the inventory is not "practicable and reasonable." Unless he can satisfy himself by alternative procedures that the opening inventory is fairly stated, the auditor will, in all likelihood, be obligated to qualify his opinion as to the fairness of the reported net income for the year because of the effect of a possible misstatement of the inventory at the beginning of the year. Under some conditions, the auditor may even conclude that he must refrain from expressing any over-all opinion on the income statement.

The typical audit procedures applicable to the accomplishment of the auditor's objectives in the examination of cost of sales and inventories are now discussed.

Establish Credibility of the Accounting Records

Tests of inventory purchase transactions have been covered previously; at this point we are concerned with audit procedures relative to inventory credits for the cost of materials placed into production and for the cost of goods sold.

Trace handling of representative transactions from origin to final account balances. Inventory credits arising from material requisitions and from sales transactions are treated in a similar fashion in the accounting system. For cost of sales, the basic document is a copy of the invoice or shipping order form on which the cost of each item sold has been noted based on standard cost sheets or on actual costs obtained from the stock ledger records. For inventory transfers for materials placed into production, the basic document is the material requisition, the quantity extended by actual or standard costs to obtain dollar amounts for general ledger entries. Final transfers to finished goods would be on the basis of cost accumulations for material, labor, and overhead.

Postings of credits to stock ledger records for quantities (and dollar amounts if actual costs are maintained) may occasionally be tested, but such a test of the subsidiary records is generally considered unnecessary. More important is the testing of dollar amounts shown by the records utilized in accumulating the amounts for general ledger entries for inventories and cost of sales. Invoices, showing cost of sales, and materials requisitions should be examined on a test basis in support of the accumulations, and unit cost figures should be traced to their source.

Totals of these supporting records may be proven by the auditor if internal control is weak, but a more important step is to trace the totals obtained to entries in the general ledger accounts affected by the transactions. Any entries to these accounts not originating in the records being tested should be fully investigated and should be tested if the amounts involved are material.

The auditor should note whether serially numbered material requisitions and invoices are used and whether the serial numbers have been accounted for, in order to gain assurance that all transactions are reflected in the records. Accounting for the serial numbers of such documents is important to the general accuracy of the accounting records and the usefulness of the records to management in controlling operations.

Entries under the retail inventory method. In the audit of department stores or other businesses using the retail inventory method, certain additional verification of control account entries is necessary. Because inventories and cost of sales are both priced according to percentages developed by statistical records of all purchases, the need for tests of these records should be apparent. Each invoice should bear the buyer's notation of the price at which the goods are to be sold. This price is multiplied by the quantity purchased to obtain the total selling price of the goods. The total cost of each purchase and the total selling price are then entered in the statistical record. The percentage developed from the totals of this record is used to figure the cost applicable to the total sales for a period and to reduce the retail value of the physical inventory to the approximate cost of the inventory.

The auditor's test verification should cover all steps through the calculation of the mark-on percentage and the application of this percentage to the sales for one or more selected months in deriving the cost of sales credit to inventory. Month-to-month variations in the mark-on percentage should be carefully investigated, as should variations of individual purchases from a normal range of this percentage. The auditor should extend his verification to include a visit to the marking room and the sales floor to satisfy himself that the selling price marked on the invoice is actually used in preparing the price tags placed on the merchandise. The auditor should also make tests of the details supporting mark-ups and mark-downs of the selling prices after goods have been entered in the statistical record. It should be noted that proper use of the retail method and the taking of mark-downs as needed place the inventory on a basis equivalent to the lower of cost or market.

Ascertain Reasonableness of Account Balances

Cost of sales figures should bear a close relationship to sales on a continuing basis. Working paper schedule 10 shows cost of sales related to sales in terms of gross margin percentage, which is the complement of the cost of sales ratio. The percentage is computed for each of the three product lines as well as for the company as a whole, and the percentages for both the current and the preceding year are compared. Changes in the percentages should be investigated and accounted for.

For instance, a decrease in the rate of gross or net margin for the current year as compared with preceding years is usually a danger signal. Investigation might show that selling prices had been declining in the latter part of the year—a situation which should suggest to the auditor that inventory pricing should be carefully scrutinized for any write-downs to market values which might be required. On the other hand, if the decreased margin percentage can be accounted for by rising material costs in the face of constant selling prices, the auditor will usually be justified in closing his investigation.

Assuming, however, that the auditor discovers no change in the relationship of cost and selling prices, he will have to look elsewhere for the cause of the decrease. The inventory cut-offs are probably the next area that would warrant investigation. Failure to adjust for merchandise charged to purchases but not received in time to be inventoried might prove to be the explanation. Another possibility would be an error in the cost of sales cut-off under the perpetual inventory plan. Goods may have been entered as cost of sales, although shipment and recording of the sale did not occur until the following period.

The cut-off of sales is still another area which might hold the answer to the decreased margin percentage. Further investigation of this cut-off might disclose that goods which had been shipped and reflected in cost of sales for the current period had not been taken into sales and receivables until the following period.

If neither price changes nor cut-off errors yield the explanation for the decreased rate of margin, the auditor may then turn his attention to the client's physical inventory figures. Under the periodic inventory method an understatement of the inventory would result in an overstatement of cost of sales and an understatement of gross margin. The possibility that some merchandise had been overlooked or that an error had been made in counting, pricing, extending, or totaling the inventory would then have to be considered. If this possibility is raised before the auditor has completed his work on the inventory, his tests can be extended and slanted toward disclosure of a possible understatement under the concept of relative risk. If the perpetual inventory method is followed, errors in the physical inventory will affect net income through the inventory variation account.

Changes in the application of generally accepted accounting principles, such as from Fifo to Lifo inventory valuation, must also be considered as a possible cause of a change in the relationship of cost of sales to sales. It is important that the auditor become aware of any such modification in inventory costing because the lack of consistency must be disclosed in the opinion paragraph of the auditor's report.

An accounting error could similarly cause a change in the cost of sales percentage. If investigation discloses such an error, an adjustment of the records would usually be in order.

The analysis on schedule 10 shows an increase in margin, which is explained as being the result of an increase in the selling prices of automated machines associated with the generally increased demand for such machinery. Related inventory expenses, such as standard cost variances, inventory shortages, mark-downs, and warehouse or stockroom expense, should also be reviewed in relation to the volume of inventory movement and in the light of any conditions known to exist. Schedule $\frac{C\text{-}1}{1}$ makes use of the relationship between the inventory shortage of raw materials and the amount of materials handled, and schedule C analyzes the relative changes of the three cost elements in work in process and finished goods. The auditor's permanent files on the engagement might well carry a chart or table summarizing such relationships over a period of years as a means of pointing up long-term trends. Inventory turnover is an especially useful figure for such a record.

Analysis and review of the relationship between two different figures permit each figure to reinforce the other. If the figures are developed independently, as in the case of sales and cost of sales or other expenses, continuation of a reasonably constant relationship between the figures provides a basis for concluding that the figures have not been distorted. Additional independent figures are sometimes available in the form of physical volume of inventory and physical movement. If only a limited number of raw materials and finished products are involved, as in a steel mill, a coal yard, or a carbonated beverage plant, records of physical quantities purchased and sold are usually maintained. By converting these quantities into dollar amounts at average prices, the auditor has a further check on sales, purchases, cost of sales, and ending inventory.

As a final test of the records, major accounts should be scanned for any unusual entries, which should be investigated to determine whether the charges or credits are appropriate to the accounts in which they have been entered.

Review Cut-off of Recorded Transactions

Inventory cut-off errors will affect net income, either through the cost of sales figure or through the inventory variation between book and physical inventory. Although the cut-off of purchases has already been discussed, additional comments are included below so that the discussion at this point will be complete concerning all aspects of inventory cut-offs.

PERIODIC METHOD

	Correct	$500 Purchase Recorded but Goods Not Included in Ending Inventory	$500 Included in Ending Inventory but Purchase Not Recorded
Sales	$15,000	$15,000	$15,000
Cost of sales			
Beginning inventory	$ 3,000	$ 3,000	$ 3,000
Purchases	10,000	10,000	9,500
Cost of goods available for sale	$13,000	$13,000	$12,500
Ending inventory	2,500	2,000	2,500
Cost of sales	10,500	11,000	10,000
Gross margin	$ 4,500	$ 4,000	$ 5,000

PERPETUAL METHOD

	Correct	$500 Purchase Recorded but Goods Not Included in Ending Inventory	$500 Included in Ending Inventory but Purchase Not Recorded
Sales	$15,000	$15,000	$15,000
Cost of sales and inventory variance			
Beginning inventory	$ 3,000	$ 3,000	$ 3,000
Purchases	10,000	10,000	9,500
Cost of goods available for sale	$13,000	$13,000	$12,500
Cost of sales (predetermined)	10,200	10,200	10,200
Gross margin	$ 4,800	$ 4,800	$ 4,800
Book inventory, end of period	$ 2,800	$ 2,800	$ 2,300
Physical inventory	2,500	2,000	2,500
Inventory variance	(300)*	(800)*	200†
Net margin	$ 4,500	$ 4,000	$ 5,000

* Shortage.
† Overage.

Purchases cut-off. A faulty purchases cut-off may act to affect the financial statements in either of two ways. If goods have been received and included in the physical inventory but the purchase has not been recorded, net income will be overstated, retained earnings will be overstated, and accounts payable will be understated. If goods for which the purchase has been recorded are not included in the physical inventory, net income will be understated, as will retained earnings and the inventory figure in the balance sheet. The over-all effects will be the same under either the perpetual or the periodic inventory method, but details within the income statement will vary. A cut-off error under the periodic inventory method will misstate cost of sales through a misstatement of either purchases or ending inventory. Under the perpetual inventory method errors affecting purchases or ending inventory will not affect the cost of goods sold figure, but will change the inventory variance figure. The simple examples shown on page 290 illustrate the effect of cut-off errors.

The reader should note that the cost of sales figure in the perpetual inventory method differs from the cost of sales shown in the "correct" column of the example illustrating the periodic method. The difference is explained by the fact that the periodic method offers no opportunity to determine whether goods which were available for sale and not on hand at the end of the period were lost or were actually sold. Therefore, the figure which is labeled "cost of sales" is actually a combined figure for both cost of sales and cost of merchandise which has not been accounted for. The resulting figure is far less informative than the figures developed under the perpetual inventory method.

Adjustments to correct the cut-off of purchases. Businesses seldom experience a clean cut-off of purchases in the normal course of operations at the year end. Instead, adjustments to both the book records and to the physical inventory are usually necessary to place the two on a common basis. The necessary adjustments may be readily determined if the accounting system reflects good internal control. In Chapter 9, mention was made of files for unmatched receiving reports, unmatched invoices, and prepaid invoices which have been paid before the goods have been received. The information provided by these files at the close of the year can be used in making needed adjustments to both book and physical inventory figures. Such use is illustrated below, based on the use of the perpetual inventory method.

	Accounts Payable	Inventory Per Books	Physical Inventory
Balance, December 31	$15,000	$32,000	$30,000
Add			
Unmatched receiving reports	2,000	2,000	
Prepaid invoices			1,000
		$34,000	$31,000

Deduct		
Inventory shortage		3,000
Adjusted physical inventory, as above		$31,000
Add		
Merchandise in transit (Unmatched invoices)	4,000	4,000
Adjusted figures for statement purposes......	$21,000	$35,000

Included in the merchandise in transit figure would be any invoices received after the balance sheet date if the invoices show that the merchandise had been shipped f.o.b. shipping point on or before the close of the year. If, however, the merchandise had been received and counted in the physical inventory, then the adjustment necessitated by the unmatched receiving report would be the only adjustment necessary.

Cost of sales cut-off. As discussed in the chapter on sales and receivables, the sales cut-off will affect net income, and therefore the recording of sales and receivables must be made in accordance with the date on which goods have been shipped. There is, however, no significant problem with respect to the recording of the corresponding entry for cost of sales. If the goods in question are on hand at the balance sheet date, they will be included in the physical inventory and therefore appear on the financial statements as an asset. If the goods have left the premises, they will not be included in the physical inventory, and because the goods are therefore not accounted for as being on hand, their cost will appear as a charge against revenues. Under the periodic inventory method, goods no longer on hand will appear as cost of sales, and income will be correctly stated if the sale has been recorded.

When the general ledger inventory records are kept on a perpetual basis, cost of sales is determined independently and is not merely a difference figure representing the goods available for sale which were not accounted for in inventory at the end of the year. Under this method costs are determined relative to each sale, and the inventory account is relieved of these costs. These costs are charged to cost of sales, and of course the entry for the cost figure should be made at the same time as the entry for the sale, even though the two entries are made independently. If a sale is recorded in one period but the cost of sales entry is not made until the following period, the result is obviously an understatement of cost of sales in the first period and an overstatement in the following period. Although this shift will affect gross margin percentages for each of the two periods, there will be no effect on net income if a physical inventory is taken at the end of the first period. The goods that have been sold and delivered will still be in the book inventory but will not appear in the physical inventory. Because the physical inventory represents the true asset figure, the book inventory must be adjusted downward. This adjustment will give rise to a debit to the account

"Inventory shortage," or "Inventory variance," which will offset the under-statement of the cost of sales figure. If this shortage figure is deducted immediately below the gross margin figure on the income statement, the resulting net margin figure will be correct. In the following period the cut-off error will cause an opposite reaction: cost of sales will be overstated, gross margin understated, and the inventory variance will show an inventory overage which will offset the understatement of gross margin.

Audit tests of the cost of sales cut-off. As stated above, there is no cost of sales cut-off problem with respect to records kept under the periodic inventory plan. When perpetual inventory controlling accounts are main-tained, the auditor should satisfy himself that the outward movement of merchandise and the recording of both the sale and the cost of the sale occur in the same period. The audit technique is dependent upon the date of shipment as shown by records prepared by the shipping department. This date should be compared with the date on which the transaction was included in the sales and cost of sales records. If either of the recording dates does not fall in the same fiscal period in which shipment was made, the need for a possible adjustment is indicated. If even a single cut-off error is noted, the auditor's tests should usually be expanded to determine whether other errors may have occurred. If the amounts disclosed by these tests are material, adjustment should be made. The reader should note, however, that a $1,000 error in the sales cut-off will be relatively more material than a $1,000 error in the cost of sales cut-off. The explanation for this apparent enigma is that the sales cut-off error will affect net income whereas the cost of sales error will not, because it will be offset by a com-pensating error in the inventory variance (assuming, of course, that the physical inventory count was made at the end of the year). This difference in materiality of the two types of cut-off errors also suggests that the auditor's tests of the cost of sales cut-off need not be as extensive as those of the sales cut-off.

Cut-off tests and relative risk. Relative risk is an important consideration in planning cut-off tests. If there is any reason why a client might wish to understate or overstate income, the auditor should ordinarily expand his tests and be particularly careful in reviewing those instances which would produce the desired result for the client. For instance, if it is known that a client plans to sell stock or bonds to raise additional capital, the auditor should recognize the possible existence of a desire on the part of the client to overstate income in order to improve the market for the securities. Conversely, a scheduled decrease in income tax rates for the following year would suggest the desirability of shifting income to the low-tax year by understating income for the current year. To disclose a possible understate-ment of income the auditor should watch for goods shipped in the current year but billed in the following year, or goods received in the following year but recorded as a purchase in the current year. Overstatement of income would result if the preceding situations were reversed.

Although only purchases and sales have been referred to in the discussion of cut-off errors, the reader should recognize that similar cut-off problems are involved concerning purchase returns, or concerning transfers from raw materials to work in process and from work in process to finished goods, as well as in transfers from central warehouse inventories to branch inventories.

REVIEW QUESTIONS

1. What are the minimum standards of disclosure and statement presentation proposed in this chapter with respect to cost of sales and inventories?
2. What are the auditor's objectives in substantiating the dollar amount of cost of sales and inventories to be shown in the financial statements?
3. How does the effect of errors in the cut-off of purchases vary as between the perpetual and the periodic inventory method?
4. How does the auditor verify the purchases cut-off?
5. Does securing a proper cost of sales cut-off under the periodic inventory method involve any problem?
6. What are the various causes which the auditor might find to be responsible for a change in the rate of gross margin realized by a client?
7. Is it correct to say that as a general rule the auditor verifies the client's inventory figure?
8. In tracing representative transactions from origin to final account balance, what documents would be examined in connection with credits to various inventory accounts?
9. Why, from the standpoint of the inventory records, is it important to account for the serial numbers of invoices and material requisitions?
10. Explain briefly how the independent auditor should test the client's records with respect to developing the mark-on percentage in a retail inventory system.

QUESTIONS ON APPLICATION OF AUDITING STANDARDS

11. The Mackey Company desires to value its inventories at the lower of cost or market but wishes to figure its cost of sales on a cost basis and to show market losses as a separate item on the income statement. Also, it wishes to have the balance sheet contain an inventory figure that agrees with the inventory figures used in the schedule of cost of goods sold.
    (a) How can the company's preferences be accomplished?
    (b) Suggest reasons for the company's preference for the determination of cost of sales.
    (c) What peculiar result would be produced in the income statement if an inventory market loss of $15,000 at the end of one year were followed by a loss of $10,000 at the end of the next year?
12. The Brandywine Company normally uses about 200,000 gallons of spirits per year as one of the basic ingredients in the product it manufactures, ordering

the spirits on a 10-day delivery basis. At December 31, the company had outstanding a firm purchase commitment for 50,000 gallons of spirits at a price of $1.00 per gallon. The company follows the recommendations of the A.I.C.P.A. Committee on Accounting Procedure in pricing its inventories.

(a) Assuming that the market price for spirits at December 31 is $1.10 per gallon, how should the purchase commitment be shown in the financial statements (if at all)? Justify your answer.

(b) How would your answer to part (a) be changed (if at all) if the market price were $.90 instead of $1.10 at the balance sheet date? Justify your answer.

(c) If the conditions under (b) prevailed, give the journal entry to record the purchase of the 50,000 gallons in the following year.

13. A recent income statement for a well-known department store listed the following item among its expenses: "Increase in reserve for possible future decline in market value of inventories." Discuss.

14. A balance sheet shows two inventory reserves; one is deducted from inventory, the other is shown as a part of the stockholders' equity.

(a) Give the probable reason for the creation of each reserve.

(b) State the manner in which each reserve should be disposed of when no longer needed.

(c) Is the title "reserve" in accordance with good terminology usage in each instance? Explain.

15. Should the auditor give an unqualified opinion on financial statements in which a large credit balance in the material price variance account has been taken to the income statement and inventories have been priced at standard cost? Explain.

16. "Breakdown of established procedures intended to accomplish maximum control over inventories under the retail method can result in an overstatement of the amount of inventory shortage but no corresponding misstatement of net income for the year." Explain.

17. Explain why the usual way of accounting for inventories under the retail method results in valuing the inventories at the lower of cost or market. What change would have to be made to cause the inventory to be valued at cost?

18. What would be the effect on a client's financial statements under the retail inventory method if at the beginning of the year a change was made from recording purchases at gross and showing an income from purchase discounts, to recording purchases net of discounts—but the statistical record used to develop cost-retail percentages was prepared as before, showing purchases at gross?

19. In the audit of a client who is following the retail inventory method, the auditor should make a month-to-month comparison of departmental mark-on percentages and review some of the larger individual purchases for abnormal mark-on percentages. If the auditor is concerned about a possible overstatement of inventories, should he watch for low and declining mark-on percentages or high and rising percentages? Explain.

20. For each of the following situations, indicate whether the stated facts would *overstate, understate,* or have *no effect* on net income for the year ended December 31. The client is on a perpetual inventory system; the physical inventory was taken December 31 and the book inventory adjusted to agree with the physical inventory without taking the following items into consideration:

(a) There was a file of unmatched receiving reports at December 31.

(b) The client accounts for purchase discounts using the method that shows "purchase discounts lost." The ending inventory was costed by using the prices shown on vendor invoices.

(c) No cost of sales entry was made for goods sold and shipped to a customer on December 31.

(d) Vendor invoices were on hand at December 31, but had not been recorded because the goods had not been received. The invoice terms were all f.o.b. shipping point.

(e) At the close of the preceding year, goods had been received but the entries to record the purchases were not made until the current year.

21. You are engaged in your first examination of a client's financial statements for the year ended December 31, 1967. The client has already made the necessary book entries to record the physical inventory at the end of the year. In the course of your test of cut-offs at the beginning and end of the year, you discover that—

   Invoices totaling $5,653.95 were entered in the voucher register in January, 1967, but the goods were received in December, 1966. The client did not consider these items in recording the physical inventory.

   Sales of $10,243.50, which cost $7,519.80, were made in December, 1967, and the goods shipped then, but the related book entries were not made until January, 1968. No consideration was given to this fact in recording the physical inventory.

   Give the adjusting entries that should be made in your working papers under the assumption that—

   (a) The general ledger inventory is maintained on a *perpetual* basis.

   (b) The general ledger inventory is maintained on a *periodic* basis.

22. Your client's fiscal year closes on December 31, but the physical inventory was taken at November 30 and the general ledger perpetual inventory account was adjusted downward at that date to bring it into agreement with the physical inventory amount. The client did not give any consideration at either November 30 or December 31 to unmatched receiving reports in the accounts payable department files. The total amounts were:

November 30	$3,269.20
December 31	3,892.15

   Give the adjusting entries, if any, that you would make in your working papers.

23. Your client has already adjusted the general ledger perpetual inventory account to agree with the physical inventory; the client's fiscal year ends December 31. In reviewing cost of sales entries for January, you discover an item costing $1,500 that was actually shipped in December. Give the adjusting entry and reversing entry (if any) you would make under each of the following assumptions:

   (a) The physical inventory was taken on November 30.

   (b) The physical inventory was taken on December 31.

   (Assume that the client's books have not yet been closed.)

24. Your client takes a physical inventory on *November 30,* adjusts the perpetual inventory control account for any shortage, and then uses the *December 31* balance of the inventory account in its financial statements for the year. It is thus necessary for you to make cut-off tests at both November 30 and December

31. In connection with the two purchases listed below covered by such cut-off tests, no adjustment had been made by the client.

Amount	Date	Invoice Terms F. O. B.	Date Goods Received	Date Invoice Entered in Voucher Register
$241.61	11/28	Shipping Point	12/3	11/29
163.95	12/27	Destination	12/30	1/2

Give the adjusting entries (if any) that you would make in your working papers, disregarding the question of materiality.

25. In your review of voucher register entries for unrecorded liabilities, you may find entries supported by vendors' invoices that are dated prior to the close of the year, but which would nevertheless not require an auditor's adjustment. Suggest as many different reasons or situations as possible that would make it unnecessary for an audit adjustment to be made.

26. Is there a difference in the materiality of cost of sales cut-off errors (perpetual inventory system) occurring at the date the physical inventory is taken, when the inventory is counted a month prior to the balance sheet date, as compared with when the inventory is counted at the balance sheet date? Justify your answer.

PROBLEMS

27. The following data all relate to inventory item No. 2468, which you are examining in connection with your examination of the financial statements of the Randolph Corporation as of November 30, 1967.

Average cost per unit	$1.00
Quantity on hand—	
per your audit test count after close of business November 15, 1967	250
per perpetual inventory record, close of business November 15, 1967	100
per perpetual inventory record, close of business November 30, 1967	250

Purchases	Purchase "A"	Purchase "B"
Invoice date	Nov. 10	Nov. 28
Received	Nov. 14	Nov. 29
Date of entry in		
Voucher register	Nov. 14	Dec. 3
Perpetual record	Nov. 16	Dec. 3
Quantity	200	300

Sales	Sale "C"	Sale "D"
Date shipped	Nov. 14	Nov. 28
Date of entry in General ledger (Cost of sales entry)	Nov. 14	Dec. 1
Perpetual record	Nov. 16	Nov. 29
Quantity	10	20

Concerning item No. 2468, and without regard to materiality, answer the following questions, supporting your answers with any pertinent calculations:

(a) What adjusting entry should be made for the indicated overage or shortage of item No. 2468?

(b) What adjusting entries, if any, affecting the inventory account should be made as of November 30, 1967?

28. You are engaged in an audit of The Wayne Mfg. Co. for the year ended December 31, 1967. To reduce the workload at year end the Company took its annual physical inventory under your observation on November 30, 1967. The Company's Inventory account, which includes raw material and work-in-process, is on a perpetual basis and the first-in, first-out method of pricing is used. There is no finished goods inventory. The Company's physical inventory revealed that the book inventory of $60,570 was understated by $3,000. To avoid distorting the interim financial statements the Company decided not to adjust the book inventory until year end except for obsolete inventory items.

Your audit revealed the following information regarding the November 30th inventory:

1. Pricing tests showed that the physical inventory was overpriced by $2,200.

2. Footing and extension errors resulted in a $150 understatement of the physical inventory.

3. Direct labor included in the physical inventory amounted to $10,000. Overhead was included at the rate of 200% of direct labor. You determined that the amount of direct labor was correct and the overhead rate was proper.

4. The physical inventory included obsolete materials recorded at $250. During December these obsolete materials were removed from the inventory account by a charge to Cost of Sales.

Your audit also disclosed the following information about the December 31st inventory:

1. Total debits to certain accounts during December are listed below:

	December
Purchases	$24,700
Direct labor	12,100
Manufacturing expense	25,200
Cost of sales	68,600

2. The cost of sales of $68,600 included direct labor of $13,800.

3. Normal scrap loss on established product lines is negligible. However, a special order started and completed during December had excessive scrap loss of $800 which was charged to Manufacturing Expense.

Required:

(a) Compute the correct amount of the physical inventory at November 30, 1967.

(b) Without prejudice to your solution to part "a," assume that the correct amount of the physical inventory at November 30, 1967 was $57,700. Compute the amount of the inventory at December 31, 1967.

(c) Compute the amount of the over- or underabsorbed overhead at December 31, 1967.   (Uniform C.P.A. Examination)

29. You have been engaged for the audit of the Y Company for the year ended December 31, 1967. The Y Company is engaged in the wholesale chemical business and makes all sales at 25% over cost.

Portions of the client's sales and purchases accounts for the calendar year 1967 are shown following:

Sales

Date	Reference	Amount	Date	Reference	Amount
12/31	Closing entry	$699,860	Balance forward		$658,320
			12/27	SI#965	5,195
			12/28	SI#966	19,270
			12/28	SI#967	1,302
			12/31	SI#969	5,841
			12/31	SI#970	7,922
			12/31	SI#971	2,010
		$699,860			$699,860

Purchases

Date	Reference	Amount	Date	Reference	Amount
Balance forward		$360,300	12/31	Closing entry	$385,346
12/28	RR#1059	3,100			
12/30	RR#1061	8,965			
12/31	RR#1062	4,861			
12/31	RR#1063	8,120			
		$385,346			$385,346

RR = Receiving report
SI = Sales invoice

You observed the physical inventory of goods in the warehouse on December 31, 1967 and were satisfied that it was properly taken.

When performing a sales and purchases cut-off test, you found that at December 31, 1967 the last receiving report which had been used was No. 1063 and that no shipments had been made on any sales invoices with numbers larger than No. 968. You also obtained the following additional information:

1. Included in the warehouse physical inventory at December 31, 1967 were chemicals which had been purchased and received on receiving report No. 1060 but for which an invoice was not received until 1968. Cost was $2,183.

2. In the warehouse at December 31, 1967 were goods which had been sold and paid for by the customer but which were not shipped out until 1968. They were all sold on sales invoice No. 965 and were not inventoried.

3. On the evening of December 31, 1967 there were two cars on the Y Company siding:
   (a) Car #AR38162 was unloaded on January 2, 1968, and received on receiving report No. 1063. The freight was paid by the vendor.
   (b) Car #BAE74123 was loaded and sealed on December 31, 1967, and was switched off the Company's siding on January 2, 1968. The sales price was $12,700 and the freight was paid by the customer. This order was sold on sales invoice No. 968.

4. Temporarily stranded at December 31, 1967 on a railroad siding were two cars of chemicals enroute to the Z Pulp and Paper Co. They were sold on sales invoice No. 966 and the terms were f.o.b. destination.

5. Enroute to the Y Co. on December 31, 1967 was a truckload of material which was received on receiving report No. 1064. The material was shipped F.O.B. destination and freight of $75 was paid by the Y Co. However, the freight was deducted from the purchase price of $975.

6. Included in the physical inventory were chemicals exposed to rain in transit and deemed unsalable. Their invoice cost was $1,250 and freight charges of $350 had been paid on the chemicals.

Required:
   (a) Compute the adjustments which should be made to the client's physical inventory at December 31, 1967.
   (b) Prepare the auditor's worksheet adjusting entries which are required as of December 31, 1967. (Uniform C.P.A. Examination)
30. The cost-of-goods-sold section of the income statement prepared by your client, Biltwell Bird Cage Co., for the year ended December 31, appears as follows:

Inventory, January 1	$ 3,215.80
Purchases	21,172.15
Cost of goods available for sale	$24,387.95
Inventory, December 31	4,321.80
Cost of goods sold	$20,066.15

Although the books have been closed, your working paper trial balance is prepared showing all accounts with activity during the year. This is the first year your firm has made an examination. The January 1 and December 31 inventories appearing above were determined by physical count of the goods on hand on those dates, and no reconciling items were considered. All purchases are f.o.b. shipping point.

In the course of your examination of the inventory cut-off, both at the beginning and end of the year, you discover the following facts:

Beginning of the Year

1. Invoices totaling $364.15 were entered in the voucher register in January, but the goods were received during December.
2. December invoices totaling $796.16 were entered in the voucher register in December, but goods were not received until January.

End of the Year

3. Sales of $564.20 (cost, $423.10) were made on account on December 31 and the goods delivered at that time, but all entries relating to the sales were made on January 2.
4. Invoices totaling $591.40 were entered in the voucher register in January, but the goods were received in December.
5. December invoices totaling $421.10 were entered in the voucher register in December, but the goods were not received until January.
6. Invoices totaling $1,215.40 were entered in the voucher register in January, and the goods were received in January, but the invoices were dated December.

Required (make corrections of prior years' income through the Retained Earnings Account):
   1. The adjusting entries to be made in your work papers assuming the company is on a periodic inventory basis.
   2. The adjusting entries to be made in your work papers assuming the company maintains the inventory control account on a perpetual basis. The book inventory figure at December 31 was $4,321.80, and the physical inventory agreed with that figure.

3. Corrected cost-of-goods-sold schedules under the assumptions in (1) and (2) above.

31. The Blank Corporation, which uses the conventional retail inventory method, wishes to change to the last-in, first-out retail method beginning with the accounting year ending December 31, 1967.

Amounts as shown by the firm's books are as follows:

	At Cost	At Retail
Inventory, January 1, 1967	$ 5,210	$ 15,000
Purchases in 1967	47,250	100,000
Mark-ups in 1967		7,000
Mark-downs in 1967		2,000
Sales in 1967		95,000

You are to assume that all mark-ups and mark-downs apply to 1967 purchases, and that it is appropriate to treat the entire inventory as a single department.

Required:

Compute the inventory at December 31, 1967 under:

(a) Conventional retail method.

(b) Last-in, first-out retail method, effecting the change in method as of January 1, 1967.   (Uniform C.P.A. Examination)

32. You are requested by a department store client to study the inventory shortage results as shown by the departmental retail inventory control book (generally referred to as "retail synopsis ledger"). After investigation you discover the following:

1. Merchandise was erroneously sold for $20 when it should have been sold for $23.

2. Certain salespeople recorded simply the net sales value for items sold to employees instead of showing gross sales price less employee's discount.

3. Some buyers were marking merchandise higher or lower than the original retail price indicated on the invoices without preparing price change reports.

4. There were other buyers who were putting through a "mark-up" on items which had been previously "marked down" for a special sale.

5. In the actual taking of the inventory you noticed that buyers distributed the inventory sheets, their salespeople counted and listed the items and the buyers collected the sheets and turned them into the controller's office the following day.

6. Items set aside in the department representing merchandise sold on "layaway" terms were listed on the inventory sheets by the salespeople.

Required:

(a) Explain briefly the principle of the retail inventory method as it pertains only to retail inventory control.

(b) Explain the application of this principle to each of the above situations, stating whether or not each of these would have any effect on the comparisons of book and physical inventory balances and, if so, in what way would such effect operate.   (Uniform C.P.A. Examination)

33. You are making an examination of the statements of the Modern Department Store at December 31. The following figures are presented to you at the time you commence your examination:

Book Inventory January 1:
  Cost $110,406.19
  Selling 154,305.91
Transactions for the Year:
  Purchases
    Cost 421,401.40
    Selling 604,367.18
  Sales 586,565.94
  Mark-ups (selling) 1,052.03
  Mark-downs (selling) 7,831.20
Physical inventory December 31 (selling) 162,325.87

In the course of your examination, you discover the following:

1. Mark-downs totaling $1,256.00 were shown on price tags, but not recorded on the books.
2. Merchandise with a sales value of $786.00 was out of the store on demonstration at the inventory date, and not included in the physical inventory.
3. The purchases figure includes invoices for merchandise costing $3,624.-98, but the merchandise had not been received. The invoices were dated December.
4. Merchandise with a sales value of $2,152.00 was counted in the inventory, but the invoices had not been received or recorded at December 31.
5. Invoices totaling $10,325.72 were on hand for merchandise shipped to your client in December, but the invoices were not recorded and the merchandise had not been received at December 31.
6. Merchandise totaling $2,376.52 was on hand and included in the inventory, but had already been sold and the sale was recorded in December.
7. All electric light bulbs are stocked on a consignment basis. The inventory of light bulbs totaled $1,271.90, and was included in the physical inventory.

Required:

1. Computations to arrive at the book inventory figure at cost and at selling price before considering items 1 to 7 above.
2. The inventory figure which should appear in your client's balance sheet, after considering items 1 to 7. (All goods are purchased f.o.b. shipping point.)
3. The income statement for the store through net margin on sales, in form ready for typing.
4. A statement as to how the auditor would likely have uncovered the information in items 1 to 7 above.

Auditing cost of sales
and inventories (concluded)

13

The physical inventory, taken once a year and sometimes oftener, is the basis for adjusting book inventory quantities and dollar amounts for the differences that are almost certain to creep into the records as a result of physical movements of stock that are not reported for proper accounting, or of errors in recording the transactions that are reported. The resulting adjustments are necessary to maintain the effectiveness of detailed records in controlling inventory quantities, as well as to produce statements that present fairly the financial position and the results of operations. It is the bearing of the physical inventory on the financial statements of a concern that prompts most businesses to take their annual physical inventory at the end of their fiscal year, or within a month or two before that date.

The annual taking of the physical inventory and the pricing, extending, and totaling of the resulting quantity figures is usually a costly and time-consuming process. The large number of detailed operations involved would present a practical impossibility if the auditor were to attempt to satisfy himself on the fairness of the final inventory figure by independently verify-ing an adequate proportion of the multitudinous individual operations. Instead of such a detailed approach to the verification of the physical inventory, the auditing profession has developed a more practical approach involving the two objectives of evaluation and compliance.

In terms of evaluation, the auditor carefully reviews beforehand the client's plans for the physical inventory. At this time the auditor makes any suggestions that appear reasonable for improving or strengthening the plans in order to provide maximum assurance that the final figures will be suffi-ciently reliable. Then, at all stages of the taking and computing of the inventory, the auditor makes sufficient tests to satisfy himself that the proposed plans have been carefully followed. If the auditor is satisfied as to both the planning and the execution of the inventory process, he can accept the final inventory figure with reasonable assurance that it is fairly stated.

Thus it may be said that the auditor does not attempt to verify the figure for inventory, but instead he establishes the fairness of the figure through reviewing the representations of management as to how the figure was derived. If the auditor's evaluation of management's plans for taking the inventory reveals deficiencies which are not corrected, or if the auditor's tests of compliance with the established plan reveal important deviations, then management's representations lose part of their validity. The auditor must counter this loss of validity either by extending his tests so as to obtain more direct verification of the inventory figure or by qualifying his certificate to show that he was not able to satisfy himself that the inventory is fairly stated.

The situation is closely related to the auditor's approach in establishing the validity of accounts receivable. In a small organization with little or no internal control, the auditor determines the validity of the receivables by mailing confirmation requests to practically every account in the receivables ledger. By contrast, in a large organization such as a public utility which has both an elaborate system of internal control and a satisfactory internal auditing program, the auditor may send negative confirmation requests covering as little as five per cent of the total dollar balances, or even less. The auditor here is relying primarily on management's representations as to accounts receivable, assuming that his appraisal of internal control and tests of compliance prove that management's representations can be relied upon. In this situation, the limited confirmation of receivables is undertaken not primarily as a proof of validity of the receivables but as a further indication of the effectiveness of internal control. This same approach applies to the examination of inventories, assuming that internal control is adequate.

The importance of the internal control element should be carefully noted in the following discussion of each of the three remaining objectives of the auditor's inventory examination. The objectives focus on the three principal steps which the client employs in arriving at a final inventory figure: counting the items on hand, valuing them, and computing their dollar total.

Establish the Physical Existence of the Inventory and the Reasonableness of Inventory Quantity Figures Determined by the Client

Establishing the physical existence of the goods underlying a client's inventory figure and ascertaining the reasonableness of the client's count of quantities are actually two separate objectives, but they are treated as one because they both deal with the physical stock of items on hand. As has been pointed out previously, these two objectives were made a part of generally accepted auditing standards as a direct result of the McKesson and Robbins investigation, so that if an auditor does not satisfy himself on these matters he must include a statement to that effect in his short-form audit report accompanying the statements.

The auditor is not expected to serve as stocktaker, nor must he verify all or most of the quantities determined by the client. Instead, the auditor's function is to observe the inventory-taking as a means of ascertaining the credibility of management's representations as to how inventory quantities were determined. There is no implication that an auditor is expected to assume the role of an appraiser or a materials expert. This point often creates an understandable doubt as to whether the auditor's additional procedures have any real value if the auditor admittedly is not an expert in materials.

The matter may perhaps be clarified by the use of two simple illustrations. In observing the inventory-taking at an oil refinery, for example, the auditor may be told that a storage tank contains crude oil. The auditor can readily ascertain that the tank actually does contain something and that the contents bear evidence of being something like crude oil, rather than water or some other less valuable liquid. The remaining problem then becomes one of determining the amount of basic sludge and water (B S & W) and the specific gravity of the oil, because its value is determined by this factor. The auditor should be sufficiently informed about the industry to know that this problem exists, but he need not know how to make the necessary tests and calculations to arrive at the final figure. He can be reasonably satisfied if he sees that the tests are made and reviews the calculations by which the final figure is determined.

The inventory of work in process in a manufacturing plant also presents problems, although the auditor's solution will necessarily involve different techniques than were suggested in the case of the crude oil. Again, the auditor may not be able to identify readily the basic raw material, except perhaps to know whether it is steel, brass, aluminum, or some other basic metal. Prices vary considerably, of course, according to the grade and specifications of the metal, so further identification is necessary. The necessary information may be shown on the inventory description of the item by the shop employee doing the counting. To substantiate this information, the auditor can refer to the engineering specifications for the part, the description of the material on the production order and inventory requisition, or possibly the standard cost sheets if a standard cost system is used. Because all these sources are independent of the production department, the auditor has an adequate basis for determining whether materials in process have been properly represented on the final inventory records.

Unless job cost records are maintained, the description of work in process must also show what operations have been performed on each lot of materials. Again, the auditor may be able to ascertain in a general way what operations have been completed by inspecting the parts but he will probably not be able to tell whether all operations of a related sequence have been performed, such as whether a hole which has been bored had also been reamed. He can further validate the listed inventory information, however, by asking a shop employee who is in the area or by referring to the production records. In summary, then, if the auditor is satisfied that good internal control has been incorporated into the inventory procedures, and if his tests show that the resulting inventory information is reliable, he has an adequate basis for judging the existence of the inventory and the fairness of the dollar total even though he is neither an appraiser nor a materials expert.

The problems and difficulties that can arise out of work in process inventories are clearly evident in the Drayer-Hanson investigation by the SEC, which is reported in *Accounting Series Releases Nos. 64* and *67*. Company oversight not detected by the auditor resulted in an $85,000 overstatement of a $244,000 work in process inventory.

Inventory Taken at the Balance Sheet Date

Most businesses, and particularly the smaller ones, take their physical inventory at the close of business on the balance sheet date. Operations may be halted early on that day to permit the counting of inventory on hand, or the count may be made the next day before operations are resumed. Although in many instances habit alone may account for taking inventory at the close of the year, there is often little choice in the matter. If a business maintains no perpetual inventory records, or if lack of internal control limits the reliability of the records which are maintained, the only way to obtain an inventory figure which will not distort financial position or operating results is to take the inventory at the statement date. The auditor's responsibility in connection with the inventory is to satisfy himself that it actually exists and that the quantities have been reasonably determined by the client. The procedures which the auditor employs in accomplishing these objectives fall under three main headings: evaluation, compliance, and verification.

Evaluation. Because the auditor accepts the final inventory figure largely on the basis of the client's representations, the auditor must decide in advance how reliable those representations are likely to be. If investigation shows any weaknesses in the client's proposed physical inventory procedures which are not corrected, the auditor will have to plan to expand his own work to compensate for the deficiencies. The major points which the auditor should watch for in evaluating the client's plans for taking the inventory are listed in the section of Chapter 11 dealing with internal control.

Ideally, the client should reduce all plans and instructions concerning the inventory to written form. By so doing there is less chance for misunderstandings to arise, and the added assurance that the instructions will be thoroughly understood is in itself an important element of internal control. The written instructions also simplify the auditor's task of evaluating the client's plans. If only oral instructions are issued, the auditor should discuss the inventory procedures with the various individuals involved. The purpose of such discussion should be to enable the auditor to determine how the inventory is to be taken and to ascertain whether the individuals involved understand what they are to do and how they are to do it.

Because the preliminary evaluation of the client's inventory plans is so important, the need should be apparent for the client to select the auditor and complete the audit arrangements well in advance of the close of the client's fiscal year.

Compliance. Although it is important that adequate internal control be incorporated into the client's plans for taking the physical inventory, it is equally important that the actual work be done exactly as planned. To establish the compliance of the client's employees with the inventory plans which the auditor has reviewed and approved, the auditor must be on hand during the actual inventory-counting process. The purpose of his presence is not, as is often supposed, to *take* the inventory, nor is it to *supervise* the taking of the inventory. Instead, the sole purpose is to permit the auditor to *observe* the work being done by the client's employees in order to satisfy himself that there is full compliance with the inventory instructions.

Among the things which the auditor should be particularly careful to watch for in this process of observation are:

1. Have production and movement of material been halted as planned, or if activity is not to be halted, have precautions been taken to assure that all items on hand will be counted once and only once?

2. Have the receiving and shipping rooms been cleared of materials, and if not, have the materials been either included or excluded from the count as required by the inventory instructions and the circumstances involved?

3. Are materials neatly stored or piled to permit accurate counts?

4. Are the employees actually attempting to obtain accurate counts? The auditor should especially note whether this is true of items which are difficult to count or must be measured, as a bolt of cloth, as employees may be tempted to make guesses in such instances.

5. If a blind second count is specified, are the employees actually making an independent second count? Sometimes access may be available to the figures for the first count, and these may be recorded without attempting to make a second count or to verify the first count. In one instance where most of the inventory was represented by neatly stacked cartons of merchandise, it was noted that the first-count crew would usually count the number

of cases up, across, and back in each stack and then figure the total by writing down the multiplication on one of the cartons. Some of the crews supposed to make independent second counts were observed merely copying down the totals arrived at by the first crew when the figuring had been done on one of the cartons.

6. Is counting actually being done in each of the areas in which goods are stored or are in process of manufacture? If count tags are left with the items counted until a given area or department has been fully counted, the auditor should note that, when the inventory supervisor authorizes the tags to be "pulled," he inspects the department to be sure that everything has been counted and that the counting has been done accurately and according to instructions.

7. Are first and second counts being compared as required and recounts made when discrepancies are noted?

8. Are all inventory tags or sheets being accounted for?

The over-all purpose of the above observations is to enable the auditor to satisfy himself that the supervision of the inventory work has been adequate and that all employees have appeared to understand their duties. In other words, the auditor should determine that all evidence points to the likelihood that an accurate inventory has been taken.

At times the auditor may not be able to be present to observe the taking of the physical inventory, as for instance if he is not engaged as auditor until after the close of the year. In such situations a vital link in the chain of verification procedures is missing, and the loss may be so important that the auditor will be unable to express an opinion on the fairness of the inventory figure. There is a possibility, however, that the auditor may be able to satisfy himself by alternative means. The auditor's approach under such circumstances will ordinarily be somewhat as follows. He should first review the inventory plans and instructions as he would under normal circumstances. Then, from inquiry of the persons who supervised the inventory-taking and did the actual counting, the auditor should attempt to determine whether a satisfactory inventory was taken. To corroborate the opinion he forms from these inquiries, the auditor should inspect the actual physical inventory records, being careful to note the presence of the initials of persons who did the work, evidence that recounts were made when necessary, and any other indications which would point to the validity and reliability of those records. Finally, the auditor should test the reliability of the physical inventory figures by tracing those figures to the perpetual inventory records to ascertain whether the perpetual records were adjusted when necessary. Then, taking current balances based on these adjusted figures, the auditor should verify the current balances by making test counts of a substantial portion of the inventory items. Such tests should be much more extensive than the tests discussed in the following section on verification. The usual tests for verification purposes are intended to provide a further basis for the auditor's conclusions based on the observation of the inventory-taking; but when the auditor was not present at the inventory date, the tests must be adequate to serve as a substitute for the usual observation. As a final check on his conclusions reached in this manner, the auditor should carefully investigate inventory variances and variations in gross margin. Even though such procedures may be adequate to enable the auditor to express a favorable opinion on the financial statements, the auditor would nevertheless be required to point out in the scope paragraph of his report that his examination was not made in accordance with generally accepted auditing standards with respect to the observation of the physical inventory, but that he was able to satisfy himself on the inventory figure by applying alternative procedures.

The above comments concerning alternative procedures are predicated on the existence of good internal control, including adequate perpetual inventory records. If these factors are not present, the auditor will ordinarily have no way satisfactorily to verify the balance sheet inventory figure at the later date, and he will be required to qualify his opinion. He will explain that as a result of being unable to carry out the customary auditing procedures, his opinion on the financial statements is exclusive of the inventory figure. Should inventories be a significant factor in the financial statements, the auditor may be forced to withhold any over-all expression of opinion on the statements.

Verification. In addition to his evaluation of the inventory plans and his observation of the inventory-taking to ascertain compliance with those plans, the auditor should make some independent verification tests of the inventory figures. These tests will ordinarily be performed in conjunction with the observation of the inventory-taking. The auditor should actually count some of the inventory items. If the client's count sheets or count tags are available, the auditor should compare his counts with those records as soon as possible so that any discrepancies can be investigated on the spot. If the auditor's counts reveal that the client's employees have been inaccurate in their work, the auditor may have to request that the entire inventory be recounted. Similar tests should then be made of the new figures to prove their reliability.

The auditor's test counts should ordinarily be recorded in his working papers, as on schedule C-5, with as much related information as possible recorded concerning each count. Such information usually includes the identifying stock number of the item, complete description of the item, its location, and the tag or sheet number on which the item was recorded by the employee who made the count. The working paper record is important for two reasons. First, it provides the means of verifying that the actual counts are reflected in the client's final inventory tabulation. In most instances the auditor will not be able to control the inventory records during the process of pricing and extending the figures. By tracing the counts recorded in his working papers to the counts shown in the completed inventory tabulation, the auditor gains assurance that no figures were changed during the period the records were not under his control. This assurance is limited, of course, if test counts have been made of only a small proportion of the inventory items. The auditor will make such limited counts, however, only when there is adequate internal control, and there will therefore be little likelihood that any of the count figures will have been altered. When internal control is weak, the auditor should endeavor to count most of the inventory items of high total value. Under these circumstances any effort by the client to change materially the inventory quantities will be readily apparent when the auditor traces his count figures into the final inventory tabulations. The auditor should also review the inventory tabulations for any major items which he has no record of having counted. These should be fully investigated, because they may well be fictitious items added by the client. Further protection against manipulation of inventory figures by the client can be gained by careful investigation of any variations in the rate of gross margin.

The second purpose in making a working paper record of the auditor's test counts is to provide evidence of the extent of the tests which were made. This information is particularly important in connection with the final review of the audit by the manager or principal in charge, as it will be one of the bases for determining whether the examination has been made in accordance with generally accepted auditing standards. To facilitate this type of over-all review, the auditor should summarize his tests in a form similar to that shown on schedule C-1. The summary should show the percentage of the total inventory test-counted by the auditor in terms of both the number of inventory items and the total dollar value of the inventory.

No generalization can be made as to how extensive the auditor's test counts should be. In a large business with good internal control and a homogeneous inventory composed of items of relatively small value, the auditor's tests will often cover as little as one per cent of the inventory. At the other extreme, in the case of a small business with little or no internal control and the bulk of the inventory value represented by only a few items, the auditor should count all the major inventory items and quite a few of the lesser ones. By concentrating on the major items, the auditor's tests may well cover ninety per cent or more of the total dollar value of the inventory while covering as little as fifty per cent or less of the total number of items represented in the inventory. Variations will also occur in the number of staff men assigned to the work on inventory quantities. If internal control is good, two or three men may be adequate to observe and test the counting of an inventory composed of several thousand items with a total value of several million dollars. The same number of men might be required to provide adequate coverage in the case of a small retail store or manufacturing plant if internal control is weak, even though the inventory may total only a few thousand dollars.

Physical existence. Closely associated with the problem of verifying that the inventory has been carefully and accurately taken is the problem of ascertaining in a general sense the basic existence of the inventory shown by the client's records and displayed in the financial statements. At the time when the auditor has physical contact with the inventory, he should attempt to satisfy himself in a general way that the inventory includes the types of items that he would expect the client to have in stock and that the quantities bear a reasonable relationship to the total dollar valuation of the inventory as shown by the accounting records. The conclusions to be reached by this procedure are necessarily tenuous, but the auditor should be able to detect gross discrepancies. A $10,000 inventory carried on the books at $100,000 should be quite apparent if a conscious attempt is made to match book figures and the volume of physical goods on hand.

As a further test of physical existence of the inventory, test counts may be supplemented by "eye tests" of additional items. These items would be sighted by the auditor, but rather than verify the accuracy of the count of the items, the auditor would merely attempt to determine in a general way that the quantity counted appeared to be present. Such eye tests would not necessarily disclose a discrepancy of 100 pieces out of a total of 1,000 (if such discrepancies are widespread, they should become apparent from the observation and test counts to establish the accuracy of the client's counts), but they would show whether the inventory item was present and in quantities not grossly out of line with the client's figures. The net result of such eye tests, which can be fairly extensive because they can be made quickly, would be substantially to increase the auditor's conviction of the physical existence of the inventory.

Inventory Taken at a Single Date Preceding or Following the Balance Sheet Date

Many businesses prefer to take inventory a month or two before the balance sheet date. The advantage of this arrangement is that the release of financial statements need not be delayed by the lengthy period usually required to investigate inventory-count differences and to complete the pricing, extending, and footing of the inventory. In the case of a well-known department store, however, at one time the fiscal year ended on December 31, but the physical inventory was not taken until the fifteenth of January. By that time stocks had been placed in a more orderly condition following the hectic Christmas rush, and January clearance sales had reduced the number of items in stock.

Evaluation and compliance. The problems and procedures are practically identical when the complete physical inventory is taken at one time, regardless of whether that event occurs on the last day of the fiscal year or at some date within a period of a month or two. Additional consideration must be given, however, to the adequacy of internal control. The auditor is forced to rely entirely on the records to reflect changes in inventory between the count date and the balance sheet date, and internal control is the principal basis for assessing the probable accuracy of these records. Careful evaluation and adequate compliance tests are therefore of utmost importance.

Provisions must be made for a clean cut-off at both the count date and the balance sheet date, and the auditor should ascertain that these provisions have been carried out. One other problem is added as a result of the time intervening between the date of the physical count and the date of the balance sheet. If a client's operations are such that inventory shortages cannot be avoided, as, for instance, in a department store, net income and the ending inventory will be overstated unless provision has been made for shortages arising after the book inventory has been adjusted to agree with the physical inventory at the count date. These comments are based on the presumption that although shortages cannot be eliminated, they can be kept under control and within reasonable limits. If excessive or erratic shortages have occurred, internal control must be presumed to be inadequate to warrant accepting book figures as evidence of inventory changes during the interim between the physical count and the balance sheet date.

Verification. The heavy reliance the auditor must place on the book records to reflect the actual movement of stock after the count date suggests the need for testing the record of transactions occurring between the count date and the balance sheet date. In formulating the audit program for these tests, the auditor may well consider the factor of relative risk. Should conditions suggest that the client might seek to increase net income for the year, an understatement of cost of sales entries during the period following the inventory count would accomplish that purpose. Under these circumstances the auditor's test comparisons between the record of goods shipped and the entries relieving inventory of the cost of those goods should emphasize tests from the shipping records to the book entries. The reverse would be true if an understatement of income were the more likely possibility. The auditor should then concentrate on the selection of specific cost of sales entries to be traced to the shipping records, as fictitious cost of sales entries not supported by actual shipments would thus be revealed.

The rate of gross margin realized from sales recorded between the inventory date and the close of the fiscal year provides another means of detecting any manipulation of the records. A rate in excess of that realized during the preceding portion of the year would suggest a possible understatement of cost of sales whereas a lower rate of gross margin would suggest the opposite possibility. If an unexplained variation exists, test comparisons between the records of sales and cost of sales would be in order.

The situation is somewhat different if the physical inventory is taken after the close of the year. To illustrate, the following example shows that an understatement of the recorded purchases during the intervening period could be used to conceal an inventory shortage and thus in turn to overstate net income.

	December 31	Purchases	January 15
Inventory control account	$34,400	$12,000	$46,400
Merchandise actually in stock	33,400	13,000	46,400

When the physical inventory is taken at January 15 and compared with the inventory balance per books, no shortage would be indicated. Unless the auditor detected the understatement of purchases, he would assume the $34,400 book inventory figure at December 31 to be correct and therefore properly used for statement purposes.

The above discussion emphasizes primarily the importance of tests designed to indicate to the auditor whether the book records accurately reflect the actual receipt and shipment of goods. Complete conformity of the book records with the facts is particularly important at cut-off dates, and tests should cover a short period before and after the date of the inventory count as well as a short period before and after the balance sheet date. As an over-all indication of the accuracy of the inventory figure at the balance sheet date, the auditor should determine whether any unusual changes have occurred in the inventory figure between the count date and the balance sheet date.

Other verification procedures to be followed when the physical inventory is not taken at the balance sheet date would be similar to those followed when the dates of the balance sheet and the physical inventory coincide.

Inventory Taken Piecemeal Throughout the Year

If an accurate inventory count is desired, it will usually be necessary to close down operations during the taking of the inventory. Businesses can avoid such disruptions, however, if internal control is adequate and the perpetual inventory records have been accurately maintained. Under such conditions it is possible to form an inventory team which will count inventory throughout the year, planning the work so that every item in stock is counted at least once during the year. As counts are made, they are reconciled with the perpetual inventory records, and the perpetual records are adjusted if a difference exists. The final inventory at the year end is then based on the adjusted perpetual records. This arrangement for taking the physical inventory obviously requires reasonably accurate perpetual inventory records. If any inventory items are highly susceptible to variances, those items should be counted as close to the balance sheet date as possible to minimize the number of variances that will occur between the count and the balance sheet date.

A slight variation of the above method of counting inventory continuously throughout the year is to count an inventory item whenever a new order is placed. Because stocks will then be near their lowest point, there will be fewer items to count, reducing the counting time and the possibility of error. Whether this method is followed or whether the continuous counts are made according to a predetermined schedule, the auditor's procedures will fall under the same three headings as when the entire inventory is taken at the balance sheet date, even though the actual procedures differ somewhat. The three headings are, of course, evaluation, compliance, and verification.

Evaluation. Regardless of whether the client takes the inventory at the year end or on a continuous basis throughout the year, the auditor must place considerable reliance on management's representations. He must therefore carefully evaluate management's plans and instructions for taking the inventory. In addition to watching for those provisions mentioned in connection with the year-end inventory, which are a prerequisite for any satisfactory inventory plan, the auditor should note that adequate consideration is to be given to the cut-off of the perpetual inventory record before a count figure is compared with the book balance. If goods have been received or issued but the posting of the transaction has not yet been made to the perpetual record, the count and book figures cannot be compared until they both are placed on an identical basis. For instance, assume that 100 units have been removed from stock and sold but that the sale has not yet been posted to the perpetual inventory record. Unless all the facts are taken into consideration, there will be an apparent shortage of 100 units. If the perpetual record is adjusted downward to agree with the number of items shown by the count, subsequent posting of the sale will further reduce the balance, and the record will show 100 fewer units than are actually owned. The error will remain in the record, of course, until another comparison of book and physical inventory is made. In the interim, statements prepared from the book figures will show inventory understated by the cost of the 100 items and net income understated by a similar amount.

In addition to being certain that the cut-off problem is given full consideration, the auditor should ascertain that the instructions require careful investigation of all major differences before book figures are adjusted to agree with the physical count made by the inventory team. Often such investigation will reveal that a cut-off discrepancy has been overlooked, that the items were miscounted, that items in a second location were not included in the count, or perhaps that the wrong items were counted. The importance of revealing and correcting any such errors should be obvious.

The client's year-end use of the perpetual inventory records must also be studied by the auditor. The cut-off of purchases and sales is again important, because the general ledger inventory controls will be adjusted to agree with the detailed perpetual inventory records. Before the two sets of records can be compared, both sets must reflect all transactions occurring prior to the end of the year, but no transactions occurring after that date. Once this point is established, the balances representing quantities on hand at the end of the year can be transcribed from the perpetual records to the inventory listing sheet. If dollar balances are maintained in the perpetual records, the balances can be listed on an adding machine to arrive at the final inventory figure. Errors made in this listing process are more readily detected if the inventory is broken down by subcontrols which can be balanced separately, but in the absence of such a possibility a second listing of the balances should provide adequate proof of accuracy.

Compliance. All the important steps discussed in the preceding section must be reviewed or observed by the auditor to ascertain that the client's plans and the features of internal control are actually in effect. Most important, of course, is the matter of whether the prescribed counts are being made as directed and whether all items will have been counted at least once in the year preceding the balance sheet date. On one or more occasions during the year the auditor should visit the client's premises, preferably unannounced, and accompany the inventory crew for the purpose of observing the manner in which the counting is being done. He should note such things as whether an effort is being made to obtain accurate counts, whether the cut-off is verified before the perpetual records are adjusted to agree with the physical count, and whether adequate investigation is made of any significant differences before the perpetual records are adjusted. In general, the auditor should be satisfied that the inventory crew understands its responsibilities and is attempting to carry them out in a satisfactory manner.

Verification. In connection with his observation of the work of the inventory-count crew, the auditor should make independent verification of some of their count figures. These test counts should be recorded in the auditor's working papers and traced to the client's perpetual inventory records. As a further verification of inventory quantities, the auditor should count, at a time near the balance sheet date, a few of the items which were counted by the inventory crew earlier in the year. Comparison of these counts with the perpetual inventory records should then be made to determine the accuracy with which these records have been maintained subsequent to their adjustment to agree with the physical counts. If substantial differences are disclosed by this step, the auditor may not be justified in accepting a final inventory figure based solely on the perpetual inventory records.

The auditor should also satisfy himself that all inventory items have been counted at least once during the year, with needed adjustments recorded on the inventory records at that time. The relative size of the individual adjustments should be noted, for a large number of material adjustments would place the reliability of the inventory records in a questionable light. Finally, tests should be made of the year-end listing of inventory quantities on the inventory listing sheets, or of the trial balance of dollar inventory amounts shown by the perpetual records, in order that the auditor may be satisfied that the figure used to adjust the general ledger inventory balance is fairly stated.

Inventories not in the Custody of the Client

When inventories are stored in public warehouses, shipped on consignment, or held by the vendor for the convenience of the client, the auditor should obtain written confirmation of those inventories directly from the custodians, in addition to inspecting such available evidence as warehouse certificates. This requirement is a further reflection of the strengthening of auditing standards that occurred after the McKesson and Robbins fraud. The A.I.C.P.A. bulletin *Extensions of Auditing Procedures* sets forth this requirement and states further that if the amount of inventories in the hands of others is a significant proportion of the client's assets, then supplemental inquiries should be made to satisfy the auditor of the *bona fides* of the situation.

The extent of the supplemental inquiries would, of course, vary according to the auditor's judgment as to the requirements of each situation. In some cases reference to a directory of bonded public warehouses would be sufficient supplementary verification of the existence of warehouses confirming inventories in their custody. Further verification would include reference to audited financial statements as evidence that a warehouse has been properly bonded or that a consignee or vendor holding inventory for the client is solvent. An actual visit to the premises on which the inventories are stored would offer maximum assurance that the situation had been properly represented to the auditor. In connection with such a visit the auditor should note that his client's inventory is properly segregated and identified. Test counts of a few of the items would also be in order, although these recommendations would obviously be inapplicable if fungible goods were involved.

Even when such verification has been made, the auditor should still inspect warehouse receipts, because the absence of such receipts usually indicates that the inventory has been pledged as collateral.

Determine that Inventory Items Have Been Fairly Valued in Accordance with an Acceptable Method Which Has Been Consistently Applied

The assignment of dollar values to the units of inventory determined by physical count is usually referred to as "pricing" the inventory. When an inventory is priced at the lower of cost or market, two distinct sets of prices are involved. The first figure to be determined will usually be the cost figure, and the auditor must satisfy himself that cost figures have been derived by some acceptable method which has been consistently applied. Should the client wish to change the method of costing, say from first-in, first-out, to last-in, first-out, the ending inventory should be priced on both bases. Then when the auditor qualifies his opinion because of the change in the method of costing, he can also set forth the actual dollar effect of the change on the financial statements. After the cost figures have been determined, consideration must be given to the substitution of market values if they are lower than cost.

As to the auditor's responsibility for inventory pricing, the reader should recall that the auditor is primarily concerned with establishing the reasonableness of the client's representations as to the final inventory figure and the manner in which it was determined. Thus the auditor's examination of inventory pricing will ordinarily be limited to a review of the client's methods, coupled with sufficient tests to assure the auditor that the methods represented by the client as being in use were actually used. Only when the auditor finds that there is insufficient basis for accepting the client's representations will he undertake to make an extensive verification of inventory pricing.

Cost. The auditor's first step, as might be expected, will ordinarily be to ascertain what method of determining cost has been used, that is, Fifo, Lifo, average, standard, retail inventory method, or net selling price, and whether purchases are recorded at full invoice cost or net of cash discount. If the method used in costing the current inventory differs from that used in costing the previous inventory, that significant fact should be noted so that it will not be overlooked when the certificate is prepared. Next, the client's completed inventory sheets should be reviewed and items selected for the pricing test as specified by the audit program. Full data on the items selected should be listed in the working papers, as illustrated in schedule C-5. Ordinarily an effort will be made to select items of high total value, thus giving maximum coverage with a minimum of items, but a representative group of items of lesser value should also be selected for verification. Depending on the internal control and the resulting reliability of the client's records, the stability of prices, the relative importance of the individual inventory items, and any other modifying factors, the pricing test may cover as little as one per cent of the total inventory value or as much as ninety per cent or even more.

To illustrate how the pricing verification of a test item selected as prescribed above might be handled, let us take a typical example and follow it through. Our client manufactures screw machine products and compiles costs on a job-order basis. Inventories are accounted for under the first-in, first-out plan. The following item has been recorded in the audit working papers for pricing verification after having been selected from the client's inventory sheets on a test basis:

Stock Number	Description	Quantity	Unit	Cost	Extension
418	1/4″ × 2″ alloy studs	13	Gross	$2.66	$ 34.58
		50	Gross	2.58	129.00

The first step in the verification process should be to ascertain whether the cost shown agrees with the cost information recorded in the client's perpetual inventory record of finished goods. Reference to this record reveals that the most recent lot of these studs to be completed was produced under Job Order 3416 for 50 gross at a cost of $2.58 per gross. The preceding lot completed was J.O. 3351 for 100 gross at a cost of $2.66 per gross. This information establishes the correctness of the inventory pricing to this point, but further verification of the cost figures must be made.

Because the two job lots represented in the ending inventory bear similar costs, and assuming that these costs are in line with the inventory record of costs on jobs completed earlier in the year, further verification of only one of the two jobs should be adequate. As job number 3416 was completed most recently and constitutes the bulk of the 63 gross on hand, selection of that job would be most logical.

The required records to complete the verification may be "pulled" by the auditor, but if the client is willing to have his employees do the work, the audit fee will be lessened thereby. Retracing the client's costing process, the first record to be consulted would be the job cost sheet for J.O. 3416, which appears on page 320.

The first point the auditor should note in reviewing the cost sheet is that the unit of count shown therein agrees with the unit of count on the inventory sheet. An inventory count shown as 63 each but priced at the cost per dozen or per gross will substantially overstate the final inventory value. On the other hand, an item counted in dozens or gross but priced at the cost for each item will have the opposite effect.

Each of the figures shown on the cost summary should be traced to supporting records in order to establish that final-inventory cost figures have been derived from properly maintained factual records. Stated in another way, the auditor's purpose is to ascertain that there is a complete set of connecting links beginning with payment for the goods or services used and ending with the final financial statement figure for inventory.

Materials. Requisition number 2953 may be inspected in support of the material cost, but because verification must go beyond the requisition, reference can be made directly to the perpetual inventory card, which should show the withdrawal of 120 10′ × ¼″ alloy rods. The following abstract of the perpetual inventory card shows that the withdrawal was correctly priced:

Date	Req. or P.O. No.	Price	Received	Issued	Balance
12/2		$.574			50
12/5	604A	.586	300		350
12/8	2940	.574		50	
		.586		50	250
12/15	2953	.586		120	130

Errors in pricing, particularly under first-in, first-out, can occur readily, however, and the auditor should be alert to such possibilities. For instance, in pricing and posting requisition 2940 the inventory clerk might easily overlook the fact that 50 units were still on hand at the old price of $.574. Had the entire issue of 100 been priced at the new figure of $.586, fifty of the units would have been overpriced $.012 each or a total of $.60. As a result, the raw material inventory would have been understated and the finished goods inventory overstated in the amount of $.60. Upon sale of the studs, net income resulting from the sale would be understated by the same amount. This error, in itself, would be insignificant, but as an indication that similar pricing errors might be present throughout the inventory it would achieve greater importance. If other tests showed similar errors, the auditor would have to conclude that the client's inventory pricing method had not been properly applied. Because such a conclusion would make the client's representations as to the pricing of inventory invalid, the auditor would have to consider the probable over-all effect of such errors on the final inventory figure. Should he conclude that inventory and net income might be materially distorted, he would have to request the client to recheck all inventory items for such errors and make an adjustment for the total amount disclosed. If the client declined to make the recheck and adjust the figures, the auditor would have to qualify his opinion with respect to the inventory figure in the financial statements.

Returning to the verification of the inventory pricing of the 63 gross of studs in the finished goods inventory, the final step in the verification of material costs should be to verify the price of $.586 by consulting the vendor's invoice covering the purchase of materials recorded on December 5, which included the 120 rods used in producing the finished studs. A separate section of the perpetual inventory card, not shown above, would contain a record of the purchase orders placed, giving the name of the vendor. With this infor-

JOB ORDER COST SHEET		JOB ORDER NO.
		3416

STOCK NUMBER	418	COST SUMMARY	
DESCRIPTION	1/4" x 2" alloy studs	MATERIAL	$ 70.32
		LABOR	27.30
		OVERHEAD (115% X $ 27.30)	31.39
QUANTITY ORDERED 50 gross	DATE 12/14	TOTAL	$ 129.01
QUANTITY COMPLETED 50 gross	DATE 12/18	UNIT COST PER gross	2.58

MATERIAL

DATE	REQUISITION NO.	QUANTITY	DESCRIPTION	UNIT COST	TOTAL COST
12/15	2953	120	10' x 1/4" alloy rods	$ .586	$ 70.32
			TOTAL MATERIAL		

LABOR

DATE	CLOCK NUMBER	HOURS	RATE PER HR.	TOTAL	DATE	CLOCK NUMBER	HOURS	RATE PER HR.	TOTAL
12/16	128	8	$ 2.38	$ 19.04					
12/17	128	2	2.38	4.76					
12/18	387	2	1.75	3.50					
							TOTAL LABOR		$ 27.30

Figure 13-1

mation the appropriate invoice can be located in the paid invoice file and the price verified against this externally created document.

The amount of work implied in the verification of this one item should suggest the practical need for accepting the client's representations on inventory pricing, rather than making a complete verification of inventory pricing. The few tests actually made are then solely for the purpose of establishing the reliability of the client's representations.

Labor. The cost sheet shows all the details necessary to permit verification of the labor cost charged to the job. Assuming that the payroll week ends on December 18, the individual time cards supporting both labor charges should be filed with the time cards for that week. The cards should show that each worker worked on job 3416 for the number of hours shown on the cost sheet. To complete the verification, cards showing rate per hour authorized for each of the two workers can be inspected in the payroll department. Proof of the extension of the hours and rate verified as suggested above can then be made.

Overhead. The overhead of $31.39 allocated to the production of the lot of 50 gross of studs represents the application of the plant overhead rate of 115 per cent to the labor cost of producing the studs. The auditor should, of course, verify this calculation. But more important is the verification of the manner in which the 115 per cent rate was computed. In most instances the rate is set at the beginning of the year based on past experience. The auditor should determine the reasonableness of such an estimate by relating total labor cost for the year to total factory overhead cost for the year, noting that no change has been made in the classification and treatment of the various factory overhead items. In most instances the actual burden rate so calculated will differ slightly from the predetermined rate used during the year. Inventory pricing of the individual items is seldom corrected for this difference. Instead, if the difference is not large, the corresponding over- or underapplied overhead expense is merely treated as a profit and loss item of the current year. Should the overhead variance be too significant to permit such a treatment, distortion of the financial statements can be avoided if the variance is "spread back" by a pro rata allocation to inventory and cost of sales, as illustrated on schedule C-7. It is not proper, however, to use this treatment if the variance represents idle capacity, for such "costs" should not be included in inventory.

Inventories priced at standard cost. Many businesses keep their records on a standard cost basis to obtain added operating information and to simplify the accounting process. Some minor variations in audit procedure are necessitated by such records, but no major problems should result. The auditor's first concern when standard costs are used will ordinarily be to ascertain the methods used by the client in establishing the standards, and then to review these findings in relation to the variances from standard produced by the year's operations. If the variances are not excessive and bear a reasonable relationship to previous experience, the auditor can be fairly certain that operations have progressed smoothly and that the standards reflect current prices and production techniques. A few tests of the records should bear out this conclusion.

Excessive variances point to an opposite conclusion. Large price variances indicate that the standards do not reflect current prices, and large use variances suggest production changes that have not been embodied in the standards being used. Because production changes are ordinarily made for the purpose of increasing efficiency, excessive usage variances will tend to be credit balances. To obtain a fairly stated inventory figure, large variances should be apportioned between inventory and cost of sales and treated as corrections of those figures in the financial statements. Usage variances resulting from inefficiency in the plant would be an exception to the above recommendation. Such variances reflect actual losses and should be taken to the income statement as period expenses. Any variances which are not excessive may be treated as income statement items, regardless of cause, as net income will not be materially affected.

Apart from the question of how to treat variances from standard, the auditor's problem is simply one of testing final inventory prices against the client's book of standard prices and rates, and testing a representative group of entries in which actual costs are converted to standard. The purpose of testing these entries is to show whether the standards being used are current and to ascertain whether variances are being correctly recorded.

To illustrate the latter procedure, two typical situations are described. The first relates to the test verification of an entry to record the purchase of raw materials at standard. An entry is first selected from the voucher register for the purchase of some item of raw materials which is known to be represented in the final inventory. The credit to vouchers payable should be the total invoice price, the debit to raw materials should be the standard cost of the purchased materials, and any difference between these figures should be shown as a debit or credit in the variance column. Inspection of the appropriate invoice should show that the vouchers payable credit agrees with the invoice cost of the materials. Reference to the standard cost rate book should show whether the raw materials debit was based on the appropriate standard cost. Any difference between actual and standard can then be computed and traced to the recorded variance. Any excessive variances should be noted in the working papers, because such variances indicate outmoded standards and a situation which the auditor must watch carefully.

Labor time variance has been selected for the second illustration of how the auditor verifies standard cost records. If employees are paid on a piecework basis, the piecework rate will usually be the standard labor cost figure. A variance will result only if an employee does not earn the guaranteed daily minimum pay. The foreman or supervisor will then prepare a labor ticket authorizing the payment to the employee of the amount of money necessary to bring the employee's earnings up to the guaranteed minimum. This amount is, of course, the labor time variance. The auditor should satisfy himself that the piecework rate on which the employee was paid agrees with the standard labor cost shown in the rate book used in pricing the inventory. The auditor should then calculate the variance between the worker's piecework earnings and his guaranteed daily minimum.

A standard labor hour plan is sometimes used instead of a piecework plan. Under such an arrangement, if the employee has produced at less than standard but has been guaranteed eight hours' pay, the auditor should verify the conversion of the pieces produced to standard labor hours, the calculation of the difference between guaranteed and standard hours, and the application of the agreed-upon hourly rates to that difference to determine the labor time variance.

Pricing verification of work-in-process inventories. Work-in-process inventories present no problem if the client is using a standard cost system. During his observation of the physical inventory count, the auditor should note that count tickets accurately list the parts or materials which are represented in each lot of work-in-process items selected for test. Because additional parts or materials may have to be added before the product is complete, failure to specify what items have already been added to the lot might result in the assumption that all necessary parts or materials were present, with inventory overstated as a result. Similarly, each operation which has been completed should be listed on the count ticket so that the final inventory figure will include only the cost of those operations.

When job costs are used, the materials which have been issued to each job can be ascertained much as was suggested above under standard cost procedure. The cost of labor which has been added to a job must, however, be accepted largely on the basis of the labor cost shown on the job cost summary, subject to verification of the year-end cut-off of these charges. The over-all reasonableness of the costs shown for each job in process can be tested by reviewing the total costs on the jobs when they are finally completed. If total costs are in line with costs on similar jobs completed at prior times, the presumption should be warranted that costs charged against uncompleted jobs at the balance sheet date are fairly stated.

Pricing verification under the retail inventory method. The pricing of inventories maintained under the retail method begins at the time that the client takes the physical inventory, and the auditor's inventory observation should be extended to include observation and test verification of the recording of retail prices on the inventory tags or sheets. The source of such figures for inventory purposes is, of course, price tags or other price marking of the merchandise on hand. Further tests of the system should be made by testing merchandise prices against the retail figure noted on purchase invoices and performing other tests of the system as discussed on p. 287.

Market. The following excerpts from the pronouncements of the American Institute of Certified Public Accountants summarize current thinking pertaining to the pricing of inventory at less than cost:

A departure from the cost basis of pricing the inventory is required when the utility of the goods is no longer as great as their cost. Where there is evidence that the utility of goods, in their disposal in the ordinary course of business, will be less than cost, whether due to physical deterioration, obsolescence, changes in price levels, or other causes, the difference should be recognized as a loss of the current period. This is generally accomplished by stating such goods at a lower level commonly designated as *market*.

The rule of *cost or market, whichever is lower* is intended to provide a means of measuring the residual usefulness of an inventory expenditure. The term *market* is therefore to be interpreted as indicating utility on the inventory date and may be thought of in terms of an equivalent expenditure which would have to be made in the ordinary course at that date to procure corresponding utility.*

In the light of these comments, if the auditor intends to assert that his client's financial statements have been prepared in accordance with generally accepted accounting principles, his verification of inventory pricing must go beyond the figures for inventory cost. Two problems are evident in this additional matter of reducing inventory to market value when utility has diminished. The first is the recognition of such a situation when it occurs, and the second is the determination of the market value figure to be used to reflect the decreased utility.

Ascertaining the existence of declines in market value. The problem of detecting decreased market values is one of the best illustrations of the fact that a competent audit must go well beyond the confines of the client's accounting department. Determining the existence of unrecorded obsolescence is an example. Certain industries operate under conditions of constant style or model changes, and knowledge that such a situation exists should place the auditor on his guard in watching for market declines. In other cases change takes place very slowly, but the auditor should always watch for products which have been dropped from the client's line of merchandise or are beginning to move very slowly. Careful review of perpetual inventory records will usually reveal such instances. Further investigation is warranted whenever the inventory quantity of an item becomes excessive in relation to recent withdrawals or sales. If such conditions become widespread in the client's business, they will also be evident in reduced inventory turnover calculated on an over-all basis. Constant or increasing inventory figures in the face of declining sales are almost a sure sign that an inventory problem exists.

The auditor must also be alert to evidence of obsolescence or physical

* *Accounting Research and Terminology Bulletins,* pp. 30–31.

deterioration during the period of observing the physical inventory count. Crushed boxes, broken pieces, scratched or oxidized metal surfaces, and dusty items stored in inaccessible locations are all signs that a write-down to market value may be in order.

Direct observation of existing conditions should always be supplemented by discussion with any employees or officials who should be acquainted with the condition of the inventory. These would include the supervisor of the stockroom, the purchasing and sales managers, the treasurer, and even the president.

Most of the officials just mentioned should also be able to supplement the auditor's knowledge of current market prices of both purchased materials and the concern's finished product. General conclusions about price levels must, however, be confirmed by test comparisons between current prices and those in effect six months or a year before.

Determining market price. If the auditor's inquiry and observation have shown that the reduction of inventory items to market value is a problem, the auditor's next step is to determine whether the client has properly computed and used the reductions to market value. The total inventory should be figured both at cost and at the lower of cost or market. By computing both totals the client can separate the effect of inventory write-downs from the inventory variance resulting from other causes. Such information gives the client better control and enables the auditor to obtain a clearer picture of what has actually occurred.

The bulletin on inventory pricing released in 1947 by the Committee on Accounting Procedure of the American Institute of Certified Public Accountants* pointed up certain shortcomings in the generally accepted method of determining market price at that time and presented a method for determining market price which was more equitable and precise. Prior to the issuance of that bulletin, "market" was generally taken to be current replacement cost by either purchase or reproduction. Although the committee agreed with such a basis in general, it added two important exceptions to the use of replacement cost. The exceptions were not original with the committee, but they were seldom observed by accountants and auditors in their work.

One exception dealt with the situation wherein decreasing sales prices for a product were not accompanied by corresponding price decreases in the market in which the product or raw materials for its manufacture were purchased. Under the old basis of valuing inventory at replacement cost, an inventory item might be carried at a figure little changed from its original cost, although sale of the item to a customer might return less than that amount after considering costs of making the sale. The result, of course,

* Now included as Chapter 4 in *Accounting Research and Terminology Bulletins,* American Institute of Certified Public Accountants.

would be to carry inventory at a figure which would include an unrealized loss. Such a situation violates the general rule that all losses should be provided for, and accordingly fails to recognize the reduction in the residual usefulness of the inventory item. Although replacement costs seldom move downward at a slower rate than selling prices, such a condition occurs occasionally, and the Committee on Accounting Procedure recommended that the exceptional situation be provided for by adding a stipulation to the general use of replacement cost. It was recommended that inventory be valued at net realizable value should that figure be less than replacement cost. Net realizable value was defined as estimated sales value less any costs of completion or disposal.

The second exception to the use of replacement cost also deals with an abnormal situation. Occasionally replacement costs may fall while sales prices remain constant or fall at a slower rate. Under such circumstances use of replacement cost results in the recognition of a loss in one period and the production of an abnormally large profit in the following period when the sale occurs. To avoid such shifting of profits between periods the committee recommended that inventory not be reduced to a price lower than net realizable value less the normal margin of profit.

Testing reductions of inventory to market value. The auditor must, of course, ascertain that market prices used to value inventory below its original cost have been properly determined by the client. The auditor's first step should be to determine current replacement cost for those items which he selects for test. (The test should include some items which the client has continued to carry at original cost.) Information on current replacement cost may be obtained from many possible sources, although ordinarily only one best source will be used in connection with any single item.

For materials traded on organized commodity exchanges, market quotations at the close of business on the balance sheet date are obviously the best indication of current replacement costs. For other materials, current price lists issued by principal suppliers should be consulted if available. When price lists are not available, the cost of the latest purchase of the inventory item may be used if the elapsed time from the date of purchase to the balance sheet date is not too great, and if price changes during the intervening period would tend to be insignificant. In the absence of a recent purchase and any other information, written requests to one or more vendors for current price quotations may be in order. Ordinarily the auditor need not be concerned about net realizable value and normal profit margins, but these figures also must be verified on a test basis when abnormal price movements have occurred.

Proper handling of mark-downs under the retail inventory method will automatically reduce inventory to the lower of cost or market. Merchandise should be reviewed to ascertain that all price changes have been noted on the price tags, and mark-downs taken subsequent to the balance sheet date should be reviewed for price changes that may actually apply to the year being examined. Sale advertisements appearing after the balance sheet date should also be reviewed in relation to the pricing of the merchandise at the balance sheet date.

The considerations pertaining to the use of market price in valuing inventory apply also to firm purchase commitments not protected by firm sales contracts. Losses on such commitments should be recognized just as if the goods were actually on hand. The account credited when such losses are recognized may be classified as a current liability. As has been previously stated, the total amount of purchase commitments should be disclosed by a balance sheet footnote if the commitments are abnormal.

Determine that Clerical Operations Have Been Performed with Sufficient Accuracy

The last objective to be discussed in connection with the auditor's verification of inventory is the final link in the chain of verification that begins with the physical quantities of goods in the inventory and ends with the final dollar total shown in the client's financial statements. The objective deals with the verification of the relatively mechanical processes involved in arriving at the final dollar figure for inventories: transcribing, extending, and footing.

Transcribing. If the physical counts are recorded on count sheets that provide space for pricing and extending dollar amounts, no transcribing of count figures is required. In most instances, however, individual count tickets for each inventory item will be used in order to facilitate the counting process. Another advantage of using tickets is that they may be sorted by department, by class of material, or in sequence according to the stock or part number of each item, thus making it easier to price the inventory. Once the sorting has been accomplished, the information from the tickets can be copied onto the final inventory sheets.

It is this copying process which the auditor must test, because he must be satisfied that the count tickets which he observed being prepared were actually the source of the information shown on the count sheets and that the transcribing of information from tag to sheet was accurately performed. Perhaps the first test to be made by the auditor should be the comparison of the counts recorded in his working papers with the corresponding information shown on the inventory sheets. Needless to say, no differences should be found in making this test. If differences do occur, careful investigation is essential, and satisfactory explanations must be obtained. For instance, the explanation that an additional quantity of an item was found in another location and added to the original count should be fully investigated by the auditor. The auditor should visit both the original and the new locations, count the quantities then on hand, and reconcile them with the quantities represented as being on hand at the count date.

In addition to tracing his own counts to the inventory sheets, the auditor should test some of the actual count tickets against the information recorded on the sheets. If a large inventory is involved and internal control is satisfactory, a test of as few as 100 items selected at random may be adequate. Statistical techniques can be helpful in determining sample size and interpreting the results of such tests. If the conditions underlying the preparation of the inventory sheets are not ideal, the need for more extensive tests should be evident. Very weak internal control and the existence of inventory items of substantial value might easily warrant tests covering ninety per cent or more of the total dollar value of the inventory.

Extensions and footings. Auditors often employ comptometer operators to verify extensions and footings on the inventory sheets in order to obtain maximum coverage at minimum expense. On the other hand, some businesses employ outside concerns to foot and extend their inventory. In such cases the auditor may accept a statement from the computing concern asserting that the work had been done and guaranteeing its accuracy. Only very limited tests by the auditor would then be necessary.

The usual situation, however, finds the auditor making the tests himself, the tests ranging all the way from statistically sound minimum samples to almost 100 per cent verification, depending on the circumstances. As the coverage increases in scope, the auditor in effect assumes additional personal responsibility for the accuracy of the final inventory figure. To keep the cost of such verification at a minimum, the auditor will usually concentrate on the inventory items of largest value so that by verifying as few as fifty per cent of the inventory items, he may often be able to verify as much as ninety per cent of the dollar value. Such selection protects the auditor against the possibility of overlooking a material overstatement of inventory. The auditor must also testify as to the over-all accuracy of the client's records, however, and as a consequence inventory items of lesser value must also be included in the auditor's sample.

The concentration on items of larger value suggests that the auditor is principally concerned with the possible overstatement of inventory. Even though the relative risk in most situations tends to point toward that possibility, the conditions are sometimes reversed. If relative risk suggests that the inventory may be understated, a more extensive sampling of items of lesser value is in order, particularly if such items involve a large count quantity or a high unit price.

As a supplement to the precise verification of extensions or page totals, auditors often use the technique of "scanning" to increase their protection against material misstatement of the inventory resulting from calculation errors. Inventory extensions can be scanned quite rapidly for obvious errors in calculation or misplaced decimal points. Similarly, items comprising a page total can be quickly scanned to ascertain that the total appears correct to the nearest hundred or thousand dollars.

If each inventory page is separately totaled and then the totals are recapped, the auditor will usually make a 100 per cent verification of the recapitulation of the page totals. Occasionally, however, an inventory may involve a thousand or more pages, and in such cases the inventory will usually be broken down by department. The auditor may then satisfy himself by selecting at random several departmental inventories and proving the recapitulation of page totals for those departments for his test. Of course all departmental totals should be traced to the final, over-all inventory recapitulation, which should be footed by the auditor.

If the final inventory sheets have been prepared by punched-card equipment or by computer, the tests of extensions and footings can be held to a minimum, or eliminated entirely if the auditor can test or control the actual machine operations.

SUMMARY

Internal control

Duties which ideally should be performed by different individuals—
Receiving
Storing
Manufacturing
Shipping
Stock ledger entries
General ledger entries
Physical inventory-taking

Statement presentation

Cost of sales should not be netted against sales.
Inventory expenses such as shortages, mark-downs, and standard cost variances may be combined with cost of sales in published financial statements.
The basis of valuing inventories and the method of determining cost should be stated.
When inventories are valued at cost, market value should be shown parenthetically, and vice versa.
The effect of any change in method of valuing inventories should be disclosed, and will necessitate qualification of the auditor's certificate.

Liens against the inventories must be disclosed.

Classes of inventory should be shown, if material.

Material or abnormal purchase commitments should be disclosed and any losses on such commitments should be recognized.

Inventory price declines that may occur after the balance sheet date should be provided for only by appropriating retained income.

Audit objectives and procedures

Establish credibility of the accounting records.

Trace handling of representative transactions, from origin to final account balances.

Ascertain reasonableness of account balances.

Account for changes in percentage relationship of cost of sales to sales.

Compute inventory turnover and account for changes.

Relate inventory expenses such as shortages, mark-downs, or standard cost variances to volume of goods handled, and account for unusual entries.

Review cut-off of recorded transactions.

Test entry date against date of receipt or shipment of goods for transactions occurring near end of fiscal year or date of physical inventory.

Establish physical existence of inventory and reasonableness of inventory quantities.

Evaluate the client's inventory-taking instructions.

Observe the taking of the inventory for compliance with instructions and to establish existence of the inventory.

Make test counts of inventory items, tracing them to completed inventory records.

Confirm inventories not stored on client's premises and make such supplemental inquiries as may be necessary.

Determine that inventory items have been fairly valued in accordance with an acceptable method of costing consistently applied.

Test cost figures against supporting records such as perpetual inventory records, vendors' invoices, job cost sheets, or standard cost rate books.

Ascertain the existence of any declines in market value under lower-of-cost-or-market pricing.

Determine that clerical operations have been performed with sufficient accuracy.

Test transcribing of count information from count cards to inventory sheets.

Test extensions, footings, and final recapitulation of the inventory.

REVIEW QUESTIONS

1. Summarize briefly the manner in which the auditor satisfies himself as to the physical existence of the inventory and inventory quantities.
2. Why should the auditor record his test counts of inventory quantities in the working papers?
3. How is the problem of cut-offs changed when inventories are counted continuously during the year rather than all at the end of the year?
4. What additional problems are created if the physical inventory is taken prior to the balance sheet date rather than at the balance sheet date?
5. What should the auditor do if part of a client's inventory is stored in a public warehouse?
6. When a client decides to change the method of costing inventory, why should the closing inventory in the year of change be costed under both the old and the new bases?
7. List the various records and supporting documents which might be examined in support of the pricing of an inventory item manufactured under a job cost system.
8. How should the auditor verify the pricing of materials when standard cost records are used?
9. When the utility of goods in inventory has decreased, how is the utility measured at the balance sheet date?
10. How can perpetual inventory records be used in ascertaining that a decline in market value may have occurred?
11. What sources may the auditor use to obtain information about the current replacement cost of inventory items?
12. In making tests of clerical accuracy, why does the auditor concentrate on items of a high dollar value?

QUESTIONS ON APPLICATION OF AUDITING STANDARDS

13. Quality Department Store uses the retail inventory method in maintaining its general ledger records on a perpetual basis and carrying inventories on the basis of cost or market, whichever is lower. Explain why the failure of a department to report mark-ups (increases in the selling prices recorded on merchandise price tags) would overstate the ending inventory at cost (after adjustment for shortage), but understate the amount of inventory shortage by an even larger amount.
14. Suggest the various steps that should be taken by an auditor in order to ascertain whether any inventory items should be written down to market value.
15. During the last two months of your client's fiscal year the sales price of the principal product has been declining, but raw material and manufacturing costs have remained relatively constant.
    (a) Is it likely that an inventory write-down will be necessary? Why?
    (b) What figures would you need in order to determine the amount of any necessary write-down?
16. Your client operates a smelter and uses large quantities of ore in the operation. The ore is unloaded from gondola cars and placed in large piles by means

of a conveyor system. Perpetual inventory records are maintained showing the amount of ore placed in each pile and the withdrawals from the pile. Withdrawals are made from one pile at a time, and the pile is exhausted before any withdrawals are made from another pile. How will you satisfy yourself as to the client's inventory quantity of ore, assuming surveys are not feasible?

17. Suggest possible causes for an excess of applied factory overhead over the amount of factory expenses for the year and also for the reverse situation. For each cause indicate how the variance should be shown in the financial statements.

18. Inventories at your client's 100 branch stores are taken by store employees who call the quantity of each item on hand and its retail price into a microphone, and the information is then recorded on magnetic tape. The department number is called onto the tape at the beginning of each section of the inventory, but no other descriptive information is recorded. At the home office, the tapes are played back to calculator operators who make the necessary extensions, accumulating the extensions in the calculator and recording the totals obtained for each department. The department figures at retail are subsequently reduced to cost through the application of normal retail inventory techniques. Prepare a memo covering the work performed by you and your assistants in satisfying yourself as to inventory quantities, prices, and extensions through the point at which the inventory figures are recorded by the calculating machine operators.

19. Explain why a company's job cost records lose some of their value as evidence to the independent auditor if the records are not tied in with the general ledger, and why they will still retain some usefulness in spite of this limitation.

20. In attempting to verify the inventory cost of an item at $1.00, you locate the most recent purchase invoice, with terms of 2/10, n/30. Explain why a chart of accounts should be consulted before you can ascertain whether the item has been correctly priced.

21. You are supervising the regular examination of financial statements of the Stratford Corp. and have assigned your assistant to examine purchase invoices in support of the client's inventory pricing. When part way through with the assignment the assistant asks you what he should do about an invoice that he wishes to see that has been removed to the company's relatively inaccessible transfer file storage area in connection with the company's regular policy of transferring such records after they have become a year old. How would you reply, and what question would you also ask the assistant?

22. C.O.D. merchandise is normally released to the carrier on one day, and the collections are not received until one or two days later. A company may record such sales upon release of the merchandise to the carrier and set up a C.O.D. receivable, or it may simply make a memo of goods released, and record the sale when the cash is received.

   (a) What bearing, if any, would information as to a client's procedures on C.O.D. sales have on your examination of the entry and supporting details recording the physical inventory?

   (b) Which of the two C.O.D. methods would you recommend that a client use? Why?

23. If both accounts receivable and inventory are subject to approximately the same degree of internal control, would the confirmation of accounts receivable and test counts of inventory quantities be likely to be equally extensive? Explain.

24. Your client's physical inventory shows 134 gadgets on hand which have been priced at $15.45. The invoice for the latest purchase of gadgets covers the purchase of 40 at a price of $15.45. Inventory is costed on a first-in, first-out basis.

(a) Would you consider the above invoice to be adequate evidence that the inventory of gadgets had been correctly priced in a period of rising prices? Explain.

(b) In a period of falling prices, what information would be needed in addition to the latest purchase invoice to properly price the inventory at the lower of cost or market in accordance with the recommendations of the American Institute of Certified Public Accountants?

PROBLEMS

25. The president of Rab Co., your client, asks for your assistance because he believes a former employee has stolen a large quantity of finished goods. The employee, who disappeared on May 1, 1968, was the production manager and had access to all production and inventory records. The president requires the information to file a claim with the insurance company.

The Rab Co. manufactures two types of kitchen chairs, All Steel and Open Seat. The legs and frames of the chairs are made of $\frac{7}{8}''$ metal tubing which is purchased in both random mill lengths and precut 72" lengths. Each chair has four 24" legs. The All Steel chair frame is made from a 72" length of tubing; the Open Seat chair frame requires a 36" length of tubing. The scrap loss in cutting random mill lengths has averaged 3%. Other fabrication losses are negligible.

Under your observation a physical inventory is taken promptly and, by applying cut-off techniques, you determine the following physical inventory at May 1, 1968. Other chair components are not subject to verification. Your audit working papers for the 1967 audit reveal the inventory quantities at December 31, 1967.

Raw materials:	5/1/68	12/31/67
72" lengths of tubing	8,500	13,500
Random mill lengths	34,800 feet	9,800 feet
Work-in-process:		
Individual legs	9,700	2,900
All Steel chair frames	800	1,300
Open Seat chair frames	100	300
Finished goods:		
All Steel chairs	5,500	10,700
Open Seat chairs	1,300	900

Your examination reveals metal tubing purchases during 1968 amounted to 202,000 pieces of 72" lengths and 125,000 feet of random mill lengths.

You determine that 100,000 chairs were shipped to customers during 1968. Of this number, 10,000 were Open Seat chairs selling for $3.75 each. The All Steel chair sells for $5.00 each. Your audit work papers show that Rab Co. has generally added 25% to its manufacturing cost to arrive at selling prices.

Required:

For insurance claim purposes, compute the amount of the dollar loss sustained by Rab Co., assuming that the types of chairs missing were in the same ratio as the sales.   (Uniform C.P.A. Examination)

26. The Paris Company manufactures and sells four products, the inventories of which are priced at cost or market, whichever is lower. A normal profit margin rate of 30% is usually maintained on each of the four products.

The following information was compiled as of December 31.

Product	Original Cost	Cost to Replace	Estimated Cost to Dispose	"Normal" Selling Price*	Expected Selling Price
A	$35.00	$42.00	$15.00	$70.00	$ 80.00
B	47.50	45.00	20.50	95.00	95.00
C	17.50	15.00	5.00	35.00	30.00
D	45.00	46.00	26.00	90.00	100.00

* "Normal" selling price = original cost ÷ (100% − the normal 50% gross margin rate).

Required:

(a) Why are expected selling prices important in the application of the lower-of-cost-or-market rule?

(b) Prepare a schedule containing unit values (including "floor" and "ceiling") for determining the lower of cost or market on an individual product basis. The last column of the schedule should contain for each product the unit value for the purpose of inventory valuation resulting from the application of the lower-of-cost-or-market rule.

(c) What effects, if any, do the expected selling prices have on the valuation of products A, B, C, and D by the lower-of-cost-or-market rule?

(Uniform C.P.A. Examination)

27. The following figures are from work papers covering a December 31 examination. The inventory is priced on a first-in, first-out basis.

Item	Per Inventory Quantity	Price	Total	Per Invoices Examined Invoice Date	Quantity	Price
A	150	$1.40	$210.00	12/15	300	$1.50
B	2,000	.28	560.00	12/20	500	.28
C	104	.75	78.00	5/17	300	.75
D	2,980	.25	745.00	2/5	3,000	.25

State whether you would question the inventory price used by the client, the auditor's verification, or both, under the following circumstances (give reasons):

(a) Material prices have been rising steadily.

(b) Material prices have been declining but sales prices have remained steady.

(c) Material prices and sales prices have been declining.

28. Your client, the Big Essex Agency, sells new and used cars and has a service department. At audit date, April 30, the used car inventory consisted of four cars.

	1	Used Car Number 2	3	4
Allowed on trade-in	$1,700	$2,400	$1,000	$1,400
Overallowance (1)......................	300	300	200	200
Service Department charges for work on car (2)	60	—	40	160
National Auto Dealers Association estimate of market value (at retail)				
At time of trade-in	1,600	2,200	875	1,200
At audit date....................	1,550	2,200	850	1,150
Probable sale price if sold during May (3)	1,600	2,150	825	1,300

(1) During the year, new cars were being sold at less than list where no trade-in was involved. The amounts in this line represent the discount that would have been allowed on the new car sold had that new car been sold for cash with no trade-in.

(2) The service department makes necessary repairs on used cars taken in trades and bills the used car department at cost plus a $33^{1}/_{3}$ per cent markup. The amounts in this line are the bills from the service department.

(3) With the exception of cars 2 and 4, which are still on hand, the used cars were sold for cash during the first week of May, at the amounts shown on this line.

Discuss the various factors which should be considered in assigning a value to the inventory of used cars. Indicate the computations needed to arrive at an acceptable inventory value for each car as at April 30.

(Uniform C.P.A. Examination)

29. Under your guidance as of January 1, 1965 the Little Corner Sporting Goods Store installed the retail method of accounting for its merchandise inventory.

When you undertook the preparation of the Store's financial statements at June 30, 1965, the following data were available:

	Cost	Selling Price
Inventory, January 1...........................	$26,900	$ 40,000
Markdowns		10,500
Markups....................................		19,500
Markdown cancellations		6,500
Markup cancellations		4,500
Purchases	86,200	111,800
Sales		122,000
Purchase returns and allowances	1,500	1,800
Sales returns and allowances..................		6,000

Required:

(a) Prepare a schedule to compute the Little Corner Sporting Goods Store's June 30, 1965 inventory under the retail method of accounting for inventories. The inventory is to be valued at cost under the Lifo method.

(b) Without prejudice to your solution to part "a," assume that you computed the June 30, 1965 inventory to be $44,100 at retail and the ratio of cost to retail to be 80%. The general price level has increased from 100 at January 1, 1965 to 105 at June 30, 1965.

Prepare a schedule to compute the June 30, 1965 inventory at the June 30 price level under the dollar-value LIFO method.

(Uniform C.P.A. Examination)

30. In connection with the annual examination of financial statements of the Super Power TV Co. as of December 31, you are assigned to the verification of the accounts related to production costs, cost of sales, and finished goods inventory. The company assembles TV chassis from parts which it purchases from various suppliers. There is no sub-assembly work, and all chassis assemblies started each day are finished the same day. Since there is no work in process inventory, production costs are charged directly to Finished Goods Inventory, and the cost of chassis sold during each month is credited to this account.

Production is scheduled in lots of 500, and memorandum records are kept on the costs of each lot. All entries for production costs and cost of sales (which are figured on a FIFO basis) are made to Finished Goods Inventory by means of monthly standard journal vouchers. The numbers of these journal vouchers are as follows:

J 1	Parts and materials used
J 4	Payroll distribution (direct labor)
J 5	Overhead applied to production
J 8	Cost of sales

By questioning various company officials and analyzing available records, you are able to acquire the following information concerning the current year's operations:

1. At considerable cost to the company, a new automated assembly line was installed during July. The new line reduced the amount of direct labor required, and reduced material costs also, through the use of printed circuits.

2. The new line was installed during the first two weeks of July, when the plant and shipping room were shut down for vacation. (Vacations were taken on a staggered basis last year, and the plant was not shut down.)

3. Over-all cost reductions resulting from the new line were passed on to customers through reduced selling prices, resulting in a definite improvement in sales.

4. Overhead was applied to production during the first half of the year at the same rate of 123 per cent of direct labor cost which was used last year. The rate was refigured to give effect to the decreased labor costs and increased overhead resulting from the new automated production set-up, and 140 per cent was used for the remainder of the year.

5. During the year, 11,927 chassis were produced and 12,062 were recorded as sales.

Your working papers for other phases of your examination reveal the following information:

1. The individual items of overhead expense were in line with last year except for increased depreciation and certain indirect labor costs associated with the installation of the new assembly line. Actual overhead expenses, as shown by your analysis and the general ledger control account, were $493,523.41.

2. Your observation of the physical inventory taken at December 31 revealed 255 completed chassis on hand in the finished goods storage area, and 158

chassis in the shipping room, packed and ready for shipment. The last production order completed for 500 units showed average costs of $96.17 per unit, based on the new 140 per cent overhead rate. This figure is to be used in pricing the inventory of completed sets, subject to any adjustments you might recommend.

3. Your verification of the cut-off of sales and cost of sales showed that the 158 chassis packed for shipment were included in sales and cost of sales for the year. The billing price of these chassis to customers was $155.00 each.

Your working papers for last year reveal the following information:

	No. of Chassis	Average per unit	Total Dollars
Inventory January 1	364	$97.52	$ 35,497.28
Charges for production			
Material		22.47	237,521.72
Labor	10,571	33.93	358,689.76
Overhead (123% of labor)		41.74	441,188.40
	10,935	98.12	$1,072,897.16
Credits for Cost of Sales	10,518	97.94	1,030,183.12
	417		$ 42,714.04
Adjustments for Inventory Shortage	12		2,999.74
Inventory December 31	405	98.06*	$ 39,714.30
Adjustment for unapplied overhead			1,125.72
Inventory December 31, per balance sheet	405	100.84	$ 40,840.02

* Average cost, last lot of 500 chassis completed.

Adjustment for Unapplied Overhead

Actual overhead expense	$ 470,812.58	
Overhead applied at 123% rate	441,188.40	
Unapplied overhead	$ 29,624.18	

		% of Total
Total cost of sales	$1,030,183.12	
Less beginning inventory	35,497.28	
Current production in cost of sales	$ 994,685.84	96.2
Ending inventory	39,714.30	3.8
Total current production cost accounted for	$1,034,400.14	100.0
Distribution of unapplied overhead to—		
Cost of sales	$ 28,498.46	96.2
Inventory	1,125.72	3.8
	$ 29,624.18	100.0

Cost of sales, last year, by months—

Jan.	$ 96,952.30
Feb.	95,920.56
Mar.	99,047.54
Apr.	93,857.07
May	82,507.87
June	64,999.95
July	61,968.20

Aug.	71,158.67
Sept.	82,476.13
Oct.	89,761.83
Nov.	94,920.54
Dec.	96,612.46
	$1,030,183.12
Adjustment for underabsorbed overhead	28,498.46
Final cost of sales, last year	$1,058,681.58

The Finished Goods Inventory account for the current year is given below.

Finished Goods Inventory

Date	Description	Ref.	Debit	Credit	Balance
Jan. 1					$40,840.02
31		J1–1	$22,156.39		
		J4–1	33,926.47		
		J5–1	41,729.56		
		J8–1		$ 95,001.52	43,650.92
Feb. 28		J1–2	21,516.96		
		J4–2	33,076.81		
		J5–2	40,684.48		
		J8–2		96,160.07	42,769.10
Mar. 31		J1–3	22,095.48		
		J4–3	33,729.63		
		J5–3	41,487.44		
		J8–3		104,296.96	35,811.69
Apr. 30		J1–4	21,716.98		
		J4–4	33,229.86		
		J5–4	40,872.73		
		J8–4		106,587.07	25,044.19
May 31		J4–5	34,761.14		
		J1–5	22,823.41		
		J5–5	42,756.20		
		J8–5		97,318.63	28,066.31
June 30		J1–6	21,783.17		
		J8–6		77,623.19˙	
		J4–6	33,288.48		
		J5–6	40,944.83		46,459.60
July 31		J1–7	10,274.33		
		J4–7	15,325.71		
		J5–7	21,455.99		
		J8–7		42,866.54	50,649.09
Aug. 31		J1–8	20,614.82		
		J4–8	30,486.90		
		J5–8	42,681.66		
		J8–8		86,891.63	57,540.84
Sept. 30		J1–9	22,234.65		
		J4–9	32,204.88		
		J5–9	45,086.83		
		J8–9		99,635.74	57,431.46
Oct. 31		J1–10	23,427.28		
		J4–10	33,718.92		
		J5–10	47,206.49		
		J8–10		107,745.62	54,038.53

Date	Description	Ref.	Debit	Credit	Balance
Nov. 30		J1–11	24,118.49		
		J4–11	34,684.57		
		J5–11	48,558.40		
		J8–11		117,696.95	43,703.04
Dec. 31		J1–12	25,515.37		
		J4–12	36,583.76		
		J5–12	51,217.26		
		J8–12		129,758.18	27,261.25

From the information given, prepare your working papers covering production costs and cost of sales for the current year, and prepare any adjusting or reclassification entries that are necessary.

31. The complete audit program for the verification of the raw materials inventory of the Madison Manufacturing Co. is given below. In addition, certain data are given covering company figures and audit work which has already been completed.

Using the information given, you are to prepare the final work sheet covering the verification of inventory, showing the results of your examination of inventory items not yet verified, and including the totals carried forward from work sheets previously completed. If no further information is given concerning any point in the audit program, assume the work was completed and no exceptions were found.

Also, prepare a summary showing the extent and results of all inventory work which was performed.

1. Observe taking of physical inventory by client on December 31, noting that all procedures covered by client's printed instructions are followed.
2. Make independent counts of about 2 per cent of the inventory items, and record in our work papers for tracing to the final inventory sheets. Select items of substantial value.
3. Select 25 material requisitions and 25 purchase transactions from the last 3 days of current period and the first 3 days of following period, for examination of cut-off on raw materials.
4. Verify pricing, which is on an average cost basis, on all items counted by us, on all other items with a value of $500 or more, and in addition select two other items from each page of the client's inventory. Verify by examining average cost shown by perpetual inventory records, and noting cost per unit on most recent purchase. For every third item selected for price test, examine the vendor's invoice in support of the most recent purchase. If most recent purchase is below previous average cost, investigate reason for difference and make note in our papers if it appears the item should be priced at market rather than cost.
5. Discuss price situation generally with purchasing manager as to raw materials and with sales manager as to finished product, to ascertain whether any general write-down of inventory costs may be necessary.
6. Careful watch should be maintained for obsolete or unusable parts.
7. Check clerical accuracy by verifying extensions and footings of every third inventory sheet. Scan other sheets for extension or footing errors.
8. Prepare entry to adjust book inventory to agree with physical inventory. Ignore errors disclosed by our examination unless they are material.

Information concerning work done or to be done:

Items selected for pricing test from last three pages of the inventory—

Part No.	Quantity	Cost	Total
2204	162	$4.39	$ 711.18
2210	1,864	.13	242.32
2213a	415	1.19	493.85
2213b	764	1.13	863.32
2220	13 doz.	2.34	30.42
2234	265	3.82	1,012.30
2241	549	.98	538.02
2246	175	2.14	374.50
2249	318	1.83	581.94
2264	65	.39	25.35
2277	204	.81	165.24

(Above part numbers which were counted during physical inventory—2213b, 2234.)

Average costs on above items as shown by perpetual inventory records (costs are per unit of one unless otherwise indicated)—

2204	$4.39		2241	$ .98
2210	.13		2246	2.14
2213a	1.19		2249	1.83
2213b	1.13		2264	.39
2220	2.34		2277	.81
2234	3.82			

Data from vendors' invoices covering items to be traced thereto—

Part No.	Voucher No.	Date	Quantity	Price
2213a	14891	12/13	300	$1.19
2234	14906	12/15	500	3.84
2249	12246	9/17	1,000(a)	1.80

(a) These items were bought at a special close-out price—regular price from new supplier will be $1.95.

Totals of worksheets covering remainder of the inventory:

	No. of Items	Dollar Value
Items selected for price test	118	$41,964.92
Items tested to vendors' invoices	39	14,251.83
Items test counted included in above figures	33	18,249.51
Differences disclosed—		
Inventory overstated		1,321.15
Inventory understated		926.57

Other data—		
Raw materials inventory	Last Year	This Year
Per books	$67,964.84	$87,465.19
Per physical		
Dollar value	60,364.29	78,216.45
No. of items	1,529	1,603
Raw materials used	$694,205.46	$851,319.82
Results of test of clerical accuracy		
Total dollar value of pages verified		$ 24,816.92
Errors disclosed by above test		
Inventory overstated		433.41
Inventory understated		926.53
Errors disclosed by scanning		
Inventory overstated		521.19

Cash systems; internal control

14

Practically all business transactions sooner or later involve the receipt or disbursement of cash. The systems problem of handling the resulting high volume of transactions is compounded by the fact that the attractiveness of cash is likely to snap the resistance of any person whose moral fiber has even the slightest flaw.

Objectives of Internal Control

The system of internal control over cash and cash transactions should provide assurance that:

1. Advance planning is adequate to anticipate and provide for cash needs that exceed cash available from normal operations, and to utilize cash available in excess of anticipated needs.

2. Independent accountability is established for all cash that is collected.

3. Disbursements are made only for authorized purposes by a limited number of designated persons.

4. A record is created of every disbursement that is made.

5. Cash balances are adequately protected from theft or misappropriation.

The cash budget, or cash forecast, is the obvious means of controlling the amount of cash available for the purposes of the business. Proper accounting for cash transactions and balances is highly dependent on the use of bank accounts for all but petty cash transactions. The chart shown in Fig. 14–1 illustrates how cash receipts may be controlled by proper division of the various responsibilities involved, and presented in Fig. 14–2 is a similar chart pertaining to the control of cash disbursements. The various activities portrayed on these charts are described under the departmental headings that are given. Cash receipts are discussed first.

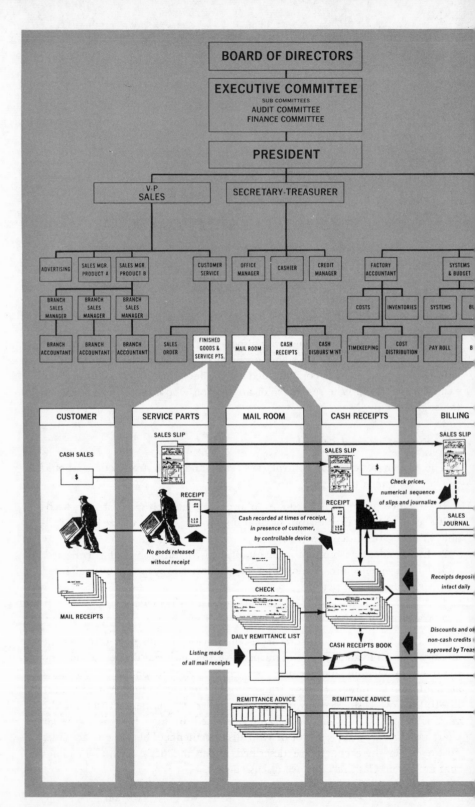

Figure 14-1

342

CASH RECEIPTS

PROCEDURAL FLOW CHART SHOWN IN RELATION
TO ORGANIZATION CHART TO PORTRAY
THE CONTROL OBTAINED THROUGH SEGREGATION
OF FUNCTIONAL RESPONSIBILITY

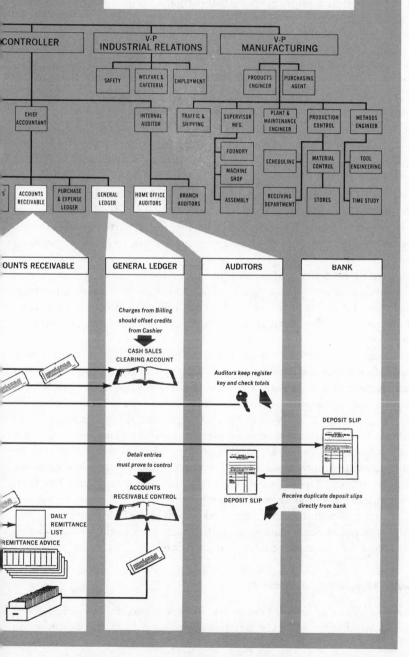

Figure 14-1 (Continued)   343

Mailroom. Most sales activity occurs on a credit basis, with subsequent payment for the purchases made by check mailed to the vendor. The secretary or mailroom employees who first handle incoming mail can usually identify remittances without opening the envelopes, and these should be separated from orders, correspondence, or other items. The internal control chart indicates that a list of the remittances should be made in the mailroom to establish control over the checks received, but such a list should be unnecessary if most of the checks are accompanied by remittance advices, which will usually be the voucher half of a voucher check. If no remittance advice is enclosed, the amount of the check can be noted on the envelope in which the check was received, thus providing a record comparable to a remittance advice, as the remitter's name and address will usually be printed on the envelope.

The check amount should be compared with the amount shown on the remittance advice to be certain that the two agree. Control over subsequent handling of the checks is then established by sending the remittance advices to the accounts receivable section for posting and the checks to the cashier for deposit. The amount deposited, plus any cash discounts, should then equal the credits posted to the accounts receivable ledger and to the general ledger control account. A person in the accounting department who has no responsibility for handling cash should compare the total of a receipted deposit ticket with the total receipts entered in the cash receipts journal for the day. (The reader should recall that entries to the cash receipts journal may be made as a separate operation, as a by-product of the detailed posting of cash receipts credits to the accounts receivable records on an accounting machine, or from the remittance cards prepared under a punched-card system.)

The procedures that have been described produce effective control over the cash after it leaves the mailroom, but adequacy of control over mailroom employees may well be questioned. First of all, *someone* must handle both the checks and remittance advices, for they arrive together, thus seemingly making it possible for a check to be abstracted and the remittance advice destroyed. Two controls are actually present, however. The first is the fact that the checks will be made payable to the company and hence will be difficult to convert into cash. Second, control exists through the accounts receivable records. The absence of a credit for a payment that has been abstracted will cause the account to become delinquent. The collection follow-up which would then be instituted would reveal that payment had actually been made, and examination of the paid check in the customer's files would reveal the full story of what had happened.

Accounts Receivable Department

The application of credits to accounts receivable records has already been described in Chapter 7. If credit terms allow cash discounts, however, an additional step should be taken before credits are posted to the receivables records: each remittance advice should be compared with the date of the corresponding sales entry in order to ascertain whether payment was made within the specified discount period. Also, the amount of discount taken should be verified in order to determine that the amount deducted by the customer is correct.

Cashier

The cashier merely reviews checks for date (postdated checks cannot be deposited) and payee, lists them on a deposit ticket, endorses the checks, and makes the deposit at the bank. A receipted copy of the deposit ticket should be sent by the bank directly to the accounting department representative who compares the day's posting total with the amount of the deposit.

To maintain proper internal control, no person with accounting responsibilities should handle cash, and conversely, people who handle cash should have no responsibility for accounting records—in fact, they should not even have access to accounting records. Unless such access is denied, the possibility exists that a collection from a customer could be withheld and concealed by posting a fictitious credit to the customer's account, or even by removing the ledger page and destroying it.

Cash sales

The internal control chart Figure 14-1, portrays an excellent form of control over receipts from cash sales in that the sale is first recorded on the cash register, and evidence of such recording in the form of a cash register receipt is necessary to obtain release of the goods. More commonly, however, the same person will make the sale, handle the cash, and initiate the accounting record. There is thus little assurance that all sales will be recorded. In some instances, additional personnel can be brought into the handling of the sale transaction to increase internal control. A few department stores use the "cashier-wrapper" system, in which the salesperson brings the customer's merchandise and cash to a central desk, where another person or persons record the sale, make change, and wrap the merchandise. Under such an arrangement, any attempt to withhold proceeds of a cash sale would necessitate either an easily detected violation of established procedures, or collusion, but an important question is whether the added protection is warranted in view of the increased expense that it entails.

The most common way of controlling over-the-counter sales is by means of cash registers operated directly by the clerk making the sale. Through "locked-in" totals, these machines establish control over all transactions recorded in the machine. Any or all of three separate devices are used to assure that sales will be recorded in the correct amount and that no sales will be omitted. One is the familiar bell which signals that a sale has been

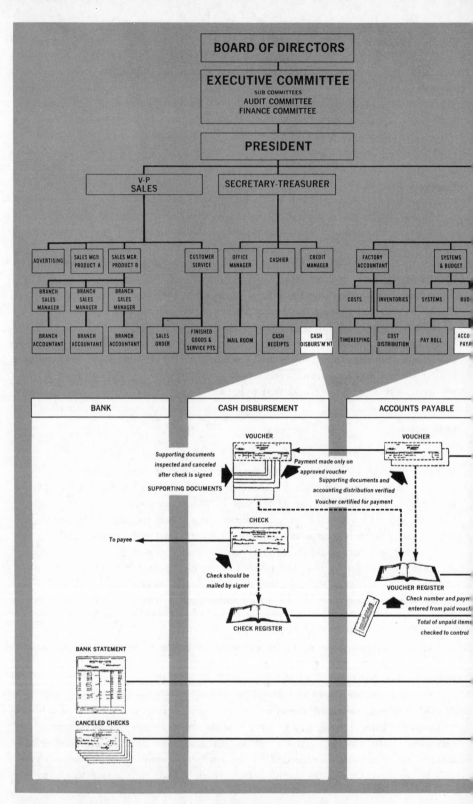

Figure 14-2

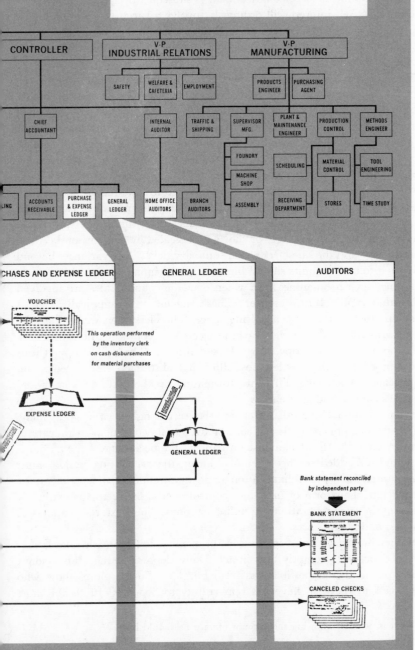

CASH DISBURSEMENTS

PROCEDURAL FLOW CHART SHOWN IN RELATION
TO ORGANIZATION CHART TO PORTRAY
THE CONTROL OBTAINED THROUGH SEGREGATION
OF FUNCTIONAL RESPONSIBILITY

CONTROLLER

V-P
INDUSTRIAL RELATIONS

V-P
MANUFACTURING

SAFETY

WELFARE &
CAFETERIA

EMPLOYMENT

PRODUCTS
ENGINEER

PURCHASING
AGENT

CHIEF
ACCOUNTANT

INTERNAL
AUDITOR

TRAFFIC &
SHIPPING

SUPERVISOR
MFG.

PLANT &
MAINTENANCE
ENGINEER

PRODUCTION
CONTROL

METHODS
ENGINEER

FOUNDRY

SCHEDULING

MATERIAL
CONTROL

TOOL
ENGINEERING

MACHINE
SHOP

...LING

ACCOUNTS
RECEIVABLE

PURCHASE
& EXPENSE
LEDGER

GENERAL
LEDGER

HOME OFFICE
AUDITORS

BRANCH
AUDITORS

ASSEMBLY

RECEIVING
DEPARTMENT

STORES

TIME STUDY

...CHASES AND EXPENSE LEDGER

GENERAL LEDGER

AUDITORS

VOUCHER

*This operation performed
by the inventory clerk
on cash disbursements
for material purchases*

EXPENSE LEDGER

GENERAL LEDGER

*Bank statement reconciled
by independent party*

BANK STATEMENT

CANCELED CHECKS

Figure 14-2 (Continued)

347

completed and the cash drawer opened. Another is the visible record at the top of the machine which proclaims to all who may be concerned the exact amount at which the sale has been recorded. The third is the printed receipt which the customer is trained to demand to establish proof of payment in the event a refund or a price adjustment is subsequently requested. Because the customer's self-interest will ordinarily involve a careful inspection of the cash register receipt, the receipt must disclose the actual facts of the transaction, and these facts will be irrevocably recorded in the registering mechanism of the machine.

The vital segregation between accountability and custodianship of the cash takes place after the sale is recorded. The salesclerk makes a "blind" count* of the contents of the cash drawer at the end of the day and turns the cash and this count record over to the central cashier. Someone who has no contact with the cash (usually the manager, the bookkeeper, or a member of the accounting department) then "reads" the cash register by inserting a key which is necessary to cause the machine to print the daily or cumulative total on the locked-in audit tape. The locked-in tape record of the day's transactions is then removed and used to establish the amount of cash which the cashier should have received from the salesclerk. A running record should be maintained of cash overages or shortages revealed by comparison between the audit tape and the salesclerk's cash summary ticket. Any variances beyond established tolerance limits should be investigated immediately.

Another device sometimes used when over-the-counter sales are involved is the autographic forms register. These machines automatically feed a three-copy form into an open writing space. The clerk then writes the sales check, turns a crank, and the machine ejects two copies of the sales check and deposits the audit copy into a locked drawer. The audit copy is thus tamper-proof, and there is less possibility that abstracted cash receipts can be concealed by showing different information on the customer's copy and the store's copy of the sales check.

As an additional over-all check on the recording of cash sales, many organizations supplement direct control over cash collections with careful inventory control. All merchandise on hand at the beginning of the accounting period, or added to the inventory during the accounting period, must be accounted for by merchandise on hand at the end of the period or by cash receipts. This form of inventory control over cash receipts is extremely important in such operations as filling stations, liquor stores, bars, sales branches, and chain stores.

Another important point in the control of receipts from cash sales is that they be deposited promptly and intact. Daily deposits reduce the amount of cash on hand and possible loss from burglary. Furthermore, those who have access to the cash have less opportunity to "borrow" funds for short

---

* That is, without knowing the amount of cash he should have.

periods of time and less flexibility in concealing shortages by substituting later receipts.

Receipts should be deposited intact, because disbursements made from cash receipts are difficult to control and they increase the opportunity for defalcation. An abstraction of cash receipts can be concealed by overstating disbursements or recording fictitious disbursements.

Cash Disbursements

Authorization for cash disbursements should originate outside the disbursement unit which is under the treasurer's jurisdiction. The steps leading up to such authorization have been presented in Chapter 9, which dealt with purchases and accounts payable. Under the procedures described, prenumbered voucher-checks are under the control of the accounts payable section, and all information shown on the face of the checks is inserted by the accounts payable section in the course of its operations. The responsibilities of the cash disbursements section (or the treasurer himself, in the case of smaller concerns) are therefore as follows:

1. Review the supporting documents submitted with the check in order to ascertain that the disbursement is for goods or services rendered to the company and that the check is drawn for the correct amount and to the order of the person or firm indicated by the supporting documents.

2. Sign the check. Signature may be handwritten with pen and ink or, if volume warrants, printed by a check-signing machine. The amount of the check may also be "protected" (shredded into the paper) by use of a check protector, or a machine may be used that combines both signing and protecting and simultaneously lists the checks for a cash disbursements record. Machine signatures are controlled by a key that locks and unlocks the machine and by a nonresettable counter that records the number of signatures.

3. Cancel the supporting documents by perforation or a "paid" stamp so they cannot be submitted for disbursement a second time—either intentionally or by accident.

4. Prepare a check register, or cash disbursements journal, as a record of all disbursements and the source of general ledger postings for disbursements.

5. Mail the checks to the payees. Under no circumstances should the checks be returned to the person or department originally preparing the checks, for to do so would greatly facilitate the making of fraudulent disbursements.

Punched-card disbursements. Under punched-card procedures, the payables cards due to be paid on a given day are sorted by vendor number, and name-and-address cards are match-merged into the deck. In this case, however, these cards are filed *behind* the related payables cards. The cards are then listed on voucher-check continuous forms. The payables cards are listed on the voucher half of the form, showing the vendor's invoice number and amount to inform the vendor what items are being paid. The forms then space up and the total is printed on the check portion of the form along with the name and address of the vendor. At the same time, the vendor number and the check amount are summary-punched into a "check card." The check cards are listed to obtain a check register.

Imprest fund disbursements. The disbursement procedures that have been presented provide excellent control, but the relative cost of such controls is likely to be excessive when small amounts are disbursed. Consequently, the disbursement of minor sums is frequently accomplished under reduced controls through an imprest fund. The fund may be on deposit in a bank subject to disbursement by check, or it may kept on hand in the form of a petty cash fund. There are several advantages to depositing the fund and making disbursements by check—advantages which are equally applicable to the basic funds and disbursements of a business:

1. Only authorized persons can withdraw deposited funds, whereas cash on hand is subject to unauthorized withdrawal by any employee who is able to gain access to the funds.

2. Paid checks returned by the bank with the bank statement represent a complete record of every disbursement, including any which were unauthorized; cash funds paid out or withdrawn provide no such automatic record.

3. Endorsement of a check by the payee provides an automatic receipt for each disbursement.

4. The possibility of loss through burglary is eliminated if funds are on deposit.

For every imprest fund disbursement that is made, an invoice or receipt written in ink should be retained. For disbursements such as travel expense advances, the duly authorized requisition for the disbursement would constitute the supporting record. All such documents should be submitted with the request for reimbursement of the fund and at that time subjected to the normal audit procedures of the accounts payable process. The reimbursement check should be drawn to the order of the petty cash custodian, or to the fund itself, and not to the order of the company. If reimbursement checks drawn in the latter fashion are accepted for cashing or for deposit, there is a possibility that checks from customers drawn to the order of the company may be similarly accepted, thereby facilitating conversion of those checks to the benefit of the defrauding employee.

A definite policy should be established limiting the types and amounts of disbursements which the petty cashier is authorized to make. Under no circumstances should employees be permitted to borrow from the fund. If the petty cashier is authorized to cash checks, the individuals or groups entitled to this service should be specified, but payroll checks should be specifically excluded from the authorization. Although frequently the petty cashier is authorized to endorse checks which have been cashed, and in turn to cash the checks at the bank, a better procedure is to deposit the checks with the regular daily receipts and draw a transfer check to reimburse the petty cash fund. This arrangement permits a constant check on whether the petty cashier's authority to cash checks has been exceeded.

Bank Reconciliations

Once each month steps should be taken to ascertain that the balance shown by the bank is in agreement with the balance shown by the company's records, except for properly recognized reconciling items. Reconciliation of the two balances should reveal any bookkeeping errors made by the bank or the company, as well as unauthorized withdrawals such as forged or raised checks, and reconciliation is important for these reasons. The chart on page 374 shows the preparation of the reconciliation by the internal auditors, but reconciliation is a routine operating function more appropriately performed by a person in the accounting department who has no responsibility for recording cash transactions. The alternative arrangement would be in line with the recommendation of the Institute of Internal Auditors that the internal auditor should not be assigned any routine operating responsibilities, so that in carrying out his objective of ascertaining compliance with established procedures he is free to make an independent review of the reconciliation work.

It is essential that responsibility for preparing bank reconciliations not be delegated to employees who handle cash receipts or cash disbursements, or who have access to unissued checks. Such a rule precludes the possibility of these employees attempting to conceal the theft of funds by manipulating figures on the bank reconciliation.

Another vital rule is that bank statements and accompanying paid checks should be delivered in sealed envelopes directly to the person responsible for preparing the reconciliations of bank balances with ledger balances. Restricting initial access to bank statements and paid checks to this person is important, because it prevents other employees from attempting to conceal shortages or unauthorized transactions by altering the bank statement or the accompanying paid checks. Methods of perpetrating fraud involving such practices are discussed in Chapter 16.

When the above precautions and the steps enumerated below are carefully followed in conjunction with the preparation of the bank reconciliation, the bank reconciliation becomes an important check on the employees who handle cash receipts and cash disbursements. The reader should recognize that the following steps go beyond the mere mechanical procedures involved in constructing a bank reconciliation, and therefore accomplish much more:

1. Account for all check numbers; inspect voided checks.

2. Compare paid checks with the cash disbursement records as to number, date, payee, and amount; list checks that are outstanding.

3. Ascertain that all checks are properly endorsed and show additional endorsements only when circumstances are known to justify such endorsements.

4. Verify that checks have been signed only by authorized persons.

5. Refer checks which have been outstanding beyond a specified period to a designated person who should authorize a journal entry transferring the amounts to a liability account or to income.

6. Compare deposits per books and per bank statement as to amount and report any delay in deposits reaching the bank.

7. Trace bank transfers to determine that dates and amounts correspond for both accounts involved.

Completed bank reconciliations should be reviewed and approved by a responsible official, such as the manager, the controller, or the treasurer.

Rotating bank accounts to eliminate reconciliation. An interesting innovation in the approach to the bank reconciliation problem has been receiving considerable attention recently. It involves the use of "rotating" bank accounts and eliminates the sorting of checks and the need to match the checks against the disbursement records in order to determine the checks that are outstanding. The technique does not, however, eliminate the desirability of performing the seven steps listed above, but these steps need not be performed regularly if cash is subject to strong internal control.

To operate the rotating account system, two separate bank accounts are maintained, usually in the same bank, and the checks written against one account should be readily distinguishable from those checks written against the other. For a full month, only the checks for one of the accounts are used and all deposits are made to that account. At the end of the month, the ledger balance of the first account is transferred to the second account, and for the following month only the checks for the second account are used and all deposits are made to that account. By the end of the second month, sufficient time should have elapsed to permit all checks written against the first account to have cleared. If all checks have, in fact, cleared and no other reconciling items have occurred, the bank statement should show a zero balance by the end of the second month. The zero balance proves, as effectively as any reconciliation, that all items have cleared, that they cleared at the same amount at which they were originally recorded by the company, and that, except for rare offsetting errors, no errors were made by the company or by the bank with respect to the account in question.

If any checks written against the account have been raised, or if fraudulent checks with forged signatures have been paid by the bank, an overdraft will signal the event as soon as all checks have cleared. On the other hand, there is always a possibility that a few checks may still be outstanding at the end of a month's time, but it is not likely that the checks will be large, and the balance that will then be remaining in the bank account should also be small. When a balance remains, there is no way of telling whether the bank balance and the company's records are absolutely correct; but if the amount is small, any error will also be small in all probability. Under these circumstances, the cost of a regular bank reconciliation which would have to be prepared in order to prove whether or not an error has occurred will hardly justify the knowledge that is gained.

A large bank balance at the end of the second month would, of course, warrant further investigation. The regular bank reconciliation procedures can then be employed in order to ascertain the cause of the balance, which may prove to be the result of a single outstanding check or an error on the company's books or an error by the bank.

Punched-card bank reconciliations. The major task in the preparation of a bank reconciliation is the development of the list of outstanding checks. The task is readily mechanized, however, if punched-card equipment is available. Assuming that paper checks are used, a "finder" card is punched with the check number for each paid check returned with the bank statement. The finder cards are then sorted into sequence by check number and are collated against the file of check cards prepared as a by-product of the check-writing operation. Matching check cards are selected from the check-card file, the remaining check cards representing the checks that are outstanding. These are then listed to obtain the detail and total of the outstanding checks for the bank reconciliation.

If punched-card checks are used, it is unnecessary to punch finder cards, as the checks themselves can be used in the collating process. It may be desirable, however, to first prove the accuracy of the bank statement by tabulating the checks without disturbing their order and balancing this total against the total bank-statement debits. The latter figure is readily calculated by adding the beginning balance and deposits shown on the statement and subtracting the ending balance. If the checks do not balance against this figure, the individual checks should be compared with the debit amounts listed on the statement to locate the bank error. The amount of the error would also be revealed by the bank reconciliation, but the actual error would still have to be identified. The comparison of checks and statement charges would then be exceedingly difficult because the checks would no longer be in the same order in which they were listed on the bank statement.

Bonding

Fidelity bonds covering employees handling the liquid assets of a business can help protect the business in the event that internal control breaks down, is inadequate, or is negated through collusion. Such bonds may carry with them added assurance that the covered employees have been above reproach in any previous employment, for bonding companies generally investigate all employees on whom bonds are requested in order to keep the risk of loss to a minimum. The mere fact that an employee is highly trusted is not a substitute for bonding: most thefts are committed by trusted employees, as they have the greatest opportunity to steal! Note, however, that a defalcation must be discovered in order for fidelity bond protection to become effective, thus emphasizing the importance of reconciliations prepared by employees having no access to cash, and of other internal control procedures that will reveal manipulations.

Management Reports

The major problem concerning cash is to maintain a sufficient balance to pay all bills on the discount date or when they are due and yet not let an excessive cash balance develop. Advance planning in the form of a cash budget or forecast is essential for this purpose, but the actual results should be reported in comparison with the budgeted figures to show whether progress is being made according to plan.

Day-to-day control of the cash balance is also important; it depends on expected cash receipts and disbursements for the near future. These figures are directly related to accounts receivable and accounts payable, for which the desired information can be reported on a daily basis as follows:

	Accounts Receivable	Accounts Payable	Cash
Balance Yesterday	$ 10,221.18	$ 7,421.90	$ 5,019.23
Today's—Charge sales	1,823.51		
—Invoices registered		1,118.20	
	$ 12,044.69	$ 8,540.10	
—Accounts receivable collections	1,625.73		1,625.73
			$ 6,644.96
—Accounts payable paid		1,720.80	1,720.80
Balance today	$ 10,418.96	$ 6,819.30	$ 4,924.16

To show a longer-term view, thus smoothing out daily fluctuations, the above figures can be reported on a month-to-date or quarter-to-date basis. Budget comparisons are also useful in evaluating the results attained.

A useful supplement to the daily cash disbursement figure is an indication as to whether disbursements are being made in accordance with credit terms. The management-by-exception principle is observed by reporting cash discounts lost or payments made after their due date.

Another aspect of cash reporting is the fact that when extensive cash transactions occur, as in a retail store, cash variances are likely to develop. Avoiding such variances is a practical impossibility, and the only alternative is to maintain careful watch over the variances that do develop to see that they do not become excessive. The net cash overage or shortage for the day should be reported, but the individual variances that produced the net figure should also be presented. Large individual variances, even though resulting in a small net variance, are significant because they evidence loose control or inaccurate cash handling. Also, in the long run, the shortages will probably far outweigh the overages. One way to stress the problem is to report a gross cash variance, calculated by adding together the absolute amounts of individual overages and shortages. Such a figure gives a better clue to the basic accuracy of cash handling; the net overage or shortage shows how much inaccurate handling has cost the business.

The monthly reconciliation that should be prepared for each bank account is not actually a report, but each reconciliation should be reviewed and approved by some designated officer—often the treasurer, the controller, or the manager of the business unit. Such a requirement insures that the reconciliations are prepared regularly and presents an opportunity to detect obvious errors or an attempt to conceal a defalcation.

Internal Auditing

An effective program of internal audit of the cash function should include most of the following steps, to be performed on a regular basis at least once a year:

1. Examination of transactions and records to show whether established procedures are being followed and internal checks are functioning as intended.

2. Surprise count of all cash on hand.

3. Confirmation of bank balances and verification of reconciling items on the bank reconciliations prepared by regular accounting personnel. (The bank statement and paid checks for the following month should be obtained directly from the bank by the internal auditor and used in proving reconciling items.)

4. Test of cash receipts and cash disbursements against supporting data and reconciliation with receipts and withdrawals per bank statement.

5. Comparison of paid checks with the check register, noting that all checks are accounted for, signed by an authorized official, and properly endorsed.

6. Proof of footings of the cash receipts and cash disbursement records.

REVIEW QUESTIONS

1. What are the objectives of internal control over cash and cash transactions?
2. What can be done to establish control over incoming remittances, other than to prelist these items in the mailroom or by the person who opens the mail?
3. Why is it difficult for the person who opens mail and first handles incoming remittances to abstract any of the funds?
4. What steps should be taken by the accounts receivable department before ¬posting remittance advices when cash discounts are involved?
5. How is the cash received from cash sales usually controlled?
6. What are the responsibilities to be carried out relative to cash disbursements under the direction of the person who is authorized to sign checks?
7. What are the two types of cards necessary to prepare voucher-checks under punched-card procedures? Which type of card should precede the other?
8. What are the advantages of making imprest fund disbursements by check?
9. What is the best way to handle checks cashed through a petty cash imprest fund? What checks should not be cashed through the fund?
10. Should bank reconciliations be prepared by the internal auditor? Explain.
11. What is a "finder" card in punched-card reconciliation procedures, and how is it used?
12. What information should be presented to management to aid in the day-to-day control of cash balances?
13. What cash auditing steps should be performed on a regular basis by the internal auditor?
14. What steps should a concern take to prevent "duplicate payment" of invoices?

QUESTIONS ON SYSTEMS APPLICATIONS

15. State the various internal control measures that might reasonably be taken to prevent the following manipulations from occurring. A clerk removes invoices and related receiving reports from the paid file, prepares checks to pay the invoices again, has the treasurer sign the checks, and then cashes the checks by forging the payee's endorsement. The duplicate checks are not entered in the cash disbursement record, but totals in the disbursement record are overstated to include the amounts of the checks. After the checks clear the bank, the checks are removed from the checks supporting the bank statements and destroyed.
16. A company's plan of internal control specifies that a "disbursement auditor" should examine every disbursement voucher and determine that it is correctly prepared and properly supported before approving the voucher for preparation of the check. State the specific steps that the disbursement auditor should follow before approving a petty cash reimbursement voucher.
17. The treasurer of the Voorhees Company insists that the invoices supporting checks which he is to sign be marked "paid" before they are presented to him. What is his apparent reason for the request that the invoices be marked "paid"? Is the method effective? Explain.
18. Discuss briefly what you regard as the more important deficiencies in the system of internal control in the following situation, and in addition include what you consider to be a proper remedy for each deficiency:

    The cashier of the Easy Company intercepted customer A's check payable to the company in the amount of $500 and deposited it in a bank account which was part of the company petty cash fund, of which he was custodian. He then drew a $500 check on the petty cash fund bank account payable to himself, signed it and cashed it. At the end of the month while processing the monthly statements to customers, he was able to change the statement to customer A so as to show that A had received credit for the $500 check that had been intercepted. Ten days later he made an entry in the cash received book which purported to record receipt of a remittance of $500 from customer A, thus restoring A's account to its proper balance, but overstating cash in bank. He covered the overstatement by omitting from the list of outstanding checks in the bank reconcilement, two checks, the aggregate amount of which was $500.   (Uniform C.P.A. Examination)

19. A small retail store uses a cash register that has a single non-resettable register for recorded amounts, and four different classification keys to identify different types of transactions as they are recorded on the locked-in audit tape. The machine adds only, and cannot subtract. The keys are used to identify the following types of transactions recorded on the machine:

> #1 Cash Sales
> #2 Charge Sales
> #3 Accounts receivable collections
> #4 Paid out

Devise a cash register analysis and reconciliation form to be prepared at the end of the day that starts with the cash register reading at the end of the day and develops a figure for cash over or short and total sales for the day. Supply your own figures to complete the form.

20. The bank charged a check for $1,000 to the account of the Sanders Co., although the check was drawn by the Saunders Co. Would the bank error be detected sooner by the Sanders Co. under regular bank reconciliation procedures or under rotating bank account procedures? Explain.

PROBLEMS

21. The Patrick Company had poor internal control over its cash transactions. Facts about its cash position at November 30 were as follows:

The cash books showed a balance of $18,901.62, which included undeposited receipts. A credit of $100 on the bank's records did not appear on the books of the company. The balance per bank statement was $15,550. Outstanding checks were: No. 62 for $116.25, No. 183 for $150, No. 284 for $253.25, No. 8621 for $190.71, No. 8623 for $206.80, and No. 8632 for $145.28.

The cashier abstracted all undeposited receipts in excess of $3,794.41 and prepared the following reconciliation:

Balance, per books, November 30		$ 18,901.62
Add: Outstanding checks:		
8621	$ 190.71	
8623	206.80	
8632	145.28	442.79
		19,344.41
Less: Undeposited receipts		3,794.41
Balance per bank, November 30		15,550.00
Deduct: Unrecorded credit		100.00
True cash, November 30		$ 15,450.00

Required:

(a) Prepare a supporting schedule showing how much the cashier abstracted.

(b) How did he attempt to conceal this theft?

(c) Taking only the information given, name two specific features of internal control which were apparently missing. (Uniform C.P.A. Examination)

22. The total cash disbursements for the month of April as shown by the bank statement received by the X Co. is $25,219.85. Given the following information, not all of which is applicable to the problem, compute the total cash disbursements for April that would be shown in the cash account of the X Co., and prepare a reconciliation between the total disbursements per bank and per books.

(a) Checks outstanding at March 31 totaled $568.19.

(b) Checks outstanding at April 30 totaled $915.89.

(c) In March, an X Co. check for $129.75 was charged by the bank as $192.75. The bank corrected this mistake by issuing a credit memo in April, entered as a deposit.

(d) A check of the Z Co. in the amount of $78.90 was erroneously charged by the bank against X Company's account in April.

(e) A check for $45.87 issued by X Co. in January has never cleared the bank and has been presumed lost. A stop payment order was issued to the bank and the X Co. wrote off the check by entering it in red in its check register for April.

(f) An X Company check for $157.25 was certified by the bank in March and paid by the bank in April.

23. The Standard Mercantile Corporation is a wholesaler and ends its fiscal year on December 31. As the Company's C.P.A. you have been requested in early January 1968 to assist in the preparation of a cash forecast. The following information is available regarding the Company's operations:

1. Management believes the 1967 sales pattern is a reasonable estimate of 1968 sales. Sales in 1967 were as follows:

January	$ 360,000
February	420,000
March	600,000
April	540,000
May	480,000
June	400,000
July	350,000
August	550,000
September	500,000
October	400,000
November	600,000
December	800,000
Total	$ 6,000,000

2. The accounts receivable at December 31 total $380,000. Sales collections are generally made as follows:

During month of sale	60%
In first subsequent month	30%
In second subsequent month	9%
Uncollectible	1%

3. The purchase cost of goods averages 60% of selling price. The cost of the inventory on hand at December 31 is $840,000 of which $30,000 is obsolete. Arrangements have been made to sell the obsolete inventory in January at half of the normal selling price on a C.O.D. basis.

The Company wishes to maintain the inventory as of the 1st of each month at a level of three months sales as determined by the sales forecast for the next three months. All purchases are paid for on the 10th of the following month. Accounts payable for purchases at December 31 total $370,000.

4. Recurring fixed expenses amount to $120,000 per month including depreciation of $20,000. For accounting purposes the Company apportions the recurring fixed expenses to the various months in the same proportion as that month's estimated sales bears to the estimated total annual sales. Variable expenses amount to 10% of sales.

Payments for expenses are made as follows:

	During Month Incurred	Following Month
Fixed expenses	55%	45%
Variable expenses	70%	30%

5. Annual property taxes amount to $50,000 and are paid in equal installments on December 31 and March 31. The property taxes are in addition to the expenses in item "4" above.

6. It is anticipated that cash dividends of $20,000 will be paid each quarter on the 15th day of the 3rd month of the quarter.

7. During the winter unusual advertising costs will be incurred which will require cash payments $10,000 in February and $15,000 in March. The advertising costs are in addition to the expenses in item "4" above.

8. Equipment replacements are made at the rate of $3,000 per month. The equipment has an average estimated life of six years.

9. The Company's income tax for 1967 is $230,000. A Declaration of Estimated Income Tax was filed for 1967. The Declaration estimated the Company's total 1967 tax as $210,000 and payments of $110,000 were made as prescribed by income tax regulations. The balance of the tax due will be paid in equal installments.

For 1968 the Company will file a Declaration estimating the total tax as $220,000.

10. At December 31, 1967 the Company had a bank loan with an unpaid balance of $280,000. The loan requires a principal payment of $20,000 on the last day of each month plus interest at ½% per month on the unpaid balance at the first of the month. The entire balance is due on March 31, 1968.

11. The cash balance at December 31, 1967 is $100,000.

12. The client understands that the ethical considerations involved in preparing the following statement will be taken care of by your letter accompanying the statement. (Do not prepare the letter.)

Required:
Prepare a cash forecast statement by months for the first three months of 1968 for the Standard Mercantile Corporation. The statement should show the amount of cash on hand (or deficiency of cash) at the end of each month. All computations and supporting schedules should be presented in good form.

(Uniform C.P.A. Examination)

24. You are auditing the Alaska Branch of Far Distributing Co. This branch has substantial annual sales which are billed and collected locally. As a part of your audit you find that the procedures for handling cash receipts are as follows:

Cash collections on over-the-counter sales and C.O.D. sales are received from the customer or delivery service by the cashier. Upon receipt of cash the cashier stamps the sales ticket "paid" and files a copy for future reference. The only record of C.O.D. sales is a copy of the sales ticket which is given to the cashier to hold until the cash is received from the delivery service.

Mail is opened by the secretary to the credit manager and remittances are given to the credit manager for his review. The credit manager then places the remittances in a tray on the cashier's desk. At the daily deposit cut-off time the cashier delivers the checks and cash on hand to the assistant credit manager who prepares remittance lists and makes up the bank deposit which he also takes to the bank. The assistant credit manager also posts remittances to the accounts receivable ledger cards and verifies the cash discount allowable.

You also ascertain that the credit manager obtains approval from the executive office of Far Distributing Co., located in Chicago, to write off uncollectible accounts, and that he has retained in his custody as of the end of the fiscal year some remittances that were received on various days during the last month.

Required:

(a) Describe the irregularities that might occur under the procedures now in effect for handling cash collections and remittances.

(b) Give procedures that you would recommend to strengthen internal control over cash collections and remittances.

(Uniform C.P.A. Examination)

Auditing cash

15

Although cash is seldom a significant portion of a company's assets, a relatively large share of the total audit time is often spent in the examination of this item. This disparity between the financial significance of cash and the time devoted to its examination is explained in part by the close relationship between cash and other statement items. Almost all assets, liabilities, incomes, and expenses clear through the cash account, thus causing it to function much as the eye of the needle, and the careful examination of cash lends additional validity to the other statement items.

The relative risk associated with cash also helps to explain the disproportionate amount of time likely to be devoted to its examination. Cash is the most liquid of all company assets and is therefore most likely to tempt the employee or officer whose moral resistance might be overcome by the need or desire for added financial resources.

The auditor must be careful, however, not to be carried away in making his examination of cash. As no valuation problem is involved, cash can be accounted for to the penny, but the auditor should resist the temptation to carry his verification to such an extent merely because the possibility exists. Placed in proper perspective, cash is but one of many items making up the financial position of a business. For the auditor to be warranted in expressing his opinion on cash as a part of the financial position of a client, the auditor has only to be satisfied that cash is fairly stated in accordance with generally accepted accounting principles applied on a basis consistent with that of the preceding year. A precise accounting for every penny of cash is neither required nor desirable, although some auditors and textbook authors occasionally overlook this fact.

In the case of small businesses where internal control is difficult or impossible to maintain, the examination of cash may be extended beyond the limits suggested above. The additional procedures will be related primarily to the detection of any fraud which might exist and are strongly reminiscent of the days when the counting of cash and the search for defalcations were the auditor's primary functions.

The extension of the auditor's examination should preferably be undertaken only if the client is concerned about the possibility of some form of fraud or defalcation having occurred and if he specifically requests and authorizes the additional work with full recognition that the fee for the examination will be proportionally increased. In some instances, however, the auditor may take the initiative and incorporate procedures related to fraud detection in his examination without specific authorization from the client. This approach is sometimes used if internal control is weak and the auditor feels that the client is unable to accept or comprehend the fact that the usual examination of financial statements is not designed to detect fraud except if it be so significant that the financial statements would be materially affected. Under these circumstances the auditor may conclude that it is the better part of valor to attempt to seek out any fraud that may have occurred rather than to apply only normal examination procedures and hope to justify at a later date that his examination was not intended to disclose fraud in the accounts, should fraud be discovered after he has completed his examination.

A key factor in any such decision is the now familiar item of relative risk. The client's position, too, may be affected by an awareness of this factor. For instance, the client who does not understand the limited purpose of an examination of financial statements may conclude that it is quite improper for the auditor not to count a $150 cash fund at a given location, and yet give no thought to the fact that the auditor did not inspect one hundred times as much inventory stored at the same location. Similarly, the auditor's failure to detect a cash defalcation having no material effect on financial position or operating results might well evoke more criticism than the auditor's failure to detect the unrecorded retirement of a major plant asset. Such situations evidence a need for an extensive program to educate clients and statement users, but progress along these lines is slow at best. Until the educational process is more complete, practical considerations will often suggest that the auditor protect himself by extending the scope of his examination beyond minimum requirements in formulating his opinion on a client's financial statements.

STANDARDS OF STATEMENT PRESENTATION

Ordinarily all cash will be shown on the balance sheet as one figure, described simply as "Cash" or "Cash on hand and in banks." Only in rare cases will the amount of cash on hand be of sufficient importance to warrant being shown as a separate figure. Similarly, little is added to the usefulness of a statement by breaking down the cash in banks figure among the various banks. The amount of cash shown, however, must be "free" and available immediately for general business purposes. This requirement indicates that any of the following items which are material in amount must be shown separate from the cash figure, either as another form of current asset or under a noncurrent classification, depending on the exact nature of the item:

1. Amounts represented by certificates of deposit or savings deposits. Even though savings deposits can usually be withdrawn on demand, the bank retains the right to require a stated number of days' notice before paying out the funds.

2. Funds for plant expansion, sinking funds, or any other funds which are to be used for non-working capital purposes. The mere fact that the fund is held by the company rather than by a trustee is unimportant; the intended use to be made of the fund is the governing factor.

3. Minimum or "compensating" bank balances which must be maintained in accordance with bank loan agreements. As an alternative, the restricted amount may be shown parenthetically or by footnote.

4. Balances in closed banks. Even though such balances now occur only infrequently, the fact still remains that a bank is much like a parachute: neither is any good unless it opens. Claims against closed banks which were uninsured and claims arising from deposits in excess of the $10,000 insurance limit should be reduced to an estimated recovery value and classified as noncurrent assets.

5. Foreign balances which are not to be used in connection with foreign operations and which cannot be converted readily into domestic currency because of exchange restrictions.

6. Expense advances to employees for travel or other purposes. These advances are not available for general purposes and are essentially prepaid expenses.

7. Deposits of any form, such as deposits on contracts, deposits with utilities, or escrow deposits.

Custom with respect to the presentation of bank overdrafts has undergone a period of change which is about completed. At one time standard practice required that overdrafts be shown as a liability. Current practice is more realistic and recognizes that if bank balances are readily transferable, overdrafts may be netted against balances in other banks. A minimum balance to be maintained in connection with a loan would not, of course, be readily transferable, and therefore an overdraft could not be offset against such an amount.

AUDIT OBJECTIVES AND PROCEDURES

The discussion of the objectives and procedures related to cash is divided into two parts. The first part, presented in this chapter, reflects generally accepted auditing standards as they pertain to the examination of cash under conditions of good internal control when the financial statements are being examined for the purpose of expressing an opinion on the statements. Under these circumstances, the auditor is concerned primarily with the question of whether cash is fairly stated as a part of the over-all financial position of the client. The detection of fraud is not germane to such an examination except to the extent that fraud might reach proportions that would materially affect the client's financial position. In that event, normal balance sheet auditing procedures should be adequate to reveal what has happened, provided the fraud involves a misstatement of the cash figure itself.

Unauthorized disbursements fraudulently concealed by charges to expense accounts, or abstracted cash receipts concealed through manipulation of income or expense accounts, would affect only the income statement. Normal audit procedures would not be likely to disclose the fraud under these circumstances (still assuming good internal control as the basis for employing only normal audit procedures), but it is interesting to note that broadly speaking the statements will not really be misstated by fraud perpetrated in this manner. Concealing the loss within the income statement causes net income to be reduced by the fraud loss, just as it would be reduced by any other kind of loss. The only actual misstatement would be in the detailed items affected, and the effect of such misstatement would be much less material than a misstatement of net income.

If the auditor is specifically authorized to extend his procedures so as to detect any fraud that may have occurred, or if he feels that he should use extended procedures because the risk of fraud is substantial as a result of weak internal control, then the material in the following chapter is pertinent. The more common methods of concealing cash defalcations are described in considerable detail, and the procedures designed to detect such manipulations are presented and discussed.

Inasmuch as cash presents no valuation problem, the objectives relating to the substantiation of the amount of cash for statement purposes are fewer in number than those having to do with the examination of receivables or inventories. These objectives are listed below:

1. Establish credibility of the accounting records.
2. Ascertain reasonableness of the cash balance.
3. Review cut-off of recorded transactions.
4. Determine that all cash is where it is supposed to be.

Establish Credibility of the Accounting Records

The procedure involved in the attainment of this objective pertains primarily to the records of cash in banks, but at least one petty cash reimbursement should be subjected to a similar examination.

Trace handling of representative transactions from origin to final account balance. The extent of tracing to be done is a direct function of the amount of internal control that is evident. The first step would be to prove the footings of the cash receipts and cash disbursement records for one or more months and trace the totals to entries in the ledger accounts that are affected. For clients with a large volume of transactions and good internal control, the proof of footings can usually be safely eliminated, but not if the records are handled by employees who have any contact with cash or checks.

Then, for selected entries, supporting documents should be examined. In the case of cash disbursements, source records would include vouchers, invoices, receiving reports, and paid checks. Cash receipts source records would include remittance advices accompanying orders or payments of account balances, receipts issued for over-the-counter payments, sales checks, or cash register tapes. Additional audit procedures to be employed when internal control is weak, or when the auditor is authorized to search for irregularities, are discussed in the next chapter.

Although ordinarily no entries will appear in imprest fund accounts, the auditor should review the supporting data for at least one reimbursement of each fund during the year. In making such a review the auditor should be particularly careful to note that transactions in the funds have been limited to those types that have been specifically authorized, and that each disbursement has received the proper approval.

Review of Cash Balance for Reasonableness

The factor of reasonableness has less bearing on the examination of cash than for most other financial statement items for two reasons: the cash balance is highly fluid and is less directly related to changes in other accounts, and the book figure can be more readily substantiated than most other items because there is but a single item to contend with. As a result of the concentration of the asset, the auditor can more readily satisfy himself directly that the asset is fairly stated, and he therefore has less need for the indirect assurance offered by the existence of reasonable relationships between figures.

Nevertheless, the auditor should not completely disregard the question of reasonableness. If cash on hand or in the bank appears to be either deficient or excessive in relation to the apparent needs of the business, the matter might well be brought to the attention of management under the concept of constructive auditing. Whether the problem appears to be too little or too much cash, in the last analysis it tends to resolve into a financial matter: how to obtain the additional funds that may be needed, or how to make better use of excessive cash balances. The auditor's training and experience should be more than adequate to enable him to give competent advice to his client on such a matter.

Review Cut-Off of Recorded Transactions

The cut-off of cash transactions is important with respect to proper statement of the cash figure, as well as other balance sheet or income statement figures. Furthermore, attempts at "window dressing" (explained later) are likely to involve the cash account.

Cut-off of cash receipts. The auditor must satisfy himself that the cash receipts records have not been held open to include cash collections received after the balance sheet date. This point is particularly important if cash sales are involved, because income will be affected. If all cash collections pertain to accounts receivable, the financial picture is changed only slightly by improperly moving up receivables amounts into cash. Holding open the cash receipts book under these circumstances may, however, be merely a prelude to holding open the cash disbursements book as well, which has a more serious effect on financial position.

Occasionally a client will hold the cash receipts record open to receive payments which have been dated and mailed by customers before the balance sheet date. This practice may appear to have some merit, particularly in the eyes of the client, but the fact remains that such receipts were unavailable for general use by the business on the balance sheet date because the business did not have possession of the funds. Consequently, if material amounts are involved, the auditor has no choice but to insist that the client reverse the recorded collections and restore the amounts to receivables or, should income be involved, eliminate the amounts entirely from the current period.

There are two conclusive procedures which the auditor can apply to determine that the cut-off of cash receipts has been properly handled. If the auditor is at the client's premises at the close of business on the last day of the fiscal year or at the beginning of the following day, a count of all undeposited cash receipts will establish the proper cut-off of cash. Based on his count, the auditor will know how much cash was actually received up to the close of business, and any attempt by the client to include in the records cash received after that point will be immediately apparent to the auditor. Should the auditor wish to avoid making a time-consuming cash count, an alternative is to place the undeposited receipts under his control until they reach the bank. Control can be established by sealing the cash in an envelope or pouch which can then be locked in the client's safe until the bank deposit is ready to be made. With such precautions no additional cash subsequently received can be added to the deposit without the auditor's knowledge, and the bank's entry for the deposit on the bank statement will establish the amount of cash which was held by the client at the close of the year.

It will seldom be feasible, however, for the auditor to be present at each client's office on the balance sheet date. Nor will the auditor's presence be necessary in most instances. Instead, the auditor can usually make satisfactory verification of the cut-off of cash receipts through a careful examination of deposits in transit listed on the client's year-end bank reconciliation. All such deposits in transit, if valid and including only cash received up to the close of the fiscal year, should be credited by the bank on the next business day following the close of the client's fiscal year. A deposit not reaching the bank on this time schedule carries a strong presumption that cash received subsequent to the balance sheet date has been included.

Other evidence that ought to suggest the possibility that the cash cut-off is not as it should be would include exceptionally heavy cash receipts or sales recorded at the end of the fiscal year, light cash receipts or sales recorded for the early days of the following year, and an unusually low accounts receivable balance at the year end.

Cut-off of cash disbursements. The auditor must be particularly careful to watch for any evidence that the cash disbursements record has been held open. The resulting simultaneous reduction of cash and accounts payable will improve the current ratio—a very understandable objective if financial condition and credit standing are weak or if a bond indenture specifies a minimum current ratio which has not been maintained. If the client could not reduce liabilities at the balance sheet date because sufficient cash was not available, the auditor should realize that the required cash could have been "generated" by holding open the cash receipts book.

Evidence that the cash disbursements record has been held open is less conclusive than is evidence concerning the cut-off of cash receipts. For instance, substantial disbursements at the year end coupled with limited disbursements during the first part of the following period would not necessarily mean that the cash disbursements record had been held open. Many businesses make a special effort at the end of the year to reduce their liabilities. If the cash is available, and if the checks are placed in the mail before the year end, the resulting improved financial picture is entirely proper. The auditor's problem, of course, is to satisfy himself that the checks were actually in the mail and therefore beyond the client's control by the close of the year. If he can satisfy himself on this point, the large number of outstanding checks on the bank reconciliation and the abnormally low amount of payables need cause him no concern.

If the auditor is at the client's office at the close of the year, he should note the serial number of the last check which has been written, and by inquiry, determine that this and all previous checks have been placed in the mail. Any additional checks which the client might then wish to show as disbursements of the expiring fiscal year would be readily detected by the auditor, and he would know that they had been written and mailed after the close of the year.

As the auditor will seldom be on hand at the end of the year, some other means of verifying the cut-off of cash disbursements must obviously be employed. The necessary evidence can usually be obtained by examining the checks paid by the bank during the first part of the month following the close of the year. For those checks which were outstanding at the end of the year, the auditor should note the lapse of time from the date of each check to the date the check was charged against the client's account, as indicated by the perforations which the bank makes in each check when it is paid. If this time period is longer than should be warranted for the check to reach the payee, be handled and deposited by him, and be returned to the client's bank, the auditor should suspect that the check may have been mailed after the close of the year. Should it develop that this check is but one of a block of outstanding checks which did not clear the bank within a reasonable period of time, the evidence of what has apparently occurred is quite conclusive. When the evidence is placed before the client, it should bring forth full admission from the client as to what was done, and the client should be expected to consent to correct the records so that they will reflect the true financial picture. Any tendency by the client to deny what has apparently happened should be regarded by the auditor with considerable suspicion.

Window dressing. Although window dressing does not necessarily misrepresent a client's financial position at the balance sheet date, the effect is misleading and therefore undesirable. Holding the cash books open is a method of window dressing which does actually misrepresent the facts. A form of window dressing, which strictly speaking does not misrepresent the facts, results if an officer who has borrowed funds from a corporation repays the loan shortly before the balance sheet date, and then is re-advanced those funds after the close of the year. Careful review of cash transactions and entries in accounts with officers occurring near the balance sheet date should reveal any window dressing which may have been attempted.

Determine that All Cash Is Where It Is Supposed to Be

Once the auditor has examined the supporting records and thus satisfied himself that the cash figure is fairly stated and properly reflects the client's cash transactions, his sole remaining objective is to satisfy himself that all cash called for by the records can be accounted for. The cash will ordinarily be either on hand or on deposit at one or more banks.

Cash on hand. Petty cash funds, change funds, and undeposited receipts generally comprise all or most of the cash on hand. If the amounts are material, the auditor should plan to count the cash at the close of the year. Otherwise, the imprest funds can be counted at any time that is convenient for the auditor, with the added advantage that some element of surprise is injected into the count. If undeposited receipts are not material, they need not be counted, because they can be verified through reference to the record of their deposit on the bank statement for the following period. The auditor should note, of course, that the deposit was made promptly. If the deposit was delayed in reaching the bank, the auditor should carefully investigate the possibility that the cash receipts book was held open or that the cashier included subsequent receipts in the deposit to cover up a shortage.

If cash is to be counted, the auditor must be certain that all cash and any assets which are readily negotiable or easily pledged are counted simultaneously or kept under the auditor's control until all counting is completed. By exercising this precaution the auditor can be assured that funds which have already been counted are not used to make up a shortage in another fund still to be counted. If good internal control has been violated by permitting a fund custodian to handle other funds not under company control (such as flower or party funds), these other funds should also be counted and balanced with available records. Otherwise, these funds could be used to offset a shortage in the company funds.

For his own protection, the auditor should count all funds or negotiable instruments in the presence of the custodian of the assets. If the auditor fails to exercise this precaution and the fund is revealed to be short of the required amount, the auditor will have little defense to the custodian's possible assertion that "It was all there when I gave it to you." As further protection, the auditor should have the custodian sign a receipt stating that the count was made in the custodian's presence and the funds returned to him intact at the completion of the count. Schedule A-1 contains an example of such a receipt obtained in connection with the count of a petty cash fund.

Some accounting firms go to the extreme of not permitting staff men to handle any of the client's funds. Instead, the custodian of each fund is requested to count the fund under the surveillance of the staff man. A variation of this arrangement is useful when very large amounts of cash are on hand, as in the case of a large department store. The store's internal auditors or other employees not connected with the cashier's department can be requested to count the cashier's funds under the independent auditor's supervision. Because a considerable measure of internal control is evident in such an arrangement, a limited number of accountants from the independent auditing firm can supervise and observe the counting being done by a large number of store employees.

Coins and currency. Regardless of how the actual counting of cash is to be handled, some agreement must be reached in advance on what shall be done concerning bundled currency and wrapped coins. Because the coins will seldom constitute a significant portion of the fund, the rolls of coins can usually be accepted for listing on the count sheet without opening and counting any of the rolls. If desired, a few of the rolls can be broken open and counted as a test, or the paper wrappers can be scratched open to verify that the rolls contain coins and not pieces of lead pipe of the appropriate size and weight. The auditor should, of course, note whether the diameter and length of the rolls correspond with what would be expected for the following standard contents:

Denomination	Number of Coins	Value of Roll
Dollars	20	$ 20.00
Halves	20	10.00
Quarters	40	10.00
Dimes	50	5.00
Nickels.	40	2.00
Pennies.	50	.50

Bundled currency presents more of a problem because of its greater value. If only a few bundles are involved, the auditor should probably open and count each bundle. If there are quite a few bundles, as in the case of a bank, and if internal control is adequate, the bundles may be test-counted. For smaller-denomination bills, only five or ten per cent of the bundles may be counted, but for bills of large denomination fifty per cent or more of the bundles should probably be counted.

As is shown on schedule A-1, the auditor's work sheet should show the quantity and total value of each denomination of coin and currency. Loose items should be listed separately from the wrapped or bundled items. Listing each quantity and its total value reduces the possibility of error in figuring total values for the various denominations and assists in locating counting errors if the auditor's count should not balance with the accounting records.

Checks. Customers' checks or checks cashed as an accommodation are almost certain to be encountered in making a cash count. If only a few checks are on hand, the auditor may list the checks on his worksheet, as is shown on schedule A-1. An adding-machine-tape listing of the checks will usually suffice if the checks are quite numerous. In some instances, when large numbers of checks are present, the auditor may not even count the checks. If they are part of the day's business to be deposited the next day and have been handled under good internal control, the auditor may simply permit the client's employees to prepare the regular deposit. The deposit should then be kept under the auditor's control during the count of other funds and until the deposit reaches the bank. Because the bank must prove the deposit anyway, the auditor merely asks the bank to notify him whether the actual deposit agreed with the amount shown by the client on the deposit ticket.

If the auditor plans to count the checks on hand, each check should be carefully examined in an effort to substantiate its validity and collectibility. Points to be observed would include:

1. Date: a postdated check cannot be classified as cash, and a check bearing an old date suggests that the check is possibly being held because it is uncollectible.

2. Payee: checks should be made payable to the client, except in those instances where authorization exists to accept checks payable to others as an accommodation.

3. Endorsement: checks not payable to the client should bear the endorsement of the original payee and that of the person who transferred the check to the client, if that person was not the payee. As a protective measure, all checks should be endorsed by the client "For deposit only."

4. Maker: checks which have been signed by an employee or officer should always be carefully investigated to determine whether the checks are valid and properly included in the fund being counted.

The best test of validity is depositing the checks to determine whether they can be collected. The checks should be controlled by the auditor until they reach the bank to prevent other checks from being substituted for any checks which are not valid or collectible. The bank should be requested to notify the auditor if any of the checks are not collected, or at the very least the auditor should inspect the bank statement for the following period to see if any uncollectible checks have been charged back against the client's account.

Undeposited receipts. The auditor should always ascertain that all cash on hand representing receipts from customers has been recorded in the appropriate record. If all or part of the receipts are not recorded, the unrecorded receipts which have been included in the counted cash would serve to cover up any shortage which existed. Furthermore, the receipts should be recorded *before* the auditor makes his count, so that the auditor can compare individual items in order to determine whether lapping has occurred.

Petty cash funds. If petty cash funds are counted at other than the balance sheet date, part of the funds will likely have been disbursed, and receipted petty cash vouchers or other supporting data will be present in their place. This condition should not hold true at the balance sheet date.

Any disbursements occurring before that time should be reimbursed in order to reflect the expenses in the proper period and to have the fund in cash form, thus permitting the entire balance to be classified as cash. If such reimbursement has not been made, technically the auditor should prepare an adjusting entry in order to have the statements reflect the actual conditions. As a practical matter, however, the amounts will usually not be material, and the adjustment can be passed as was done on schedule A-1.

Any disbursement vouchers which are on hand at the time of the petty cash count should be listed in the auditor's working papers. The date, recipient, purpose, and amount of each disbursement should be shown, although if a large number of disbursements has been made, an adding-machine-tape listing will usually suffice. Each voucher or invoice should be reviewed to determine that it bears a current date, has been approved or receipted as required, has not been cancelled, and is in accordance with the authorization for the operation of the fund. In addition, some auditors request a responsible official to review the list and sign a statement indicating that each item represents a valid and appropriate disbursement. This procedure was followed in the preparation of schedule A-1.

Although much discussion has been presented concerning the techniques of handling cash counts and the reasons for those techniques, the reader should not allow himself to lose sight of the primary objective in counting cash on hand: to determine that cash called for by the records as being on hand is actually there and fully accounted for. If the amounts involved are not material, it is becoming more and more common not to count such funds, especially if internal control is good and the client makes occasional "surprise counts."

Cash in bank. The auditor's first consideration in verifying cash in bank is to ascertain the actual balance on deposit. Even though this balance can be determined by referring to the bank statement, standard practice requires that independent confirmation of the bank balance be obtained directly from the bank. To facilitate obtaining such confirmation, plus important information on other relationships between the client and the bank, Standard Bank Confirmation Form—1961 is customarily used. This form, a copy of which is shown as schedule $\frac{A\text{-}2}{1}$, has been approved by the Committee on Auditing Procedure of the American Institute of Certified Public Accountants and by the National Association of Bank Auditors and Comptrollers. The printed form consists of an original and a duplicate copy. The request for the specified information must be signed by one of the client's officers whose signature is on file at the bank. A bank should not release confidential information about a customer's affairs without proper authorization, and the duplicate copy is retained by the bank to prove that it had such authorization. Other information typed on the form before it is mailed includes:

(1) the name and address of the bank (so located on the form that a window envelope can be used for mailing), (2) the date for which the information is requested, (3) the client's name, and (4) the name and address of the auditor to whom the reply is to be sent. As with all confirmation requests, mailing should be by the auditor.

The automation of bank records has made it very desirable to list all accounts and give account numbers to aid the bank in looking up the necessary information; but if the client's internal control is weak, it may be preferable to omit this information, as there will then be less likelihood that the bank will overlook any accounts carried for the client but not shown by the client's records.

The bank will also show whether an account is subject to withdrawal by check and whether the account bears interest. If the account is not subject to withdrawal by check, the auditor should determine whether the account is properly classified as cash on the balance sheet. The data on interest is further evidence of whether a balance can be withdrawn on notice and also enables the auditor to ascertain that all interest income has been accounted for. In addition to the data on bank balances, the confirmation request also covers the following points, which are of vital importance to other phases of the audit examination: any direct liability of the client to the bank on loans, acceptances, or other types of paper; any contingent liability for discounted notes or as guarantor for others; and any other direct or contingent liability, any open letters of credit, and any collateral held by the bank. The bank should, of course, date and sign the form before it is returned to the auditor.

The bank reconciliation. The verification of cash in bank is far from completed when the auditor has secured confirmation of the balance on deposit. Invariably the client's balance for the bank account will reflect transactions not yet recorded by the bank, and the bank may have recorded some transactions not yet recorded by the client. These reconciling items, which must account for the difference between the client's balance and the bank's balance, must be carefully verified before the auditor can be satisfied that the amount of cash in bank specified by the client's records has been adequately accounted for.

In most instances the client will have prepared a bank reconciliation, based on the bank statement for the last month of the client's fiscal year and setting forth the various reconciling items. The auditor should obtain this reconciliation and in the course of his verification work should prove that the reconciliation is mathematically correct. The validity and accuracy of the reconciling items must also be verified. The most obvious approach to this problem would appear to be a repetition of the processes employed by the client in constructing the reconciliation. Actually, however, this is neither the most efficient nor the most conclusive solution. A far better method is a review of subsequent events to determine whether incomplete transactions have been completed as would be expected, and to ascertain whether any incomplete transactions at the balance sheet date have been omitted from the reconciliation.

Bank cut-off statement. The principal source of information which the auditor uses in proving reconciling items is the bank cut-off statement. This is simply a bank statement covering a specified number of days following the close of the client's fiscal year. For very large businesses with considerable check activity, a five- to ten-day period may be adequate, but for smaller businesses with less internal control the statement may cover two weeks or even a full month. The request to the bank for the cut-off statement must, of course, be signed by the client. In this request, the bank will be directed to deliver to the auditor the bank statement and accompanying paid checks for the specified period. The possibility that a member of the client's organization might alter the statement or tamper with the accompanying checks makes it most desirable that the statement be delivered by the bank directly to the auditor. Should circumstances make such delivery impossible, the auditor should be particularly careful to scrutinize the bank statement for alterations, and he must determine that all debits on the statement are properly supported by paid checks or bank debit advices. This step is known as "proving" the bank statement. As a guard against the substitution of spurious checks or bank advices, each document should be inspected to ascertain that the date of payment perforated into the document by the bank falls within the period covered by the bank statement.

When internal control is adequate, procedures based on the cut-off statement should be sufficient to prove the validity of the client's reconciliation and thus substantiate the cash balance. These procedures are discussed in the following three sections. If internal control is weak, additional procedures as described in the next chapter should also be applied.

Deposits in transit. In verifying deposits in transit, the auditor should realize that a shortage of cash in bank can be concealed by an overstatement of deposits in transit. The verification procedures which are ordinarily followed should detect any possible overstatement if the procedures are properly applied. These procedures follow:

1. Trace the deposit-in-transit figure to the client's cash records to determine that the figure agrees with the amount of cash shown as received on the last business day. If more than one day's receipts are involved, thorough investigation of the situation should be made.

2. Compare the deposit-in-transit figure with the count of cash on hand, if such a count was made by the auditor at the close of the year. Cross-reference the two schedules.

3. Trace the deposit-in-transit figure to the cut-off bank statement. The

date of the bank entry for the deposit should be noted in the working papers as was done on schedule A-2. Any deposit which does not reach the bank by the next business day should be investigated. Possible causes of such a delay might include holding open the cash receipts record and using subsequent collections to make up a shortage.

4. Ascertain that all checks deposited were collectible by noting whether the cut-off statement shows any debit memos for checks charged back against the client's account.

Outstanding checks. The most troublesome and potentially dangerous item on the bank reconciliation is outstanding checks. The greatest danger is not, as the neophyte often assumes, that a check may have been included which is not actually outstanding, but that a check which *is* outstanding may have been omitted or shown at less than the actual amount. In terms of relative risk, the most likely possibility is that the ledger figure for cash may exceed the cash on deposit as a result of a defalcation. Any attempt to conceal the resulting shortage of cash through manipulation of the figure for outstanding checks on the bank reconciliation must of necessity involve an *understatement* of that figure or the *omission* of a check which is actually outstanding. If this point is not clear to the reader, he should work out a simple illustration to prove to himself that concealment of a cash shortage by means of manipulating outstanding checks must involve an understatement of the outstanding checks.

The incorrect listing of a check on the bank reconciliation can be readily detected in several ways, as will be shown presently, but disclosing that an outstanding check has been omitted is a far more difficult matter. Because the omitted check is not known to the auditor, he has no specific point at which he can begin his investigation. An omitted check may have been written months, or even years, before the beginning of the auditor's investigation. A review of all checks written since the previous audit would be required to discover the existence of an outstanding check which had been purposely omitted from the bank reconciliation. The magnitude of such an undertaking should be evident when it is realized that many businesses write thousands of checks every month. Furthermore, the results of such an investigation would not necessarily be fully conclusive. In view of such problems and limitations, it should be apparent that the auditor can hardly be expected to state that the cash figure is correct. He can, however, determine with reasonable assurance whether the figure is fairly stated, which is adequate for the needs of most third parties who refer to and rely on financial statements. The auditor's opinion that cash is fairly stated should be taken to mean that in his opinion no pronounced misstatement has occurred which would actually affect a reader's conclusions concerning the company's financial position.

The usual audit procedures employed in the search for significant amounts of outstanding checks which may have been omitted from the bank reconciliation are included below. When internal control is weak or fraud is suspected, certain additional procedures may be employed. These are included among the more detailed procedures, discussed in the next chapter, which are used in conjunction with the proof of cash. The following procedures represent a typical approach to the verification of outstanding checks under conditions of reasonably good internal control.

1. While the checks returned with the bank cut-off statement are still in order according to the dates on which they were paid by the bank, examine the checks for predating; that is, for a bank endorsement which predates the date of the check. A check evidencing such predating should suggest the possibility that kiting has occurred, or perhaps that a bill had to be paid but the check was not recorded in order to avoid showing an overdraft on the books. (See the discussion of kiting in the next chapter.)

2. Sort the paid checks into serial-number order, or have an employee of the client do so under the auditor's supervision.

3. Ascertain from the cash disbursement records the number of the last check recorded during the fiscal year under examination.

4. Review checks bearing a higher serial number to be certain they are all dated for the following year. If any of these checks are payable to cash, officers, or banks, investigate the checks to ascertain that they are proper, have not been issued as a part of window dressing, and do not relate to the fiscal year under examination. Large checks for round amounts should receive particularly close scrutiny.

5. Perform the following procedures with respect to checks bearing a date or serial number showing that they were written before the close of the client's fiscal year:

(a) Trace each check to the copy of the client's list of outstanding checks in the audit working papers. Be sure that each check is listed and that the correct amount is shown. This is the single most effective procedure for disclosing omissions or inaccuracies resulting in an understatement of outstanding checks. The procedure is, of course, based on the presumption that the payee of a check will normally cash or deposit the check as quickly as possible, and that as a result most checks outstanding at the balance sheet date are likely to clear the bank within a relatively short period of time after the balance sheet date. This presumption should hold true especially for large checks, which might materially misstate the cash figure if not properly included on the bank reconciliation.

(b) Note on the list of outstanding checks those checks which have been paid by showing the date on which each check was paid by the bank, as was done on schedule A-2. A review of these dates should indicate whether the cash disbursements record may have been held open.

(c) Trace the checks, on a test basis, to the cash disbursements record to ascertain their agreement with that record as to date, number, payee, and amount.

6. Review the list of outstanding checks for any checks which did not clear the bank during the period covered by the cut-off statement. Trace the amounts shown for these checks to the cash disbursements records to determine that the correct amounts have been listed as outstanding. If any of these checks are large in amount, also examine supporting data such as invoices to further evidence the correctness of the amount. In addition, discuss these large checks with the client to find out why they have not cleared. In some cases correspondence with the payee, in order to obtain further information, may be warranted. The need for such precaution stems from the possibility that the payee may be holding the check because the amount is in dispute. If so, there may be an additional liability which should be reflected on the client's records.

7. Prove the footing of the list of outstanding checks.

8. Review the list of outstanding checks in the working papers for the previous year's examination for checks which had not cleared the bank by the close of the examination. If these checks do not appear as outstanding at the close of the current year, they should be located in the client's files of checks paid during the current year. Inspect the checks, on a test basis if they are numerous, comparing the amounts with those shown by the outstanding-check list, and noting that endorsements are proper and that no second endorsements are given. These checks should be accounted for because old outstanding checks are not likely to be presented for payment and therefore are the ones most likely to be dropped from the list of outstanding checks in order to conceal the theft of cash. Many companies, after checks have been outstanding a specified length of time, attempt to contact the payees and induce them to deposit the checks or to request duplicates if the originals have been lost. If such efforts are unsuccessful, the checks are then written back on the books and taken up as income or as a liability. This procedure reflects much better internal control than does permitting the checks to remain listed as outstanding.

Other reconciling items. If reconciling items other than deposits in transit or outstanding checks appear on the bank reconciliation, the auditor should satisfy himself that the items are valid and have been properly shown. If the item first appears on the client's records, the auditor should ascertain that the item is recorded in the same amount by the bank in the following month or that the client's records are corrected in the following period. For instance, if the client properly prepared a check drawn on Bank A, but recorded the check as a withdrawal against Bank B, reconciling items for the same amount should appear on the bank reconciliations for both banks. When the check is finally paid, the auditor should examine both the check and the original entry to verify the facts and should note that a correcting entry has been made in the following period.

Many reconciling items will first be recorded on the bank's records. If the bank has improperly charged a check to the client's account, the error will be discovered when the client prepares the bank reconciliation. The bank will then issue an advice of correction in the following month. The auditor should note the original entry and satisfy himself that the proper correction appears in the bank statement for the following month, supported by the bank's correction advice. Service charges are another type of reconciling item which first appears on the bank's records. The auditor should inspect the bank's charge slip and then determine that the charge is recorded by the client in the following period. Technically, of course, the adjustment should be reflected in the period under examination, but when the amount is not material the auditor should waive the adjustment for practical reasons.

Rotated bank accounts. If the client rotates bank accounts, the auditor will not only have to use a different approach in substantiating the cash balance, but he will have to be particularly careful to protect himself against the possibility of manipulation involving unrecorded transfers of funds between accounts. The following procedures would be substituted for those ordinarily followed when the client prepares a regular reconciliation. The procedures are based on an assumed December 31 fiscal year.

In addition to obtaining confirmation of both bank accounts at December 31, the auditor should obtain the bank statements for both accounts for December, and the January bank statement for the account that was active in December. Preferably, all of these statements should be obtained directly from the bank. For the account that was active for December, the auditor should ascertain that the account was activated by a deposit equal to the bank balance shown by the general ledger at November 30. The deposits in the account should be compared with the daily record of cash received to establish that no unrecorded transfer of funds was made to the account to cover up a cash shortage. The December statement of the account that was inactive should reflect the withdrawal of the November 30 general ledger cash balance, and there should be no deposits recorded, except for the November 30 deposit of that day's regular collections, which normally would be in transit. The December 31 balance on deposit as shown by the bank statement should be very small, or nothing if all checks have cleared. If an overdraft has occurred or the balance is quite large, the client should investigate to determine what has happened, and the auditor should substantiate the client's findings so that he can be certain that the client's cash balance is not misstated. The same procedures used with reference to the bank statement for the account that was inactive for December should also be applied to the account that is inactive for January.

If the auditor is expected to complete the field work of his examination prior to January 31, he will have to request the bank statement for the inactive account for an earlier date. If checks are still clearing the account in considerable number at the earlier cut-off date, the auditor will probably conclude that he should ask the client to reconcile the account at that date in order that the auditor can ascertain that the balance shown by the bank statement is approximately what it should be. If the client's internal control is very good, however, the auditor should consider making his review of the records and bank statements as of November 30. With the records and cash balance substantiated as of November 30, the auditor can then review the December book transactions and bank statement entries for unusual amounts, confirm the bank balances at December 31, and ascertain that the bank balances exceed the client's ledger balances by an amount that appears to be sufficient to cover a reasonable amount of outstanding checks.

Timing. In the examination of cash, as well as in most other phases of an audit examination, part of the auditor's work can be performed in advance of the balance sheet date if internal control is satisfactory. The review of internal control is perhaps the most obvious procedure which can be handled readily on a preliminary basis. Imprest cash funds can also be counted beforehand, assuming that the amounts are not material. If regular surprise counts are made by the internal auditor, the count of these funds may often be dispensed with by the independent auditor. He should, however, review the internal auditor's working papers to verify that satisfactory counts were actually made as stated. In any case, at the year end the independent auditor should inquire to determine that all imprest funds have been reimbursed and restored to their original amount.

Bank reconciliations for the principal bank accounts can also be verified on a preliminary basis. In addition to following all year-end procedures as described previously, the auditor should make any counts of cash, notes receivable, investments, and any other negotiable assets at the date of the preliminary bank reconciliation. The purpose of such simultaneous verification is, of course, to prevent the transfer of funds from one asset to another to conceal a shortage.

Even though a complete examination of cash in bank has been performed at an earlier date, certain additional procedures will be necessary at a later time. Entries to the cash accounts during the period from the date of the preliminary verification work to the year end should be reviewed for propriety and reasonableness and traced to source records if added verification is desired. The auditor should also satisfy himself that a proper cut-off of cash receipts and cash disbursements was made. The client's bank reconciliations at the balance sheet date should be reviewed and compared with the preliminary reconciliations. Bank confirmations for the balance sheet date should be obtained and the bank balance figure compared with the corresponding figure on the client's bank reconciliation. The book balance figure on the reconciliation should be compared with the corresponding figure in the grouping sheet in the auditor's working papers.

SUMMARY

Internal control

Duties which ideally should be performed by different individuals—
    Handling sales transactions.
    Cash register readings.
    Pre-list of mail receipts.
    Deposit of cash receipts.
    Comparison of deposit total with cash register reading or pre-list total.
    Accounts receivable entries.
    General ledger entries.
    Check preparation.
    Check signing and mailing.
    Preparation of bank reconciliations.
    Custody of imprest funds.
Additional factors in attaining good internal control—
    Use of mechanical devices—
        Cash registers.
        Autographic forms registers.
        Window-posting machines.
        Check protectors.
        Check signers.
    Other internal control measures—
        Use of inventory control to establish accountability over cash sales.
        Use of prenumbered cash receipt forms and checks.
        Bonding of all employees having access to funds or records.

Statement presentation

Items not properly includable as cash—
    Time deposits.
    Funds allocated for non-working capital purposes.
    Claims against closed banks.
    Foreign balances subject to exchange restrictions.
    Expense advances.
    Deposits with firms other than banks.
Net overdrafts should be shown as a liability.

Requirements to maintain minimum bank balances should be disclosed if material.

Audit objectives and procedures

Establish credibility of the accounting records.
> Trace handling of representative transactions from origin to final balance.

Ascertain reasonableness of cash balance.
Review cut-off of recorded transactions.
> Test cut-off of cash receipts by ascertaining that deposits in transit reach the bank promptly.

> Test cut-off of cash disbursements by ascertaining that checks do not remain outstanding an unreasonable length of time.

Determine that cash is where it is supposed to be.
> Count cash on hand; undeposited collections may be controlled to the bank in lieu of counting.

> Confirm bank balances.

> Prove mathematical accuracy of client's bank reconciliations.

> Trace bank reconciliation items to cut-off bank statement obtained directly from the bank.

> Compare checks written prior to year end and clearing with the cut-off bank statement with client's list of outstanding checks supporting the bank reconciliation.

> Test outstanding checks not clearing with the cut-off statement against cash disbursements records.

> Account for checks still outstanding at close of previous audit.

REVIEW QUESTIONS

1. In what ways do the problems of satisfactorily verifying the cash account differ from those encountered in verifying most other accounts?

2. List seven different types of items which may have to be excluded from cash to assure that financial statements meet accepted standards of presentation.

3. What are the auditor's objectives in making an examination of cash, when the purpose of the examination is to enable the auditor to express an opinion on a client's financial statements?

4. What are the two principal means by which the auditor determines whether the cash receipts book has been held open?

5. Do large disbursements at the end of the year and a low balance of accounts payable necessarily mean that the cash disbursements record has been held open? Explain.

6. As an indication of the importance of cash, the audit program will normally require the expenditure of a fairly substantial amount of time for its verification, and yet the work is likely to be entrusted to the lowest-ranking man available. How can this apparent inconsistency be justified?

7. What types of items is the auditor likely to find in the petty cash fund?

8. What is the most conclusive test of the worth of checks which make up part of the balance of a petty cash fund?

9. In addition to counting the petty cash fund, what other audit procedure should the auditor employ if he is concerned about detecting employee irregularities in handling the fund?

10. How is it possible for the auditor to verify undeposited receipts as of the balance sheet date without being on hand to count the cash?

11. Why is the auditor interested in verifying the cash "cut-off"?

12. What work, in addition to verifying the balance of cash on deposit at the year end, must normally be done if internal control is weak?

13. How does the auditor verify deposits in transit and outstanding checks on a year-end bank reconciliation?

14. When checks are included in cash on hand, what points should the auditor watch if he "counts" the checks?

15. What information is a bank requested to supply on the Standard Bank Confirmation Form?

16. Why should the auditor examine all checks listed as outstanding at the close of the previous year, but which were paid after the completion of the previous audit?

17. If the auditor verifies all bank reconciliations at a preliminary date, what additional steps should be performed as of the balance sheet date with respect to cash in bank?

QUESTIONS ON APPLICATION OF AUDITING STANDARDS

18. Your client uses rotating bank accounts and transfers balances at the end of the month. You are asked to deliver your opinion report by January 20, and therefore request a cut-off statement from the bank as of January 15 for the account that was active in December. The statement shows that a substantial balance remains in the account and that checks are still clearing at the rate of several per day. You ask the client to reconcile the account for you at January 15 so that you can establish that the balance on the bank statement is adequate to cover all checks that are still outstanding, but receive the response that no one has the time to do the work. How would you proceed?

19. For what reasons should the auditor note the cancellation dates and bank endorsement dates on checks clearing with the cut-off statement?

20. What relation does the standard bank confirmation form have to the auditor's examination of receivables?

21. You count your client's petty cash fund on January 2 and find that it is short $153.69. The cashier states that this is the amount of the reimbursement due the fund as of December 31, for disbursements made prior to that date. How would you satisfy yourself as to this explanation?

22. Your review of your client's system of internal control over cash disbursements, as indicated by your answers on your internal control questionnaire, is very satisfactory. There are slight variations in the procedures for handling each of the principal types of disbursements, such as material purchases, expense disbursements, petty cash reimbursements, freight and express payments, factory payroll, office payroll, and cash dividends on capital stock. Approximately 1,500 checks are written each month. What tests would you

make of compliance with the client's system for cash disbursements, and how extensive would the tests be?

23. When the auditor cannot be present to count the undeposited cash receipts at the end of the year which comprise the deposit in transit, how can he be certain that the deposit when made did not include subsequent receipts added to make up for a cash shortage?

24. Why does controlling undeposited receipts to the bank offer the auditor more positive verification than verifying the details on an authenticated duplicate deposit ticket?

25. Why is the client required to sign the Standard Bank Confirmation Form?

26. An auditor in making his cash count at December 31 discovered that the cashier had not yet balanced his records or made up the daily deposit. Cash on hand included both currency and checks. No other cash or negotiable instruments were held by the company. The auditor recorded his count of the cash, totaling $15,394.72, and released the cash to the cashier.

    The cashier's fund was $5,000, and the auditor subsequently noted a bank deposit dated January 2 on the January bank statement in the amount of $10,394.72, whereupon he concluded that he had satisfactorily verified all cash on hand.

    (a) What opportunities were open to the cashier as a result of the manner in which the auditor made the examination?

    (b) What should the auditor have done?

27. An auditor's unqualified opinion on a client's financial statements may be taken to mean that insofar as the auditor could reasonably determine, all cash receipts and disbursements for the period have been properly accounted for. Do you agree? Explain.

28. An auditor is engaged to make an examination as of December 31 on the following January 10, and begins the examination on that date. The client has substantial excess funds invested in marketable securities. What departure from the normal auditing procedures would be necessitated by the facts stated?

PROBLEMS

29. The Rickard Company's fiscal year ended March 31, 1968. Your examination the preceding year disclosed that the internal control was weak. The staff and organization was unchanged.

    The office manager was unable to reconcile the bank statements at March 31, and opened an account called "Exchange" for $170 in order to balance his preliminary trial balance.

    In your discussions with Mr. Rickard, the owner, you learned that receipts from cash sales were deposited only once a week, in the Central Bank. All disbursements were made by checks drawn on either the Central or State Bank. The checks were drawn upon either bank regardless of the type of expenditure.

    Mr. Rickard also revealed that he attended a convention early in March and drew several checks (which have not been recorded) while entertaining prospective buyers.

    You have available the following records of the client:
    1. The cash receipts book for March 1968.
    2. The cash disbursements book for March 1968.
    3. The general ledger cash accounts.
    4. The bank reconciliation of both bank accounts at February 29, 1968.

5. The bank statement and accompanying data for March from the Central Bank.
6. The bank statement and accompanying data for March from the State Bank. As part of your confirmation procedure you requested and received directly:
7. A cut-off statement dated April 11, 1968 and accompanying data from the Central Bank.
8. A cut-off statement dated April 11, 1968 and accompanying data from the State Bank.

Required:
(a) Reconcile both bank balances to the adjusted cash balances as of March 31, 1968.
(b) Prepare all necessary *journal entries* to adjust the cash accounts at March 31, 1968. (Assume that the books have not been closed.)

1.   **CASH RECEIPTS BOOK**

					Cash	
				Accounts Receivable	Central Bank	State Bank
Date	Account Credited	LF	Amount	Credit	Debit	Debit
1968						
March 1	B. Hillman	√		686		686
2	Notes receivable	130	2,400			
	Interest income	813	24			2,424
4	Sales	401	5,497		5,497	
9	M. Walker	√		1,587		1,587
10	Purchase allowances	519	684			684
11	B. Kline	√		770		770
11	Sales	401	6,533		6,533	
14	Notes receivable discounted	131	2,000			2,000
18	Sales	401	1,629		1,629	
23	B. Mercedes	√		800	800	
25	Sales	401	1,502		1,502	
31	W. Benson	√		713		713
			20,269	4,556	16,061	8,864

2.   **CASH DISBURSEMENTS BOOK**

						Cash	
				Accounts Payable	Check	Central Bank	State Bank
Date	Account Debited	LF	Amount	Debit	No.	Credit	Credit
1968							
March 2	M. Moss	√		737	634	737	
4	Office supplies	701	73		635	73	
10	Insurance	707	217		1,080	217	
10	Note payable	230	2,800				
	Interest expense	713	14		1,081		2,814
11	Office furniture	145	210		1,082		210
14	Selling expense	509	200		636	200	
18	Queen Co.	√		1,600	637	1,600	
18	O. Randolph Co.	√		2,156	638	2,156	
23	Contribution	728	200		1,083		200

25	Sales allowances	403	17		1,084		17
28	Salaries	702	845		639		845
31	A. Hansen & Co.	✓		363	640	363	
31	I. Marlon	✓		612	1,085		612
			4,576	5,468		5,346	4,698

3.

GENERAL LEDGER—CASH ACCOUNTS:

Cash—Central Bank

1968				1968		
March 1	Balance	✓	5,843	March 31	CD	5,346
31		CR	16,061			

Cash—State Bank

1968				1968		
March 1	Balance	✓	733	March 31	CD	4,968
31		CR	8,864			

4.

RICKARD COMPANY

Bank Reconciliation
February 29, 1968

	Central Bank	State Bank
Balance per books, February 29, 1968............	$ 5,845	$ 736
Less bank charges	2	3
Adjusted balance, February 29, 1968	$ 5,843	$ 733
Balance per bank statement, February 29, 1968	$ 4,836	$ 3,237
Add deposit in transit	2,100	—0—
	6,936	3,237
Less outstanding checks:		
No. 629....................$ 17		
630.................... 52		
633.................... 1,024	1,093	
No. 1062.................... 2,402		
1074.................... 43		
1079.................... 59		2,504
Adjusted balance, as above	$ 5,843	$ 733

5.

CENTRAL BANK

Statement

Account : The Rickard Company

Date	Charges	Deposits	Balance
1968			
Feb. 29			4,836
March 1		2,100	6,936
2	1,024	52	5,860
4	73		5,497
11	150	175	11,284
14	737	6,533	17,492
		7DM	16,748
15	1,013DM		15,735

18	200	1,600	1,629	15,564
24	2,156		800	14,208
25	87		1,502	15,623
28	845			14,778
31	363DM			14,415

Cancelled checks returned with bank statement :

No.	630....$	52	No.	636....$	200
	633....	1,024		637....	1,600
	634....	737		638....	2,156
	635....	73		639....	845
	—....	150		Drawn by Mr. Rickard while	
	—....	175		attending convention.	
	7268....	87		Check written by Rickard	
				Co.	

Bank debit memoranda enclosed with bank statement :

Service charge . . . . $ 7

For certified check (No. 640) 363

Charge for note of R. Walbert discounted
by The Rickard Company and dishonored
by R. Walbert at maturity :

Face of note: . . . . $ 1,000

Interest @ 6% for 60 days   10

Protest fee   3   1,013

6.   **STATE BANK**

Statement

Account :   The Rickard Company

Date	Charges	Deposits	Balance
1968			
Feb. 29			3,237
March 1	43	59 686	3,821
2	2,402	689DM 2,424	3,154
9		1,587	4,741
11	2,814	4DM 1,454	3,377
14	217DM	2,000	5,160
18	220	686	5,626
25		1,900CM	7,526
31	17		7,509

Cancelled checks returned with bank statement :

No.	1062....$ 2,402	No.	1081....$ 2,814
	1074.... 43		1082.... 220
	1079.... 59		1084.... 17
	1080.... 217		

Debit memoranda enclosed with bank statement :

Service charge . . . . $ 4

For certified check (No. 1080) 217

Charge for an " insufficient funds " check of
B. Hillman :

Face of check . . . . $ 686

Protest fee.   3   689

This check was subsequently redeposited.

Credit memorandum included with bank statement :

For Mueller Co. non-interest bearing note
entered for collection and subsequently
collected . . . . $ 1,900

7.
CENTRAL BANK
Statement

Account : The Rickard Company

Date	Charges	Deposits	Balance
1968			
March 31			14,415
April 1		713	15,128
6	959	87EC	14,256
8	82	43	2,530 16,661
11	55	167	16,439

Cancelled checks attached to bank statement :

No. 646....$ 959   No. 650....$ 167
    647....   82   651....   55
    —   43   Check written by Rickardy
                      Company

8.
STATE BANK
Statement

Account : The Rickard Company

Date	Charges	Deposits	Balance
1968			
March 31			7,509
April 1	153	2,540	9,896
4	70		9,826
8		1,732	11,558
11	200		11,358

Cancelled checks returned with bank statement :

No. 1083....$ 200
    1090....   153
    —   70   Drawn by Mr. Rickard while
                       at convention during
                       March.

(Uniform C.P.A. Examination)

30. In connection with your audit of the ABC Co. at December 31, 1967 you were given a bank reconciliation by a company employee which shows:

Balance per bank	$ 15,267
Deposits in transit	18,928
	$ 34,195
Checks outstanding	21,378
Balance per books	$ 12,817

As part of your verification you obtain the bank statement and cancelled checks from the bank on January 15, 1968. Checks issued from January 1 to January 15, 1968 per the books were $11,241. Checks returned by the bank on January 15 amounted to $29,219. Of the checks outstanding December 31, $4,800 were not returned by the bank with the January 15 statement, and of those issued per the books in January 1968, $3,600 were not returned.

(a) Prepare a schedule showing the above data in proper form.
(b) Suggest four possible explanations for the condition existing here and state what your action would be in each case, including any necessary journal entry.

(Uniform C.P.A. Examination)

31. In connection with the regular examination of financial statements as of December 31 of the Wholesale Grocery Co., you make a count of cash on hand at 10:30 A.M. on January 2. There are no other funds or negotiable paper on hand. The receipts of December 31 have already been deposited and there has been no mail delivery as yet on January 2, so there are no collections on hand from accounts receivable.

The company cashier, J. Kurtz, has custody of the petty cash and change fund which is carried on the books at $250. He is authorized to make disbursements from the fund for miscellaneous expenses, such disbursements to be supported by properly executed bills, receipts, or other documents. He is also authorized to cash personal checks for employees up to $25, and he collects on all cash sales made. The proceeds of these sales are mingled with the petty cash fund until the end of the day, when they are segregated and merged with the regular collections and prepared for deposit. Checks in the fund are deposited about every ten days, and a credit is made to an account "checks deposited." A reimbursement check is then drawn which is charged to the checks deposited account, balancing that account. The contents of the cash drawer at the time of your count are as follows:

Currency	Coin
$ 20 bills: 2	Halves: 10
$ 10 bills: 3	Quarters: 7
$ 5 bills: 4	Dimes: 33
$ 1 bills: 12	Nickels: 21
	Pennies: 28

Checks

Date	Maker	Amount
12/28	J. Cosgrove	$ 20.00
1/2	Smith's Grocery	18.91
12/24	Wholesale Grocery Co. (payroll)	42.50
11/15	J. Kurtz	45.00
1/25	J. B. Quick	15.00
12/29	A. J. Rank	12.00

Disbursement Vouchers

Date	Receipted bills for	Amount
12/15	Light bulbs purchased	$ 3.51
12/22	Typewriter repairs	2.75
12/26	Repairing broken window	4.75
1/2	Envelope moistener	3.91

Cash Sales Checks

No.	Amount
1851	$ 7.53
1850	18.91
1853	6.13

You are requested to prepare a worksheet which is to include the following:
1. Count of the above fund.
2. Record of the completion of any other procedures necessary to complete your verification of the fund.
3. Any points you should raise with the senior concerning items in the fund, changes in methods, and so forth.
4. Any journal entries you would recommend (ignore materiality considerations).

Cash defalcations and the
detailed cash audit

16

Presumably the moral standards of most people in the business world are reasonably good where the handling of money is concerned, and in many situations internal control is present to help individuals resist the temptations offered by the ever-present sums of money that are a consequence of business activity. Yet, business losses resulting from theft or embezzlement by employees are estimated to amount to as much as a half-billion dollars per year! And there is no sure way of ascertaining that the trusted employee will always merit the trust that has been placed in him. One study* has shown that employees have commenced to steal from their employers as soon as three days after employment, but the average dishonest employee has been employed six and one-half years before beginning to steal, and in one instance an employee did not begin to steal from his employer until twenty-nine years had elapsed!

In the face of such conditions, the auditor can hardly ignore the possibilities of employee defalcations under conditions of poor internal control, and he owes it to himself and to his client to—

a. Encourage the client to correct the weaknesses that exist in the system of internal control, after showing the client how improvement might best be accomplished, and

b. Extend the scope of his examination as a means of disclosing any losses that may have occurred.

The ability of cash to command any of the limitless variety of material goods understandably makes it the prime target of the embezzler. A study by a national public accounting firm of the defalcations occurring among

* *Crime Loss Prevention*, rev. ed. Chicago: Continental Casualty Company, 1948, p. 6.

its clients bears out this conclusion. Eighty-eight per cent of the defalcations related to cash, and the remaining cases involved inventory. More of the individual instances involved cash receipts rather than cash disbursements, but the opportunities for theft through the cash disbursements route were presumably more extensive, as over eighty per cent of the dollar losses of cash occurred in the area of cash disbursements.* The most reasonable inference from these figures is that it is more difficult to prevent the embezzlement of cash receipts, but the theft of large amounts of receipts is more likely to become apparent, thus limiting the size of the individual losses▮

The Techniques of Defalcation

If the auditor is to be successful in ferreting out cash losses that may have beset his client, he must be well informed about the more common methods by which funds can be abstracted and the shortage concealed. Such knowledge suggests where the auditor should look and what he should look for, particularly in those situations where internal control is weak and there is consequently an increased opportunity for employee theft to occur.

Cash receipts can be abstracted and the resulting shortage concealed by any of the following means:

1. Withholding all or part of the proceeds of a cash sale and either recording no amount on the cash register or sales check or recording less than was actually collected. For instance, the customer's copy of a sales check made out for $10.00 is easily corrected to reflect an actual sale of $70.00 or $40.00.

2. Withholding collections from customers on accounts receivable, recording the collection, and concealing the resulting cash shortage by:
   (a) Underfooting the cash receipts column in the cash book and overfooting the sales discount column by a similar amount.
   (b) Recording discounts on collections when the full invoice amount was actually remitted because the discount period had expired, or overstating the amount of discount taken.
   (c) Overstating cash disbursements. (See the material below on cash disbursements.)
   (d) Manipulating the bank reconciliation by:
   　(1) Overstating deposits in transit.
   　(2) Understating outstanding checks.
   　(3) Falsifying additions or subtractions on the reconciliation.
   (e) Kiting. (See the discussion below.)

3. Withholding collections from customers on accounts receivable, making

* Charles A. Stewart, "The Nature and Prevention of Fraud," *The Journal of Accountancy*, February, 1959, p. 42.

no book record of the collection at the time. The customer can be prevented from learning that he has not received credit by:

(a) Withholding any statements or credit follow-ups which would normally be sent.

(b) Lapping. (See the discussion below.)

(c) Subsequently placing a fictitious credit to the customer's account, indicating:

   (1) The account was written off as a bad debt.

   (2) A merchandise return or allowance was granted.

   (3) The account was paid. The records can be kept in balance by making an offsetting debit to a fictitious account receivable or by crediting the general ledger controlling account for receivables and debiting some general ledger account other than cash. As an alternative, no offsetting entry need be made and the trial balance of accounts receivable can be manipulated to conceal the lack of agreement with the accounts receivable control.

4. Recording sales on account at less than the correct amount but billing customer for the full amount. The difference can then be withheld when the account is paid.

Cash in petty cash funds and cash in bank can be obtained and the shortage concealed by the following means:

1. Removing cash from the petty cash fund and either allowing the fund to remain short or:

(a) Raising vouchers being submitted to the general cashier for reimbursement of the petty cash fund.

(b) Writing fictitious vouchers, forging approvals.

(c) Changing dates on vouchers which have previously been reimbursed and submitting them for a second reimbursement.

2. Preparing checks payable to self and forging the signatures or using blank checks which have been signed in advance. The paid checks are then destroyed when they are returned by the bank and cash is credited to relieve the ledger account of the misappropriated funds by:

(a) Overfooting cash disbursements and underfooting purchase discounts. If expenses are debited through the cash disbursements record, balance can also be maintained by overfooting expense totals.

(b) Raising the entry for another check and also raising the amount of the check after it has been paid by the bank.

3. Preparing checks payable to others, forging the endorsements, and cashing the checks or depositing them in a special bank account opened

for that purpose. Authorized signatures can be obtained on the checks by:

(a) Submitting fictitious invoices and other supporting data.

(b) Submitting invoices which have previously been paid. (The fraudulent check can be destroyed after it has been paid, and the original check substituted in its place, after changing the date and the number of the check.)

4. Overpaying a vendor's invoice and appropriating the vendor's refund check.

5. "Padding" the payroll by continuing to prepare checks for employees who have been terminated or by adding fictitious employees to the payroll. Endorsements can be forged on the checks when they are cashed. 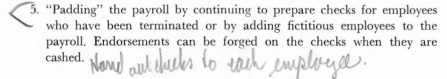 *Hand out checks to each employee.*

Kiting

The manipulation involved in kiting is one that employs the "float" period (the time that it takes for a check to clear the bank on which it is drawn) to conceal a cash shortage within the business, or to prevent an actual overdraft from being detected by the bank that is involved. When kiting is used to conceal a shortage of cash in bank, its detection will reveal that a defalcation has occurred, as well as the fact that the client's financial position is overstated. The manner in which this form of manipulation is accomplished is shown by the following example. A company located in Kansas City has a sales branch in New York. All collections in New York are deposited in a special bank account there. Only the treasurer of the company, who is located in Kansas City, is authorized to sign checks transferring funds from the New York account to the regular account in Kansas City. Just before the end of the year the two bank accounts appear as follows (ignoring reconciling items):

	Kansas City	New York
Balance per bank	$15,000	$10,000
Balance per books	20,000	10,000

The Kansas City bank account is short $5,000, representing collections which the cashier has withheld. To conceal the shortage, the cashier draws a transfer check on December 31 to transfer $5,000 from New York to Kansas City. The treasurer signs the check because the check appears to be a regular check drawn in the normal course of business. The cashier then deposits the check in the Kansas City bank but enters the check in the company records for January. The check will thus appear as a deposit on the Kansas City bank statement on December 31, but because of transit time will not appear as a withdrawal on the New York bank statement until several days later. The result is that at December 31 the Kansas City bank would show $20,000, the amount called for by the books, the New York bank would still show the $10,000 called for by the books for that account, and no shortage would appear to exist. The shortage will reappear, of course, as soon as the transfer check is paid by the New York bank.

The auditor's best course of action in seeking to detect the existence of kiting is to prepare a schedule of all interbank transfers made during the last few days of the current year and the first few days of the following year. The transfer check in the above example would be shown on a schedule of interbank transfers in this manner:

Check No.	Kansas City Bank	New York Bank	Date Withdrawn		Date Deposited	
			Per Books	Per Bank	Per Books	Per Bank
4297	$5,000	($5,000)	1/2	1/3	1/2	12/31

This schedule shows at a glance that something is amiss.

Other means of detecting kiting can be used either in lieu of or to supplement the analysis of interbank transfers. In the case just discussed, a comparison of deposits recorded by the bank and shown on the books for the last few days of the year would show a bank deposit for which there would be no corresponding book entry. If such a discrepancy is not the result of kiting, the explanation is probably that an employee is replacing money which was "borrowed" from the bank account at an earlier date. Such a practice is, of course, equally as objectionable as kiting. Another procedure is to examine all checks paid by each bank during the first few days following the close of the year. Checks dated before the close of the year should agree with corresponding entries in the cash disbursements record and should be listed as outstanding on the bank reconciliation. The check in question, bearing a date of December 31, would appear in neither place.

It might seem that the preceding method of detection would break down if the check were simply dated "January 2." Such a possibility is unlikely because the bank should refuse to accept such a check for deposit on December 31, although it is quite possible that the bank would not notice the postdating of the check. If the check *did* pass the bank, the auditor can still uncover the irregularity. Banks always endorse customers' checks by stamping both the bank name and the date of the transaction on the back of each check. Thus the auditor has only to take the checks paid by the New York bank during the first few days of January and compare the date on the face of each check with the date of the earliest bank endorsement appearing on the reverse side. Any bank endorsement which predates the date of the check is a danger signal.

An additional form of kiting, used to "pad" a concern's cash position and operating results, involves recording a transfer check as an income item, offset by a disbursement entry that is deferred until the following fiscal period.

In some instances the float period is used, not to conceal a book short-age, but as a means of concealing an actual overdraft from the bank, and in effect using the bank's credit without authorization and without payment of interest. For instance, a company may have two bank accounts in widely separated places, each account having a balance of $1,000. The company must pay a $5,000 debt, and does so by drawing a check on Bank A. To prevent the bank from dishonoring the check for lack of sufficient funds, a check for $4,000 is drawn on Bank B and deposited in Bank A. This check will in turn overdraw the account in Bank B, so a check for $4,000 is drawn on Bank A and deposited in Bank B to cover the original transfer check drawn on Bank B. The process must be repeated constantly until sufficient funds can be deposited to permit all checks to be covered. Although this might seem to be a very unlikely course of action, a case is reported in which a small businessman in Missouri concealed overdrafts totaling $35,000 in this manner. The largest case on record occurred in Iowa and eventually concealed overdrafts of $265,000, with checks totaling $37 million being involved in the kiting operation!

Lapping

Lapping is another form of embezzlement in which the embezzler must "keep running to keep even." As stated in the chapter on receivables, lapping of collections on accounts receivable can be detected by confirming account balances with customers. Lapping may also be disclosed by a careful examination of the cash records if customers pay by check, and provided they do not pay in round amounts as in the case of installment accounts. When each check received is for a different amount, the check received from A and appropriated by an employee will not be covered exactly by the check received from B a day or two later. Thus the entry in the cash receipts record crediting A for the check received from B will not agree with the amount of the check. The difference can be made up by depositing additional cash if B's check is smaller, or by making an additional credit to some other account if B's check is larger than the credit which must be made to A's account.

Whereas the total of the day's collections shown by the cash receipts record and the total of the deposit ticket showing the amount of cash deposited will agree when lapping has occurred, the individual amounts listed on the deposit ticket will not agree with the individual amounts shown by the cash receipts book. An item-for-item comparison of these two records will therefore show whether lapping has occurred. As there is a possibility that a duplicate deposit ticket in the client's possession may have been altered to conceal an irregularity, a copy of any deposit ticket to be used by the auditor should first be sent to the bank with a request that the bank compare the ticket with its copy. If the two copies agree, the bank will "authenticate" the deposit ticket with a stamp showing that it agrees with the copy in the bank's records.

A word of caution is warranted about placing too much reliance on bank deposit tickets, even if they have been authenticated by the bank. Most banks prove each customer's deposit in total only, as a part of a "central proof" operation. Thus it is quite possible that a deposit ticket could show details which differed from the actual checks deposited and the discrepancy would be discovered by the bank only if the deposit did not prove, necessitating a comparison of the bank's listing with the depositor's listing. Consequently, there is a possibility that an employee who is familiar with both auditing procedures and banking procedures might contrive to destroy the effectiveness of the detailed comparison of an authenticated deposit ticket with the cash receipts record.

Detection of Fraud and the Four-Column Bank Reconciliation

The reader should be able to devise procedures which will reveal most of the forms of fraud that have been discussed. Some of these procedures will be performed in connection with the examination of accounts other than cash. The procedures relating specifically to the detailed examination of cash receipts and cash disbursements are usually performed in conjunction with the preparation of a four-column bank reconciliation, an operation that is sometimes referred to as a "proof of cash." A simple example of this type of reconciliation is given below, and a more complete example appears on schedule A-3.

	Balance November 30	December Deposits	December Withdrawals	Balance December 31
Transactions per bank	$2,800	$1,500	($1,800)	$2,500
Deposits in transit				
November 30	300	(300)		
December 31		250		250
Outstanding checks				
Checks written prior to December 1	(1,100)		900	(200)
Checks written in December			(700)	(700)
Transactions per books	$2,000	$1,450	$1,600	$1,850

The reconciliation is usually prepared covering a period of one month although a longer period can be used. The reader should note that reconcilement is effected between bank and book figures at the beginning and close of the period, as well as for receipts and disbursements during the period, and when, on occasion, the reconciliation is made for the last month of the year, it obviates the need for separate verification of the year-end reconciliation. Use of the form in connection with a detailed examination of cash for a given period has these advantages:

1. All balances, transactions, and reconciling items are logically arranged for review.

2. The figures in the reconciliation become the starting point for the specific verification procedures.

3. The source and disposition are shown for every reconciling item, and any differences between bank and book figures are forced out into the open.

In preparing the reconciliation, the figures for the two balance columns are obtained from reconciliations prepared by the client. The figure for total deposits per bank can be readily determined by preparing an adding-machine tape of the deposits shown on the bank statement. The figure for withdrawals per bank can then be inserted by "plugging" the difference to complete the line for transactions per bank. The figures for transactions per books should be obtained from the general ledger account for the particular bank account being examined. Reconciling items originating or clearing through the columns for deposits and withdrawals can then be inserted as called for by changes in the reconciling items at the beginning and end of the period. For example, of the $1,100 in checks outstanding at November 30, only $200 remain outstanding at December 31. Therefore, $900 in checks must have been paid by the bank in December, and because these checks were entered in the books prior to December, the amount becomes a reconciling item in the column for withdrawals. To show that the amount is to be deducted from withdrawals per bank in order to reconcile to withdrawals per books, the amount is not encircled.

With the completion of the reconciliation form, the more important process of verifying the figures can begin. Each figure should be keyed to a description in the working papers of the actual verification work which was performed. The following are typical verification procedures:

BALANCES

1. Trace bank balances to the bank statement for the period involved. Also, carefully examine the bank statement for erasures or alterations. Request confirmation of the bank balances as an added precaution.

2. Verify book balances against the balances shown in the general ledger.

3. Prove the footing of all four columns of the reconciliation.

RECEIPTS AND DEPOSITS

1. Prepare an adding-machine tape to obtain the total figure for deposits per bank. Note thereon the date each deposit was recorded by the bank and the date the cash was recorded on company records. Investigate any deposits not reaching the bank by the next business day.

2. Subtract from the total of the above tape the deposit in transit at the beginning of the period, and add the deposit in transit at the end of the period. The new total should agree with the recorded deposits per books, unless other reconciling items are present.

3. Obtain authenticated duplicate deposit tickets for one or more days' deposits, including the deposit at the close of the period, as a test for lapping. Compare each deposit ticket, item for item, with the recorded cash receipts items.

4. Prove the footings of all columns of the cash receipts book for one or more days.

5. Trace the recorded cash receipts, for the days selected under item 4, to documents supporting the individual entries. Such documents may include customers' remittance advices, carbon copies of cash receipts forms, cash register tapes showing totals for the day, cash register reconciliation forms showing resulting cash overages or shortages, and adding-machine tapes totaling sales checks issued for the day. In the last instance, the sales checks should be re-added to prove the validity of the client's tape, and all sales check numbers should be accounted for, beginning with the last number of the previous day and ending with the first number of the following day.

6. Verify sales discounts taken by customers during the period under review. Calculate the amount of the discount to which the customer is entitled, and by reference to the original sales invoice or the debit entry in the customer's account, determine that payment was made within the discount period.

DISBURSEMENTS

1. Ascertain that all checks paid by the bank during the period are present.

(a) Prepare an adding-machine tape of the checks, and balance the total with the figure for bank withdrawals in the bank reconciliation form. This proof of disbursements per bank, coupled with certain other procedures stated below, obviates the need to prove the footing of the client's cash disbursements record. In preparing the tape of the checks, a subtotal should be taken after listing the last of the checks written prior to the period being examined. This subtotal will be the source of the figure for checks outstanding at the beginning of the period but paid during the period (the figure of $900 in the sample reconciliation presented earlier).

(b) Inspect the payment date perforated into each check to determine that the check was actually paid during the period under examination.

2. Trace to the list of checks outstanding at the beginning of the period each check paid during the period which was issued prior to the period.

Ascertain that each of these checks is listed correctly and that none has been omitted from the list of outstanding checks. Place a tick mark alongside each amount so verified on the list of outstanding checks.

3. Verify against the cash disbursements record the amount of each outstanding check not shown as paid in the preceding step, and trace the amount to a copy of the client's list of checks outstanding at the close of the period. Every outstanding check not paid during the period *must* be shown as outstanding at the end of the period.

4. Compare each check paid during the period with its cashbook entry as to date, number, payee, and amount, and determine that the check bears an authorized signature, that it is properly endorsed, and that any second endorsements, particularly by an officer or employee, can be reasonably explained. For each check written and paid during the period being examined, place a small tick mark alongside the appropriate entry in the cash disbursements record.

5. Trace the amount of each cash disbursement entry not tick-marked as a result of the previous step to the list of checks outstanding at the close of the period, noting that each unpaid check is listed correctly and that none has been omitted. (These five procedures will establish the validity of the client's list of outstanding checks at the close of the period.)

6. Prove the footing of the list of outstanding checks at the close of the period, and ascertain that the total agrees with the corresponding figure in the bank reconciliation form.

7. Account for all check numbers, commencing with the last check issued at the close of the previous period and ending with the first check issued at the beginning of the following period. Inspect all voided checks, making certain that the checks have been mutilated to prevent their use. Any check numbers not represented by paid or voided checks *must* be listed as outstanding at the close of the period.

8. Determine (usually on a test basis) the validity of the disbursements listed in the cash disbursements record during the period by examining invoices, receiving reports, payroll records, or other supporting documents.

   (a) The vendor's name and the amount on each invoice should agree with the corresponding entry, and the invoice should be addressed to the client.

   (b) Each invoice should be noted for any evidence that it may have been paid previously; hence an invoice bearing an old date should always be regarded with suspicion.

   (c) Invoices should bear evidence that required approvals were given.

   (d) Any disbursements to officers, employees, or banks should receive particularly close scrutiny.

   (e) Reimbursements to petty cash funds should be reviewed in detail; supporting vouchers should be totaled and inspected for propriety and necessary approvals.

(f) Inter-bank transfers should be scheduled in the manner recommended on page 393.

If the procedures which have just been discussed are thoroughly understood and carefully applied, they should be adequate to disclose most efforts designed to conceal the embezzlement or theft of cash. The principal exceptions would be cash that is withheld at the time a sale is made, with no recording of the sale or recording at a reduced amount, and kickbacks by suppliers representing billings to the company in excess of the correct amounts. The cash-sales problem points up the undesirability of having one person in control of all phases of a transaction. The kickback from the supplier illustrates the problem of collusion and suggests the importance of intimate acquaintance with operating figures on the part of owners and managers.

Generally speaking, the detailed audit of a client's cash transactions should give the auditor reasonable assurance that (a) cash receipts have been fully accounted for, (b) cash disbursements have been made only for authorized and valid purposes, and (c) cash balances are intact. The auditing procedures involved should be used as a supplement to regular year-end procedures only if internal control is weak or when the additional verification is specifically requested by the client.

REVIEW QUESTIONS

1. Explain what is meant by lapping.
2. By what means can the auditor disclose the existence of kiting?
3. What records will the auditor have to obtain from the client in order to prepare and verify a four-column bank reconciliation?
4. Of what value is an authenticated duplicate deposit ticket to the auditor?
5. The auditor "examines" checks paid by the bank in support of disbursements recorded in the books. Explain in detail how the auditor "examines" the checks.
6. Why does the auditor prepare a schedule of inter-bank transfers?
7. If a collection from a customer is recorded but withheld from the day's cash deposit, by what means can the resulting shortage be concealed?
8. When verifying a four-column bank reconciliation, how does the auditor satisfy himself that he has been given all checks paid by the bank during the period covered by the reconciliation?
9. How does the auditor proceed in accounting for all checks issued during the period covered by the four-column bank reconciliation?

QUESTIONS ON APPLICATION OF AUDITING STANDARDS

10. Given the following figures for the line "Transactions per Bank" on a four-column bank reconciliation, show how the following reconciling items would be displayed on the reconciliation—i.e., in which column or columns the reconciling amount would be shown, and whether it would be added or subtracted (figure encircled).

	Balance 4/1	Receipts	Withdrawals	Balance 4/30
Transactions per bank	$2,000	$3,500	($3,800)	$1,700

(a) As a result of a footing error in March, cash receipts were understated $100 in that month. An entry correcting the error was made in April.

(b) A check for $50 written in April and clearing the bank in April was not recorded in the cash disbursements record until May.

(c) A customer's check for $200 received in April and deposited was charged back by the bank as NSF in April. The client was still holding the check at April 30, and had made no book entries concerning the check.

11. Justify your conclusion as to which of the following frauds would have a more material effect on the financial statements, assuming that the fraud was not discovered and that the loss is fully covered by fidelity insurance:

 (a) Collections totaling $10,000 were withheld during the year, and the abstraction of these receipts concealed by underfooting the total of outstanding checks at the year end by the same amount.

 (b) Purchase documents totaling $10,000 were submitted for payment a second time, and endorsements were then forged on the checks to obtain the money.

12. You are engaged in an examination of a client's financial statements as of May 31, and have ascertained that your client's excellent internal control has been sustained since your previous examination. Justify your decision as to which (if any) of the following procedures you would employ in your examination:

 (a) Account for the serial numbers of all checks written during May.

 (b) Trace all checks dated May 31 or prior and returned with the June 15 cut-off statement to the client's list of outstanding checks at May 31.

 (c) Request the bank to authenticate duplicate deposit tickets for May 29, 30, and 31 and compare these deposit tickets in detail with the cash receipts book.

 (d) Account for all checks outstanding at May 31 last year that did not clear with the cut-off statement.

13. The last check entered in the check register for December is No. 2804, but in reviewing checks received with the cut-off statement you note that check No. 2805, payable to The Bank of the Kaw (one of the client's depositaries), is dated December 31. What type of manipulation should be suspected, and what steps should indicate whether manipulation or an honest mistake is involved?

14. Suggest a reason for the suggestion that in preparing the four-column bank reconciliation the auditor add up the deposits on the bank statement and "plug" the difference to get withdrawals, rather than add the withdrawals and plug the deposit figure.

15. What procedures in connection with verifying the four-column bank reconciliation will reveal the fact that a check charged on the bank statement for the period under examination has been abstracted from the accompanying file of paid checks?

16. What forms of manipulation are each of the following procedures designed to detect?

 (a) In connection with the current audit, account for all checks outstanding at the close of the audit for the preceding year which did not clear the bank by the completion of the audit.

(b) Investigate large checks outstanding at the audit date and not clearing the bank with the cut-off statement for the subsequent period.

(c) Compare daily deposit totals per books and per bank for the last week of the year.

(d) Compare all checks returned with the cut-off bank statement and ·dated on or before the audit date with the list of outstanding checks at the audit date.

(e) Note the length of time required by the checks examined under (d) to clear the bank.

(f) Examine checks clearing the bank during the subsequent period for endorsements which predate the date of the check.

(g) Obtain directly from the bank the cut-off statement for the subsequent period.

17. Preparation of checks, recording disbursements, and reconciling the bank account are all handled by J. M. Carter of the Cordo Company. Carter notes that a check for $100 has been outstanding for over one year and probably will not be cashed. He therefore takes a check from the back of the checkbook and writes it payable to himself for $100, forges the treasurer's signature, cashes the check, and attempts to conceal the disbursement by omitting the original check from the list of outstanding checks on subsequent reconciliations and destroying the fraudulent check.

(a) What is the principal internal control weakness which should be corrected?

(b) What audit procedures would disclose the manipulation?

PROBLEMS

18. From the following information, prepare a four-column bank reconciliation for the month of January, supplying any missing figures.

Per January bank statement	
Balance, January 1	$4,000
Deposits, January	9,000
Balance January 31	3,000
Outstanding checks	
December 31	1,500
(Of these checks, $1,000 cleared the bank in January)	
January 31	2,000
(Including December checks still outstanding)	
Deposit in transit December 31	500
Check from Customer A received January 3, charged back by bank as NSF January 5, redeposited January 7 and cleared. Only book entry is for the receipt of the check from Customer A on January 3.	100

19. The following information was obtained in an audit of the cash account of Tuck Company as of December 31. Assume that the C.P.A. has satisfied himself as to the validity of the cash book, the bank statements and the returned checks, except as noted.

1. The bookkeeper's bank reconciliation at November 30.

```
Balance per bank statement ..........................  $ 19,400
Add deposit in transit  .............................     1,100
   Total  ...........................................    20,500
Less outstanding checks
                        #2540        $140
                         1501         750
                         1503         480
                         1504         800
                         1505          30               2,300
Balance per books  ..................................  $ 18,200
```

2. A summary of the bank statement for December.

```
Balance brought forward  ............................  $ 19,400
Deposits  ...........................................   148,700
                                                        168,100
Charges  ............................................   132,500
Balance, December 31  ...............................  $ 35,600
```

3. A summary of the cash book for December before adjustments.

```
Balance brought forward  ............................  $ 18,200
Receipts  ...........................................   149,690
                                                        167,890
Disbursements  ......................................   124,885
Balance, December 31  ...............................  $ 43,005
```

4. Included with the cancelled checks returned with the December bank statement were the following:

Number	Date of Check	Amount of Check	
#1501	November 28	$75	This check was in payment of an invoice for $750 and was recorded in the cash book as $750.
#1503	November 28	$580	This check was in payment of an invoice for $580 and was recorded in the cash book as $580.
#1523	December 5	$150	Examination of this check revealed that it was unsigned. A discussion with the client disclosed that it had been mailed inadvertently before it was signed. The check was endorsed and deposited by the payee and processed by the bank even though it was a legal nullity. The check was recorded in the cash disbursements.
#1528	December 12	$800	This check replaced #1504 that was returned by the payee because it was mutilated. Check #1504 was not cancelled on the books.

Number	Date of Check	Amount of Check	
⎯	December 19	$200	This was a counter check drawn at the bank by the president of the Company as a cash advance for travel expense. The president over-looked informing the bookkeeper about the check.
⎯	December 20	$300	The drawer of this check was the Tuck Company.
#1535	December 20	$350	This check had been labeled NSF and returned to the payee because the bank had erroneously believed that the check was drawn by the Luck Company. Subsequently the payee was advised to redeposit the check.
#1575	January 5	$10,000	This check was given to the payee on December 30 as a postdated check with the understanding that it would not be deposited until January 5. The check was not recorded on the books in December.

5. The Tuck Company discounted its own 60-day note for $9,000 with the bank on December 1. The discount rate was 6%. The bookkeeper recorded the proceeds as a cash receipt at the face value of the note.

6. The bookkeeper records customers' dishonored checks as a reduction of cash receipts. When the dishonored checks are redeposited they are recorded as a regular cash receipt. Two NSF checks for $180 and $220 were returned by the bank during December. The $180 check was redeposited but the $220 check was still on hand at December 31.

   Cancellations of Tuck Company checks are recorded by a reduction of cash disbursements.

7. December bank charges were $20. In addition a $10 service charge was made in December for the collection of a foreign draft in November. These charges were not recorded on the books.

8. Check #2540 listed in the November outstanding checks was drawn two years ago. Since the payee cannot be located, the president of Tuck Company agreed to the C.P.A.'s suggestion that the check be written back into the accounts by a journal entry.

9. Outstanding checks at December 31 totaled $4,000 excluding checks #2540 and #1504.

10. The cut-off bank statement disclosed that the bank had recorded a deposit of $2,400 on January 2. The bookkeeper had recorded this deposit on the books on December 31 and then mailed the deposit to the bank.

Required:

Prepare a four-column reconciliation (sometimes called a "proof of cash") of the cash receipts and cash disbursements recorded on the bank statement and on the Company's books for the month of December. *The reconciliation should agree with the cash figure that will appear in the Company's financial statements.* (Uniform C.P.A. Examination)

20. Glatfelt Rural Electric Power Cooperative issues books of sight drafts to the foremen of its ten field crews. The foremen use the drafts to pay the expenses of the field crews when they are on line duty requiring overnight stays.

   The drafts are prenumbered and, as is clearly printed on the drafts, are limited to expenditures of $300 or less. The foremen prepare the drafts in duplicate and send the duplicates, accompanied by expense reports substantiating the drafts, to the general office.

   The draft duplicates are accumulated at the general office and a voucher is prepared when there are two or three draft duplicates on hand. The voucher is the authority for issuing a company check for deposit in an imprest fund of $5,000 maintained at a local bank to meet the drafts as they are presented for payment. The Cooperative maintains a separate general ledger account for the imprest fund.

   The audit of the voucher register and cash disbursements disclosed the following information pertaining to sight drafts and the reimbursement of the imprest fund:

   1. Voucher #10524 dated 12/31, paid by check #10524 dated 12/31, for the following drafts:

Draft #	Date	Crew #	Explanation	Amount
6001	12/24	3	Expenses, 12/22-24	$160
2372	12/28	6	Expenses, 12/26-28	310
5304	12/30	7	Cash advance to foreman	260
			Voucher total	$730

   2. Voucher #10531 dated 12/31, paid by check #10531 dated 1/3, for the following drafts:

Draft #	Date	Crew #	Explanation	Amount
4060	12/29	1	Expenses, 12/27-29	$150
1816	1/3	4	Expenses, 1/1-3	560
			Voucher total	$710

   3. Voucher #23 dated 1/8, paid by check #23 dated 1/8 for the following drafts:

Draft #	Date	Crew #	Explanation	Amount
1000	12/31	9	Expenses, 12/28-31	$270
2918	1/3	10	Expenses, 12/28-31	190
4061	1/7	1	Expenses, 1/4-6	210
			Voucher total	$670

   4. All of the above vouchers were charged to Travel Expense.

   5. Examination of the imprest fund's bank statement for December, the January cut-off bank statement and accompanying drafts presented for payment disclosed the following information:

      a. Reimbursement check #10524 was not credited on the December bank statement.

      b. The bank honored draft #2372 at the established maximum authorized amount.

c. Original drafts drawn by foremen but not presented to the client's bank for payment by 12/31 totaled $1,600. This total included all December drafts itemized above except #4060 and #2372, which were deducted by the bank in December.

d. December bank service charges listed on the December bank statement but not recorded by the client amounted to $80.

e. The balance per the bank statement at December 31 was $5,650.

Required:

(a) Prepare the auditor's adjusting journal entry to correct the books at December 31. (The books have not been closed.) A supporting working paper analyzing the required adjustments should be prepared in good form.

(b) Prepare a reconciliation of the balance per bank statement and the financial statement figure for the imprest cash account. The first figure in your reconciliation should be the balance per bank statement.

(Uniform C.P.A. Examination)

21. The senior accountant in charge of the engagement to which you are assigned (The Anderson Company) hands you the following ledgers, journals, and other records and instructs you to make a thorough review of the December transactions and the December 31 and November 30 bank reconciliations. He cautions you that the audit is being made because fraud is suspected on the part of the bookkeeper-cashier, and that therefore you should be extremely alert.

You may assume that the books (ledger and journals) correctly reflect all transactions of the business which took place up to and including November 30. Thus the cash account shows the amount of cash for which the bookkeeper-cashier is accountable at November 30. Also, there have been no bank errors. The bank statement at all times reflects the amount on deposit for which the bank is legally liable. All sales are made on account, and all disbursements are first recorded as a liability through the voucher register.

Should you find any discrepancies you are to prepare a report, *in form for typing, which will be delivered to C. D. Anderson,* owner of the business. The report should give:

1. A description of each and any discrepancy found, and the total of the discrepancies if there is more than one.

2. Any adjusting entries that should be made, assuming the books have not been closed.

Bank Reconciliation 11/30				Cash Receipts—December	
Balance per bank			$2,398	Date	Amount
Outstanding checks	#124	$10		12/2	$32
	#126	12		12/5	19
	#127	9		12/17	18
	#128	5	31	12/29	24
		—		12/31	30
			$2,367		—
Deposits in transit		$25			$93
		20	45		
		—			
			$2,412		

Check Record—December		Cash Account—December						
Number	Amount	12/1	Balance	$2,412	12/31	Checks	$ 246
129	$ 25	12/31	Deposits	93	12/31	Bal.	2,259
130	20						
131	30			$2,505			$2,505
132	19	1/1	Balance	$2,259			
133	28						
134	14						
135	10						
136	5						
137	17						
138	23						
139	19						
140	8						
	$246						

Bank Statement—December

Date		Withdrawals	Deposits	Balance
12/1				$2,398
12/1	#124	$10	$20	2,408
12/3	127	9		2,399
12/3	129	25	32	2,406
12/6	130	20	19	2,405
12/9	131	30		2,375
12/11	125	18		2,357
12/14	133	28		2,329
12/18	128	15	18	2,332
12/21	132	19		2,313
12/25	134	14		2,299
12/27	136	5		2,294
12/29	139	19		2,275
12/30			24	2,299

Bank Reconciliation 12/31

Balance per bank			$2,299	
Outstanding checks	#126	$12		
	135	10		
	137	17		
	138	23		
	140	8	70	
			$2,229	
Deposit in transit			30	(credited by bank 1/2)
Balance per books			$2,259	

Payroll systems:
internal control; auditing

17

Payroll expenses for wages and fringe benefits constitute a major operating item for most businesses; as such, systems and internal control considerations warrant close attention. The area does not, however, present a problem of similar magnitude to the independent auditor because the expense element is usually well controlled by management; the combined internal control over payroll and the disbursement of cash is usually quite good, and the related balance sheet liability for the various accruals tends to be nominal and to present little difficulty in valuation. The influence of the balance sheet aspect of the item on the determination of the proper amount for income statement purposes is thus nominal. Systems considerations are discussed first, but the audit of the system and statement figures is also included in this chapter.

Objectives of Internal Control

Control of payroll expenses and the prevention of fraud are evident in the following list of objectives, which are intended to give assurance that:

1. Payroll expenses are reported on a responsibility basis, preferably in comparison with standard or budgeted amounts.
2. Compensation is closely related to the work done through a program of job evaluation and classification.
3. Only qualified persons are added to the payroll.
4. Hours worked, rate of pay, gross pay, and deductions are all correctly computed.
5. Employees whose services are terminated are immediately removed from the payroll.

The means of accomplishing these objectives are the subject of the chart on pages 410–11 and the ensuing discussion of the systems responsibilities assigned to the various departments.

Employment (Personnel) Department

The employment department plays an important part in payroll activities, commencing with screening and engaging new employees and extending through to the termination of an employee's services. Employment agencies and classified advertisements are the principal sources of prospective employees. Applicants should be interviewed and tested to provide an indication of their competence and suitability for employment. Those who appear satisfactory are then usually referred for final acceptance to the line supervisor under whom they will be expected to work.

Before or immediately after a final favorable decision is reached, former employment should be verified. Former employers should be asked to state why the person left their employ, whether the person's work was satisfactory, and whether they would be willing to re-employ the person. An important aspect of such investigation is the matter of gaps, particularly for extended periods, in the person's employment record. Assertions that the applicant was unemployed or engaged in further education or training should be verified, to guard against an omitted listing of employment from which the applicant was discharged for cause, or failure to report a period spent in prison.

If the applicant is to be employed, he should complete form W-4, "Employee's Withholding Exemption Certificate," and sign authorizations for any amounts to be deducted from his pay, such as insurance, union dues, or savings. The appropriate information from these records, plus a rate card showing the person's rate of pay, should be forwarded to the payroll department. If address plates are used in the payroll process for repetitive printing of name, department, employee number, and other information, a plate should be prepared for the new employee. Preparation of the employee's first time card would complete the preliminary steps.

If a program of job evaluation is in effect to assure that pay scales are in accordance with the employee's qualifications and the type of work he is doing, this program may be under the jurisdiction of the employment department, or possibly under the industrial engineering section of the manufacturing department.

The employment department should also play a key part in the procedures when employment is terminated. An "exit" interview is important in determining why an employee is quitting, or in explaining the reasons for a temporary layoff or permanent dismissal. In order to assure that such an interview is not bypassed by the employee, it is common to require completion of the interview before the requisition is drawn for the check for wages earned since the last full pay period. At the same time, the payroll department should be notified that the employee is to be removed from the payroll, thus providing protection against payroll padding: any payment involving a nonexistent person, former employee, or present employee who did not actually perform any work.

Timekeeping Department

Timekeeping is commonly a responsibility that is under the factory or cost accountant. From the standpoint of internal control, timekeeping should not be a responsibility of line supervisors or of employees who have payroll responsibilities, in view of the opportunities for padding that would be presented.

Most systems require two different types of time records—attendance time, showing the total number of hours at work; and job time, showing what jobs the employee performed while at work. Attendance time cards are headed up with employee name, number, and other information shortly before the payroll period by means of addressing equipment and then placed in timecard racks near the plant and office entrances.

As an employee reports for work, he selects his own card, punches in on a nearby time clock, and then places his card in a slot bearing his name in an "in" card rack. Time recording should be supervised by plant security guards, who should be responsible for enforcing the rule that an employee should punch only his own card. Punching another person's card in addition to his own should constitute cause for dismissal, as the presumption would be that the other card was punched in order to defraud the company by indicating that an absent employee was at work.

Through the use of both an "in" and an "out" timecard rack, the timekeeper can readily note, after the regular starting time, which employees are late or absent for purposes of special reports to be prepared.

In the case of construction or other types of field work, attendance records may be kept in a time book by the foreman, or if the job is large enough, a timekeeper will check the men in and out and make test checks during the day to be sure that the men are still on the job.

Job time may be kept by each worker on a form with provision for job number or description and start and stop time for a series of jobs, or separate prepunched cards may be used for the information on each job. Sometimes the timekeepers record job time, with workers reporting to their timekeeper each time they start a new job. Special elapsed-time recorders may be used to record job time, thus eliminating the manual subtraction of start time from stop time to obtain the amount of time spent.

When compensation is on a piecework basis, the number of pieces may be counted and reported by the employee, by a timekeeper, or by an inspector. Other plans involve automatic counting devices that are attached

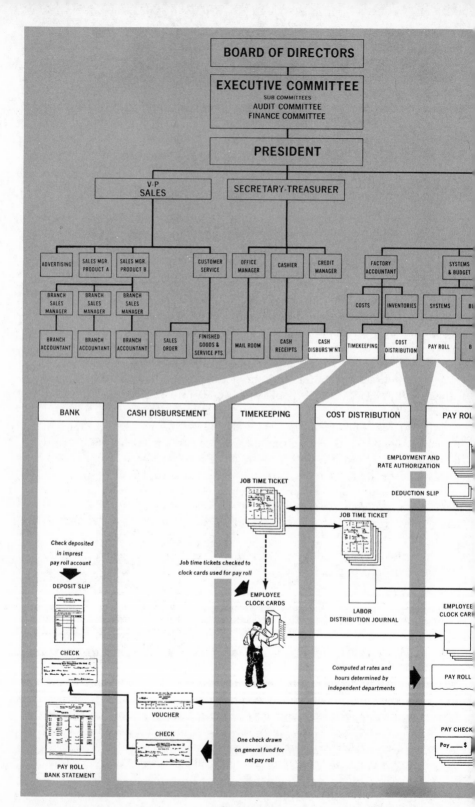

Figure 17-1

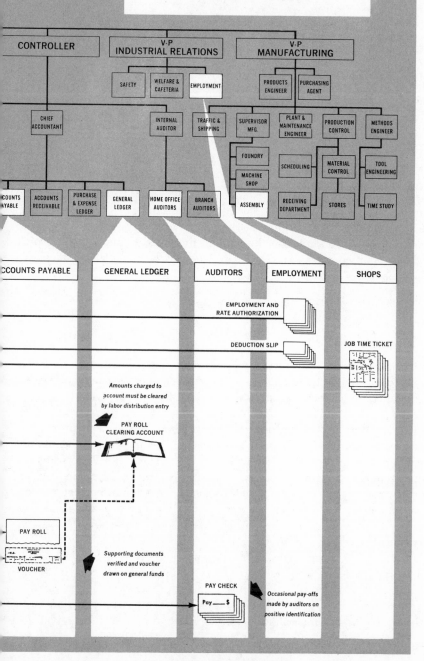

PAY ROLL

PROCEDURAL FLOW CHART SHOWN IN RELATION
TO ORGANIZATION CHART TO PORTRAY
THE CONTROL OBTAINED THROUGH SEGREGATION
OF FUNCTIONAL RESPONSIBILITY

CONTROLLER

V-P INDUSTRIAL RELATIONS

V-P MANUFACTURING

SAFETY | WELFARE & CAFETERIA | EMPLOYMENT

PRODUCTS ENGINEER | PURCHASING AGENT

CHIEF ACCOUNTANT

INTERNAL AUDITOR | TRAFFIC & SHIPPING | SUPERVISOR MFG. | PLANT & MAINTENANCE ENGINEER | PRODUCTION CONTROL | METHODS ENGINEER

FOUNDRY

SCHEDULING | MATERIAL CONTROL | TOOL ENGINEERING

MACHINE SHOP

ACCOUNTS PAYABLE | ACCOUNTS RECEIVABLE | PURCHASE & EXPENSE LEDGER | GENERAL LEDGER | HOME OFFICE AUDITORS | BRANCH AUDITORS | ASSEMBLY | RECEIVING DEPARTMENT | STORES | TIME STUDY

CCOUNTS PAYABLE | GENERAL LEDGER | AUDITORS | EMPLOYMENT | SHOPS

EMPLOYMENT AND RATE AUTHORIZATION

DEDUCTION SLIP

JOB TIME TICKET

Amounts charged to
account must be cleared
by labor distribution entry

PAY ROLL
CLEARING ACCOUNT

PAY ROLL

VOUCHER

Supporting documents
verified and voucher
drawn on general funds

PAY CHECK

Pay ____ $

Occasional pay-offs
made by auditors on
positive identification

Figure 17-1 (Continued)   411

to the machines, or the use of production tickets that are prepared at the time a production order for the lot is prepared.

Payroll Department

The payroll department has the responsibility for calculating earnings for the payroll period and preparing checks and related payroll records. This activity is ordinarily a part of the general accounting work under the chief accountant, as suggested by the chart, Figure 17–1.

Because supervisory employees are held responsible for payroll costs charged to them on a responsibility basis, it is desirable that they have an opportunity to review and approve attendance and job time. records before these records are released to the payroll department for processing. The first step in payroll calculation should be to balance job and attendance time for each employee. Hourly rates can then be inserted on the records, or can be verified if the rates have already been recorded by the employee. Hours and rate can then be extended to obtain total earnings and the charge to each job. Premium pay for overtime or any shift differential is also calculated at this point. Because the overtime premium (the extra half-time paid in addition to the straight-time rate for overtime) is preferably accounted for as an overhead charge to be spread over all work, the calculation is best handled as follows:

$$
\begin{array}{llll}
46 \text{ hrs.} & @ & \$2.00 = & \$92.00 \\
6 \text{ hrs.} & @ & \$1.00 = & \underline{6.00} \\
& & \text{Total earned} & \underline{\underline{\$98.00}}
\end{array}
$$

If overtime is directly attributable to a particular job, however, the premium may be charged directly to that job rather than charged as general overhead.

The attendance clock card is often used as a form of payroll "worksheet" by recording on the card the various tax deductions and other authorized deductions. Withholding tax deductions can be computed or obtained from a table, after considering the number of exemptions to which the employee is entitled as shown on the payroll department records. Social Security tax (often referred to as F.I.C.A. tax or F.O.A.B. tax) is calculated at the current rate on earnings not in excess of the maximum subject to tax. If an employee's earnings have exceeded the maximum taxable, that fact can be ascertained from the earnings record prepared by the payroll department.

If an accounting machine with calculating ability is used, the payroll can be completed by working directly from the attendance card, including the making of extensions, without further intermediate steps. Three separate payroll records are necessary, and they can be prepared simultaneously with one writing on an accounting machine. The records are:

1. Payroll journal (or register) listing all employees for the payroll period and showing for each employee his name and payroll number, hours worked, gross earnings, the various deductions made from his pay, and his net pay. Net pay is calculated by one register of the accounting machine by subtracting the various deductions from gross earnings. Other registers are used to develop columnar totals for the entire payroll for gross earnings, each type of deduction, and net pay. These totals are used to prepare the payroll voucher, which is the vehicle for recording payroll information in the general ledger and for authorizing the payroll disbursement.

2. Check and earnings statement for each employee. The earnings statement is in the form of a stub attached to the check and contains the same information recorded on the payroll journal, detailing the factors entering into the calculation of net pay. The check is drawn for the amount of the net pay shown on the earnings statement.

3. Earnings record for each employee. This is a continuous record for the year, showing the earnings and deductions for each pay period. The record must be maintained in order that required quarterly reports on earnings can be prepared for F.I.C.A. and unemployment tax purposes, as well as the annual W-2 form showing total earnings and income taxes withheld. Because the figures are needed on a cumulative basis, they may be totaled at the end of each quarter, or if the accounting machine used in preparing the payroll has sufficient register capacity, "to date" totals can be maintained by picking up the previous "to date" figures each time a posting is made. Under such an arrangement, the program control of the accounting machine will cause a figure such as gross earnings to be simultaneously recorded in three registers: the register that computes net pay, the register that accumulates gross earnings for all employees for the payroll period, and the register that develops the new gross earnings to date figure for the employee. To prove the pickup of previous "to date" totals, sometimes a special proof total is also maintained. For example, if gross earnings and withholding tax are the only figures maintained on a "to date" basis, the proof total would be the sum of these two figures. The proof of pickup would involve programming a separate register to add together the pickup of gross earnings to date and withholding tax to date, and to subtract the pickup of the proof total. A zero balance standing in the proof register following this operation would indicate that the pickup was made correctly, making it possible for the operator to go on to the next step. Any balance in the proof register at this point would cause the machine to lock, forcing the operator to correct the error that was made.

The earnings record is also used as a convenient repository for various data needed for payroll preparation: rate of pay, number of exemptions for withholding tax calculation, and various deductions that the employee has authorized to be made from his pay.

Treasury Department

Payroll disbursements are frequently made through a special payroll account maintained at the bank on an imprest basis. Better control is possible in this way, as raised or forged checks will become apparent more quickly (by throwing the account into an overdraft), and the heavy volume of payroll checks is not intermingled with general disbursement checks. A payroll voucher becomes the basis for drawing a transfer check, which is used to place an amount of cash in the payroll account equal to the total net pay for the period. The voucher is based on totals shown in the payroll journal and results in an entry on the order of the following, which would be made through the voucher register:

```
Payroll account                                          XXX
    Vouchers payable (net pay) ......................        XXX
    Withholding taxes payable .......................        XXX
    F. I. C. A. taxes payable .......................        XXX
    Other liability accounts for amount withheld  ........   XXX
```

The payroll journal is, in effect, a disbursement record for the individual payroll checks drawn against the payroll imprest account. These checks are signed by the treasurer or by a check-signing machine that is under his control. The signed checks are then handed to the paymaster, who is under the treasurer and is charged with distributing the checks to the employees. The paymaster constitutes a vital link in the chain of internal control, particularly with respect to preventing payroll padding. He should be satisfied as to the identity of each employee who receives a check, and no person should receive more than one check. It is particularly important that the check for an employee not be handed to his supervisor or any other person, as that would facilitate any attempt at payroll padding.

Control over unclaimed checks for absent employees is also important. The paymaster should prepare a list of these checks, handing the checks and one copy of the list to the cashier or another person designated to hold the unclaimed checks until they are claimed. An employee who was absent should obtain a form, signed by his supervisor or timekeeper, evidencing that he was absent on payday and authorizing delivery of his check to him.

The other copy of the list of unclaimed checks should be given to a designated person in the accounting department. From time to time this person should account for each check shown on his copy of the list by examining either a check that is still on hand or a delivery-authorization form showing that the check was given to the employee upon his return to work.

Cost Accounting

To this point, the discussion has been concerned almost exclusively with the credit, or disbursement, side of payroll procedures. There remains the matter of the payroll distribution: allocating the payroll amount to the various expense accounts affected. In a simple situation where employees always work within the same department and departmental expense distribution is all that is necessary, these figures can be readily obtained by grouping the employees by department on the payroll journal and obtaining an expense total for each department. Under these circumstances, the debit for the payroll expense would be directly to the respective departmental payroll expense accounts, rather than to a payroll account, as was suggested earlier.

If workers shift from job to job and prepare job time records covering their activities, these records, after being balanced with the attendance time records, become the basis for the payroll distribution entry. The records are sorted according to account number, totaled, and a journal entry prepared to charge the expense accounts affected and to credit the payroll account, which was charged for the gross payroll amount in connection with the payment procedures.

Standard cost variances are developed from tickets authorizing payment for nonstandard amounts, such as for idle time, setup, rework, time in excess of the standard established, or a rate other than the standard rate. Approval of these tickets by the supervisor as soon as the variance has occurred presents an excellent opportunity for controlling direct labor on an exception basis.

Alternative Payroll Records

In very small businesses, a payroll book may perform most of the functions of the various records that have been described. A page is devoted to each employee, with a line for each payroll period. Hours worked can be recorded each day, then totaled at the end of the period, extended, and deductions and net pay shown. The book serves as both a payroll journal and an employee's earnings summary.

Another approach utilizes a form of bookless bookkeeping. Payroll checks, with an earnings statement stub across the top, are supplied in sheets of three or four, in an original and two copies. The earnings information, employee name, and check amount are filled in, by the use of a ball-point pen or a typewriter. The original check with earnings statement attached goes to the employee; the duplicate copy is separated from the others making up the sheet and placed in a special file for the employee, constituting the earnings record for payroll tax information; and the triplicate copy is filed in sheet form, constituting the payroll journal record.

Punched-Card Records

Procedures for handling salaried payroll by punched card are relatively simple because each employee receives the same amount each pay period. Identifying information, plus gross earnings, the various deductions, and net pay are punched in master cards. The master cards are used as input to the tabulator to print checks and earnings statements. Next, summary cards containing earnings and deduction totals to date are merged with the master cards. With the merged cards as input to the tabulator, a payroll journal is prepared, and current and previous earnings and deductions are combined to summary-punch new summary cards showing earnings and deductions to date.

For hourly payroll, one plan utilizes attendance cards which are punched cards reproduced from a master file. Time is clocked in and out on the card in either printed or punched-hole form. At the end of the pay period, total hours worked are figured by a clerk and recorded in written or mark-sensed form for subsequent punching. For time recorded in punched-hole form, the electronic calculator figures the time worked and punches the total into the card.

Job time cards may be key-punched from handwritten job time records or prepunched job cards can be used, with subsequent punching employed to punch employee number and elapsed time from handwritten information. At the close of the payroll period, the punched attendance and job cards are sorted together according to employee number and zero-balanced on the tabulator in order to detect any errors or lost cards.

The attendance cards are separated from the job cards, and the calculating punch is used to extend hours and rate, figure any overtime earnings, and calculate withholding and F.I.C.A. taxes, punching the results into the cards. The cards are then merged with employee deduction cards, and the payroll work is completed following procedures similar to those described for salaried payroll.

The job cards are sorted and tabulated to obtain a variety of figures and reports, such as employee efficiency, variance totals classified by type and by department in which incurred, indirect expenses, and costs by job or part number.

Advanced systems that involve the use of an electronic computer record information on magnetic tape or even directly in the computer memory, from input stations located throughout the plant. These stations read employee-identifying information from a card or the employee's badge inserted in a reading slot. Job number is recorded by depressing keys. From that point, all processing is handled automatically by the computer.

Management Reports

The materiality of labor costs in most types of operations, coupled with the fact that labor is so subject to vacillation, usually results in a wide variety of reports intended to assist in the control of that element of expense. Related personnel statistics may touch on such matters as labor turnover, absenteeism, lost time from illness or accident, overtime, and number of employees added or removed from the payroll, classified by reason in the latter instance.

Responsibility reporting should be the basis for the presentation of all labor-cost information. The variances reported under standard cost plans are also important to effective reporting, because they highlight the exceptions that have occurred, and the classes of variances indicate the causes for the deviations from standard.

Indirect labor has tended to grow in importance relative to direct labor, largely as a result of the influence of automation in reducing direct labor while requiring additional indirect workers to service the machines. As a result, indirect labor expense, which was once considered "just another overhead expense," has become of sufficient importance to warrant utilization of all applicable control techniques. Especially important of these are budgeting and the comparison of actual and budgeted results with the comparative figures classified on a responsibility basis. For any indirect labor that bears a close relationship to direct labor, the percentage relationship of the figures should always be shown.

If indirect labor is chargeable to other departments, as in the case of repairs and maintenance, the expense should be reported both in terms of the department supervising the work and the department for which the work was done. Many tasks performed by indirect labor are largely repetitive, and in such instances time and motion study, the setting of standards, and reporting of variances from standard are being applied with considerable success.

Internal Auditing

The internal auditor's principal concern in his examination of payroll procedures and labor expense should be the minimization and control of such expenses. To this end he should review the form and use of the various operating reports prepared, the setting of standards and budgets, and the procedures and related internal control pertaining to payroll preparation. Sufficient tests of the payroll records should be made to satisfy the internal auditor that the system is being followed in practice. Payroll data should be tested against timecards, piecework records, approved rates of pay, and authorizations for payroll deductions. Calculations and footings should also be tested. Particular attention should be paid to the presence of approvals that are required, and the internal auditor should accompany the paymaster when paychecks are being distributed in order to note whether proper procedures are being followed.

In the course of his work, the internal auditor should watch for possible wages and hours law violations, failure of employees to observe regulations concerning the punching of timecards, and any other payroll deficiencies. Figures reported to management should be traced on a test basis to the underlying records as evidence that the reports are being correctly prepared. If the reports include explanations for variances from standard, the propriety and reasonableness of the explanations should be tested against the available facts.

STANDARDS OF STATEMENT PRESENTATION

There are no particular problems of presentation of payroll expenses and liabilities in the financial statements. The standards of presentation given in Chapter 10 concerning éxpenses and liabilities are fully applicable to payroll amounts. In a multiple-step income statement, salaries and wages will appear under several classifications: direct labor, overhead expenses, and selling, general, and administrative expenses. Payroll taxes and other payroll-related expenses are shown as overhead charges if related to production payrolls, or under the selling and administrative expense classifications when they pertain to those categories.

The liability for accrued wages may be shown under the sub-captions "Accrued liabilities" or "Other liabilities," or simply as "Salaries and wages payable" in the general listing of liabilities. The liability for taxes withheld from employees' wages is often classified under the caption "Accounts payable—other." The liability for payroll taxes assessed against the company may be shown as an accrued liability or grouped with the liability for amounts withheld from employees.

AUDIT OBJECTIVES AND PROCEDURES

The objectives in the examination of payroll expenses and liabilities are similar to those for other expenses and liabilities but are fewer in number:

1. Establish credibility of the accounting records.
2. Ascertain reasonableness of account balances and consistent application of appropriate expense classifications.
3. Review year-end cut-off of payroll transactions.

Establish Credibility of the Accounting Records

Tests of representative payroll transactions constitute the principal means of establishing the credibility of the accounts, at the same time providing necessary information about the operation of the system of internal control.

Trace handling of representative transactions from origin to final account balances. As a rule, the auditor's tests will be limited to one payroll period, but they may be extended if internal control is weak.

Factory payroll. The tests of the details of the factory payroll for a selected pay period should usually cover a group of workers selected at random from all departments. If all departments pay on approximately the same basis, however, the auditor may select the entire group of workers from one or two departments. For the workers selected for the test, the auditor should trace the figures for hours worked or pieces produced as shown by the payroll register to the source records. The source records might be time cards timekeeper's reports, job time tickets, or inspection reports showing number of pieces completed. Because the job tickets will probably be filed away by job number, they are not likely to be readily available for use by the auditor as a double check of the workers' time. The additional proof is not necessary, however, particularly if the payroll department compared both attendance and job time records when the payroll was prepared.

Hourly wage rates should be compared with rate authorization records. The payroll department should have the authorizations in its files, but if a duplicate record is maintained in the personnel department, the auditor's verification is strengthened if the comparison is made against the record which is outside the payroll department. The wage rates should also be tied in with the provisions of any union contracts which have been signed. The entire contract should be read, and any provisions which affect the client's financial liabilities to the workers should be noted in the working papers. Included might be provisions relating to the payment of overtime or shift premiums, vacation pay, allowance for uniforms or safety devices, sick benefits, or insurance premiums to be paid by the employer. All these provisions would, of course, affect payroll figures, and the auditor should satisfy himself that they have been properly carried out.

If payment is made on a piecework basis or on a standard-hours plan, the rates used should be traced to the company's official rate books or standard cost sheets.

The auditor's next step should be to verify the extension of hours or pieces times the rate to obtain the figure for gross earnings. Overtime or shift premiums and special allowances would also enter into the picture at this point and should be verified.

Deductions would be the next items to be verified. The verification of the Federal withholding tax would involve reference to the W-4 form filed by the employee and to a table of withholding tax figures. The amount of F.I.C.A. tax withheld should be verified by applying the current rate to the gross earnings. If the wages are shown to be exempt because the worker has already earned $6,600 in the year, the employee's earnings for the year to date should be verified by a reference to the individual earnings summary for that employee. Other deductions for such items as insurance, savings bonds, and union dues should be traced to the copy of the authorization for those deductions signed by the employee.

To complete the verification of the payroll register, the worker's net pay should be calculated, and then the register should be footed and cross-footed. The totals should be traced to the general ledger postings. Paid payroll checks will have been tested against the payroll register in connection with the examination of cash disbursements.

The total payroll amount will usually be charged to a payroll account and then distributed to the appropriate accounts by a separate journal entry showing the classification of the payroll charges. The payroll distribution figures should be tested against timecards, job tickets, or other records showing to what accounts the worker's time should be charged.

The above tests are most efficiently carried out by working directly from the client's records. In that case, the only working paper will be a memorandum describing the work that was done, as on schedule 20–1.

Office payroll. The procedures for testing the office payroll are quite similar to those discussed above for factory payroll, although office workers do not usually punch timecards. One procedure is to have them write their time in and time out opposite their names on a time sheet. If no record of attendance is kept, the supervisor should be required to prepare an absence report or time-off report if the payroll department is to dock the employee for the time missed.

Information for the distribution of payroll charges to the proper expense accounts is usually obtained simply by grouping the employees by department on the payroll register. The subtotal for each group then becomes the expense charge to that department.

Officers' salaries. Officers' salaries should be authorized by the board of directors. A schedule similar to 40–1 should be prepared listing each officer's salary. The schedule should carry a cross reference to the work paper schedule containing the abstract of the minutes of the directors' meeting at which the salaries were approved. The total officers' salaries should be reconciled with the corresponding charges to the various expense accounts.

Observation of payoff. In situations where internal control is weak, or where the auditor may wish to obtain additional evidence that payroll disbursements are being made only to persons actually working for the client, the auditor should observe the distribution of pay checks or pay envelopes. If the company is so large that it is not practicable for the auditor to observe the distribution of the entire payroll, one or more complete departments can be selected for the test.

The auditor should not announce in advance his intentions to observe the payoff. Rather, he should wait until the payroll checks or envelopes are ready to be distributed, and he should assume control over the checks or envelopes at that time. Before the distribution begins, the auditor should compare each worker's pay with the amount shown by the payroll register, and he should be certain that a check or envelope is present for each entry on the payroll register. The footings of the payroll register should be verified as further evidence that everything is proper.

The auditor should then turn the pay checks or pay envelopes over to the custody of the paymaster, but he should keep them under his observation and control. If company procedures require that an employee present proper identification before his pay is released to him, the auditor should be sure that the required procedure is being followed. If such a procedure is in effect, and if the auditor is satisfied that each employee receives only one check or envelope, he can be relatively certain that no irregularities exist with respect to any of the items he has observed being distributed.

In smaller companies the paymaster may be expected to know each employee personally, so that no further identification is required. In such cases the auditor should have an additional company employee, who has no connection with payroll, be present to further identify each employee as he receives his pay. If this arrangement is not followed, the auditor should at least note that no employee presents himself a second time and receives a second check or envelope. If there is any doubt in the auditor's mind about the identification of an employee, the auditor should not hesitate to ask for adequate evidence of his identity.

When employees are paid in cash, the auditor should note that each employee signs a receipt before his envelope is released to him. In some cases the receipt may be the stub of his timecard which the employee has retained. These should not be signed in advance, but if this sound rule has not been followed, the auditor should ask each employee to sign the receipt a second time, in the presence of the auditor. To be certain that no payroll manipulations have occurred involving "shorting" employees' pay envelopes, the auditor should ask each employee to count his pay while he is still in the auditor's presence.

If there are any unclaimed pay checks or envelopes, the auditor should prepare a list of them, seal the unclaimed wages in an envelope, and release the sealed envelope to the person who normally holds those items until they are claimed. Then, as the employees call for their pay, the auditor should be notified so that he can release each individual's pay upon proper identification of the employee. Should this procedure be too cumbersome, or should some wages still be unclaimed after a reasonable period of time, the auditor can proceed in a different manner. His purpose should be to establish the fact that the unclaimed wages belong to a person who was a bona fide employee of the company during the payroll period involved. This fact can usually be sufficiently proved by reference to personnel records and inquiry of appropriate company officials and other employees. To further verify the situation, the auditor, with the company's permission, may mail any remaining pay checks to the respective employees after verifying the addresses.

Ascertain Reasonableness of Account Balances and Consistent Application of Appropriate Expense Classifications

The most common means of approaching the problems of reasonableness and consistency is through comparisons of current figures with annual figures for prior years, as well as through comparisons on a month-to-month basis. For example, schedule C analyzes the changes in labor and the other elements that comprise the various inventory balances in order to highlight any significant changes in the relationships of these figures. Schedule 20 compares the amount of labor and other elements in cost of sales for the current and the preceding year. The month-to-month type of comparison is illustrated on schedule 20-1. All of the accounts charged with factory payroll expense are listed and the monthly charges to these accounts are shown. The most convenient method of preparing such a schedule is to summarize the monthly journal entries that distribute factory payroll expense.

Payroll taxes offer yet another means of establishing the reasonableness of recorded payroll expense. Schedule CC-2 shows how entries to the various payroll tax accounts may be summarized, supported by examination of tax returns and paid checks, and then related to total payroll expense as well as to the recorded payroll tax expense. The fact that payroll tax figures are audited by both the individual employees (through the year-end W-2 tax report) and the government and bear a direct relationship to payroll expense makes it possible to obtain an important independent verification of the reasonableness of payroll expense.

Other useful evidences of the reasonableness of payroll figures are budget and standard cost variances when these are available. Nominal variances afford assurance that the payroll amounts are reasonable and that there has been no major inconsistency in payroll classification.

The auditor should also take note that known changes in payroll costs, as when a labor contract has been revised to provide increases in wages or fringe benefits, are reflected accordingly in the accounting figures.

Review Year-End Cut-Offs of Payroll Transactions

Because the time required for payroll processing makes it impossible to pay employees on the last day of the payroll period, a company will always have a liability for accrued wages and for other related payroll transactions as well. These liabilities must be properly reflected in the accounts in order that the various payroll expenses for the year may be properly stated and hence fair presentation of both income statement and balance sheet amounts relative to payrolls require that the year-end cut-off of transactions be properly handled.

Accrued payroll. Some concerns use time records to compute the actual amount of accrued wages earned by each employee between the close of the last payroll period for which payment has been made and the end of the fiscal year. These amounts are accumulated to develop the figures for the year-end adjustment for accrued wages. The auditor should make sufficient tests of these calculations to assure himself that the work was properly done. He should also make an over-all test of the amount of accrued wages payable by allocating the total of the first payroll for the following period. The allocation between amounts earned prior to the close of the year and amounts earned in the following year can be made on the basis of the number of days involved.

Many concerns do not make a precise calculation of accrued payroll but merely estimate the amount by using the allocation method described above. This arrangement is satisfactory, but in reviewing the calculations the auditor should be satisfied that an allocation based on the number of days is sufficiently representative. Abnormal amounts of overtime occurring just before or just after the end of the year, or excessive absences on a particular day, could easily cause the allocation figure to be misstated. One quick way of checking for the possible existence of such distortions is to compare the total amount of the allocated payroll with payrolls immediately preceding and following that period.

Commissions or bonuses earned at the balance sheet date but not yet paid must, of course, be determined by actual calculation. The auditor should test sales figures against supporting records, establish the correctness of the rate of payment used, and test the extension of the two figures. Most importantly, the liability should bear a reasonable relationship to the liability at the close of the preceding year, and to any changes in contract terms or the volume of sales, profits, or other basis of such payments.

Accrued vacation pay. Some companies accrue the cost of employee vacations in order to avoid distortion of monthly operating statements during vacation months. Other companies may find it necessary to make the accrual because their union contract specifies that employees earn one day's vacation pay for every stated number of days worked, and are entitled to this pay after it is earned even in the case of dismissal or voluntary termination of employment. Under these conditions an actual liability exists and must be reflected in the financial statements.

The auditor should always read carefully all union contracts in order to become acquainted with any provisions in the contracts pertaining to vacation pay or other obligations upon the company that may have a direct bearing on the financial statements. The employer's computation of the liability existing at the balance sheet date should then be reviewed by the auditor for accuracy and reasonableness in relation to the contract terms and further tested by an over-all computation of the estimated liability based on total payroll expense, number of employees, and average vacation period.

Accrued pension payments. Pension agreements should be read by the auditor and pertinent provisions abstracted for retention in the permanent working paper files. Pension fund contributions required for the year under examination but not yet remitted to the trustee or insurance company handling the fund should appear as a current liability in the financial statements. The auditor should also consider the desirability of requesting confirmation that all payments to the fund have been made as required.

Unfunded pension plans present a particularly difficult problem to the auditor, and he may find it necessary to obtain the opinion of an actuary that the liability shown by the client is adequate to cover the pension rights that have become vested in the employees at the balance sheet date.

Accrued payroll taxes. If an analysis of payroll taxes similar to that shown on schedule CC-2 has been made, little more needs to be done to establish a proper cut-off. Examination of the tax return and paid check related to the year-end liability amount adds further support that the amount is properly stated.

Liability for amounts withheld from employees. Any amounts withheld but not remitted at the balance sheet date are a liability and must be included in the balance sheet. Payroll tests should indicate whether the various deductions have been properly authorized and correctly computed. Deductions not remitted at the balance sheet date should be traced to payroll totals and to reports and paid checks covering their subsequent remittance to the proper parties.

SUMMARY

Internal control

Duties which ideally should be performed by different individuals—
    Employment

Work supervision
Timekeeping
Payroll preparation
Disbursement of funds
Distribution of checks or pay envelopes to employees
General ledger accounting and reporting
Cost accounting and reporting

Statement presentation

General standards for reporting expenses and liabilities apply to payroll items.

Payroll taxes and fringe-benefit costs should be reported as overhead expenses if related to production payrolls, or as selling and administrative expenses when they pertain to those categories.

Liability for accrued wages may be reported as a separate current liability or under the sub-caption of "Accrued liabilities" or "Other liabilities."

Liability for amounts withheld from employees may be reported as "Accounts payable—other."

Audit objectives and procedures

Establish credibility of the accounting records.

Trace handling of representative transactions from origin to final account balances.

Observe payoff if internal control is weak.

Ascertain reasonableness of account balances and consistent application of appropriate expense classifications.

Make month-to-month and year-to-year comparisons.

Review variances from budget or standard.

Tie together payroll taxes and the reported wage amounts on which they should be based.

Account for the effect of any changes in wage rates or fringe benefits as shown by union contracts or otherwise known to have been initiated by the client.

Review year-end cut-off of payroll transactions.

Make over-all test of accrued wages by allocating year-end payroll on the basis of number of days to the close of the fiscal period.

Review calculations underlying amounts of accrued vacation pay and pension contributions.

Trace amounts for accrued payroll taxes and amounts withheld from employees to tax returns or remittance notices and paid checks.

REVIEW QUESTIONS

1. Why do payroll expenses, despite the substantial amounts usually involved, present little problem to the independent auditor in most situations?
2. What are the objectives of internal control over payroll expenses?
3. What important step relative to internal control should be taken by the employment department when an employee's services are terminated?
4. Differentiate between attendance time and job time.
5. What different departments will ordinarily be involved with payrolls when there is good internal control?
6. What are the principal reasons for maintaining an earnings record for each employee?
7. In preparing payroll records on an accounting machine, an employee's gross earnings may be simultaneously recorded in three different machine registers. What function would be served by each of these registers?
8. What is the reason for requiring that the paymaster deliver a payroll check only to the employee named as payee?
9. What use is made of the various copies of the payroll check and earnings stub under a plan of bookless bookkeeping?
10. Responsibility reporting would require that certain indirect labor payroll charges be reported in two different ways. Explain.
11. What are the independent auditor's objectives in the examination of payroll expenses and liabilities?
12. Explain how payroll taxes can be helpful to the independent auditor in his examination of recorded payroll expense.
13. How should wage rates be verified in connection with a test of factory payroll?
14. Explain in detail how the various tax deductions from workers' pay should be verified.
15. What should the auditor do about unclaimed pay checks at the completion of his observation of a payoff?

QUESTIONS ON SYSTEMS APPLICATIONS AND APPLICATION OF AUDITING STANDARDS

16. Assume that the account "Salesmen's Salaries" shows a total of $14,895.23 for the month of October. What can be done in internal reporting to help management properly interpret the meaning and significance of this figure?
17. Briefly describe and distinguish between four different manual methods of preparing payroll records.
18. Most businesses must pay time and one-half for work in excess of 40 hours during a work week. Under what circumstances should method (a) be used in computing payrolls? Method (b)?

$$
\begin{array}{llll}
\text{(a)} & 40 \text{ hrs.} \times \$1.00 = & \$40.00 \\
& 4 \text{ hrs.} \times \$1.50 = & \underline{6.00} \\
& & \underline{\$46.00} \\
\\
\text{(b)} & 44 \text{ hrs.} \times \$1.00 = & \$44.00 \\
& 4 \text{ hrs.} \times .50 = & \underline{2.00} \\
& & \underline{\$46.00}
\end{array}
$$

19. Explain why the paymaster should not be permitted to hold unclaimed wages until the employee calls for them, but rather, should list the unclaimed wages and turn them over to someone else for distribution to the employees.

20. What records and supporting data would be used in making a complete examination of payroll for one week?

21. What audit procedures would disclose that the payroll was padded by retaining on the payroll employees who had resigned?

22. Your client's bookkeeper has discovered that most employees do not reconcile total withholding tax shown on their W-2 forms with the amounts withheld during the year. Accordingly, the bookkeeper would understate the amount of withholding tax posted to various employees' cumulative earnings records and increase the tax posted to his own summary record by the same amount. Following the end of the year he would then claim a refund for the excess withholding tax shown on his own W-2. Should the customary examination of financial statements disclose the manipulation? Explain. What procedures would disclose the manipulation?

23. Why should the working papers contain the auditor's explanations and comments concerning variations in various payroll expenses as compared with the preceding year?

PROBLEMS

24. The Kowal Manufacturing Company employs about fifty production workers and has the following payroll procedures.

The factory foreman interviews applicants and on the basis of the interview either hires or rejects the applicants. When the applicant is hired he prepares a W-4 form (Employees' Withholding Exemption Certificate) and gives it to the foreman. The foreman writes the hourly rate of pay for the new employee in the corner of the W-4 form and then gives the form to a payroll clerk as notice that the worker has been employed. The foreman verbally advises the payroll department of rate adjustments.

A supply of blank time cards is kept in a box near the entrance to the factory. Each worker takes a timecard on Monday morning, fills in his name, and notes in pencil on the timecard his daily arrival and departure times. At the end of the week the workers drop the timecards in a box near the door to the factory.

The completed timecards are taken from the box on Monday morning by a payroll clerk. Two payroll clerks divide the cards alphabetically between them, one taking the A to L section of the payroll and the other taking the M to Z section. Each clerk is fully responsible for her section of the payroll. She computes the gross pay, deductions and net pay, posts the details to the employees' earnings records, and prepares and numbers the payroll checks. Employees are automatically removed from the payroll when they fail to turn in a timecard.

The payroll checks are manually signed by the chief accountant and given to the foreman. The foreman distributes the checks to the workers in the factory and arranges for the delivery of the checks to the workers who are absent. The payroll bank account is reconciled by the chief accountant who also prepares the various quarterly and annual payroll tax reports.

Required:
List your suggestions for improving the Kowal Manufacturing Company's

system of internal control for the factory hiring practices *and* payroll procedures.   (Uniform C.P.A. Examination)
25. You are engaged in auditing the financial statements of Henry Brown, a large
independent contractor. All employees are paid in cash because Mr. Brown
believes this arrangement reduces clerical expenses and is preferred by his
employees.

During the audit you find in the petty cash fund approximately $200 of
which $185 is stated to be unclaimed wages. Further investigation reveals that
Mr. Brown has installed the procedure of putting any unclaimed wages in the
petty cash fund so that the cash can be used for disbursements. When the
claimant to the wages appears, he is paid from the petty cash fund. Mr. Brown
contends that this procedure reduces the number of checks drawn to replenish
the petty cash fund and centers the responsibility for all cash on hand in one
person inasmuch as the petty cash custodian distributes the pay envelopes.

Required:
   (a) Does Mr. Brown's system provide proper internal control of unclaimed
       wages? Explain fully.
   (b) Because Mr. Brown insists on paying salaries in cash, what procedures
       would you recommend to provide better internal control over unclaimed
       wages?   (Uniform C.P.A. Examination)
26. During your audit of the accounts of the Gelard Manufacturing Corporation,
your assistant tells you that he has found errors in the computation of the wages
of factory workers and he wants you to verify his work.

Your assistant has extracted from the union contract the following description of the systems for computing wages in various departments of the Company. The contract provides that the minimum wage for a worker is his base
rate, which is also paid for any "down time," time when the worker's machine
is under repair or he is without work. The standard work week is 40 hours.
The union contract also provides that workers be paid 150% of base rates for
overtime production. The Company is engaged in interstate commerce.

   1. *Straight piecework.* The worker is paid at the rate of $.20 per piece
produced.

   2. *Percentage bonus plan.* Standard quantities of production per hour are
established by the engineering department. The worker's average hourly production, determined from his total hours worked and his production, is divided
by the standard quantity of production to determine his efficiency ratio. The
efficiency ratio is then applied to his base rate to determine his hourly earnings
for the period.

   3. *Emerson Efficiency System.* A minimum wage is paid for production up
to $66\frac{2}{3}\%$ of standard output or "efficiency." When the worker's production
exceeds $66\frac{2}{3}\%$ of the standard output, he is paid at a bonus rate. The bonus
rate is determined from the following table:

Efficiency	Bonus
Up to $66\frac{2}{3}\%$	0%
$66\frac{2}{3}\%$ — 79%	10%
80% — 99%	20%
100% — 125%	40%

Your assistant has prepared the following schedule of information pertaining
to certain workers for a weekly payroll selected for examination:

Worker	Wage Incentive Plan	Total Hours	Down Time Hours	Units Produced	Standard Units	Base Rate	Gross Wages Per Books
Long	Straight piecework	40	5	400	—	$1.80	$82.00
Loro	Straight Piecework	46	—	455(1)	—	1.80	91.00
Huck	Straight piecework	44	4	420(2)	—	1.80	84.00
Nini	Percentage bonus plan	40	—	250	200	2.20	120.00
Boro	Percentage bonus plan	40	—	180	200	1.90	67.00
Wiss	Emerson	40	—	240	300	2.10	92.00
Alan	Emerson	40	2	590	600(3)	2.00	118.00

(1) Includes 45 pieces produced during the 6 overtime hours.
(2) Includes 50 pieces produced during the 4 overtime hours. The overtime, which was brought about by the "down time," was necessary to meet a production deadline.
(3) Standard units for 40 hours production.

Required:

(a) Prepare a schedule comparing each individual's gross wages per books and his gross wages per your calculation. Computations of workers' wages should be in good form and labeled with the workers' names.
(b) All the above errors, as well as others, were found in a weekly payroll selected for examination. The total number of errors was substantial. Discuss the courses of action you can take.

(Uniform C.P.A. Examination)

27. You are auditing the financial statements of the Soo Company for the year ended December 31, 1967. Following are transcripts of the Company's general ledger accounts for salary expense and payroll taxes.

Salary Expense

Date	Explanation	Fol	Debit	Credit	Balance
12/31/67	Weekly payrolls (Total of 12 monthly summary entries)	CD	$44,470		$44,470

Payroll Taxes Expense

Date	Explanation	Fol	Debit	Credit	Balance
1/10/67	Quarterly remittance	CD	$4,100		$ 4,100
4/20/67	Quarterly remittance	CD	3,801		7,901
7/14/67	Quarterly remittance	CD	3,327		11,228
10/18/67	Quarterly remittance	CD	3,320		14,548

Payroll Taxes Withheld

Date	Explanation	Fol	Debit	Credit	Balance
1/1/67	Balance forward			$3,200	$3,200

Employer Payroll Taxes Payable

Date	Explanation	Fol	Debit	Credit	Balance
1/1/67	Balance forward			$900	$900

The following additional information is available:

1. Copies of the quarterly tax returns are not available because the typist did not understand that the returns were to be typed in duplicate. The pencil drafts of the tax returns were discarded.

2. Your audit of the payroll records revealed that the payroll clerk properly computed the payroll tax deductions and the amounts of quarterly remittances. You are able to develop the following summary:

Quarter	Gross Salaries	Payroll Taxes Withheld F.I.C.A.	Income	Net Salaries
First	$13,600	$425	$2,600	$10,575
Second	12,000	375	2,280	9,345
Third	12,800	325	2,400	10,075
Fourth	18,700	225	4,000	14,475

3. The Soo Company did not make monthly deposits of taxes withheld. You determine that the following remittances were made with respect to 1967 payrolls:

	4/20/67	7/14/67	10/18/67	1/12/68
F. I. C. A. $(6\,^{1}/_{4}\%)$	$ 850	$ 750	$ 650	$ 450
Income Tax	2,600	2,280	2,400	4,000
State Unemployment Insurance (2.7%)	351	297	270	162
Total	$3,801	$3,327	$3,320	$4,612

4. The effective Federal Unemployment Tax rate for 1967 is .8%. The laws of the state in which Soo Company does business do not provide for employee contributions for state unemployment insurance.

Required:

(a) Prepare a worksheet to determine the correct balances at December 31, 1967 for the general ledger accounts, Salary Expense, Payroll Taxes Expense, Payroll Taxes Withheld, Employer Payroll Taxes Payable. (Disregard accrued salaries at year end.)

(b) Prepare the adjusting journal entry to correct the accounts at December 31, 1967.   (Uniform C.P.A. Examination)

Depreciation and plant accounting systems: internal control; auditing

18

The importance of capital goods in a highly developed economy such as that of the United States suggests that depreciation expense and plant asset accounting would represent major problems to both the company accountant and the independent auditor. The magnitude of the problem for the independent auditor is lessened, however, by the following factors.

First, as implied by the term "fixed assets," the turnover of such assets is much slower than the turnover of current assets. As a result, the items carried over from year to year require less audit work once the entry for the original acquisition cost has been verified. A second factor is the relatively large dollar value of the average unit of property or equipment, which reduces the number of transactions to be examined for a given total dollar value as compared with inventory, for example. A third factor is the fact that errors in the amount at which property, plant, and equipment are stated will be less material in their effect on the financial or operating picture than would be true of an error in stating any of the current assets. Current assets and the current ratio are much more important to creditors and stockholders than are noncurrent asset figures. Also, net income will ordinarily not be affected to the same extent by an error in the figure for plant assets as by an error in current assets. Cut-off errors will seldom affect net income, and the effect of any errors made will be spread in part over net income for each of the years the asset is used. Fourth and last, the relative risk of errors occurring through fraud is lessened by the fact that plant assets are less useful and less tempting to the employee who might be inclined to defraud his employer.

Objectives of Internal Control

As suggested by the final factor listed above, the prevention of fraud is of secondary importance in the internal control maintained over plant assets. The major objectives are:

1. To control plant expenditures through some form of capital budgeting.

2. To maintain accountability and utilization controls over plant assets subsequent to acquisition.

3. To provide adequate historical information for such matters as calculating and allocating depreciation charges, recording retirements, preparing tax returns, establishing the amount of insurance coverage, and filing insurance claims.

The procedures to accomplish these objectives begin with the steps to be followed in acquiring a new asset and continue through to the eventual retirement of the asset.

Authorization of Expenditures

The usual business approach to the control of expenditures is through budgets. Most business budgeting is of the "forecast" type, which makes possible an over-all plan and measurement of actual results against the plan on an after-the-fact basis. The budget may be exceeded without authorization, but the person responsible is expected to be able to justify excesses that occur. Governmental budgeting, on the other hand, is of the "authorization" type which sets absolute limits which cannot be exceeded. This is the only way that the authorizing body can exercise effective control and keep expenditures from exceeding the revenues that will be available. The special problems involved in budgeting plant expenditures tend to make governmental-type authorization budgeting more advantageous in the plant expenditure area than the more permissive forecast budgeting that is used to control most business expenditures.

The capital-budgeting approach to the authorization of plant expenditures is based on the fact that invariably expenditure proposals will exceed the funds available to finance the expenditures from such sources as the recovery of depreciation charges and retained earnings. Under these circumstances, all possible expenditures should be considered, and those that are essential or offer the greatest promise of return on investment are selected in an amount equal to the availability of funds. Return-on-investment percentages and payout periods for remaining proposals can then be considered in the light of the cost of borrowing additional funds and the over-all financial planning of the concern to reach a decision on whether any of these proposals can be authorized. On occasion, a project that appears to be less profitable than others may be approved under long-run considerations such as the need for a balanced line of products or the desire to have products of advanced design even though immediate acceptance may be limited.

There may be several different levels of approval for the authorizations that are made. Requests for minor expenditures not in excess of a stated amount may be screened by a single official, such as the plant superintendent or controller. Approved items may then be combined into a single blanket request for authorization. The blanket request and proposals in excess of the stated cut-off point would then be submitted to a capital-budgeting committee, composed possibly of the plant superintendent, chief engineer, controller, and treasurer. These proposals would have to be fully supported with estimates of cost and savings and any other justification for the expenditure. Very large requests, particularly those involving an entirely new product or program, might also be subject to approval by the board of directors.

Accounting for Expenditures

The capital-expenditure budget resulting from the process described in the preceding section provides the means for over-all control of plant expenditures. Monthly comparisons of budgeted and actual expenditures would show in general how effectively such expenditures were being controlled, but more detailed information would be required to permit corrective action to be taken where necessary. The usual solution to this problem is a work-order system whereby actual expenditures are accumulated under a separate work-order number for each approved project. Periodic reports of budgeted and actual expenditures for each work order will then show how each work order is progressing and whether costs are being kept within the budget limits.

Expenditures must also be properly classified to show whether they should be capitalized or expensed. Strict accounting theory can well be sacrificed in part to considerations of expediency in classifying the expenditures. A minimum limit for items to be capitalized will result in some true capital items being charged to expense; but if the limit is intelligently set, the distortion of net income will be slight and the savings in recordkeeping costs will be substantial. Small tools are frequently expensed when purchased under such a plan, although the toolroom may well keep unit records on the tools to control their use.

One factor in setting a minimum limit for expenditures to be capitalized would be the size of the company. The figure might be $50 for a small company but several hundreds of dollars for large companies. Such a limit must not be used to circumvent company policy. Orders for large quantities of small items which are normally capitalized should not be broken down into smaller orders for the purpose of having the purchases expensed as being under the minimum figure.

Plant Records

After items of property or equipment have been acquired, a detailed accounting record of them should be maintained in a plant ledger with a separate page for item. A sample plant ledger form is shown each in Fig. 18–1.

PUMPHREY MANUFACTURING CO. - Plant Record Card

Description Metal-turning lathe model 58CA Serial number BW 808954

Manufacturer Bryan-Wicks Tool Co.

Purchased from Mfr. ☒ New ☐ Second-hand Date installed 7-22-1 Date first operated 8-12-1

Location Main building Floor 3 Department Finishing Center No. 402

Removed to (location & date)

Control account Machinery

Depreciation	Date	Rate%	Date	Rate%	Date	Rate%
	8-1-1	8⅓	6-2-6	10 on balance		

Appraisal Record

Date	Reference	Page	Amount

Nature of Retirement

Date retired 8-8-7

How disposed of Improved Model 60CA will take the place of this item. Sold to Farnham Bros., Inc. of Detroit, through B.W.T. Co.

Accounting Record

Detail	Date	Ref.	Amount Dr.	Amount Cr.	Balance
Investment					
Invoice cost	7-8-1	8329	2 897 40		2 897 40
Freight	7-11-1	8526	180 54		
Cartage	7-22-1	8943	28 10		
Installation	7-22-1	8944	50 12		3 156 16
Added safety rails	3-4-5	2387	250 00		3 406 16
Retirement					
Proceeds	8-16-7			1 500 00	1 906 16
Depreciation					
Before Jan. 1, 7	8-22-7	J 4010		1 445 36	460 80
Jan. 1 – Aug. 31	"	"		144 80	316 00
Loss or gain (loss)	12-10-7	J6364		316 00	-0-

Plant-record-unit form (front)

DETAILS OF DEPRECIATION

PARTICULARS	DATE			REF.	DR. OR CR.	DETAILS	BALANCE
Provision 19 x 1 (5 months)	12	31	x1	J 381	Cr.	109 59	109 59
– 2	–	–	x2	J 5840	–	263 01	372 60
– 3	–	–	x3	J 47a	–	281 16	653 76
– 4	–	–	x4	J 562	–	287 20	940 96
– 5	–	–	x5	J 87AJ	–	287 20	1 228 16
– 6	–	–	x6	J 4250	–	217 20	1 445 36
– 7 (8 months)	–	–	x7	J 6365	–	144 80	1 590 16
Carried to P&L	–	–	–	J 4010	Dr.	1 590 16	0

Plant-record-unit form (reverse)

FIGURE 18-1. PLANT-RECORD-UNIT FORM (E. L. KOHLER, *A DICTIONARY FOR ACCOUNTANTS*, 3RD ED., ENGLEWOOD CLIFFS, N. J.: PRENTICE-HALL, INC., 1963, P. 377)

The functions of such a record are as follows:

1. It establishes accountability over each plant asset. An identifying serial number shown on each machine and recorded on each plant ledger page facilitates the taking of a physical inventory of plant assets. Such an inventory is essential to determine whether items have been dismantled, scrapped, or sold without proper treatment in the accounting records and whether theft or other losses have occurred.

2. It provides a means whereby depreciation charges can be accurately

Lapsing Schedule

Date	Description	Life	Cost	1966	1967	Annual Depreciation 1968	1969	1970	1971
2/1/66	1966 Chevrolet sedan............	4 yrs.	$2,185.60	$273.20	$546.40	$546.40	$546.40	$273.20	
3/21/66	National Cash Register	10 yrs.	921.87	46.10	92.19	92.19	92.19	92.19	$92.19
8/14/66	Refrigerator display case	10 yrs.	795.75	39.79	79.58	79.58	79.58	79.58	79.58
5/5/68	1966 Chevrolet sedan traded in on '68—see below		(2,185.60)			(273.20)	(546.40)	(273.20)	
5/5/68	1968 Chevrolet sedan	4 yrs.	2,321.57			290.20	580.39	580.39	580.39
			$4,039.19	$359.09	$718.17	$735.17	$752.16	$752.16	$752.16

determined. Also, information is provided for the adjustment of monthly or annual depreciation charges for assets which have been sold or retired, or have become fully depreciated, and properly to account for the mandatory investment credit allowance under Federal income tax procedures.

3. All information is readily available as to original costs and accumulated depreciation so that appropriate entries may be made when an asset is disposed of. The reader should recognize how difficult it is to obtain such information in the absence of a plant ledger.

4. The record of experience with each machine, showing period of use and major repairs and improvements, provides a useful guide to the purchase of additional or replacement equipment.

To be certain that the plant record is being accurately maintained, regular trial balances should be taken of both cost amounts and accumulated depreciation.

Alternative Records

So far as accounting needs alone are concerned, a small firm which does not feel that a formal plant ledger is warranted can obtain adequate information by use of what may be referred to as a "lapsing schedule." An example of such a schedule follows on page 435, with a few illustrative entries shown.

The schedule is based on taking straight-line depreciation at one-half the annual rate in the year of purchase and in the year of disposition. Depreciation for each year of anticipated use is pre-figured and entered in the proper column at the time of purchase. When an asset is retired, the cost amount is entered as a deduction in the cost column, and any depreciation which has not yet been charged to expense is deducted in the depreciation columns which are involved, as when the 1966 Chevrolet was traded in. This same information can then be used to prepare the corresponding general ledger entry. The total of the cost column should at all times balance with the corresponding general ledger account. The depreciation columns provide the necessary information concerning the amount of depreciation to be charged each year.

Depreciation

The widespread acceptance of the concept of depreciation of plant assets and accounting for the resulting charge against operations on a systematic basis represented a significant accounting advance that occurred early in the present century. Depreciation accounting is accepted today as essential to the proper determination of income.

Of the two fundamentally different approaches to the recording of depreciation, the unit depreciation method is most widely used. Although the composite-rate method is simpler to apply, the results are less accurate because it is an averaging method. The handling of retirements under the two methods is quite different. Under a unit approach the actual depreciation to the date of retirement is taken into consideration in figuring gains or losses. Under the composite method, because it is based on averages, retirements are always assumed to be fully depreciated, and no gains or losses are recognized except in unusual cases.

The more common bases for calculating the periodic depreciation charge are listed below. The methods have widely divergent effects on the determination of income and the net carrying value of depreciable plant assets.

1. Straight line (units of time).
2. Hours used or units of output.
3. Sum of years' digits.
4. Fixed percentage on diminishing balance (the Internal Revenue Code now recognizes an approximation of this method which uses a rate double the straight-line rate).
5. Replacement method.
6. Retirement reserve method.
7. Sinking fund method.

Although depreciation is almost always a fixed expense and thus not subject to the requirements of responsibility reporting, depreciation charges should be accumulated on a cost-center basis in order to obtain appropriate overhead charges. Allocation to nonmanufacturing functions is also important in order to arrive at the full costs of providing those functions.

Retirements

All maintenance or special work done in the factory should be authorized by work orders. If this plan is followed and the work orders are carefully analyzed in the accounting department when expenses are incurred against them, the accounting department is put on notice whenever a work order is for dismantling a machine or moving it to the shipping dock for eventual disposition. The accounting department can then make the appropriate general ledger and plant ledger entries concerning the retirement. Such an arrangement makes it impossible for the plant personnel to dispose of any assets without the accounting department being put on notice that such an event has occurred.

Maintenance Expenditures

Maintenance expenditures have increased along with the increased investment in plant assets brought about by the trend to automation. The resulting amounts are of sufficient magnitude to necessitate the application of effective control measures, and there is the further problem of the different accounting treatment that should be accorded to maintenance and ordinary repairs charges, as against expenditures that should be capitalized because they pertain to extraordinary repairs and betterments.

Maintenance work should be under work-order control, with recurring activities such as preventive maintenance charged against a standing work order, the charges in turn being allocated on a consistent basis to the departments or cost centers. Other maintenance and repair work should be done on special work orders. These work orders and their charges can then be analyzed in the accounting department and charged on a responsibility basis against the department or cost center for which the work was done, or capitalized if the work represented extraordinary repairs or betterments. Frequently, the charges are also posted to a maintenance-history record on the reverse side of the plant ledger record, thus giving a history for each machine which can be consulted when a decision must be made to retire or replace the machine.

Maintenance charges should also be accumulated and reported for all maintenance activity in order to facilitate over-all control of repair and maintenance work, as well as to develop an overhead charge to be added to the labor cost for the work done for other departments. In some instances, the volume of repetitive activity has become so great that standards have been established for much of the work, and variances from standard can then be reported as an aid to control.

Punched-Card Records

Unit plant records can be readily maintained in punched-card form. In addition to identifying information, date of purchase, and related matters, the card should show total cost, the amount of the monthly or annual straight-line depreciation charge, and cumulative depreciation that has been charged. For each accounting period, the periodic-charge amounts can be accumulated by the tabulator according to the expense code to which the depreciation is charged. At the same time, for each card the periodic charge is added to the cumulative amount of depreciation and a new card is summary-punched, thus carrying forward the fixed information and the depreciation charged off to date.

Repair-history records can be prepared by posting annual total costs incurred relative to each piece of equipment to the corresponding ledger record, or by simply updating to-date totals maintained on summary cards.

The value of punched-card records is particularly evident with respect to obtaining a trial balance of the plant ledger and listing all assets owned, in sequence by location, to facilitate physical-inventory verification.

Management Reports

Many of the internal reports that would be useful to management in controlling property, plant, and equipment have already been mentioned. Included would be a monthly report showing budgeted and actual plant expenditures for the month and for the year to date. Supplementing this report should be a list showing the status of all plant acquisitions approved for the year. For each item the estimated cost, actual cost to date, and amount over or under the estimate should be shown. Notations can be added showing expected starting or completion dates if known, percentage complete at the time of the report, and reasons for any large variances between actual and estimated costs.

Another report might schedule all additions and deductions made to the various plant accounts and the related depreciation accounts. In addition, a departmental breakdown showing depreciation charges for the month and year to date compared with the previous year will usually be helpful. Proceeds from disposition of plant assets and resulting gains or losses could also be shown in this report. Any adjustments resulting from the taking of a physical inventory of plant assets should be clearly labeled.

Because maintenance and repair expenditures are closely related to the complete picture of the plant assets and their physical condition, a schedule of those expenses should accompany the above reports. A supplementary report detailing the expenses according to individual work orders should also be useful.

Internal Auditing

Following the typical pattern, the internal auditor should review the policies and practices concerning plant assets and make adequate verification for statement purposes. Included would be all aspects of the acquisition, care, depreciation, and disposal of the assets.

Budgeted plant expenditures should be reviewed for reasonableness. Tests should be made of the accounting for charges against the various work orders, and invoices and other supporting data should be examined. Reported figures comparing budgeted and actual expenditures should be verified, and excessive variances from budgeted amounts should be investigated. The internal auditor should also satisfy himself that proper distinction was maintained between capital and revenue charges.

The plant ledger should be balanced with the related general ledger accounts, and depreciation rates and the monthly or annual depreciation charges should be reviewed. Entries recording the retirement or disposal of plant assets should be verified. The auditor should check to see that all related figures have been removed from the records and that any gain or loss has been properly treated.

The physical inventory of plant assets is a very important phase of plant accounting, and the internal auditor should review the instructions for taking the inventory to be certain that they are satisfactory. He should also observe and make tests of the actual inventory process in order to satisfy himself that the inventory was correctly taken and proper adjustments made to the plant ledger.

Finally, the internal auditor should make an over-all appraisal of the plant asset situation for the purpose of recommending any improvements. Included would be the physical care and protection being given to such assets, the procedures for authorizing purchases or retirements, maintenance policies, adequacy of records being maintained, policies concerning depreciation charges and minimum amounts to be capitalized, and the various reports which are issued.

STANDARDS OF STATEMENT PRESENTATION

Basis of Valuation

As in the case of inventories, to avoid any misunderstanding by persons reading a financial statement, the basis of valuation for all plant assets should be stated. The generally accepted basis of valuation is cost less depreciation, and the Committee on Accounting Procedure and the Accounting Principles Board of the American Institute of Certified Public Accountants have several times reaffirmed their preference for that method. The effects of inflation and changing price levels have, however, brought considerable pressure for a change of position, and the price-level question will in all likelihood be a major issue in the deliberations of the Accounting Principles Board, as successor to the Committee on Accounting Procedure.

For the present, any departure from historical costs in financial statements accompanied by an auditor's opinion would require that the opinion be qualified on the basis that the statements do not reflect generally accepted accounting principles. As recommended by the Committee on Accounting Procedure, the auditor might, however, encourage the use of supplementary financial statements based on current price levels. Such supplementary statements could then be used to explain and justify the fact that all profits reported on an historic basis are not available for dividends, wage increases, price reductions, or tax payments.

Liens

Any liens on plant assets resulting from chattel or other mortgages must be clearly stated in connection with the particular assets involved, to show that they would not be available to general creditors upon liquidation. The liabilities which are secured by such assets should also carry some notation indicating the security which is involved.

Depreciation Not to Be Netted Against Asset Balances

The amount of accumulated depreciation is a useful figure to the person reading a financial statement, and it should not be buried by showing assets only at their net carrying value. The accumulated depreciation figure gives some idea of how modern a plant a company owns. When related to the annual depreciation charge, the figure can be used to give some indication of when additional funds may be needed for plant replacement.

Classification

Two problems of classification are involved in the presentation of plant assets. The first is related to the fact that only productive assets should be classified as plant assets. Thus any land, buildings, or equipment which are held for investment purposes or future use must be shown under a separate caption if material, rather than under the plant classification. Also, any idle or abandoned assets should be shown under some other caption, and they should be fully described to show the true facts. Standby equipment should not be confused with items which are idle or abandoned. Standby equipment is a part of the regular productive plant, even though used only on very rare emergency occasions.

The second problem of classification involves an adequate breakdown of the productive plant to give a clear picture of just what types of assets are owned. Land should always be classified separately, particularly because it is not subject to depreciation. If a company owns depletable mining lands and owns material amounts of other land which is not subject to depletion, those two groups should be shown separately.

Other productive assets should also be broken down into separate classifications based on materiality of the amounts involved, differences in the basic nature of the assets, and differences in depreciation rates. Thus any or all of the following classifications might be used, depending on the amounts involved: buildings, machinery and equipment, automotive or transportation equipment, tools, dies, jigs, and patterns. Construction work in progress might be another important classification in some instances. These classifications are only suggestive, and many others could be used. For instance, electric utilities may classify their plant assets under the headings of generating, transmission, distribution, and administrative facilities.

Fully Depreciated Assets

If material amounts of fully depreciated assets are owned and in use, the statement reader should be put on notice, for these assets are contributing to the production of income without any corresponding charge for depreciation. Also, these assets may require replacement in the near future. Some companies write off fully depreciated assets against the accumulated depreciation. In such cases the information as to the cost of fully depreciated assets currently in use may be given parenthetically or as a footnote. If both the assets and the accumulated depreciation are being carried in the accounts, the assets can be shown under a separate classification. If they are included with the figures for other similar assets, that fact can be footnoted or a parenthetical comment can be made, as in the following example:

Machinery and equipment, at cost (including $154,250 of fully depreciated facilities)

Disclosure of Amount of Depreciation Charged Against Income

The amount of depreciation charged during the year may be important for several reasons. First, as stated earlier, the figure is useful to the statement reader in estimating the approximate age of the plant and the probable date when replacement may be necessary. Also, depreciation is usually a substantial fixed charge, and the figure may be important in estimating net income under various rates of operation. Lastly, because depreciation is a noncash expense, the figure gives some indication of the cash inflow which is available for purchasing replacements, expanding plant facilities, or financing other activities. If the amount of depreciation expense is not shown as a separate item in the income statement, the total amount of depreciation charged should be reported parenthetically or by footnote.

AUDIT OBJECTIVES AND PROCEDURES

The independent auditor's approach to the examination of plant assets differs materially from the approach followed in verifying current asset figures. In the case of cash, receivables, and inventories, the auditor deals primarily with those items which constitute the ending balance of the account. He attempts to satisfy himself that there are sufficient assets to justify the statement figure. Although the auditor has this same concern with respect to the figures for plant assets, the long life and low turnover of such assets make it possible to reach a conclusion in a different manner. Once the balances of the various property accounts have been verified in connection with an initial audit, the auditor in his subsequent examinations has only to examine those transactions which have taken place during the intervening period. This indirect approach is not practical for current assets because they usually undergo a complete turnover between audits.

The objectives given below in substantiating the amount of plant assets and depreciation in the financial statements thus differ somewhat from the listings presented in earlier chapters for other statement items. Almost all of the auditor's work in a sense is largely an expansion of procedures intended to establish the credibility of the accounting records. The latter objective is not stated as such, however, but instead the various objectives pertaining to the different types of entries in the plant asset accounts are listed as the focal points for the various audit procedures. Also, the matter of cut-offs is not of sufficient importance to warrant listing as a separate objective, but the question is referred to under some of the other objectives. The objectives are:

1. Tie in supporting records with statement amounts for plant assets and depreciation.

2. Ascertain that additions to plant asset accounts have been correctly recorded and that capital and revenue charges have been properly distinguished.

3. Ascertain that retirements of plant assets have been correctly recorded, with proper recognition of any gains or losses.

4. Establish reasonableness of depreciation charges, both current and accumulated amounts.

5. Establish existence of plant assets.

6. Determine ownership of plant assets and the existence of any liens.

Tie in Supporting Records with Statement Amounts for Plant Assets and Depreciation

Trial balance of the plant ledger. When the client has taken trial balances of the individual plant ledger balances for cost and accumulated depreciation on the balance sheet date or shortly before, the auditor should make some examination of the trial balances to prove their authenticity. Tests to be made need not be nearly as extensive as those that would be made of an accounts receivable trial balance, however. The explanation lies in the reduced relative risk that the plant ledger trial balances would be intentionally misstated and the fact that transactions during the year are quite thoroughly examined.

The auditor's first step after obtaining the trial balances should be to compare the totals with the balances of the general ledger accounts for asset cost and accumulated depreciation. Next, test comparisons should be made of trial balance amounts with the corresponding plant ledger figures. These comparisons ordinarily need not be extensive enough to establish the accuracy of the trial balance. In most cases it will be sufficient if the tests are adequate to establish that the auditor has in fact been given a trial balance which is based on the amounts in the plant ledger. Under these circumstances, an adequate test may consist merely of selecting several groups of items from the trial balance tape and comparing each figure in each group with the corresponding figure in the plant ledger. Any unusually large figures appearing on the trial balance should also be verified. In most cases such tests would not have to exceed ten per cent of the total dollar amount of the assets.

Although as a rule a trial balance should be refooted by the auditor, relative risk suggests that such a procedure is seldom necessary in the case of a plant ledger trial balance. If the auditor is being assisted by a comptometer operator, however, the cost of proving the footing of the trial balance may be nominal and thus warrant the additional assurance to be gained.

Trial balance of construction work in process. Large commercial companies and most public utilities do much of their own construction work on additions to plant and equipment. During the construction period expenditures relating to such projects are commonly charged to a construction work-in-process account. The balance of this account should be supported by the charges made against the individual work orders for the work being done, and the auditor should prove the trial balance of these charges. He should then review the open work orders for any which are essentially repair or maintenance projects, and all charges to such work orders should be transferred to appropriate expense accounts. For cut-off purposes, any work orders covering plant assets which have been completed should be noted and the balances transferred to the appropriate plant accounts. Depreciation should be provided for on any assets placed in use before the end of the year.

Charges against the open work orders should be substantiated in the same manner as additions to the various other plant accounts. Matters concerning the related procedures are discussed under the appropriate heading in the following section, which deals with the second of the auditor's objectives.

Ascertain that Additions to Plant Asset Accounts Have Been Correctly Recorded and that Capital and Revenue Charges Have Been Properly Distinguished

The broad area of plant additions includes the acquisition of new assets, improvements to existing assets, and overhauling or replacement of parts of existing assets when such work has the effect of increasing the expected useful life of the assets. Expenditures designed to increase the useful life of assets are frequently charged against accumulated depreciation.

Schedule major additions. In the examination of additions, the auditor's first step will usually be to analyze all charges to asset or accumulated depreciation accounts on a work sheet similar to schedule U-1, which is in turn cross-referenced to UV. Each major plant expenditure should be listed with adequate identifying and explanatory information. A few smaller items should also be individually listed to make the auditor's verification representative, but most of the smaller items can be grouped together in one balancing figure as in U-1. As always, the auditor's intent should be to cover the major part of the dollar total while examining only a minimum number of individual items.

Supporting data. The various documents supporting the items listed or described above should then be pulled from the files by the auditor, or preferably by one of the client's employees. Included will be disbursement vouchers with supporting invoices and receiving reports, and journal vouchers. The journal vouchers will usually be supported by work orders, which may in turn have underlying data in the form of invoices, material requisitions, and labor tickets. Reference should also be made to the initial approval of major expenditures by the appropriate authority, such as a capital expenditures committee or the board of directors.

If construction work has been done by independent contractors, architects' certificates should be available showing percentage completion and stating that the work has been satisfactory. Such certificates should be available in support of both progress and final payments.

The supporting data should be compared with the listed amounts on the auditor's worksheet and the worksheet figures tick-marked to show that the amounts are correct. The auditor should also review the supporting data for proper approvals and indication of receipt of materials at this time. If there is any question about the actual amount disbursed in any given case, the paid check is further evidence of the amount involved.

The supporting data should be watched for any indication that only part of a total amount due may have been paid. For example, a construction contract may entitle the purchaser to withhold a stated percentage of each progress payment until the job has been completed and accepted. Such amounts should be capitalized and recorded as a liability.

Amounts properly capitalized. In accordance with generally accepted accounting principles, only expenditures which will benefit future years should be capitalized. When the auditor reviews the data supporting additions to plant asset accounts, he should note whether generally accepted accounting principles were adhered to in treating the amounts as asset additions. Tick-marks should be used to indicate that such a review was made and that tick-marked items have been properly capitalized.

Amounts capitalized should be recorded net of any cash discounts allowed for prompt payment. The investment credit reducing the liability for Federal income taxes may also be shown as a deduction from the related asset, under the theory that the credit is a form of "discount" designed to encourage plant expenditures. Transportation and installation costs are properly included in the total amount capitalized. If assets have been constructed by the client, all material and labor costs are properly included in the amount to be capitalized. There is no set rule as to the proper treatment of overhead charges on such jobs. Certainly any overhead expenses directly attributable to a given project should be capitalized. If normal overhead items also benefit the project, regular overhead can be added to the total construction cost at the normal rate. Any properly capitalized expenditures relating to leased property should be carefully noted, inasmuch as they should be classified as leasehold improvements on the balance sheet, rather than being included with the client's regular plant asset classifications.

As an expedient, purchases of small tools can be charged directly to expense if net income is not distorted by such treatment. Some companies, however, follow the more elaborate method of treating small tools on a perpetual inventory basis.

In accordance with *Opinion of the Accounting Principles Board Number 5* property leases that in substance represent installment purchases of the property should be stated in the balance sheet at the discounted amount of future payments specified for the lease. The asset amount should then be amortized over a period appropriate to the nature and use of the asset.

Maintenance and repairs. The procedures described above should be adequate to assure the auditor that the total additions to plant assets have been correctly stated and reflect transactions which were properly capitalized. But to satisfy himself that proper distinction has been maintained between capital and revenue charges, the auditor must also direct his attention to the accounts that contain the revenue charges related to plant assets. These will usually be the repair and maintenance accounts.

Tests of the data supporting entries to these accounts should be made, but they need not be nearly as extensive as the tests of capitalized amounts. The reduced need for testing is justified largely by the fact that the individual charges will tend to be relatively small. As a result, a test of a few carefully selected items should suffice, particularly if the client has good internal control. If a properly qualified person in the accounting department designates how each expenditure is to be recorded, the results of his decisions can be accepted provided that those items tested show his judgment to be sound.

Among the items to be "carefully" selected should be any large or otherwise unusual amounts detected in the course of the auditor's over-all review of the repair expense accounts. If the auditor detects any material variations in repair expenses from year to year or from month to month, the causes for those variations should be sought out by inquiry and by tests of unusual items which appear to have increased the total amount. The auditor should also scan the detailed record of charges for the year, seeking any items which appear unusual or out of line. (See schedule U-2.)

In setting the scope of his examination pertaining to the classification of capital and revenue charges, the auditor may well be guided by the relative risk factor in making his decision. In a year of poor earnings, or in a year when a high earnings figure might help assure the success of additional financing, the auditor should concentrate his examination (although not exclusively) on the review of charges to the asset accounts to detect any attempt to inflate earnings by capitalizing charges which should be expensed. Conversely, in a year when high earnings might make the negotiation of a reasonable labor contract more difficult, or in a year when income tax reductions have been announced to be effective in the following year, the auditor might well broaden his examination of expense charges on the theory that the client might endeavor to conceal part of the income for the year by overstating such charges.

Ascertain that Retirements of Plant Assets Have Been Correctly Recorded, with Proper Recognition of Any Gains or Losses

Schedule major retirements. All major retirements and a representative sample of smaller ones recorded during the year should be scheduled for verification as was done on U-3. The verification tests should be designed to assure the auditor that asset and depreciation accounts were relieved of the proper amounts, that any proceeds of sales were fully accounted for, and that resulting gains or losses were properly treated. The cost of assets retired should be substantiated by reference to detailed plant ledger cards, or, in the absence of a plant ledger, by reference to the entry for the original purchase in the general records. The accumulated depreciation should likewise be traced to the plant ledger card, but in addition it should be independently verified by the auditor, based on the original cost, period of use, and established rate of depreciation. Trade-in allowances received should be proven against the purchase documents for the new asset acquired. Substantial proceeds from sales of usable assets should be traced to the record of cash receipts. Proceeds of sales of scrap from junked machinery are not usually considered in figuring the gain or loss on disposition, but are merely recorded as other income. The total amount of gain or loss on disposition, reflecting the net effect of original cost, accumulated depreciation, and proceeds of sale, should be cross-referenced to the appropriate income or expense account, as was done on U-3. Gains or losses which are material and would therefore distort net income are properly taken directly to the retained earnings account.

Unrecorded retirements. One of the most troublesome problems in the audit of plant accounts is the possibility of unrecorded retirements. The problem exists not so much because clients find this a convenient way to overstate assets or manipulate net income, but because the necessary retirement entries are so easily overlooked. Someone in the factory, for instance, decides that a machine has served its useful life, and the machine is consigned to the scrap heap. Factory personnel naturally are most concerned about their own production problems and decisions and may not realize that many of their decisions may have accounting implications. Consequently the machine goes to the scrap heap and its cost stays on the records. If the machine is not yet fully depreciated, depreciation continues to be charged, a loss remains unrecognized, and the asset account and the related depreciation account are overstated.

If the machine has been traded in or sold for cash, the supplementary transactions give the accounting department a chance to detect the retirement, but even this opportunity may be overlooked. In smaller businesses the relatively untrained bookkeeper may not recognize the implications of such transactions.

For the larger business, where adequate internal control is practicable, the means of assuring that the accounting department will be put on notice that retirements have occurred have already been discussed. The first of these is the requirement that all handling of machinery be authorized and accounted for on work orders. This requirement then gives the accounting department an opportunity to note what has occurred and to make the additional entries which are required. The second is the physical inventory of plant assets, which will reveal any retirements which have inadvertently been overlooked.

Regardless of the internal control, the independent auditor should make some investigation to satisfy himself that material amounts of unrecorded retirements do not exist. The investigation can, of course, be very limited when internal control is adequate.

Some of the techniques which the auditor can employ in his search for unrecorded retirements are:

1. Question management and supervisory personnel in the factory about retirements which they know have occurred.

2. Review work orders, tracing any indicated retirements to the records to confirm that they have been recorded.

3. Investigate major plant additions to ascertain whether they represent additional facilities or replace old assets which have been retired.

4. Review miscellaneous income accounts for possible proceeds of sales of machines which have been scrapped or junked. (Because there is seldom satisfactory control over such proceeds, the auditor should also attempt to satisfy himself that the proceeds of known dispositions of plant assets have been accounted for.)

5. Investigate the possibility that major changes in plant layout or in the type or design of the product being produced may have resulted in the retirement of some plant assets.

6. Review plant ledger records on a test basis to ascertain that all items not noted as being on hand at the time of the last physical inventory have been removed from the accounts.

7. If insurance coverage on buildings or contents has been reduced,

investigate the possibility that part of the plant assets may have been sold or otherwise disposed of.

The reader should be careful not to assume that all the above procedures would be used in every audit. Rather, each situation must be appraised and only those procedures which appear warranted in the particular case should be applied. Then, too, part of the procedures should become almost automatic. For instance, any time the auditor learns that a product change has occurred, he should immediately begin to wonder whether the change may have made obsolete some of the client's inventory or plant equipment. Such automatic reactions are the sign of a person who has the aptitude and innate inquisitiveness of the successful auditor.

Establish Reasonableness of Depreciation Charges, Both Current and Accumulated Amounts

The question of the reasonableness of depreciation amounts can be broken down into three subsidiary considerations—adequacy, consistency, and accuracy.

Adequacy. The primary responsibility for the adequacy of depreciation charges rests with management. The auditor's concern should be to ascertain whether management has made an intelligent and conscientious effort to arrive at a meaningful life estimate in setting depreciation rates. In the evaluation of rates arrived at by management, "guideline" rates published by the Internal Revenue Service, as *Revenue Procedure 62–21*, or the now superseded *Bulletin F*, offer a useful reference point. The old *Bulletin F* rates were based largely on engineering studies and covered hundreds of different types of real and personal property. By contrast, the guidelines refer to relatively few very broad classes of assets and tend to be somewhat more liberal than the *Bulletin F* rates. The differences in rates are in part the result of the fact that the guidelines are based primarily on economic studies rather than engineering studies.

In the last analysis, however, the auditor's own appraisal of the adequacy of the client's depreciation rates and the amount of accumulated depreciation is most important. Even though the auditor is not an expert in this field, general knowledge, common sense, and careful observation should be sufficient to permit him to reach some useful conclusions. For instance, large amounts of fully depreciated assets, or excessive recurring losses on assets retired, carry strong implications about the adequacy of depreciation charges.

The auditor's objective is not to satisfy himself that the client's life estimates agree with his own to the nearest year. If the client has attempted to arrive at reasonable estimates, the auditor needs merely to be satisfied that the estimates are in fact reasonable. If the client has estimated a life of 50 years for a building and the auditor is convinced that a life of 60 years would be more correct, there is hardly a reasonable basis for disagreement. But if the auditor's estimate is 25 years, or 100 years, then certainly the matter should warrant further investigation and discussion.

In general, however, the auditor's review will be less detailed than is implied above. He should satisfy himself that asset classifications cover items which have a similar life expectancy, and that the rates applied to each group are in line with his judgment. He should also form some idea of the age and condition of the entire plant and be satisfied that the accumulated depreciation is roughly indicative of the age and physical condition of the plant.

Consistency. The matter of consistency relates to changes in the method or rates used in figuring depreciation. Reference to the work papers for the preceding year and a knowledge of what was done in the current year should indicate whether the client has made any significant changes. Revised depreciation rates based on a sound reappraisal of life estimates ordinarily need not concern the auditor. A qualified opinion on the financial statements may be required, however, if rates have been revised without cause or if a new method of depreciation has been adopted, and if net income is materially affected as a result.

Accuracy. The auditor's third consideration, accuracy, simply involves the mathematical computation involved in applying depreciation rates to the respective asset figures. Note should be made here that depreciation has been properly figured on additions and retirements during the year. Occasionally depreciation will be figured to the nearest month in such cases, but most companies follow a policy of taking one-half of the annual depreciation in the first and last years. Another variation is to take a full year's depreciation the first year and none the last, or vice versa. Any of these plans should be acceptable if consistently followed. The auditor should also be satisfied that no depreciation is being charged on fully depreciated assets.

The manner in which the auditor's working papers might show the verification of depreciation is suggested on schedule V-1.

Establish Existence of Plant Assets

The auditor's procedures to establish the existence of the recorded plant assets are much less extensive than those pertaining to the existence of current assets. The explanation lies in the factors mentioned at the beginning of this chapter—relative risk and materiality. Typical procedures relating to the verification of the existence of plant assets are suggested in the following sections.

Current additions. The auditor should physically inspect all major additions recorded during the year and a few of the smaller ones as well. In inspecting the assets he should note whether they bear a reasonable relationship to the recorded description and cost.

Over-all review. In a general way, the auditor should be satisfied that the physical facilities he has observed in his "get-acquainted" tour of the plant bear out the balances carried in the ledger. He should be able to recognize the difference between a million-dollar plant and a hundred-thousand-dollar plant, but his over-all appraisal can hardly be more precise than that. His main concern should be to detect any obvious overstatement of plant assets.

Branch plants of considerable size will usually be visited every year, and all regular procedures carried out. For smaller units, such as branch sales offices or retail stores, rotating visits over a two- to ten-year period are common. New units, or those having major capital additions, should be visited during the year, if at all possible, to verify the existence of tangible assets in support of book figures. For those branches which are not visited in any one year, sales and expense reports and active bank accounts present useful evidence of the continued existence of assets at those branches.

Small tools. If small tools are carried as an asset, the account balance will be either an approximate figure which is never changed, or it will be based on an inventory of the tools on hand. In the first instance, the auditor need only satisfy himself that small tools do exist in the plant and that the figure used is reasonable. If an inventory is taken, the same procedures employed in the verification of merchandise inventory should be followed, except on a more limited basis.

Remotely located equipment. Unlike manufacturing companies, whose plant assets are usually clustered at one or more locations, some concerns will have plant assets distributed over a wide area. Examples of companies with operations of this type would include public utilities, motor carriers, construction contractors, and juke box and vending machine operators.

The internal control in most public utility concerns is usually adequate to permit the auditor to accept the existence of the plant assets and additions thereto without inspection of the assets, except for such major items as generating or pumping stations. For other items, the review of additions and retirements through test inspection of closely controlled work orders, plus the existence of carefully maintained detailed plant records, should give the auditor adequate assurance of the existence of his client's plant assets. Further assurance can be gained by relating revenues and sales statistics to the total plant investment and comparing the resulting figures with those for previous years.

Because motor carriers' principal productive assets are their trucks, and most of these will be on the road, the auditor may be faced with a difficult problem in attempting to satisfy himself as to the existence of the major portion of such companies' equipment, which will be a significant item on the balance sheet. Important evidence of the existence of these assets should, however, be present in the office in the form of certificates of title, license registration receipts, and insurance policies containing detailed listings of the insured equipment. Detailed records showing gasoline and oil consumption and repair expenses would also support the existence of the equipment called for by the general records.

In the case of construction contractors, it will usually be desirable for the auditor to visit several locations at which work is in progress and satisfy himself by actual inspection that the specified equipment is actually present. Internal control will seldom be adequate to assure the auditor of the existence of the assets called for by the general records without at least some test inspections of the equipment.

Vending machine and juke box operators present a particularly difficult problem of asset verification. Internal records showing the amount of inventory or number of records placed in each machine and the resulting periodic collections of cash receipts should be of some help, particularly if the cash receipts figures can be tied in with daily deposits. In addition, it would be well for the auditor to make further tests by accompanying several route men and noting not only the existence of the machines listed for the route, but also the inventory stored in the machines and the cash collected.

Returnable containers. Certain companies, such as beverage and chemical concerns, often have a substantial investment in returnable containers. The existence of containers on hand can be readily verified, but those containers "with the trade" present a considerable problem. Although the asset account may correctly show all containers shipped to customers, there is no assurance that all those containers will be returned. Those which customers have lost, broken, or appropriated for other uses can no longer be shown as an asset and must be written off the books.

To estimate how many containers held by customers are likely to be returned, statistics are usually developed by occasional tests. A cut-off date is selected, and a record maintained of all containers returned after that date which were shipped on or before that date. This record will then show the number of containers with the trade at that date, and the records can be adjusted for those containers which were not returned.

The figure for containers with the trade is directly related to the volume of business being done, and is usually stated as representing X number of days' sales prior to the cut-off date. This figure for the number of days' sales represented in the inventory of containers with the trade varies but slightly from year to year, and consequently an inventory of containers with the trade can be estimated at any time by determining the amount sold in the specified number of days preceding the date for which the figure is desired. Trade associations in industries where this problem is prevalent frequently develop average statistics, thus obviating the need for many companies ever to make such a test.

For the auditor whose client owns returnable containers, the audit procedures to be followed are quite simple. The maximum asset value for containers must not exceed the cost of containers on hand plus those estimated to be with the trade, determined as suggested above. Each of these figures should be independently tested or calculated by the auditor. The auditor should note that accumulated depreciation on containers lost has been removed from the accounts and that any liability for deposits on containers has been adjusted to correspond with the number of containers estimated to be with the trade and to be returned. The net effect of the cost, accumulated depreciation, and deposits pertaining to containers lost will then be the net gain or loss to be recognized on such containers.

Determine Ownership of Plant Assets and Existence of Liens

The absence of any rental payments is in itself indication that a client must own the plant assets which he is using. Further evidence should be available, however, and should be examined by the auditor. For real property there should be a deed which has been duly recorded, an abstract of title, and an attorney's title opinion or a title guarantee policy. Although these are highly technical legal documents, the auditor should at least note that each shows the client to be the legal owner of the property.

Some authors have recommended that the auditor should also examine the public records for actions affecting the client's property, thus further verifying ownership and the absence of any liens. Such an examination is rarely made, however. Adequate alternative evidence of ownership is usually available. If there is a question concerning the client's title to any property, or if there is a possibility that a lien may exist against the property, any search of the public records should be made by a person with legal training. An attempt by the auditor to make such a search might well result in a wrong conclusion that could be both embarrassing and costly to the auditor. There is no acceptable substitute for an attorney's opinion in such matters.

Readily accessible evidence that can be examined to show acquisition and ownership of specific items of property would include contracts, invoices, and paid checks. Tax bills present further evidence of ownership. The bills should be addressed to the client, and the description and location of the property as shown on the bills should agree with the property carried as an asset by the client. Insurance carried on property is also an indication of ownership. Insurance policies should be inspected by the auditor in order to determine that they relate to the assets in question.

Liens. Most property liens will be disclosed through the examination of liabilities, but the auditor should also be alert for evidence of the existence of liens during other phases of his examination. For instance, a purchase contract examined to establish ownership of an asset may prove to be a conditional sales contract with part of the balance still unpaid. The examination of insurance policies may also disclose the existence of a lien. Sometimes such policies must be deposited with the mortgagee to show that his security is adequately protected. Thus the absence of any insurance policies should always suggest the possible existence of a lien. The fact that a policy is on hand and not deposited with someone else is not, however, sufficient basis for concluding that no mortgage lien exists. Careful study of the policy may reveal an endorsement assigning the proceeds of any claims to a mortgagee.

Paid tax bills are sometimes presented to a mortgagee as evidence that taxes have been paid, and the absence of such bills carries much the same significance as missing insurance policies. The paid tax bills should also be examined as evidence that no liens have resulted from unpaid taxes.

Making an Initial Audit

The preceding comments have been predicated upon the assumption that the auditor made a similar examination in the preceding year. Only the entries for additions, retirements, and depreciation for the current year were subjected to scrutiny, as the previous examination would have covered the balances in the accounts at the end of that year. But what does the auditor do when he is making an examination for the first time for a client who has been in business for fifty years or more? It will obviously be impractical to make an examination of the changes in the plant accounts during each of the preceding years.

If another independent auditor examined the financial statements for the preceding year, there might appear to be no problem. That is not quite true, however, because the new auditor, in expressing an opinion on the financial statements, must take full personal responsibility for that opinion. Yet he can take considerable assurance from the situation if his predecessor took no exception to the figures for property, plant, and equipment in expressing his opinion. If the new auditor knows that his predecessor was competent and reliable, only limited tests of plant transactions for previous years should satisfy him that he can accept the opening balances in the plant accounts. But if the previous auditor is unknown to him, or if no previous audit has been made, the examination of previous transactions should be much more extensive. The form of the examination to be made is suggested below. The examination will invariably be on a test basis, but the extent of the tests will be influenced by internal control and the factors just discussed.

Procedures when client maintains plant ledger. The auditor's work is both simplified and reduced if the client maintains a plant ledger which has recently been adjusted to agree with an inventory of plant assets. The first steps would be, of course, to verify a trial balance of the ledger and to determine that the assets listed were shown to be on hand by the physical inventory. Next, a sizable proportion of the major assets and a representative proportion of the less costly items should be selected for verification. Expenditures should be verified in much the same manner as in a repeat audit, and the accumulated depreciation should be verified. Then, as a supplement to these procedures, the auditor should review all past debits and credits to the various general ledger accounts. Any entries which appear to be unusual in any way should be investigated. Particularly important would be any entries suggesting an appraisal write-up or a major adjustment to past depreciation. All relatively large amounts should be investigated, including entries for the retirement of assets. If any purchases of assets are disclosed which were not covered in the tests based on the plant ledger, these purchases should be verified and carefully studied. Depreciation charges for preceding years should be related to those for the current year, and material year-to-year variations should be investigated.

Procedures when no plant ledger is maintained. The absence of a plant ledger suggests that internal control is likely to be limited and must be compensated for by more extensive testing. Furthermore, the auditor will be forced to be less selective in his testing because there is no ledger record showing which assets are still in use. Plant additions will have to be selected at random from the general ledger record. Because many assets acquired years previously may still be in use, additions in the early years will have to be tested almost as extensively as those in later years, even though many of the acquisitions selected may already have been retired. Entries for retirements will have to be given considerably more attention than when there is a plant ledger. The double check on retirements afforded by the plant ledger and a physical inventory will be missing and must be compensated for by additional audit work. If major amounts of unrecorded retirements exist, the situation must be disclosed and corrected to avoid overstatement of asset and accumulated depreciation figures. Unrecorded retirements may also cause current depreciation charges to be overstated and losses or gains to remain buried in the balance sheet accounts.

Timing of the Examination of Plant Assets

Even in a small business with little or no internal control, part of the examination of plant assets can be made prior to the balance sheet date. Because the major portion of the examination consists of a review of internal control and an analysis of transactions occurring since the previous examination, the work can be started at any time. At the end of the year, then, only transactions occurring since the date of the preliminary work would have to be examined.

SUMMARY

Internal control

Capital expenditures should be budgeted and controlled through a system of authorization and reporting.

Detailed plant records or lapsing schedules should be maintained.

A system of factory work orders should be used as a means of controlling maintenance expenditures and gaining notice of retirements.

A physical inventory of plant assets should be taken every two or three years.

Statement presentation

The basis of valuation for plant assets should be stated.

Any liens should be disclosed.

The amount of accumulated depreciation and the depreciation charge for the current year should be shown.

Plant assets should be broken down into separate classifications if material amounts are involved.

The amount of fully depreciated assets should be disclosed.

Audit objectives and procedures

Tie in supporting records with statement amounts for plant assets and depreciation.

Test trial balances of plant ledger asset cost and accumulated depreciation, and of construction work in process.

Review construction work-in-process items for completed jobs and charges that should be expensed.

Ascertain that additions to plant asset accounts have been correctly recorded and that capital and revenue charges have been properly distinguished.

Schedule major additions and a sample of lesser additions.

Trace scheduled amounts to supporting data such as authorizations, invoices, and receiving reports.

Determine that amounts were properly capitalized and should not have been expensed.

Review maintenance and repair charges for reasonableness and possible amounts that should have been capitalized.

Ascertain that retirements of plant assets have been correctly recorded, with proper recognition of any gains or losses.

Schedule major retirements.

Verify cost, accumulated depreciation, proceeds, and gain or loss.

Investigate possibilities of unrecorded retirements.

Establish reasonableness of depreciation charges, both current and accumulated amounts.

Review rates and amounts for adequacy, consistency, and accuracy.

Establish existence of plant assets.

Inspect major additions during the year.

Relate record of plant assets to physical assets on an over-all basis.

Determine ownership of plant assets and existence of liens.

Inspect contracts, deeds, title guarantee policies, paid tax receipts, and other related documents.

REVIEW QUESTIONS

1. What factors simplify the verification of property, plant, and equipment, as compared with the verification of current assets?
2. What are the objectives of internal control over plant assets?
3. How should capital expenditures be reported to give management maximum information for use in controlling such expenditures?
4. What are the functions of a detailed plant ledger?
5. How can information on the amount of accumulated depreciation be useful to the user of financial statements?
6. What classification problems exist in properly showing plant assets in the balance sheet?
7. How does the usual examination of property, plant, and equipment differ from the examination of current assets?
8. What are the independent auditor's objectives in the examination of plant assets?
9. How does the auditor proceed in substantiating additions to plant assets?
10. In what way does relative risk affect the auditor's verification work pertaining to the maintenance of proper distinction between capital and revenue charges?
11. What figures should be verified in connection with major retirements of plant assets recorded during the year?
12. Under a good system of internal control, how can a company guard against unrecorded retirements of plant assets?
13. What procedures can the auditor employ to discover retirements which have not been recorded?
14. How is an auditor's initial examination simplified if the client maintains a plant ledger?
15. What procedures does the auditor follow in establishing the existence of plant assets?
16. If returnable containers are lost by a customer, what accounts will be affected, assuming the customer paid a deposit on the containers and the containers are estimated to have a life of four years?
17. What possible significance should the auditor attach to the fact that a fire insurance policy is not on hand?

QUESTIONS ON SYSTEMS APPLICATIONS AND APPLICATION OF AUDITING STANDARDS

18. Your client has consistently used the straight line method of depreciating plant assets, but beginning January 1 of the year under examination has used the "double declining balance" method for both book and tax purposes on all assets acquired after that date. Only minor additions were made during the year, and the effect was to increase depreciation expense from $46,254 as it would have been computed using straight line depreciation for all assets, to $48,625. What effect, if any, should the above facts have on your audit report on the client's financial statements?

19. One of the supporting schedules in the auditor's working papers for his examination of property, plant, and equipment would be "Additions to Plant Assets."
    (a) Tick marks would be used to show the audit steps performed with respect to various figures on the schedule. Give the "legend" or explanation for three tick marks that would appear on the "Additions" schedule.
    (b) What would be the titles of other supporting schedules for property, plant, and equipment?

20. Would depreciation expense ordinarily be subject to responsibility reporting? Justify your answer.

21. In his search for unrecorded liabilities, the independent auditor discovered an invoice for $750 for the overhaul of a company truck. The invoice was dated December 29, covered work completed at that time, but the entry for the item was dated January 5 in the voucher register for January. Explain why the auditor would have to inquire into the details of exactly what was done on the truck in order to properly assess the materiality of the unrecorded liability.

22. An analysis of the accumulated depreciation account reveals a charge covering the cost of tuck pointing a building. What assumption is indicated by the treatment of the charge? Do you agree with the treatment used? Explain.

23. List the three basic types of entries with which the auditor is concerned in relation to the objective of determining that plant assets have been properly valued. Under each type, list the various items of evidence to which the auditor might have occasion to refer in the course of his examination.

24. Suggest contrasting reasons on the part of internal and independent auditors for their concern over rates of depreciation.

25. Suggest accounts other than those directly related to plant assets in which the auditor's work might have some bearing on plant asset figures.

26. Your client revalued all plant assets to reflect current price levels and created a "Revaluation Surplus" classified in the equity section of the balance sheet. It is proposed that depreciation will be charged on the new valuations for the plant assets, and that a transfer will be made each year from revaluation surplus to earned surplus in an amount equivalent to the excess of depreciation charged over depreciation figured on original cost. Do you agree with the proposed yearly entries? Why? Will your short-form audit report be affected by the client's proposed yearly entries? Explain.

27. What audit procedures would you apply in examining an account titled "Construction Work Orders in Progress"?

28. The football stadium at a midwestern university was built as a war memorial, from the gifts of students, alumni, and friends of the university. Title is held

by the Athletic Association, and since the structure had no cost to the Association, no depreciation was charged. If you were engaged for an examination of financial statements of the Association, would you be willing to give an unqualified opinion under the circumstances, or would you insist that depreciation be recorded before you would be willing to give an unqualified opinion? Justify your position.

29. Many banks depreciate their physical facilities at a rapid rate, and it is not uncommon to find a bank balance sheet on which the banking facilities are listed at a value of $1. Would you expect to be able to give an unqualified opinion in such a case? Explain.

PROBLEMS

30. You have been engaged to audit the December 31, 1967 financial statements of The Smith Equipment Corporation which was formed in 1946 and sells or leases construction equipment such as bulldozers, road scrapers, dirt movers, etc. to contractors. The Corporation at year end has 50 pieces of equipment leased to 30 contractors who are using the equipment at various locations throughout your state.

The Smith Equipment Corporation is identified as the owner of the leased equipment by a small metal tag that is attached to each machine. The tag is fastened by screws so that it can be removed if the machine is sold. During the audit you find that the contractors often buy the equipment that they have been leasing, but the identification tag is not always removed from the machine.

The Corporation's principal asset is the equipment leased to the contractors. While there is no plant ledger, each machine is accounted for by a file card that gives its description, cost, contractor-lessee and rental payment records. The Corporation's system of internal control is weak.

You were engaged upon the recommendation of the president of the local bank. The Smith Equipment Corporation, which had never had an audit, had applied to the bank for a sizeable loan; the bank president had requested an audited balance sheet.

You barely know John Smith, the principal stockholder and president of The Smith Equipment Corporation; he has a reputation for expensive personal tastes and for shrewd business dealings, some of which have bordered on being unethical. Nevertheless, Mr. Smith enjoys a strong personal allegiance from his contractor-lessees, whose favor he has curried by personal gifts and loans. The lessees look upon Mr. Smith as a personal friend for whom they would do almost anything. Often they overlook the fact that they are dealing with the Corporation and make their checks payable to Mr. Smith, who endorses them over to the Corporation.

Required:

(a) List the audit procedures that you would employ in the examination of the asset account representing the equipment leased to the contractors.

(b) Although your audit procedures, including those you described in answering part "a," did not uncover any discrepancies, you have been unable to dismiss your feeling that Mr. Smith and some of the contractor-lessees may have collaborated to deceive you. Under this condition discuss what action, if any, you would take and the effect of your feeling upon your auditor's opinion. (Assume that you would not withdraw from the engagement.)   (Uniform C.P.A. Examination)

31. In your examination of the financial statements of Gaar Corporation at December 31, 1967 you observe the contents of certain accounts and other pertinent information as follows:

BUILDING

Date	Explanation	LF	Debit	Credit	Balance
12/31/66	Balance	X	$100,000		$100,000
7/ 1 /67	New boiler	CD	16,480	$1,480	115,000
9/ 1 /67	Insurance recovery ..	CR		2,000	113,000

Allowance for Depreciation—Building

Date	Explanation	LF	Debit	Credit	Balance
12/31/66	Balance—15 years ⓐ				
	4% of $100,000 ..	X		$60,000	$60,000
12/31/67	Annual depreciation ..	GJ		4,440	64,440

You learn that on June 15 the Company's old high-pressure boiler exploded. Damage to the building was insignificant but the boiler was replaced by a more efficient oil-burning boiler. The Company received $2,000 as an insurance adjustment under terms of its policy for damage to the boiler.

The disbursement voucher charged to the building account on July 1, 1967 is reproduced below:

To : REX HEATING COMPANY

List price—new oil-burning boiler (including fuel oil tank and 5,000 gallons fuel oil)	$16,000
Sales tax—3% of $16,000	480
Total	16,480
Less :	
Allowance for old coal-burning boiler in building—to be removed at the expense of the Rex Heating Company.......................	1,480
Total price	$15,000

In vouching the expenditure you determine that the terms included a 2% cash discount which was properly computed and taken. The sales tax is not subject to discount.

Your audit discloses that a voucher for $1,000 was paid to Emment Co. on July 2, 1967 and charged to the repair expense account. The voucher is adequately supported and is marked "installation costs for new oil-burning boiler."

The company's fuel oil supplier advises that fuel oil had a market price of 16¢ per gallon on July 1 and 18¢ per gallon on December 31. The fuel oil inventory at December 31 was 2,000 gallons.

A review of subsidiary property records discloses that the replaced coal-burning boiler was installed when the building was constructed and was recorded at a cost of $10,000. According to its manufacturers the new boiler should be serviceable for 15 years.

In computing depreciation for retirements Gaar Corporation consistently treats a fraction of a month as a full month.

Required:
Prepare the adjusting journal entries that you would suggest for entry on the books of Gaar Corporation. The books have not been closed. Support your entries with computations in good form.   (Uniform C.P.A. Examination)

32. (a) In considering the merits of using price indexes for the purpose of converting the accounting data as reflected in the conventional historical cost accounts, some people have suggested that *these price-level adjustments should be confined to the fixed assets and related depreciation.* What can be said in favor of such a proposal? Against it?

(b) The price index rose from 125 to 175 during the previous year and from 175 to 225 during the current year. The dollar sales during the previous year were $240,000 and during the current year were $300,000.

   (1) For comparative income statement purposes you are to convert the sales figures for both years to the price level existing at the end of the current year. You are to assume that sales were made uniformly throughout both years, and that the change in price level was also uniform.

   (2) What additional information is revealed by a comparison of the converted figures? How do you interpret them?
                                            (Uniform C.P.A. Examination)

33. The federal income tax returns of X Company for the years 1959 and 1960 have been examined by the Internal Revenue Service. The company has calculated depreciation on a four-year life. Salvage value was not used in the calculation and was not questioned by the Internal Revenue Service auditor. The only change has been the disallowance of the use of the sum-of-the-years-digit method for computing depreciation because two automobiles were not held for three years. In the tax audit, to which the client and the IRS supervisor agreed, a change was made to the straight-line method of computing depreciation.

The income including gains on sale of automobiles has been $5,000 in each of the years 1959, 1960 and 1961 after providing depreciation on the sum-of-the-years-digit method. Effective tax rates on such income were 30 per cent, and 25 per cent on capital gains, in each year.

Depreciation and federal income taxes have been provided for the year 1961 based on the company's method. The company wishes to keep its books on the same basis as that used for tax purposes.

Required:
Prepare adjusting entries on the clean surplus theory (all inclusive income statement), as of December 31, 1961 for each account affected by the change of depreciation method except that no accrual for interest should be made. The books have not been closed. (Support each item with organized computations.)
The company owns or has owned the following automobiles:

Car	Purchased	Sold	Cost	Sales price
A	3/31/59	6/30/61	$2,400	$1,500
B	9/30/59	On hand	3,200	
C	4/30/60	12/31/61	3,600	2,000
D	7/31/61	On hand	4,800	

Depreciation has been computed to the nearest month.
                                            (Uniform C.P.A. Examination)

34. The Vorta Corp. purchased a new milling machine on January 1, 1966, to be paid for in ten installments, due on January 1 of each year including the year of purchase. The machine is estimated to have a life of 20 years. The annual payments were calculated as follows:

List price of machine	$ 0,000
Interest	
Total	$10,000
Annual installments (10)	$ 1,000

The Vorta Corp. has made no entries for the purchase of the machine and has followed the practice of charging the annual payments as rent expense.

Prepare any adjusting entries you would make in connection with a first audit as of December 31, 1967.

35. In connection with a first examination of the Soda Pop Company as of December 31, you have obtained the following information:

Balances, December 31	
Bottles	$ 3,122.51
Cases	3,617.00
Accumulated depreciation—cases	1,827.82
Deposits	3,931.75
Sales, December	4,187.20
Sales, year to date	88,629.18
Depreciation on cases	904.25

A physical inventory of cases and bottles on hand at December 31 was as follows:

Cases...	1,923
Bottles	46,152

Cases are to be depreciated at the rate of 25 per cent per year, with depreciation charged for one-half year for cases purchased during the year and one-half year for cases lost or destroyed during the year. Cases costing $419 were purchased during the year.

Deposits are charged as follows:	
Case	$0.27
Bottles (24 per case @ $0.02 per bottle)	0.48
Total deposit, full case	$0.75

Average costs:	
Bottles	$1.75 per 100
Cases	0.50 each
Selling price of Pop—$0.80 per case	

Through the trade association for the carbonated beverage industry you are able to ascertain that companies, on the average, find that the inventory of containers with the trade at any one time which will be returned for deposit refund amounts to about 21 days' sales (based on 24 business days per month).

Prepare a work sheet for your examination of the above accounts, showing any adjusting entries you would recommend.

36. In the course of a regular annual audit of the Bean Manufacturing Corporation you are assigned to the audit of machinery and equipment. A transcript of the ledger account appears below:

MACHINERY AND EQUIPMENT-ACCT. 83

Jan. 1, 1967 Balance	$209,628.12	Apr. 25, 1967 CR 12 $75.00	
Apr. 18, 1967 VR 23	31,994.45		
July 28, 1967 J 8	6,681.81		
Sept. 9, 1967 VR 41	14,189.00		
Nov. 11, 1967 VR 52	7,261.88		

You have examined the invoices for September 9 and November 11 and have no questions as to them. In support of the entry of April 18, 1967, you find an invoice, Figure 18–2, reproduced below. In support of the entry of July 28, 1967, you find a journal voucher which is also reproduced.

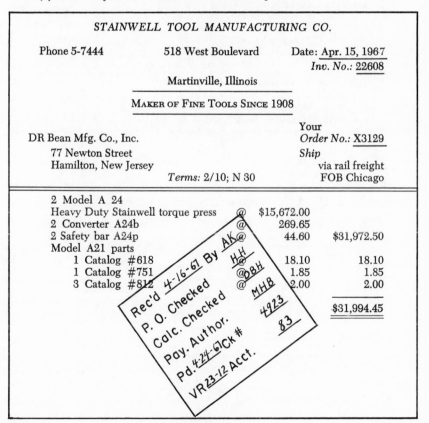

STAINWELL TOOL MANUFACTURING CO.

Phone 5-7444   518 West Boulevard   Date: Apr. 15, 1967
                                                          Inv. No.: 22608

Martinville, Illinois

MAKER OF FINE TOOLS SINCE 1908

DR Bean Mfg. Co., Inc.   Your
                                                Order No.: X3129
77 Newton Street   *Ship*
Hamilton, New Jersey   via rail freight
                    Terms: 2/10; N 30   FOB Chicago

2 Model A 24
Heavy Duty Stainwell torque press   @ $15,672.00
2 Converter A24b   @   269.65
2 Safety bar A24p   @   44.60 $31,972.50
Model A21 parts
    1 Catalog #618   18.10   18.10
    1 Catalog #751   1.85   1.85
    3 Catalog #812   2.00   2.00
                                                        $31,994.45

Rec'd 4-16-67 By AK
P. O. Checked HH
Calc. Checked DBH
Pay. Author. MHB
Pd. 4-24-67 Ck # 4923
VR 23-12 Acct. 83

FIGURE 18-2

Required:

After applying usual auditing procedures to the information available, state
the adjustments of the Machinery and Equipment account or questions for further investigation which are suggested by the ledger transcript and supporting
documents. Describe the nature of each adjustment or item questioned, and

JOURNAL VOUCHER 52-7-8
CONSTRUCTION OF CONVEYOR

Machinery and equipment		$6,681.81	
Drafting department salaries			$ 198.00
Repair department wages			611.95
Factory direct labor.................................			386.60
Purchases			5,485.26
To record cost of conveyor as follows :.................			
John Redfield, draftsman, 43 hours @ $2...............		$ 86.00	
Wm. White, draftsman, 56 hours @ $2...............		112.00	
		$ 198.00	
Repairmen assigned to construction :			
D. Baker 94 regular hours	@ $2.12	$ 199.28	
42 overtime hours	@ $3.18	$ 133.56	
E. Miller 71 regular hours	@ $2.26	$ 160.46	
35 overtime hours	@ $3.39	118.65	
		$ 611.95	
Factory workers assigned to construction :			
R. Fischer 94 regular hours	@ $1.20	$ 112.80	
35 overtime hours	@ $2.30	$ 80.50	
J. Smith 94 regular hours	@ $1.20	$ 112.80	
35 overtime hours	@ $2.30	80.50	
		$ 386.60	
Purchases VR 34-18.................................		$ 921.85	
VR 35-4		2,876.50	
VR 35-13.................................		235.42	
VR 35-37.................................		689.17	
VR 36-11.................................		319.40	
VR 36-22		442.92	
		$5,485.26	

(Uniform C.P.A. Examination)

troller. Segregation of this responsibility and that of custody of the securities is of utmost importance, because independent accountability is thus established over the securities and the income which they produce. Further control over security transactions is possible if the accounting department ascertains that each transaction has been properly authorized.

Accounting control over income from securities is essential if assurance is desired that all income has been deposited in company bank accounts. In the case of investments in bonds, many concerns make monthly standard journal entries accruing all interest earned and amortizing any premium or discount. Such entries facilitate the preparation of monthly statements, and by recording the entries in the ledger rather than as worksheet adjustments, an account for accrued interest receivable is established. This account then shows the amount of interest income the treasurer must account for and results in a far superior situation to that where the treasurer is solely responsible for reporting to the accounting department the amount of interest income he has received and deposited.

Dividends from corporate stocks are more difficult to control. No accrual entry for the dividends can be made, as even though a company may have a definite program for payment of dividends, conditions may result in dividend rates being raised or lowered, and regular dividends may be omitted or extra dividends declared. Perhaps the best means of securing adequate accountability over dividends when only a few stocks are held is to place the stocks in safekeeping. The usually superior internal control of the safekeeping agent then replaces that of the owning company, and if the agent reports all dividends received directly to the accounting department, independent accountability is fully operative. For businesses which do not keep stocks in safekeeping, a representative of the accounting department should periodically compare dividends received with a published record of all dividends that have been declared and paid.

In instances where several securities are held and transactions are frequent, a subsidiary ledger record for each security should be maintained. As in the illustration on page 468, such a record usually provides for the showing of complete identifying information for each security, a record of each purchase and sale transaction, and a record of all income received.

Bonding

As in the case of employees or officers handling cash, those handling securities or the income from the securities should be bonded. The large risks ordinarily involved when securities are held in the owner's custody make it essential that all persons having access to the securities be adequately bonded. The cost of such fidelity insurance can be avoided, of course, if the securities are placed in safekeeping.

RECORDS OF STOCKS AND BONDS

(FRONT)

NAME OF SECURITY

| PAR VALUE OR DENOMINATION $ | | DATE OF ISSUE | DATE OF MATURITY |

| DIVIDENDS OR INTEREST RATE | PAYABLE |
| STOCK DIVIDENDS | | DIVIDENDS CUMULATIVE |

TAX STATUS		RIGHTS
CALLABLE AT $	WHEN CALLABLE	CONVERSION PRIVILEGES
REGISTERED IN NAME OF		WHERE LOCATED

OTHER DATA

PURCHASES

| DATE | SOUGHT FROM OR SOLD TO OR NAME OF BROKER | MEMO. | CERTIFICATE OR BOND NO. | QUAN. | AMOUNT |

SALES

| QUAN. | COST | SOLD FOR | PROFIT OR LOSS | QUAN. | AMOUNT |
BALANCE

RECORD OF DIVIDENDS OR INTEREST
NAME OF SECURITY

(BACK)

| DATE | MEMO | AMOUNT | DATE | MEMO | AMOUNT | DATE | MEMO | AMOUNT |

Courtesy Charles R. Hadley Company

Management Reports

At least once a year, and in some cases as often as once a month, a report should be prepared listing all securities held and showing their cost and market value. Such a report is vital in analyzing and appraising a company's investment position. Supplementing this report, an analysis may be given of all security transactions occurring since the date of the previous report. A schedule showing the return on each investment and the over-all return on all investments will also prove highly useful in most instances.

Internal Auditing

One of the most important services that the internal auditor can perform when investments are held is to make occasional surprise counts of the investments. Those securities which are not on hand should be confirmed. Only in this way can the independent records establishing control over the custodian of the securities be made fully effective. Without such counts there is no assurance that the securities are on hand and have not been converted for personal gain. If there is no internal auditor, some employee or officer outside of the treasurer's department should count the securities and balance the count against the ledger records at least once a year.

Other important procedures applied by the internal auditor in making an examination of investments would include a review of purchases and sales since the previous examination. Supporting data, such as brokers' advices, should be examined in support of recorded costs for purchases and in support of the proceeds of sales. Prices may also be verified against market quotations, and the authorization for each purchase and sale should be inspected. Particular note should be made that any gains or losses on sales have been properly recorded.

The internal auditor should also verify the income from investments. All dividends and interest due should have been recorded, and the cash should have been received shortly after the dividend or interest payment date. Amortization of premium or discount should be verified, as should the accrual of interest at the end of the year.

STANDARDS OF STATEMENT PRESENTATION

Investments involve most of the problems of statement presentation mentioned in the previous chapters pertaining to other types of assets. One problem that seldom affects most other assets, however, is invariably present when investments appear among a client's assets: should the investments be classed with current assets, or must they be included under a noncurrent classification?

Classification as Current or Noncurrent

be excluded from the current section of the balance sheet. They may be shown under a separate "Investments" caption or they may be classed under "Other Assets," depending on the materiality of the amounts involved. Investments which are not readily marketable would include mortgage notes, other long-term notes, securities of close-held corporations, advances to affiliated companies, and the cash surrender value of life insurance policies.

Occasionally investments which are readily marketable must nevertheless be classified as noncurrent. Any investments which are held for nonworking capital purposes would fall in this category. Examples would include investments in pension funds, sinking funds, or plant expansion funds, as well as investments in subsidiary or affiliated companies, loans or advances to such companies, and investments held for long-term production of income.

The preceding comments should suggest that only readily marketable securities being held for working capital purposes may properly be classified as current assets. Obviously included in this category would be the temporary investment in marketable securities of idle funds during the slack period of a seasonal business. In some cases, however, even securities which have been held for several years may be shown as current assets if intentions are to use the securities for working capital purposes whenever the need arises.

Financial institutions such as banks and insurance companies ordinarily do not have a problem in classifying investments. The major portion of their resources is usually invested in such assets, and all of the investments are considered to be security for the claims of depositors or policyholders. Classifying the investments by type is much more meaningful than any attempt to classify them as current or noncurrent, and such classification takes the place of the customary classifications found on balance sheets of industrial and trading concerns.

Indication of Basis of Valuation

Because investments may be valued in any of several acceptable ways, explicit information should be given to show how securities have been valued in each instance. For marketable securities carried as a current asset, the most common method of valuation is cost, but preferably the market value of the securities should be stated parenthetically, regardless of whether market is above or below cost. Marketable securities may also be properly carried at the lower of cost or market, in which case the higher of the two figures should be given parenthetically. A write-down to market should always be made if there is a material, permanent decline in the value of a security.

Long-term investments shown under a noncurrent classification are normally valued at cost. Market value of the securities may be stated parenthetically if the client so desires, but the information is not considered as essential as in the case of securities classified as current assets. If market value of the long-term investments has declined materially as a result of the unsatisfactory financial position of the issuing company, the loss should be recognized by reducing the carrying value of the securities. No write-down should be made, however, to reflect temporary declines associated with price fluctuations of the security market as a whole.

Investment securities held in a self-administered pension trust may properly be carried at market value, particularly if the trust indenture so requires. The current valuation figure is quite important relative to the valuation of the shares of officers and employees entering, leaving, or continuing under the trust arrangement.

As recommended in *Accounting Research Bulletin No. 51*, investments in the stock of nonconsolidated subsidiary or affiliated companies are preferably handled by recording, as income and an increase in the investment, the parent's share of the subsidiary's net income and reducing the investment for dividends received. Another alternative is to take the adjustments of the investment account directly to retained income or a special reserve account.

Because each of the methods described above for valuing investments may be used if desired, the auditor's problem is not primarily one of inducing the client to follow an acceptable method of valuation. The main consideration is to determine that the client has clearly indicated in the balance sheet the basis of valuation being followed. The variety of acceptable methods makes such information essential to the reader or analyst who is attempting to interpret the company's financial position or results of operation. Also, of course, the auditor must carefully comment in his report on any change between years in the method of valuing investments, unless such change will not materially distort the comparability of the client's financial statements.

Other Balance Sheet Considerations

The following points should also be considered in meeting accepted standards of statement presentation:

1. If investments are a significant portion of the total assets, as in the case of financial institutions, information should be given showing the

major types of investments, listed in the order of their liquidity. The following classifications are frequently used:

United States government securities
  Short-term notes, bills, and certificates
  Bonds

Corporate bonds
Long-term notes
Mortgages
Advances to affiliates or subsidiaries
Preferred stocks
Common stocks

2. Full disclosure must be made if any securities have been pledged as collateral or are otherwise subject to lien.

3. Investments in affiliated or subsidiary companies should be listed separately from other investments and the nature of the relationship to such companies should be stated.

4. A company's own bonds or stocks held in the treasury or in special funds are preferably shown as offsets to the total amount of bonds or stocks issued. If the client wishes to follow the less desirable alternative of showing such securities as assets, full disclosure should be made of the fact that the company's own securities are involved. Similarly, on the equity side of the balance sheet, reference should be made concerning any of the issued securities which are being carried as assets. Securities held in special funds or acquired for resale under stock option plans are sometimes suggested as instances warranting an asset classification.

Income Statement Considerations

The ownership of securities entails certain problems of presentation of the resulting income in the income statement.

1. Unless investments are a principal source of income, as in the case of financial institutions, the income should be classified as "Other Income."

2. If significant amounts are involved, interest income and dividends received should be displayed separately as the lesser stability of income from dividends may be an important factor in making a projection of estimated future earnings.

3. Gains or losses resulting from the disposition of securities should be shown apart from the interest and dividends received, for such gains or losses may be nonrecurring. In situations where such nonrecurring items would materially alter the net income reported, they are preferably taken directly to retained earnings.

for the day as further verification of the unit cost. The paid check resulting from the client's payment for the purchase is also very useful evidence of the cost. Ordinarily no reference to the paid check should be necessary when the broker's advice is available, but if the investment is some form of mortgage note or unsecured note, the paid check may be the only satisfactory evidence available.

Sales. When sales of investments occur, the auditor must be careful to note that the investment account was credited with the cost of the securities sold, and not with the proceeds of the sale. It is a natural mistake for the bookkeeper who only rarely handles such transactions to credit the full proceeds to the investment account, ignoring any accrued interest received and any gain or loss on the sale.

If a partial sale of investments acquired over a period of time occurs, some method of determining the cost of the securities sold must be consistently followed. Ordinarily, one of the two methods acceptable for tax purposes wil be used—specific identification of the cost of the certificates delivered, or first-in, first-out. The proceeds of the sale used in determining the gain or loss should ordinarily be the net proceeds after deducting the expenses of the sale. Sales of investments and the proceeds from such sales should be verified in much the same manner as purchases. Evidence that the proper amount of cash was actually received will be in the form of an entry on a deposit ticket or on the bank statement. As there will be no special identifying information for such entries, identification must be made on the basis of the dollar amount involved.

Cut-off of purchases and sales. To assure correct and full disclosure of the facts as they actually exist at the balance sheet date, the auditor should satisfy himself that a proper cut-off was observed in recording all transactions occurring shortly before or shortly after the balance sheet date. In the case of purchases of securities through a broker, ordinarily payment does not have to be made until several days after the purchase is consummated by the broker. The actual delivery of the stock or bond certificate to the client may not occur until several weeks later as a result of the time required to record the name of the new owner on the records of the transfer agent and to issue a new certificate in the client's name. Thus it is quite possible that a purchase may have been made shortly before the balance sheet date and yet no record would appear until after that date. By examining the supporting data for such purchases, particularly the broker's advice of purchase, the auditor can ascertain exactly when the purchase occurred. If the purchase was consummated before the close of the year and material amounts were involved, adjustment should be made to show the investment as an asset, and the resulting liability for the purchase cost should also be shown.

A similar situation may arise in the case of securities sold shortly before the balance sheet date. The cash proceeds will ordinarily not be received until several days after the sale date, and the actual certificates sold do not have to be delivered to the broker until three days after the sale. Thus it is quite possible that a sale may have occurred before the balance sheet date in spite of many indications to the contrary. Again, review of the facts and evidence related to a sale recorded shortly after the balance sheet date should reveal the true situation. If the sale was actually made prior to the end of the year, the investment account should be reduced and a nontrade receivable shown for the amount of the proceeds. The realization of either a gain or loss on the disposition will be an important factor in determining whether failure to record the transaction in the proper period will materially affect the financial statements.

Market value. As stated earlier, investments classified as current assets should either be valued at the lower of cost or market, or at least have their market value shown parenthetically. Market value is also important in the case of long-term investments, because any permanent declines of a material amount should be reflected in the financial statements. For securities actively traded on the securities exchanges, closing prices at the end of each day are ordinarily available in large-city newspapers or in various financial news publications. If no sale took place on the day in question, quoted bid figures, or the average of bid and asked figures, can be used as an indication of market value. In the case of securities which are traded "over the counter," the auditor can usually get recent sale prices and bid and asked figures from a security dealer who handles the securities in question. If such information is not available, reference should be made to the financial statements of the company issuing the securities. The auditor should be able to determine in a general way by careful study of the statements whether the securities are likely to have declined in value below their original cost.

In using published market quotation figures, the auditor must take great care to be sure the published description of each security agrees exactly with the securities owned. This is particularly important in the case of United States Government securities. There are bills, notes, bonds, and certificates of indebtedness, and often many different issues of each, distinguishable only by the interest rate or the maturity date. The auditor must also be sure that he interprets the price quotations properly. Corporate stocks and bonds are quoted in steps of one-eighth. United States bonds are quoted in thirty-seconds, but a price of 101 $16/32$ is often printed as 101.16. Thus the proper market value of a $10,000 bond would not be $10,116, but $10,150. State and municipal securities are usually quoted on a yield basis, such as 2.05 per cent, and bond tables must be used to convert the yield figures into market values.

Total market value of the securities is customarily used, rather than figuring each item at the lower of cost or market as in the case of inventories.

One author has recommended that when market prices of securities held are in excess of cost, provision should be made for the amount of taxes which would be payable upon sale of the securities. This would be particularly important in the case of stockbrokers, who normally carry their securities at market, and investment companies, which show unrealized appreciation on their investments.

If the client has already figured the market value of securities owned, the auditor should verify the prices used against published quotations and verify all extensions and footings involved in arriving at the final figure. If the client has not done this work, the auditor can do it, although the value of a double check of the figures is lost. In such cases the client should at least review and approve the auditor's figures.

Working papers. Schedule N-1 illustrates the manner in which the auditor customarily summarizes changes in the client's investment account and indicates the verification work which he has performed. The beginning balance for each security, both face value (or number of shares) and cost, should be compared with the closing balance shown in the working papers for the preceding year. Purchases and sales should be recorded on the schedule from an analysis of the general ledger account, or balanced with transactions in the general ledger account if the information is taken from the detailed securities ledger. Verification of the recorded purchases and sales should be made as suggested above, and tick-marks with an explanatory legend should be used to show what has been done. The columns for net proceeds and gain or loss on sale are merely memorandum columns. The cost of securities sold recorded in the sales column, plus or minus the figure in the memo column for gain or loss, should equal the net proceeds of the sale. The total of the memo column for gain or loss should agree with and be cross-referenced to the trial balance figure for net gain or loss arising from sales of securities.

The cost amounts in the column for balances at the close of the year should be totaled and cross-referenced to the trial balance figure for investments. The description and the face amount or number of shares of each security on hand at the end of the year should be verified by the count of securities, as mentioned later.

In the case of long-term bonds which are to be held for more than a year, provision must be made in the working papers for a record of premium or discount amortized during the year. These amounts should be verified or calculated by the auditor and treated as an adjustment of the carrying value of the investments and of the cash interest income recorded. The general rule, based partly on conservatism, is that premium amortization should be based on the call date of the bonds if such a provision exists, whereas amortization of discount should always be figured based on the maturity of the bonds. The rule also gains justification from the fact that bonds are more likely to be called before maturity if the bonds are selling at a premium than if they are selling at a discount.

Verification of entries in the investment account. As in the case of the examination of other accounts, the auditor should satisfy himself that entries to the general ledger control account for investments reflect bona fide transactions and that the postings originated from the regular books of original entry. In the typical commercial audit involving relatively few investment transactions, the manner of preparing and verifying the working paper analysis of the investment account as described above fully covers the matter of establishing the credibility of the accounting records.

In the examination of financial organizations having large numbers of securities transactions made under good internal control, entries to the investment control accounts should be traced to source records for one or two months to establish the validity of the entries in the controlling accounts. As a further test of the client's records, the individual transactions listed in the source records should be traced to the postings to the individual securities ledger sheets. These postings should be tick-marked, and on completion of this work the ledger should be reviewed to ascertain whether all entries dated in the month chosen for examination have been tick-marked. If entries to the securities ledger are to be random-tested rather than verified in their entirety for a stated period, then some tests should be made working from entries in the securities ledger and tracing the entries to the source records to ascertain that they appear in those records. Only in this manner can the auditor detect fictitious entries in the securities ledger.

Establish Existence and Ownership of Investment Assets

Investments which are in the client's possession should be examined in support of the ledger records of those investments. Direct confirmation should be obtained covering all investments not on hand, and as is later pointed out, notes receivable should be confirmed with the individuals or firms who have issued the notes.

Physical examination. One of the most important procedures in establishing the existence of the client's investment assets is the physical inspection of the certificates or documents evidencing those investments. Because most documents of this type are easily negotiated or pledged as collateral for borrowed funds, the safeguards pertaining to the count of liquid assets in the chapters on receivables and cash apply with equal force to the count of investments. In other words, all liquid assets must be counted simultaneously or kept under control until the counting has been completed, in order to preclude any attempt to conceal a shortage by substitution of an asset already counted. Also, it is desirable that the auditor obtain a signed statement that all the investments counted were returned to their custodian at the completion of the count made in his presence.

If the count cannot be made on the balance sheet date, additional audit time will be consumed. Cash in bank will have to be reconciled at both the balance sheet date and at the count date. Furthermore, all investment transactions occurring between the count date and the balance sheet date will have to be verified to establish the amount of investments at the balance sheet date. These problems can be eliminated if the client keeps the investment certificates in a public safe deposit vault. Operators of such vaults maintain records of all entries to the boxes stored in the vault. Thus if the auditor counts the investment certificates after the balance sheet date, the same certificates can be presumed to have been present at the balance sheet date if the vault operator certifies that his records show that no access was given to the client's deposit box between the balance sheet date and the time of the auditor's count. If the auditor plans to delay the count of investments and proceed on this basis, the client should be cautioned that the loss of control will entail additional audit work if anyone obtains access to the box before the auditor makes his count.

The count of securities held by a large financial institution may extend over several days. In such instances all securities should be placed under the auditor's seal and the auditor should maintain a record of all securities added or withdrawn during the period the securities are under his control.

Making the count. At the beginning of the investment count both the client and the auditor should be in full accord on what is to be counted. Subsequent disclosure that the client's representative did not present all the securities in his custody to the auditor may necessitate a complete recount of all liquid assets at a later date. If the auditor is not sufficiently informed at the time of making the count to recognize the omission and ask for the additional securities, part of the blame for the additional work is his.

If the auditor is not making a surprise count of investments, he will usually find it advantageous to prepare, before beginning the count, a list of all securities held. The listing may well be made on the regular worksheet for investments, as was done in the case of schedule N-1 at the close of the chapter. A tick-mark is then used to show that each security has been counted. Preparing the list from the records in advance of the count not only speeds the making of the actual count but gives immediate notice if anything has been omitted from the count.

In counting securities the auditor should note carefully that the description of each certificate he examines agrees exactly with the description in the records of the company. Many companies have several outstanding issues of stocks or bonds which are similar in appearance and description. If the records show 100 shares of cumulative $4\frac{1}{2}$ per cent preferred stock, the auditor must be sure that he has examined a certificate of that description and not one representing 100 shares of the same company's $5 noncumulative participating preferred. Similarly, close attention must be given to the company name on the certificate. The securities of ABC Co. may have vastly different value from those of ABC, Inc. Some documents may be difficult to identify. A promissory note may be incorporated with a complicated collateral agreement that is ten pages in length. Similar to the note agreement in appearance, and kept in the same place for safekeeping, may be a warranty agreement or a perpetual-care agreement for a cemetery lot. Accurate and careful description of each item counted is especially important in the case of a surprise count, when the record made by the auditor during the count must later be checked out against the client's record.

If coupon bonds are encountered, all unmatured coupons should be attached to the bonds. The coupons are payable to bearer and are fully negotiable; hence missing coupons will cause a bond to diminish in value. On the other hand, matured coupons which have not been clipped suggest that interest payments are in arears and that the bond may not be paid in full at maturity.

Ownership. If the auditor is to be fully satisfied that all investments owned by the client are fully accounted for and have been submitted to him for examination, he must attempt to ascertain the true owner of all securities presented to him for count. Unless care is exercised on this point, the auditor may be misled into improperly accepting the securities as being the client's when in fact they may be securities which have been pledged by a customer as collateral, borrowed from other portfolios which the client holds as trustee, or borrowed from an outside source. The possibility of concealing a shortage by substituting other securities held by the client should show the importance of determining what securities are held by the client in a bailment capacity and fully accounting for those securities as well as the securities owned by the client. Information on the securities held by the client but owned by others should be established independently by requesting information on collateral pledged when notes or other receivables likely to be secured are confirmed in connection with the verification of the receivables.

Of considerable importance in the determination of ownership of a security being examined is the name of the registered owner shown on the certificate. The name should, of course, be that of the client. Possibly the only permissible exception is where a company carries its securities in the name of an individual who acts as nominee in order to avoid revealing the identity of the company as owner. The auditor should also note whether the certificates examined have been endorsed. Endorsement increases the possibility for misuse of the securities. The absence of any endorsement is fairly conclusive evidence that the securities have not been temporarily converted to some individual's use in the past. These comments do not apply, of course, to bearer bonds.

The most positive identification which can be made of the certificate being examined is its serial number. Serial numbers can be obtained from the client's records, from the working papers of the previous year in the case of a repeat audit, or from copies of brokers' delivery advices. These numbers should then be compared with the numbers on the certificates counted by the auditor. By making effective use of these numbers the auditor can protect himself against the substitution of borrowed securities to conceal a shortage, and he can detect a temporary conversion of the securities accomplished by a sale of the securities and repurchase before the time of the auditor's count.

Serial numbers are seldom tendered such consideration, however, in the audit of financial institutions holding substantial amounts of investments. In such cases internal control is usually adequate to preclude any question being raised about the certificates being examined.

Confirmation. As a general rule stocks or bonds which have been counted need not be confirmed. This is particularly true of securities traded on a recognized exchange. The number of parties and the precautions involved in the transfer of security certificates in such cases presents substantial assurance to the auditor that the certificates he is examining are valid. Even more important, however, in assuring the authenticity and validity of such a certificate is the physical make-up of the certificate itself. The color engraving and paper used are specialties of a limited number of concerns, and these concerns are careful to accept only work which is properly authorized. The slightest indication that any fraud might be involved in an order for such engraving work would bring immediate rejection of the order and possible police investigation.

The effect of such precautions in the engraving and printing of security certificates and the manner in which securities are purchased and sold afford the auditor reasonable justification for accepting the certificates on their face, much as government currency is accepted. When these protective features are wholly or partially absent, then, of course, confirmation must be obtained from the issuer to compensate. This would be true in the case of unlisted stocks or bonds issued by unknown companies and purchased from the issuer or from another party without the services of a regular security dealer being involved. For the same reason, and also because the documents are less formal, confirmation would be required on any notes which are held. Such confirmation is doubly important because it may reveal payments made which have not been recorded by the client's employees, possibly as the result of a misappropriation.

Of course, any investment document which is not available for count at the count date must be confirmed with the holder at that date to establish the existence of the investment. Investigation as to the reason that the note or certificate is held by someone else may lead to disclosure that it has been pledged as collateral, a situation which has important balance sheet connotations, as noted previously. Usually, however, the evidence of the investment will be absent because the certificates are being held in safe-keeping or under a trust agreement, or because they are being transferred to the new owner after purchase, or because they have been sent out for collection. Confirmation of securities held by a trustee under a sinking fund or pension trust agreement is especially important. The auditor should request sufficient information to enable him to ascertain that the trustee is operating in accordance with the terms of the trust agreement, and the list of securities held may reveal that some of the client's own securities are in the fund.

If the certificates prove to be in transit at the count date, the auditor should note carefully the transit period involved after the certificates arrive. An abnormally long period might indicate that the certificates had actually been received earlier, and were utilized for some fraudulent purpose at the count date. If important securities are in transit to the client at the count date, the auditor may wish to control the client's incoming mail until the certificates arrive. In this manner the auditor can determine the exact date of arrival and can note the postmarks and the sender's return address as further verification of the true facts.

Account for All Income from Investments

In the examination of financial organizations holding large amounts of securities, internal control will usually be adequate to assure that all income from the investments has been properly accounted for. Some tests should be made, however, of the record of income received. The purpose of such tests is not primarily to show directly that all income has been recorded, but rather to show that the system of internal control is functioning and that accrual has been made of income earned at the end of the year.

For businesses which hold securities incidental to their principal activities, internal control over the income from the securities is often nonexistent, and the auditor should compensate for this deficiency by completely accounting for all income earned during the year. The following comments are predicated upon such a situation.

Bonds. The description in the audit working papers for each bond investment should include all information necessary to verify the income from the investment. Most important, of course, will be the interest rate and the interest dates. Working with this information, the auditor can schedule his verification of income through the use of four additional columns on his schedule of investments. As shown on schedule N-1, these columns would be:

1. Interest accrued at the beginning of the year.
2. Interest earned during the year.
3. Interest received during the year.
4. Interest accrued at the end of the year.

In effect, these columns represent an analysis of an accrued interest receivable account maintained on a perpetual basis. The first column should agree with the final column in the audit working papers for the preceding year. The interest earned for each type of bond held should be calculated as based on the interest rate and the period the bonds have been held. The figure should be inserted in the second column. Each interest payment which should have been received is then scheduled in the third column and traced to the appropriate entry in the cash receipts record. The dates of entry should be carefully noted to show that there was no undue delay in recording the receipt of the interest. Accrued interest purchased should be entered in the third column as a negative figure. Accrued interest received at date of sale should be entered in the same manner as for any interest received.

The next step is to add across the figures in the first two columns, subtract the figures in the third column, and enter the difference in the fourth column. This final amount is, of course, the amount of interest accrued at the end of the period, and the amount should be verified by a calculation of the actual interest accrued at the end of the year. The total of this column should agree with and be cross-referenced to the trial balance figure for accrued interest receivable. The total of the interest-earned column, after adjustment for amortization of premium or discount as shown in the investments schedule, should agree with and be cross-referenced to the interest income account, as was done on schedule N-1.

The above steps represent a complete verification of interest income, subject only to the possibility that all interest may not have been paid. Interest in default should be verified by reference to a published investment service or by contacting the debtor company, thus assuring the auditor that the failure of the records to show the income is not the result of a misappropriation. If there is assurance that delinquent interest payments will be brought up to date in the near future, the interest should be accrued and reported as income. If no such assurance exists, no accrual should be made, and of course the carrying value of the investment itself should be carefully reviewed to indicate the possible need for a substantial write-down.

Stocks. Although there are no accruals to be verified in the case of stock investments, the verification of income received is more difficult than for bonds. Reference must be made to a published service, such as *Standard & Poor's Annual Dividend Record,* to ascertain what dividends have been declared on each company's stock and when those dividends were paid. Such publications also show the record date for each dividend— a factor of great importance if stocks have been bought or sold in the interim between the date a dividend has been declared and the date it is paid. The relationship between the record date and the date of purchase or sale will determine whether the client should have received the dividend.

OTHER TYPES OF INVESTMENTS

Investments in Subsidiaries or Affiliated Companies

When a controlling interest is held in a corporation whose activities are closely related to those of the parent company, ordinarily consolidated financial statements should be prepared in order to present the clearest picture of financial position and results of operations. If a controlled subsidiary is not to be consolidated, the burden of proof that the omission is proper and does not obscure the true financial picture should be on those who desire not to include the subsidiary in the consolidated statements. The auditor must be careful to ascertain that the reasons given are sound.

Subsidiaries to be consolidated present no particular auditing problems if the auditor has also examined the financial statements of the subsidiaries. If the subsidiaries have been examined by other competent independent accountants, the auditor of the parent company should be justified in accepting the subsidiary statements without comment. Some protection is gained, however, if the auditor expressing his opinion on the consolidated statements indicates in his certificate that figures for consolidated subsidiaries were accepted on the basis of the reports of other independent accountants.

When subsidiaries or affiliates are not consolidated, the auditor must be satisfied that the investment account has been consistently maintained in accordance with a generally accepted method. In many cases the cost method will be followed, but methods which compensate the carrying value of the investment account for changes in the book value of the parent's equity in the subsidiary are preferable. Regardless of the method followed, the auditor's main concern should be to see that the carrying value of the investment does not materially exceed the underlying worth of the investment. His conclusions must come from a careful analysis of the financial statements of the subsidiary if no market value figure is available. The reliance to be placed on the financial statements will depend on whether they have been examined by the auditor or by another independent public accountant.

Advances to nonconsolidated subsidiaries or affiliates present some additional problems. In the first place, written confirmation of the indebtedness should be obtained from the related company. Second, the terms of the advance must be noted to ascertain whether the advance can be classified as a current asset or must be classified as noncurrent. Last, the auditor must attempt to determine whether the advance is likely to be repaid in accordance with the established terms. This problem may involve not only reviewing supporting financial statements but also determining how the advance was utilized and the probable results of such utilization. Advances designed to permit expansion of manufacturing facilities or development of a patent obviously cannot be repaid in the immediate future. The question of eventual repayment will hinge on the profitability of operations with the additional plant, or the progress being made on the patent development. Thus the auditor may touch upon a wide variety of matters in satisfying himself that an advance to a subsidiary or affiliate is properly classified in the financial statements and is carried at an acceptable dollar amount.

Mortgage Notes

Mortgage notes are customarily carried at cost as adjusted for the amortization of any premium or discount, and of course must be classified as a noncurrent asset if the terms exceed the operating cycle of the business. The notes should be examined at the same time that other liquid assets are counted. Each note should be payable to the client or be accompanied by an assignment by the original payee. Also to be examined in support of the notes are such documents as the mortgage agreement or trust deed, title policy, letter of title search or abstract of title, appraisal report, fire insurance policies, and tax receipts. The balance due on the mortgage should be confirmed with the debtor. Confirmation is especially important, as most mortgage notes are liquidated by regular periodic payments, and the auditor should ascertain that all payments made have been accounted for. Payments are customarily applied first against interest which is due, and the auditor should review the allocations made between interest and principal. Supplementing this review, the auditor should calculate the approximate amount of interest income based on the average balance during the year and compare this figure with the recorded income.

Verification of the acquisition of a mortgage note should be similar to such verification for other investments. Of major importance will be the authorization for the acquisition and the paid check. In the case of the audit of a bank or a building and loan association, appraisal reports should be on hand evidencing that the maximum loan percentages set by law have not been exceeded.

To justify showing a mortgage note at cost less payments on principal, the auditor should be satisfied that the client can be expected to realize the full amount due. Of first importance here is the credit-worthiness of the mortgagor. Regularity of past payments is a good indication, but in special cases the auditor should attempt to ascertain the mortgagor's ability to pay. The auditor should also make some investigation of the secondary protection which the mortgagee holds in the form of the mortgaged property. Reference to a title policy or an attorney's letter of title search should indicate whether the mortgagor had clear title which he could then mortgage. The mortgage agreement should be noted for evidence that it has been properly recorded in the public records to protect the interests of the mortgagee. In the event of any question about such legal matters, opinion of the client's attorney should be obtained. Examination of insurance policies shows whether the mortgagee is adequately protected in the event of a fire or windstorm loss. The policies should be sufficient in amount to give full protection to the mortgagee and should contain endorsements assigning the proceeds of the policies to the mortgagee. Examination of paid tax bills provides evidence that no unpaid taxes have become prior liens against the property. Appraisal reports should provide some indication of the amount likely to be realized if mortgage payments are in default. If no recent report is available, inspection of the property may be warranted in order that the auditor may form some opinion of its present worth.

Cash Surrender Value of Life Insurance

A business may carry life insurance on an officer, partner, or key employee to compensate for the loss arising from the death of such person, or to provide funds to enable the business to purchase the deceased person's interest in the business. The latter arrangement is often of great importance in making it possible for the estate of the deceased person to be able to pay estate and inheritance taxes assessed against the estate. The business, on the other hand, cannot be forced into a position where it must accept a new part owner who is not fully acceptable to the surviving owners.

The auditor's concern when such policies exist is to satisfy himself that the interrelated items of premium expense and cash surrender value are fairly stated. In addition, if a strict accrual basis of accounting for the premiums is followed, there may also be a prepaid expense account for a portion of the premium. If the insurance is carried with a mutual insurance company, there may be an asset representing dividends left to accumulate, although ordinarily the dividends earned are likely to be used to reduce the premium payment for the following year.

The growth in the cash surrender value of the policy serves to reduce the true expense of the policy below the yearly cash outlay. The auditor should therefore ascertain that the balance of the account for the cash surrender value has been correctly figured and that the increase during the year has been credited to the premium expense account. The insurance policy will list the amount of cash surrender value at the end of each policy year. Although the true cash surrender value at any time prior to the end of the year will reflect a discount factor, the amount of the difference will not be material, and can be ignored if the client's fiscal year does not coincide with the policy year.

In addition to verifying the premium expense and cash surrender value by reference to the insurance policy, the auditor should obtain confirmation of the cash surrender value of the policy from the insurance company. To simplify the insurance company's compliance with the auditor's request, the amount of the cash surrender value may be requested as of the last premium payment date. This figure will usually represent a close enough approximation of the value at the balance sheet date to be entirely satis-factory for audit purposes.

The insurance company should also be requested to confirm that all premiums have been paid to date, the amount of any accumulated dividends and the interest thereon, the amount of any loans outstanding against the policy, and the name of the beneficiary of the policy. If the beneficiary is not the client company, the cash surrender value is not an asset of the company, and the premiums paid by the company become extra compensa-tion to the insured person.

SUMMARY

Internal control

Duties pertaining to securities which ideally should be performed by different individuals—

    Authorization of purchases and sales.

    Custody of the securities.

    Handling of the accounting records of the securities and related income.

Statement presentation

Securities should be classified as noncurrent assets if—

    Not readily marketable.

    Held for other than working capital purposes.

The basis of valuation should be stated, with market value given parentheti-cally if the securities are stated at cost, and cost given parenthetically if the securities are stated at market value.

If significant amounts of securities are held, the major types should be separately classified.

Liens against the securities must be disclosed.

Investments in affiliated or subsidiary companies should be separately classified.

The client's own securities held in the treasury or in special funds should be shown as offsets to the issued securities.

Income from investments should be classified as other income, except for financial institutions.

Interest, dividends, and gains or losses from sales should be shown separately, if material.

Audit objectives and procedures

Tie in supporting records with statement amounts for the asset and income.
   Prepare a trial balance of asset and income amounts.
Determine that the recording of asset transactions has resulted in appropriate year-end valuations.
   Verify recording of purchase and sale transactions, including gain or loss.
   Review cut-off of purchase and sale transactions.
   Ascertain market values.
Establish existence and ownership of investment assets.
   Make physical count of certificates or notes evidencing investments.
   Verify ownership through name in which securities are registered or accounting for serial numbers.
   Obtain written confirmation of investments for which certificates are not on hand.
Account for all income from investments.
   Verify interest received on bonds or notes against terms of the investment; verify accrued interest and amortization of premium or discount.
   Verify dividends on stocks against published dividend record.
Other types of investments.
   Examine statements of subsidiaries, or obtain audited statements; ascertain that carrying value of nonconsolidated subsidiaries is fairly stated.
   Examine mortgage agreements, title policies, insurance policies, tax receipts, and appraisal reports in support of mortgage notes; ascertain value of the security given; confirm the remaining balance on the note with the debtor.
   Confirm cash surrender value, absence of loans, payment of premiums, and name of beneficiary on life insurance policies.

REVIEW QUESTIONS

1. What are the objectives of internal control over investments?
2. Give examples of investments which are not readily marketable. How should these investments be classified in the balance sheet?
3. Is it possible that investments which have been held for several years might nevertheless be classified as current assets? Explain.

4. Why is it essential that the auditor insist that financial statements show the basis on which investments have been valued?

5. How do the procedures differ in controlling interest income from bonds and dividend income from common stocks?

6. What are the independent auditor's objectives in the examination of investments and investment income?

7. What additional audit work may be required if investments cannot be counted on the balance sheet date and cannot be kept under the auditor's control until the count is made?

8. Does the fact that certain securities are in the client's possession necessarily prove that the securities are owned by the client? Explain.

9. How are the serial numbers on stock or bond certificates useful to the auditor?

10. How should the auditor proceed if, in response to a confirmation request directed to a transfer agent, the agent replies that the securities had been forwarded to the client the day prior to the date the auditor made his cash and security counts?

11. What procedures are ordinarily followed in verifying a purchase of investment securities?

12. Should the entire amount of the net proceeds of a sale of securities ordinarily be credited to a single account? Explain.

13. In what ways may the market value of securities be determined?

14. Which columns in the auditor's schedule of bond investments and income can be cross-referenced to trial balance figures?

15. How would the audit procedure differ in the case of an advance to a consolidated subsidiary and a nonconsolidated subsidiary?

16. List the possible items of evidence which might be examined in support of a mortgage note.

17. What accounts might the auditor find in connection with a life insurance policy carried by a client on one of its officers?

QUESTIONS ON APPLICATION OF AUDITING STANDARDS

18. Of what significance would it be to an auditor making a securities count that bonds are "bearer" bonds rather than "registered" bonds?

19. Your client made the following entry for the purchase of a bond:

12/1/67	Bond investment	1,038	
	Cash		1,038

To record purchase of $1,000, 6% bond, including accrued interest of $10. Interest dates 4/1 and 10/1; maturity 4/1/71.

Assuming that the client made no other entries with respect to this bond, what adjusting entry or entries would you recommend be made at 12/31/67, the close of the client's fiscal year?

20. Your client holds two 4 per cent $10,000 bonds, each of which matures in 15 years from the current date. The bonds were each purchased on the open market subsequent to the issue date at costs as shown below:

A Co. Bonds $7,000
B Co. Bonds 9,850

    (a) Was the market rate of interest presumably more or less than 4 per cent at the date the bonds were purchased? Explain.

    (b) Should the discount on the bonds be amortized? Why?

21. You are making an initial examination of your client's financial statements. Certain securities were held as an investment at the beginning of the year, but all have been sold during the year. State what procedures you would follow with respect to these securities, and state why you would use the procedures.

22. Your client is the beneficiary of an estate administered by a local attorney who is also serving as administrator for a number of other estates. In making an examination of the estate, what problem are you confronted with in verifying the existence of securities in the estate? How can such a problem be solved?

23. Your client invests idle cash resulting from the seasonal nature of the business in marketable securities. There are normally from two to six different issues involved and from five to ten purchase and sales transactions per year. You have previously recommended to your client that a separate subsidiary record be maintained for each issue held, but he has stated that there seems to be little justification for such a record since all the information is already in the control account. What advantages should your client be able to realize by maintaining such a record?

24. What information appearing on the face of a bond certificate will be useful to the auditor in computing the income from that bond for the year? The bond was purchased at a premium.

PROBLEMS

25. You are in charge of the audit of the financial statements of the Demot Corporation for the year ended December 31, 1967. The Corporation has had the policy of investing its surplus funds in marketable securities. Its stock and bond certificates are kept in a safe deposit box in a local bank. Only the president or the treasurer of the Corporation has access to the box.

    You were unable to obtain access to the safe deposit box on December 31 because neither the president nor the treasurer was available. Arrangements were made for your assistant to accompany the treasurer to the bank on January 11 to examine the securities. Your assistant has never examined securities that were being kept in a safe deposit box and requires instructions. He should be able to inspect all securities on hand in an hour.

Required:

    (a) List the instructions that you would give to your assistant regarding the examination of the stock and bond certifications kept in the safe deposit box. Include in your instructions the details of the securities to be examined and the reasons for examining these details.

    (b) When he returned from the bank your assistant reported that the treasurer had entered the box on January 4. The treasurer stated that he had removed an old photograph of the Corporation's original building. The photograph was loaned to the local chamber of commerce for display purposes. List the additional audit procedures that are required because of the treasurer's action. (Uniform C.P.A. Examination)

26. You are engaged in the audit of the financial statements of the Sandy Core Company for the year ended December 31, 1967. Sandy Core Company sells lumber and building supplies at wholesale and retail; it has total assets of $1,000,000 and a stockholders' equity of $500,000.

The Company's records show an investment of $100,000 for 100 shares of common stock of one of its customers, the Home Building Corporation. You learn that Home Building Corporation is closely held and that its capital stock, consisting of 1,000 shares of issued and outstanding common stock, has no published or quoted market value.

Examination of your client's cash disbursements record reveals an entry of a check for $100,000 drawn on January 23, 1967 to Mr. Felix Wolfe, who is said to be the former holder of the 100 shares of stock. Mr. Wolfe is president of the Sandy Core Company. Sandy Core Company has no other investments.

Required:
   (a) List the auditing procedures you would employ in connection with the $100,000 investment of your client in the capital stock of the Home Building Corporation.
   (b) Discuss the presentation of the investment on the balance sheet, including its valuation.

27. You are engaged as the auditor for an employees' profit-sharing pension trust which has been in existence for a number of years. Each qualified employee has an equity in the trust which the employee is entitled to receive when he leaves the company. The membership of participating employees changes each year because additional employees qualify while others are retired. The amount of equity received varies with length of service from zero for the first five years up to 100 per cent with ten years of service. The trust agreement does not state how the fund's assets should be valued.

The trust's assets consist of the following:

	Cost	Market
Cash	$ 50,000	$ 50,000
Rental properties (building)	100,000	250,000
Stocks	1,000,000	1,250,000
Bonds	500,000	400,000

   (a) You are requested to give the trustees your recommendations for the valuation of the trust's assets in certified financial statements and the reasons for your recommendations.
   (b) Would your opinion be a standard opinion or would you vary it, and, if so, how?
   (c) The trustees inform you that the trust has entered into a ten-year lease on the rental property. The trust is to receive annual rents of $21,000 for ten years and the lessee has the option to purchase the building for $125,000 at the end of the lease. The lessee has installed an expensive air conditioning system, and has expended substantial sums for remodeling and modernization. The trustees would like your recommendations for valuing the building in the accounts this year and in the future, and your suggestions for the proper accounting entries to record the yearly $21,000 payments.
   (d) What disclosure, if any, of the lease should be made in the financial statements?   (Uniform CPA Examination)

28. For several years you have made the annual audit for the Edgemont Company This company is *not* a dealer in securities. A list of securities presently held is kept but an investment register is not maintained. When making the examination, the following worksheet was prepared.

Column Number	Column Heading
	Description of Security
1	(name, maturity, rate, etc.)
	Balance at Beginning of Year
2	Face value or number of shares
3	Cost or book value
	Additions during Period
4	Date
5	Face value or number of shares
6	Cost
	Deductions during Period
7	Date
8	Face value or number of shares
9	Cost or book value
10	*Proceeds on Disposals* (net)
11	*Profit or (Loss) on Disposals*
	Balance at End of Year
12	Face value or number of shares
13	Cost or book value
14	Market value
	Interest and Dividends
15	Accrued at beginning of year
16	Purchased
17	Earned
18	Received
19	Accrued at end of year

Required:

Draw a line down the middle of a lined sheet(s) of paper.

(a) On the left of the line, state the specific source(s) of information to be entered in each column, and where required, how the data of previous columns are combined.

(b) On the right of the line, state the principal way(s) that such information would be verified.   (Uniform CPA Examination)

29. You are to make an examination of the bond investment account of the Sanders Company in connection with an examination of the financial statements as of December 31, 1967. This is the first time such an examination has been made. Your working papers should include provisions for analyzing all 1967 transactions, including those affecting profit and loss.

Transcripts of the accounts and a summary of pertinent information on brokers' advices of purchase or sale are given below.

Investment Account

1967		Debit	Credit	Balance
Jan. 1	Balance			$29,950.00
	10M Underhill Co. . .			
	($10,550.00)			
	20M Carlyle, Inc. . .			
	($19,400.00)			
Feb. 15	20M Arthur Corp. . .	$20,550.00		50,500.00
Sept. 1	Carlyle, Inc.		$9,816.67	40,683.33

Interest Income

1967

Feb.	3	Carlyle, Inc.	$ 200.00	$ 200.00
June	5	Underhill Co.	250.00	450.00
July	2	Arhur Corp.	200.00	650.00
Aug.	4	Carlyle, Inc.	200.00	850.00
Dec.	3	Underhill Co.	250.00	1,100.00

Brokers' Advices

Date	Quantity	Description	Price	Interest	Amount
PURCHASES					
11/30/65..	10M	Underhill Co. 5's J&D, June, 68/73	$103	$250.00	$10,550.00
2/1/66....	20M	Carlyle, Inc. 2's F&A, Feb., 1971	97	......	19,400.00
2/15/67 ..	20M	Arthur Corp. 2's J&J, July, 1970	102½	50.00	20,550.00
SALES					
9/1/67....	10M	Carlyle, Inc. 2's F&A, Feb., 1971	98	16.67	9,816.67

1. Set up a worksheet to analyze the year's transactions, beginning with a
corrected balance at 1/1/67, and showing all 1967 entries as they *should
appear*. Use the following column headings:

A. Investment account
    1. Balance 1/1/67
        (a) Face
        (b) Premium or (discount)
    2. Purchases
        (a) Face
        (b) Premium or (discount)
    3. Sales
        (a) Face
        (b) Premium or (discount) } The total of these three
        (c) Profit or (loss) (memo only) } columns will be the net
                                cash proceeds of the sale.
    4. Amortization
    5. Balance 12/31/67
        (a) Face
        (b) Premium or (discount)

B. Accrued Interest Receivable
    1. Accrued at 1/1/67
    2. Accrued during 1967
                (The total of this column plus or minus the
                total Amortization column above is the inter-
                est income for the year.)
    3. Received during 1967 (Show the accrued interest purchased on
        the Arthur Corp. bonds as a negative figure in this column.)
    4. Accrued at 12/31/67.

2. Prepare adjusting entries to correct the books at December 31, 1967, to
agree with your worksheet, assuming the books have not been closed.

Explanations for each entry should show clearly how the amounts were determined. Correct income of prior years through retained earnings.

30. Your client, the Roberts Mfg. Co., carries a $50,000 ordinary life policy on the life of its president, Wm. A. Roberts, allowing dividends to accumulate with the insurance company. The insurance is carried with the Sasnak Mutual Insurance Co. Write the confirmation request letter you would ask the client to sign (to be mailed to the insurance company) concerning the insurance policy.

Other expenses, losses, assets and liabilities: internal control; auditing

20

The miscellaneous items not directly related to the expenses, assets, and liabilities discussed in the preceding chapters are brought together at this point.

Objectives of Internal Control

The assets with which we are concerned are not claims against others arising out of income-producing transactions but rather are the cost residuals of benefits or services paid for prior to the time that the benefits or services are received. In general, they are referred to as prepaid expenses, deferred charges, and intangibles. The internal control objectives are to gain assurance that:

1. All expenditures for such assets are justified in terms of expected return.
2. Expired costs are matched against the revenues that they have produced.

Of the various liabilities that may be incurred by a concern, relatively few, such as accounts payable and payroll liabilities, have been discussed previously. For all liabilities, however, the objectives of internal control are to give assurance that:

1. The authority to incur liabilities is restricted to a limited number of designated persons.
2. Liabilities being liquidated were properly authorized and incurred for the benefit of the concern.
3. Accruals are recorded when benefits or services have been received in order to recognize the related expense and liability.

Because the problems and the accounting procedures for many types of miscellaneous assets and liabilities are relatively similar, only a few different assets and liabilities are discussed in the next section.

Prepaid Insurance

Authorization of expenditures for insurance involves the broader problem of insurance coverage. Each time a policy is renewed, and sometimes more often, a company's insurable risks should be reviewed to determine whether there has been any change which would warrant adding or eliminating insurance on some of these risks. For those risks for which it is decided to continue insuring, conditions should be studied to determine whether there has been any change in the amount of the insurable risk. The steady decrease in the purchasing power of the dollar has particularly aggravated this problem in terms of property insurance, and replacement costs of assets should be considered in relation to the amount of insurance coverage to be acquired. Liability insurance is also subject to the effect of inflationary trends. Under-insurance forces the company to become partially self-insured in contra-distinction to the presumed intention to transfer all such risks to insurance companies. Overinsurance, on the other hand, entails a needless waste of company resources.

A properly designed insurance register should be helpful in summarizing the information on existing insurance coverage for such over-all appraisals as suggested above. It should also provide the data for the monthly or annual journal entry to record expired insurance as an expense. The balances of unexpired insurance premiums then become the supporting details for the general ledger account for unexpired insurance.

Supplies

The responsibilities for purchasing supplies and maintaining adequate quantities on hand are similar to those pertaining to regular inventory items, and should be treated in much the same way. Companies vary widely, however, with respect to accounting for the supplies and controlling the issuance of supplies. Some companies follow all the procedures used in controlling the regular merchandise or materials inventories. Such control tends to be necessary if supplies are a significant item in company operations, and if supplies used are charged to various departmental accounts.

Other companies omit maintaining the general ledger records on a perpetual basis but keep detailed records of quantities to aid in purchasing and to establish control over supplies in the storeroom. A physical inventory is then taken at the end of the year to determine the allocation of the balance of the supplies account into asset and expense portions. Perhaps the most common treatment, however, is to maintain no control over the supplies after they are purchased, and to charge all purchases directly to expense.

In such cases the cost of supplies used should not be a material item, and if this is true the failure to account for fluctuations in year-end supply inventories will not have a significant effect on either the results of operations or financial position.

Expense Advances

The control over expense advances for travel or other purposes should be similar to the control over imprest fund operations. The original advances should be duly authorized, and the expenditures which are subsequently reported should be audited in the same manner as any cash disbursement. Unexpended balances may be allowed to stand charged against the individual if additional expenses will be incurred in the near future. Otherwise, the balance of the advance should be refunded to the company and the individual's account closed out.

Postage

Internal controls over postage have been strengthened greatly by the increasing use of postage meters. There is then less opportunity for dishonest employees to divert to personal use funds intended for the purchase of stamps. More important, the loss of stamps by theft or misappropriation is precluded. Further advantages of the use of postage machines are reductions in the cost of sealing and stamping envelopes and a more convenient means of determining departmental charges when such allocations are made. Reading the registering dials before and after stamping a given batch of mail and making a simple subtraction to determine the exact amount of postage used are the only steps that are necessary.

Notes and Bonds Payable

The authority to borrow money should be restricted to only two or three officers of the company, with the signatures of two officers required on any notes. The authority should be granted by the board of directors, and the officers should be limited as to the maximum amount for which they can obligate their company. Larger borrowings should be made only under specific authorization of the board of directors.

If only occasional loans are made, the general ledger account may well contain all needed information. For concerns which borrow frequently from other sources, including individuals (a commercial finance company would be an example), preprinted, serially numbered notes should be used, and a note register showing all pertinent information should be maintained. These comments also apply to bond issues, when the company handles all the details. Preferably, however, a bond issue should be handled through a trustee and with a separate registrar. These agents can then control the issuance of the bonds and the remittance of proceeds, with the company maintaining a double check on their activities.

All interest payments should be subjected to close scrutiny before they are approved, to be certain that interest is being paid only on known liabilities. If coupon bonds are involved, those coupons which have been paid should be counted, reconciled with the amount of cash disbursed, and then mutilated to prevent their re-use. If the bonds are registered as to interest, address plates can be used to prepare the periodic interest checks. The employees responsible for the file of plates should have no responsibilities pertaining to cash. Again, however, when large amounts are involved, the best arrangement is to handle the payments through an independent disbursing agent. Only one interest check will then be required.

The repayment of loans involves the same precautions as apply to the payment of interest. Each disbursement should be ascertained to cover a known and recorded liability before it is approved. Release of the check should then be made only upon presentation of the note or bond being paid. The retired instrument should be marked paid, or mutilated, and retained in the files as evidence that the debt has been paid. When bonds have been paid through a trustee, the trustee may merely submit a cremation certificate listing the bonds which have been paid and destroyed.

Any checks issued for payment of interest or principal which are not claimed should be kept under close control. The best plan is to cancel such checks and reinstate the liability pending submission of a claim for payment or the eventual transfer of the unclaimed amounts to income.

Management Reports

Most of the miscellaneous assets are of insufficient importance to warrant the preparation of periodic reports. Insurance is an exception, because top management should be kept informed about coverage and the amount of expense being incurred. All of the miscellaneous assets will be reported in the regular balance sheets that are prepared; but if this is the only report, some responsible officer, such as the controller, should regularly review the transactions and balances shown in the ledger accounts. The review should give assurance that these asset accounts are not becoming a dumping place for suspense or other items that do not belong there.

The situation is much the same in reporting on liabilities. The amount of activity in accounts payable warrants the preparation of daily reports of such activity, but for other liabilities, their listing in the balance sheet should be sufficient.

The charges to expense resulting from the write-off of assets or the incurrence of liabilities should be reported on a responsibility basis whenever applicable; other expenses will be reported as an item of factory overhead (rent or royalties, for example), selling or administrative expense, or "other expenses," as in the case of interest or amortization of goodwill. The liability resulting from income received in advance will gradually be transferred to income and so reported as it is earned.

Internal Auditing

For miscellaneous assets, the internal auditor should review charges to the accounts to determine that the expenditures were properly authorized, that they represent justifiable expenditures of company funds, and that the charges have been properly accounted for. Decisions underlying these expenditures are fully within the internal auditor's province, and his attention is properly directed to such questions as whether insurance coverage is adequate but not excessive, whether supply quantities kept on hand are reasonable, and whether postage expense is being properly controlled.

Liabilities require constant evaluation of the procedures intended to control the incurrence and liquidation of the various liabilities, plus compliance tests to show whether the established procedures are being followed. The internal auditor should also verify that the amounts of the various liabilities are correct and that no liabilities exist that have not been recorded. Contracts and minutes of meetings of the board of directors or of special committees should be reviewed for any liabilities that may have been incurred. Alertness is especially required for the possible existence of liabilities for such things as product or performance guarantees, large purchase commitments, and lawsuit claims.

STANDARDS OF STATEMENT PRESENTATION

Those assets of the prepaid expense variety are now recognized as being appropriately classified as current assets. Most of these will not extend beyond one year, or beyond the period of the operating cycle if it is longer than one year, and as a consequence are closely related to current operations and the working capital picture. Businesses with short operating cycles will nevertheless frequently have some prepayments which will extend beyond one year, such as the premium on a three- or five-year insurance policy. If the amounts involved are significant, they should be shown under a noncurrent classification, but they will be minor in most cases and can therefore be properly included in the current section with the prepayments for one year or less.

Prepaid expenses are usually grouped together and shown as a single item, but if any items are sufficiently large to attain individual significance, they should be listed separately. As there is hardly any basis for valuing prepayments at a figure other than cost, such a basis of valuation is usually understood and need not be set forth in the statements.

Deferred charges are much like prepaid expenses, but they usually cover longer periods of time and thus are not to be included in the current asset classification. The use of a separate classification for deferred charges is seldom warranted, and they are therefore frequently listed under the heading of "Other assets." The item of unamortized bond discount may be shown as a deduction from the liability for bonds payable.

Intangible assets are frequently the least liquid of assets, and as a result they will usually be the last item on the balance sheet if the amount is sufficiently material to warrant a separate classification. Because intangibles are sometimes stated at figures other than cost, even though cost is the only acceptable basis of valuation, the basis of valuation used should always be stated. Also, as there is no uniformity on the matter of amortizing certain intangibles, those intangibles which are being amortized should be so described. A typical description would be "Goodwill—at cost less amortization."

The make-up of existing liabilities is usually of considerable importance to creditors or prospective lenders who may be studying a balance sheet. Knowledge of the various types of current liabilities may give some indication of how those liabilities are likely to fall due during the coming year or the operating cycle, and whether there are any which can be readily postponed or extended. Perhaps even more important, the types of liabilities may give some indication of the concern's credit-worthiness. Only good credit risks are likely to obtain unsecured bank loans. Those whose credit standing is weaker may have to give collateral security in obtaining a loan from either a bank or a commercial finance house. The security given may also give a clue as to credit standing. Some companies may pledge government securities in obtaining a loan. These companies are obviously in a very sound position and are borrowing from the bank because it is more advantageous than selling the securities and then replacing them when the added funds are no longer needed. Certain types of inventory loans (such as dealer floor plan financing*), or equipment loans (such as equipment trust certificates), are quite common in many businesses and carry no stigma. Loans secured by regular inventory or by pledging receivables are, however, likely to be an indication of financial weakness.

The above comments suggest some of the reasons for certain statement practices concerning liabilities which have become relatively traditional. These and other considerations are reflected in the following list of points which should be observed if the presentation of liabilities in the statements is to meet adequate standards.

1. Any liability which is material in amount should be shown separately and carefully described.

---

* A type of financing used by automobile or other kinds of dealers in which inventory purchases are financed by loans secured by the inventory items while they are in the dealer's hands. The loans are then repaid out of the proceeds as the inventory items are sold.

2. The arrangement of liabilities in the current section should follow the traditional pattern. This pattern is indicated in the following listing, which, for illustrative purposes, contains many more individual items than would usually be shown for any one concern.

Bank loans
Demand loans
Term loans, privately placed
Notes payable, sold through note
  brokers
Notes payable to trade creditors
Trade acceptances
Notes payable to officers
Trade accounts payable
Other accounts payable

Accounts receivable credit balances
Accrued liabilities
Income taxes payable
Dividends payable
Sinking fund requirements due within
  one year
Current serial bond maturities
Deposits, such as returnable container
  deposits
Deferred credits
Subordinated debts

3. Material amounts of accounts or notes payable to parent or subsidiary companies, stockholders, directors, officers, or employees should be shown separately from payables to third parties.

4. For secured liabilities the description should preferably include identification of the assets pledged, supplementing the reference to the lien which should appear on the asset side of the balance sheet.

5. Assets and liabilities should not be offset. This rule requires that material amounts of accounts payable debit balances be reclassified to the asset side of the statement and precludes deducting a liability from an asset by which it is secured; for instance, the deduction of secured installment notes from the cost of the equipment purchased. One exception to the rule of offsets is recognized: U.S. Treasury tax notes may be deducted from the liability for Federal income taxes, provided both amounts are shown.

AUDIT OBJECTIVES AND PROCEDURES

The auditor's objectives in his examination of other expenses, losses, assets, and liabilities are:

1. Determine that nonoperating, nonrecurring losses are not combined with operating expenses for reporting purposes.

2. Ascertain that all losses have been recorded.

3. Establish the propriety and validity of amounts originally debited to the asset accounts.

4. Determine that asset amounts are being amortized or allocated on a systematic basis to obtain proper matching of expenses with the revenues that they have produced, and that future periods will benefit from remaining amounts being carried forward as assets.

5. Establish that recorded liabilities are correctly stated.

6. Ascertain the existence of any unrecorded liabilities.

To summarize, the stated objectives reflect the auditor's concern as to whether the various expenses, assets, and liabilities are fairly stated. The succeeding discussion is not, however, organized primarily in terms of the specific objectives but rather is related to the various expenses, assets, and liabilities commonly encountered. The comments given reflect the objectives but are stated in terms of the specific types of assets and liabilities involved because the problems and procedures tend to vary substantially depending on the particular type of item being examined.

Assets Versus Liabilities

One general comment is perhaps in order before proceeding to the detailed discussion: there are significant underlying differences in the auditor's approach to the examination of assets as against the examination of liabilities. These differences emanate from the following contrasts between the two financial items.

1. Management fraud, designed to improve the apparent financial position of a company, is accomplished by an *overstatement* of assets but by an *understatement* of liabilities. An overstatement of an asset necessitates an overt act in the form of a fictitious entry, and by verifying asset entries and balances the auditor can, as a rule, quite readily detect the fictitious amount. The understatement of a liability, on the other hand, requires no action at all. A transaction which has given rise to a liability need merely be ignored in the records to achieve the desired effect. The auditor's problem is then much more difficult, for he has no convenient starting point for his examination designed to disclose a possible unrecorded liability. Instead, his approach must be indirect and much more circuitous. The problem is exemplified by situations mentioned in earlier chapters involving the problem of ascertaining the possible existence of unrecorded outstanding checks or of unrecorded retirements of plant assets.

2. Defalcations by employees present less of a problem in the case of liability accounts because defalcations usually involve the abstraction of assets, and manipulations to conceal the resulting shortage are thus centered in the asset accounts. Some possibility for fraud does exist in the case of liabilities, nevertheless, because employees who are authorized to obligate their company by borrowing money may appropriate the proceeds of a loan and make no book record of the liability. Because such opportunities are limited to a very few employees, the problem is therefore less extensive than in the case of assets, which may be accessible to a considerable number of employees.

3. Most liabilities are a statement of fact, whereas most assets involve valuation problems based on individual judgment. Only some of the contingent liabilities, such as a provision for costs to be incurred in connection with product guarantees, involve a valuation problem.

The loss problem. Losses, unless material, nonoperating, and nonrecurring, should be reported in the income statement. It might thus seem that the examination of losses is essentially a part of the examination of the income statement, and that is true for losses that have been recorded. But a more important problem may be that losses have occurred that have not been recorded. The auditor must gain an awareness of any unrecorded losses and see to it that material amounts are reflected in the financial statements in order that financial position and results of operations may be fairly presented.

The best source of possible information about unrecorded losses is a careful study of the asset and liability accounts that would also be affected by the events or transactions that have produced the losses. Thus the examination of receivables, inventories, plant assets, investments, or other assets may reveal losses that are still incorporated in the balances of those accounts. Unrecorded losses involving liabilities, on the other hand, would be divulged by procedures designed to uncover the existence of any unrecorded liabilities. Such procedures are developed in considerable detail later in this chapter.

Preferably, however, the auditor should not make a specific search for losses and then put the matter out of his mind. There are many points in the course of an examination where indications of losses may crop up, and the possibility of a loss that should be recorded should always be kept in mind. For instance, the examination of purchases may reval that substantial purchase commitments at fixed prices are outstanding. At another point, the examination of sales and of inventory pricing may reveal that a general price decline is occurring. The combination of these relatively unrelated bits of information leads to the possibility that there may be losses from the purchase commitments that must be recorded. Similarly, discussion with production and customer service personnel may reveal that a new, more liberal policy is being implemented concerning work to be done under the company's product guarantee to its customers. The added expenses should be anticipated by an increase in the liability provided for product guarantees. Another possibility is that a contractor has underestimated a job bid on a fixed-price basis. Although costs incurred to date may be less than the estimated total, if the costs necessary to complete the job will cause the total cost to exceed the contract fee, the resulting loss should be recognized at once.

We turn now to the problems of auditing the miscellaneous grouping of assets, liabilities, and related expenses or losses.

Prepaid Insurance

Prepaid insurance is probably the most common of the assets covered in this chapter. Equally common is the tendency to overaudit the insignificant amount likely to be represented in prepaid insurance premiums. The audit of this amount lends itself very readily to the preparation of very complicated and professional-looking working papers; and because the possibility to do so is present, it is sometimes difficult to resist verifying the amount of prepaid insurance down to the very last penny.

By way of contrast, the following procedures will usually suffice when good internal control is present. The work is based on the information contained in the client's insurance register, but the auditor should not recopy all the information from the insurance register to his working papers. Instead, he should work from the register in making his audit, and his work papers need then include only a statement of what he did and the conclusions he reached. He should note whether the amount of insurance coverage appears reasonable and adequate, and he should note that prepaid amounts appear proper in relation to the premiums paid and the period covered by those premiums. The various insurance policies in effect should be examined. Further support of the data recorded in the insurance register is gained in connection with the examination of the policies, but information about such other matters as property liens is usually of much greater importance. (See the discussion about such liens in Chapter 18.)

There are two reasons for reviewing the client's insurance coverage. One is to cast some additional light on the balances shown in the property accounts. A $10,000 fire policy on a building carried at $100,000 should suggest that something may be wrong with the property figure. The second reason is to gain some indication of the adequacy of the coverage. If rising property values have reduced the effectiveness of insurance amounts established some years previously, the auditor may perform a most valuable "extra" service by bringing the situation to the client's attention. This is particularly true of policies which contain a coinsurance clause. Of course, any alert insurance agent should have brought up the matter long before, but the client may merely have thought the agent was trying to increase his income by selling more insurance. The auditor's independent appraisal of the situation might well be more convincing than the insurance agent's recommendations. Here is an excellent illustration of the importance of the provision in the code of professional ethics prohibiting a public accountant from sharing in the commissions from the added insurance.

The auditor should summarize the information about insurance coverage in his working papers if he has been requested to submit a long-form report on his examination which is to be used for credit purposes. Most creditors prefer to have information on such coverage, and the working papers can then be used in supplying the desired information for the report.

If the client does not maintain an insurance register, the auditor may wish to prepare and work from a schedule such as is illustrated by schedule L-1. Note that even under inadequate internal control it should not be necessary for the auditor to analyze all entries in the prepaid insurance account, examine supporting data for the debits, and reconcile credits with the expense accounts. The materiality of the amounts simply does not warrant such extensive verification. Two things the auditor should be careful to watch for, however, are the disposition of dividends received from mutual companies and the reduced coverage that results if a claim is paid on a policy and no additional premium is paid.

Workmen's compensation insurance functions on a slightly different basis as compared with most other forms of insurance. An estimated premium is paid in advance, but the final determination of the premium is based on actual payroll disbursements as defined by the policy. As of the balance sheet date the amount of premium earned should be calculated based on the prescribed payroll figures. If this figure is less than the amount paid in advance, the balance on deposit represents a prepaid expense. If the premiums earned exceed the amount deposited, an accrued liability must be shown. The auditor need simply review these calculations if they have already been made by the client.

Fidelity bonds also warrant a brief comment. If the policy contains any provisions or special requirements pertaining to an independent audit, the auditor should be certain that his examination meets all the stated requirements. Because these requirements may exceed the scope of the examination planned by the auditor, he should review the fidelity bond provisions before he begins his examination. In this way he can avoid the possible risk of having to repeat part of his examination on an expanded basis, with the attendant embarrassing explanations to be made to the client.

Prepaid Taxes

Most taxes accrue rather than being prepaid. Property, franchise, and vehicle taxes are some of the principal exceptions. Such taxes vary only slightly in amount from year to year, however, and many companies avoid additional accounting costs by following the expedient of charging the payments directly to expense because any distortion of the financial statements will be negligible.

When prepaid amounts are deferred to future periods, the deferred amount should be based on the time period covered by the tax. This period is open to several interpretations in the case of property taxes, but the preferred method is to write off the taxes in relation to the fiscal period of the taxing body to which they are paid. The theory here is that some direct benefits are received by the taxpayer as the taxing body expends the revenues it receives in the fiscal year.

Receipted tax bills, and in some cases paid checks as well, should be examined in support of major tax payments. The calculation of any deferred amounts should then be reviewed by the auditor, as was done on L-2.

Prepaid Interest

Reference to loan agreements and to confirmations requested on payables should provide the auditor with adequate information to verify any prepaid interest. Most interest accrues, however, and is paid at the end of the period rather than in advance.

Prepaid Rent

The review of leases should provide the necessary information to verify any prepaid rent. If rent is regularly paid one month in advance, there need be no objection to charging each payment to expense and ignoring the one month's prepayment. Prepayments covering a longer period may well be material, however, and should be properly accounted for. Material amounts pertaining to periods beyond one year should not be classed as a current asset.

Expense Advances

If substantial expense advances appear on the balance sheet, two approaches may be followed in verifying the amounts. The most direct way is to obtain written, or possibly oral, confirmations from the individuals holding the advances. An alternative approach is to examine vouchers or paid checks in support of the amounts and dates of the original advances, and then examine the subsequent expense reports when they are received. Any unusual amounts should be carefully investigated and possibly discussed with some official.

Prepaid Commissions

The verification of prepaid commissions is quite similar to the verification of expense advances, and both types of approach may be used. In this case, however, the report closing out the advance would be a sales report showing that the salesman had earned the commission. Any advances to salesmen no longer employed by the company should be subjected to very close scrutiny. At best, the amounts may be valid but doubtful of collection, but a more serious possibility is that the amounts are the result of defalcation activities.

Prepaid Advertising and Promotion

When expenditures have been made for advertising or promotional material, and the benefits will not be realized until the following period, the expenditures are properly treated as a prepaid expense. By study of invoices and an over-all review of the situation, the auditor should be able to ascertain that the amounts involved are properly treated as prepaid expenses. Mail order houses ordinarily defer part of the production costs with respect to catalogs which are still in use or perhaps have not even been distributed as yet to customers. Expenditures for institutional advertising expected to have an over-all, long-term favorable effect should not, however, be capitalized.

Postage

The verification of postage on hand is a simple matter if the client uses postage meter machines, as the auditor has only to read the descending register dials. If the postage is in the form of stamps, the auditor may not feel justified in counting the stamps if the total amount is reasonable and in line with that for the previous year. If a count does appear to be necessary, it can be limited to stamps of larger denominations, plus full sheets of stamps of smaller denominations.

Supplies

When supplies are carried as an asset, the amount should be based on a physical inventory taken by the client. The auditor's procedures should be similar to those used in connection with the merchandise inventory but applied on a much less extensive basis in view of the usual immateriality of the amount of supplies.

Deposits

Businesses occasionally are requested to deposit funds to assure payment or performance of services. For instance, airlines customarily require deposits from businesses in connection with the issuance of credit cards, and contracts often specify the deposit of a performance guarantee. Deposits should be verified by written confirmation if material amounts are involved. Otherwise, the figures can be accepted if they fit in with known facts and the amounts appear proper.

Unamortized Bond Discount

Verification of the amount of unamortized bond discount should begin with the original recording of the discount at the time the bonds were sold. If the bonds were sold through an underwriting syndicate, the statement rendered by that group will show the proceeds to the company of the bond issue. The difference between this amount and the face amount of the bonds will represent the figure for the discount. Other evidence of the proceeds of the bond issue would be cash book entries and deposit entries on the bank statement. The amortization of the discount over the life of the bonds should also be verified, so that the auditor can be satisfied that the remaining balance and the charge to interest expense for the year are correct. The balance of unamortized discount should, of course, be reduced for any discount relating to bonds that have been retired or are held in the treasury.

If bonds are refunded through the cash proceeds of a new bond issue, the unamortized bond discount of the old issue can be deducted for tax purposes only in the year of refunding. If the client then chooses, for accounting purposes, to charge the unamortized discount to retained earnings, or to continue to write it off on the same basis as before, an adjustment must be made to avoid distorting net income. Without the adjustment, the deduction for tax purposes will reduce the amount of income tax and cause an increase in net income, even though the causal factor is essentially either an expense or a loss. The solution is to show a debit adjustment to income tax expense to bring the total for that item up to the figure it would have been had there been no tax deduction for the unamortized bond discount. The offsetting credit should be either to the unamortized bond discount account, or to retained earnings if the discount has been charged to that account. The rule reflected by such an adjustment is that the tax effect of any item should follow the item itself. Thus if the unamortized discount is charged as a loss against income for the period, reduction in income taxes can also be shown in the income statement. If the loss is charged against retained earnings, the tax reduction should be credited to that account. If the discount is allowed to remain as a deferred charge, then the reduction in tax liability should be credited to the unamortized discount account. A complete discussion of this problem may be found on pages 87–92 of *Accounting Research and Terminology Bulletins, Final Edition,* issued by the Committee on Accounting Procedure of the American Institute of Certified Public Accountants.

Plant Rearrangement Costs

When plant rearrangement costs have been carried forward as a deferred charge, the auditor should test the charges to the account against the supporting records and satisfy himself that all charges do, in fact, relate to the rearrangement process. Repairs or other expense items should not be included in the cost of rearrangement. Theoretically, the rearrangement costs should not be capitalized unless the original costs of installation of the machinery are written off. As a practical matter, however, the original costs will seldom be readily determinable, and management may be opposed to showing any current expense or loss charges as a result of the rearrangement in view of the fact that the work is intended to produce future benefits. Under these circumstances, and considering the fact that material amounts will seldom be involved, the auditor need not take exception to the capitalization of the rearrangement costs, but he should see that the costs are amortized over a three- to five-year period.

Leaseholds

When a premium is paid in order to acquire a favorable lease, or when a large advance payment of rent must be made in order to obtain a new lease, these amounts should be charged to a leasehold account. This account may be considered to represent either a deferred charge to future operations or an intangible asset, representing the cost of obtaining the right to use the leased property. In either event, the auditor should verify the original amount charged to the account, and he should be satisfied that the amount is being properly amortized over the life of the lease.

Improvements made by the lessee to leased property revert to the lessor at the termination of the lease. The cost of such improvments, described as leasehold improvements, may be carried as a separate item under property, plant, and equipment. If, however, it is felt that this classification would be misleading, in spite of the description used, then the amount can be classified as an intangible asset. The theory would be that the property, plant, and equipment classification is improper because no tangible asset is involved. What the lessee owns is merely the intangible right to use the improvements during the life of the lease. Regardless of the exact balance sheet treatment of the item, the auditor should ascertain that proper classification has been made of any expenditures related to leased property noted in his examination of additions to plant assets, and he should see that all leasehold improvements are being amortized over a period which is not longer than the life of the lease, plus renewal options.

Goodwill

The proper handling of goodwill is indeed a controversial matter. Most accountants agree that only purchased goodwill should be recorded as an asset, but the determination of the cost of the asset may be quite problematical in so-called "basket" purchases, and no goodwill should be recorded if the client has merely paid an excess price for certain plant assets or patents. The excess should be included as part of the cost of the assets purchased.

There is considerable disagreement over whether purchased goodwill should be carried as an asset so long as operations are profitable, or whether it should be amortized by charges to expense, and, if so, over how long a period. Because there are firm defenders of both alternatives, it may said that there are two generally accepted methods of handling goodwill. Conservatism, however, tends to favor the write-off of goodwill over a reasonably short period of time.

The auditor should take a firm stand against the arbitrary recognition of goodwill (no matter how obvious its existence might be), and against the treatment as goodwill of major advertising expenditures designed to improve a company's reputation or to introduce a new product. When there has been an actual purchase of goodwill, the auditor must satisfy himself that the amount to be shown on the balance sheet has been reasonably determined. Even if the figure for goodwill is specified in the contract for the purchase, the figure may merely represent the difference between the book value of the assets being sold and the total price for the going business. On the books of the purchaser, the tangible assets acquired should be recorded at their estimated fair market value at the time of purchase, and not at the same figure at which they were carried by the seller. The difference between this fair market value and the total purchase price will then be the amount of goodwill to be recognized. Although the auditor is not expected to be an appraiser, he should at least satisfy himself in a general way that the fair market values are reasonable and that a sincere effort was made to arrive at a representative figure.

As to the amortization of goodwill, about the only thing the auditor can do is to see that amortization, if figured, is consistent from year to year. Any balance in the goodwill account, regardless of whether amortization is being taken, should be allowed to remain as an asset only if sufficient profit is being earned to show that goodwill actually does exist.

Organization Costs

Although organization costs warrant approximately the same accounting treatment as goodwill, it is perhaps more common to amortize organization costs. Most accountants and businessmen would probably prefer to expense such costs at the time they are incurred, but the financial condition of a new business can seldom absorb such a charge in the first year. As a consequence, organization costs are usually capitalized and then amortized over a five- or ten-year period. Expenses in connection with subsequent issues of stock should not be added to this account but should be shown as an expense, or deducted from the proceeds of the sale of the stock. Organization expenses incurred prior to August 16, 1954, are not deductible for income tax purposes, but expenses incurred after that date may be deducted if amortized over a period of not less than sixty months.

The verification of unamortized organization costs would follow the general plan suggested in preceding sections.

Research, Experimental, and Exploration Costs

Expenditures made with the hope that they will result in future benefits present a particularly knotty accounting problem. A business obviously will not make such expenditures unless benefits are expected, and yet experience shows that only a small proportion of the projects will actually be successful. Lacking the ability to foresee the future, most businesses take a conservative viewpoint and expense all, or most, of their research, experimental, or exploration expenditures, and such treatment has the further advantage of an immediate tax benefit. The oil industry in particular has extensively followed this practice with respect to exploration expenses and "intangible" drilling costs. The intangible costs include such expenses of operating a drilling rig as labor, drilling bits, fuel, lubricants, and depreciation of the rig. The drilling rigs themselves, pipe, and other items that can be re-used are capitalized and subjected to depreciation write-offs.

Expensing charges that will produce benefits in future periods is, of course, not in accord with the accepted accounting principle of matching costs and revenues, but when such expenditures have been made eligible for immediate deduction for income tax purposes, there has usually been a demand to follow the same treatment for accounting purposes. The objections stemming from the basic conflict with accounting theory are the resulting understatement of current income and the omission of an asset from the balance sheet. Even more seriously, the opportunity of management to control such expenditures carries with it an equal opportunity to control the reported net income for the enterprise. For instance, an oil-producing company that expenses intangible drilling costs and shows a satisfactory income from its regular producing operations can "drill up" all its regular income by the simple expedient of drilling more than the usual number of new wells.

One justification for tolerating a practice that is not strictly in conformity with sound accounting theory is that in most instances the research, exploration, or intangible drilling costs have tended to be fairly constant from year to year, and have therefore produced only minor distortion on the income statement. The oil industry has been an exception to this generalization, however, and the situation has been further confused by the fact that not all companies have elected to expense their intangible drilling costs as these are incurred.

In permitting such a situation to develop, the accounting profession has, in effect, abdicated part of its responsibility to the users of audited financial statements. On the other hand, it is difficult to change the situation now because there would be strong reaction from those who would be forced to change methods of long standing, or who greatly prefer the freedom of choice of methods and the opportunity to retain control over reported income figures. It is to be hoped, however, that the profession will move in the direction of bolstering the meaningfulness and utility of audited financial statements.

For the present, if a client is engaged in a substantial special research project when ordinarily very little research is conducted, the auditor should probably insist that the client capitalize the costs, unless it should appear that the project may be unsuccessful. For successful projects the capitalized costs should, of course, be amortized over the periods in which benefits are expected. In those cases where clients have followed the practice of expensing research and development costs and the yearly expenditures are fairly constant, no action by the auditor is warranted as long as the profession does not change its present position. On the other hand, if the client's practices during a given year produce a substantial distortion of net income, the auditor should give serious consideration to the question of whether the statements present *fairly* the results of operations.

Patents

In instances where patents result from previous research expenditures, it would appear that the expenditures should have been capitalized. As suggested in the preceding section, however, companies which engage in such activities as a regular practice in order to keep abreast of competition seldom capitalize the expenditures. In those cases where the costs have been capitalized, the auditor should test the detailed figures against supporting evidence to determine that the resulting total is made up of items which are correct in amount and which actually apply to the project. If a patent is acquired by outright purchase, the contract of sale should be examined if one exists, and the paid check resulting from the transaction should also be examined. Such items as attorneys' fees relating to the acquisition of a patent or to the successful defense of a patent infringement suit are also properly capitalized and should likewise be subjected to audit verification.

The valuation of patents acquired in exchange for capital stock should be closely scrutinized. In one instance a business acquired patents and patent applications from predecessor companies through issuance of capital stock, part of which was eventually to be donated back to the company, and valued the patents and patent applications at the par value of the issued stock. The patent amounts constituted the principal assets of the new company, which proposed to raise funds through the public sale of stock. The financial statements showed how the patents and patent applications had been acquired, and on this basis the company's auditors issued an unqualified opinion on the statements. The Securities and Exchange Commission refused to accept the statements with the patents valued in the manner described above and censured the auditors, a national public accounting firm, for approving the company's statements.

As evidence of ownership of patents the patent letters should be examined, and there should be no payment of royalties for the use of the patented items or processes. Although patents have a legal life of seventeen years, their economic life is usually much shorter. Amortization should be based on the shorter of the two periods, and the auditor should carefully review the decision reached in this respect.

Copyrights

Most of the points mentioned in connection with patents apply also to copyrights. The legal life of copyrights is twenty-eight years, and they can be renewed for another twenty-eight years, but their economic life is usually much shorter. Many publishers write off all copyright costs over the first printing of a book, or over the first year of publication.

Trademarks

Trademarks are not subject to a maximum legal-life period, and their acquisition costs are usually nominal unless a trademark with an established reputation is acquired. The nominal costs are best expensed as they are incurred. Material amounts are ordinarily capitalized, and although they can be allowed to stand as long as the trademarked item is successful, amortization over a reasonable period is usually in order.

Franchises

The life of a franchise is usually definitely stated in the franchise agreement, and any costs incurred should be written off over that life period. The existence of the franchise, the costs of its acquisition, and the basis chosen for amortization of the costs should all be verified by the auditor.

Notes Payable

The auditor should ascertain that notes issued during the year were properly authorized, and he should trace the proceeds of large notes into the cash records and into the bank. If notes have been paid off during the year, the paid notes should be examined, and possibly the paid checks evidencing such payment should also be examined if internal control is weak. Interest expense for the year should be reconciled with the amount of notes outstanding. Such a test may reveal that interest is being paid on notes which have not been recorded because the proceeds have been misappropriated. Any accrued interest payable at the balance sheet date should be verified by calculation.

Notes payable should always be confirmed, and a request should be made for a list of any collateral pledged to secure the notes. Confirmation is important because external evidence is not available in support of the figures, as it is in the case of accounts payable. Also, because fewer employees are normally involved in the issuance of a note than in the purchase of materials, internal control is of necessity weaker.

The Standard Bank Confirmation form, illustrated in schedule $\frac{\text{A-2}}{1}$, includes a request for information on all direct obligations to the bank. The form should be sent to every bank with which the client has done business during the year, and the replies should be carefully examined for any indication that notes are outstanding. Information on such notes should be cross-referenced to the schedule of notes payable as shown on $\frac{\text{A-2}}{1}$ and AA.

Bonds and Mortgages Payable

The basic audit procedures for bonds and mortgages payable are about the same as those presented above for notes payable. Mortgages, of course, involve a lien on certain assets, and the auditor must be sure that the lien is clearly noted in the financial statements. Bonds may or may not involve a lien, a fact to be determined by examination of the trust indenture concerning the bonds.

Bonds are not confirmed with the actual holders, but with the trustee for the issue, and with the registrar if a separate registrar is named. The confirmation request should also ask for a statement showing whether all interest due has been paid. The proceeds of any bond issue should be traced to the cash records and into the bank. If the bonds have been sold through an underwriter, the statement rendered by the underwriter will provide useful evidence of the amount of cash to be accounted for. Because bonds will usually sell at a premium or discount, rather than at par, verification of the proceeds of sale is important to the verification of any premium or discount resulting from the sale. In verifying the balance of unamortized premium or discount, the auditor should determine that any amounts related to bonds retired or held in the treasury have been removed from the account.

Of utmost importance to the examination of bonds payable is the trust indenture under which the bonds are issued. The indenture should be closely studied by the auditor, and all pertinent facts should be summarized and placed in the permanent file. The following list suggests some of the more important matters which may be ascertained from the indenture. Many of these matters, it should be noted, have a direct bearing on financial statements.

1. Descriptive title of the issue.
2. Maximum amount of bonds authorized.
3. Interest rate and dates.
4. Maturity date.
5. Date and price, if bonds may be called before maturity.
6. Name of trustee and registrar.
7. Possible restrictions on use of bond proceeds.
8. Assets pledged as security.
9. Any special obligations concerning pledged assets, such as carrying a minimum amount of insurance and making necessary repairs.
10. Restrictions on payment of dividends during the period the bonds are outstanding. (Such provisions usually state that only profits above a certain amount each year shall be available for the payment of dividends. A requirement may also be made that dividends can be paid only if working capital or the current ratio exceeds a certain figure.)
11. Convertibility provisions. (Such provisions will necessitate reserving shares of unissued stock to accommodate bondholders who may exercise the convertibility privilege.)
12. Provisions for repayment. (Some stated or calculated amount may be required to be paid into a sinking fund or used to retire bonds purchased on the open market.)
13. Name of trustee to whom sinking fund payments are to be made.
14. Restrictions on additional borrowing while the bonds are outstanding.

If the auditor finds that any provisions of the trust indenture have not been carried out or have been violated, notice should be given to both the client and the trustee, and appropriate comments should be made in the financial statements.

Consignment Accounts Payable

Amounts owing to consignors for merchandise sold should be verified by reference to the consignment agreement and to the client's records of consigned merchandise received, sold, and on hand. The quantities of consigned merchandise on hand should be verified during the taking of the physical inventory. The consignor may be asked to confirm the quantity of goods shipped to the client and any payments received, but the amount owed to the consignor for goods sold before the close of the year must be determined from the client's records.

Income Taxes Payable

Taxes on income are now one of the major taxes paid by successful corporations, and those taxes have a material effect on both balance sheets and income statements. To be able to express an informed opinion on a client's financial statements, the independent accountant must therefore be well informed about our highly complicated tax laws so that he can ascertain that a proper provision has been made for income taxes payable. Most public accountants are, of course, thoroughly familiar with the income tax laws because one of the principal services to their clients concerns income tax matters. In practically all small- and in most medium-sized audits the auditor is likely to be requested to prepare the client's income tax return. Larger concerns usually have well-trained tax people on their own staff and therefore often prepare their own tax returns. Even when the auditor does not prepare the client's tax return, tax knowledge is still important because the auditor must review the client's tax accrual to satisfy himself that balance sheet and income statement figures are fairly stated.

The income tax liability account should be analyzed, and paid checks should be examined as evidence that taxes for the previous year have been paid. The current year's tax provision should then be reviewed, making certain that gross revenues have been determined in conformance with the tax laws, that nondeductible expenses have been eliminated in figuring taxable net income, and that gains and losses of the current and prior years have been properly treated. As he is making this review, the auditor should always be alert for any opportunity to effect a tax saving, even though he does not prepare the tax return. Suggested opportunities for tax saving are one of the finest stimulants to good client relationships. The auditor should also bring up any opportunities by which sound tax planning may aid in reducing future taxes. Many auditors encourage clients who do not employ a tax man on their staff to contact them at any time during the year when important contracts or financial transactions are contemplated, to permit the auditor to study the tax effect of the proposed action. Frequently a variation in the proposed plan can be made to effect substantial tax savings.

In a first audit the auditor should review all tax returns which have not yet been reviewed by a revenue agent, to insure that there have been no substantial underpayments of taxes due which would result in an additional liability to be shown. In repeat audits, the auditor should review any revenue agent's reports rendered since the previous year. Such reports show whether additional taxes are due or whether past returns have been satisfactorily closed.

State income taxes, although at a much lower rate, involve the same problems and verification procedures as do Federal income taxes. A complicating feature arises when a corporation earns its income in several states and is subject to income taxes in each of the states.

Tax effect of differences between accounting income and taxable income.
When differences exist between accounting income and taxable income,
failure properly to handle the provision for income taxes may cause a distortion of net income. The most common instance of this situation today
arises out of the use of one of the so-called "fast" depreciation methods
for income tax purposes, along with continued use of straight-line depreciation for accounting purposes. In the first few years following the adoption
of a method such as double-declining-balance or sum-of-digits for figuring
depreciation for tax purposes, the depreciation deduction for tax purposes
will exceed the straight-line depreciation used for accounting purposes. A
similar situation will result in future years if substantial net additions to
the plant investment occur.

If the income tax expense under such conditions is shown as the amount
of the actual taxes payable for the year, the amount will be less than the
taxes that would otherwise be payable on the reported net income, and
the effect will be to increase the after-tax net income. It is maintained
that this increase is purely illusory, because a few years later the tax-
deductible depreciation will become smaller than the book depreciation,
and the taxes actually payable will then be greater than the taxes that
would be payable on the reported income. The A.I.C.P.A. Committee on
Accounting Procedure has in effect concluded that it is artificial and misleading to permit reported income to rise on this basis, only to fall at a later
date, and has set forth its recommended solution to the problem in *Accounting Research and Terminology Bulletins,* Final Edition.

The committee's recommendation is based on the presumption that
income taxes are subject to allocation between periods much as is any other
type of expense. On this basis the increased taxes payable in later years
when tax depreciation is less than book depreciation should be allocated
as expense charges to the earlier years when tax depreciation exceeds book
depreciation. In making an additional charge for income tax expense in
the years when the actual tax liability is reduced, the subsequent liability
for increased taxes is thereby established in the records, and when the
increased taxes are later paid they are charged to this special liability
account, with no effect on the income statement. As a practical matter,
however, this tax "liability" may never have to be paid, for if new assets are
constantly added, the extra tax depreciation during the early life of those
assets will offset the reduced tax depreciation on older assets, and the book
and tax depreciation will remain approximately equal.

The final result of allocating to current years the increased taxes that
may have to be paid in later years is to show in each year income tax
expense that corresponds with the taxes that would normally be payable
on the income that is reported in the income statement. The effect of
changes in the actual taxes payable produced by differing amounts of book
and tax depreciation is thereby prevented from affecting the reported net

income. To generalize, it may be said that in years when tax depreciation exceeds book depreciation, the income tax expense reported in the income statement will exceed the actual taxes payable for that year, and the reverse would be true when tax depreciation is less than book depreciation. The liability for the income taxes charged as expense in one year but expected to be paid in later years should appear on the balance sheet below the current liabilities and may be simply described as "Deferred income taxes," or a longer, more revealing description can be used, such as, "Income tax savings expected to be payable in future years."

The problem of the proper treatment of the tax effect of differences between book and taxable income also arises in connection with extra-ordinary, nonrecurring gains or losses that enter into the income tax computation but are taken directly to retained earnings for statement purposes. The taxes related to the retained earnings entry should not affect the amount of tax expense reported in the income statement but should be allocated to the retained earnings account, so that the special item taken to retained earnings will appear net of its tax effect. The general rule applied in both this and the depreciation situation is that the tax effect of an item should be treated in the same way as the item itself in order to avoid distortions of the net income figure appearing on the income statement.

The reduction of income taxes payable resulting from the investment credit is intended to encourage investment by reducing the cost of such investment. Accordingly, the tax reduction should not increase income for the year, but should be taken up ratably over the life of the related asset. The credit may be made to the related asset or to a deferred income account. Such treatment reflects the preference expressed by the Accounting Principles Board in its *Opinion No. 2,* but in *Opinion No. 4* the Board agreed that the frequent practice of taking the credit immediately to income is also acceptable.

Deferred Income

If income has been received in advance, the auditor must satisfy himself that the full amount received has been treated originally as a deferred credit, and that the correct amounts are transferred to income as the income is earned. The actual method of verification will vary with each situation and the type of records kept. For instance, a motion picture theater may sell special coupon admission books. The books should be serially numbered, thus enabling the auditor to determine how many were sold and whether the proceeds were properly accounted for. Debits would be made to the liability account for the coupons turned in each day, and the auditor should test a few of those entries against the supporting coupons.

As a rule, not all the coupons will be redeemed, and consequently part of the deferred income over and above the amount relating to coupons redeemed can be taken into current operations. If separate accounts are maintained for coupon books sold during each year, the balances of accounts which are one or two years old will readily indicate about what proportion of the tickets will be redeemed. Provision can then be made each year to take into income the value of coupons not expected to be redeemed. The auditor should, of course, review such calculations to be sure that they are being handled correctly.

In some situations the problem may be considerably more complicated, as when subscriptions to magazines or newspapers are paid in advance. *A.I.C.P.A. Auditing Case Study No. 2* reports the procedures followed in the audit of a newspaper publisher. The auditor supervised the running of a listing of all address plates used in the mailing of mail subscriptions at the balance sheet date. Each plate included the expiration date of the subscription, and the client's employees computed on the listing the liability to each subscriber for the unexpired portion of the subscription. The auditor tested these computations and the footing of the amounts, and the total was then used to adjust the balance of the unearned subscription liability account to reflect the actual liability at the balance sheet date.

Contingent Liabilities

Many different types of items fall under the heading of "Contingent Liabilities," representing liabilities which may or may not materialize and liabilities which are indeterminate in amount. The classification includes such items as public liability claims, patent infringement claims, liability in connection with notes receivable discounted or accommodation endorsements, costs to be incurred under product guarantees, possible future payments in connection with long-term leases or purchase commitments, additional tax assessments, and possible refunds to be made based on contract-price redetermination or renegotiation. *Accounting Research Bulletin No. 50* contains an extensive discussion of the general problem of contingencies.

Claims Subject to Litigation

The client's attorney is the best source of information about existing or pending litigation. He should be requested to reply in writing, stating any litigation or other disputes of which he is aware, and indicating the extent of possible losses which might result. In providing for such losses in the accounts, allowance must be made for any recoveries to be expected on insurance carried against such losses.

Presentation in the financial statements of the contingent liability concerning claims being litigated often involves a severe straining of auditor-client relationships. The client may be strongly opposed to admitting any possible loss because he may feel that the admission might prejudice his case, and he might even object to any mention of the existence of the claim in the financial statements. The auditor, on the other hand, must be satisfied that the statements give full disclosure of all pertinent facts. If full disclosure is not made, he would ordinarily be forced to qualify or withhold his opinion on the financial statements.

One method of presentation is to mention the existence and amount of the claim by footnote to the balance sheet, supplemented by a statement as to the attorney's opinion if he believes that no actual liability will result or if he believes that final settlement or judgment will involve a figure substantially below the amount of the claim. On the other hand, if it is likely that ultimate disposition of the claim will be unfavorable to the client, the loss and liability should be reflected in the accounts rather than by footnote.

Notes Receivable Discounted and Accommodation Endorsements

The contingent liability on any notes receivable discounted with the client's bank will be reported by the bank on the Standard Bank Confirmation form used to confirm the balance on deposit with the bank. As a further check on such liability, the auditor should review credits to the notes receivable account for any indications that notes may have been discounted rather than collected at maturity.

Other than through inquiry and review of the minutes of directors' meetings, the bank confirmation form presents about the only opportunity for the auditor to learn of the existence of any accommodation endorsements.

Service Guarantees

Many products are sold under a guarantee of free service or replacement during a stated period. Costs likely to be incurred under such guarantees should be anticipated in the year the product is sold rather than recorded as an expense when any service or replacement costs may be incurred. Experience will usually suggest the relationship between such estimated future expenses and sales for the year. The auditor should review the client's calculation of the year's provision for the future expenses and the basis for the calculation. He should also make tests of the actual expenses charged against the estimated liability account to satisfy himself that only appropriate items are being charged. Any substantial month-to-month variation in such charges should be carefully investigated. As a final test, the auditor should note whether the balance of the liability account varies in proper relationship to sales of the guaranteed product. An increasing balance during a period of constant sales would suggest that the provision is too high. A decreasing balance in the face of increasing sales should suggest the opposite conclusion.

Model changes, new products, or a substitution of new parts or materials should cause the auditor to question whether past experience should still be used as the basis for providing for future expenses under guarantees.

Sale-Leaseback Agreements and other Long-Term Leases

Long-term leases can be expected to involve a substantial liability for future rent payments, and depending on economic trends, may become either advantageous or burdensome to the lessee. As a consequence, the existence of such agreements, if material, should be reported in the financial statements along with an indication of the amounts of the annual payments and the period of time the lease is to run.

The urgent need for additional working capital to finance expanded operations and increased costs has resulted in numerous sale-leaseback transactions, which have in turn increased the need for adequate disclosure. When such transactions occur, full disclosure of the terms of the agreement should be made in the year of sale, in addition to the customary reference to the obligation concerning future rentals to be paid. As an alternative, the present value of the liability and the related asset can be included in the balance sheet, with each figure properly described to indicate the nature of the item that is involved. The auditor should, of course, carefully study the lease agreement in support of the information and figures presented in the balance sheet. *Opinion No. 5* of the Accounting Principles Board requires that leases be recorded as a purchase at the discounted amount of the future lease rental payments if the payments run well ahead of any reasonable measure of the expiration of the service potential of the asset, so that an equity is created in the property.

Ascertaining the Existence of Unrecorded Liabilities

The auditor is likely to employ many procedures in seeking out the possible existence of unrecorded liabilities. The more commonly used procedures are suggested here, but the list should not be taken to be all-inclusive. Some of the procedures have already been mentioned at other points, but they are restated to show that they have a bearing on the possible disclosure of unrecorded liabilities. In a first audit, the same procedures should be applied to the records for the preceding year. The auditor is not concerned with the unrecorded liability itself in this case, but with the possible effect of any such items on the income for the year being examined.

Review of subsequent transaction. All liabilities are eventually reflected in the records, either through payment or by other means. This fact, combined with the usual auditing situation which involves procedures that must be carried out following the close of the client's fiscal year, makes it possible for the auditor to capitalize on the advantages of hindsight in his quest for information about unrecorded liabilities. The review of following-year entries in the voucher register and cash disbursement record has already been discussed relative to disclosure of unrecorded accounts payable. Other records that should be consulted for leads on unrecorded liabilities would be the general journal and minutes of directors' meetings. Major contracts signed in the interim between the balance sheet date and the completion of the audit field work should also be reviewed from the standpoint of uncovering any liabilities that existed at the balance sheet date.

Confirmations. The Standard Bank Confirmation form (see $\frac{A\text{-}2}{1}$) should be sent to all banks with which the client has done business during the year. The replies will list any direct or contingent liabilities to those banks, and an opportunity therefore exists to detect any liabilities not recorded in the client's records. A similar opportunity exists for disclosing unrecorded liabilities through confirmation of accounts payable or by analysis of vendors' statements. Although the requests for confirmation or a statement of the account are sent primarily to vendors with whom there is a large year-end balance, the auditor should review purchasing activity for the year and send requests to any vendors with whom a substantial volume of business was done during the year, even though there may be no year-end balance.

Consignment sales. The review of subsequent transactions may reveal a payment to a consignor for goods sold prior to the end of the year. The auditor should seek to make the necessary adjustment if the liability is material and was not recorded. The auditor should also examine the inventory record of consigned goods for the purpose of noting whether any goods have been sold but no liability recorded.

Information from client's attorney. Most businesses of medium size or above retain counsel to handle any legal matters which may arise. The attorney should be requested to notify the auditor, in writing, of any lawsuits or claims pending against the client, and he should also be requested to state his opinion of the probable outcome of such matters. The request to the attorney should also ask for information on any other liabilities of an unusual nature of which he has notice and for the amount of any fees or reimbursable expenses which may be due from the client.

If the client does not engage an attorney on a retainer basis, a clue to the possible existence of any pending legal matters may be gained from an analysis of any expense accounts to which legal fees may be charged. The payment of any such fees should be a signal for the auditor to investigate the situation to determine whether any liability exists or may be likely to result.

Client's representations. Until liabilities are made a matter of record, information about them may be solely within the knowledge of officers of a business. Because those officers are primarily responsible for the information in the financial statements of the business, it is both proper and customary to ask the officers for any information about possible unrecorded liabilities. Any liabilities known to them but which through oversight had not been recorded would be brought to light in this manner. The reader should not assume, however, that a statement from the officers relieves the auditor of any responsibility for discovering unrecorded liabilities. There is always a possibility that information may be intentionally withheld from the auditor or unintentionally overlooked, so the auditor must still make all the usual tests, thus indicating the reliability and accuracy of the representations made by the client's officers.

To avoid any possibility of error or misunderstanding, the representations should be made in writing. A possible form for such a representation is given below. Note the list of contingent liabilities which is included to assist the officers in recalling any such liabilities which might exist.

Date ————————————

To (name of auditor):

To the best of our knowledge all known or ascertainable direct liabilities of the company at (date) have been recorded in the accounts at that date, with the exception of minor items which are carried forward from month to month in ordinary operations.

The company had no material contingent liabilities that were not provided for in the accounts at (date), except as set forth below:

	Amount if
Kind of Contingent Liability	*Determinable*
Upon customers' or other notes that were	
dicounted, sold, or otherwise transferred	
Upon drafts negotiated	
For Federal or state income taxes	
For accommodation endorsements	
For guarantees of notes or securities of other issuers	
For guarantees of company products or services	
Under repurchase agreements	
Upon leases	
Under contracts or purchase agreements	
Under profit sharing arrangements	
Under pending lawsuits	
For all other contingent liabilities of any nature	

The company has entered into purchase commitments that approximated $———— at (date), which have arisen in the ordinary course of operations and contain no unusual amounts.

(Signed)

————————————————————
(President or other principal officer)

————————————————————
(Treasurer or chief financial officer)

————————————————————
(Controller or chief accounting officer)

Revenue agents' reports. The auditor should always ascertain whether an agent of the Internal Revenue Service has examined and closed any income tax returns during the period since the auditor was last in the client's office. If any returns have been examined, the agent's report should be reviewed to see whether any additional taxes have been assessed.

Interest expense. A reconciliation should be made between interest expense and the amount of interest-bearing obligations outstanding during the year. There is always a possibilty that interest is being paid on an unrecorded note, the proceeds of which have been appropriated by some officer or employee.

Notes and bonds. If serially numbered notes or bonds are issued by the client, all serial numbers should be accounted for in order to detect any instruments which have been issued but not recorded. When notes or bonds are shown by the records to have been liquidated, the paid documents should be inspected by the auditor. The absence of the document evidencing the original liability would suggest that the recorded payment may have been for some other purpose and that the original obligation is still outstanding. In cases where there may be any question, the paid check can be examined as further evidence of what actually happened to any payments made.

Review of cash receipts record. The auditor should review cash receipts for the audit period for any large receipts. Such receipts should be traced into the accounts to verify that the corresponding credit has been properly recorded, regardless of whether the cash represents the proceeds of a note or loan or the result of some other form of transaction.

Receiving records. All merchandise received prior to the balance sheet date should either be paid for or reflected in the total for accounts payable. Only in special cases will it be necessary to make a special review of the receiving records, however, because the verification of the inventory cut-off and the review of subsequent transactions should reveal any significant amounts of materials which have been received but not recorded as a liability.

Review of directors' and stockholders' minutes. Minutes of directors' and stockholders' meetings may contain authorizations to borrow money, reference to contracts which may obligate the company, or mention of claims or lawsuits pending against the company. As a consequence, such minutes should be carefully read and pertinent information abstracted in the working papers to permit subsequent comparison with ledger entries concerning the actions taken and any resulting liabilities.

Review of operations. The client's operations should be studied for any types of transactions which might involve liabilities not recorded at the balance sheet date. As an obvious illustration, any company with a weekly payroll is almost certain to have a liability at the end of the year for accrued wages. Other liabilities whose existence should become apparent with a thorough understanding of the client's operations would include container deposits, accrued royalties, accrued interest payable, service guarantees, accrued commissions, consignment accounts payable, and reimbursement for expenditures made by officers or employees.

Expense comparisons. A month-to-month comparison of expenses which revealed reduced expenses in the final month of the year might suggest that there is a liability for unpaid expenses.

Knowledge of tax laws. Even though the auditor cannot be an expert in all possible taxes to which the client might be subject, he should at least be familiar with the principal types of taxes and should note that all such taxes have been paid or accrued. Among the more common taxes are city, state, and Federal income taxes, gross earnings taxes, payroll taxes, excise taxes, sales taxes, stock transfer taxes, and franchise taxes.

Review of company contracts. All major contracts entered into by the client should be reviewed by the auditor for any direct or contingent liabilities that may have been created. Labor contracts, especially, should be reviewed, because they may contain provisions obligating the client for insurance benefits, pension payments, or vacation pay based on the number of months worked in a given period with payment to be made even if an employee leaves the company.

Workmen's compensation insurance. As noted earlier, compensation insurance is usually handled by making an advance deposit based on estimated payrolls, with either a refund or additional payment being made later based on actual payrolls. When the policy year terminates on or shortly after the balance sheet date, there is always a possibility that actual payrolls have exceeded the original estimate and that an additional premium may be due.

SUMMARY

Internal control

Expenditures of any type should be properly authorized and approved, and expenditures related to the various asset items discussed in this chapter are no exception.

Adequate records should be maintained to assure proper accounting for the assets and the charge-off of the assets to achieve proper matching of costs and revenues.

The right to obligate a concern should be limited to a minimum number of employees, and should be granted only by specific authorization.

The principles of good internal control over cash disbursements should be closely followed in the liquidation of all liabilities.

Accrued assets and liabilities and the related income and expense should be recognized whenever statements are prepared.

Statement presentation

Prepaid expenses are properly classified as current assets.

Deferred charges and intangible assets, which usually cover a period of more than a year, should not be classified as current assets; they are frequently classified as "Other Assets."

Each type of liability, if material, should be separately described.

The order in which liabilities are presented should follow customary practice.

Obligations to affiliated companies, stockholders, and officers should be distinguished from obligations to third parties.

Secured liabilities should carry an indication of the assets pledged.

Assets and liabilities should not be offset, with the exception of U. S. Treasury obligations that are to be used in payment of Federal income taxes.

Contingent liabilities should be shown short or by footnote, if they cannot be reasonably estimated and recorded in the accounts.

The description of long-term liabilities should include call date and price, maturity date, and interest rate.

Treasury bonds should be deducted from the liability for bonds issued.

Audit objectives and procedures

Determine that nonoperating, nonrecurring losses are not combined with operating expenses for reporting purposes.

Compare and analyze account balances.

Ascertain that all losses have been recorded.

Scrutinize asset and liability accounts for unrecorded losses.

Establish the propriety and validity of amounts originally debited to asset accounts.

Examine invoices, paid checks, tax returns, or other supporting documents.

Ascertain that future benefits are anticipated from the amounts charged.

Determine that asset amounts are being amortized on a systematic basis to obtain proper matching of expenses with revenues.

Review basis of amortization and calculation of amounts.

Determine that remaining balances are justified by future benefits that are anticipated.

Establish that recorded liabilities are stated correctly.

Request statements from vendors or use statements that the client has received and reconcile with recorded liabilities.

Confirm interest-bearing obligations.

Relate interest expense to the recorded liability and verify accrued interest payable.

Trace proceeds of loans or other forms of borrowing into the cash records and examine paid checks and cancelled notes in support of major repayments.

Analyze bond trust indentures for provisions affecting the financial statements or limiting what the client is permitted to do.

Review calculations concerning consignment accounts payable and test figures against source records.

Test detailed computations for accrued expenses and deferred income, and make over-all reviews to establish reasonableness of the amounts.

Test client's computations relating to income and other taxes payable, and examine tax returns and paid checks in support of payments made.

Obtain attorney's opinion on contingent liabilities arising out of present or prospective litigation.

Review notes receivable transactions for possible contingent liability on notes receivable discounted; examine bank confirmation reply.

Determine liability on long-term leases and ascertain that proper disclosure is made on the balance sheet.

Ascertain the existence of unrecorded liabilities.

(The following procedures should also be applied to the records for the preceding year in a first audit.)

Review subsequent transactions as recorded in the voucher register, check register, and general journal.

Request written confirmation of obligations from banks and principal vendors, unless vendors' statements are on file.

Review consignment account sales reports rendered after close of year for sales occurring prior to year end.

Request opinion from client's attorney concerning lawsuits or claims pending, and for amount of fees or expenses owed to the attorney by the client.

Obtain representation letter from client covering liabilities.

Review Internal Revenue Service revenue agents' reports on examinations of past income tax returns.

Reconcile interest expense and outstanding interest-bearing obligations.

Account for serially numbered unissued notes or bonds, and examine paid instruments in support of liquidated obligations.

Review cash receipts records and trace recording of unusual amounts of cash received.

Review receiving records for period prior to year end to ascertain that a liability has been recorded for all materials received.

Review minutes of meetings of directors and stockholders.

Review operations for any types of transactions that might involve a liability at the balance sheet date.

Make month-to-month expense comparisons to indicate possible unrecorded liabilities for expenses.

Ascertain that a liability has been recognized for all taxes to which the business is subject.

Review company contracts.

Ascertain whether premiums earned on workmen's compensation insurance may have exceeded the original premium deposit.

REVIEW QUESTIONS

1. What are the objectives of internal control over (a) other assets and (b) other liabilities not discussed in earlier chapters?
2. Briefly describe three variations in the method of accounting for supplies and handling the related detailed records.
3. What are the internal control advantages of using a postage meter machine?
4. What internal control measures should be placed in effect when numerous notes payable are issued each year?
5. Of the various other assets and liabilities, which is most likely to be subject to regular internal reporting? Why?
6. What is the internal auditor's main concern with respect to the assets discussed in this chapter?
7. Since prepaid expenses will not be converted into cash, are they properly shown as a current asset? Explain.
8. What points should be considered in the proper presentation of payables in the balance sheet?
9. What are the independent auditor's objectives in the examination of other expenses, losses, assets, and liabilities?
10. How is the auditor's verification of prepaid insurance simplified if the client maintains a satisfactory insurance register?
11. Why should the auditor review the amount of the client's insurance coverage?
12. What auditing procedures may be used in connection with expense advances?
13. How should the auditor proceed in verifying unamortized bond discount?
14. What possibility should the auditor watch for when a company follows the policy of expensing such items as research, experimental, or exploration costs?
15. Why should notes payable paid during the year be examined?
16. List 10 possible provisions which appear in a bond trust indenture which would be of interest to the auditor.
17. What procedures may be employed in verifying the amount of the contingent liability provided for service guarantees?

QUESTIONS ON SYSTEMS APPLICATIONS AND
APPLICATION OF AUDITING STANDARDS

18. Given the following information, prepare the journal entry to properly record the liability and expense for Federal income taxes. Assume a rate of 50% on net income and 25% on capital gains and losses, and that generally accepted accounting principles are to be followed with respect to income tax allocation.

$ 100,000	net income before tax
$ 50,000	gain on sale of building, taken directly to Retained Earnings in accordance with the current operating performance concept of income
$ 40,000	accelerated depreciation to be deducted for purposes of computing income taxes
$ 20,000	straight line depreciation deducted in arriving at net income shown above

19. Explain the following statement: "With today's substantially increased replacement cost of plant and equipment, the requirement that depreciation for income tax purposes be based on historical cost changes the income tax partly into a confiscatory tax on capital."

20. Explain the following statement: "Responsibility reporting necessitates that supplies be accounted for on a perpetual basis."

21. If a company issues numerous notes payable, why should the notes be pre-numbered? At what point in the accounting process should the numbers be accounted for?

22. Suggest procedures to be followed by the internal auditor under each of the objectives of evaluation, compliance, and verification, in conjunction with the examination of a company's insurance program.

23. A client maintains a complete insurance register, and you are instructed to make your examination of prepaid insurance against this record. Write a memorandum covering the work you would have done in connection with such an examination.

24. List six different prepaid expenses or deferred charges, and for each indicate from what documents you would obtain evidence as to
    (a) The amount of the original disbursement.
    (b) The period over which the amount should be written off.

25. Would you consider examination of cancelled checks to be adequate verification that taxes had been fully paid? Justify your answer and state what additional procedures you would use if you consider the cancelled checks to be insufficient.

26. Through discussion with your client's purchasing manager, you learn that the previous supplier of the electric motors used in the washing machines which it manufactures and sells has been forced to suspend deliveries as a result of a strike by its employees. For the past three months all motors used have been obtained from a small, little-known manufacturer of electric motors. The motors are not believed to be as good as the ones regularly used, and the company is eager to obtain motors from the regular supplier as soon as they are available. What bearing should the above information have on your examination?

27. Your client has acquired a piece of property subject to an existing mortgage (the mortgage was not assumed), and since he is not legally obligated by the

mortgage, proposes to deduct the mortgage from the cost of the property in preparing his financial statements. Would this treatment affect your opinion as expressed in your short-form audit report? Explain.

28. What auditing procedures should be undertaken by an independent auditor in connection with outstanding bonds that have been reacquired on the open market and retired?

29. Your client has a series of coupon bonds outstanding. Coupons may be presented to the company cashier for payment. The cashier immediately marks all such coupons "paid" and periodically presents them to the accounting department for reimbursement. The accounting department verifies the number of coupons before approving the reimbursement. After the reimbursement has been made, the coupons and the covering voucher are placed in the paid voucher file.

In the course of your examination you note that, whereas in the past about 97 per cent of the coupons were redeemed for each interest period, in recent periods the redemption rate has risen to 98.5 per cent.

Based on the information given,

(a) What may have been happening?

(b) How would you prove your contention?

(c) What recommendations would you make to the client?

PROBLEMS

30. You have assigned your assistant to the examination of the Cap Sales Company's fire insurance policies. All routine audit procedures with regard to the fire insurance register have been completed (i.e., vouching, footing, examination of cancelled checks, computation of insurance expense and prepayment, tracing of expense charges to appropriate expense accounts, etc.). Your assistant has never examined fire insurance policies and asks for detailed instructions.

Required:

(a) In addition to examining the policies for the amounts of insurance and premium and for effective and expiration dates, to what other details should your assistant give particular attention as he examines the policies? Give the reasons for examining each detail. (Confine your comments to fire insurance policies covering buildings, their contents, and inventories.)

(b) After reviewing your assistant's working papers, you concur in his conclusion that the insurance coverage against loss by fire is inadequate and that if loss occurs the Company may have insufficient assets to liquidate its debts. After a discussion with you management refuses to increase the amount of insurance coverage.

1. What mention will you make of this condition and contingency in your short-form report? Why?

2. What effect will this condition and contingency have upon your opinion? Give the reasons for your position.

(Uniform C.P.A. Examination)

31. A new client, Carr Corporation, requested you to review the account titled "Insurance." Carr Corporation commenced business on January 1, 1966 and wants to correct the financial statements for 1966 and 1967. They were prepared by the bookkeeper who failed to take cognizance of any adjustments in

the account. There were appropriate business reasons for the variance in inception dates for various policies. Data from examination of the account and insurance policies follow:

Insurance

Debits:

1966

January 3	Annual premium of insurance policy on life of officer. Date of policy is January 1, 1966	$ 6,000
January 20	Deposit on workmen's compensation insurance premium for 1966. Coverage is from January 1 to December 31....	1,900
July 15	Premium on fire insurance on building and contents covering period from August 1, 1966 to July 31, 1969........	3,600
September 15	Premium on employees' fidelity bonds covering period from September 1, 1966 to August 31, 1967..............	1,800
October 30	Cash shortage of employee to be reimbursed by insurance company......................................	500
		$ 13,800

Credits:

1966

October 1	Reduction of fire insurance rate on building covering period from October 1, 1966 to July 31, 1969	$ 340
December 31	To profit and loss	13,460
		$ 13,800

Debits:

1967

January 3	Annual premium of insurance policy on life of officer....	$ 6,000
January 16	Adjustment of 1966 workmen's compensation insurance premium...	300
January 17	Premium on fire insurance on addition to existing building during construction period, January 15 to May 15, 1967	500
January 18	Deposit on workmen's compensation insurance premium for 1967	2,200
February 1	Premium on automobile insurance November 1, 1966 to October 31, 1967	3,000
May 10	Additional premium on fire insurance policy covering building addition from May 15, 1967 to July 31, 1969	2,650
June 1	Premium on marine insurance policy for goods shipped to Europe	150
September 15	Premium on employees' fidelity bonds covering period from September 1, 1967 to August 31, 1968..............	1,800
November 10	Embezzlement by employee to be reimbursed by insurance company...	1,100
		$ 17,700

Credits:

1967

March 1	Payment of cash shortage by insurance company........	$ 500
December 12	Damages collected in full settlement for European shipment jettisoned during storm	1,700
December 31	To profit and loss	15,500
		$ 17,700

1. On December 31, 1967 the premium on automobile insurance had not been paid or recorded. The insurance agent reported there would be no change in the premium.
2. The cash surrender value of the insurance policy on the life of the officer amounted to $1,200 on December 31, 1967 and was not recorded. On December 9, 1967 the client, in accordance with its election, received a cash dividend of $360 on the life insurance policy which was credited to miscellaneous income.
3. The actual workmen's compensation premium for 1967 was determined to be $1,900.

Required:
(a) Prepare a worksheet which will properly identify and distribute all amounts related to insurance for 1966 and 1967.
(b) Prepare the worksheet entry to correct the financial statements for 1966.
(c) Prepare the worksheet entry to correct the financial statements for 1967.

(Uniform C.P.A. Examination)

32. The Baker Co. asks your help in determining the amount of loss and in filing an insurance claim in connection with a fire which destroyed part of the company's inventory and some of the accounting records. You are able to obtain the following information from the records available:
(a) The fire occurred on July 15.
(b) The last physical inventory was taken on the previous January 31st, and the inventory at that time, at cost, was $23,421.52.
(c) The annual premium of $160 on the insurance carried was due and paid on May 1. The face amount of the policy is $15,000, and the policy carries an 80 per cent coinsurance clause.
(d) Accounts payable were $12,234.16 on January 31, and $14,105.22 at the time the fire occurred.
(e) Payments to vendors from January 31 to the date of the fire amounted to $71,319.87.
(f) All sales are on account, and accounts receivable were $15,001.97 at January 31 and $11,905.80 at the date of the fire.
(g) Collections on receivables from January 31 to the date of the fire amounted to $97,355.92.
(h) Most articles sell at approximately 25 per cent in excess of cost. An inventory of merchandise not destroyed by the fire amounted to $16,098.62 at cost on July 15.

33. The Lewis Company, a manufacturer of heavy machinery, grants a four year warranty on its products. The Estimated Liability for Product Warranty account shows the following transactions for the year:

Opening balance	$ 45,000
Provision	20,000
	65,000
Cost of servicing claims	12,000
Ending balance	$ 53,000

A review of unsettled claims and the Company's experience indicates that the required balance at the end of the year is $80,000 and that claims have averaged 1½% of net sales per year.

The balance in Accrued Federal Income Taxes is $27,000, which adequately covers any additional liability for prior years' income taxes and includes a $25,000 provision for the current year. For income tax purposes only the cost of servicing claims may be deducted as an expense.

The following additional information is available from the Company's records at the end of the current year:

Gross sales	$ 2,040,000
Sales returns and allowances	40,000
Cost of goods sold	1,350,000
Selling and administrative expense	600,000
Net income per books before income taxes	50,000

Required:

Prepare the necessary adjusting journal entries giving effect to the proper accounting treatment of product warranty and Federal income taxes. Support each entry with clearly detailed computations. The books have not been closed. The Company has not allocated income taxes in the past. Assume a rate of 50% for income tax calculations.   (Uniform C.P.A. Examination)

34. The Trumb Radio Corporation, a client, requests that you compute the appropriate balance for its *Reserve for product warranty* for a statement as of June 30, 1967.

Using the data below, draw up a suitable working-paper schedule, including the proposed adjusting entry. Assume that proper recognition of costs for financial accounting will be allowed for income tax purposes.

The Trumb Radio Corporation manufactures television tubes and sells them with a six-month guarantee under which defective tubes will be replaced without a charge. On December 31, 1966 the *Reserve for product warranty* had a balance of $510,000. By June 30, 1967 this reserve had been reduced to $80,250 by charges for estimated net cost of tubes returned which had been sold in 1966.

The company started out in 1967 expecting 8 per cent of the dollar volume of sales to be returned. However, due to the introduction of new models during the year, this estimated percentage of returns was increased to 10 per cent on May 1. It is assumed that no tubes sold during a given month are returned in that month. Each tube is stamped with a date at time of sale so that the warranty may be properly administered. The following table of percentages indicates the likely pattern of sales returns during the six-month period of the warranty, starting with the month following the sale of tubes.

Month following sale	% of total returns expected
First	20
Second	30
Third	20
Fourth through six—10 per cent each month	30
Total	100

Gross sales of tubes were as follows for the first six months of 1967:

Month	Amount
January	$ 3,600,000
February	3,300,000
March	4,100,000
April	2,850,000
May	2,000,000
June	1,800,000

The company's warranty also covers the payment of freight cost on defective tubes returned and on new tubes sent out as replacements. This freight cost runs approximately 10 per cent of the sales price of the tubes returned. The manufacturing cost of the tubes is roughly 80 per cent of the sales price, and the salvage value of returned tubes averages 15 per cent of their sales price. Returned tubes on hand at December 31, 1966, were thus valued in inventory at 15 per cent of their original sales price.　　　(Uniform C.P.A. Examination)

35. The following covenants are extracted from the indenture of a bond issue. The indenture provides that failure to comply with its terms in any respect automatically advances the due date of the loan to the date of noncompliance (the regular due date is 20 years hence). Give any audit steps or reporting requirements you feel should be taken or recognized in connection with each one of the following:

(1) "The debtor company shall endeavor to maintain a working capital ratio of 2 to 1 at all times, and, in any fiscal year following a failure to maintain said ratio, the company shall restrict compensation of officers to a total of $100,000. Officers for this purpose shall include Chairman of the Board of Directors, President, all vice presidents, Secretary, and Treasurer."

(2) "The debtor company shall keep all property which is security for this debt insured against loss by fire to the extent of 100 per cent of its actual value. Policies of insurance comprising this protection shall be filed with the trustee."

(3) "The debtor company shall pay all taxes legally assessed against property which is security for this debt within the time provided by law for payment without penalty, and shall deposit receipted tax bills or equally acceptable evidence of payment of same with the trustee."

(4) "A sinking fund shall be deposited with the trustee by semiannual payments of $300,000, from which the trustee shall, in his discretion, purchase bonds of this issue."　　　(Uniform C.P.A. Examination)

36. From the following accounts and supplementary information prepare work papers showing your verification work and any adjusting entries covering your audit of bonds payable in connection with your first examination of Simpson, Inc., as of December 31, 1967.

6% 25-year Debenture Bonds, Due January 1, 1988

January 1, 1963	CR	$	$ 500,000.000	$ 500,000.00

Bond Premium

January 1, 1963	CR	$	$ 25,000.000	$ 25,000.00

Treasury Bonds

October 1, 1967	CD	$ 104,500.00	$	$ 104,500.00

Bond Interest Expense

January 1, 1967	CD	$ 15,000	$	$ 15,000.00
July 1, 1967	CD	$ 15,000		30,000.00

The treasury bonds were purchased at a price of 103 plus accrued interest through a broker. The bonds are not to be reissued, and the client asks you to prepare an adjusting entry writing off the bonds.

Owners' equity:
internal control; auditing

21

The number of transactions affecting the owners' equity accounts of a concern is usually limited. As a consequence, there is little need for an elaborate accounting system, and the independent auditor's work is correspondingly simplified. The examination of owners' equity accounts as a rule requires only a small proportion of the total audit time, but the few transactions that occur may involve substantial amounts and should be scrutinized closely.

Objectives of Internal Control

Internal control over transactions affecting owners' equity accounts should give assurance that:

1. Proper authorization exists for all such transactions.
2. Accountability for the transactions is independent of the handling of funds and certificates of ownership.
3. Detailed information is available concerning the equity of individual owners.

In attaining these objectives, most smaller concerns handle the transactions themselves, but for large corporations it is quite common to delegate to independent registrars and transfer agents part or all of the responsibility for handling equity transactions and keeping the detailed records. Through such delegation, the concerns gain the benefit of the good internal control exercised by the trust departments of companies that handle such work and in addition have the advantage of utilizing an organization equipped to accomplish the necessary work efficiently and with full knowledge of the specialized legal requirements involved.

Responsibilities of the Board of Directors

The starting point for a good system under any circumstances is the proper authorization of transactions and accounting entries. The board of directors, as well as the stockholders in some instances, should authorize capital stock transactions. For both sales and repurchases of stock, the number of shares and the price per share should be set. The board should also authorize the method of payment for shares sold if payment is not to be made immediately or is to be made with assets other than cash.

Other responsibilities which should be retained by the board of directors include the determination of amounts at which certain transactions should be recorded, the authorization of transfers between equity accounts, and the declaration of dividends. When stock is issued in exchange for property, the valuation of the property and the amount of the equity created by receipt of the property should be set by the board. When no-par stock is issued, any allocation of the proceeds to an account other than capital stock should be made by the board. Transfers between equity accounts, as in the creation or extinction of retained earnings reserves and the restatement of any equity accounts, should also be authorized by the board. Dividends must be declared by the board. The declaration of a dividend includes setting the record and payment dates for the dividend.

When a corporation handles all stock transactions itself, the board of directors should designate the officers who are authorized to sign and countersign new stock certificates, the officer who is to maintain stockholders' records (usually the secretary), and the officer or officers authorized to sign dividend checks. One of the officers authorized to sign stock certificates should be designated as custodian of unissued certificates. If outside agents are to handle the stock transactions, the board should, of course, name those agents.

Records Maintained by the Corporation

As stated above, when the company handles its own stock transactions, one officer should be designated custodian of unissued stock certificates. He should receive delivery of the prenumbered certificates directly from the printer and should immediately ascertain that all certificates are accounted for. The officers authorized to sign stock certificates should do so only after satisfying themselves that the stock has been fully paid for or that a previously outstanding certificate has been surrendered.

The stock certificates are usually prepared in a form similar to a checkbook, with each stub showing the certificate number, and with spaces provided for entering the number of shares, the name of the person to whom issued, and information about previously issued shares when the new certificate is issued in exchange for another certificate on a stock transfer. A state tax in some states must be paid on issuance of stock certificates, and stamps purchased for the payment of such taxes should be affixed to the certificate stubs. When shares are repurchased or certificates are submitted to be reissued to a new owner, the old certificates should be cancelled to preclude their re-use and should be attached to the appropriate stub. Thus only stubs for issued and outstanding certificates will not have an unissued or cancelled certificate attached.

A stockholders' ledger should be maintained in addition to the certificate stubs, if there are many stockholders. Such a record facilitates payment of dividends and makes stockholder information more readily accessible. The record also serves as an independent check on the certificate stubs. The record may be maintained by the secretary of the corporation, or possibly by the accounting department, but in the case of large concerns the records may be kept by a separate stock transfer department.

Dividends are preferably paid by checks drawn on a separate dividend-disbursing account. The checks should be prepared from the stockholders' ledger, or from an address plate file showing all needed information. Before signing the checks, the treasurer should calculate the total dividend payable, based on the dividend rate set by the board of directors and the number of shares outstanding. He should then balance the total checks written with this figure. The checks should be mailed without being returned to the person preparing the checks. Dividends should not be paid on treasury shares.

Independent Registrar and Transfer Agent

All corporations whose stock is listed on securities exchanges are required to utilize the services of an independent registrar, thus protecting stockholders against excessive or fraudulent issues of stock certificates. Such companies also, as a rule, appoint an independent transfer agent, because such a specialist is better prepared to handle the keeping of stockholders' records and the transfer of stock ownership. Additional internal control is also achieved in this way.

The responsibility of the registrar is to see that certificates issued by a corporation are in accord with the authorization granted by the corporate charter issued by the state of incorporation, and with the authorizations of the board of directors. A stock certificate becomes valid only after it is signed by the registrar. He should approve certificates only up to the maximum number of shares authorized, and he should approve a new certificate on transfer of ownership only upon presentation of the old certificate.

The transfer agent also has a record of the number of shares of stock outstanding. His main concern, however, is not in limiting the number of shares issued, but in maintaining records showing who owns the outstanding shares and in effecting transfers of stock ownership. The transfer agent supplies the corporation with a certified list of shareholders on the dividend record dates to serve as the basis of preparing invididual dividend checks, and on the dates of annual meetings to show the number of votes to which each shareholder is entitled. The transfer agent may also serve as dividend-disbursing agent, in which case a single check is forwarded to the agent to cover the individual dividend checks prepared and mailed by him.

Management Reports

As might be expected, periodic reports showing balances and changes in the equity accounts are of little significance to successful business operation. In most instances periodic balance sheets supplemented by a statement of changes in contributed capital and retained earnings will meet all requirements for such information. To supplement such reports, however, the treasurer or controller should regularly review all entries to the equity accounts to establish their propriety.

Internal Auditing

One of the principal responsibilities of the internal auditor should be verification of all entries in the equity accounts to permit him to be certain they have been properly authorized, are stated at the correct amount, and reflect generally accepted accounting principles. Such a review will obviate the need for the treasurer or controller to make a similar examination.

If the company maintains all capital stock records itself, the internal auditor should account for all stock certificates, making certain that certificates issued since his previous audit are properly supported by the receipt of assets or cancellation of previously outstanding certificates, and that the proper tax stamps have been affixed. The number of shares shown as outstanding by the general ledger should be balanced with the stock certificate stubs and with the stockholders' ledger. Dividends paid should be verified in total against the directors' declaration, and the individual payments should be tested against the stockholders' ledger.

If an independent registrar and transfer agent are employed, confirmation should be obtained as to the number of shares outstanding. Dividends paid should be tested against the certified list of shareholders submitted by the transfer agent, unless, of course, the transfer agent also acts as dividend-disbursing agent.

For companies which maintain their own stock transfer departments, periodic surprise audits of the department are in order. All certificates on hand should be counted and balanced with the records, and tests should be made of the records to show whether all transactions have been properly recorded.

STANDARDS OF STATEMENT PRESENTATION

Capital Stock

To enable the statement reader or financial analyst to obtain all information which may affect any conclusions reached, complete data about the capital stock of the company should be given in the stockholder's equity section, as follows:

1. Description of each class of stock outstanding.
2. Preferences of any preferred shares as to dividends or liquidation and any other rights or privileges, such as convertibility. (If preferred stock carries a redemption or liquidation price which is in excess of par or stated value, the aggregate of that excess should be mentioned to show the effect on common stock equity.)
3. Indication of whether stock is par or no-par.
4. Par value of stock, or stated value, if applicable.
5. Number of shares authorized, issued, held in the treasury, and outstanding.
6. Information concerning shares reserved for stock subscribed but not issued, for outstanding options or stock purchase warrants, or for issuance to bondholders or preferred stockholders on exercise of the right to convert into common stock.
7. The amount of any discount or premium resulting from the sale of outstanding shares.

Treasury Stock

Shares of stock held in the treasury should not be listed as an asset except in very rare instances, and then only if the nature of the items is clearly revealed. Similarly, dividends on treasury shares should not be recorded and shown as income.

Three ways of treating treasury shares appear to have some acceptance, both in theory and as demonstrated by published corporate statements. Based on findings published by the A.I.C.P.A. in its annual study, *Accounting Trends and Techniques,* the least popular of the three alternatives is to deduct the cost of treasury shares from retained earnings. Although this treatment may appear to mix the proverbial apples and oranges, there is sound theoretical justification for such treatment. Corporate stockholders have been given limited liability in exchange for a promise to protect creditors by not withdrawing originally contributed capital. Thus any payment to a stockholder to reacquire shares issued to him is proper only to the extent that the assets paid out originated from retained earnings rather than from the original payment for the stock. In some states the acquisition of treasury stock is legally restricted to the amount of retained earnings, thus justifying the deduction of treasury stock from retained earnings. But even in states where such a restriction does not exist, proper recognition of the inherent obligation to maintain paid-in capital intact as a form of protection to creditors should warrant a similar treatment of the cost of treasury stock in the financial statements.

Of the two remaining possibilities for displaying treasury stock in the financial statements, the trend is toward more widespread use of the method which shows the cost of treasury stock as a deduction from total paid-in capital and retained earnings. The gaining popularity is probably attributable to the simplicity of the accounting entries under this method and the clarity of the treatment to the average investor not trained in accounting or the use of financial statements.

A third method of presentation is the so-called "constructive retirement" method whereby treasury stock is carried at par or stated value and is shown as a deduction from the total shares of stock issued. Under this method, as is also true when reacquired shares are actually retired, gains resulting from a repurchase price less than the original issuance price should be credited to a contributed capital account and not to retained earnings. If the repurchase price exceeds par or stated value, any such excess up to the amount of any premium received on the original sale of those shares should be charged against the original premium received. Any amount by which the repurchase price exceeds the original issuance price should be charged either against any previous gains from treasury stock transactions or against retained earnings.

A few companies show shares of their own stock as an asset, but invariably the shares are being held in a special fund, such as a pension fund, or have been acquired to meet the requirements of a bonus or stock option or stock purchase plan.

Under any of the methods of treating treasury stock, upon resale of the stock, amounts received in excess of cost should be treated as contributed capital and not taken to the retained earnings account. Losses may be charged against any previous credits arising from treasury stock transactions, but after these are exhausted, losses should be charged against retained earnings.

Contributed Capital in Excess of Par or Stated Value

Under the theory that contributed capital should be maintained intact for the protection of creditors, any contributed capital amounts other than those shown as capital stock should be shown in such a way that the amounts will not appear to be available for dividends or be confused with retained earnings. Typical items of contributed capital which would be classified under this heading would include amounts received on capital stock in excess of par or stated value, gains on treasury stock transactions, amounts arising from recapitalization, and donations. The best procedure is to list each type of item separately with a full description, but if the amounts are not material they may be combined under a single heading. Any changes in these contributed amounts during the year should be set forth in a separate statement.

Unrealized Appreciation

Although accountants continue to look with disfavor on revaluing assets to reflect appreciated value or replacement value, a few business concerns have nevertheless revalued some of their assets. The resulting increase in the stockholders' equity should be shown as a separate item with clear indication that it is unrealized. Every effort should be made to prevent the statement reader from assuming that the item is available for dividends.

Retained Earnings

The term "retained earnings" has been used throughout this book in recognition of the recommendations of the Committee on Terminology of the American Institute of Certified Public Accountants to eliminate the use of the term "surplus." The recommendation was made in view of the misapprehensions often resulting when the term "surplus" is encountered by investors who are not familiar with the technical meaning of the term. Substitute terms other than "retained earnings" which have been used include "earnings reinvested in the business," "retained income," "accumulated earnings retained and used in the business," and "undivided profits."

Analysis of changes in retained earnings. A separate statement may be used to give a complete picture of changes in retained earnings, or the analysis of the changes may be combined with the income statement. In the latter instance, the balance of retained earnings at the beginning of the year should be added to the net income figure before any other items are shown If the only changes are the net income for the year and the dividends paid, the analysis of changes in retained earnings may be shown as a part of the balance sheet presentation of retained earnings. Of the three alternatives, the combined statement of income and retained earnings is frequently recommended because some of the changes in retained earnings may be closely related to net income. A good example would be a correction of prior years' earnings. The principal disadvantage of the combined statement is that the important figure of net income for the year is buried within the statement.

Treatment of gains and losses arising from extraordinary, nonrecurring

transactions. There are two generally recognized concepts of income center-
ing on the treatment of extraordinary, nonrecurring gains or losses. Under
the "all-inclusive" or "historical" concept it is held that, to give a true
picture of income over the years, all gains or losses should be reflected in
the income statement before arriving at the figure for net income. Any
extraordinary, nonrecurring gains or losses should, however, be reported
separately, immediately before the net income figure, and should be clearly
labeled. The figure immediately preceding any such items will thus be net
income from normal operations, whereas the final figure will simply be the
final net income for the year.

Under the "current operating performance" concept of net income it is
held that because the net income figure is used in evaluating past performance and estimating future prospects, the inclusion of extraordinary, nonrecurring gains or losses in the computation of net income would tend to
distort the net income figure and lead to false conclusions. Thus the
recommendation is made that extraordinary, nonrecurring gains or losses
which are material in relation to net income should be taken directly to
retained earnings. As an acceptable alternative, they can be reported on the
income statement *after* the figure clearly labeled as net income. The final
figure on the income statement would then be described in some such
fashion as "Balance of net income transferred to retained earnings, after
special loss item."

The Committee on Accounting Procedure has stated that extraordinary,
nonrecurring charges or credits should be excluded from the determination
of net income, if the materiality of the items is such that to include them
would impair the significance of net income. Studies of published reports
show that the committee recommendation is not being followed consistently,
but a sufficient number of statements reflect such items in the statement of
retained earnings to warrant the observation that the burden of proof is on
the person who does not follow the committee preference. The committee
also expressed a preference for taking special items directly to retained
earnings rather than showing them on the income statement following the
net income figure. This preference is based on possible misconceptions that
the last figure on the income statement is the net income for the year, even
though the statement clearly shows that another figure is actually the net
income for the year.

Examples of items properly charged or credited to retained earnings would
include premiums paid on the redemption of preferred stock, adjustments
applicable to prior years, write-offs of intangible assets (material amounts
only, not regular amortization), unusual gains or losses of a material amount,
recapitalization expenses, and adjustments of the carrying value of investments in subsidiaries. As stated in the preceding chapter, any effect which
such items have on income taxes payable should also be taken to retained
earnings rather than be allowed to affect net income.

An alternative to taking items representing adjustments of prior years' income directly to retained earnings is to restate the income statements for the years involved and "spread back" the adjustments. Because the revised figures for the prior years presented on a comparative basis will not agree with the figures originally reported, the revised figures should be footnoted with a full explanation concerning the nature of the revision and the amount involved.

Reserves. The A.I.C.P.A. Committee on Terminology has recommended that the term "reserve" be used only in connection with appropriations of retained earnings, and that recommendation has also been followed in this book. So-called asset valuation reserves and liability reserves have been given titles which do not involve the use of the term "reserve." Inasmuch as the term "reserve" is restricted to appropriations of retained earnings, it therefore follows that such reserves should not be provided by charges against income. This point is particularly important with respect to reserves for possible future inventory price declines, general-purpose contingency reserves, or any other provisions for indefinite possible future losses or expenditures. Because such amounts are indeterminate, they would have the effect, if charged against income, of arbitrarily reducing net income. Preferably, all items entering into the determination of net income should be based on objective measurements. Although admittedly many estimates are included in the classification, there are, nevertheless, objective bases for the estimates, as in the case of depreciation or a provision for expenses related to product guarantees. General-purpose contingency reserves, on the other hand, at best represent pure conjecture, and they are highly subject to individual opinions and desires.

The reasoning behind the manner in which true reserves should be created also affects the proper method of disposing of the reserves. The only permissible charges against the reserves should be for transfers restoring any unneeded amounts to retained earnings. Income should not be relieved of costs or losses applicable to the current period by charging such items against a reserve, even though the reserve may have been provided in anticipation of such items. If the items are material and of a nonrecurring, extraordinary nature, they should be taken directly to retained earnings. If a reserve had been provided in anticipation of such items, the reserve can then be restored to retained earnings. Costs or losses which were definitely anticipated in an earlier period should have been provided for by a charge to income at that time, but then the contra credit should not have been to an account which included the term "reserve" in its title.

Restrictions on retained earnings. Any limitations on the availability of retained earnings for the payment of dividends should be disclosed in the balance sheet. Disclosure may be made by footnote or by showing restricted amounts separately from those amounts available for dividends. Restrictions may result from the provisions of a bond indenture or a loan agreement, legal requirements relating to the acquisition of treasury stock, cumulative preferred dividends in arrears, or voluntary action by the board of directors. In the latter case, the restriction is usually accompanied by an appropriation of retained earnings set up in the form of a reserve.

"Dating" retained earnings. When a deficit has been eliminated by a reduction in contributed capital through a quasi-reorganization, any retained earnings arising after the reorganization should be "dated" for the next five to ten years by including a comment such as, "Retained earnings since June 25, 1966." In this way the reader is put on notice that operations prior to that date resulted in a deficit absorbed by a reduction of contributed capital.

Owners' Equity in a Partnership or Sole Proprietorship

Customarily, earnings and drawings are combined with the previous balance of the owners' equity in a partnership or sole proprietorship, and a single total is shown on the balance sheet, but each partner's equity should be shown separately. There appears to be considerable merit, however, to following a plan similar to that used in accounting for stockholders' equity in a corporation. Although the same legal reasons do not exist for showing retained earnings as a separate figure for a partnership or proprietorship, valuable additional information can be given in that manner. The size of the retained earnings figure gives some indication of whether the business has prospered in the past and shows whether the business has been expanding. Expansion by retention of earnings is usually taken as a sign of health and vigor in a business.

AUDIT OBJECTIVES AND PROCEDURES

The auditor's objectives in the examination of amounts related to owners' equity are:

1. Establish credibility of the accounting records.
2. Tie in supporting records with the statement amounts.
3. Determine that all legal requirements have been observed and that the rights of various parties have been respected.

Establish Credibility of the Accounting Records.

Entries in any of the owner's equity accounts occurring since the previous examination should be detailed in the auditor's working papers and the credibility of the records established by verifying the propriety and accuracy of the recorded amounts. The working-paper analysis makes available in the auditor's files a complete history of all changes in the owners' equity.

Capital stock transactions. All capital stock transactions should be traced to authorizations in the minutes of the board of directors. This would include sales of unissued stock, the exchange of unissued stock for property, the issuance of shares in connection with a stock dividend or a stock split, and the acquisition or disposition of treasury shares. Where specific dollar amounts have been set by the board for such transactions, the recorded transactions should, of course, agree with those figures. Any amounts received in excess of par or stated value should be determined and traced to entries in the appropriate accounts.

Any proceeds of sales of unissued or treasury shares should be traced to entries in the appropriate asset accounts and to deposits in company bank accounts if cash was received. The amount should also be verified against any supporting data available, such as an underwriting agreement or stock option agreement.

When treasury stock has been purchased, if a price has been specified by the board of directors the auditor should determine that the transaction was effected at that price. As further evidence of the purchase cost, paid checks should be examined, and if the purchase was effected through a security dealer, the advice of purchase should also be noted. Proceeds of sales of treasury stock should be verified in a comparable manner. The auditor should also note that any gains or losses arising from treasury stock transactions are recorded on a generally accepted basis. Gains should not be taken to the retained earnings account either directly or through the income statement. Losses should first be offset against previous gains resulting from transactions in the same class of stock, and any remaining amounts should be charged against retained earnings.

Stock dividends representing less than twenty or twenty-five per cent of the number of shares of stock outstanding necessitate special treatment. Such dividends are unlikely to affect the market value of the outstanding stock, and recipients quite frequently assume that the shares received represent a distribution of corporate earnings in an amount equivalent to the fair market value of the shares received. In view of these circumstances, the Committee on Accounting Procedure has recommended that when such proportionately small stock dividends are issued, retained earnings should be capitalized in an amount that is not less than the market value of the stock issued. The requirement is intended to prevent amounts from remaining in retained earnings, available for subsequent distribution, which the stockholder may assume have already been distributed to him, as represented by the market value of the stock he received as a dividend. On the other hand, if sufficient shares are issued so that the share market value of the stock is likely to be materially reduced, the minimum amount to be capitalized as described above does not apply. The distribution will then be more likely to be recognized as a form of stock split rather than as a distribution of income.

Retained earnings. It might seem, after the auditor has verified every other figure on the balance sheet, that retained earnings would simply be the balancing figure and would require no further verification. Under the double-entry system, however, the verification of all entries to the retained earnings account provides a valuable double check. For instance, a debit to an asset account may have been balanced by a credit to retained earnings. If the entry was improper, and if the debit was overlooked because it was buried among a large number of other debits, the transaction would still be brought to light through a careful analysis of entries to the retained earnings account. Another reason which makes the analysis of all entries to retained earnings of extreme importance is that the account is the basis for dividends, and it must therefore reflect only realized income from transactions other than the purchase or sale of the company's own stock. Finally, verification of all other balance sheet accounts, plus verification of all entries to retained earnings except net income, results in a highly important verification or confirmation of the key figure, net income for the year.

Credits to retained earnings. The principal credits to retained earnings should be for net income for the year, extraneous, nonrecurring gains taken directly to retained earnings, and reserves which are unneeded and are therefore being restored to the retained earnings account. Each of these can be readily verified as to amount, and the return of reserve to retained earnings should be traced to authorization by the board of directors.

Dividends. Of the possible debits to retained earnings, dividends can be expected to occur most frequently. The auditor should verify that dividends were paid on dates specified in the minutes of the board of directors. If the fiscal year closes between the date of the directors' meeting at which a dividend was declared and the date specified for payment, the auditor should ascertain that the dividend payable has been set up as a current liability. The amount of each dividend should be verified by applying the per-share amount declared to the number of shares outstanding at the record date, as was done on schedule TT-2. The data concerning the authorization of the dividend should be cross-referenced to the appropriate reference in the abstract of the minutes of the board of directors' meetings.

Reserves. Debits to retained earnings for the creation of reserves may either be authorized specifically by the board of directors, or they may result from a contractual agreement, as in the case of a loan agreement or a provision in the trust indenture covering bonds payable. Because the board would have approved such an agreement, no further approval would be necessary to set up the required reserve. In addition to verifying any entries to create or increase a reserve against the authorization for such entries, the auditor should satisfy himself in a general way that all reserves are serving a useful purpose and are reasonable in amount. Although any unnecessary or excessive reserves would not be likely to necessitate any qualification of the auditor's opinion, the auditor might wish to advise the client about the matter in the hope of inducing the client to make adjustments which would make the reserves more meaningful and realistic. As stated earlier, reserves established to provide for general contingencies or possible losses should be provided by an appropriation of retained earnings rather than by a charge against income. If losses do occur, they should not be charged against such reserves, but rather they should be treated in the customary manner, and any reserve balances no longer required should be returned to retained earnings.

In a first audit, all material entries affecting retained earnings since the inception of the business should be verified for approvals, accuracy of amount, and propriety.

Tie in Supporting Records with the Statement Amounts

Corporate charter. In an initial audit the corporate charter should always be read, and any matters having accounting implications should be abstracted and retained in the permanent file. Such matters would include a description of the various classes of stock which the company is authorized to issue, any special privileges or rights of the individual classes, and the number of shares of each class of stock which the corporation is authorized to issue. Such information is, of course, essential in determining the propriety of the client's presentation of capital stock amounts in the balance sheet.

Records of shares issued. When the issuance of stock certificates and the maintenance of stockholders' records are handled by the client rather than by an independent agent, the auditor will have to do considerably more work before he will be in a position to form an opinion on the client's statement figures. Typical procedures involving reference to supporting records would include preparing or verifying a trial balance of the stockholders' ledger and balancing the trial balance total with the general ledger record of the number of shares outstanding. Also, the stock certificate book should be examined and a total obtained of the number of shares shown as outstanding by each stub not accompanied by a cancelled or unissued certificate. This figure, likewise, should agree with the general ledger record. In examining the stock certificate book the auditor should be careful to note that no unissued certificates have been removed from the center or back of the book. When internal control is negligible and relatively few certificate changes have occurred, the auditor may find it desirable to account fully for each certificate issued since his previous examination. On transfers of ownership, this would involve examining the cancelled certificates surrendered in effecting the change.

If the client has engaged an independent transfer agent and/or registrar, written confirmation should be obtained of the number of shares of stock authorized and the number of shares of stock issued and outstanding. The transfer agent should also be asked to state the number of shares held in the name of the corporation to aid in the verification of any treasury stock. The auditor should examine any shares held in the treasury to verify their existence and to establish that the shares have not been placed to an unauthorized use.

Determine That Legal Requirements Have Been Observed and Rights of Various Parties Respected

Both legal requirements and questions of the rights of various groups who may have opposing interests are likely to be involved in almost any transaction affecting the stockholders' equity in a corporation. Even though the auditor is not expected to be an expert on such matters, he should at least recognize the more common requirements and problems and ascertain that they have been properly met or solved. If there are matters about which the auditor is in doubt, he should certainly seek the opinion of the client's attorney. Among the points which the auditor should be especially careful to watch for are the following:

1. Has the business been legally incorporated?

2. Have provisions of the corporate charter been adhered to concerning such matters as the type of activity the company is entitled to engage in and the classes of stock and number of shares which the company is authorized to issue?

3. Have any state stock transfer taxes been paid and the tax stamps properly handled?

4. Can unissued stock be sold at a discount?

5. Is the corporation permitted to re-acquire or retire outstanding stock?

6. Have any legal or contractual restrictions on the payment of dividends been observed? These might result from the acquisition of treasury stock, bond indenture agreements, or cumulative preferred dividends in arrears.

7. Have any restrictions on the use of retained earnings for the payment of dividends been mentioned in the balance sheet?

8. Has all contributed capital been separately accounted for and retained intact for the protection of creditors, unless distributions are permitted by state law?

Audit of Partnerships and Sole Proprietorships

One of the most important points that the auditor should watch for in the audit of an unincorporated business is the proper separation of business and personal transactions. Such transactions must be properly handled if the true income of the business is to be determined. Personal expenses paid from business funds should be charged against the owner's equity rather than as an expense of the business. Conversely, business expenses paid from personal funds must be brought into the business records. Tax considerations tend to foster the payment of personal expenses from business funds, particularly in the case of social activities which may have some limited business connection. Borderline cases are usually decided in favor of the treatment which will result in the lowest tax, with the additional advantage of pleasing the client. Excessively liberal treatment of such items may, however, work to the disadvantage of both the auditor and the client. The auditor's independence may be questioned, with a corresponding detrimental effect on his professional reputation. At the same time, the client's tax return is likely to be subjected to a more critical review if it becomes apparent that the client has taken excessive expense deductions.

In the examination of a partnership, the auditor should satisfy himself that the provisions of the partnership agreement have been carried out as they pertain to the distribution of net income and the maintenance of partners' capital and drawing accounts. Points likely to be covered in the agreement would include the basis of distributing profits, including any provisions for salaries or interest, maximum drawings permitted during the year, minimum capital balances to be maintained, additional capital to be contributed, and the treatment of loans by the partnership to or from the partners.

SUMMARY

Internal control

All transactions affecting the owners' equity of a corporation should be authorized by the board of directors, and the board should determine, when necessary, the dollar figures at which the transactions are to be recorded.

Preferably, stock issues and transfers, as well as stockholders' records, should be handled by an independent registrar and transfer agent.

If the company handles stock transactions itself, the following duties should be performed by separate individuals:

Custody of unissued stock certificates.

Countersignature of certificates as issued.

Posting of stockholders' ledger.

Statement presentation

Capital stock should be fully described, including indication of any preferences, par or stated value, and number of shares authorized, issued, outstanding, and reserved for special purposes.

Premium or discount on stock issued should be shown as a separate item but closely related to the capital stock amount.

Treasury shares should not ordinarily be carried as an asset, but the following methods of presentation are acceptable:

Deduct at cost from total capital stock and retained earnings.

Deduct at cost from retained earnings.

Deduct at par from capital stock issued.

Dividends should not be paid on treasury shares.

Gains on treasury stock transactions should not be included with retained earnings.

Increases in owners' equity resulting from asset write-ups or adjustment of depreciation for price-level changes should be separately presented and indicated as not available for dividends.

A supporting schedule should show the details of all changes in accounts during the year.

Material, extraordinary, nonrecurring gains and losses should be taken directly to retained earnings.

Appropriations of retained earnings may be identified as "reserves."

Restrictions on the availability of retained earnings for dividend distribution should be disclosed.

Retained earnings should be dated following a quasi-reorganization.

Audit objectives and procedures

Establish credibility of the accounting records.

Prepare an analysis of all changes in equity accounts.

Examine authorization for all transactions in minutes of board of directors.

Inspect supporting data for proceeds of sale of unissued or treasury stock, and trace proceeds to cash records and bank account.

Inspect paid checks in support of treasury stock purchases, and ascertain that purchases are at amounts specified by the board of directors.

Ascertain that the proper amount of retained earnings was capitalized in connection with stock dividends.

Review all entries to retained earnings for correct amount, conformity with generally accepted accounting principles, and board of directors' authorization if that is necessary.

Tie in supporting records with statement amounts.

Read corporate charter and excerpt pertinent provisions for permanent file.

Balance total shares outstanding as shown by the stockholders' ledger and stock certificate stubs with the capital stock account in the general ledger, or obtain confirmation of the number of shares outstanding from the independent registrar and transfer agent.

Determine that legal requirements have been observed and rights of various
parties respected.

Establish that the company is legally incorporated.

Ascertain that provisions of the corporate charter have been adhered to.

Verify proper handling of stock transfer taxes.

Ascertain that statutory or contractual requirements have been followed
in such matters as sale of stock at a discount, acquisition of outstanding stock, and declaration of dividends.

For partnerships or sole proprietorships, ascertain that personal and
business transactions have been kept separate and properly accounted
for.

For partnerships, ascertain that provisions of the partnership agreement
have been followed in the distribution of net income and the maintenance of minimum capital balances.

REVIEW QUESTIONS

1. What are the objectives of good internal control over owners' equity transactions?
2. Contrast the typical approach to internal control over capital stock transactions and records for a small corporation and for a large corporation.
3. What information should be shown on the stock certificate stubs?
4. Describe the responsibilities of a registrar and a transfer agent.
5. State the procedures which the internal auditor might perform in verifying
transactions and records concerning the stockholders' equity when the corporation handles the transactions and records.
6. What information should be included in the balance sheet concerning capital
stock?
7. Describe the three acceptable ways of showing treasury stock in the balance
sheet.
8. List the more common situations which would give rise to amounts of contributed capital in excess of par or stated value.
9. What disadvantage exists in the use of the combined statement of income and
retained earnings?
10. Describe and distinguish the two basically different concepts of income.
11. How should the creation and disposition of general purpose contingency reserves
be handled? Why?
12. In what ways may restrictions on retained earnings arise which would have
to be disclosed in the balance sheet?
13. What are the auditor's objectives in verifying the amount at which the owners'
equity is stated in the balance sheet?
14. What supporting records should be examined in support of the balance sheet
amount for capital stock when the client maintains the stock records?
15. Why is the verification of entries to the retained earnings account extremely
important?
16. For what points should the auditor watch to ascertain whether transactions

affecting the stockholders' equity have been in accordance with legal requirements and the rights of various groups?

17. What problem is often faced in the audit of unincorporated businesses?

QUESTIONS ON APPLICATION OF AUDITING STANDARDS

18. Prepare a memorandum covering your examination of capital stock on a repeat examination for a company that does not have an independent registrar and transfer agent. No shares of stock were reacquired or sold by the company during the year, although several changes of ownership occurred as a result of transactions by stockholders. A stockholders' ledger is maintained.

19. In the course of your December 31, 1967 audit of a client's machinery account, you discover that the following machine was sold for $10,000 cash on July 1, 1967:

Cost January 1, 1963 .... $100,000
Straight-line depreciation on 10-year estimated life
    recorded to December 31, 1967............................   50,000

Federal income taxes on recorded income for 1967 have already been recorded at the prevailing 50% rate, but capital gains and losses are subject to a 25% rate. The only entry made for the sale of the machine on July 1, 1967 was as follows:

Cash $10,000
Machinery $10,000

Give the adjusting entry or entries to correct the accounts in the auditor's working papers under each of the following assumptions:

(a) The client follows the all-inclusive concept of income.

(b) The client follows the current operating performance concept of income.

20. Your client handles all records pertaining to its capital stock, including the issuance of the stock certificates. During the year under examination, a 5% stock dividend was declared and issued. List the audit steps that you would apply in order to satisfy yourself concering this transaction.

21. Your client's records indicate that a gain was realized during the year you are examining, as a result of the sale of treasury shares that were purchased earlier in the same year.

(a) What audit procedures would you employ in satisfying yourself that the gain was properly recorded?

(b) How should the gain be shown in the financial statements?

22. You are engaged in making the audit of a corporation whose records have not previously been audited by you. The corporation has both an independent transfer agent and a registrar for its capital stock. The transfer agent maintains the record of stockholders and the registrar checks that there is no overissue of stock. Signatures of both are required to validate certificates.

It has been proposed that confirmations be obtained from both the transfer agent and the registrar as to the stock outstanding at the balance sheet date. If such confirmations agree with the books, no additional work is to be performed as to capital stock.

If you agree that obtaining the confirmations as suggested would be sufficient in this case, give the justification for your position. If you do not agree, state specifically all additional steps you would take and explain your reasons for taking them. (Uniform C.P.A. Examination)

23. What factors should be considered in determining whether the following items are proper charges to retained earnings for the year under examination?

Unabsorbed factory overhead due to plant shutdown for 2 months	$22,800
Damages in settlement of patent infringements occurring over the past 6 years	36,000
Cost of replacing defective parts in machines sold the previous year ..	7,800
Fire loss in excess of insurance carried........................	10,200

24. List the various circumstances which might result in a restriction of the availability of retained earnings for dividend distributions. For each, state how the auditor would ascertain that such a restriction existed.

25. Your client has retired a bond issue in the year under examination, and asks your recommendations as to what disposition to make of the sinking fund reserve which is no longer required. What would you advise?

PROBLEMS

26. You are a C.P.A. engaged in an examination of the financial statements of Pate Corporation for the year ended December 31, 1967. The financial statements and records of Pate Corporation have not been audited by a C.P.A. in prior years.

The stockholders' equity section of Pate Corporation's balance sheet at December 31, 1967 follows:

Stockholders' equity :

Capital stock—10,000 shares of $10 par value authorized; 5,000 shares issued and outstanding	$ 50,000
Capital contributed in excess of par value of capital stock	32,580
Retained earnings	47,320
Total stockholders' equity................................	$129,900

Pate Corporation was founded in 1961. The Corporation has ten stockholders and serves as its own registrar and transfer agent. There are no capital stock subscription contracts in effect.

Required:

(a) Prepare the detailed audit program for the examination of the three accounts comprising the Stockholders' Equity section of Pate Corporation's balance sheet. (Do not include in the audit program the verification of the results of the current year's operations.)

(b) After every other figure on the balance sheet has been audited by the C.P.A., it might appear that the retained earnings figure is a balancing figure and requires no further verification. Why does the C.P.A. verify retained earnings as he does the other figures on the balance sheet? *Discuss.* (Uniform C.P.A. Examination)

27. On February 1, 1968 when your audit and report is nearly complete, the president of the Sundex Corporation asks you to prepare statistical schedules of comparative financial data for the past five years for inclusion in the Company's annual report. Your working papers reveal the following information:

1. Income statements show net income amounts as follows:

> 1963—$20,000*
> 1964—(17,000) (loss)
> 1965— 30,000
> 1966— 38,000
> 1967— 42,000**

* Includes extraordinary gain of $8,000.
** Includes an unfavorable income tax adjustment of $5,000 applicable to 1965.

2. On January 1, 1963 there were outstanding 1,000 shares of common stock, par value $100, and 500 shares of 6% cumulative preferred stock, par value $50.
3. A 5% dividend was paid in common stock to common stockholders on December 31, 1964. The fair market value of the stock was $150 per share at the time.
4. Four hundred shares of common stock were issued on March 31, 1965 to purchase another company.
5. A dividend of cumulative preferred stock was distributed to common stockholders on July 1, 1965. One share of preferred stock was distributed for every five shares of common stock held. The fair market value of the preferred stock was $55 per share before the distribution and $53 per share immediately after the distribution.
6. The common stock was split 2-for-1 on December 31, 1966 and December 31, 1967.
7. Cash dividends are paid on the preferred stock on June 30 and December 31. Preferred stock dividends were paid in each year except 1964; the 1964 and 1965 dividends were paid in 1965.
8. Cash dividends on common stock are paid semiannually. Dividends paid per share of stock outstanding at the respective dates were:

	June 30	December 31
1963	$ .50	$ .50
1964	None	None
1965	.75	.75
1966	1.00	.50*
1967	.75	.75**

* After 2-for-1 split.
** Before 2-for-1 split.

Required:
  (a) In connection with your preparation of the statistical schedule of comparative financial data for the past five years
    1. Prepare a schedule computing the number of shares of common stock and preferred stock outstanding as of the respective year-end dates.

2. Prepare a schedule computing the current equivalent number of shares of common stock outstanding as of the respective year-end dates. The current equivalent shares means the number of shares outstanding in the respective prior periods in terms of the present stock position.

3. Compute the total cash dividends paid to holders of preferred stock and to holders of common stock for each of the five years.

(b) Prepare a five-year summary of financial statistics to be included in the annual report. The summary should show by years "Net Income (or Loss)," "Earnings per Share of Common Stock" and "Dividends per Share of Common Stock." Include any explanatory footnotes considered necessary.   (Uniform C.P.A. Examination)

28. You are a senior accountant responsible for the annual audit of Black, Inc., for the year ended 12/31/67. The information available to you is presented below. You may assume that any pertinent information not presented below has already been checked and found satisfactory.

(1) Excerpts from Trial Balance 12/31/67

	Debit	Credit
Surplus .... $		$40,000
Inventory reserve		7,500
Capital stock (600 shares).......................		60,000

(2) The books have not been closed but all adjusting entries which the company expects to make have been posted. Their trial balance shows a $15,000 net profit for the year.

(3) Selected Ledger Accounts

Surplus

8/ 6 /67	CD62	$ 160	12/31/66	Balance	$52,960
10/10/67	J34	10,000	4/29/67	CR8	200
12/31/67	J40	3,000			

(Note: The balance at 12/31/66 agrees with last year's working papers and represents the net difference over the years between credits from the profit and loss account and debits for dividends.)

Inventory reserve

9/26/67	CD78	$500	6/30/67	J19	$ 5,000
			12/31/67	J40	3,000

(4) Analysis of Selected Cash Receipts

Date	Page	Account credited	Explanation	Amount
4/29/67	8	{ Capital stock	Sold $100 par stock @ $102	$10,000
		{ Surplus		200
10/10/67	20	Building	See J34	20,000

(5) Analysis of Selected Cash Disbursements

Date	Page	Account debited	Explanation	Amount
8/6/67	62	Surplus	Freak accident to company truck not covered by insurance; repair by Doe & Co.	$ 160
9/26/67	78	{ Inventory reserve	Purchase of materials (X Co.) to be used on orders taken prior	500
		Purchases	to 6/30/67. $500 is price increase since 6/30/67.	6,300

(6) Selected Entries in General Journal

Date	Page	Entry and Explanation	Debit	Credit
6/30/67	19	Inventory loss (P & L)	$ 5,000	
		Inventory reserve		$ 5,000
		Provision voted by Board of Directors for estimated future price increases in materials needed to complete orders on hand. (Note: Orders do not represent contractual obligations.)		
10/10/67	34	Reserve for depreciation	50,000	
		Surplus	10,000	
		Building		60,000
		Sale of main office bldg., moved to rental quarters downtown. (See CR20)		
12/31/67	40	Surplus	3,000	
		Inventory reserve		3,000
		Provision to value materials inventory at lower of cost or market in accordance with company pricing policy.		

Cost $30,000
Market 27,000
$ 3,000

You are to prepare the following in good form:

(a) Schedule of recommended adjusting entries to be placed on the books to state the Stockholders' equity accounts in accordance with accepted accounting principles.

(b) Statement of Retained Earnings for 1967.

(c) Stockholders' equity section of balance sheet.

(Uniform C.P.A. Examination)

29. (a) The board of directors of Tabac, Inc., not a closely-held corporation, declared an "ordinary stock dividend" equal to 5 per cent of the corporation's outstanding common stock, to be issued to common stockholders of record as of April 15, 1967. The corporation's treasury stock was to be used for this purpose to the extent available. The market value of the common stock just prior to the declaration was $64 per share and remained at substantially that figure for more than a month after the issuance of the dividend shares.

The corporation's equity accounts at the dates of declaration and record included the following balances:

Preferred stock, $5 cumulative (no par), authorized 25,000 shares; in treasury 130 shares; outstanding 10,402 shares	$1,053,200
Common stock (par $50), authorized 50,000 shares; in treasury 880 shares; outstanding 27,780 shares	1,433,000
Paid in surplus—amounts contributed in excess of par value of common shares	251,464
Retained earnings	963,425
Treasury stock, $5 cumulative preferred (at cost)	14,922
Treasury stock, common (at cost)	40,920

At the time of declaration, the board directed that retained earnings in the amount of the aggregate par value of the dividend shares be transferred to the appropriate permanent capital accounts.

You are to:

(1) Prepare an entry which will record the net effect of the board's actions.

(2) The Institute's committee on accounting procedure has made certain recommendations for the consideration of boards of directors in situations similar to that outlined in this problem. Discuss the Tabac board's action relating to the retained earnings transfer in the light of the committee's recommendations. Include in your discussion the gist of such of the committee's recommendations as pertain to the retained earnings transfer, the reasons advanced by the committee for its recommendations, and the propriety of the board's transfer at par value.

(3) Assuming that the entry in (1) had not been made and that the board had followed the committee's recommendations, prepare an entry which will give effect to the issuance of the dividend stock in accordance with the recommendations.

(b) Assume the same facts as set forth in *a*, except that the dividend declaration equalled 40 per cent (instead of 5 per cent) of the outstanding common shares and had resulted in a substantial reduction in the market value of the common shares of Tabac, Inc.

What are the committee's recommendations in such a case? Does the board's transfer of retained earnings on a par value basis conflict with or conform to these recommendations? *Explain.*

(Uniform C.P.A. Examination)

30. The Jordan Company handles the issuance and transfer of its capital stock, maintaining in addition to the general ledger account a stockholder ledger, and a stock certificate book in which stubs are provided to record the necessary information concerning the outstanding certificates. Cancelled certificates are attached to the stubs.

Based on the following accounts and supplementary information, prepare audit work papers showing the extent of your examination of the following accounts. You are making a regular repeat examination of the financial statements as of December 31.

Capital Stock, Authorized 50,000 Shares
$10 Par Value

Jan. 1	Balance forward	$	$	$250,000
July 1	Stock dividend J7-13		125,000	375,000

Capital Paid in on Capital Stock in Excess of Par Value

| Jan. 1 | Balance forward | $ | $ | $ 37,500 |
| July 1 | Stock dividend J7-13 | | 18,750 | 56,250 |

Retained Earnings

Jan. 1	Balance forward	$	$	$364,208
Mar. 31	Dividend paid CD 37	12,500		351,708
July 1	Stock dividend J7-13	143,750		207,958
Sept. 30	Dividend paid CD 96	18,750		189,208
Dec. 31	Profit and loss J12-15		51,297	240,505

Excerpts from minutes of Board of Directors:

Meeting Date	Action Taken
March 15	Approved cash dividend of 50¢ per share payable March 31 to stockholders of record March 25.
June 13	Approved stock dividend at rate of one share for two shares held payable July 1 to stockholders of record June 25. Amount per share capitalized to be equal to proceeds per share on all stock outstanding.
Sept. 15	Approved cash dividend of 50¢ per share payable September 30 to stockholders of record September 25.

On June 25 there were 27 stockholders. Last stock certificate issued during the year was No. 103. The working papers for the previous year state that stock certificate No. 73 was the last certificate issued, and all subsequent numbers were in the certificate book and unissued.

Other audit considerations;
electronic data processing

22

The preceding chapters have covered the essential aspects of the auditor's examination of a client's balance sheet and income statement for the purpose of expressing an informed opinion on the acceptability of those statements. In this chapter certain miscellaneous audit procedures necessary to complete the audit are covered, and a general over-all review is given of the auditor's objectives and his approach to the audit engagement. The final portions of the chapter deal with certain internal and professional considerations relating to the audit engagement and conclude with a brief discussion of the problems of auditing records maintained under electronic data-processing methods.

COMPLETING THE AUDIT

Verification of Postings to General Ledger Accounts

The financial statements covered by the auditor's opinion are based on the balances of the various general ledger accounts. In the course of his examination the auditor will have referred to various forms of evidence supporting entries to the general ledger accounts and the balances of the accounts. To complete his examination of the accounts the auditor should make tests which will assure him that all entries to the general ledger originated from sources which have been tested by him and which he is satisfied are accurate and appropriate.

The best way for the auditor to satisfy himself concerning the general ledger postings is to select one month of the year and trace all figures shown in such source records as journals, journal vouchers, or worksheets to the corresponding entries in the general ledger. Each ledger entry verified in this manner should be tick-marked neatly, and in such a fashion as to avoid incurring the animosity of the general ledger bookkeeper, who may take considerable pride in the neat appearance of the general ledger. Also, each entry should be reviewed in a general way to determine that it appears proper and reasonable.

After all source records have been covered by the above test, the auditor should review each general ledger account for the test month to be certain that all entries have been tick-marked. This procedure is the final and vital step in determining that all entries during the month were valid and originated from appropriate sources. Any entries not ticked should be carefully investigated, as they would suggest that unauthorized entries had been made to the ledger—possibly to cover a defalcation, to conceal an out-of-balance condition, or to manipulate the records to show a more favorable financial or operating picture.

The reader may wonder at the apparent duplication implied by the above test, because tests of entries to the general ledger were also mentioned in connection with the examination of the various balance sheet and income statement accounts under the objective relating to the credibility of the accounting records. It is true that these tests could all be made covering the same month, and the ledger entries tick-marked as described above. The difficulty, however, lies in the fact that all the work could not be done at one time. The general ledger would have to be released from the auditor's control during the course of the work, and when the work was finally finished the auditor would have no way of knowing whether the tick marks were his own or ones added by someone else to give an appearance of validity to a fraudulent entry.

Minutes of Directors' and Stockholders' Meetings

At numerous points in the preceding chapters reference was made to matters which would be found in the minutes of meetings of the board of directors or stockholders. Included were such items as authorization of plant expenditures, approval of contracts with other companies or individuals, authorization of loans or sale of capital stock, declaration of dividends, appointments of officers, and designation of compensation to officers. The importance of the actions and matters considered at stockholders' and directors' meetings suggests the need for the auditor to be fully informed about those matters if he is to be in a position to express an unqualified opinion on a client's financial statements.

To gain the required information the auditor should request permission to read the minutes, and he should abstract all matters which have a bearing on the financial statements. Those notations should then be cross-referenced to the working paper schedules which are affected, as was done on schedule XX. In a first audit for the client, the auditor should read all minutes since the inception of the business, although fewer items will be abstracted in the working papers than in the case of minutes for the current year. Matters of only momentary importance, such as the authorization of officers' salaries or short-term loans, would be ignored; however, actions authorizing new bank accounts and designating persons empowered to sign checks on those accounts, declaring dividends, authorizing the sale of stock, revaluing assets, or adjusting any account balances are examples of items which should be noted.

The importance to the auditor of having full knowledge of such matters is so great that should the client decline to permit the auditor to examine the minute books, the auditor should probably conclude that he cannot safely express a favorable opinion on the client's financial statements. The fact that other phases of his audit examination revealed no exceptions or differences would not change the situation.

A reason the client might give in denying the auditor access to the minute books might be the confidential nature of important actions recorded in the minutes. The very fact that those matters are important is, of course, the principal reason why the auditor should have knowledge of them, and the client should have no fear that the auditor will commit a breach of confidence. The auditor's professional practice is contingent, among other things, upon his ability to treat confidentially all information concerning the affairs of his client, and the code of professional ethics by which he is governed further evidences that fact (rule 1.03).

To stress the importance of making the minutes of all meetings available to the auditor, many auditors ask the secretary of the client corporation to prepare a letter addressed to the auditor listing all meetings of the board of directors and stockholders held since the auditor's previous examination. In that letter, the secretary is also asked to state that the full and complete record of those meetings has been presented to the auditor for his inspection. This minute letter should be filed with the auditor's abstract of the minutes as evidence of the client's actions. The auditor is then protected if subsequent events should prove that the audited statements were incorrect or misleading, and that the sole evidence of the true facts was contained in the minutes of a directors' or stockholders' meeting which were not presented to the auditor for his scrutiny.

The availability of some form of copying equipment in most offices suggests the possibility of obtaining an actual copy of the minutes in place of an abstract such as on XX.

Review of Subsequent Events

The auditor's certificate specifically states that it pertains to a balance sheet for a given date and the related income statement for a period ending on the balance sheet date. Nevertheless, the auditor is generally held to be responsible for disclosing events occurring after the balance sheet date which have an important bearing on the financial statements. The period of responsibility for such disclosure ordinarily extends to the date of the auditor's certificate. *Statement on Auditing Procedure No. 25* (Chapter 11 of *Auditing Standards and Procedures*) deals in considerable detail with this problem of events subsequent to the financial statements.

Types of events. Three types of events which may occur after the balance sheet date should receive the auditor's attention. The first of these types has already been referred to in the preceding chapters dealing with the examination of statement figures. Included would be such events as the subsequent collection of a large account receivable which had appeared doubtful of collection at the balance sheet date, the initiation of bankruptcy proceedings against a customer with a large accounts receivable balance on the client's books, the payment of a major liability which had not been recorded at the balance sheet date, and events covered by the usual cut-off tests. The auditor's regular examination procedures should be designed to reveal all such subsequent events, and the auditor is expected to make full use of the information. Financial statement figures should, of course, be adjusted to reflect such subsequent events.

The second type of event which might occur subsequent to the balance sheet date would not require adjustment of the statements although it would affect future statements. Nevertheless, the events should be disclosed by footnote in the current statements in view of the significance these events might have to a person attempting to reach a decision based on the financial statements. Examples would be the subsequent sale of a large bond issue with restrictive covenants, merger with another company, disposal of a large portion of the client's productive assets, or serious losses resulting from fire, flood, or other casualty.

The third type of subsequent event has no direct accounting implications, and disclosure is not usually made of such events. The auditor should, however, be fully aware of the existence of these events and should carefully weigh the need for disclosure. Examples of the type of event in question would include changes in management, product changes, strikes, unionization, and loss of important customers. There are two reasons why such events are not usually disclosed. One is that even if they occurred before the balance sheet date, they would not directly enter into the financial statements. The second reason is that mention of such events might cause the reader to puzzle over the inference intended to be drawn from the comment. For instance, the reader would probably wonder whether a reference to a change in management was intended to indicate a favorable or an unfavorable condition. Although no reference might be made to events of this type in the financial statements, the auditor should know about the events, because they are likely to explain variations in the operating and financial results during the succeeding year.

Responsibility for disclosure. When events of any of the three types occur, the primary responsibility for making any needed disclosure in the financial statements rests with management. The auditor should, however, extend certain audit procedures to cover the period between the balance sheet date and the date of his report, because he is obligated to make independent verification of the adequacy of the disclosures made by management. Should the auditor discover events which he feels require disclosure, and the client refuse to make such disclosure, the auditor should take recourse in the content of his certificate. He may disclose the events in his certificate or he may qualify his opinion concerning the fairness of the financial statements.

Audit procedures. Audit procedures to be used by the auditor in reviewing events occurring subsequent to the balance sheet date would include the following:

1. Review of bank statements for evidence of returned checks.
2. Review of accounts receivable collections.
3. Review of cash receipts book for proceeds of loans or significant sales of inventory or plant assets.
4. Review of general journal for material entries.
5. Review of any interim financial statements which the client has prepared.
6. Review of minutes of directors' or stockholders' meetings.
7. Inquiry of management concerning events which may have occurred.

As suggested earlier, the auditor's responsibility for disclosure of subsequent events extends to the date of his report in most instances, and the date of his report should therefore correspond with the date the auditor's work in the client's office was completed. If the report cannot be issued until a much later date and the auditor wishes to have the report date correspond with the actual issuance of the report, he should include a statement that his report is based on field work completed at an earlier date.

Signed Copy of Client's Financial Statements

Although the practice is not universal, it will usually be advantageous for the auditor to obtain a signed copy of the client's financial statements in their final form. The principal officer of the client, and possibly the chief accounting or financial officer as well, should sign the statements, with a notation that they are the final statements for the year. If the client does not prepare his own financial statements but relies on the auditor to do so, a copy of the statements prepared by the auditor should be accepted and signed by the appropriate officer or officers.

There are two reasons for obtaining signed financial statements. One is to impress upon the client his primary responsibility for the statements. The second is to protect the auditor from any complaint by the client that the statements in the auditor's report do not agree with those the client has prepared. In view of the second reason the auditor should, of course, make certain that the signed statements actually do agree with the statements to be presented with the auditor's report.

List of Adjusting Entries to Be Recorded by the Client

Almost invariably the auditor's examination will reveal adjustments to be made to the client's records. The auditor should prepare a copy of the adjustments shown in his working papers for use by the client in making the necessary adjusting entries. If any of the entries relate to transactions already recorded by the client in the following period, the' auditor may also find it desirable to give the client a list of reversing entries to be made. If the auditor has maintained the proper distinction in his working papers between adjusting entries and reclassification entries, only the adjusting entries need be given to the client.

In England, the auditor is required to state that the financial statements in his report agree with the client's books, and thus the client must make all adjusting entries which the auditor has made in his working papers. Although no such requirement exists in the United States, the auditor will usually be well advised to follow the requirement as nearly as possible. One difficulty often stands in the way, however. The client will usually have closed his books for the year being audited and will have begun entering transactions for the following year before the auditor has concluded his examination. Under those circumstances, adjustments affecting income or expense can be made to the retained earnings account.

The auditor may find it greatly to his advantage to verify the posting of the adjustments after they have been made. If the adjustments have not been made, or if they have been made incorrectly, the audit for the following year will be complicated accordingly.

Representation Letter

As a final step in the audit process, many auditors ask their clients to sign what is known as a *representation letter*. The representation letter is merely an expanded version of the liability letter discussed in the chapter on liabilities. Its purpose has been described as follows:

> The information shown by written representations would have to be obtained, where pertinent, either orally or in writing. Reducing it to writing provides evidence, avoids misunderstandings, and has the additional advantage of reminding the client of his primary responsibility for the correctness of the statements. There is no evidence that the representations are regarded as relieving the independent auditor of any his audit functions or responsibilities. The purpose is

rather to secure the active cooperation of the client. They complement, rather than substitute for, a proper examination, and every practicable means should be used to substantiate the information developed by the inquiries.*

The following example illustrates a possible form for such a representation letter.

January 29, 19—

Black and Decker
Certified Public Accountants
Kansas City, Missouri

This letter is furnished in connection with your examination of our financial statements for the year ended December 31, 19—. The purpose of the letter is to give you our assurance that to the best of our knowledge and belief the company's accounts and financial statements have been maintained and prepared in such a manner as to properly present the financial position and results of operations of this company. In this connection we make the following representations, which we understand have been or will be reviewed or checked by your representatives within the normal scope of your examination of our accounts:

1. The company has satisfactory title to all assets, and all mortgages or other liens outstanding against the assets have been recorded in the accounts.

2. Raw materials, work in process, finished goods, and supplies have been physically inventoried at October 31, 19—, and the accounts were adjusted to agree with the physical inventory.

3. All inventories were priced at the lower of cost or market, and adequate provision was made for obsolete or otherwise unsalable items.

4. The carrying value of all property, plant, and equipment which was retired, abandoned, sold, or otherwise disposed of at December 31, 19—, has been removed from the accounts.

5. The depreciation provided during the year and the amount of accumulated depreciation at December 31, 19—, were adequate to cover the amortization of the cost of property, plant, and equipment over the life expectancy of those assets.

6. The company had no unrecorded or contingent assets of material amount at December 31, 19—.

7. To the best of our knowledge all known or ascertainable direct liabilities of the company at December 31, 19—, have been recorded in the accounts at that date, with the exception of minor items that are carried forward from month to month in ordinary operations.

8. The company had no material contingent liabilities that were not provided for in the accounts at December 31, 19—, except as set forth below:

Kind of Contingent Liability	*Amount if Determinable*
Upon customers' or other notes that were discounted, sold, or otherwise transferred	
Upon drafts negotiated	

* *Codification of Statements on Auditing Procedure,* American Institute of Certified Public Accountants, 1951, p. 49.

For Federal or state income taxes
For accommodation endorsements
For guarantees of notes or securities
   of other issuers
For guarantees of company products
   or service
Upon leases
Under repurchase agreements
Under contracts or purchase agreements
Under profit sharing arrangements
Under pending lawsuits
For all other contingent liabilities of
   any nature

9. The company has entered into purchase commitments that approximated $350,000 at December 31, 19—, which have arisen in the normal course of operations and contain no unusual amounts.
10. Amounts due from directors, officers, or stockholders have been identified as such in the accounts.
11. The company has no shares of its capital stock reserved for officers and employees, options, warrants, conversions, or other requirements.
12. All transactions reflected in the accounting records have resulted from negotiations conducted at arm's length, and there has been no participation by management in outside concerns involved in significant purchase and sale transactions.

President (or executive officer)

Treasurer (or chief financial
officer)

Controller (or chief accounting
officer)

All accounts are stated in conformity with generally accepted accounting principles, which have been applied on a basis consistent with that of the preceding year.

Controller (or chief accounting
officer)

AUDITING REVISITED—OR ONCE OVER LIGHTLY

The preceding section concludes the discussion of the examination of financial statements by the independent auditor. The two following chapters deal with the auditor's final responsibility: preparation of the report on his examination. At this transition point it seems advisable to reconsider briefly, from an over-all point of view, what has preceded.

In making his examination of a client's financial statements the auditor's principal objective is to determine whether he is justified in giving his endorsement to those statements in his short-form report, or certificate. The primary responsibility for the accuracy and fairness of the statements rests with the client, and the client retains the final right to determine the form and contents of the statements. If the auditor is not satisfied with the statements as they have been prepared by the client, and if the client refuses to change them, the auditor's recourse is through qualification of his certificate. The client is similarly privileged to set the scope of the auditor's examination if he so desires, but he must be content with a qualified auditor's certificate if the restrictions he places upon the auditor make it impossible for the auditor to formulate a satisfactory opinion about the financial statements.

The auditor's approach to the examination should be positive; that is, he should undertake the examination with the idea of proving that the client's figures are correct and that the statement presentation is acceptable. The auditor's first step is to ascertain the manner in which the client has arrived at the final accounting figures. The intended and actual accounting and office routines as they affect the accounts are reviewed from the standpoint of internal control, which includes such matters as the division of duties among employees, internal reports to management, and, in larger organizations, internal auditing.

The soundness of the client's internal control directly affects the probable accuracy and reliability of the accounting figures, and the auditor accordingly adjusts the scope of his examination in relation to his conclusions concerning the system of internal control. In making his examination the auditor gathers necessary evidence by retracing the various steps taken by the client, usually in reverse order. That is, he traces figures from the final financial statements to supporting worksheets, then to the general ledger accounts, and in support of the general ledger entries he examines the various books of original entry. The mathematical accuracy of these books is tested, individual entries are traced to supporting documents, and finally the original authorizations for the transactions are examined to complete the chain of evidence. Physical evidence or externally created documentary evidence should also be referred to whenever possible to corroborate the book figures.

As the auditor relates supporting evidence to the transactions and account balances, he must be watchful that generally accepted accounting principles have been applied on a basis consistent with that of the preceding year, and he must be alert for facts which will affect the presentation of the accounts in the financial statements.

The auditor must be careful, too, that in making his examination he does not become overly absorbed in the mass of details which are present. In addition to proper attention to details, a successful audit requires a thorough understanding of the client's business and its operation, and of the external factors which affect the business. One of the auditor's first requests as he begins a new audit should be to have one of the company officers escort him on a tour through the plant. The purpose of such a tour should be to lend additional meaning to the accounting figures and to enable the auditor to gain a clearer picture of company operations.

Discussion with key executives should give the auditor valuable information about problems the company is facing. Such information will help to explain the variations the auditor will notice in comparing figures with previous years or in analyzing month-to-month changes. The auditor should also supplement his understanding of the client's internal affairs with a knowledge of external factors affecting the client. These would include sales trends in the industry, price trends, the vigor of competition in the industry, the availability of raw materials, long-term prospects for the industry, and new developments in product design and use of materials, to mention only a few possibilities.

If the auditor is adequately supplied with this type of information, and is thoroughly acquainted with the client's operations, he can be confident that such understanding, coupled with the careful performance of the verification phases of his examination, will give him a sound basis for the expression of an opinion on the client's financial statements.

As a final step, the working papers, financial statements, and audit report should be carefully reviewed by the principal or manager supervising the work. The reviewer should be satisfied that the examination was conducted in accordance with generally accepted auditing standards, and that the financial statements reflect generally accepted accounting principles applied on a basis consistent with that of the preceding year. The review of the working papers is particularly important, and along with the question of the adequacy of the examination that was made, the reviewer should watch for "loose ends," unanswered questions, and any suggestion of deference to the client's wishes in auditing or accounting matters. Perhaps the ultimate question in making such a review becomes, "Is there anything in the working papers that an opposing attorney in a legal action might use against us?"

PRELIMINARIES TO THE AUDIT ENGAGEMENT

As mentioned earlier, it is desirable that audit engagements gravitate to the auditor solely on the basis of his professional reputation. Such an arrangement helps to assure those desiring professional accounting services of the best possible satisfaction of their needs. A number of the rules of professional conduct of the public accounting profession are designed to help accomplish this objective. Examples (see Appendix B) include rule 3.04, which prohibits the accountant from paying commissions to persons not members of the profession for work referred to the accountant; rule 3.02, which forbids the accountant directly or indirectly to solicit clients; rule 3.01, which prohibits the accountant from advertising his services; and rule 3.03, which prohibits the accountant from making competitive bids for engagements.

Obtaining Clients

For the person who may someday hope to enter the public accounting profession as an individual practitioner, the preceding comments are likely to pose this question: "If I can't advertise, if I can't solicit clients, and if I can't compete with established accountants by bidding for the work that is available, how can I ever hope to establish a practice?" Perhaps the easiest and most obvious ways of obtaining a practice are to buy an existing practice or to obtain employment with an existing practitioner who is seeking someone to take over the practice. Usually, however, the public accountant seeking to have his own practice must plan to establish his practice the slow, hard way and accept a very meager income as he attempts to build up his prestige.

Because clients are expected to seek out the accountant, obviously the person with the greatest circle of friends and acquaintances in the business world has the best initial chances of success. To capitalize on this potential advantage, however, the individual must have demonstrated in the past, through his college record, past employment, and personal contacts, that he is a capable accountant, and he must serve his clients in such a way that opinions as to his ability are strengthened rather than weakened.

Attorneys and bankers are usually the best source of referrals to the practitioner, second only in importance to an enthusiastic group of well-satisfied clients. Contact with potential clients, attorneys, and bankers can be gained through memberships in country clubs and fraternal organizations, but these memberships are not necessarily the best way of making such contacts, and certainly they are not the only way. The active worker in a civic club is assured of gaining attention and respect for his ability, and the same is true of good workers in church organizations and fund drives for charitable or civic purposes. The young public accountant is likely to be asked to serve as treasurer or auditor of these organizations, thus presenting the best possible opportunity for demonstrating his professional skills.

Speeches before civic clubs or other groups are certainly an excellent way of presenting oneself to other members of the business community. Such opportunities cannot, of course, be solicited, but a hint can be dropped on occasion, and tax information is always in demand during the tax season. Newspaper or magazine articles can be prepared and submitted without a specific request, and if accepted are likely to result in recognition to the writer and invitations to discuss similar matters before various groups.

Establishing a Regular Source of Income

Because early progress in the profession tends to be quite slow, many practitioners begin on a part-time basis while they are holding another job. Teaching lends itself well to this type of arrangement, but even an industrial accounting job offers many free evening and week-end hours. Employment with a public accounting firm should not be considered, however, for it would hardly be ethical for a person to compete with his own employer.

For the person who plans to enter the profession immediately on a 100 per cent basis, several "bookkeeping" or "monthly write-up" jobs are almost essential to assure some steady income, even though the income may be somewhat meager. This type of work is sometimes rather disparagingly referred to as "professional bookkeeping" rather than true public accounting, and although the work requires less professional skill than many other types of public accounting services, the work is important to both the profession and its clients—and rightly so. In larger cities, another possible source of regular income is night-school teaching, and occasionally some daytime teaching may be available. In the case of bookkeeping service, however, the young practitioner must be careful not to become overly engrossed in his work. He should not get into a situation in which he may not have time to accept other types of engagements for which he is peculiarly qualified and which present a greater challenge and proportionately greater income. Also, preoccupation with a regular task may cause the individual to lose the perspective and vision required to handle major accounting problems and to neglect his reading of current literature and his activities in his professional organizations.

Fees

When a request for his services comes to the accountant, through either personal acquaintance or the recommendation of others, several things are likely to happen. First, after the nature of the required services is made known, the accountant is likely to be asked for an estimate of his fees. The accountant may properly give such an estimate if he has no knowledge that the prospective client is also considering estimates from other accountants. For his own protection, however, the accountant should make it clear that it is difficult to estimate accurately such fees in advance, and that the final fee, based on the accountant's regular per diem rates, may be more or less than the estimate. The accountant will, however, be under considerable pressure to keep the final fee from exceeding the estimate.

Per diem rates vary with the size of the firm, the locality, and the experience of the accountant. A reasonable range of fees for the junior accountant would be from $30 to $60 per day; for the senior accountant, from $40 to $100 per day; for the manager, from $50 to $150 per day; and for the partner of a well-established accounting firm, from $60 to $250 per day. For the individual practitioner who is just entering into practice, the fees would tend to be about on a par with those for the senior staff accountant. For out-of-town engagements the client is also charged for the accountant's travel and living expenses.

The reader who is planning on entering the profession as an employee of an accounting firm should not mistakenly assume that his salary will approximate the rate at which his time is charged to the client. Staff accountants' compensation tends to vary between about forty per cent and fifty per cent of their daily billing rate. The partner of the accounting firm does, of course, receive as profit some of the difference between the staff man's salary and billing rate. The bulk of the difference, however, is consumed by "lost time" when the staff man is not working on a regular engagement, the cost of staff training, vacation and sick pay, payroll taxes, and office overhead expenses.

Time Estimates

The time estimate for completing an audit engagement is an important factor in the control and supervision of the engagement and in keeping fee charges to the client at an acceptable level. The total estimate is usually built up by estimating the time to be required for each step of the audit program. In the case of a repeat engagement, the detailed time records of the work for the preceding year will be an important factor in setting the new estimates. Modifications should be made, however, if the total time for the preceding year was excessive, if special conditions present during the preceding year will no longer be a factor, or if special conditions are anticipated for the current year.

The pressure to complete a job within the time estimate, or at the lowest cost to the client, is a significant aspect of public accounting, and the prospective employee or practitioner should either be prepared to expect and accept such pressure or he should plan on entering some line of work other than public accounting. The pressure is always present and is often severe, even to the extent that promotion or professional success will usually hinge on whether the accountant can work fast enough to keep within the time estimate. The reader should not falsely assume, however, that the time estimate, once set, determines how the job is to be done. Adaptability to conditions as they actually exist is essential to the successful completion of an audit. The tail cannot be permitted to wag the dog.

If, however, time estimates are exceeded, the accountant should be prepared to give any explanation or justification which may exist for the overrun. Acceptable explanations would include an increased volume of transactions, disorderly files and records which required additional time to locate documents and substantiate account balances or entries, or an expanded scope required by unexpected deficiencies in the client's internal control. Then, too, in some cases the senior may have to report that the cause of the overrun was the inability of one of his assistants to perform the required work in a reasonable amount of time. In other cases, the manager or partner may be forced to conclude that the cause was the inability of the senior properly to organize and supervise the work.

Confirmation of Arrangements for the Conduct of the Audit Engagement

The beginning point in any audit is the initial contact between the accountant and the client. This initial contact is especially important in the case of a new client, as compared with a client who has been served for many years. In either case, however, the accountant must fully understand the needs of the client. Merely agreeing to "make an audit" is certain to result in misunderstanding, confusion, and disagreement during the conduct of the engagement. The accountant should know exactly what it is that the client wants and expects, although frequently the accountant may find that what the client actually *needs* is something entirely different.

The importance of these matters should suggest that the initial contact should usually be made between a partner of the accounting firm and the principal officer of the client. In the case of a new client, the first contact may be followed by an interval of several days during which a representative of the accounting firm will review the records and reports of the client. Only after this review is completed will any concrete recommendations or proposals be made to the client. For a recurring engagement, however, a telephone conversation may be adequate to complete all arrangements.

In either event, the understanding which is finally reached should encompass the terms of the engagement, the way in which it is to be conducted, and the fees to be charged. Because the accountant will have had more experience in these matters than his client, it is his responsibility to broaden the area of understanding to include any points which experience has taught him may be the cause of controversies at a later date. Of particular importance is the question of whether the client wants or needs an unqualified certificate covering his financial statements. If an unqualified certificate is desired, the client should understand that the auditor will then be obligated to undertake the relatively costly procedures of confirming receivables and observing and testing the taking of the physical inventory.

Once a final agreement has been reached, a formal letter confirming the arrangements is usually written to the client. A copy of the letter in the audit files then serves to inform the senior accountant about what is to be done. The example below illustrates such a letter.

October 5, 19—

Machine Products Co.
Wichita, Kansas

    This letter confirms the understanding reached yesterday between R. H. French, president of Machine Products Co., and A. B. Decker, a partner of this firm.

    We are to make an examination of the financial statements of Machine Products Co. as of December 31, 19—, and to render to you our opinion on those statements. The examination is to be conducted in accordance with generally accepted auditing standards, and will include such tests of the accounting records and such other auditing procedures as we may consider necessary. It is not contemplated that we shall make a detailed examination of all transactions, such as would be necessary to disclose any defalcations or irregularities which may have occurred. We shall, however, advise you of any findings which appear unusual or abnormal, and we shall thoroughly review the system of internal control. Our comments on your system of internal control will be furnished to you in a separate memorandum.

    Our charges for this examination will be at our usual per diem rates, plus any out-of-pocket expenses for traveling or similar items that are incurred.

    Your decision to entrust this examination to us is greatly appreciated. You may be certain that every phase of the examination will receive our most careful attention.

Very truly yours,
Black and Decker
Certified Public Accountants

By_____

    The engagement letter illustrated above is quite general. Special circumstances may make it desirable for any number of additional matters to be included in the letter, as, for example, the date the auditor's report is to be delivered, the date the client's records are to be ready for the auditor to begin his work, whether or not a long-form report is to be prepared in addition to the short-form report (certificate), limitations on the scope of the examination to be made, indication of any detailed auditing to be done, whether tax returns are to be prepared, assistance to be given the auditor by the client's staff, the estimated fee for the examination, and a list of the per diem rates to be charged.

DETAILED AUDITS

    Occasionally a client may suspect that fraud has occurred or may question the accuracy of the accounting records. Such discrepancies are not likely to be detected by the regular examination of the financial statements unless the amounts involved are material in relation to financial position and results of operations. Consequently, if the client wishes to have the full facts concerning such matters, he must specifically authorize the auditor to do the additional work necessary to obtain the desired information. On occasion, however, the auditor may suggest certain areas in which a detailed audit might be desirable, based on weaknesses he has noted in internal control or unaccountable changes in certain account balances or in the ratios of related accounts.

Essentially, a detailed audit is a thorough verification of the accounting processes associated with recording business transactions. The detailed audit may encompass all types of transactions occurring during a specific period, such as a month or a year, or only certain types of transactions, such as sales, accounts receivable charges and credits, cash receipts, cash disbursements, or some particular type of cash disbursement, like purchases, payroll, or petty cash disbursements. Also, the audit may cover each individual transaction which occurred, or it may simply cover a relatively large sample of the total transactions.

For the transactions selected for verification, each record and each step in the recording process should be verified. Included would be the evidence authorizing a transaction (such as a purchase order), the internal documents prepared in connection with the transaction, entries and footings in the books of original entry, and postings to general and subsidiary ledgers. Thus the detailed audit is much like the tests which the auditor makes in reviewing the client's system of internal control, except for the extent of the verification involved.

If the detailed audit is to be performed on a sampling basis, the auditor must be alert to any special problems created thereby. For instance, a test of entries in the subsidiary accounts receivable ledger will not reveal fictitious entries if the tests are all made from the source documents to the ledger postings. On the other hand, testing only from the ledger postings to the source documents will not show that all transactions and the related documents have been recorded.

REPORTS TO THE SECURITIES AND EXCHANGE COMMISSION

The Securities Exchange Act of 1934, as amended by the Securities Acts Amendments of 1964, requires that, with certain exceptions, a company must register with the SEC, must register all subsequent issues of securities, and must file semiannual and annual reports with the SEC if the following conditions prevail:

1. The company is engaged in interstate commerce or its securities are traded by use of the mails or by any means of interstate commerce.
2. The company has total assets in excess of $1 million.
3. The company has equity securities held of record by 500 or more persons.

These requirements cover all companies whose securities are listed on national securities exchanges, as well as major companies whose securities are traded through the over-the-counter market.

Audited financial statements must be included with most of the reports, applications, and registrations filed with the SEC. The required filings are intended to give the SEC an opportunity to review the information submitted in order to ascertain that the information is complete and does not appear to be misleading in any way. After the SEC has examined the information that has been filed, and after any deficiencies noted by the SEC have been corrected, the information filed becomes public and may be distributed by the corporation involved. These procedures reflect the principal intent of the securities acts: enforced disclosure of adequate information for use by investors. The responsibility for the fairness and accuracy of the statements rests primarily with the management of the company involved, and secondarily with the independent public accountants selected by the company to express the required opinion on the financial statements.

Registered companies are required to furnish certain annual information to stockholders in connection with proxy solicitations, or separately if there is no such solicitation. Rule 14a-3 of the Commission requires that "Any differences, reflected in the financial statements in the report to security holders, from the principles of consolidation or other accounting principles or practices, or methods of applying accounting principles or practices, applicable to the financial statements of the issuer filed or proposed to be filed with the Commission, which have a material effect on the financial position or results of operations of the issuer, shall be noted and the effect thereof reconciled or explained in such report."

Rules and Regulations Governing Reports to be Filed

The reports to the SEC, including audited financial statements, must be filed with the Commission in accordance with the various forms (S-1, 9-K, 10-K, and so on) and the instructions accompanying those forms, as prescribed by the Commission. A booklet entitled *Regulation S-X* lists the rules and regulations of the SEC pertaining to the administration of the various legislative acts under which it draws its authority. Included are rules pertaining to the form and content of financial statements and supporting schedules required in most of the registration statements and reports specified by the securities acts. Also important to the public accountant serving his client with respect to reports filed with the SEC are the Accounting Series Releases of the Commission. These releases contain the opinions of the Commission as they relate to accounting principles, independence of certifying accountants, and other matters of importance to accountants expressing an opinion on financial statements to be filed with the SEC. Also included in the series are the findings and opinions of the Commission in connection with hearings concerning the suspension or disqualification of accountants from practice before the Commission.

There is obviously a large body of material with which the accountant must be familiar if he is to serve his client effectively in connection with SEC matters. The intention of the comments included here is merely to make the reader aware of what is required in a very general way and to suggest the material that must be consulted to gain a complete picture of the requirements.

Form S-1

A registration statement is filed on Form S-1, and must include an audited balance sheet and audited income statements for the three years preceding the balance sheet date. The date of the balance sheet must be within ninety days of the date that the form is filed. Should the filing date be more than ninety days after the close of the company's fiscal year, the balance sheet may be unaudited provided that an audited balance sheet as of the end of the most recent fiscal year is also included. A summary of earnings for the period preceding the "ninety-day" balance sheet for the current and preceding years must also be included with the unaudited balance sheet.

An earnings summary, in comparative form, for the most recent five fiscal years of the company must also be included in Form S-1. The summary need not be certified, but underwriters sometimes request that the summary be certified for at least the three years corresponding with the certified income statements that must be filed.

After the registration statement is filed, the SEC has a twenty-day period in which changes in the statements or additional information can be requested. If the registration statement is not amended in accordance with the Commission's recommendations, the Commission can issue a "stop order" refusing to permit the statements to become effective until amended.

If no changes are requested, or if any required changes have been made, the registration statement becomes effective twenty days after it is filed, although by special request the statements can be made effective at an earlier date. The wording of the Securities Act of 1933 is such that a certifying accountant is held liable for material misstatements or omissions existing in the certified statements accompanying a registration statement *at the date when the registration statement becomes effective.* The effect of this arrangement is to extend the auditor's responsibility for events subsequent to the balance sheet date beyond the date of his certificate and up to the effective date of the registration statement. The review to be made during this additional period would include inquiry of appropriate officials concerning important developments which might have an effect on the financial statements, review of any statements prepared for internal purposes, and the reading of the minutes of any directors' or stockholders' meetings that were held. Any important developments discovered in this manner would necessitate an amendment to the financial statements filed with the Commission.

Forms 9-K and 10-K

Companies whose securities are registered with the SEC are subject to a continuing reporting requirement. A semiannual report must be filed on Form 9-K within forty-five days after the close of the first half of the company's fiscal year. The report calls for a limited amount of income statement information, and if this information has been included in a regular printed report to stockholders, the printed report may be filed as an exhibit to Form 9-K. The information need not be audited.

Form 10-K is more comprehensive, and must be filed within 120 days of the close of the company's fiscal year. An audited balance sheet, income statement, and statement of surplus changes are specified for inclusion in this form.

Accounting Principles Relating to Financial Statements Filed with the SEC

Fortunately, the SEC has not undertaken to dictate the accounting principles to be followed in statements filed with the Commission. Had that been done, there might have arisen two bodies of accounting principles: those acceptable to the SEC and those acceptable to the accounting profession. Although the Commission has left the general development of accounting principles to the accounting profession, in some cases where there is no uniformity of practice the Commission has specified the method to be followed in statements filed with the Commission.

The Commission's attitude with respect to accounting matters is further set forth in its *Accounting Series Release No. 4:*

> In cases where financial statements filed with this Commission...are prepared in accordance with accounting principles for which there is no substantial authoritative support, such financial statements will be presumed to be misleading or inaccurate despite disclosures contained in the certificate of the accountant or in footnotes to the statements provided the matters involved are material. In cases where there is a difference of opinion between the Commission and the registrant as to the proper principles of accounting to be followed, disclosure will be accepted in lieu of correction of the financial statements themselves only if the points involved are such that there is substantial authoritative support for the practices followed by the registrant and the position of the Commission has not previously been expressed in rules, regulations or other official releases of the Commission, including the published opinions of its Chief Accountant.

ELECTRONIC DATA PROCESSING

The tremendous growth of electronic data processing has greatly increased the probability that an auditor will find that part or all of a client's records are maintained through the use of an electronic computer. Initially, there was a tendency for auditors to treat the computer as a "black box" involving operations beyond the competence reasonably expected of a proficient auditor. Under this approach, the operations of the computer in developing the accounting records were largely ignored; auditors merely audited "around the computer." Source documents giving rise to computer input were selected on a test basis, summarized by the auditor in accordance with the various output classifications developed for the data, and then the auditor's totals were compared with the output that resulted from the computer processing. If the auditor was thus able to reconcile input and output figures, he was satisfied that the computer was producing reliable results that could be accepted for statement purposes, subject only to the usual corroborative procedures carried out with respect to year-end balances and totals.

Special Problems with "Real Time" Systems

One of the matters currently causing considerable concern in auditing circles is "real time" systems that utilize the direct introduction of data to a computer from an original source without the creation of an intervening visible record of the transaction that can be audited. The processing of the data by the computer is similarly invisible, because there is no intervening record available for use in auditing the processing that has occurred. For example, a worker may insert an identifying tag in a receptacle and depress a few buttons, causing his worker number, the job number or account number on which he is working, and the time of the day to be recorded directly on magnetic tape, or even directly into computer memory. From this point, and without visible indication of how the results were derived, the computer can produce a record showing the worker's total earnings for the payroll period involved and a listing showing the total payroll charges to the various account or job numbers for all workers for the payroll period.

Actually, such a system can be modified to produce a chronological printed record of the start or stop time of each entry of data, a printed record of all data entries grouped according to worker number to show the details supporting each worker's total earnings, and a printed record of all data entries grouped according to account or job number to support the total amount charged to each classification. Such records *could* be obtained, but their preparation would largely defeat the time and cost savings sought from the computer, and the company would gain nothing of value, because it is interested only in obtaining the final results. The auditor, of course, will miss the records, but it is unreasonable and impractical to insist that the records be prepared merely to permit him to audit a few entries here and there out of the thousands or millions of entries for a year.

In reality, however, the problem presented by these circumstances is not so new or unique as it first appears, for auditors learned many years ago how to adapt to a similar problem. Then, as now, at the heart of the problem was a computer that accepted input information directly from employees and produced classified totals that could not be conveniently verified. The earlier form of computer that presented a comparable problem was the now ubiquitous cash register, which not only is accepted by auditors without qualm, but is recommended as indispensable to the typical retail establishment.

Controls Substituted for Records

The solution to the loss of verifiable records in the case of the cash register applies equally as well to the more complex electronic computer. First of all, either machine can be relied upon to perform its work without error (except for rare malfunctioning, which ordinarily would be readily apparent), and hence there is little or no need for the auditor to make the same type of verification that is required when working with records prepared by error-prone human beings. Second, the work of the machines is less suspect than the work of a person, for the machines cannot profit from intentional misstatement of the figures they handle.

A third factor is the management review directed to the machine figures in each instance. Management responsibility for operating results necessitates careful attention to all operating data, and material errors or manipulations should become evident in the course of such review. A fourth factor in each situation is the tie-in of the machine figures with cash amounts which are separately controlled and lend further credibility to the machine figures.

Lastly, other forms of internal control offer still further indication of the reliability of the machine figures. If a retail store operates under the retail inventory system, the annual comparison of book and physical inventory figures lends further validity to departmental sales figures which represent the source of cost of sales credits to inventory accounts during the year. Similarly in payroll accounting, standard costs offer a basis for comparison of figures, so that erroneous machine figures would produce attention-getting cost variances.

There is one advantage that is usually present in computer applications, however, that cannot be readily obtained in the case of the cash register. Computer operators represent a highly specialized work force who will ordinarily have no responsibilities outside of the data-processing function, and hence they will play no part in authorizing or originating transactions, and they will have no contact with cash or other liquid assets of the business. Under these circumstances they will have little reason to tamper with figures or totals, whereas the cash register is operated by the same employee who makes the sale, handles the merchandise, and receives the cash.

The Control Group

Additional controls may also be superimposed over the data-processing function through the operation of a separate control group. The employees in this group maintain certain key control totals over payroll or other data and prove each computer run against such control totals. For example, a record would be sent to the control group covering each employee added or deducted from the payroll, and on the basis of such information the control group would maintain running totals of fixed deductions, pay rates, and a so-called "hash total" of employee payroll numbers. Proper computer programming would cause comparable totals to be developed as a by-product of the payroll run, and the control group's balancing of the computer figures with its own totals would provide further evidence that no employees were improperly added or omitted during the payroll run.

Such a control group would also establish controls over legible data to be transcribed and processed by the data-processing unit. Sales invoices, for example, if prepared on a billing machine would be controlled by a list and the total automatically prepared by the billing machine. A record of this total would be retained by the control group, and after the invoices had been transcribed by the data-processing department onto the proper computer input media and the data processed to obtain the desired final reports, the totals of these reports would be verified by the control group against its control totals. Any incoming data not accompanied by a predetermined total would, of course, first be listed by the control group to establish a total before releasing the data for transcribing and processing.

A technique known as "integrated data processing" has been developed as one solution to the cost of transcribing data and eliminating the human errors likely to creep into the transcribing process. For example, a special billing machine may be used with an attachment that automatically prepares a punched paper tape containing all the information necessary for further processing of the data. The paper tape can then be introduced into an automatic converter in the data-processing section which will convert the information to punched-card form or directly to magnetic tape.

Audit Review of Data-Processing Controls

As with internal control in general, the auditor must review data-processing controls as a basis for determining whether he can, indeed, place sufficient reliance on the final results of the system. In this connection he should ascertain that the control group is maintaining all the controls that appear to be necessary, and the control records should be tested against the evidence from which the controls were derived, as well as against the comparable figures in final reports.

The auditor may also wish to satisfy himself that one or more computer "programs" have been properly designed. Such programs may include hundreds, or even thousands, of individual steps, all stored on punched cards or reels of magnetic tape. The programs can be "printed out" and then reviewed, but seldom will this step be necessary, and furthermore, most auditors would lack the ability to interpret and evaluate the program steps. Instead, an excellent opportunity to ascertain the efficacy of a program exists when it is first placed into operation. Prudence suggests that parallel runs of data be prepared for a short period of time so that, if the program is defective, the final figures can still be obtained in the same manner as in the past, and in addition, the program can be proved by comparing the results obtained under the two processes. Under such an arrangement, the auditor can readily satisfy himself that the program is producing proper results.

Increasing contact with computerized systems and a gradual growth of knowledge about computer programming and processing have made it clear that the earlier concept of auditing around the computer is unsatisfactory and inconsistent with the trend toward increasing attention to the audit of the accounting system, as expounded in the preceding chapters of this text. Furthermore, the use of parallel runs by the client to verify computer programs is a one-time-only solution, and the life expectancy of such a proof is likely to be short, because computer programs are likely to undergo fairly constant change. Replacing the largely outmoded "around the computer" approach is the more compatible approach of auditing "through the computer." To audit through the computer, the auditor must become familiar with the flow charts that are the basis for the computer program, must evaluate the adequacy of the controls incorporated into the system, and then must prove the correspondence of the actual program with the flow charts that have been studied and the controls that have identified. A frequently employed technique to prove a program is to develop a "test deck" of input data that will test the various controls and limits purported to be incorporated into the program. The test deck is processed under the control of the program regularly used by the client in order to ascertain that transactions that violate established limits are rejected, that all exceptions are recognized and reported, and that specified control totals are developed. In so doing, the auditor can also establish that the program in use by the client is actually the program represented in the flow charts and evaluated by the auditor.

An Internal Control Checklist for Electronic Data Processing

Internal control is equally as important and equally as feasible for an electronic data-processing system as for the more traditional forms of accounting systems, and the independent auditor's review of internal control is likewise of first importance. The means by which internal control is accomplished are vastly different, however, and we are indebted to H. Bruce Joplin for the development of a questionnaire for the review of internal control over electronic data processing. The questionnaire first appeared in the magazine *Management Services* for July-August, 1964, and is reproduced below by permission.

EDP department organization

1. Is the EDP department independent of all operating units for which it performs data processing functions?
2. Are the following work units physically as well as organizationally separate?
   (a) Computer center
   (b) Control unit
   (c) Program and tape library
   (d) Systems and programing units
3. Is there a current operating manual for the department?
4. Are current organization charts and flow charts available?
5. Is there a schedule of all active programs, including a brief description of the function of each, date of approval, and identification number?
6. Is access to the computer center limited to persons having a legitimate mission therein?
7. Is access to control data restricted to employees of the control unit?
8. Is the control unit responsible for recording and expediting all data processed by the EDP section, including control over the number, due date, and distribution of reports?
9. Are approved copies of all computer programs and necessary supporting documents maintained in the library and issued to interested persons only upon written authorization?
10. Are systems and programing unit employees forbidden to operate computers on regular processing runs?

Standardization of procedures

1. Is there a standard format for the program file which should be assembled for each program?
2. Are flow charts and block diagram symbols and procedures standardized?
3. Are program testing procedures well established?
4. Are program techniques standardized for the following?
   (a) Table look-up or search methods
   (b) Use of program switches
   (c) Initialization routines
   (d) Tape record blocking
5. Are halt addresses standardized as to core location and use?
6. Are symbolic programing labels or tags standardized?
7. Have all standardized procedures been compiled in a programing manual and is the manual current?

Computer program maintenance

1. Are program changes cleared through persons of authority other than programers directly involved in the preparation of programs?

2. Are program changes documented as to the following?
   (a) Reason for change
   (b) Effect of change
   (c) Prior period adjustments necessary
3. Is there a program file for each computer program containing the following information?
   (a) Specific program name and number
   (b) The purpose of the program
   (c) Agreements as to:
      1. When source data is to be ready for processing
      2. What output is required, format, etc.
      3. When reports are due
      4. How various transactions and exceptions are to be handled
      5. What coding will be used
   (d) A narrative description of the program
   (e) A general block diagram
   (f) A detailed block diagram
   (g) Complete operating directions. These instructions should be clear and simple. They should be so complete that no oral instructions are required to operate the program. These instructions should:
      1. Identify tape units on which various input and output files will be mounted
      2. Describe any action required regarding external tape labels
      3. Specify console switch settings
      4. List all program halts with prescribed action for each
      5. Describe restart procedures if other than standard
      6. Describe any exception to other standard routines
   (h) A description of all input data required
   (i) A description of output data required: form numbers, approximate quantity, number of copies, etc.
   (j) Disposition of input material, defining exactly what is to be done with all input material; where to deliver; how long to retain
   (k) Detail layout of:
      1. Tape input records
      2. Tape output records
      3. Punched-card input and output format
      4. Printed output including samples
   (l) Layout of storage locations:
      1. Input, output, and work areas
      2. Subroutines
      3. Constants and variables
   (m) Description and example of any control card which may be necessary
   (n) A sample of the printer carriage tape
   (o) A dump of the program now in use

Input procedures

1. Is the number of basic types of input documents limited so as to facilitate control and processing efficiency?
2. Are all input documents press-numbered?
3. Are all numbered documents accounted for by the control unit?

4. Are data processed in serially numbered batches?

5. Are all source documents identified by batch number and canceled to prevent reprocessing?

6. Are data controlled by the number of documents processed and by hash totals as well as by dollar amount?

7. Does the control unit use a document register or other positive method of comparing machine run totals with control totals?

8. Is responsibility fixed, and are adequate procedures in effect, for tracing and correcting input errors?

9. Are corrections identified and recorded in such a manner that duplicate correction will not occur and subsequent audit will be possible?

10. Are all instructions to key punch operators (or bookkeeping machine operators preparing paper tapes) written in clear, concise form?

11. If the computer writes checks or other negotiable instruments, are the requisition and use of blank stock closely controlled?

Computer processing procedures

1. Do programs positively identify input data as to date, type, etc?

2. Do programs test for valid codes in input data, and are halts or printouts provided when invalid codes are detected?

3. Are changes in program rate tables and other constants initiated in writing by persons authorized to do so, and are all such changes recorded and retained for audit?

4. Are all instructions to operators set forth in writing in clear and unequivocal language?

5. Are operators cautioned not to accept oral instructions or to contact programers directly when errors are detected?

6. Is there a positive follow-up to determine if corrections are made on errors found by the machine?

7. Are all halts (except end of job) and errors recorded and the record retained for audit?

8. Is the use of external switches held to a minimum, and are the instructions for their use set forth in writing?

9. Are the situations whereby data may be inserted or extracted by the use of the console set forth in writing and limited to circumstances which cannot be handled through the stored program?

10. Are console printouts controlled and reviewed by persons (other than operators) who are familiar with the activity being performed?

11. Are console printouts labeled so as to be reasonably intelligible?

12. Are account codes, employee numbers, and other identification data designed with self-checking test digits, and does the program test for these digits?

13. Are checkpoints provided in lengthy processing runs, and are program or external restart instructions provided in case a checkpoint fails to balance?

14. Is computer usage recorded on a positive basis by program as to run-time and set-up time and by nonuse as to maintenance time and off time?

Magnetic tape use

1. Are there physical controls to prevent inadvertent erasure of tapes?

2. Are there formal procedures for preventing premature reuse of tapes?

3. Do external tape labels contain the following?

(a) Reel number
(b) Serial number
(c) Number of reels in the file
(d) Program identification number
(e) Date created
(f) Retention date
(g) Density
(h) Drive number

4. Do header labels have the following data?
   (a) Program identification number
   (b) Reel number
   (c) Date created
   (d) Date obsolete

5. Do trailer labels have the following data?
   (a) Block count
   (b) Record count
   (c) Hash totals
   (d) End of reel or end of file designation

6. Do programs test for header and trailer labels each time a new tape is accessed or the end of the reel is sensed?

7. Has a policy been established for the retirement of tape reels which have excessive read or write errors?

Physical Condition

1. Has a policy been established regarding visitors, neatness, smoking, etc., in the computer center?

2. Is the hardware serviced by qualified engineers on a regular basis?

3. Are manufacturer's cleaning recommendations for the computer center strictly followed?

4. Are manufacturer's temperature and humidity requirements maintained?

5. Are magnetic tape reels stored according to manufacturer's specifications?

Requesting Printout

As mentioned earlier, intermediate or final data processing results can be printed out for the auditor's use, but because the printouts will usually involve a special request that departs from established routine, as well as added cost and inconvenience, the requests should be held to a minimum. The most common reason for requesting such a printout is to obtain a visual record of details which the auditor wishes to subject to further verification.

A typical instance would involve detailed accounts receivable records which the auditor would require for confirmation purposes. The printout might be specified to contain only customers' names and account balances, but such limited information would make it difficult for the auditor to investigate confirmation exceptions. Thus it will usually be preferable to request that the details supporting each account balance also be shown.

Requests for such printouts should be anticipated at an early date, for it is next to impossible in many instances to obtain a printout of details for a given date after that date has passed. For instance, accounts receivable records are likely to be maintained on an "open item" basis, with only the unpaid sales transactions carried in the computer memory or on tape storage. Thus, the payment of an item is reflected by deleting the item from the record, and the only feasible time to obtain a printout of December 31 accounts receivable balances is immediately after all December 31 transactions have been processed and before any January transactions have been introduced.

The ability of the computer can be of considerable assistance to the auditor in the preparation of such printouts. Because receivables confirmation is usually conducted on a test basis, only the details on accounts to be confirmed would be required, and the computer can be programmed with little difficulty to make the selection of accounts to be confirmed in accordance with the auditor's specifications. Thus, the computer could be programmed to select all accounts with balances over a specified amount, all accounts more than three months delinquent, and a random or systematic selection of a specified number of additional accounts. Furthermore, the printout can be arranged in columns to show the aging of each selected account, and while the full accounts receivable record is being processed, the computer can also develop a count and dollar total of all accounts not selected and develop an analysis of that total by age classification. Such figures can then be related to the comparable figures for the accounts printed out as an indication that the work of the computer was properly performed, and the auditor will have proven the trial balance total and the aging without further effort on his part. The auditor should observe the console operator during the actual running of the program to satisfy himself that spurious figures have not been inserted from the console to produce results that appear to balance with control figures. Here we see yet another auditor-computer relationship established, one that is sometimes described as auditing "with the computer."

Filing of Original Documents

When original visible documents are prepared and then transcribed onto cards or magnetic tape, the auditor should not expect to find the original documents filed in the same order that would prevail under older accounting techniques, should he find it necessary to refer to such original documents. Vendors' invoices, for example, might be filed in the exact "hysterical" sequence in which they were received from the accounts payable section. The reason is that it is more economical to sort data electronically than to sort it physically. If the original documents are not to be sorted prior to being filed away, they will ordinarily be imprinted with a sequence or "locator" number assigned by machine, and this same locator number will be carried along with the related data at all times during the processing by the computer. Then if at any time a question should arise, the original document can be located simply by using the locator number shown along with the transaction details.

The preceding comments are brief in relation to the complexities of electronic data processing, but they are intended to point out some of the principal problems and possible solutions to those problems. When the auditor first encounters an electronic data-processing installation, he will obviously find it necessary to learn a great deal about electronic computers and to become acquainted with computer terminology. From this point on, sound auditing techniques, imagination, and resourcefulness should carry him through his first audit encounter with an electronic computer.

REVIEW QUESTIONS

1. If the auditor is testing postings to the general ledger for one month, working from the source records to the general ledger, what should he do after he has tick-marked all postings which he has tested from the source records?
2. In connection with a first audit, what types of items should be abstracted when reading the minutes of meetings held in prior years?
3. Why would the auditor be unable to express a favorable opinion on a client's financial statements if the auditor is not permitted to read the minutes of the board of directors?
4. Describe the three types of events which may occur after the balance sheet date and which are of significance to the auditor.
5. What procedures would be used by the auditor in reviewing events occurring subsequent to the balance sheet date?
6. Why should the auditor obtain a signed copy of the client's financial statements?
7. List the various representations which the auditor may request the client to make concerning the client's records and financial statements.
8. Summarize the rules of professional conduct which are designed to cause the person in need of public accounting service to seek the practitioner who can best fulfill his needs.
9. What information is likely to be included in the letter confirming the audit arrangements with the client?
10. How is a detailed audit performed?
11. What companies must register with the S.E.C.?
12. What responsibility does the Securities and Exchange Commission assume in connection with the financial statements of registered companies?
13. When do registration statements filed with the S.E.C. become effective?
14. Of what significance is the effective date of a registration statement to a certifying accountant?
15. Upon what factors can the auditor base his opinion concerning various figures when a computer is used and usual forms of audit evidence are unavailable?
16. Distinguish between auditing around the computer and auditing through the computer.
17. How would an auditor satisfy himself that a client's data processing control group has functioned effectively?

18. Why are documents not likely to be filed in the usual alphabetical or numerical sequence if they have been transcribed for computer processing?

QUESTIONS ON APPLICATION OF AUDITING STANDARDS

19. The representation letter that the auditor customarily asks the client to sign lists various possible liabilities and the client is asked to indicate whether, to the best of his knowledge, any such liabilities exist that have not been recorded. If the client knows of such a liability but does not mention it in the representation letter, would legal liability be incurred by the auditor if he fails to discover the unrecorded liability? Explain.

20. A note payable owed by your client is not due until two years after the current balance sheet date, but in the course of your review of subsequent disbursements you discover that the note has been paid off prematurely. Should the note be classified in the balance sheet as a current liability or as a long-term liability? Why?

21. The intent of a company with respect to a given asset or liability may properly affect the presentation or classification of the item on the balance sheet. Give four basically different examples to illustrate this point.

22. List ten different balance sheet items on which the auditor might request confirmation from a person outside the client's organization, and state who that person would be.

23. Would you expect your client's introduction of an extensive program of electronic data processing to increase or decrease the hours expended on the engagement and the total audit fee? Explain.

24. How would you satisfy yourself that the computer program used to process your test deck is the program regularly used by the client and agrees with the flow charts that you have reviewed?

25. The audit of the financial statements of a client that utilizes the services of a computer for accounting functions compels the C.P.A. to understand the operation of his client's electronic data processing (EDP) system.

    Required:
    (a) The first requirement of an effective system of internal control is a satisfactory plan of organization. List the characteristics of a satisfactory plan of organization for an EDP department, including the relationship between the department and the rest of the organization.
    (b) An effective system of internal control also requires a sound system of records control of operations and transactions (source data and its flow) and of classification of data within the accounts. For an EDP system, these controls include input controls, processing controls, and output controls. List the characteristics of a satisfactory system of input controls. (Confine your comments to a batch-controlled system employing punched cards and to the steps that occur prior to the processing of the input cards in the computer.)   (Uniform C.P.A. Examination)

26. It is customary for an auditor to make inquiries of non-accounting officers and responsible employees. State five different things about which an auditor might make inquiries that are not primarily aimed at determining the kind and degree of internal control. For each, explain the purpose of the inquiry and the title (or duties) of the person to whom the inquiry is addressed.
    (Uniform C.P.A. Examination)

27. Explain why you believe the Code of Professional Ethics prohibits competitive bidding on engagements.

28. As a commissioner of the city of Pretty Prairie, would you vote for or against a resolution authorizing the mayor to secure competitive bids for an audit of the city's records for the past year? Justify your stand.

29. E. Beaver, C.P.A., has recently established a public accounting practice and in his spare time has written an article on accounting controls for the small business which has been published by *The Journal of Accountancy*. He is considering obtaining sufficient reprints of the article to send to clients, friends, members of his Rotary chapter, and various other persons who operate small businesses. Would you recommend that he proceed with these plans? Explain.

PROBLEMS

30. Internal auditing is a staff function found in virtually every large corporation. The internal audit function is also performed in many smaller companies as a part-time activity of individuals who may or may not be called internal auditors. The differences between the audits by independent public accountants and the work of internal auditors are more basic than is generally recognized.

    Required:
    (a) Briefly discuss the auditing work performed by the independent public accountant and the internal auditor with regard to:
    1. Auditing objectives.
    2. General nature of auditing work.
    (b) In conducting his audit the independent public accountant must evaluate the work of the internal auditor. Discuss briefly the reason for this evaluation.
    (c) List the auditing procedures used by an independent public accountant in evaluating the work of the internal auditor.
                                                              (Uniform C.P.A. Examination)

31. You are the senior accountant in the audit of the Paulsen Grain Corp. whose business primarily involves the purchase, storage and sale of grain products. The corporation owns several elevators located along navigable water routes and transports its grain by barge and rail. Your assistant submitted the following analysis for your review.

Paulsen Grain Corporation
Advances Paid on Barges Under Construction—a/c 210
December 31, 1967

Advances Made:

1/15/67—CK. #3463—Jones Barge Construction Co.	$100,000	(1)
4/13/67—CK. #4129—Jones Barge Construction Co.	25,000	(1)
6/19/67—CK. #5396—Jones Barge Construction Co.	63,000	(1)
Total payments	$188,000	
Deduct cash received 9/1/67 from Eastern Life Insurance Co.	188,000	(2)
Balance per general ledger—12/31/67	-0-	

(1) Examined approved check request and cancelled check and traced to cash disbursements record.

(2) Traced to cash receipt book and to duplicate deposit ticket.

Required:

(a) In what respects is the analysis incomplete for report purposes? (Do not include any discussion of specific auditing procedures.)

(b) What two different types of contractual arrangements may be inferred from your assistant's analysis?

(c) What additional auditing procedures would you suggest that your assistant perform before you accept the working paper as being complete? (Uniform C.P.A. Examination)

32. The following events occurred in different cases, but in each instance the event happened after the close of the fiscal year under audit, but before all representatives of the auditor had left the office of the client. State in each case what notice, if any, you would take in your report on the fiscal year; the closing date in each instance is December 31, 1967.

   (1) Merchandise handled by the company had been traded in the open markets in which it procures its supplies at $1.40 on December 31, 1967. This price had prevailed for two weeks, following an official market report that predicted vastly enlarged supplies; however, no purchases were made at $1.40. The price throughout the preceding year had been about $2.00 which is the level experienced over several years. On January 18, 1968, the price returned to $2.00, following public disclosure of an error in the official calculations of the prior December, correction of which destroyed the expectations of excessive supplies. Inventory at December 31, 1967 was on a cost-or-market basis.

   (2) On February 1, 1968, the board of directors adopted a resolution accepting the offer of an investment banker to guarantee the marketing of $100,000,000 of preferred stock.

   (3) On January 22, 1968, one of the three major plants of the client burned with a loss of $50,000,000 which was covered to the extent of $40,000,000 by insurance.

   (4) The client in this case is an investment company of the open-end type. During the early part of 1967 a wholly new management came into control. By February 20, 1968 the new management had sold 90% of the investments carried at December 31, 1967 and had purchased others of a substantially more speculative character.

   (5) This company has a wholly owned but not consolidated subsidiary producing oil in a foreign country. A serious rebellion began in that country on January 18, and continued beyond the completion of your audit work. The press in this country has carried extensive coverage of the progress of the fighting.   (Uniform C.P.A. Examination)

33. In auditing the financial statements of a manufacturing company that were prepared from data processed by electronic data processing equipment, the C.P.A. has found that his traditional "audit trail" has been obscured. As a result the C.P.A. may place increased emphasis upon over-all checks of the data under audit. These over-all checks, which are also applied in auditing visibly posted accounting records, include the computation of ratios, which are compared to prior year ratios or to industry-wide norms. Examples of such over-all checks or ratios are the computation of the rate of inventory turnover and computation of the number of days' sales in receivables.

Required:

(a) Discuss the advantages to the C.P.A. of the use of ratios as over-all checks in an audit.

(b) In addition to the computations given above, list the ratios that a C.P.A. may compute during an audit as over-all checks on balance sheet accounts and related nominal accounts. For each ratio listed name the two (or more) accounts used in its computation.

(c) When a C.P.A. discovers that there has been a significant change in a ratio when compared to the prior year's ratio, he considers the possible reasons for the change. Give the possible reasons for the following significant changes in ratios:

1. The rate of inventory turnover (ratio of cost of sales and average inventory) has decreased from the prior year's rate.

2. The number of days' sales in receivables (ratio of average daily accounts receivable and sales) has increased over the prior year.

(Uniform C.P.A. Examination)

34. What modifications, if any, would you make in the manner in which the following audit was conducted in order to reduce the time spent on the audit?

You are assigned to audit the ABC Company as of June 30, 1967 and accordingly arrive at the plant accompanied by a junior assistant on the morning of July 1. You find that the June bank statements have not yet been received and are not expected to arrive until the next day. They also tell you that the physical inventory was taken on June 29 and accordingly you and your assistant spend your first day making test counts of the quantities on hand and the next day you reconcile these counts back to the quantities shown on the company's inventory count sheets, using receiving, production and shipping records. Meanwhile your assistant goes off to count the petty cash.

The company maintains a general office petty cash fund of $100.00 and ten other funds of $10.00, each maintained for specific purposes at various locations in the general office, the downtown office, the plant and the East Chicago receiving station. You instruct your assistant to count these, and when he is finished you tell him to obtain from the company the June bank statements (which have since arrived) for the two bank accounts (the general account and the imprest payroll account) which the company maintains. Following your instructions, he finds that these bank statements have been opened by the treasurer's office, and accordingly you point out to him the appropriate instructions which detail the steps to be performed in a situation where the bank statements have been opened before we receive them. The assistant then sets to work and while he is successful in effecting a reconciliation of the payroll account, he comes to you a couple of days later to state that on the general bank account his reconciliation is 10 cents off and that he cannot find the difference. Accordingly you instruct him to make a recheck, and by the end of the next day, he advises you that he has successfully run down the error. You then review his working papers and find that he has followed the instructions satisfactorily and that his working papers, including schedules of outstanding checks, adding machine tapes of deposits and withdrawals etc., are complete and properly prepared.

You next put him to work on the accounts receivable, instructing him to draw off a trial balance thereof showing the balance for each customer, and with separate columns for billings 30, 60, 90, 120 and over 120 days old. When he has completed this schedule, you tell him to draw off a list, on 14-column paper, of the names, addresses and balances receivable from all customers from whom more than $50.00 is due, and then to write up accounts receivable confirmation requests for all of the customers on the list, taking care to number these requests and place the same numbers on the list. When he has finished this, stuffed the confirmations in envelopes bearing the firm's return address, stamped them and mailed them, you then instruct him to go to the credit manager and review with him the status of all of the balances on the accounts receivable trial balance which are over thirty days old. As a second step you also tell him to draw off an analysis of the reserve for bad debts for the entire year showing the amounts credited thereto each month and scheduling in detail all accounts written off to the reserve. Having prepared such analysis, he is then to ascertain on what basis the monthly provisions to the reserve have been calculated and test-check the calculations for three months selected at random, in order to prove that the established method has been followed. When he has completed all of this, you again review his papers and having considered the balance in the bad debt reserve in the light of the credit manager's explanations of the delinquent accounts, you determine that the reserve for bad debts is adequate to care for probable losses. Since it is still fairly early in the audit, you instruct the assistant to defer checking the amounts collected on the receivables after the balance sheet date, and tell him that this will be done later on when more remittances have been received.

By this time, the general ledger bookkeeper has completed his regular June postings and has drawn off a preliminary general ledger trial balance. The bookkeeper explains to you that this trial balance will be subject to a considerable number of year-end adjustments, but since it is necessary for you to have a trial balance in order to proceed with your audit, you copy off his preliminary one, advising him that you will pick up his various year-end closing entries as post-closing adjustments, in the same manner that you record your own adjusting entries.

As stated previously the physical test of the inventory quantities was made when you first arrived on the audit, and the counts made by you were thereafter reconciled back to the company's June 29 inventory sheets. In the meanwhile the tabulation and pricing of the inventory has been completed and accordingly you instruct your assistant to sit down with a calculator and check the accuracy of every other extension in the inventory. You also tell him to run adding machine tapes in order to verify the inventory footings. When he has completed this, you instruct him to copy from the inventory sheets the descriptions, quantities, unit prices and values of two hundred large items selected at random, and verify the unit prices used by examining recent vendors' invoices in support thereof. The client maintains a voucher register showing voucher numbers, and accordingly the assistant goes through the entries in this register for the last two months, and is successful in obtaining the numbers of the most recent vouchers paid to the various suppliers from whom the purchasing agent says the various materials on the list have been purchased. He then goes and pulls these vouchers and completes this phase of the work without running into any serious discrepancies. Meanwhile, you have prepared a summary analysis for the year of the transactions appearing in the fifteen general ledger controlling accounts which the company maintains for its various classes of inventory, in order to determine the general nature of the transactions flowing through these accounts. On the basis of this work, as well as that performed by your assistant, you are able to satisfy yourself that the inventories have been correctly taken and valued.

The next step in the audit is to review the fixed assets and reserves for depreciation and accordingly you ask your assistant to prepare a list of all additions to fixed assets for the year showing voucher numbers and such other information as is available on them in the fixed assets ledger. When he has prepared this schedule you then instruct him to test check—in the same manner that he verified the inventory prices—the individual additions against supporting vouchers, picking all items over $100.00. You handle the verification of the depreciation reserves yourself, and in that connection prepare working paper schedules similar to those made up in previous years' audits, showing the fixed assets as of July 1, 1966 by years of acquisition, together with the depreciation reserve applicable to each such group. You then add the current year's additions and retirements to the schedule, apply the various depreciation percentages to the asset balances and thereby arrive at your computation of the current year's provision, which you find is substantially the same as the calculations made by the company.

By this time a week has elapsed and you feel that you have waited long enough for the completion of the verification of accounts receivable. Accordingly you instruct your assistant to go through the detailed customers' accounts and post on his trial balance all cash collected on them since the balance sheet date. When he has done this, you give him the pile of confirmation replies (which you have been picking up at our office each morning on your way to work) and tell him to schedule all the exceptions reported by the customers on a 14-column work sheet with the following headings:

Name of customer
Confirmation number
Amount per books
Amount per reply
Difference
Explanation of difference

He then takes this schedule and having investigated each exception by examining sales and cash records, and by discussions with the credit manager, indicates on his schedule how it was disposed of.

Your assistant finishes his work on receivables and starts on the accounts payable. You instruct him to go through the voucher register listing all the open items, including voucher numbers, names and amounts, and having prepared such schedule, to proceed with our standard verification procedures. You also tell him to examine all vouchers entered in July 1967 and to prepare a list of invoices bearing June or prior datings, showing in each case voucher number, vendor's name, amount, nature of material or service, receiving date, and account charged.

When all of the foregoing has been completed, you and your junior assistant turn to the income and expense accounts and verification of cash disbursements for one month. The latter phase of the work you turn over to him and instruct him to obtain all of the cancelled checks returned by the bank for the months of January and February, 1967 and trace them back to the cash disbursements records for January. You then instruct him to pull the vouchers for the same months and compare them with the voucher register. When he has completed this step, you tell him to crosscheck the voucher register to the cash disbursements book so as to obtain a complete verification of the outgoing cash transactions for the month selected by you for test purposes. For your part, you prepare the usual analyses of the miscellaneous income and expense accounts and in addition prepare summary analyses of the principal accounts (purchases, direct labor, and so forth) in cost of sales, in order to satisfy yourself as to the general nature of the transactions flowing through these accounts. Having finished this, you prepare extracts from the corporate minutes for the year, post your trial balance, schedule your journal entries, and then return to the office with your assistant to write your report.

Standards of reporting;
the short-form report

23

Throughout the audit examination the independent auditor should be guided by the report he is expected to render at the completion of his examination. Ideally, he should be able to report that his examination was made in accordance with generally accepted auditing standards, and, based on this examination, that in his opinion the client's financial statements present fairly the client's financial position and results of operations in conformity with generally accepted accounting principles applied on a basis consistent with that of the preceding year. The auditor's representations concerning the scope of his examination and his professional opinion may constitute the entire contents of the report which he renders to his client. In that case the report is known as a short-form report, or certificate. If the representations are supplemented by detailed comments analyzing the client's financial position and results of operations or setting forth the major audit procedures followed, the report is usually referred to as a long-form report. The long-form report is discussed in the following chapter.

The short-form report recommended by the American Institute of Certified Public Accountants was presented in Chapter 1. This recommended form is used almost verbatim in connection with most published financial statements. In other cases the wording is changed somewhat, or the arrangement is reversed, with the opinion preceding the information on scope. Only very rarely does the auditor's report accompanying published financial statements represent a direct departure from the recommended form. Such unanimity has been accomplished solely by voluntary means, and has been a significant factor in achieving national acceptance and understanding of the independent audit services performed by Certified Public Accountants, regardless of the identity of the individual accountant performing the service.

Significance of Exact Wording Used in the Certificate

Persons who rely upon audited financial statements should not, however, assume that a two-paragraph statement followed by the auditor's signature is a sure sign that the financial statements are reliable and may be used without question. The exact wording of the two paragraphs is extremely significant. Either of the paragraphs may contain exceptions which will drastically affect the reliability and usefulness of the financial statements. As a result of limitations placed by the client upon the scope of the auditor's examination, or as the result of conditions which make certain important audit procedures impracticable or unreasonable, the auditor may have to state that his examination was not made in accordance with generally accepted auditing standards. These limitations may make it impossible for the auditor to reach a satisfactory opinion about the statements, and he may thus be forced to qualify his opinion concerning the statements, or perhaps even state that he can express no over-all opinion.

Statements which do not present fairly the client's financial position or results of operations, in conformity with generally accepted accounting principles applied on a basis consistent with that of the preceding year, may similarly necessitate qualification of the opinion expressed by the auditor, or even result in an "adverse" opinion, as discussed later in this chapter.

Control by the Client Over the Wording of the Auditor's Certificate

Because his certificate is rendered in an independent capacity, the auditor must retain final authority over the wording of his certificate. At the same time, the client can directly control the wording of the certificate. This paradoxical situation is explained by the fact that if the client wishes to have an unqualified certificate, he must give the auditor free reign in determining the scope of the examination to be made and the form and content of the final financial statements. On the other hand, if the client requests that certain procedures be omitted from the examination, or that the financial statements be presented in a manner which is not satisfactory to the auditor, then the client must be content with a certificate which is qualified as the auditor may deem necessary.

Development of the Form of the Auditor's Certificate

An actual audit report, rendered in 1906 by a national firm of Certified Public Accountants which is still practicing, reads as follows:

In accordance with your request, we have made an audit of your books and accounts, for the year ended July 31, 1906, and submit herewith two pages of comments, and the following described exhibits and schedules, viz.:

EXHIBIT

"A" GENERAL BALANCE SHEET—JULY 31, 1906—AND 1905—AND COMPARISON
Schedule
   #1—Notes Payable—July 31, 1906
"B" SUMMARY OF INCOME AND PROFIT AND LOSS—FOR THE YEARS ENDED JULY 31, 1906 AND 1905—AND COMPARISON
Schedule
   #1—Cost of Goods Sold and Expenses
   #2—Depreciation Charges Against Income
                              Yours truly,
                              (Signed) ———————————————
                              Certified Public Accountants

The report contains no reference to an opinion or certification of the statements, but the reader is apparently expected to conclude that the financial statements have the full approval of the accountants, because the accountants have made an audit and have included the financial statements in their report on the basis of their audit.

1917. The first attempt at standardization of auditors' reports took place in 1917, when, at the request of the Federal Trade Commission, the American Institute of Certified Public Accountants prepared "A memorandum on balance sheet audits." This memorandum was forwarded by the Commission to the Federal Reserve Board, which issued the material in a widely used pamphlet entitled *Approved Methods for the Preparation of Balance Sheet Statements*. The suggested form of report included in the pamphlet reads:

I have audited the accounts of Blank & Co. for the period from ——— to ——— and I certify that the above balance sheet and statement of profit and loss have been made in accordance with the plan suggested and advised by the Federal Reserve Board and in my opinion set forth the financial condition of the firm at ——— and the results of its operations for the period.

Acceptance of the suggested form of report was far from complete, however. Many auditors used a more simplified form, and others used a long-form report in which they listed all the procedures followed. The reader of the long-form report was left to decide whether the procedures followed were adequate, or whether certain important procedures had been omitted.

1929. The experience with the Federal Reserve Board's pamphlet and the suggested form of audit report was reviewed by a special committee of the A.I.C.P.A. in 1929, and as a result certain changes were recommended in the 1917 pamphlet. The revised pamphlet was again published by the Federal Reserve Board, this time with the title *Verification of Financial Statements.* The pamphlet dealt more extensively with the auditor's responsibility in connection with his certificate, stressing the importance of the adequacy of the examination in relation to the requirements set forth in the pamphlet and suggesting a new form of certificate to be used with statements found to be "correct" in all material respects:

> I have examined the accounts of ——— for the period from ——— to ———. I certify that the accompanying balance sheet and statement of profit and loss, in my opinion, set forth the financial condition of the company at ——— and the results of operations for the period.

1934. The first standard form of audit report to receive general acceptance by the profession was suggested by the American Institute of Certified Public Accountants in 1934, in its pamphlet *Audits of Corporate Accounts.* The form of the report was quite similar in general content and purpose to the report which is widely used today, although it included phrases not presently in use and omitted other phrases which are used in today's report. The wording recommended in 1934 is as follows:

> We have examined the balance sheet of the X Company as of December 31, 1933, and the statement of income and surplus for the year then ended. In connection therewith, we examined or tested accounting records of the company and other supporting evidence and obtained information and explanations from officers and employees of the company; we also made a general review of the accounting methods and of the operating and income accounts for the year but we did not make a detailed audit of the transactions.
>
> In our opinion, based on such examination, the accompanying balance sheet and related statements of income and surplus fairly present, in accordance with accepted principles of accounting consistently maintained by the company during the year under review, its position at December 31, 1933, and the results of its operations for the year.

The reader should note some of the more important changes reflected in the above report, as compared with the 1917 report. One of these is to refer to the auditor's work as an examination of the client's financial statements rather than as an audit of the accounts. Also, a general description of the nature of the auditor's examination is included. In the opinion portion of the report the word "certify" is omitted, but the terms "fairly present," "accepted principles of accounting," and "consistently maintained" make their appearance. The latter terms represent a more direct expression of the auditor's opinion, because the 1917 report merely stated that the statements were made "in accordance with the plan suggested and advised by the Federal Reserve Board." In general, the changes reflect marked growth in the professional stature of the public accounting profession.

1939. In *Extensions of Auditing Procedure,* published by the American

Institute of Certified Public Accountants in 1939 following the McKesson & Robbins disclosures, further changes in the report were made. A phrase was added indicating that the auditor had reviewed the client's system of internal control in the course of his examination, but the phrase "obtained information and explanations from officers and employees of the company" was deleted as it was assumed to be inherent in all auditing procedures that such information and explanations would be obtained. Another addition to the scope paragraph was the indication that the examination was made "by methods and to the extent we deemed appropriate," thus emphasizing the auditor's responsibility for the procedures employed.

The principal change in the opinion paragraph was to add the qualifying term "generally" to the phrase "accepted principles of accounting." In the explanatory material relating to the revised certificate, however, a forthright statement was made concerning exceptions to the auditor's opinion. The pamphlet pointed out that:

> The independent certified public accountant should not express the opinion that financial statements present fairly the position of the company and the results of its operations, in conformity with generally accepted accounting principles, when his exceptions are such as to negative the opinion, or when the examination has been less in scope than he considers necessary. In such circumstances, the independent certified public accountant should limit his report to a statement of his findings and, if appropriate, his reasons for omitting an expression of opinion.

1941. After discussion with the American Institute of Certified Public Accountants, the Securities and Exchange Commission amended its *Regulation S-X,* effective March 1, 1941. Added to *Regulation S-X* was Rule 2.02(b), which stated that:

> The accountant's certificate (i) shall contain a reasonably comprehensive statement as to the scope of the audit made including, if with respect to significant items in the financial statements any auditing procedures generally recognized as normal have been omitted, a specific designation of such procedures and of the reasons for their omission; (ii) shall state whether the audit was made in accordance with generally accepted auditing standards applicable in the circumstances; and (iii) shall state whether the audit made omitted any procedure deemed necessary by the accountant under the circumstances of the particular case.

(The wording of this rule has since been changed in the revision of *Regulation S-X,* which became effective December 20, 1950.)

To avoid a "double standard" whereby reports to the SEC might differ from reports issued for other purposes, the Committee on Auditing Procedure of the A.I.C.P.A. recommended that the standard report be revised to include a statement to the effect that "our examination was made in accordance with generally accepted auditing standards applicable in the circumstances and it included all procedures which we considered necessary." The recommended revised report, set forth in *Statement on Auditing Procedure No. 5* issued in February, 1941, was deemed by the SEC to meet the requirements of its new rule.

1942. No changes in the wording of the standard certificate were recommended in 1942, but as a result of experience under the increased audit requirements set forth in *Extensions of Auditing Procedure,* and in view of the new rule of the SEC pertaining to auditors' certificates, *Statement on Auditing Procedure No. 12* was issued in May, 1942. The additional disclosure which was recommended concerning the omission of required auditing procedures was largely a reflection of existing practice by most accountants. The concluding paragraph of statement No. 12 reads:

> Accordingly, the committee on auditing procedure hereby recommends that hereafter disclosure be required in the short form of independent accountant's report or opinion in all cases in which the extended procedures regarding inventories and receivables set forth in "Extensions of Auditing Procedure" are not carried out, regardless of whether they are practicable and reasonable, and even though the independent accountant may have satisfied himself by other methods.

1947. After extensive study of the relatively new idea of auditing standards which stemmed from the 1941 rule of the SEC, the Committee on Auditing Procedure issued in 1947 the report *Tentative Statement of Auditing Standards—Their Generally Accepted Significance and Scope.* With the further understanding of auditing standards, it became evident that auditing *standards* were universal and did not vary with the circumstances, whereas auditing *procedures* should be varied according to the circumstances. Accordingly, the recommendation was made that the new phraseology recommended in 1941 be changed to read, "Our examination was made in accordance with generally accepted auditing standards and included all procedures which we considered necessary in the circumstances."

1948. The general membership of the American Institute of Certified Public Accountants adopted in 1948 the summary of auditing standards presented in the 1947 report on auditing standards. As this action gave official status to the meaning of the term "generally accepted auditing standards," the Committee on Auditing Procedure concluded that further modification of the recommended form of the certificate was in order. The committee recommended that reference was no longer needed to the fact that the examination included a review of the system of internal control and did not include a detailed audit of the transactions, as these points were specifically made a part of generally accepted auditing standards. Standard No. 2 under the heading "Standards of Field Work" states, "There is to be a proper study and evaluation of the existing internal control as a basis for reliance thereon and for the determination of the resultant extent of the tests to which auditing procedures are to be restricted."

The Committee did, however, suggest a modification of the wording of the final sentence of the scope paragraph which included an implication that no detailed audit had been made. The revised sentence read, "Our examination was made in accordance with generally accepted auditing standards, and accordingly included such tests of the accounting records and such other auditing procedures as we considered necessary in the circumstances."

No further changes have been recommended in the form of the standard certificate since 1948. In its present form the standard certificate corresponds with the example presented in Chapter 1 of this book.

1949. Another major action by the A.I.C.P.A. which related to accountants' reports on financial statements occurred in 1949, when *Statement on Auditing Procedure No. 23,* entitled "Clarification of Accountant's Report When Opinion Is Omitted," was adopted by the Institute membership at its annual meeting in November, 1949. Two significant points were involved. The first related to the fairly common practice of issuing clients' financial statements on the accountant's stationery, or within covers bearing the name of the accountant, but with no representation by the accountant as to the fairness of the statements, or possibly with only a nondefinitive notation that the statements were "for management purposes only." The second point related to situations in which the auditor's comments accompanying a client's financial statements indicated that an examination had been made but where there was no expression of opinion concerning the statements and no specific disclaimer of an opinion.

Because the auditor has no control over the use of financial statements accompanied by his name, both of the above practices tended to cause misunderstanding or misinterpretation on the part of third parties to whom the statements were shown. With no firsthand knowledge concerning the auditor's work, such third parties were often unclear concerning the responsibility assumed by the auditor for the representations in the financial statements. To avoid such difficulties and to recognize more adequately the responsibility of the accounting profession to third parties, the Committee recommended and the Institute adopted the recommendation that

...whenever financial statements appear on the stationery or in a report of an independent certified public accountant, there should be a clear-cut indication of the character of the examination, if any, made by the accountant in relation to the statements, and either an expression of opinion regarding the statements, taken as a whole, or an assertion to the effect that such an opinion cannot be expressed. When the accountant is unable to express an over-all opinion, the reasons therefor should be stated. When the accountant considers it appropriate to comment further regarding compliance of the statements with generally accepted accounting principles in respects other than those which require the denial of an over-all opinion, he should be careful to indicate closely the limitations of such comments.

The reason for the Committee's request that its recommendations be approved by the membership of the Institute related to a provision of *Extensions of Auditing Procedure* approved by the membership in 1939. As noted previously, that document stated that there should be no expression of opinion by the auditor if his exceptions were such as to negative an opinion or if his examination were less in scope than he considered necessary. The new action, taken ten years later, required that the auditor's representations in such situations be clarified by an unequivocal assertion by the auditor that he was not in a position to express an over-all opinion concerning the financial statements. This action has been further reflected in Rule 2.03 of the Code of Professional Ethics.

1956. Additional action was taken by the Committee on Auditing Procedure in 1956 in an effort to secure clarification of the auditor's report in situations where confirmation of receivables or observation of the client's physical inventory were not undertaken, but the auditor nevertheless was able to satisfy himself that the related statement figures were fairly stated. In dealing with this problem, *Statement on Auditing Procedure No. 26* expressed the view of the Committee that in connection with the omission of the required receivables and inventory procedures the auditor should "...not only disclose, in the general scope section of his report, whether short or long form, the omission of the procedures, regardless of whether or not they are practicable and reasonable, but also should state that he has satisfied himself by means of other auditing procedures if he intends to express an unqualified opinion."

1957. *Statement on Auditing Procedure No. 28* was released by the Committee on Auditing Procedure in 1957, dealing with the wording of the auditor's report in such special circumstances as when an opinion is expressed on cash-basis statements or on the statements of nonprofit organizations.

Generally accepted auditing standards require that the auditor's report on a concern's financial statements include an opinion as to the conformity of the statements with generally accepted accounting principles. The Committee concluded that the requirement is not applicable to statements that do not purport to set forth financial position or results of operations, as would be the case when statements are prepared on the basis of cash receipts and cash disbursements. It is desirable that such statements clearly reveal that they have been prepared on a cash basis and indicate the general nature of items that have been omitted in their preparation, such as accounts receivable, inventories, or accounts payable. Under these circumstances it should not be necessary that the auditor's report point out that the statements do not present the firm's financial position and results of operations in accordance with generally accepted accounting principles. Instead, in the opinion of the Committee, it is necessary only that the report indicate whether the statements present fairly all data on the basis indicated in the statements. The Committee also suggested that use of the terms "balance sheet" and "income statement" would appear to be inappropriate under such circumstances. The following suggested opinion paragraph incorporates the recommendations of the committee:

> In our opinion the accompanying statements present fairly those assets and liabilities recognized by ———— Company at December 31, 19——, as a result of cash transactions, and the revenues collected and expenses disbursed during the year then ended. The statements have been prepared on a basis consistent with that of the preceding year.

Should the statements not clearly indicate the basis on which they have been prepared, or be subject to misleading inferences, the Committee suggested the addition of an intermediate paragraph to the auditor's report to point out that the statements do not present financial position and results of operations.

As to reports on the statements of nonprofit organizations, the Committee indicated that if clearly defined principles applicable to the type of organization in question (such as a hospital or educational institution) have become generally accepted, no basic modification of the reports on the statements of such organizations would be necessary. The fact that the principles might vary from those applicable to concerns organized for profit would not alter the situation. (Educational institutions, for example, do not ordinarily reflect depreciation of plant and equipment as an expense, although strong arguments have been presented opposing this practice.)

1962. *Generally Accepted Auditing Standards* included a reference to cases where ". . . the accountant's exceptions as to practices followed by the client are of such significance that he may have reached a definite conclusion that the financial statements do not fairly present the financial position or results of operations. In such cases, he should be satisfied that his report clearly indicates his disagreement with the statements presented." In *Statement on Auditing Procedure No. 32,* the Committee on Auditing Procedure introduced the term "adverse opinion" to cover such situations. The Committee pointed out that a *disclaimer* of opinion would be inappropriate under those circumstances, and that instead an adverse opinion should be given. In addition, rule 2.03 of the Code of Professional Ethics was subsequently amended to include a specific reference to the adverse opinion as one of the types of opinion that might be expressed.

1964. The governing Council of the A.I.C.P.A. adopted a recommendation that Institute members see to it that departures from Opinions of the

Accounting Principles Board (including *Accounting Research Bulletins* accepted by the Board) are disclosed in footnotes to financial statements, or if not so disclosed, then in the audit report prepared for the engagement. The recommendation adopted by the Council states:

> If an accounting principle that differs materially in its effect from one accepted in an Opinion of the Accounting Principles Board is applied in financial statements, the reporting member must decide whether the principle has substantial authoritative support and is applicable in the circumstances.
>
> If he concludes that it does not, he would either qualify his opinion, disclaim an opinion, or give an adverse opinion as appropriate.
>
> If he concludes that it does have substantial authoritative support, he would give an unqualified opinion and disclose the fact of departure from the Opinion in a separate paragraph in his report or see that it is disclosed in a footnote to the financial statements and, where practicable, its effects on the financial statements.

SHORT-FORM REPORT STANDARDS

The purpose of this section is to explore and elaborate upon the use of the short-form report and its adaptation and modification to conform with generally accepted standards of reporting under varying circumstances.

General Requirements

The following points, many of which have been discussed previously, are enumerated below to indicate the standards that apply in the normal situation when the recommended form of report can be used without modification. The responsibilities involved in rendering an unqualified auditor's short-form report are also stated.

1. The report should be dated. The dating establishes the termination of the auditor's responsibility for disclosing events occurring subsequent to the balance sheet date and will ordinarily represent the date that the field work was completed in the client's office. In the case of registration statements filed with the Securities and Exchange Commission, the responsibility for disclosure extends to the effective date of the registration statements.

2. The report should be addressed to the client. When the client is a corporation, the report should be addressed to the stockholders or to the board of directors.

3. The report should disclose the exact name of the client, which in the case of a corporation would be the name specified in the corporate charter, including any abbreviations, such as "&," "Co.," "Corp.," or "Inc." In addition, it is desirable to disclose the nature of the business entity to which the financial statements pertain. This disclosure can be made parenthetically,

subsequent to the name of the business given in the opening sentence of the report, as for instance:

The Wheat State Produce Co. (a Kansas Corporation), or

Sigel & Co. (a partnership)

4. The report should identify each statement (balance sheet, income statement, statement of retained earnings, statement of funds provided and applied) to which the report pertains and the exact date of the statement or the period covered by the statement.

5. The report should indicate that the auditor's examination was made in accordance with generally accepted auditing standards.

6. The report should state that in the auditor's opinion the financial statements present fairly the financial position of the business and the results of operations in conformity with generally accepted accounting principles applied on a basis consistent with that of the preceding year.

7. The financial statements are the representations of the management of the business concern. The primary responsibility of management for the financial statements and the disclosures made therein preclude the auditor from changing or modifying the statements without the consent of management.

8. The informative disclosures in the financial statements must be adequate to meet the needs of the typical statement user.

9. The financial statements must be fully self-explanatory through the use of captions, classification of items, descriptive information, and footnotes (which are considered to be part of the statements).

10. The auditor's report should bear the manual signature of the auditor.

11. The statements and the auditor's report should be bound in such a fashion that the statements and report cannot be separated and used individually without mutilating the paper on which they are presented.

For the purpose of this discussion, as well as in the actual conduct of independent audit examinations, items 5 and 6 in the above listing are of prime importance. The auditor's representations as to the scope of his examination and his expression of opinion concerning the client's financial statements represent the core of the entire matter. When the short-form report is rendered in the recommended form and without any manner of qualification pertaining to the scope of the auditor's examination or the opinion he has reached, the report reflects the ideal situation. Deviations from the ideal situation and the effect of those deviations upon the short-form report under acceptable standards of reporting constitute the subject matter of the remainder of the chapter.

Modifications of the Standard Report

If the client requests that certain required auditing procedures be omitted, if the client's financial statements are unacceptable to the auditor and the client refuses to change the statements, or if certain required auditing procedures cannot be applied for reasons beyond the control of the client or the auditor, the form and content of the auditor's certificate must be modified accordingly. The modification may involve an exception to the assertion that the examination was made in accordance with generally accepted auditing standards, a qualification of the auditor's opinion concerning the financial statements, or a combination of both of these modifications. In other cases, the qualifications of the auditor's opinion may be so significant as to make an expression of opinion meaningless, or even misleading. Under those circumstances the auditor should clearly state that he is unable to express an opinion concerning the statements as a whole, and if appropriate he should give his reasons for this denial of an opinion. The auditor may, however, go on to indicate the scope of the examination which he made and give a "piecemeal" opinion with respect to those specific items in the financial statements on which he is in a position to express an opinion. As discussed more fully at a later point, however, the piecemeal opinion must be carefully worded so as to avoid giving the reader the impression that the auditor is actually expressing an opinion on the statements as a whole.

If the client has followed accounting practices which result in statements that are actually misleading, or if the client refuses to include informative disclosures necessary to prevent the statements from being misleading, the auditor should express an *adverse* opinion that the statements *do not* present fairly the financial position and results of operations, giving his reasons for so stating.

Effect of Limitations in Scope of Auditor's Examination

Restrictions placed on the scope of the auditor's examination either by the client or by circumstances not under the control of the client will affect the scope paragraph of the auditor's report, and in some cases will also affect the opinion paragraph—possibly even necessitating a denial of opinion. Only significant restrictions will affect the report, however. For instance, a client may rent space in another city and maintain a sales office there. The only assets maintained at the sales office are office equipment and a petty cash fund; shipments are made from the main plant, all sales and receivables records are maintained at the home office, and all salaries and expenses other than petty cash items are paid from the home office. It would certainly not be reasonable to expect the auditor to visit the sales office in order to count the petty cash fund and establish the physical existence of the equipment in the office in view of the insignificance of the items involved in relation to the over-all financial position and operating results. For the same reason, there would be no need for the auditor to take any exception in his report to the statement that his examination was made in accordance with generally accepted auditing standards, and included all procedures which he considered necessary *in the circumstances.* It is thus conceivable that the auditor *might* have insisted on counting the petty cash fund had the fund been located at the main office, even though he would not insist on doing so under the circumstances described.

Disclosure of deviation from normal auditing procedures; no effect on representations as to scope or opinion. By increasing the significance of the branch office operation set forth in the preceding illustration, a point is reached at which the auditor's report will be affected if normal auditing procedures are not followed in examining the branch operations. The exact point at which such a change would occur is difficult to determine. In each situation the auditor would have to evaluate all the pertinent facts and arrive at a decision based on his experienced judgment.

To illustrate the factors which would influence such a decision and to suggest a possible point of reference, a series of assumptions have been supplied concerning a branch operation. The assumptions are then evaluated, and a point is suggested at which the significance of the branch operation, considering the attendant circumstances, would probably affect the auditor's certificate in the absence of adequate verification of the branch figures.

1. The client requests that the auditor not visit the branch office to carry out the normal auditing procedures, because travel costs and other out-of-pocket expenses charged to the client would be excessive.

2. The branch represents a completely decentralized operation, with inventories stored at the company's local warehouse and all records pertaining to sales, receivables, and cash collections and disbursements maintained at the branch.

3. Branch activities relating to warehousing, shipping, billing, receivables, cash, payrolls, and general bookkeeping are all handled by separate individuals who report directly to the branch manager.

4. The home office keeps perpetual inventory records pertaining to inventories held at the branch, based on shipments to the branch from the main warehouse and sales reported by the branch.

5. The branch records are audited yearly by the company's internal auditor, who also observes the taking of the physical inventory at the end of the year and reconciles the quantity figures with the home office records.

6. The independent auditor confirmed the balances of branch bank accounts and traced reconciling items on the bank reconciliations to bank cut-off statements mailed directly to him.

7. The independent auditor carried out satisfactory confirmation of branch receivables based on a trial balance of the receivables submitted by the branch.

8. The independent auditor totaled the duplicate sales invoices submitted

by the branch for one month and balanced the figure with reported sales for the month. The merchandise withdrawals were tested against the home office perpetual records of branch inventory. Credits to home office inventories for merchandise shipped to the branch for the month were tested against debits to the branch inventory records.

9. The independent auditor tested the internal auditor's working papers covering the reconciliation of physical inventory quantities at the branch with the home office records and made adequate tests of inventory prices and clerical accuracy. Personal property tax assessments and insurance policies were examined in further support of the branch inventories.

10. Branch inventories had shown a reasonable relationship to sales in recent years, based on comparable home office figures, and branch expenses were about the same percentage of sales as for the home office.

11. Company inventories are approximately 40 per cent of current assets and 25 per cent of total assets. Net income has averaged about 10 per cent of total assets.

12. The independent auditor visited the branch in the preceding year and carried out all normal auditing procedures at that time. No substantial errors or differences were noted, and through past experience the independent auditor has formed a favorable opinion concerning the integrity of the management of the company and the accuracy of its accounting records.

13. The principal deficiencies in the independent auditor's examination were the absence of direct contact with accounting records maintained at the branch with respect to sales, receivables, and expenses, and with. the physical inventory. However, in view of the internal check and the other procedures applied by the auditor, he was satisfied that the branch figures were fairly stated, although such satisfaction was limited with respect to inventory quantities.

Based on the above assumptions, it is the opinion of the author that if branch inventories and other figures did not exceed more than about 10 per cent of the figures for the company as a whole, no disclosure would be necessary in the auditor's report that he did not visit the branch to carry out the customary auditing procedures. This conclusion is based on the fact that the branch figures would not under these circumstances be a significant proportion of total company figures, and the fact that the procedures which the auditor was able to apply to the branch figures would give the auditor considerable basis for believing that the branch figures were fairly stated. In view of these considerations, no useful purpose would appear to be served by commenting on the situation in the auditor's report.

As the proportion of the total company figures represented by branch inventories and operations is increased, the mounting significance of the branch figures would necessitate that the auditor disclose the fact that he had not visited the branch, even though he had satisfied himself by other means that the branch figures were fairly stated. However, as under these circumstances any existing misstatement of the branch figures would still tend to be sufficiently limited so as not to have a material effect on the client's financial position and results of operations, no actual qualification would be necessary in either the scope or opinion paragraph of the auditor's certificate. Disclosure requirements under acceptable standards of reporting would appear to be adequately met by adding the following statement at the close of the scope paragraph:

> ...In view of the expense which would have been involved, the management asked that we not visit the company's branch office and warehouse located at Portland, Oregon, to carry out our normal auditing procedures, but we were able to satisfy ourselves by other means with respect to the accounting figures pertaining to the branch.

Deviation from normal auditing procedures necessitating qualification of scope and opinion. Mere disclosure of the omission of generally required auditing procedures would be adequate until the branch figures would begin to approach 25 per cent of the total company figures. As that point would be neared, the materiality of the figures in question would suggest the need for more than simple disclosure, even though the auditor were reasonably satisfied that the figures were fairly stated. The alternative procedures with respect to inventories would not constitute the full equivalent of the procedures which would normally be applied, and a possible misstatement of the branch inventory figures could have a significant effect on over-all financial position and results of operations.

For instance, an effort by management in collusion with the internal auditor to overstate inventories at the branch might easily result in an overstatement of as much as, say, 20 per cent. It is doubtful whether the procedures applied by the independent auditor would be adequate to uncover such an overstatement, and yet, based on the eleventh assumption stated earlier, a 20 per cent overstatement of the branch inventory when those inventories were, say, 30 per cent of total inventories would produce the following results:

Overstate total inventories	6.0%
Overstate current assets	2.4
Overstate total assets	1.5
Overstate net income	15.0

In view of such a possibility the auditor could hardly discharge his responsibility by merely disclosing the fact that he had not carried out observation of the physical inventory-taking at the branch. Rather, he should qualify the assertion that his examination was made in accordance with generally accepted auditing standards. In turn, such a qualification would mean that he was unable to satisfy himself as to the over-all fairness of the inventory figure, and he should therefore qualify his opinion as to that figure. In the area involving branch inventories beginning at about 25 per cent of total inventories and approaching as much as about 40 per cent of total inventories, the following modifications of the standard report should meet acceptable standards of reporting and disclosure:

> ...Our examination was made in accordance with generally accepted auditing standards and accordingly included such tests of the accounting records and such other auditing procedures as we considered necessary in the circumstances, except as stated in the following paragraph.
>
> In view of the expense which would have been involved, the management asked that we not visit the company's branch office and warehouse located at Portland, Oregon, to carry out our normal auditing procedures. The branch physical inventory-taking process was observed by the company's internal auditor, and he reported that the work was properly handled in accordance with instructions which we had approved. We reconciled the physical inventory figures obtained by the internal auditor with perpetual inventory records maintained at the home office. Although these procedures indicated that inventory quantities stored at the Portland branch have been correctly reported, the procedures were not adequate in relation to generally accepted auditing standards, and we were unable to fully satisfy ourselves with respect to the inventory quantities stored at Portland, representing about 30 per cent of total inventories. As to all other figures pertaining to the Portland branch, we were able to satisfy ourselves by the application of either normal or alternative auditing procedures that those figures were fairly stated.
>
> Except for the $1,401,218.69 of inventories stored at Portland, Oregon, and included in the total inventories of the company, in our opinion the accompanying balance sheet and statements of operations and retained income present fairly....

The above report is obviously not entirely satisfactory from the reader's point of view because it transfers some of the responsibility to him for deciding exactly how much reliance can be placed on the financial statements. At the same time, however, the reader knows that only about 30 per cent of the inventories relate to the branch, and he knows that the auditor is satisfied as to the general accuracy of the branch figures other than inventory which are included in the company totals.

In most instances the auditor should try to avoid a qualified opinion, giving either an unqualified opinion, if warranted by his conclusions based on the application of alternative procedures, or else denying an over-all opinion on the financial statements. A qualified opinion should preferably be given only if the limitations on the scope of the auditor's examination were the result of unalterable circumstances and the alternative procedures which were practicable and reasonable did not give the auditor an adequate basis for an unqualified opinion.

Limitation of scope of examination necessitating denial of over-all opinion. Continuing with the same set of assumptions concerning the branch, when branch inventories begin to exceed as much as 40 per cent of total inventories, a significant misstatement in the branch inventory figure could distort the company's financial position and results of operations so seriously as to make the over-all picture presented by the financial statements completely meaningless. Under such circumstances a qualified opinion would quite likely mislead an outsider into placing more reliance on the financial statements than would be warranted, and the auditor should therefore protect both himself and third parties by stating in his report that he is unable to express an over-all opinion concerning the financial statements. To accomplish this objective, the report could be worded as follows:

> ...Our examination of the home office records was made in accordance with generally accepted auditing standards and accordingly included such tests of the accounting records and such other auditing procedures as we considered necessary in the circumstances.
> At the request of management, made in view of the expense which would have been involved, we did not visit the company's branch office and warehouse located at Portland, Oregon. We were thus precluded from applying auditing procedures which we considered necessary in the circumstances with respect to inventories and other figures pertaining to the branch and included in the company's financial statements.
> Although we applied certain alternative auditing procedures with respect to figures pertaining to the branch, we were unable to satisfy ourselves generally concerning those figures. In view of the materiality of branch operations with respect to the financial position and results of operations of the company as a whole, we are unable to express an opinion as to the fairness of the accompanying balance sheet of X Company as of December 31, 19—, and of the statements of operations and retained income for the year then ended.

Denial of over-all opinion accompanied by piecemeal opinion. The preceding denial of opinion perhaps seems unduly harsh in view of the substantial amount of work performed by the auditor and the information gained thereby. If it is assumed that the auditor could satisfy himself by means of satisfactory auditing procedures with respect to all branch figures except inventories, a piecemeal opinion might be given. There would still be a denial of opinion concerning the statements as a whole in view of the materiality of the branch inventory figure, but the auditor could then go on to express an opinion concerning the various figures in the statements except for inventories, cost of sales, and net income.

The scope paragraph of the report would be modified to conform with the revised assumption, and the opinion paragraph could then read somewhat as follows:

> Owing to the limited scope of our examination with respect to inventories stored at the Portland, Oregon, branch warehouse, we are unable to express an opinion concerning the accompanying financial statements as a whole. In our opinion, the financial statements do, however, present fairly the assets (except inventories of $1,923,416.51, located at the Portland warehouse),

liabilities, and stockholders' equity (except for the effect of any possible misstatement of income for the year) of X Company at December 31, 19—, and the revenues, costs (except as those costs would be affected by a misstatement of inventories at the Portland warehouse), and expenses for the year then ended in conformity with generally accepted accounting principles applied on a basis consistent with that of the preceding year.

Such piecemeal opinions must be worded with extreme care to avoid giving the reader the impression that the auditor is actually giving an opinion on the statements as a whole in spite of his earlier denial of such an opinion.

General comments concerning preceding illustrations. The use of specific percentages for illustrative purposes in the preceding examples should not lead the reader to mistakenly believe that judgment concerning auditing matters can be rendered with such preciseness. Some dividing line had to be established for illustrative purposes, and although the percentages used are believed to be reasonable in the light of the stated assumptions, other individuals might select other percentages. The percentages would, however, be unlikely to vary substantially from those supplied herein.

Furthermore, the reader should not assume that the percentages given would apply to any audit situation involving a branch which is not visited. Actually, a change in any one of the thirteen assumptions stated at the beginning of the illustration would change the points at which the various modifications of the report should become effective.

The illustration used was somewhat extreme, particularly as the significance of the branch operations was increased, but all factors other than the relative size of the branch were purposely held constant to make possible an integrated series illustrating the causal factors necessitating modification of the auditor's report. As a practical matter, a large branch would probably be visited by either the auditor himself or by a representative of his firm from another office located closer to the branch who would perform any auditing work in accordance with the instructions issued by the auditor in charge of the engagement at the client's home office. Such conditions are commonplace and indicate the reason for the growth of national public accounting firms with offices in all the principal cities of the United States and often with offices in many foreign countries as well.

Engagement of another accountant. When a branch audit situation is faced by a local accounting firm and the travel cost to the branch would be excessive, a common solution is for the firm to engage an accounting firm located near the branch to perform the work. Rule 2.01 of the Code of Professional Ethics permits a member of the A.I.C.P.A. to engage another accountant to conduct part of an examination provided the other accountant is a "...certified public accountant, or firm of public accountants, at least one of whom is a certified public accountant, who is authorized to practice in a state or territory of the United States or the District of Columbia, and whose independence and professional reputation he has ascertained to his satisfaction."

In engaging another accountant or accounting firm to handle part of an audit engagement, it is assumed that the accountant or firm is fully responsible to the accountant who initiated the arrangement. The initiating accountant is thus able to specify the verification work to be performed and should in turn be able to assume full responsibility for the reasonableness of the audited figures as reported by the other accountant. Under these circumstances no disclosure of the situation or arrangements would be required in the audit report, provided the amounts audited by the other accountant do not overshadow those audited by the certifying accountant.

Branch audited by independent accountant engaged by the client. In many cases the client, rather than the certifying accountant, will engage the accountant who is to examine and report on the figures for a branch operation or a subsidiary company. Such an arrangement changes the position of the certifying accountant slightly. If the certifying accountant is satisfied that the other accountant is of recognized standing in the profession, and if he is also satisfied that the scope of the other accountant's examination was adequate, then the report of the other accountant may be accepted on approximately the same basis as if he had been engaged by the certifying accountant. That is, no disclosure of the situation would be necessary in the report on the statements which included the branch or subsidiary figures.

Rule 2.05 of *Regulation S-X* of the Securities and Exchange Commission affords further insight into the courses of action open to the accountant when relying on the work of other accountants:

If, with respect to the certification of the financial statements of any person, the principal accountant relies on an examination made by another independent public accountant of certain of the accounts of such person or its subsidiaries, the certificate of such other accountant shall be filed...; however, the certificate of such other accountant need not be filed (a) if no reference is made directly or indirectly to such other accountant's examination in the principal accountant's certificate, or (b) if, having referred to such other accountant's examination, the principal accountant states in his certificate that he assumes responsibility for such other accountant's examination in the same manner as if it had been made by him.

It should be noted that alternative (a) in the above rule in effect makes the certifying accountant responsible for the other accountant's work, for the absence of any disclosure of the work done by the other accountant leaves the certifying accountant solely responsible for all figures in the financial statements.

To summarize, the certifying accountant's decision as to whether or not to disclose his reliance upon the work of another accountant will depend upon (1) whether the other accountant was engaged by the certifying accountant, and (2) the materiality of the figures involved. Should these circumstances or any other consideration cause the certifying accountant to be unwilling to accept the report of the other accountant on the same basis as if he, himself, had made the examination, the audit report should be modified accordingly. The following illustration suggests a possible way of handling the situation:

> ...Our examination, which did not include the company's branch located at Portland, Oregon, was made in accordance with generally accepted auditing standards, and accordingly included such tests of the accounting records and such other auditing procedures as we considered necessary in the circumstances.
> The accounts of the Portland branch, which have been examined by other independent public accountants, have been incorporated in the accompanying financial statements on the basis of the amounts shown in the report of those accountants. Net assets of the branch at December 31, 19—, amounted to $865,439.21, or 21 per cent of total net assets, and net income of the branch for the year amounted to $142,631.85, or 26 per cent of total net income.
> In our opinion (which in the case of the Portland branch is based on the report of other accountants) the accompanying financial statements present fairly. . . .

Opinion Qualified for Reasons Other Than Scope of Examination

The auditor's opinion may also be qualified if the financial statements do not permit the auditor to make the customary representations that the financial statements present the client's financial position and results of operations—

1. Fairly.
2. In accordance with generally accepted accounting principles.
3. On the basis of the consistent application of the accounting principles as compared with the preceding year.

As with most auditing matters, materiality is a factor in determining whether the auditor should qualify his opinion. Certainly no qualification would be necessary merely because the auditor found $1,500 worth of obsolete inventory items in an inventory of a million dollars; because the client, following past practice, made no accrual adjustment for utilities consumed during the final month of the fiscal year; or because an item of nonrecurring income amounting to $10,000 was included in arriving at net income for the year of $500,000. Conversely, of course, exceptions could be so significant that they would negate any over-all expression of opinion on the financial statements, and the auditor would thus be required to give an adverse opinion.

Fairness. For instance, a company may have realized excessive profits on contracts with the armed forces, with such contracts representing the bulk of its business for the year. The income as determined by the company would be subject to renegotiation, and conceivably profits might be so high that the Renegotiation Board might recapture over half of the reported profits. If the auditor, relying on past experience and his knowledge of renegotiation proceedings, concluded that renegotiation would be likely to have such an effect, he would want the statements to reflect a liability and reduction of net income for the amount estimated to be recaptured through renegotiation. If the client refused to make the requested provision for renegotiation, the statements as a whole would be misleading in view of the substantial understatement of liabilities and overstatement of retained earnings and net income. In such circumstances the significance of the auditor's qualification would negate any over-all opinion, and the only acceptable approach would be to give an adverse opinion on the statements, with the reason stated as being the omission of an appropriate provision for refunds resulting from contract renegotiation.

A different approach might be followed if there were considerable uncertainty about the amount of the possible renegotiation refund. The client should reveal the existence of the refund possibility in the financial statements—most likely by means of a footnote disclosure. The auditor's opinion then might read:

> In our opinion, subject to adjustment for renegotiation refunds referred to in Note A to the financial statements, the accompanying financial statements present fairly. . . .

It would not be appropriate, however, for the client to attempt to disclose the impact of renegotiation by footnote if there were a reasonable basis for estimating the probable amount of the refund. Such a treatment would be misleading because the statement figures would have an appearance of validity which would be unwarranted in view of the content of the footnote. Ordinarily it should not be acceptable for the client to seek to disclose by footnote information that should be disclosed by adjustment of the statements themselves.

There are, of course, many other circumstances that might lead to an exception as to the fairness with which the client's financial statements present financial position and results of operations. For example, the exception in the following excerpt from an auditor's report relates to the fairness of the accounts receivable:

> As stated in Note (1) to the consolidated balance sheet, certain receivables are from debtors having net current asset positions which do not justify classifying such receivables as current. They are, however, included in the balance sheet as current receivables on the basis of the company's opinion that they will be

realized within one year. We are not in a position to confirm this opinion. It is not possible to determine the ultimate bad debt losses at this time. Based on our review of the accounts, and on the additional bad debt provisions claimed and proposed to be claimed for Federal income tax purposes for the years 1964 and 1965 stated in Note (3) to the consolidated balance sheet, it is our opinion that generally accepted accounting practice requires substantially larger reserves than those provided for the receivables referred to in Note (1) and for the receivables classified on the balance sheet as noncurrent receivables. If the bad debt provisions claimed for tax purposes were reflected in the accounts, they would affect surplus and 1965 profits by the amounts set forth in Note (4) to the consolidated balance sheet.

In our opinion, except for the effect of the matters mentioned in the preceding paragraph, the accompanying consolidated balance sheet and statements of consolidated profit and loss and surplus present fairly. . . .

Consistent application of generally accepted accounting principles. When the client has made a material change in the basis of applying generally accepted accounting principles, the auditor's opinion will be affected accordingly. In addition, it is usually desirable to indicate the effect of the change on the financial statements and to state whether the auditor approves of the change, as in the following example:

> In our opinion, the accompanying statements of financial position and operations present fairly the financial position of ——— *Company* at January 31, 1967, and the results of its operations for the year then ended, in conformity with generally accepted accounting principles which, except for the change (with which we concur) referred to in Note A of notes to financial statements, have been applied on a basis consistent with that of the preceding year.

Note A to the financial statements fully explains the change and sets forth the effect of the change on the statement figures:

> The financial statements for the six years ended January 31, 1966 have reflected the adoption as of January 31, 1960 of the Lifo method of determining cost of inventories. At January 31, 1967, inventories in stores are stated at the lower of cost or market as determined by the retail inventory method, and certain other inventories, principally those in warehouses and in transit, are stated at invoice cost. Consequently, the earnings for the year ended January 31, 1967 reflect the use of opening inventories based on the Lifo method and closing inventories based generally on the retail method. In connection with the discontinuance of the use of the Lifo method, approval of which was obtained from the Treasury Department in May, 1966, certain changes in procedures were adopted during the year, which made it impracticable to determine the cost of inventories at the year end under that method. For this reason, only an estimate could be made of the effect of this change on the results for the year. This estimate indicates that the 1966 net earnings as reported would have been approximately $600,000 less if the use of the Lifo method had been continued.

Should a change in the method of inventory costing be adopted in a year when materials prices remained fairly constant, the effect of the change on net income would be negligible. Nevertheless, the statements should at least be footnoted to reveal the change in view of the possible material effects which might result from the change in future years. Such disclosure might come under the heading of the auditor's general responsibility to investors, as there would be no other way in which investors would become aware of the change, unless the financial statements disclosed the basis of determining inventory costs, as recommended in Chapter 12.

The opinion paragraph of the audit report must also be qualified if the client's financial statements do not reflect generally accepted accounting principles. The following excerpt from an auditor's report illustrates this point. The exception is particularly interesting because the auditor endorses the adjustment of depreciation to reflect current price levels, but must nevertheless point out that the adjustment is not in conformity with generally accepted accounting principles.

As set forth in Note 1 to the accompanying financial statements, the statement of net revenue reflects an additional charge for depreciation of $658,000; this change is equivalent to the amount by which depreciation computed on the cost of depreciable property adjusted to reflect current price levels exceeds depreciation computed on cost. Although this practice is not yet recognized as a generally accepted principle of accounting, it is our opinion that, for the Company, it results in a fair statement of net revenue for the year, and we have approved its adoption. In other respects, the financial statements, in our opinion, were prepared in accordance with generally accepted accounting principles.

The additional depreciation necessary to reflect the increase in price level was shown as a separate item in the operating expense section of the income statement and was explained by the following footnote:

The Company provides for depreciation on the historical cost of the electric properties on a straight-line basis at rates determined by engineering studies. In the years 1965 and 1966 additional amounts were provided representing the difference between depreciation computed on property adjusted to current price levels and depreciation based on the historical cost; such additional provisions amounted to $658,000 and $665,000, respectively.

Disclaimers of Opinion

These comments concerning disclaimers, or denials, of opinion are presented because there are numerous situations in which denials should be made, and full recognition of the situations and the proper action to be taken is essential to the well-being of the public accounting profession. Failure to make a clear-cut denial when such a denial is required opens the way for statement users to be misled in relying upon financial statements which do not warrant such reliance. The possible result could be to destroy public confidence in the expression of independent opinions on financial statements. Such a loss of public confidence would be a serious blow inasmuch as expressing opinions is the greatest single factor in the existence of the public accounting profession.

The fact that it is only in recent years that the profession has courageously assumed its full responsibilities in connection with the expression of opinions on financial statements indicates that the profession is young and still developing, but is fully cognizant of its responsibility to the public. As noted earlier, principal advances occurred in 1939 when the American Institute of Certified Public Accountants stated that there should be no expression of opinion when qualifications of the opinion would have the effect of negating any opinion, and in 1949 when the Institute agreed that the accountant should specifically deny any opinion in cases where an opinion could not be given.

Typical situations necessitating denial of opinion. The auditor's denial of opinion may be necessary if he has not satisfied himself as to material amounts included in the financial statements. Any of the following reasons might be involved:

1. The statements may have been prepared from the books without audit, as when they are presented for management purposes only in connection with a general bookkeeping service rendered to the client. Such statements, if presented in connection with the accountant's name, should carry a prominent notation, such as "Prepared from the books without audit."

2. The statements may have been prepared in conjunction with a partial examination of current transactions, with the intent that additional procedures applied at the end of the year would permit expression of an opinion on the annual statements. Such interim examinations are essentially a supplement to internal control, and although of great benefit to management, they would hardly warrant even a piecemeal opinion on the statements prepared in conjunction with the examination. Banks often request such statements, however, in spite of the denial of opinion, because the statements give a current picture of the borrower's affairs.

3. Circumstances may not permit the application of required procedures in the verification of material items. Occasionally alternative procedures can be applied, or a qualified opinion may be given, but ordinarily a denial of opinion on the statements as a whole will be required. Typical situations would include a first engagement, when obviously the auditor would be unable to observe the taking of the opening inventory. In some cases, however, the inventory records will be such that the auditor can satisfy himself concerning the inventory by careful review and tests of the records. Inadequate records which give the auditor no opportunity to satisfy himself on the opening inventory would necessitate a denial of opinion on the income statement if inventories were a material item, but would not affect

his opinion on the balance sheet. Other situations in which circumstances would necessitate the omission of important procedures would include the engagement of the auditor after the year-end physical inventory had been taken and the conduct of an initial examination when past records of plant assets and retained earnings had been destroyed.

4. When internal control is wholly inadequate, as will usually be true of very small businesses, it may be impracticable to compensate for the deficiency by expansion of the scope of the audit examination, and the auditor would thus be required to state a denial of any over-all opinion, although a piecemeal opinion might be given.

5. Quite frequently the client will request that certain required audit procedures not be applied. The procedures most commonly involved are confirmation of receivables, observation of physical inventory-taking, and examination of records of a branch located at a distant point. The reasons given for the request may be the cost of the additional work, the fact that the examination is made primarily for the owner (and he is satisfied that the figures are stated correctly), or a combination of both reasons. Occasionally the figures involved may not be material or the auditor may be able to satisfy himself by other means, thus permitting the expression of a qualified opinion, or possibly even an unqualified opinion. Usually, however, a denial of opinion will be necessary.

Suggested Wording of Portions of the Auditor's Report to Cover Special Situations

The following material is intended to illustrate the manner in which the auditor's certificate can be modified to meet the requirements of various situations. Both typical and unusual situations are included. The excerpts given are intended only to be suggestive of a satisfactory approach to the problems involved. Regardless of whether the auditor is faced with an entirely new situation or a situation related to one of the following examples, he should develop his own wording if modification of the certificate is required. His wording must fit the requirements of the situation exactly, for seldom is any given situation completely duplicated in practice. The examples presented are thus suggestions only, and they should serve primarily to establish a point of departure.

Comments concerning statements for previous year included with auditor's report. If the auditor previously examined the financial statements for the prior year and these statements have been included in the current report for comparative purposes, the auditor may wish to add the following sentence at the conclusion of the scope paragraph: "We made a similar examination of the financial statements for the preceding year." In addition, the opinion should specifically refer to the statement figures for both years. If the statements for the prior year were examined by another independent public accountant, the added sentence should read: "The financial statements for the preceding year were examined by other independent public accountants." If no previous examination has been made of the statements for the previous year, the auditor might disclaim any responsibility for the statements by making this comment at the conclusion of the opinion paragraph: "Financial statements for the preceding year have not been examined by us and are included only for comparative purposes."

Special considerations in reporting on the examination of a partnership or proprietorship. The preparation of the auditor's report on his examination of the financial statements of a partnership or proprietorship presents a special problem. The auditor will normally have examined only the affairs of the business enterprise, but the law does not recognize the business as an entity distinct from the personal affairs of its owner or owners. Under these circumstances, assets of the business may be attached to satisfy personal obligations of the owner, and the auditor is normally well advised to point out this possibility to the user of the financial statements on which he has expressed his opinion. The caveat may appear as a footnote to the financial statements or in the body of the auditor's report in a form similar to the following:

> The accompanying statements reflect no liability for income taxes inasmuch as such taxes are paid individually by the partners on their respective shares of the income of the partnership. No determination has been made of the extent to which the personal obligations of the partners for income taxes or other forms of indebtedness may impinge upon the assets of the partnership.

Examples of wording to cover other special situations.

CONFIRMATION OF CERTAIN RECEIVABLES NOT PRACTICABLE

> Except that it was not practicable to confirm by direct communication with debtors the current accounts due from hotel guests, as to which we have satisfied ourselves by other auditing procedures, our examination was made in accordance with generally accepted auditing standards and accordingly included such tests of the accounting records and such other auditing procedures as we considered necessary in the circumstances.

PHYSICAL TESTS OF CERTAIN INVENTORIES NOT PRACTICABLE

> Our examination was made in accordance with generally accepted auditing standards, and accordingly included such tests of the accounting records and such auditing procedures as we considered necessary in the circumstances, except that it was not practicable for us to make physical tests of the inventories of calculators and adding machines located at company field offices throughout

the United States and Canada. We satisfied ourselves with respect to such inventories by means of other auditing procedures.

CONFIRMATION OF ACCOUNTS RECEIVABLE AND
TREATMENT OF SPECIAL CHARGE

Our examination was made in accordance with generally accepted auditing standards and accordingly included such tests of the accounting records and such other auditing procedures as we considered necessary in the circumstances. It was not practicable to confirm receivables from the United States Government, as to which we have satisfied ourselves by means of other auditing procedures.

The write-off of certain deferred development expenses, amounting to $181,820 after reduction for applicable Federal income tax credit, which has been charged as a special item in the statement of consolidated income and earned surplus should, in our opinion, have been deducted prior to the determination of net income for the 1967 fiscal year under generally accepted accounting principles. In our opinion, the statements mentioned above present fairly the consolidated financial position of ——— *Corporation* at September 30, 1967 and, except as set forth in the preceding paragraph, the results of its consolidated operations for the year then ended, in conformity with generally accepted accounting principles applied on a basis consistent with that of the preceding year.

CONTINGENCIES

In our opinion, except for the effect of any renegotiation refunds that may be required for years subsequent to 1964, the accompanying balance sheet and statements of net earnings and retained earnings present fairly the financial position of ——— *Company* at December 31, 1967 and the results of its operations for the year then ended, in conformity with generally accepted accounting principles applied on a basis consistent with that of the preceding year.

LEGAL ACTIONS AND INVENTORY VALUATIONS
NECESSITATING DISCLAIMER

The legal actions referred to in note 9 to the financial statements allege, among other things, that certain material transactions (particularly those relating to purchase of television time and motion picture rights) mentioned in the accompanying notes to financial statements were not negotiated at "arm's length" and that certain present or former officers and directors of the company were interested, directly or indirectly, in the companies with which such transactions were effected. We are not in a position to pass upon the validity of such allegations, or to determine the fair values of the television time and motion picture rights acquired, or to estimate the probable recovery, if any, under said legal actions. Neither are we in a position to estimate the probable realizable value of that portion of the inventories referred to in note 3 to the financial statements.

The accompanying financial statements are in agreement with the books of the companies and, except for the matters referred to in the preceding paragraph, in our opinion, have been prepared in conformity with generally accepted accounting principles applied on a basis consistent with that of the preceding year after revision as explained in note 2. However, having regard to the possible material effect of these matters upon the financial position and results of operations of the company we are precluded from expressing an opinion with respect to the fairness of the presentation until such matters have been resolved.

The Auditor's Certificate of the Future

Until generally accepted auditing standards are more universally followed by the profession and more thoroughly understood by persons who rely on audited financial statements, no departure is warranted from the current suggested short form of report. So long as there is no complete certainty as to exactly what an auditor did and what conclusions he reached, the auditor and the person using his report are both better protected by a careful and precise recitation of the facts as in the current scope and opinion paragraphs.

Further growth and development of the public accounting profession should, however, result in almost universal meaning and application for generally accepted auditing standards and generally accepted accounting principles. When this millennium is reached, the two-paragraph certificate should be as superfluous as the explanation that sterling silver is silver which meets the standard of 0.925 fineness for manufactured articles. At such a time the certificate may simply read: "We endorse the accompanying (or above) financial statements without qualification." If, then, qualification is necessary, the additional wording will clearly indicate some departure from normal, whereas today an exception in the auditor's report is often not apparent without careful reading of the report.

Under these ideal conditions, two of the present rules in the Code of Ethics of the American Institute of Certified Public Accountants will become of even greater importance. These rules are:

Rule 2.02. In expressing an opinion on representations in financial statements which he has examined, a member or associate may be held guilty of an act discreditable to the profession if

(a) he fails to disclose a material fact known to him which is not disclosed in the financial statements but disclosure of which is necessary to make the financial statements not misleading; or

(b) he fails to report any material misstatement known to him to appear in the financial statement; or

(c) he is materially negligent in the conduct of his examination or in making his report thereon; or

(d) he fails to acquire sufficient information to warrant expression of an opinion, or his exceptions are sufficiently material to negative the expression of an opinion; or

(e) he fails to direct attention to any material departure from generally accepted accounting principles or to disclose any material omission of generally accepted auditing procedure applicable in the circumstances.

Rule 2.04. A member or associate shall not permit his name to be used in conjunction with any forecast of the results of future transactions in a manner which may lead to the belief that the member or associate vouches for the accuracy of the forecast.

REVIEW QUESTIONS

1. Does the fact that an auditor's certificate accompanies a set of financial statements mean that the statements can be safely relied upon? Explain.
2. How can an auditor be said to be independent when the client can control the wording of the auditor's certificate?
3. What was the stand taken by the American Institute of Certified Public Accountants in the pamphlet *Extensions of Auditing Procedure* concerning exceptions to the auditor's opinion?
4. Why did the Committee on Auditing Procedure recommend a change in the phrase "generally accepted auditing standards applicable in the circumstances"?
5. What conditions led to the recommendations made in the report "Clarification of Accountant's Report When Opinion Is Omitted"?
6. List the standards relating to the preparation of the short-form report in the standard form when no exceptions are present.
7. What basically different modifications of the auditor's report may be required, depending on the circumstances?
8. Define a piecemeal opinion, and state when it would be used.
9. Will limitations on the scope of the auditor's examination affect his opinion? Explain.
10. What is the danger in giving a piecemeal opinion?
11. When a branch or subsidiary included in the final statements has been audited by another accountant, will it make any difference in the certifying accountant's report whether the other accountant was engaged by the certifying accountant or by the client? Explain.
12. Can a footnote to the financial statements be used to disclose material items which could be reflected in the statements themselves? Explain.
13. Under what circumstances should the auditor render a denial of opinion?
14. If the auditor did not observe the taking of the physical inventory of a manufacturing concern and applied no alternative procedures, could he properly issue an opinion qualified as to inventories? Explain.
15. Why might the auditor render a denial of opinion after an audit of a small business having extremely weak internal control?
16. How should the short-form audit report be modified if the client follows a cash basis of accounting?
17. What is an adverse opinion, and when should it be used?
18. What disclosure is required if the client's accounting is not consistent with an opinion of the Accounting Principles Board?

QUESTIONS ON APPLICATION OF AUDITING STANDARDS

19. The officials of Maverick, Inc., have decided that the funds expected to be recovered in the following year equivalent to depreciation charges will be available for general working capital purposes, and therefore they have set up a current asset at the end of the present year to reflect this situation. You are the company's independent auditor. Will this situation affect your audit report? How? Why?
20. Criticize the following auditor's report:
    In my opinion the accompanying financial statements present fairly the

financial position of Boswell Products, Inc., as of April 30, 1968, and the results of its operations for the year then ended. My opinion is based on an examination that was made in accordance with generally accepted auditing standards and included such tests of the accounting records and such other auditing procedures as I considered necessary in the circumstances, except that the company's customers were not requested to confirm accounts receivable balances, and I did not observe the taking of the physical inventory at April 30, 1968.

21. Public utilities, such as gas or electric companies, ordinarily do not accrue the revenue arising from services supplied to customers but not yet billed to them.
    (a) Does this situation warrant any modification of the short-form audit report? Explain.
    (b) Should there be any modification of the short-form report if a utility following the above plan switched from monthly to bi-monthly billing? Why?

22. If the auditor accedes to the client's request not to confirm receivables, does this necessarily constitute a loss of independence? Explain.

23. Can an auditor properly say that he has examined a client's December 31 financial statements when his physical inventory observation and receivables confirmation procedures were carried out at October 31? Explain.

24. What is your opinion of a financial statement footnote that reads: "No provision has been made for renegotiation refunds."

25. You are engaged to examine the financial statements of the annual fair presented by your county. A major source of revenue of the fair is the 10% of gross receipts which each concessionaire is required to pay to the fair organization. Each concessionaire makes a daily remittance of the amount due, accompanied by a signed statement of the amount of gross receipts for the day. Will the fact that it is not feasible for you to audit the concessionaires' daily receipts necessitate a qualification of your opinion? Explain.

26. Discuss the advisability of shortening the auditor's short-form report in accordance with the following suggestions:
    (a) The report would consist of only the following statement: "In our opinion the accompanying balance sheet and income statement present fairly the financial position of XYZ Corporation at ————, and the results of its operations for the year then ended."
    (b) The "report" would consist simply of the auditor's signature followed by the letters C.P.A., placed on each statement.

27. Account for the trend away from the detailed recitation of audit procedures which was formerly quite common in the auditor's report.

28. State with reasons whether the following portions of an auditor's certificate would be acceptable in connection with the examination of (a) a department store and (b) a city bus transportation company:
    "Our examination was made in accordance with generally accepted auditing standards except that we did not observe the taking of the physical inventory, but in all other respects our examination included such tests of the accounting records and such other auditing procedures as we considered necessary in the circumstances.
    "In our opinion, except for the fact that we were not able to satisfy ourselves with respect to the inventory at the end of the year, the accompanying balance sheet and statements of operations and retained income present fairly the financial position of Zim Incorporated at December 31, ————, and the results of its operations for the year then ended in conformity with generally accepted

accounting principles applied on a basis consistent with that of the preceding year."

29. You are engaged at the end of a client's fiscal year to make an initial examination of the client's financial statements. The client does not take an annual physical inventory, but makes counts of the various items during the year and at that time makes any adjustment of the inventory records necessitated by the physical count.

    (a) What effect, if any, will this situation have on the scope paragraph of your report?

    (b) State in what ways the opinion paragraph might be affected by this situation, and state briefly the considerations which would govern the possible effects on the opinion paragraph.

30. The term "generally accepted auditing standards" which appears in the short-form report relates primarily to judgments and decisions which the auditor must make throughout the audit. Illustrate this point by listing the decisions the auditor would be likely to make in connection with confirmation of accounts receivable.

31. Your client has realized a gain of $1,857 on the sale of a building in the year under examination, and insists that the amount be included in income for the year. Net income for the year before taxes and without including the gain was $6,438. Income for the past six years has averaged $53,241 per year. Would you qualify your certificate? Explain.

32. Your client, the Caveat-Emptor Company, operates a chain of twenty-seven self-service food markets. The stores were formerly all owned by your client, but during the past year the press for additional working capital to finance expanded operations led to sale and leaseback of fifteen of the stores on thirty-year leases, at an average annual rental of $6,000 per year.

    (a) What effect will these transactions have on the balance sheet other than through removal of the applicable asset and depreciation amounts?

    (b) Write the portions of your certificate that should be modified if the client refuses to follow your recommendations for part (a) above.

PROBLEMS

33. The following year-end financial statements were prepared by the Colesar Corporation's bookkeeper. The Colesar Corporation operates a chain of retail stores.

COLESAR CORPORATION
Balance Sheet
June 30, 1967

Assets

Current assets :	
Cash	$ 90,000
Notes receivable	100,000
Accounts receivable, less reserve for doubtful accounts	75,000
Inventories	395,500
Investment securities, at cost	100,000
Total current assets........................	760,500

Property, plant and equipment:

Land, at cost (note 1)	$175,000	
Buildings, at cost less accumulated depreciation of $350,000	500,000	
Equipment, at cost less accumulated depreciation of $180,000	400,000	1,075,000
Intangibles		450,000
Other assets:		
Prepaid expenses		6,405
Total assets		$2,291,905

Liabilities and Owners' Equity

Current liabilities:			
Accounts payable		$ 25,500	
Estimated income taxes payable		160,000	
Contingent liability on discounted notes receivable		75,000	
Total current liabilities		260,500	
Long-term liabilities:			
5% serial bonds, $50,000 due annually on December 31			
Maturity value	$850,000		
Less unamortized discount	35,000	815,000	
Total liabilities		1,075,500	
Owners' equity:			
Common stock, stated value $10 authorized and issued, 75,000 shares)		750,000	
Retained earnings			
Appropriated (note 2)	$110,000		
Free	356,405	466,405	1,216,405
Total liabilities and owners' equity			$2,291,905

COLESAR CORPORATION
Income Statement
as at June 30, 1967

Sales			$2,500,000
Interest income			6,000
Total revenue			2,506,000
Cost of goods sold			1,780,000
Gross margin			726,000
Operating expenses:			
Selling expenses			
Salaries	$95,000		
Advertising	85,000		
Sales returns and allowances	50,000	$230,000	
General and administrative expenses			
Salaries	84,000		
Property taxes	38,000		
Depreciation and amortization	86,000		
Rent (note 3)	75,000		
Interest on serial bonds	48,000	331,000	561,000
Net income before taxes			165,000
Provision for federal income taxes			160,000
Net income			$ 5,000

Notes to financial statements:
Note 1. Includes a future store site acquired during the year at a cost of $75,000.
Note 2. Retained earnings in the amount of $110,000 have been set aside to finance expansion.
Note 3. During the year the Company acquired certain equipment under a long-term lease.

Required:
Identify and discuss the defects in the above financial statements with respect to terminology, disclosure, and classification. Your discussion should explain why you consider them to be defects. Do not prepare revised statements. (You should assume that the arithmetic is correct.)

(Uniform C.P.A. Examination)

34. You are finishing your examination of the financial statements of Ash Corporation for the year ended September 30, 1967. The Corporation's report to stockholders, which will include your short-form opinion, will contain the consolidated financial statements of Ash Corporation and its substantial subsidiary, Worth Corporation. This is your third annual audit of Ash Corporation, and you find that the following changes from the prior year have occurred:

1. Worth Corporation, which is located in another state, was acquired as a subsidiary during 1967. Another independent auditor, who was engaged by the client, rendered an unqualified opinion on the Worth Corporation financial statements for the year ended September 30, 1967. While you are willing to use his report for the purpose of expressing your opinion on the consolidated statements, you are unwilling to assume responsibility for the performance of the work which served as the basis for his opinion.

    You have reviewed the accounting procedures employed by the client to prepare the consolidated statements and approve of them. The Corporation has appended to its financial statements a footnote that explains adequately the time of acquisition and the method of consolidation.

2. In accordance with your suggestion, on October 1, 1966 for the 1967 fiscal year Ash Corporation had begun the procedure of estimating its total social security taxes expense for the calendar year and then allocating the total to monthly costs and expenses on the basis of the proportion of total estimated annual payroll actually earned each month. In prior years this tax expense was charged to costs and expenses in the same months that the related taxable wages were paid. The unallocated social security taxes expense on taxable wages earned through September 30, 1967 amounted to $20,000 before consideration of income tax effect. (The income tax rate is 50%.) Worth Corporation uses the same method of accounting for social security taxes as Ash adopted.

3. For 1967 Ash Corporation changed its policy of taking a complete physical inventory at September 30 to taking physical inventories of half of the inventory on July 31 and the other half on August 31. You were consulted on this change and approved it. Your observation of the two physical inventories and your other procedures produced no exceptions as to quantities.

4. A new customer of Ash Corporation is a retail chain store company whose accounting system makes it unable to confirm the $56,000 balance of its account. You examined related remittances by this customer totaling $50,000 in post-balance-sheet-date audit procedures and satisfied yourself

regarding the balance by examination of shipping documents with the
exception that there is a $200 charge in dispute, which you considered
immaterial. The $56,000 is net of a credit memorandum for $150.

5. Your post-balance-sheet-date audit procedures disclosed that Ash Corporation is considering shutting down on December 31, 1967 a division that
has been a marginal operation. Because of the possible effect upon stockholder and employee relations, management prefers not to make a disclosure of its consideration of the proposed shutdown in the annual
report which will probably be mailed to stockholders on November 15.

6. A number of substantial claims and lawsuits, which were given widespread publicity, were filed in 1967 against Ash Corporation for damages
alleged to have resulted from the use of certain products sold in 1966.
The line of products was discontinued early in 1967. The Corporation's
attorney is unable to predict the outcome of these claims and lawsuits.
The management of the Corporation believes that losses, if any, incurred
in excess of the product liability insurance coverage would not have a
material effect upon the Company's financial position.

The scope of your examination of Ash Corporation was not limited
by the client in any way. No other items of importance were uncovered
by your examination.

Required:

(a) Prepare the additional footnotes that you would suggest that the client
should append to the financial statements. (Give the exact wording of
the footnotes. Do not discuss what should be included in the footnotes.)

(b) For each of the listed changes that you think does not require disclosure,
justify your belief in one sentence.

(c) Assuming that the client adopts your recommended footnotes, prepare
your short-form auditor's report (scope, opinion, and middle paragraph,
if any) for your examination.   (Uniform C.P.A. Examination)

35. You have been engaged by the Board of Directors of The Products Company,
a medium-sized manufacturer, to examine its balance sheet as of December 31,
1967, and the related statement of income and retained earnings for the year
then ended. You have made a similar examination for the preceding year. At
the conclusion of your examination you will be expected to issue a short-form
report (certificate) relating to the financial statements.

In the conduct of your examination you encounter the following situations:

(1) In response to a request for positive confirmation of its outstanding
balance, one of the company's customers, a large mail order concern
whose balance represents almost one-half of total accounts receivable
and 20 per cent of total current assets, replies that its records are not
maintained in a manner permitting confirmation.

(2) It is the company's practice to store most of its finished goods in public
warehouses from which shipments to customers are made. At December
31, 1967, the date of the examination of inventory quantities, the inventory in these warehouses is substantial in relation to the company's total
assets. One warehouse alone, which is located in a distant city and which
is operated by a company not known to you, holds one-third of the
company's finished goods.

(3) The company has advised you that it is the defendant in litigation
brought by a competitor for patent infringement. Counsel for the com-

pany advises of the amount of the damages sought by the competitor which is in excess of the company's net worth. Counsel also states that in his opinion, judgment will be in favor of your client.

(4) For the entire year under examination, the company, in accordance with your recommendation made last year, charged its expenditures for research to miscellaneous income deductions. Previously such expenditures, which are material in amount in relation to the company's operations, had been recorded as deferred charges. The amounts so recorded in previous years are being amortized over five-year periods.

Considering the specific facts recited above, and assuming that any additional audit procedures you recommend result in substantiating the facts as presented, you are to *state* and *justify fully* for each of the above situations:

(a) The additional audit procedures, if any, which should be followed.

(b) The disclosures, if any, which should be made in the financial statements or in footnotes thereto.

(c) The qualifications, comments, or references, if any, you should include in a short-form report in addition to the items in (b) above.

(Uniform C.P.A. Examination)

36. You have accepted an engagement to audit the financial statements of the Hopewell Mfg. Company. You determine that this is the company's first audit and that, in past periods, unaudited statements had been submitted to a local bank that is granting a substantial line of credit to the Company.

The prior periods' unaudited statements had reported fixed assets at an appraised amount with a corresponding credit to an appraisal capital account. The financial statements on which you rendered your short-form report state the fixed assets at cost, make no reference to the appraisal values, and exclude the appraisal capital account. You expressed an unqualified opinion in your report.

After your report is submitted to the bank president, he advises your client that the line of credit will be reduced substantially if your report is submitted to the bank's board of directors because the net worth of the Company in the financial statements in your report does not warrant the present line of credit. The bank president returns your report to the client and suggests that the financial statements be revised.

Your client confronts you with this situation and insists that you revise the financial statements in your report so that the line of credit will not be reduced.

Required:

1. What possible courses of action are open to you so that the line of credit will not be reduced? Discuss.

2. Under what conditions, if any, may the client submit additional financial statements prepared on the same basis as the prior year statements to supplement your report? Discuss.

3. Would it be proper for the C.P.A. to prepare and to label these additional statements "prepared without audit"? Discuss.

(Uniform C.P.A. Examination)

37. Juffy Clerical Services is a corporation which furnishes temporary office help to its customers. Billings are rendered monthly based on predetermined hourly rates. You have examined the company's financial statements for several years. Following is an abbreviated statement of assets and liabilities on the cash basis as of December 31, 1967.

Assets

Cash	$20,000
Advances to employees	1,000
Equipment and autos, less allowance for depreciation	25,000
Total assets	46,000

Liabilities

Employees' income taxes withheld.....................	8,000
Bank loan payable	10,000
Estimated federal income taxes on cash basis profits	10,000
Total liabilities................................	28,000
Net assets	$18,000

Represented by :

Common stock	$ 3,000
Cash profits retained in the business	15,000
	$18,000

Unrecorded receivables were $55,000 and payables were $30,000.

Required:

(a) Prepare the opinion you would issue covering the statement of assets and liabilities as of December 31, 1967, as summarized above, and the related statement of cash income and expenses for the year ended that date.

(b) Briefly discuss and justify your modifications of the conventional opinion on accrual basis statements.   (Uniform C.P.A. Examination)

Long-form reports

24

The auditor may have occasion to render many types of reports other than the short-form report, or certificate. These would include reports setting forth the exceptions or errors noted in the course of his examination, recommending changes in the accounting system to increase efficiency or improve internal control, or reporting on the results of any special examination or investigation for which the auditor was engaged. The reports are often presented in letter form, although a formal report may be submitted if the client or the auditor so desires.

If the person who engaged the auditor is both owner and manager of the business which was audited, any special reports should be addressed to him. If the owner is not active in the management of the business, the special reports may be addressed to the owner, the manager, or both, depending on the circumstances. In the case of large corporations, such special reports are usually addressed to a top management official rather than to the directors or stockholders, as is usually true of an audit report.

Strictly speaking, none of the above types of reports should be referred to as long-form reports; they are merely special reports. The true long-form report is closely related to the auditor's examination of financial statements and is rendered either in place of the short-form report or as a supplement to it.

Reasons for Preparation of Long-Form Reports

For maximum effectiveness, a long-form report should be written for a single purpose only, and the contents should then be selected in the light of that purpose. One important reason for the preparation of long-form reports is to supply adequate information to banks or other lending agencies in connection with new or continuing loans.

The other principal reason is to provide owners and management officials with a studied analysis of a company's financial position and results of operations to assist them in directing and managing the affairs of the business.

In many cases, of course, both lending agencies and owners or managers may be satisfied with the auditor's short-form report. Lending agencies are usually willing to accept a short-form report if the borrower is a large concern or has a high credit rating and the loan is well secured. Persons associated with the concern being audited will ordinarily be satisfied with a short-form report if adequate internal reports are available.

A long-form report is likely to be submitted to a lending agency in the case of smaller concerns or marginal credit risks, because the added information will aid in reaching a sound credit decision. The need for additional information will also be the governing factor in submitting long-form reports to owners or managers. Thus smaller businesses are the usual recipients of such reports, because they are seldom in a position to employ an accountant with sufficient training and ability to provide adequate internal reports.

The function of the auditor's long-form report under such circumstances is to expand and supplement the bare facts presented in the financial statements so as to convey a more meaningful interpretation of the company's financial position and operating results. The long-form report thus analyzes a concern's financial and operating data much as the optical prism diffracts a beam of light into its color spectrum, and, indeed, the A.I.C.P.A. has chosen the prism as its emblem, symbolizing the importance of the accountant's function as the interpreter of business facts.

Determining Whether a Long-Form Report Should Be Prepared

As noted in an earlier chapter, the form of report to be prepared is a matter which should preferably be determined at the time when other basic details concerning the audit engagement are settled. The letter to the client confirming the engagement should then set forth all such matters on which an agreement has been reached. In discussing the question of the type of report to be rendered, the auditor should attempt to determine the needs of the client as specifically as possible. He should then be in a position to recommend the type of report which will best meet those needs.

Although the time spent in preparing a long-form report is included in the audit fee, the auditor's recommendation that a long-form report be prepared should neither be intended nor interpreted as a means of selling additional services and earning a higher fee. When the auditor recommends a long-form report, he should be convinced that such a report is needed and that the additional expense is fully justified.

Occasionally, the auditor may detect a need for a long-form report after the engagement has begun, even though the client has insisted that only a short-form report is required. In such a situation, if the auditor is firmly convinced that he has judged the problem accurately, he may proceed to prepare the needed type of report on his own initiative. If the auditor has decided wisely, the value of the report should be readily apparent to the client, and his satisfaction with the report will provide a clue as to whether the auditor should venture to include the cost of preparing the report in his bill for services rendered.

The Auditor's Opinion and the Long-Form Report

Occasionally a long-form report may be prepared without an examination of the client's financial statements. In such cases the report and any financial statements should clearly indicate that the report and statements have been prepared from the books without audit, or some similar form of disclaimer of opinion should be given. If an examination has been made and the auditor is in a position to express an opinion on the financial statements, the opinion may be stated in a short-form report and incorporated in the long-form report by reference to the opinion in the shorter report. Preferably, however, the long-form report should contain the customary two-paragraph statement concerning the scope of the examination and the auditor's opinion.

Until recent years the opinions in long-form reports customarily covered only the financial statements in such reports. This practice did not, however, appear to be fully consistent with the requirements of generally accepted auditing standards, for the fourth standard of reporting includes the statement, "In all cases where an auditor's name is associated with financial statements the report should contain a clear-cut indication of the character of the auditor's examination, if any, and the degree of responsibility he is taking." The inconsistency in many long-form reports with respect to this standard stemmed from the fact that the reports included financial data, supplementary information, and statistical analyses in addition to the basic financial statements, with no indication of the responsibility assumed by the auditor for such information.

In *Statement on Auditing Procedure No. 27,* issued in 1957, the Committee on Auditing Procedure pointed out the desirability of including a brief statement in the auditor's report to give a clear indication of the degree of responsibility assumed by the auditor for the fairness of such information. As an alternative, the Committee indicated the possibility of footnoting the supplementary information to show the responsibility assumed by the auditor. In line with the Committee's recommendation, the auditor should state either that the supplementary information was subjected to the same auditing procedures as the basic statements and that in his opinion is fairly stated in relation to the basic financial statements as a whole, or that the information has not been audited and is presented as obtained from company reports, analyses, or inquiry of various employees, with no assumption of responsibility by the auditors for the fairness or accuracy of the information.

Writing Long-Form Reports

The only tangible evidence the client receives of the many hours spent by the auditor in making his examination is the auditor's report. The report also represents the principal basis the client has for judging the ability and competence of the auditor whom he has engaged. In this position as the focal point of the auditor's work, the report obviously deserves maximum care and attention in its preparation. After the auditor has devoted many hours to making a thorough and competent examination, he should not risk destroying the effect of his work through a carelessly or hurriedly written report. In terms of building a clientele of enthusiastic supporters, an additional hour or two spent in perfecting a good report will produce a greater return for the auditor than almost anything else he can do.

Of particular importance in assuring that a report will be well received is to limit the report to information that will be of importance and interest to readers, and to present and interpret this information in text, statements, and exhibits that offer high readability. The rounding of dollar amounts to eliminate pennies, or even to show the figures rounded to the nearest hundred or thousand dollars is helpful, and percentages should not be carried out beyond two significant digits.

Organization. Very few good reports have been prepared by simply writing as ideas come to mind. The best procedure is to jot down all possible items which might be included, organize them about a logical framework, and then discard those which contribute little or nothing to the presentation of the principal ideas to be communicated.

The "newspaper" technique of organization is ideal for audit reports. The objective is to arrange the material in descending order of importance, with the conclusion or principal idea or facts set forth at the outset, possibly on a separate page of "highlights." Supplementary information or supporting facts are then detailed, still under the rule that the most important things should come first. The value of such an arrangement lies in immediately attracting the reader's interest and attention and then inducing him to read on to learn the pertinent details. These details should also be arranged with the most important items first, followed by any others necessary to complete the picture. In this way, the reader can stop at any time he feels he has gained sufficient information, and he will have missed none of the principal ideas or facts.

If the arrangement of material in descending order of importance is not followed, there is always a possibility that the reader may lose interest and stop reading before reaching the most important items. If the reader continues in spite of the temptation to stop, when he does reach the important material he is likely to feel that the writer had no real understanding of his needs and problems. There is no other possible explanation for finding the major items buried at various places throughout the report. To illustrate this point, the reader is asked to compare the following examples:

1. A 10 per cent decrease in net sales, a 12 per cent decrease in cost of sales, and a decrease in operating expenses from 28 per cent of net sales to 26 per cent of net sales resulted in increased net income for the year as compared with the previous year. The net income for the current year was $1,254,631.82, as compared with $1,193,927.85, or an increase of 5 per cent.

2. Careful buying and control of expenses in the face of declining sales enabled the company to realize net income of $1,254,631.82, an increase of 5 per cent over the preceding year. Cost of sales was reduced 12 per cent while sales were declining 10 per cent, producing additional margin of $35,246.15. Operating expenses were reduced $25,457.82, decreasing from 28 per cent of net sales last year to 26 per cent of sales this year.

Style. A report should be written in a formal style, of course, but it need not be ponderous or sonorous. Short sentences which come right to the point are much easier to read than long, involved sentences which may have to be analyzed before the meaning is clear. Similarly, one- and two-syllable words and short paragraphs with a liberal sprinkling of captions aid the reader in comprehension.

One writer* has analyzed a number of examples of accountants' writing and found them deficient in most of the above respects. In evaluating such writing he used as his standard an analysis of an editorial in *The New York Times*, which he judged to be an example of good writing. The following tabulation summarizes the results of his analysis:

Clauses, average words	11
Sentences, average words	21
Paragraphs, average words	75
One-syllable words	63%
Two-syllable words	20%
Larger words	17%

Writing is not, of course, necessarily good merely because it matches the above statistics. But good writing which exceeds the average number of words in the three categories, or has a high proportion of multisyllabic words, can probably be made better. Bringing it closer to the standard

* John Mantle Clapp, *Accountants' Writing*, Copyright, 1948, The Ronald Press Company.

based on the editorial passage from *The New York Times* would be certain to improve it.

Excessive use of accountants' jargonese is another fault that the report writer should studiously avoid. Unlike the doctor or the lawyer, the auditor must communicate his ideas to his client. The doctor may state that the patient is suffering from arteriosclerosis combined with the effect of a gangrenous cholecystitis, but if he can proceed to cure the patient, the exact nature of the ailment is probably relatively unimportant to the patient. But the auditor doesn't have the opportunity to effect the cure—his services usually close with the diagnosis of the business ailment. Accordingly, he can expect a certain amount of difficulty if he reports to the business executive that: "The nominal burden rate used during the year resulted in unabsorbed burden which relieved the principal by-products of a fair apportionment of indirect costs. The resulting inflated realization figures induced a reduction of the sale price and actually caused the by-products to have a decremental effect on net income rather than an incremental effect."

A technical term may often provide a tempting short cut in expressing a given idea, but if the auditor wishes to communicate the idea to the client, he will do better to exchange his professional jargon for general business terminology of broader usefulness.

Mechanics. Although basically mechanics are less important than organization and style, errors in mechanics are more obvious and thus are most likely to add definiteness to an unfavorable impression. Spelling errors are the most apparent defect in writing, and they are likely to bring the reader to an abrupt halt in his thinking and cause a lowering of his esteem for the writer. Fewer people may recognize grammatical errors, but such errors are equally as damaging as spelling errors when they are detected.

Surveys designed to disclose the deficiencies of college graduates entering the public accounting profession almost invariably show that the inability to write well is a principal shortcoming. Although the inability to write in a clear, readily understood fashion is undoubtedly the leading cause of such unfavorable reactions, grammatical and spelling errors are probably also an important factor. They are certainly the least excusable inasmuch as they are the easiest to correct.

Preparing the report for delivery to the client. The auditor will usually be well advised to discuss the preliminary draft of any report with appropriate officials in the client's organization. Such discussions will often reveal changes which the auditor can make to cause the report to be more useful or more acceptable to the client. These comments apply particularly to reports which are to be submitted to creditors or other third parties.

When the staff auditor releases the report for typing, he must be certain that his draft is in the exact form which he expects the finished report to take. Dollar signs and rulings should be shown where necessary, and no abbreviations should be used unless they are to appear in the completed report. The actual typing of the report requires highly skilled and exacting work. Tabular, or statistical, typing must be carefully planned to get all the necessary material for a statement or schedule on one page and to have the material well located within the available space.

The typed report should be proofread, and all mathematical calculations should be verified. Some firms then have the finished report "referenced." This process involves verifying figures in the body of the report by reference to corresponding figures in the financial statements. All other figures in the report and in the financial statements are then referenced against the original figures in the working papers. Such referencing should not be looked upon as simply a mechanical procedure. The person who does the work should have a good knowledge of accounting, and often the work is assigned to members of the regular audit staff. Referencing is the final check of the over-all acceptability of the report and financial statements. If errors are undetected in this process, the client is likely to be the only person who will find them. Such a situation obviously would immeasurably weaken the effectiveness of the report and create a poor impression of the quality of the auditor's work.*

Reports for Banks or Other Credit Agencies

Bank credit men or others concerned with the lending of funds need considerably more information than is shown in the typical set of financial statements. Also, their needs for information are often different from the needs of business management, although the difference is largely a matter of emphasis. To acquaint businessmen and accountants more fully with these needs, Robert Morris Associates, which is the national association of bank loan officers and credit men, published a pamphlet entitled *Financial Statements for Bank Credit Purposes*. It sets forth standards for statement presentation and disclosure which are similar to the standards of statement presentation listed in earlier chapters of this book. The pamphlet also sets forth various types of supplementary information which are useful to persons who approve the granting of loans or other types of credit. The types of supplementary information recommended are summarized in the following sections.

Receivables. If notes receivable are significant in amount, they should be itemized showing date of origin, maker, maturity, and any security given. If a large number of notes is involved, a summary should be given aging the notes by date of origin and classifying the notes as current or past due

---

* Possible variations in the above procedures might include having the report referenced before it is typed (in order to eliminate correction of the numerous finished copies), and having the report read critically by a "report editor" to help achieve high standards of uniformity and excellence in all reports.

and secured or unsecured. The amount of notes taken for past-due accounts should also be shown.

Trade accounts receivable should be aged either according to date of sale or according to whether they are not yet due, past due from 1 to 30 days, 30 to 60 days, 60 to 90 days, and so on. Selling terms should be stated, and any important deviations from those terms should be indicated. If there is a concentration of receivables in a relatively few large accounts, the names of the largest debtors and the amounts owed by them should be listed. Amounts receivable other than from trade customers should be itemized to indicate their nature, liquidity, and value.

If provision is made for doubtful accounts, the basis of determining the provision should be given. An analysis should also be provided showing the changes in the provision account during the year.

Inventories. In addition to classifying inventories by stage of manufacture, if appropriate and practical they should also be classified by location, department, or product. If the Lifo method of inventory valuation is used, the year of adoption should be stated. The amount of any inventory write-downs during the year should be given, and the amount and description of any slow-moving inventory items should be stated.

Cash surrender value of life insurance. Information should be provided showing the names of insured, insurer, and beneficiary, and the face amount and cash surrender value of each life insurance policy.

Property, plant, and equipment. The asset accounts and the related amounts of accumulated depreciation should be analyzed showing beginning balance, additions, reductions, and ending balance. The manner in which depreciation is computed should be outlined and the rates used for the various classes of assets listed. Any information resulting from independent appraisals should be given.

Other assets. Material amounts of prepaid expenses or deferred charges should be itemized to indicate their identity. Tax refund claims should be listed according to the nature of the refunds, the years to which they apply, and their current status. The basis for amortization of any intangible assets should be noted.

Current liabilities. For notes which are material in amount, names of payees and maturity dates should be given. Important amounts payable to other than trade creditors should be itemized and described. Trade accounts payable should be aged by date of origin, and customary purchase terms should be stated. Any accounts which are past due should be shown separately. The terms under which any customers' deposits have been received should be indicated.

Other liabilities. In addition to the normal information included in the financial statements concerning long-term liabilities, the names of the payees should be given for any significant individual obligations. The provisions of any covenants relating to long-term liabilities should be summarized and a statement included as to the compliance with such covenants. A definite statement should be made concerning the existence or absence of any contingent liabilities and full information given on any such liabilities which do exist. Any commitments relating to purchases of machinery or construction of buildings should be disclosed.

The latest year for which income tax returns have been reviewed and closed should be stated. Any additional tax assessments should be reported, even though they are being contested.

Reserves. A summary of changes in any reserve accounts should be provided, and the nature and purpose of all reserves should be clearly indicated.

Income statement. Revenues and expenses should be reported in adequate detail. Disclosure should not be limited by combining material amounts with other items, or offsetting incomes and expenses. If practical, unit figures should be given for sales and cost of sales, and breakdowns by division, department, or product should be included. The amount of unfilled sales orders on hand should be given.

Other information. It is desirable to include summaries showing the month-end balances of the following accounts: cash, trade receivables, inventories, notes payable, and trade payables. Monthly cash and charge sales figures are also useful to the banker in estimating the amount and duration of seasonal borrowing.

Information is often desired concerning the method and extent of confirmation of receivables and the extent of tests of inventory quantities and prices. Also, the auditor's specific opinion may be requested concerning the adequacy of provisions for losses on doubtful accounts and income taxes.

Insurance policies in effect should be summarized as to type, and information supplied concerning coverage limits and the book value of insured assets, preferably broken down by locations. Coinsurance should be so indicated.

A brief description of any pension plan should be given.

Any material or unusual contractual agreements should be disclosed, including any sale and leaseback transactions.

Consolidated statements should be supported by schedules showing the details of the consolidation.

The items of information listed in the preceding pages and suggested for possible inclusion in a long-form report prepared for credit purposes are numerous indeed. Yet the reader should note that the auditor should be able to obtain most of this information directly from his working papers.

The information is almost entirely of a type which the auditor should consider in arriving at his opinion concerning the client's financial statements

Budgets. With respect to budgets, the pamphlet states, "Budgets have a definite value to the businessman for planning and control, and are often required for bank credit purposes, particularly in connection with term loan applications." In this connection, it might be noted that one of the banker's principal concerns is how a loan, if granted, can be repaid. If clients regularly prepare budgets, the cash budget, together with the supplementary information listed in the preceding sections, will usually supply the principal answers which the banker is seeking.

If the client who is seeking a loan does not prepare a regular budget, the auditor will be well advised to offer his assistance to the client in preparing a cash forecast showing how the loan is expected to be repaid. The forecast should not ordinarily be included in the auditor's report, but rather should be submitted to the banker by the client as a separate document. The prospective borrower who can show the banker exactly what he plans to do with the money he wishes to borrow and how he expects to repay it is certain to receive a more favorable reaction from the banker than the one who is sure of only one thing: that he needs some money. Even though the auditor cannot express an opinion on a cash forecast, the banker will usually be more inclined to accept the forecast if he knows that the auditor has assisted in its preparation.

General Comments Concerning Long-Form Reports for Credit Purposes

The various items summarized above from the Robert Morris Associates pamphlet represent an all-inclusive list of informative data which might be covered in preparing a long-from report for credit purposes, with the possible exception that no reference is made to inclusion of a statement of sources and uses of funds. This statement has become so important that it is often considered a basic statement along with the balance sheet and income statement. In each particular case the auditor should evaluate the client's situation from the point of view of what information would be of value to the credit man and then include only such information in the report he prepares.

The comment in the pamphlet recommending the inclusion in the long-form report of certain information about the scope of the auditor's examination seems to be a carryover from the days when there were no generally accepted auditing standards. The present level of development of the public accounting profession should obviate the need for such a recommendation. Credit agencies should be willing to accept the professional judgment of the Certified Public Accountant if he states that his examination has been made in accordance with generally accepted auditing standards and accordingly inlcuded such tests of the accounting records and such other auditing procedures as he considered necessary in the circumstances. Such a statement is backed by the C.P.A.'s most valuable asset—his professional reputation. Also, the competence of the C.P.A. to judge the adequacy of his examination is implicit in his possession of a C.P.A. certificate, which is issued only to persons who have received adequate training and have demonstrated a high degree of proficiency in auditing and accounting matters. The adequacy of an examination made in accordance with generally accepted auditing standards is reasonably assured by the research and educational activities of the American Institute of Certified Public Accountants in developing and establishing such standards.

Another factor which makes information about the scope of the auditor's examination superfluous is the fact that the adequacy of the examination can be judged only in the light of full information about the client's accounting system and records. Only the auditor would be sufficiently acquainted with such factors as the degree of internal control to be able to evaluate the adequacy of the procedures which were applied.

REPORTS FOR MANAGEMENT

A long-form report prepared for credit purposes may not serve equally well as a report for management. A good report for management purposes should include much more information about operations, whereas the detailed breakdowns and comments pertaining to the various assets and liabilities should be eliminated except for special conditions which would be important to management. Changes in financial position should represent important information to both management and creditors, however, and thus both types of reports should include comparative balance sheets and a statement of funds provided and applied.

Management-type reports are becoming less common because in this area of service to the client many auditors have recognized that the greatest opportunity for service lies in the direction of correcting the conditions that have necessitated such reports. Even in the small business that may be unable to justify the employment of a person capable of preparing a satisfactory report for management there is often a better alternative than the repeated preparation of reports by the auditor. A special report is usually necessary because the accounting system is not producing directly the information needed by management. The logical alternative is thus to determine what information is desired, and then to modify the system and the statement and report format so that the required figures will be generated as a part of the normal operation of the system, leaving only the simple clerical task of transferring the figures to the appropriate locations in the statement or report forms. Such an arrangement is not only more economical but infinitely more helpful to management because the information needed is available monthly rather than once or twice a year.

Chapter 25 contains excerpts from actual reports recommending changes of the type suggested here. To exemplify the objective of such recommendations, one accountant has stated that he would feel that he had failed his client if he found it necessary to prepare a report analyzing financial position and operations after the first examination.

External Comparisons

A question that usually plagues most management officials is how well their company is performing on a relative basis. Effective budget and standard cost figures help to answer this key question; but even where such information is available, management is likely to be wondering how well its own operations compare with those of its competitors. If a competitor publishes an annual report, some comparative information will be available, but it is usually limited to over-all figures and little is given about operating details.

Frequently, however, the desired detail data are compiled for all concerns in a given trade or industry by a trade association, a government agency, or a private concern. The published reports give averages or industry totals that can be most useful as a basis for comparison, and the independent auditor may well give consideration to including such comparative information in his long-form report, thereby helping management or others to answer some of the questions about relative performance. In terms of general sources for the comparative data, the Small Business Administration publishes a considerable amount of data, and Dun & Bradstreet publishes annually a most comprehensive analysis. Dun & Bradstreet reports figures for twelve retail lines, twenty-four wholesale lines, and thirty-six manufacturing lines. Fourteen different ratios based on balance sheet and income statement figures are presented for each type of concern, with the ratios detailed for the upper quartile, median, and lower quartile for each classification. Supplementary tables show trends by reporting the median ratios for the most recent five years for each of the ratios for each industry.

A COMBINATION REPORT FOR BOTH CREDIT AND MANAGEMENT PURPOSES

Although it has been pointed out that a report should be tailored to the needs and interests of the reader for maximum effectiveness, there has been a recent development that involves preparing a single standardized report intended for use by both the creditors of a concern and its management. The standardized report has been developed by the Midwest C.P.A. firm, McGladrey, Hansen, Dunn & Company.

The background of the reporting innovation developed by this firm involves a number of interesting considerations, among them the fact that in many situations there is a need on the part of both creditors and management for a detailed report. Because it is seldom feasible or desirable to prepare a separate report for each group, the accounting firm developed a report format that incorporates most of the information desired by both groups, so that a single report will suffice in practically all cases.

The second consideration that influenced the firm in developing a standardized report is the practical conclusion that it is unrealistic to expect that each year's report on a continuing engagement will be a newly created masterpiece designed solely to fit the situation at the particular moment of time. In fact, most reports tend to be closely patterned after the previous year's report, with different figures and possibly some modification to accommodate changed circumstances. Continued originality in such situations is beyond reasonable expectations.

A standardized report format has been the solution of McGladrey, Hansen, Dunn & Company to these dilemmas. The standardized format is adapted to all situations in which a long-form report is prepared by the firm and is expected to yield the following advantages in addition to resolving the above-mentioned problems. More attention was given to the design of the standardized format than can reasonably be expected to be given to the writing of the report for an individual engagement, thus yielding a superior report. Also, the standardized format facilitates a reader's comparison with previously reported data. The standardized reports should be especially useful to banks because familiarity with the format should simplify an analyst's use of each new report that is received and facilitate the making of intercompany comparisons.

" Model Corporation " Financial Report

The following material is selected from the report manual of McGladrey, Hansen, Dunn & Company and is reproduced with the firm's permission. The manual gives the format for the annual financial report for "Model Corporation." Included in the report are the regular two-paragraph auditors' short-form report and the formal audited financial statements of the corporation. The next item in the report is the firm's statement of responsibility for the supplementary data included in the report, and then the actual supplementary material is presented.

AUDITORS' STATEMENT OF RESPONSIBILITY
FOR SUPPLEMENTARY DATA

The following information is not an integral part of the basic financial statements, but is submitted for supplementary analysis purposes. Except as otherwise noted on the individual pages, it has been tested in connection with our original examination of the basic financial statements, and, subject to those exceptions, in our opinion, is fairly stated in all respects material in relation to the financial statements taken as a whole.

COMPARATIVE FINANCIAL STATISTICS

Income Statistics

	May 31		
	19___	19___	Etc.
Net sales	$	$	$
Salaries, officers			
Income before taxes on income (and extraordinary items)			
Income before extraordinary items			
Extraordinary items			
Net income, including extraordinary items			
Dividends paid			
Gross profit %			
% of income before extraordinary items to sales			
% of income before extraordinary items to stockholders' equity			

Balance Sheet Statistics

Cash and marketable securities	$	$	$
Receivables, net			
Inventories			
Prepaid expenses and miscellaneous			
Total current assets	$	$	$
Current portion of notes and contracts	$	$	$
Other current liabilities			
Total current liabilities	$	$	$
Working capital	$	$	$
Ratio of current assets to current liabilities	to 1	to 1	to 1
Investments	$	$	$
Property and equipment, net			
Long-term debt, net of current portion			
Total stockholders' equity			
Retained earnings			

Per Share Statistics*

Earnings per common share (before extraordinary items but after provision for preferred dividends)	$	$	$
Extraodinary items per common share			
Dividends per common share			
Book value per common share			

 * Adjusted for (2 for 1 stock split) (50% stock dividend) of February _____, 19___ .

COMPARATIVE SUMMARY OF SOURCES AND USES OF FUNDS

	Year Ended May 31	
	19_____	19_____
Sources of Funds		
Income before extraordinary items	$	$
Depreciation, etc. not requiring funds this year		
Funds provided by operations	$	$
Increase in long-term borrowings		
Increase in current borrowings		
Sale of common stock at a premium		
Sale of investments, less gain included above		
Reduction in inventories		
Reduction in trade receivables		
Collections on sale of branch plant		
Miscellaneous		
Uses of Funds		
Dividends paid	$	$
Purchases of property and equipment, net		
Reduction in long-term debt		
Reduction in current borrowings		
Repurchase of capital stock		
Increase in long-term investments		
Increase in inventories		
Increase in current receivables		
Cost of extraordinary flood damage, net of insurance proceeds		
Miscellaneous		
	$	$
Net increase (decrease) in cash and marketable securities	$	$
Balance of cash and marketable securities at May 31	$	$

ORGANIZATION, NATURE OF BUSINESS AND HISTORY

Management and Ownership	Shares Owned	
	Preferred	Common
George Model, Director and Chairman of Board	xxx	xx
Donald Model, Director and President	xx	xx
Paul Jones, Director and Vice President		xx
Robert Brown, Director and Treasurer		xx
William Smith, Secretary		xx
Mary Model, Director	xx	xx
Agnes Model	xx	xx
Major Outsider	xx	xx

Affiliations

The Company is affiliated through control of the common stock by similar interests as follows:

	Model Corporation	ABC Company	DEF Company
Percent of common stock owned:			
George Model	55%	56%	26%
Agnes Model	10	15	27
Donald Model	10	14	46

ABC Company manufactures automobile upholstery materials. There are no regularly recurring intercompany dealings. Further information about this company is shown in the balance sheet detail.

DEF Company is an equipment distributor which handles this Company's products among others; sales to it are on the same terms and at the same prices as to other customers.

Nature of Business

The Company manufactures and sells earth-moving machinery and attachments, principally scrapers, bulldozers, etc. The Company also purchases and distributes gasoline engines and electric motors.

The trade name Model is used on the products manufactured by the Company except for private-label products produced under the customer's trade name.

About one-fourth of the sales are to Caterpillar Tractor Company, one-fourth to other manufacturers and most of the balance are direct to independent dealers.

The trade territory includes the entire U. S. and western Canada, but is largely concentrated in the middle western U. S.

General office and factory, Clientown, U. S. A., owned; factory warehouse, Clientown, U. S. A., lease expires December 31, 19__, option to renew for ten years.

Branch sales offices are maintained in Denver, Colorado, lease expires December, 31, 19__; Cleveland, Ohio, lease expires April 30, 19__.

History and Predecessor Organizations

19__ Business started as jobber of mill supplies under an individual proprietorship.

19__ A partnership formed between J. J. Officer and A. B. Officer, his son, and manufacturing operations were commenced in a rented plant.

19__ Incorporated under the name Model Corporation taking over certain assets and assuming certain liabilities of the partnership through a tax-free exchange of stock with the partners.

19__ Acquired by purchase the stock of A. B. Competitor, a manufacturer of bulldozers, and liquidated the company, which had been in business since 19__. Began manufacture of scrapers.

19__ Control of the Company was acquired by George Model.

19__—Addition to factory of 90,000 square feet. A few units of a new pick-up model #31 were manufactured and sold on an experimental basis. Road graders were dropped from the product line.

Arrangements were concluded late in the year to supply a substantial amount of equipment to Caterpiller Tractor Company under private label during the coming year.

Incorporation Data

Date and state, incorporated in Delaware December 8, 1940; Charter renewed December 8, 1960.

Existence, perpetual (charter expires December 8, 1980).

Annual meeting, third Tuesday in January.

Capital stock:
Preferred, callable at $105 and accumulated dividends. Nonvoting unless dividends two years in arrears.
Common, pre-emptive rights as to any additional stock issued.

BALANCE SHEET DETAIL

Cash

	May 31	
	19—	19—
Petty cash	$	$
Change funds		
Checking accounts		
Savings accounts		
Certificates of deposit, current		
Savings and loan deposits		
	$	$

Marketable Securities

	May 31			
	19—		19—	
	Market	(Amortized) Cost	Market	(Amortized) Cost
U. S. Treasury Bonds, 2½%, Due 72-78, Face $10,000.00	$	$	$	$
General Motors Co., Common stock, 100 shares				
	$	$	$	$
Total cash and marketable securities		$		$

Trade Receivables

	May 31			
	19—		19—	
	Amount	Percent	Amount	Percent
Regular accounts, billed in				
May	$	%	$	%
April				
March				
December, January and February				
Prior to February				

Special advance datings		**		
Total accounts	$	* 100%	$	100%
Customers' notes				
Total trade receivables	$		$	
Less allowance for doubtful accounts***				
Net trade receivables	$		$	

Terms of sale are: manufacturers, 1%, 10 days, net 30; dealers, 2%, 15 days, net 30; special discounts and datings are granted to meet competition and to stimulate sales during the normally slack season.

* Included in the May 31, 19___ regular accounts is a total of $_____ due from _____ Co. which is aged as follows:

** Special advance datings are due as follows:

	Year Ended May 31	
*** Analysis of allowance for doubtful accounts:	19—	19—
Balance, beginning	$	$
Addition to allowance for year		
Recoveries of accounts previously written off		
Accounts written off during year	$	$
Balance, end of year	$	$

The addition to the Allowance for Doubtful Accounts is determined on the basis of establishing an ending balance equal to varying percentages of outstanding accounts depending on age (plus a special provision for specific accounts).

Other Receivables

	May 31,	
	19—	19—
Accounts, affiliates	$	$
Accounts, officer		
Notes, officers', current maturities		
Income tax claim		
Debit balances in accounts payable		
Accrued interest		
Accrued rent		
	$	$

Inventories

Product (Location) (Division) May 31, 19—:	Finished Goods	Work In Process	Production Materials	Production Supplies	Total
A	$	$	$	$	$
B					
C					
D					
May 31, 19—	$	$	$	$	$
May 31, 19—	$	$	$	$	$

Prepaid Expenses

	May 31	
	19—	19—
Commissions	$	$
Rent		
Insurance		
Advertising and office supplies		
	$	$

Investment in ABC Company, An Affiliate

	May 31	
	19—	19—
Investment in stock :		
7% cumulative nonparticipating preferred, $100 par :		
Cost	$	$
Dividends paid to _____ 19—		
Number of shares owned at May 31 :		
19—, 120 shares; 19—, 100 shares		
Common stock, $100 par :		
Cost		
Book (market) value at May 31 :		
19—,$;19—,$		
Number of shares owned at May 31 :		
19—, 75 shares; 19—, 65 shares		
Percent of total common owned at		
May 31 : 19—, 12%; 19—, 10%		
Dividends received during year ended		
May 31 : 19—,$; 19—,$		
Loans and advances, noninterest-bearing, due on demand		
	$	$

This company manufactures automobile upholstery materials. There are no substantial intercompany sales. Further information is included in the Notes to Financial Statements.

Rental Properties

	May 31	
	19—	19—
Fort Lauderdale, Florida, apartment house, 32 units, acquired 19— :		
Original cost	$	$
Depreciated cost		
Balance owed on mortgage		
Net equity above mortgage		
Net income after depreciation (and interest on mortgage)		
% of net income to net equity	%	%
Depreciation taken for year, on declining-balance (straight-line) method	$	$
Net income before depreciation		
% of net income before depreciation to net equity	%	%

Other Investments and Long-term Receivables

	May 31,	
	19—	19—
Long-term receivables, instalment contract for sale of St. Louis, Missouri warehouse, dated 9/1/19—, original amount $100,000.00, payable $10,000.00 annually with interest at 5%, secured by mortgage on property sold:		
Unpaid balance	$	$
Less amount included in current assets		
	$	$
Cash value of life insurance, see schedule below		
	$	$

Schedule of life insurance policies:	Face Amount	Net Premium Cost Year Ended May 31		Cash Value, May 31	
		19—	19—	19—	19—
Insurer and insured:					
New York Life Insurance Co., George Model, officer	$	$	$	$	$
Northwestern Mutual Life Insurance Co., I. Cook, employee					
	$	$	$	$	$

Model Corporation is beneficiary on both of the above policies.
Details as to indebtedness secured by the above policies are shown in the Notes to Financial Statements.

Property and Equipment

	Assets at Cost				
	Balance May 31, 19—	Acquisitions	Eliminations	Balance May 31, 19—	Estimated Life in Years
Land	$	$	$	$	
Land improvements					
Building					
Machinery and equipment					
Patterns					
Furniture and fixtures					
Trucks					
Construction in progress					
	$	$	$	$	

| | Accumulated Depreciation | | | Depreciated |
	Balance May 31, 19—	Depreciation For Year*	Elimina- tions	Balance May 31, 19—	Cost May 31, 19—
Land	$	$	$	$	$
Land improvements					
Building					
Machinery and equipment					
Patterns					
Furniture and fixtures					
Trucks					
Construction in progress					
	$	$	$	$	$

* Depreciation for the year has been computed by the following methods:
  Straight-line $
  150% declining-balance
  200% declining-balance
  Sum-of-digits

                              $

Goodwill

| | May 31 | |
	19—	19—
Cost	$	$
Amortization to date		
Amortized cost	$	$

This amount represents the excess of the amount paid for the business of the Extinct Manufacturing Company over the value of the tangible assets acquired, primarily to obtain the benefit of that company's contacts with distribution outlets. The cost allocated to goodwill is being amortized over five years, which is the estimated period benefited.

Other Intangibles

	Total	Patents	Organization Expense
Life used for amortization		*	5 Yrs.
Original cost	$	$	$
Amortization to May 31, 19—			
Amortized cost at May 31, 19—	$	$	$
Amortization for year ended May 31, 19—			
Amortized cost at May 31, 19—	$	$	$

* Various lives, depending on the period of estimated useful life to this company.

Other Assets

Advances to officers

	Interest			May 31	
Due From	Rate	Maturity	Security	19—	19—
George Model	3%	Demand	Unsecured	$	$
Paul Jones	5	*	**		
				$	$
Less amount included in current assets					
				$	$

　　* Payable $2,000.00 semiannually on June 30 and December 31.
　**　Secured by first mortgage on residence in Clientown, U. S.A., purchased by Jones September 12, 19— for $

Notes and Contracts Payable

					May 31	
Payee	Interest Rate	Maturity	Security	Original Amount	19— Balance	19— Owed
Clientown Bank and Trust Company	5%	May 20, 19—	None	$	$	$
Ace Machinery Company	6	*	*			
					$	$

　　* The contract payable to the Ace Machinery Company represents the balance due on automatic steel handling machinery and is payable in monthly instalments of $＿＿＿＿＿＿ plus interest.

Accounts Payable and Accrued Expenses

	May 31	
	19—	19—
Accounts, trade	$	$
Accounts, affiliates		
Accounts, officers		
Property taxes		
Payroll and withholding taxes		
Sales and excise taxes		
Salaries and wages		
Bonuses, officers		
Commissions		
Vacation pay		
Dividends		
Interest		
Pension and profit-sharing plan		
Estimated liabilty on product warranties		
	$	$

Other Current Liabilities

	May 31	
	19—	19—
Rent collected in advance	$	$
Customers' deposits on orders		
Provision for liability on product warranties		
	$	$

Long-term Debt

			May 31	
		Original	19—	19—
	Rate	Amount	Balance Owed	
First-mortgage bonds, due serially $ annually on July 1 from 19— to 19—*	%	$	$	$
SBA loan, due $ on _____ 19—and $ on _____ 19—(Note 1)				
			$	$
Portion payable within one year				
Long-term portion			$	$

* Information as to restrictive covenants, collateral security and other features of this indebtedness is presented in Note_____ of the Notes to Financial Statements.

INCOME STATEMENT DETAIL

Cost of Goods Sold

	Year Ended May 31	
	19—	19—
Production materials:		
Inventory, beginning	$	$
Purchases, net		
Freight in		
	$	$
Inventory, ending		
Production materials used	$	$
Direct labor	$	$
Manufacturing expenses:		
Indirect labor:		
Supervision	$	$
Transportation		
Other indirect		
Total indirect labor	$	$
Production supplies		
Depreciation		
(Gain) loss on sale of machinery and equipment	( )	( )
Etc.		
Etc.		

Scrap (sales)	( )	( )
Total manufacturing expenses	$	$
Total manufacturing costs	$	$
Work in process variation:		
Inventory, beginning	$	$
Inventory, ending		
(Increase) decrease	$	$
Cost of goods manufactured	$	$
Finished goods variation:		
Inventory, beginning	$	$
Inventory, ending		
(Increase) decrease	$	$
	$	$

Other Operating Revenue, Net

	Year Ended May 31	
	19—	19—
Equipment rental income, net	$	$
Royalties		
Commissions		
Storage fees		
Coke and candy machine sales, net of cost of sales		
Miscellaneous		
	$	$

Selling Expenses

	Year Ended May 31	
	19—	19—
Officers' salaries (and bonuses)	$	$
Salesmen's salaries		
Travel expense		
Advertising		
Etc.		
	$	$

General and Administrative Expenses

	Year Ended May 31	
	19—	19—
Officers' salaries (and bonuses)	$	$
Office salaries		
Telephone and telegraph		
Amortization of organization expense		
Amortization of goodwill		
Provision for doubtful accounts		
Depreciation		
(Gain) loss on sale of office equipment		( )
Etc.		
	$	$

Financial and Other Nonoperating Income Net

	Year Ended		May 31	
	19—		19—	
Financial expense:				
Interest expense	$		$	
Amortization of deferred bond expense		$		$
Financial and other nonoperating income, net:				
Rental property income, net*	$		$	
Dividend income				
Interest income				
		$		$
*Rent income		$		$
Rental property expenses:				
Insurance	$		$	
Property taxes				
Depreciation				
Repairs				
Rental property income, net		$		$

Federal and State Income Taxes

	Year Ended May 31	
	19—	19—
Estimated federal income tax, current year	$	$
Estimated state income tax, current year		
Addition to (reduction of) deferred taxes on income*		
Adjustment for income taxes allocated to extraordinary items		
Amount previous year's estimate (over) under actual		
Additional income tax assessed for year ended October 31, 19—		
Refund of income tax paid for year ended October 31, 19— (based on operating loss carrybacks)		
	$	$

* See note 1 of the Notes to Financial Statements.

SCHEDULE OF INSURANCE COVERAGE

	May 31, 19—
Factory and Office Building:	
Fire and extended coverage, 80% coinsurance	$
Sprinkler leakage	
Boiler explosion	
Elevator liability	
Plate glass insurance	
Contents, Stock, Fixtures and Machinery:	
Fire and extended coverage, 80% coinsurance	
Sprinkler leakage	

Automobiles and Trucks:
  Bodily injury liability
  Property damage
  Fire and theft
  Collision
  Nonownership
Other Business Insurance:
  Business interruption (U. and O.)
  Public liability
  Product liability
  Fidelity bonds
  Holdup, messenger
  Robbery
  Safe burglary
  Workmen's compensation   Statutory

The foregoing summary of insurance protection is presented on the basis of unaudited information obtained from policies on file in the Company's office. The adequacy of the coverage was not investigated by the auditors.

Comments on " Model Corporation " Report

Also included in the report manual for the Model Corporation report is a final section, "Auditors' Summary of Certain Auditing Procedures." The inclusion of such a summary is discretionary with the partner of the firm responsible for the engagement and depends generally on preferences expressed by bankers who will receive the report.

Of particular interest in the preceding suggested form for supplementary data is the page of comparative financial statistics used to introduce the supplementary data. The report manual recommends that as many as ten years' data be included if available, to more clearly show long-term trends. This page is a variation of the "highlights" page that is frequently given as an opening page in long-form reports. A very useful item that may be included on the page of statistics if available is high and low market prices for the client's capital stock.

Although the schedule showing sources and uses of funds is presented as part of the supplementary data, an optional treatment recognized by the firm is to present the information as one of the major financial statements along with the income statement and balance sheet, as suggested by *Opinion No. 3* of the A.P.B. If the optional presentation is utilized, the statement should be named in the auditor's report on his examination in the same manner as the other statements covered by his report. The schedule of sources and uses of funds, it should be noted, accounts for changes in the total of cash and marketable securities, rather than the traditional changes in working capital. This arrangement has a number of advantages. It stresses the change in the vital amount of liquid funds available for the payment of liabilities rather than the relatively meaningless figure for working capital. It also moves changes in other current asset items and all current liability items into the statement proper. Changes in these items are equally as important in their effect on the firm's ability to pay its debts as are the changes in the customary non-working capital items, and they are more likely to receive the attention that they warrant if they are included in the statement proper rather than in a supporting schedule. Another advantage of the cash and marketable securities approach is that it does away with the troublesome and confusing presentation of the amount of long-term installment debt that becomes current during the year.

Modifications of the statement form given that might further aid in readability and interpretation would be to show dividends paid as a deduction from net income, thus presenting as a specific figure the amount of income retained in the business, which can in turn be supplemented by a percentage figure to highlight the effect of the concern's dividend policy. Similarly, depreciation and purchases of property and equipment could be juxtaposed to show more clearly how much of these expenditures is financed by depreciation recoveries and to show the net effect of these two items. In a like manner, deducting the increase in accounts payable from the increase in inventories shows how much of the inventory increase has been financed by suppliers rather than by the company's own funds.

On a more general basis, it should be noted that the supplementary data for Model Corporation are oriented more toward creditors than toward management. The emphasis could be altered slightly, if desired, by placing the income statement detail ahead of balance sheet detail. More interpretive data and information on income statement changes could also be given by revising the comparative money columns on the income statement to read as follows:

Year Ended May 31, 1968	% Change from 1967	% of Net Sales 1968	1967

In the above format, previous-year figures are not shown, on the assumption that the reader will be interested in the figures only as a basis of comparison. Because he is really interested primarily in determining what changes have occurred, the rate of change is shown and the previous-year dollar figures used in calculating the rate of change are omitted. Amounts are given further interpretation by showing the percentage relationship to sales for figures for the current and preceding years. Direct comparison is used in this case because it is much easier for the reader to determine the relative change in percentage figures than the change in dollar amounts.

REVIEW QUESTIONS

1. How much responsibility should the auditor assume for the fairness or accuracy of supplementary information or statistical analyses included in a long-form report?

2. How frequently is it desirable for the independent auditor to prepare a long-form report for management purposes for a given client?

3. What types of reports is the auditor likely to prepare other than the short-form report, or certificate?

4. Why are long-form reports prepared?

5. Does a long-form report always include the auditor's opinion with respect to the financial statements? Explain.

6. What is meant by the term "newspaper" technique as related to the organization of a long-form report?

7. Why should long, involved sentences be avoided in writing the long-form report?

8. Can the auditor, in his writing, expect to use technical terms as freely as do doctors or lawyers? Explain.

9. What is meant by having a report referenced?

10. What recommendations were made by the Robert Morris Associates concerning the information to be given about trade receivables in a long-form report to be used for credit purposes?

11. What information did the R.M.A. pamphlet recommend be shown concerning property, plant, and equipment?

12. What information can the banker be given in a long-form report which would aid him in estimating the amount and duration of seasonal borrowing?

13. "Including a summarization of the scope of the auditor's examination in a long-form report for credit purposes is both useless and unnecessary." Explain.

14. What are the advantages of using a single standardized report format for a report designed for use by both a concern's creditors and its management?

QUESTIONS ON APPLICATION OF AUDITING STANDARDS

15. In accordance with a provision in the bond indenture underlying your client's outstanding bonds, the client is not permitted to reduce working capital below $250,000 at any time, and you are required to include in your report a statement as to whether the client has complied with this requirement. What steps would be necessary in order for you to comply with this requirement?

16. One of the more confusing aspects of the traditional form of statement of sources and application of funds to the non-accountant is the adding back of depreciation to net income to show funds provided by operations. Suggest alternative means of presentation that can be used to avoid this problem and indicate the relative advantages and disadvantages of each.

17. In the course of your regular audit examinations you have observed a long-term trend of decreasing inventory turnover. Would you present figures in your long-form report that would tend to highlight this situation? Explain.

18. The short-form audit report of Zinn and Co. contains an unqualified opinion on the financial statements of Kass Manufacturing Co. The statements indicate accounts receivable of $256,291, with a provision for doubtful accounts of $10,765. Zinn and Co.'s long-form report contains an aging of accounts receivable showing $42,524 of the accounts to be past due, and lists the customers' names of major accounts along with the account balance in each case and an indication of any portion of the account that is past due. The account

of Topp Distributing Co. is stated to include an amount of $16,451 that is three months past due. Comment.

19. Write a comment to be included in your client's report explaining why dividend payments on the capital stock have not kept pace with the increase in income in the years since 1960. Your client is a typical manufacturing concern, with total assets of $2,500,000, and its experience in the period since 1960 has been typical.

20. In connection with the opening of wage negotiations with your client, the labor union has published the following statistics:

	1956	1966
Average weekly pay	$ 60	$ 90
Annual company profits	30,000	100,000

Your client feels that these figures present a misleading picture of the situation and asks you for your opinion on the matter.

21. A company seeking a short-term bank loan will normally be expected to present a plan for the liquidation of the loan. Would it be proper for the auditor to assist a client in preparing a cash forecast to show the company's plans for repaying the loan? Should the forecast be included in the auditor's long-form report to be presented to the bank? Explain.

22. You are preparing your long-form report in connection with the examination of State Gas Company at December 31, 1967. The report will include an explanation of the 1967 increase in operating revenues.

The following information is available from the company records:

	1966	1967	Increase (Decrease)
Average number of customers	27,000	26,000	(1,000)
MCF sales	486,000	520,000	34,000
Revenue	$ 1,215,000	$1,274,000	$ 59,000

Required:

To explain the 1967 increase in operating revenues, prepare an analysis accounting for the effect of changes in:

1. Average number of customers.
2. Average gas consumption per customer.
3. Average rate per MCF sold (MCF = thousand cubic feet).

(Uniform C.P.A. Examination)

PROBLEMS

23. To obtain a more realistic appraisal of his investment, Martin Arnett, your client, has asked you to adjust certain financial data of The Glo-Bright Company for price level changes. On January 1, 1965 he invested $50,000 in The Glo-Bright Company in return for 10,000 shares of common stock. Immediately after his investment the trial balance appeared as follows:

	Dr.	Cr.
Cash and receivables	$ 65,200	
Merchandise inventory	4,000	
Building	50,000	
Accumulated depreciation-building		$ 8,000
Equipment	36,000	
Accumulated depreciation-equipment.....		7,200
Land...................................	10,000	
Current liabilities		50,000
Capital stock, $5 par..................		100,000
	$165,200	$165,200

Balances in certain selected accounts as of December 31 of each of the next three years were as follows:

	1965	1966	1967
Sales	$39,650	$39,000	$42,350
Inventory.............................	4,500	5,600	5,347
Purchases	14,475	16,350	18,150
Operating expenses (excluding depreciation)..	10,050	9,050	9,075

Assume the 1965 price level as the base year and that all changes in the price level take place at the beginning of each year. Further assume that the 1966 price level is 10% above the 1965 price level and that the 1967 price level is 10% above the 1966 level.

The building was constructed in 1961 at a cost of $50,000 with an estimated life of 25 years. The price level at that time was 80% of the 1965 price level.

The equipment was purchased in 1963 at a cost of $36,000 with an estimated life of ten years. The price level at that time was 90% of the 1965 price level.

The LIFO method of inventory valuation is used. The original inventory was acquired in the same year the building was constructed and was maintained at a constant $4,000 until 1965. In 1965 a gradual buildup of the inventory was begun in anticipation of an increase in the volume of business.

Arnett considers the return on his investment as the dividend he actually receives. In 1967 Glo-Bright paid cash dividends in the amount of $8,000.

On July 1, 1966 there was a reverse stock split-up of the Company's stock in the ratio of one-for-ten.

Required:

(a) Compute the 1967 earnings per share of common stock in terms of 1965 dollars.

(b) Compute the percentage return on investment for 1965 and 1967 in terms of 1965 dollars. (Uniform CPA Examination)

24. The Specialties Co., Inc. is engaged in manufacturing and wholesaling two principal products. As their accountant, you have been asked to advise management on sales policy for the coming year.

Two different plans are being considered by management, either of which, they believe, will (1) increase the volume of sales, (2) reduce the ratio of selling expense to sales, and (3) decrease unit production costs. These proposals are as follows:

Plan 1—Premium Stamp Books

It is proposed that each package of Product A will contain 8 premium stamps, and each package of Product B will contain 4 premium stamps.

Premium stamp books will be distributed to consumers, and when a book is filled with stamps (100 stamps) it will be redeemed by the award of a cash prize in an amount indicated under an unbroken seal attached to the book at the time of distribution. Every 10,000 books distributed will provide for prizes in accordance with the following schedule:

Number of Books	Prize for Each	Total prizes
1	$150.00	$ 150
5	50.00	250
14	20.00	280
50	10.00	500
160	5.00	800
1,020	1.00	1,020
8,750	.40	3,500
10,000		$6,500

This schedule is fixed and not subject to alteration or modification. The cost of this plan will be as follows:

Books, including distribution cost	$ 15 per 1000 books
Stamps	$ 1 per 1000 stamps
Prizes	$650 per 1000 books

The premium stamp book plan will take the place of all previous advertising, and previously established selling prices will be maintained.

Plan 2—Reduced Selling Prices

It is proposed that the selling price of Product A will be reduced by $8\frac{1}{3}\%$ and of Product B by 5% and to increase the advertising expenditures over those of the prior year. This plan is an alternative to Plan 1, and only one will be adopted.

Management has provided you with the following information as to the previous year's operations, and as to anticipated changes:

Prior year's operations:	Product A	Product B
Quantity sold	200,000 units	600,000 units
Production cost per unit	$.40	$.30
Selling price per unit	$.60	$.40

Selling expenses were 18% of sales, of which one third was for advertising. Administrative expenses were 5% of sales.

Expected changes:	Product A	Product B
Increase in unit sales volume:		
Plan 1	50%	50%
Plan 2	40%	25%
Decrease in unit production cost:		
Plan 1	5%	10%
Plan 2	$7\frac{1}{2}\%$	$6\frac{2}{3}\%$
Advertising:		
Plan 1	None	None
Plan 2	8% of sales	7% of sales
Other selling expenses:		
Plan 1	15% of sales	12% of sales
Plan 2	12% of sales	12% of sales

Premium book expenses:

Plan 1	As indicated	
Plan 2	None	None

Administrative expenses:

Plan 1	4% of sales	4% of sales
Plan 2	Same dollar amount as prior year	

Required:

Prepare a schedule for submission to management comparing operations of the previous year with those under both proposed plans.

(Uniform C.P.A. Examination)

25. The manager of The Thomas Manufacturing Company has reviewed the annual financial statements for the year 1967 and is unable to determine from a reading of the balance sheet the reasons for the changes in working capital during the year. He asks you for assistance and presents the following balance sheets of The Thomas Manufacturing Company.

	December 31, 1967	December 31, 1966	Increase (Decrease)
Goodwill	—0—	$ 200,000	$(200,000)
Buildings	$ 810,000	560,000	250,000
Land	140,000	150,000	(10,000)
Machinery	330,000	200,000	130,000
Tools	40,000	70,000	(30,000)
Bond investment	18,000	15,000	3,000
Inventories......................	210,000	218,000	(8,000)
Accounts receivable..............	180,000	92,000	88,000
Notes receivable—trade...........	21,000	27,000	(6,000)
Cash in bank	—0—	8,000	(8,000)
Cash on hand	2,000	1,000	1,000
Unexpired insurance—machinery....	1,200	1,400	(200)
Deferred bond discount	2,100	2,500	(400)
	$1,754,300	$1,544,900	$ 209,400
Capital stock....................	$ 700,000	$ 400,000	$ 300,000
Bonds payable	150,000	100,000	50,000
Accounts payable.................	58,000	52,000	6,000
Bank overdraft	4,000	—0—	4,000
Notes payable—trade.............	9,000	10,000	(1,000)
Bank loans—short term	5,500	6,800	(1,300)
Accrued interest	10,000	6,000	4,000
Accrued taxes	5,000	3,000	2,000
Allowance for bad debts	4,500	2,300	2,200
Allowance for depreciation	271,200	181,000	90,200
Retained earnings................	537,100	783,800	(246,700)
	$1,754,300	$1,544,900	$ 209,400

You are advised that the following transactions took place during the year:

1. A 2 per cent dividend was declared and paid, on the outstanding capital stock at the first of the year.
2. There were no purchases or sales of tools.
3. Stock was sold during the year at 90; the discount was charged to the Goodwill account.
4. Old machinery which cost $4,500 was scrapped and written off the books. Accrued depreciation on such equipment was $3,300.
5. The Income Statement for the year, 1967, was:

Sales (net)		$1,250,000
Operating charges:		
Material and supplies	$250,000	
Direct labor	210,000	
Manufacturing overhead	181,500	
Depreciation	123,500	
Selling expenses	245,000	
General expenses	230,000	
Interest expense (net)	7,500	
Total		1,247,500
Net profit to retained earnings		$ 2,500

(There were no unusual items in any of the company's listed income and expense accounts statements shown above.)

Required:
  (a) An application of funds statement for The Thomas Manufacturing Company, supported by a schedule of working capital changes.
  (b) A cash flow statement, supported by a schedule detailing the cash provided or applied by profits or losses from operation.

(Uniform C.P.A. Examination)

26. The president of your client, the Collins Manufacturing Corp., has asked that you prepare a detailed report for him to be used at the next meeting of the board of directors. The report is to be addressed to the board. The president states that he is not interested in details concerning your examination, but in an analysis of the company's operations. He is particularly interested in having you show why the company had to borrow from the bank in the face of increased profits over the preceding year. Condensed balance sheets and income statements for the company are presented below, along with certain additional information. The statements need not be reproduced in your report.

COLLINS MANUFACTURING CORP.
Comparative Balance Sheets, December 31

Assets

	This Year	Last Year
Cash	$ 93,628	$ 87,425
Receivables	275,931	241,639
Inventories	421,658	336,918
Plant and equipment	384,123	406,831
Less accumulated depreciation	(204,963)	(215,869)
Other assets	15,629	13,804
	$986,006	$870,748

Equities

	This Year	Last Year
Bank loan	$ 50,000	$ —
Accounts payable	165,913	148,319
Accrued liabilities	76,904	68,419
Capital stock	400,000	400,000
Retained earnings	293,189	254,010
	$986,006	$870,784

COLLINS MANUFACTURING CORP.
Comparative Income Statements, Year Ended December 31

	This Year	Last Year
Sales		
Gimmicks	$463,807	$428,931
Doodads	604,361	$321,173
Total	$1,068,168	$750,104
Expenses		
Cost of sales—gimmicks	$ 329,686	$301,873
Cost of sales—doodads	334,956	182,939
Administrative expenses	52,316	43,281
Selling expenses	113,814	84,616
Interest	1,241	—
Income taxes	136,976	73,904
Total	$ 968,989	$686,613
Net Income	$ 99,179	$ 63,491
Depreciation included in expenses	$ 27,555	$ 24,316
Dividends declared and paid	60,000	60,000
Cost of fully depreciated machinery retired	38,461	—

Management advisory and other
public accounting services

25

The area of management advisory services has been receiving growing attention from public accountants in recent years. The services involved are essentially of the consulting variety and are directed primarily at the typical problems faced by business management in such areas as accounting, finance, administration, production, sales, purchasing, transportation, and personnel. The increasing interest and activity of public accountants in the provision of such consulting services to company managements may be attributed to several factors:

1. The development of such highly specialized techniques as operations research, statistical sampling, electronic data processing, and production control has made it difficult for most businesses to maintain staffs with competence in all of these areas. Such businesses have naturally sought outside assistance as they have become interested in these advanced techniques, and for reasons to be explored shortly, public accountants have been a logical choice to provide the desired assistance.

2. In periods of continued prosperity, businesses become more expansive in their thinking and more willing to accept the risks of experimentation with new ideas. Coincidentally, profitable operations provide funds which can be used for such experimentation.

3. The education and training of the people entering public accounting have gradually been broadening, thus facilitating the entrance of public accounting firms into the field of business consultation.

4. Consulting services in the management field are a natural outgrowth of the auditing work performed for clients.

5. The fees for consulting work are attractive, because they are based in part on the savings or other benefits produced.

Public Accountants a Logical Choice for Management Services

There are various reasons why management may reasonably be expected to turn to the public accounting firm that conducts the annual audit when seeking consulting assistance. Perhaps most importantly, the auditing firm and the quality of its work are already known to management as a result of an extended period of contact. An outside management consulting firm can be judged only on the basis of its own assertions as to its competence or on the recommendation of others who may have engaged the firm and been satisfied with the results.

Another reason for securing management consulting services from the public accounting firm that conducts the regular audit examination is the familiarity that the firm will already have gained with the client's organization, operations, and problems. A firm that does only management consulting work would have to acquire a similar amount of background information, but acquiring the information would entail added expense and inconvenience to the client.

Management advisory services are also often a natural outgrowth of the performance of the auditing function—particularly if a "constructive auditing" approach has been employed. As discussed more fully later in this chapter, a constructive approach yields suggestions to management for improving organization, operations, or accounting. Management then frequently turns to the accounting firm for assistance in implementing such suggestions.

Perhaps one of the major factors pointing to the choice of a concern's public accountants for management consulting service is the presence of what amounts to a practical guarantee that the work will be satisfactory. A management consulting firm is engaged on a one-time basis, and after it has presented its recommendations and collected its fee, its responsibility is ended. The public accounting firm, however, has to "live with its recommendations," for it can hardly risk losing an audit client as a result of faulty management advisory services. Its representatives will therefore be returning under a corresponding pressure to remedy any shortcomings that may appear as a result of recommendations by management services personnel.

Another desirable feature of engaging a concern's auditors or any firm of Certified Public Accountants is the fact that such firms operate under strict rules of professional conduct, whereas management consultant firms do not. The advantage here lies in freedom from high-pressure sales methods and assurance that the firm has succeeded through reputation for good work, rather than through the development of clever advertising and promotional activities.

The Introduction of Nonauditing Services into Public Accounting

The reader should recall that at the turn of the century the auditing profession in the United States was still largely engaged in a routine mechanical form of auditing and the typical auditor who was performing such work naturally had only a limited horizon that seldom included a recognition or understanding of the problems of management. The obvious familiarity of the practitioner of that day with accounting systems did, however, frequently lead to engagements to design and install accounting systems. As the amount of such work and the size of accounting firms increased, the opportunity arose for individuals within firms to specialize in systems work, and from such a beginning has developed the more comprehensive activity of management advisory services.

It is interesting to note that although accounting systems work was performed by accounting firms well in advance of the introduction of the first income tax law in 1913, services in the area of taxation expanded more quickly and soon exceeded systems work as a source of fee income. Taxes were more compatible with the earlier public accountant's penchant for detail, and there was no other group so well qualified to assist in the problems arising from the new tax based on income. By contrast, management engineering firms stood ready to aid the company that needed help with its accounting system, and these engineering firms aggressively sought such engagements. There was also a widely held belief that accounting systems were merely one branch of the whole field of systems, which was essentially an engineering matter.

Accounting firms continued to do an increasing amount of systems work, however, largely as a direct result of their auditing activities, and other types of related services were occasionally performed at the request of regular clients. But World War II marked a major turning point in the situation as a result of such developments as operations research, electronic computers, and statistical techniques. Business concerns sought an increasing amount of outside assistance, and accounting firms began to employ specialists to aid in the increasing variety of services being performed.

Professional Developments

In 1953 the A.I.C.P.A. appointed a Committee on Management Services to explore this area of service to clients, to develop ways of furthering recognition of C.P.A.'s as competent advisers to management, and to assist C.P.A.'s in providing more competent management advisory services. In 1956 this committee released a pamphlet entitled *A Classification of Management Services by CPA's*, which was designed to show the broad scope of the field of management services. The pamphlet included a list of services intended primarily to be illustrative, but representing services that had actually been performed by at least a few C.P.A.'s. The six-page list was classified under eight major headings covering the principal functional areas of business, plus the over-all area of general management and administration. Included under these headings were such services as assistance in development of management policies, development of complete plans of internal reporting, advice as to sources of capital and types of securities to be issued, assistance in long-range financial planning, survey of production planning and methods of production and quality control, advice on product prices, and assistance in the preparation of job classifications and job evaluations.

Another development in the area of management services has been the publication by the Institute of a series of bulletins dealing with various types of management services and designed to assist the C.P.A. in increasing his competence in these areas. These bulletins and other related materials have been drawn together in a 418-page *Management Services Handbook,* which is supplemented by a series of "Technical Studies in Management Services." Specific problem areas are treated in depth in these studies, and case studies describing actual engagements in the area are included. Study No. 1 is entitled *Cost Analysis for Product Line Decisions;* Study No. 2 is entitled *Cost Analysis for Pricing and Distribution Policies.*

Professional Considerations in Providing Management Services

As has already been indicated, management services may extend into areas that are quite unrelated to accounting. The extension of the accountant's services beyond the area of accounting should cause no concern, provided that the following limitations are not violated:

1. There must be competence in all engagements that are undertaken, both on the part of staff employees performing the work and on the part of the principal of the accounting firm responsible for supervising the work.

2. Engagements should not extend into areas that are legally forbidden, such as law or medicine.

3. The rules of professional conduct applicable to the practice of accounting in general must also be observed in such nonaccounting work.

4. Services should not extend beyond the presentation of recommendations or the giving of advice; making actual decisions for management would jeopardize the independence of the practitioner and his firm in performing independent auditing services.

Referring Clients to Other Accountants

Should a client seek services which the accountant lacks competence to perform, the accountant may properly assign the work to a person on his staff who has the necessary competence, provided that the accountant concludes that he is capable of supervising the work done and evaluating the results. Lacking such a person on his own staff, the accountant may either attempt to work out a plan to perform the work in cooperation with another firm of accountants possessing the required competence, or he may refer the client to another firm of public accountants or to a management counsulting firm which he is confident can provide the desired services competently and successfully.

Accounting firms are understandably reluctant to refer a client to another accounting firm, because this involves an admission of the other firm's broader qualifications. But the partners of a small accounting firm can hardly be expected to possess competence in a wide variety of technical specialties or to have persons on their staff who are trained in such specialties, and a client should be expected to recognize these realities.

Another reason for hesitancy about referring a client to another accounting firm is that the client may become so well satisfied with the new accountant's work that he may also transfer his auditing and tax work to the new accountant. Such defection is unlikely, however, if the referring accountant has consistently provided his client with the highest quality of service that is available. Further protection to the referring accountant is embodied in rule 5.02 of the A.I.C.P.A. Code of Professional Ethics, which stipulates, "A member or associate who receives an engagement for services by referral from another member or associate shall not discuss or accept an extension of his services beyond the specific engagement without consulting with the referring member or associate.

Selection and Training of Staff for Management Services

Accounting firms have followed three general courses of action in building up a management services staff. Perhaps the preferred approach is to select men from the audit staff who have demonstrated ability and interest in management services and to permit them to specialize in such work. The preliminary audit experience is most valuable because it affords contact with a wide variety of businesses, the procedures they have developed, and the problems they face. Also, audit experience and acquaintance with audit working papers facilitate the use of audit files in gathering information and assure careful recognition of the implications of continued relations with the client through the performance of audit and tax services. Lastly, the audit staff man is likely to have become a C.P.A. by the time he begins to specialize in management services, and if he possesses the other necessary qualifications he is thus in a position to progress into the partnership ranks of the firm, which would be closed to the non-C.P.A.

When men transfer from the audit staff to management services, they are usually encouraged to develop some specialty within that area and are frequently given additional training through special schools within the firm or through technical or graduate courses in regular educational institutions. Such specialized training might be in mathematics, production control, industrial engineering, statistics, tabulating machines, electronic computers, or many other areas.

A second source of management services staff is persons who have trained directly for fields such as have just been mentioned. A frequent problem in using men with such specialized technical training is that they are likely to lack a management viewpoint and be insensitive to the problems and considerations of management. Such a gap is frequently bridged, however, by having the management services man work as a team with a man from the audit staff who has become familiar with the client company and its procedures and problems.

A third source of staff is men with experience in industry in some related area. These men should be well acquainted with the practical problems associated with their particular area and should have had ample opportunity to acquire the desired management viewpoint. Such staff appointments represent an interesting reversal of the usual movement from public accounting to industry.

Management Services a Natural Outgrowth of Changed Auditing Concepts

As we have seen, independent audits are a vital factor in a capitalistic economy because they help to assure that capital will flow to the most productive opportunities and thus provide the maximum amount of goods for the economy at large. With unaudited financial information there is always a possibility that the information may be misleading and cause capital to flow to relatively unproductive uses, at a resulting loss to both the investor and the economy.

In the above sense, audits actually serve a useful function for *society*, but until recent years the *individual business* that engaged the auditor and paid his fee was likely to consider him little more than a parasite—an organism that obtains its living at the expense of some other living organism, usually contributing nothing in return. Today, however, many progressive accounting firms have taken a new approach to their auditing work— one that places them in a classification that is far removed from that of the parasite. The term "constructive auditing" has been used to characterize this new approach, which is sometimes stated to have as its goal the development of constructive suggestions during an audit that will more than repay the client for the cost of the audit. From the standpoint of the client, the examination by an auditor who adheres to this approach may be looked upon as being much like a regular medical examination. The auditor is somewhat of a "business physician," who is prepared to diagnose and prescribe remedies for the ills that he may encounter.

If, then, the accounting firm is prepared to serve the client in the area of management services, it is only natural that the client would be likely to turn to the accounting firm for assistance in providing some of the more technical remedies that the auditor may have prescribed.

Examples of Audit Recommendations Related to Management Services

As the auditor is conducting his reviews, analyses, and investigations relative to the independent audit, he will be well advised to note possibilities for improvements and money-saving changes in the client's way of doing things. The principal areas for potential savings and improvements will normally include:

1. Plan of organization and delegation of responsibility
2. Internal reporting
3. Management controls
4. Protection against fraud
5. Clerical savings
6. Mechanical and electronic data-processing equipment
7. Tax savings

During the progress of the audit, careful notes should be kept of recommendations that might be made, and then after thorough study and evaluation, the auditor should present the recommendations to the client in carefully written form. The addressing of this supplementary report is most important and will vary with the situation. Ideally, the report should be addressed to the highest-ranking officer consistent with the significance of the recommendations, provided that he can be expected to be interested in the recommendations and that he has the necessary initiative and authority to make the changes that are required.

To illustrate the possible breadth, depth, and intensity of such recommendations and to show how the recommendations might be worded, excerpts are reproduced below from three such reports prepared in conjunction with actual audit examinations. All information that would tend to identify the clients involved has been carefully disguised. The recommendations are not solicitations for additional work; on the other hand, it is quite likely that the clients might turn to the accounting firm for assistance in carrying out some of the recommendations.

NANNELL INDUSTRIES, INC.

Mr. S. J. Nannell, President,
    Nannell Industries, Inc.:

This memorandum has been prepared as a result of the work we have performed in connection with our initial examination of the company's financial statements. This examination has afforded us the opportunity to observe and study the accounting policies and procedures and the organization of the company, and to become familiar with certain of the company's basic operating and financial problems. The knowledge gained in this process has enabled us to present various suggestions to the company with respect to taxes, controls and procedures during the course of our work. It also prompted our proposal to make a highspot review of procedures at three of the principal plants in order to obtain a better understanding of the problems which we felt were present with respect to inventory control and production scheduling, and to develop specific suggestions for more effective management control.

We found the company's accounting system to be fundamentally sound and generally well organized to provide essential information to management for effective operating and financial control of the company's business. At the same time we observed certain areas where procedural modifications or revisions might facilitate the development of information, provide additional information or enable management to perform its function to better advantage.

Although certain of the suggestions previously offered to the company were formalized in memorandums, many suggestions have been made verbally during conferences with various members of the company's management. It is appropriate that the more significant suggestions be summarized for the information and use of the entire management of the company. This memorandum has been prepared for this purpose, as well as to offer certain suggestions not previously presented.

It should be recognized that our suggestions for the most part represent by-products of observations made during the audit. Accordingly, in most instances we have made no detailed review of them, since this was not contemplated in the work being performed. Consequently, even though we consider each of these suggestions to have merit, they should be evaluated carefully and studied further in reaching final decisions regarding their disposition.

We would welcome the opportunity to discuss any of these suggestions with you in more detail.

Very truly yours,

Summary of Results of Highspot Review

Before the completion of our examination, arrangements were made for qualified administrative services personnel to make a highspot review of the operating divisions located in Kansas City, Wichita, and Springfield. The specific objectives of this review were—

1. To supplement the information obtained during the audit by affording these people an opportunity to obtain first-hand knowledge of the operating characteristics and problems of each division and to obtain a more thorough understanding of the policies and practices governing each division.

2. To determine the methods and procedures used for data processing and reporting.

3. To evaluate the information obtained in this review and to pass on our observations to management for further consideration.

Our observations have been discussed with management, and a tentative draft of our comments delivered. This portion of the memorandum will be used to finalize these comments. The points discussed in this section are—

I. The greatest potential for improving operations of the company lies in the area of inventory control and production scheduling. Because of customer service, unbalanced inventories, and high set-up costs, the Instruments Division has the most acute problem.

II. There appear to be potential savings to the company in the data processing field. The potential lies in two areas:
  a. Streamlining the existing system.
  b. Centralizing data processing.
The company apparently has not decided in which of these areas to concentrate. Management should make this decision so the efforts of all concerned can be directed toward a common goal; however, substantially the same evaluation process is necessary to streamline the existing procedures as is required to study the feasibility of centralized data processing. Management should consider that a properly executed feasibility study will produce—
  a. The basis for making a decision as to whether or not to centralize.
  b. The information essential for streamlining the system regardless of the outcome of the decision.

III. Summary techniques could be utilized to reduce the volume and increase the usability of top management reports.

I. INVENTORY CONTROL

Of all the areas reviewed, inventory control offers the greatest potential for savings to the company. These savings could be in the form of clerical cost reductions and reduced inventories for given levels of operation.

The inventory control systems used have certain characteristics which impair their effectivenes. These characteristics can be summarized as follows:

1. Selective controls are not used for various kinds of inventory. This generates clerical effort which does not produce control.

2. Management policy in respect to inventories is not adequately defined. As a result, inventory decisions are made at a fairly low level; in many cases, the clerical level.

3. Inventory status information is not available for management to use in—
  a. Reviewing the effectiveness of policy and revising where necessary.
  b. Insuring itself that the established policies are being followed.

Selective Controls

"Selective Controls" in inventory is a term used to describe techniques which apply the principle that the dollars and effort spent in controlling inventories should be in direct ratio to the value of the inventory being controlled. Generally, in a manufacturing organization, an analysis of the inventory will show—
  70% of the value in 10% of the quantity of items;
  25% of the value in 25% of the quantity of items;
  5% of the value in 65% of the quantity of items.

By concentrating control on only 35% of the items in inventory, 95% of the dollars can be effectively controlled, and the majority of the items which represent the least value can be controlled by less expensive methods.

II. MANAGEMENT REPORTING

The accounting sections at each location prepare reports on a timely and accurate basis. The presentation of operating information is along responsibility lines which should be useful to operating management in controlling expense. There are, however, two observations in regard to the operating reports which merit consideration.

1. Reporting along responsibility lines is generally more effective if only

controllable costs are included. At least, unnecessary clerical cost is avoided by eliminating the need for allocations of expenses which have little, if any, meaning in relation to the controllable items.

2. It appears that there are several reports which could be obtained as a by-product of the normal accounting routine instead of upon special analysis. For example, an Engineering Labor Analysis is prepared in Kansas City covering engineering personnel in three divisions. Approximately fifty hours per month of clerical time are spent in analyzing time reports submitted by engineering personnel and in preparing the report. Many companies have found that by using the reported activities as expense classifications that this type of report can be prepared as a by-product of normal payroll processing. Another example, among others, is a statement of sales and expenses by salesmen which is prepared in the sales department in Kansas City. The accounting department handles the information necessary for these reports, and some duplication of effort could be eliminated if accounting's procedures could be modified to build these reports. Other similar reports of lesser magnitude are: labor analysis, advertising expenditures, advertising supplies, etc.

Top management receives practically every detail report issued, plus numerous special analyses. Effective summary reports can frequently highlight for management the areas to which its attention should be directed.

CONSOLIDATED UTILITIES, INCORPORATED
Materials and Supplies

The investment of $1,500,000 in operating and construction materials and supplies represents 57% of the total current assets of the company at September 30. Assuming the cost of money to be 6%, the company is paying, in interest alone, a total of $90,000 per year to maintain this stock. Interest, of course, is only one factor of the expense involved.

A comparison of the percentage of materials and supplies to utility plant with two other decentralized utility companies in this area follows:

	Consolidated Utilities, Incorporated	Company A	Company B
Investment in utility plant	$47,445,000	146,584,000	$36,416,000
Investment in materials and supplies	1,500,000	1,471,000	490,000
Percentage of materials and supplies to plant	3.16%	1.00%	1.35%

Although the necessary investment for any company in materials and supplies must be determined by that company's individual situation, the above comparison indicates that the company's investment in materials and supplies may greatly exceed the amount required for efficient operation. If materials and supplies on hand could be reduced to an amount comparable to those of Company A and Company B above, a substantial amount of funds could be released for investment in revenue-producing properties and would tend to further defer the necessity of additional financing.

Control Of Investment By Centralized Accounting

An effective method of controlling the investment in operating materials and supplies is the use of centralized stores accounting. With stores records centrally located, it is possible for the purchasing department to have current information available at all times as to the quantities of each type of material on hand at each location, thus permitting transfers of materials in oversupply at one location to eliminate shortages in other locations. With a decentralized system, such as that used by the company, it is much more difficult to avoid ordering additional materials when an adequate supply is already on hand.

Other advantages to centralized stores accounting include:

(1) Better storage and care of materials.

(2) Permits conversion of stores accounting to punch cards.

By releasing storekeepers from accounting work, they would have more time to devote to their primary function of properly caring for and protecting the company's assets. In large storerooms the elimination of stores accounting in the field might result in a reduction of storeroom employees needed.

The company is converting revenue accounting to a punch-card operation and will undoubtedly wish to extend the use of this equipment to other areas in due time. Conversion of stores accounting to punch cards is much more feasible where the stores accounting system is centralized.

Issue Tickets Should Be Prepared At The Time
Materials Are Issued

In those divisions which we have visited in the last two years the major variations between stores items on hand and the perpetual records have been caused by failure to prepare issue tickets for material taken out on jobs. The reason for this situation is that in some instances line foremen wait until the close of a job to prepare issue tickets, instead of doing this at the time material is removed from stores. The delay in preparing issue tickets by line foremen and other personnel responsible causes difficulty in both stores and plant accounting, because frequent adjustments to work orders occur in connection with:

(1) Physical counts of materials and supplies to reflect materials actually on hand, and

(2) Field inventories of completed projects to reflect issues equal to the number of units actually installed.

A rigid program of requiring issue tickets to be prepared when material is taken from stores would:

(1) Assure proper distribution of material costs.

(2) Reduce the size and number of physical inventory adjustments.

(3) Eliminate the large differences which occur when completed projects are inventoried.

(4) Allow maximum use of perpetual inventory records.

THE THORNWOOD WATERWORKS COMPANY

This memorandum sets forth various accounting procedures now in effect and suggestions which, we believe, will increase office efficiency, strengthen accounting controls, and provide more meaningful financial statements. These comments are based upon a limited review of the Company's accounting system and internal control which came to our attention during our recent visit to the Company's offices. We have attempted to make these suggestions as comprehensive and practicable as possible, with the hope they will be of help to you.

In general, the condition of the Company's records is good. The bookkeeper is competent in many respects but cannot record transactions which are not mechanical in nature. The Company's former auditor prepared many of the entries, closed the books, and prepared the monthly financial statements. A program should be undertaken to expand the duties of the bookkeeper, but until such time as she can perform the entire accounting function, she should receive outside assistance in order that the books and monthly financial statements will properly reflect the financial position and operating results of the Company.

Machine Billing Should Be Considered

The Company has approximately 3,300 customers, each of which is billed monthly.

There are three meter readers who commence reading about the 15th of each month. Upon receipt of the meter-books the revenue accounting clerks extend the consumption and compute the bill using applicable rate schedules. Each customer's bill is manually prepared on a *typewriter*.

After preparation, the bills are taped and compared to a tape of the meter books. Bills are stuffed into envelopes and mailed on the last day of the month.

The accounts receivable record consists of a hand-posted ledger that contains individual ledger sheets for each customer. Prior to the mailing of the bills, the current month's charges are manually posted to the accounts receivable ledger.

Subsequent cash receipts are also hand posted.

As a means of reducing the time required each month to read meters, prepare bills and post accounts receivable ledgers, the Company should consider the following:

1. An Addressograph machine to print customer's name and address on bills. A postcard-type bill and "stub" receivable record would be very practical.

2. Mechanical preparation of bills on a billing machine would be economically feasible. This would eliminate the manual posting of accounts receivable records since the billing and posting are performed simultaneously by the machine. Taping of detail bills would also be eliminated, as a billing machine provides controls for these totals, i.e., the proofs are automatic. Errors in billing, footing, etc., would be kept at a minimum.

3. Cycle billing of customers' accounts would spread the work load of the meter readers, bookkeepers, and cashiers more evenly throughout the month. The month-end rush as now experienced would thus be avoided.

4. Bi-monthly billing has become very common among water utilities in recent years. This procedure provides for a bill every *two* months and consequently reduces expenses such as meter reading, postage, clerical time, billing supplies, etc. More working capital will be required initially to install such a system; also, as the average water bill becomes higher, uncollectible revenues may increase.

Adoption of the above procedures would require fewer personnel than is presently required to perform the billing and accounts receivable functions. It is conceivable that a substantial saving could be effected as it is possible that one meter reader and one bookkeeper could be eliminated.

Preparation Of Sewer Tax Bills

The City of Thornwood imposes a sewer tax upon water customers of the Company which approximates 125% of the water bill. The tax is billed separately by the City from data extracted from the accounting records. This operation normally requires that City employees visit the Company offices several days each month.

In addition to improving oprations it is conceivable that the installation of mechanized billing could generate additional revenue for the Company. Water bills which include sewer tax are normal for many utilities. While we cannot say at the present time, it appears that the City of Thornwood might be receptive to having the Company do its sewer tax billing. There are savings which would accrue to the City such as:

1. Savings on postage of $100 per month.
2. Savings on the cost of the forms on which bills are rendered.
3. Savings on employees' time, due to the elimination of the preparation and collection of bills.
4. Sewer tax revenue would be current. The month lag would be eliminated.

The increase in billing time required to show the sewer tax, in addition to the charges for water, would be nominal. The major increase in costs to the Company would be in the processing of cash collections; however, using the bill-stub approach, the increase in clerical work in this area should be minimized.

To determine the feasibility from the Company's standpoint, it will be necessary to measure the cost aspects more closely. If the Company decides it can perform these functions, it should then determine on what basis it would charge the City for services rendered. It would seem that either a percentage of collections or a flat monthly rate would be acceptable. The Company should decide whether or not to explore this possibility further before determining the type billing machine to be used, inasmuch as a slightly larger machine would be necessary for billing two services. In the event the City of Thornwood were to agree to such a program, there is no doubt that the Company could recover the cost of mechanizing its billing more rapidly.

Management Services by the Local Practitioner for Small Clients

Much of what has been said about management services has obviously been in terms of larger public accounting firms and medium- and large-size clients. Yet small clients also need management services, and the individual practitioner or small partnership should stand ready to meet that need. True, the firm cannot maintain a staff of specialists for that purpose and, indeed, will seldom find it possible to have even one person who specializes in management services. On the other hand, small clients will seldom require highly technical assistance. Most of the problems likely to exist in a small business can usually be capably handled by the public accountant himself merely through application of what he should have learned through intimate contact with the affairs and practices of his many clients over a period of years.

The more common needs of the small business are likely to include such elementary matters as:

1. Developing a good classification of accounts to assure adequate and useful operating and financial information.

2. Attaining maximum internal control commensurate with the limited number of employees.

3. Instituting simple cost-saving clerical procedures such as "write-it-once" systems whereby several forms are prepared with a single writing

(pay check, earnings statement, employee earnings summary, and payroll register, for example), supplemented by such basic types of simple machines as cash registers, dual-register adding machines, and stencil-type addressing equipment.

4. Inaugurating basic inventory control records involving the retail inventory method or Kardex unit inventory records.

5. Developing a simple cost accounting system that can aid in cost control and yield useful product cost information.

6. Instituting elementary budgeting and cash forecasting procedures.

7. Assisting in financial planning and obtaining needed financing.

The individual practitioner or small local partnership is often engaged in doing a large amount of detail work for clients, with much of the work likely to be sub-professional. The practitioner must constantly strive to avoid becoming hopelessly entangled in the morass of detailed work in such circumstances, and a conscious effort must be made to recognize the opportunities that are always present for constructive service and to capitalize on those opportunities. In so doing, the practitioner is raising the level of his practice and providing invaluable and otherwise unattainable services for his clients. Only the public accountant is likely to have sufficient knowledge of the businessman's affairs, plus the training and insight necessary to provide such services.

Frequently the practitioner serving the small client finds that the most important service he can provide for the client is what has sometimes been called "public controllership." The small businessman, operating without specialists in his employ, is usually sorely in need of someone to oversee the accounting work, about which the businessman is likely to know little or nothing, interpret the periodic statements of operations and financial position, counsel the businessman on financial matters and financial planning, point out trouble spots and problem areas as they may develop, and evaluate the tax implications of present and proposed plans of action.

Tax Services

Tax work represents a major phase of the practice of most public accountants. Although much of the tax work is done for clients for whom regular examinations are made, in many cases the accountant's sole service to the client may be the preparation of the client's tax returns. The preparation of the tax return is likely to be relatively more expensive in such cases, because the review or analysis of many accounts normally made as a phase of the regular audit examination will have to be made as an incidental step to the preparation of the return.

One of the most vital phases of tax work is tax planning, and this type of work presents the public accountant with an excellent opportunity to demonstrate in a tangible manner the value of his services. Tax figures based on alternative plans show the client exact savings in dollars and cents, and most accountants increase their income by basing their fees for tax matters on the savings which have been demonstrated as well as on the time spent.

If the accountant is to be of maximum service to his client in tax planning, the client should be encouraged to consult the accountant before entering into any important contracts or transactions. Tax considerations are always present in such matters, and often the transaction can be handled in a way which will effect substantial tax savings.

The accountant is also often asked to prepare the personal income tax returns of partners or officers of the client firm, and here again tax planning should be brought into the picture. Estate taxes are an important consideration in such planning, as are the various means of splitting income to reduce the total taxes paid on a given amount of income.

Many accounting firms have brought men to their staffs who are both lawyers and C.P.A.'s to specialize in tax work. Legal training has proven to be especially useful in view of the importance of knowledge of the law and court decisions in connection with tax matters. When a firm has a tax specialist, other staff members are usually expected to continue to do the bulk of the work in the preparation of schedules and returns, with the tax man serving in a consulting capacity when difficult or questionable matters arise. The tax man is then the logical person to carry out such research as the problem may necessitate.

Quite commonly the tax man will also review all tax returns after they have been prepared—particularly the more involved returns. The purpose of such review will not be to establish the mechanical accuracy of the returns (although such review should be made by others), but rather to ascertain that major items have been properly handled in relation to the applicable laws and regulations, and particularly to consider major tax-saving alternatives that may have been overlooked in the preparation of the return. The tax specialist should also be a central figure in all tax-planning work being performed for clients.

The presence of lawyers on the staffs of C.P.A.'s and the fine line that divides accounting practice and legal practice in tax matters has led to occasional conflict between the legal profession and the accounting profession, and local bar associations have sometimes sought to restrict the tax work being done by accountants through test cases in the courts. In an effort to resolve some of the conflict that developed, a National Conference of Lawyers and Certified Public Accountants was formed, and in 1951 the conference released its "Statement of Principles Relating to Practice in the Field of Federal Income Taxation." This statement of principles has been quite successful in accomplishing its intended purpose and in general sets forth the areas open exclusively to lawyers or to C.P.A.'s, as well as the areas in which both may properly practice. The statement also points out the importance of having *both* a lawyer and a C.P.A. serve the client in matters that involve both law and accounting.

The reader should keep firmly in mind, however, that a lawyer on the staff of a public accounting firm should not endeavor to provide legal services to the firm's clients, and in this connection Rule 4.03 of the A.I.C.P.A. Code of Professional Ethics provides: "A member or associate in his practice of public accounting shall not permit an employee to perform for the member's or associate's clients any services which the member or associate himself or his firm is not permitted to perform." Neither this rule, nor any other rule of the A.I.C.P.A., specifically prohibits the joint practice of law and accounting by a person who is qualified in both fields, but such joint practice is generally frowned upon and discouraged. Furthermore, the two fields are so complicated and subject to constant change that one person can hardly maintain satisfactory proficiency in both fields, and any attempt to do so can be only at the expense of the quality of service rendered to clients.

Bookkeeping Service

The large national public accounting firms usually avoid performing bookkeeping services (sometimes referred to as "write-up work") for their clients because their organization and mode of operation are not well adapted to providing such services. Also, the remuneration for such service is substantially less than for most other public accounting services because less professional skill is required. On the other hand, most local accounting firms and individual practitioners are likely to have a certain amount of such work. Often, particularly for newcomers to the profession, such services may represent the backbone of the accountant's practice.

The service rendered is usually the preparation of adjusting entries and monthly statements, but often the accountant will also prepare the books of original entry and post the general ledger as well. The goal of every practitioner should be to spend as little time as possible on such bookkeeping service for clients, from the standpoint of both the development of his practice and service to his clients, for the well-qualified practitioner can be of greater service to his clients in a multitude of other ways. Nevertheless, businessmen need such service, and they should be encouraged to look to a C.P.A. for the most competent attention to their needs. One solution to the problem is for the C.P.A. to employ clerical help that has had bookkeeping training or experience to do the work, so that the practitioner can limit himself to supervision of the work. In many instances bookkeeping machines have been purchased to facilitate the work and to improve the accuracy and appearance of the final results.

Another development in this class of work in large communities has been the establishment of data-processing centers to handle the preparation of records and statements automatically from punched cards or punched paper tape at a minimum of time and expense. Some public accountants have acquired their own facilities to handle this type of work. Recently, another step forward in the mechanization of bookkeeping service has been made possible by the development of an adding-machine attachment that will punch paper tape, which in turn can be used in a tape-to-card converter to punch tabulating cards automatically. Under this method, original transactions are listed on the adding machine with necessary identifying information such as type of transaction, account number, customer number, or employee number, indicated by numerical coding. The regular adding-machine tape provides a visible record that is useful for verifying the work and establishing predetermined proof totals to control subsequent phases of the work. The punched-tape attachment simultaneously produces the tape that is subsequently used at a data-processing center to automatically prepare the entry cards which are in turn used to prepare journals, ledgers, and statements on tabulating machines or electronic computers. General ledger work, accounts receivable, sales analysis, payroll, and any other accounting operations can all be handled in this manner.

A different approach to the problem of placing data in a form suitable for input to data-processing equipment is the use of an "optical font" for the printing of cash register audit tapes. The tapes can then be read directly into data-processing equipment by an optical scanning device for preparation of a great variety of sales analyses, including unit sales figures for numbered items.

Nationally franchised bookkeeping service organizations such as Mail-Me-Monday sometimes present an additional service feature by combining operating data for businesses of given types and sizes and including this comparative information on the monthly statements prepared for each client.

Regardless of the exact method by which bookkeeping service is performed, a major consideration in offering such service is that regular contact is established between the accountant and the client. The accountant thus becomes the logical person to turn to if the client needs audited financial statements, tax advice, financial advice, or assistance with operating problems of his business. Indeed, the accountant's close contact with the client's business should make it possible for the accountant to anticipate these needs even before they become apparent to the client and to supply advice that will keep many problems from ever occurring in the first place.

REVIEW QUESTIONS

1. Why are businesses increasingly being forced to turn to outside consultants for solutions to some of their problems?

2. Why is it frequently possible for fees for consulting work to produce a greater return to an accounting firm than fees from auditing work?

3. Assuming that a public accounting firm possesses the necessary competence, why is it reasonable to expect audit clients to turn to that firm for consulting assistance, rather than to seek an outside consulting firm?

4. Indicate the areas within which C.P.A.'s have actually performed management services.

5. What limitations should a C.P.A. observe in extending his services outside the area of accounting?

6. Why are public accountants who provide auditing services often reluctant to refer clients to other accountants for management services that they are not able to perform themselves?

7. How does the Code of Professional Ethics help to protect a C.P.A. referring a client to another C.P.A. for special services that the first C.P.A. is not competent to provide?

8. Why is it desirable to select men who have had audit staff experience in choosing men to specialize in management services work?

9. How can a public accounting firm utilize the services of a highly trained mathematician in the management services area if the mathematician has had little experience in business?

10. What is meant by the term "constructive auditing"?

11. Under what circumstances is the public accountant likely to find a need for "public controllership" services? What types of activity are likely to be involved?

12. Why is it desirable to have income tax returns that are prepared by the audit staff man reviewed in the office by a tax specialist?

13. Why should the practitioner seek to reduce the amount of his time spent on bookkeeping service work?

14. How is bookkeeping service work being automated?

QUESTIONS ON APPLICATION OF AUDITING STANDARDS

15. Although your client has not discussed the problem with you, you have concluded that his business is in dire need of additional liquid funds. You have noted that payables are being liquidated well after discount dates have expired and that most equipment is being leased rather than purchased, as would be the case in most businesses of this type. The problem is being aggravated by a continued comfortable increase in volume, which has necessitated carrying larger inventories and receivables and leasing additional equipment at rates well in excess of normal depreciation charges. The owner of the business has already invested all his available liquid funds in the business. Suggest possible recommendations that you might make to aid your client, and indicate other possibilities that seem inapplicable in this situation, stating your reasons for concluding that they are inapplicable.

16. Your client distributes a product at retail through ten retail salesmen who operate the company's delivery trucks. Each truck carries about $1,000 in inventory, and the inventory stored at the company's main office and plant varies between $40,000 and $60,000 depending on the season. The office and plant were constructed at a cost of $100,000 ten years ago, and furniture and equipment is being carried at a depreciated cost of $10,000. In your examination of prepaid insurance you note that the delivery trucks are adequately

covered, but that the only other principal form of insurance carried is fire and extended coverage on building and contents in the face amount of $150,000. What recommendations, if any, would you make to your client?

17. The principal advantage that a client should expect from a management services survey of its accounting system is a reduction in the cost of operating the system. Do you agree? Explain.

18. Assume that you are in public accounting practice and a prospective client asks you to prepare his tax return from the trial balance of his business accounts, plus totals that he has derived from his personal records. What would you do?

19. Your client expenses all office and factory supplies as they are purchased. The supply rooms are open to those who need supplies, and they merely help themselves to the amount needed. Would you consider a recommendation to your client that the system of handling supplies be changed in any way? Explain.

20. A small client for whom you prepare quarterly statements and various tax returns calls you to say that his bookkeeper is leaving the job because she is getting married. He asks you to interview applicants for the job and to give him your recommendations. What is your answer to this request?

21. Is it permissible within the C.P.A.'s code of ethics for the C.P.A. to recommend one business machine to a client over another machine? May the C.P.A. accept a fee from the business machine manufacturer for making such a recommendation? Explain.

22. Your client's operations are such that there is always an inventory shortage at the end of the year. The client objects to the fact that monthly income statements tend to show relatively good operating results, and then the statements for the year are in direct contrast to the monthly figures as a result of the inventory shortage developed when the physical inventory is taken at the end of the year. What recommendation would you make to your client?

23. What reasons would you advance to your client for changing his fiscal year closing from a calendar year basis to a natural business year basis?

24. Suggest the advantages to your client (a department store) of preparing and mailing customers' statements on a cycle basis rather than at the end of the month.

25. What advantages and disadvantages would have to be weighed in reaching a decision as to whether to recommend that a public utility client change from monthly to bi-monthly billing?

26. Your client makes extensive use of punched-card accounting methods, and has followed a policy of verifying all of the key punch work done by its four key punch operators. The result has been that an equal number of verifiers has been necessary. Suggest how statistical sampling techniques might be useful to this client.

PROBLEMS

27. The president of Beth Corporation, which manufactures tape decks and sells them to producers of sound reproduction systems, anticipates a 10% wage increase on January 1 of next year to the manufacturing employees (variable labor). He expects no other changes in costs. Overhead will not change as a result of the wage increase. The president has asked you to assist him in developing the information he needs to formulate a reasonable product strategy for next year.

You are satisfied by regression analysis that volume is the primary factor affecting costs and have separated the semivariable costs into their fixed and variable segments by means of the least-squares criterion. You also observe that the beginning and ending inventories are never materially different.

Below are the current year data assembled for your analysis:

Current selling price per unit	$ 80.00
Variable cost per unit:	
Material	$ 30.00
Labor	12.00
Overhead	6.00
Total	$ 48.00
Annual volume of sales	5,000 units
Fixed costs	$51,000

Required:

Provide the following information for the president using cost-volume-profit analysis:

(a) What increase in the selling price is necessary to cover the 10% wage increase and still maintain the current profit-volume-cost ratio?

(b) How many tape decks must be sold to maintain the current net income if the sales price remains at $80.00 and the 10% wage increase goes into effect?

(c) The president believes that an additional $190,000 of machinery (to be depreciated at 10% annually) will increase present capacity (5,300 units) by 30%. If all tape decks produced can be sold at the present price and the wage increase goes into effect, how would the estimated net income before capacity is increased compare with the estimated net income after capacity is increased? Prepare computations of estimated net income before and after the expansion.

(Uniform C.P.A. Examination)

28. When you had completed your audit of The Scoopa Company, management asked for your assistance in arriving at a decision whether to continue manufacturing a part or to buy it from an outside supplier. The part, which is named Faktron, is a component used in some of the finished products of the Company.

From your audit working papers and from further investigation you develop the following data as being typical of the Company's operations:

1. The annual requirement for Faktrons is 5,000 units. The lowest quotation from a supplier was $8.00 per unit.

2. Faktrons have been manufactured in the Precision Machinery Department. If Faktrons are purchased from an outside supplier, certain machinery will be sold and would realize its book value.

3. Following are the total costs of the Precision Machinery Department during the year under audit when 5,000 Faktrons were made:

Materials	$67,500
Direct labor	50,000
Indirect labor	20,000
Light and heat	5,500
Power	3,000
Depreciation	10,000
Property taxes and insurance	8,000
Payroll taxes and other benefits	9,800
Other	5,000

4. The following Precision Machinery Department costs apply to the manufacture of Faktrons: material, $17,500; direct labor, $28,000; indirect labor, $6,000; power, $300; other, $500. The sale of the equipment used for Faktrons would reduce the following costs by the amounts indicated: depreciation, $2,000; property taxes and insurance, $1,000.

5. The following additional Precision Machinery Department costs would be incurred if Faktrons were purchased from an outside supplier: freight, $.50 per unit; indirect labor for receiving, materials handling, inspection, etc., $5,000. The cost of the purchased Faktrons would be considered a Precision Machinery Department cost.

Required: (The following requirements are of approximately equal weight.)

(a) Prepare a schedule showing a comparison of the total costs of the Precision Machinery Department (1) when Faktrons are made, and (2) when Faktrons are bought from an outside supplier.

(b) Discuss the considerations in addition to the cost factors that you would bring to the attention of management in assisting them to arrive at a decision whether to make or buy Faktrons. Include in your discussion the considerations that might be applied to the evaluation of the outside supplier. (Uniform C.P.A. Examination)

29. The Gercken Corporation sells computer services to its clients. The Company completed a feasibility study and decided to obtain an additional computer on January 1, 1968. Information regarding the new computer follows:

1. The purchase price of the computer is $230,000. Maintenance, property taxes and insurance will be $20,000 per year. If the computer is rented, the annual rent will be $85,000 plus 5% of annual billings. The rental price includes maintenance.

2. Due to competitive conditions, the Company feels it will be necessary to replace the computer at the end of 3 years with one which is larger and more advanced. It is estimated that the computer will have a resale value of $110,000 at the end of the 3 years. The computer will be depreciated on a straight-line basis for both financial reporting and income tax purposes.

3. The income tax rate is 50%.

4. The estimated annual billing for the services of the new computer will be $220,000 during the first year and $260,000 during each of the second and third years. The estimated annual expense of operating the computer is $80,000 in addition to the expense mentioned above. An additional $10,000 of start-up expenses will be incurred during the first year.

5. If it decides to purchase the computer, the Company will pay cash. If the computer is rented, the $230,000 can be otherwise invested at a 15% rate of return.

6. If the computer is purchased, the amount of the investment recovered during each of the three years can be reinvested immediately at a 15% rate of return. Each year's recovery of investment in the computer will have been reinvested for an average of six months by the end of the year.

7. The present value of $1.00 due at a constant rate during each year and discounted at 15% is:

Year	Present Value
0—1	$ .93
1—2	.80
2—3	.69

The present value of $1.00 due at the end of each year and discounted at 15% is:

End of Year	Present Value
1	$ .87
2	.76
3	.66

Required:

(a) Prepare a schedule comparing the estimated annual income from the new computer under the purchase plan and under the rental plan. The comparison should include a provision for the opportunity cost of the average investment in the computer during each year.

(b) Prepare a schedule showing the annual cash flows under the purchase plan and under the rental plan.

(c) Prepare a schedule comparing the net present values of the cash flows under the purchase plan and under the rental plan.

(d) Comment on the results obtained in parts "a" and "c." How should the computer be financed? Why?   (Uniform C.P.A. Examination)

30. A client submits the following details about The Appliance Business to be formed: Estimated sales in terms of units by months:

January	100
February	160
March	180
April	220
May	380
June	360

Each appliance will be sold for $200. It is anticipated that 25% will be sold for cash and the balance on an installment contract. The installment contract requires a down payment of 10% and ten monthly payments of $20 each which include the finance charge. The finance charge is assumed to be earned in proportion to the collections on installment contracts.

The appliances cost $125 each. Their purchase can be financed by paying 20% down with a noninterest bearing floor-plan note for the balance. This balance must be paid at the end of the month in which the appliance is sold. An average inventory of 200 units should be maintained. The same purchase terms will be available for all replacements.

The installment contracts will be pledged as collateral for loans of 60% of the unpaid balance. These loans will be reduced, monthly, by 60% of all installment collections received. The client agrees to maintain a minimum bank balance of $15,000.

Salesmen will be allowed a commission of $20 per unit to be paid the month of the sale. Other variable expenses will be approximately $30 per unit sold. Other fixed expenses are estimated at $1,200 per month. Interest expense on bank loans will be 6% per annum on loans outstanding at the end of the previous month.

Assume that payments to the manufacturer and monthly advances from the bank will be consummated on the last day of each month. Bank interest will be payable monthly following the date the loan is received. For budgeting purposes all computations should be to the nearest ten dollars.

From the foregoing information you are to prepare a cash budget by months, with appropriate supporting schedules, which will summarize cash receipts, cash disbursements, and additional cash investments required to comply with the terms of the bank loan.   (Uniform C.P.A. Examination)

Statistical sampling techniques
and the auditor

26

Auditing practice has long encompassed the technique of sampling, although auditors customarily refer to their sampling activities as "testing" or "test checking." These terms are, however, somewhat broader in their technical connotation than "sampling," for the use of the auditing terms often includes verification activities that are performed during the sampling process. For instance, the instruction to "test inventory extensions" is properly interpreted to require the proving by calculation of the accuracy of the extensions of those inventory items selected for the sample.

In most testing, or sampling, the sample is chosen from a series of items (the "population") with the expectation that the sample will be representative of the population; that is, that the sample will reflect approximately the same qualities or characteristics as are present in the population as a whole. Then, from a study of the qualities or characteristics of the sample, an inference can be made about the qualities or characteristics of the entire population. In auditing practice, this process of sampling and deriving an inference about a population has traditionally been handled on a judgmental basis, with the auditor's judgment the basis for determining sample size, the selection of the items for the sample, and the conclusion about the population inferred from the results of the sample. Today, however, statistical techniques are available to implement the auditor's judgment in this area. It is important to note, in this connection, that these statistical techniques *implement* the auditor's judgment; they do not *supplant* his judgment, as some persons have erroneously assumed. The auditor's use of statistical techniques may be likened to the physician's use of the electrocardiograph. The machine does not make any decisions for the physician; it merely provides additional information that the physician can use in making his diagnosis of the patient's condition.

Historical Development

The application of statistical techniques to audit sampling is of relatively recent origin. The many applications that are currently being made are essentially experimental, although operational applications are becoming more common. A simple application of statistics was proposed in 1933,* but the first treatise dealing extensively with the subject did not appear until 1950, and it was not until 1956 that the American Institute of Certified Public Accountants appointed a committee to give further consideration to the problem. There are several major works available on the subject today, and the reader who seeks more information and insight into the subject than is presented in this relatively elementary introduction will be well advised to consult any of these volumes, as well as the growing number of articles that have been appearing in accounting periodicals.

Much of the current interest in statistical sampling stems from the intensive research on the subject conducted during World War II. The first extensive interest in the application of statistical techniques to the sampling problem in auditing involved the acceptance sampling techniques of statistical quality control, and most frequently the specific method of "sequential sampling." At present, it may be said that there are three main types of statistical sampling techniques that seem to be useful in auditing: acceptance sampling, discovery sampling, and estimation sampling. Acceptance sampling is discussed first, and then the closely related subject of discovery sampling is covered, with the discussion of estimation sampling reserved for the final portion of the chapter.

Theory Underlying Acceptance Sampling

The theory of probability as it relates to acceptance sampling is perhaps best explained through the use of the classical illustration of a bowl containing white balls and black balls. For our purposes, assume that the bowl contains 10,000 balls, of which 9,000 are white and 1,000 are black, or in terms of percentages, 90 per cent of the balls are white and 10 per cent are black.

A random sample of the contents of the bowl can be taken by drawing one ball from the bowl, recording its color, replacing the ball, stirring the contents, and repeating the process until a desired number of balls has been drawn. If the process is stopped after 100 draws, it is theoretically possible that all 100 balls selected would be white, or that all 100 balls selected would be black. As a matter of fact, however, we would expect the tabulation of our selection to show that the distribution of black balls

---

* Lewis A. Carman, "The Efficacy of Tests," *The American Accountant,* December 1933, pp. 360–366.

and white balls approximates more nearly the distribution of the full 10,000 balls in the bowl. In other words, the sample would probably show 90 white balls and 10 black balls, or a distribution varying only slightly from this 90–10 relationship.

If 100 balls were to be drawn as described above, and that sampling process were to be repeated 1,000 times, the statistician could compute in advance the likely over-all results of the thousand samples. This type of computed forecast is based upon probability, and the statistician says in effect that the probable results of taking the thousand samples will be those shown in the table below.

This table bears out the earlier statement that we could hardly expect to draw 100 white balls in a sample of 100, nor 100 black balls in a sample of 100. The table also shows that we would probably draw in the neighborhood of 10 black balls in our sample of 100. Although we would draw exactly 10 only about 13.2 per cent of the times (132 times in 1,000), we would draw 8 to 12 black balls (10 plus or minus 2) about 59.6 per cent of the times, and 6 to 14 black balls (10 plus or minus 4) about 87 per cent of the times.

Probable Results, Based on the Binomial Distribution, of Drawing 1,000 Samples of 100 Each from a Population Containing 10 Per Cent Black Balls

Number of Black Balls in Sample of 100	Number of Times in 1,000 the Stated Number of Black Balls Will Probably Appear	Cumulative Number of Times in 1,000 that Stated Number of Black Balls or Fewer Will Probably Appear
0	0*	0
1	0*	0
2	2	2
3	6	8
4	16	24
5	34	58
6	60	118
7	89	207
8	115	322
9	130	452
10	132	584
11	120	704
12	99	803
13	74	877
14	51	928
15	33	961
16	19	980
17	11	991
18	5	996
19	3	999
20	1	1,000
21	0*	1,000

* There is some chance that the stated number of black balls may be drawn but, because that chance is less than $\frac{1}{2}$ in 1,000, the stated number of black balls is not likely to appear in only 1,000 draws.

An Application of Acceptance Sampling

With these facts at hand, we can illustrate the application of acceptance sampling. Let us take a bowl containing 10,000 balls, without knowing how many of the balls are white or how many are black. We shall assume that the presence of black balls is undesirable, and that we are willing to accept the bowl of balls only if we can be relatively certain that not more than 10 per cent of the balls are black. If we take a random sample of 100 balls (following the process of selecting a ball, noting its color, returning the ball to the bowl, stirring the contents, and then repeating the process) we can make some useful inferences about the relative proportion of black balls in the bowl for the purpose of determining whether to accept the bowl of balls.

Assume that our sample of 100 produces 2 black balls. It should be apparent that there is little basis for concluding, on the strength of our sample, that the bowl contains the same proportion of black balls noted in our sample. Reference to tables similar to the table on page 690 would show that if exactly 2 per cent of the balls in the bowl were actually black, only about 271 times out of 1,000 samples of 100 could we expect to obtain samples containing exactly 2 black balls. Furthermore, the tables would show that it would be possible to obtain a sample containing 2 black balls if the bowl contained as few as 10 black balls (1/10 of 1 per cent) or as many as 1,200 black balls (12 per cent).

To this point, our inferences about the possible percentage of black balls are relatively useless, for they tell us only that the percentage probably ranges between 1/10 of 1 per cent and 12 per cent, and that the likelihood is not strong (271 chances in 1,000) that the percentage is exactly 2 per cent. Nevertheless, although we are unable to ascertain what *is* the actual percentage of black balls, we are in a much better position to infer what the percentage *is not*. For instance, using the table on page 690, we can see that if as much as 10 per cent of the balls in the bowl were actually black, we could expect to find a sample of 100 containing 2 black balls or less only about 2 times in 1,000. Because this would be an extremely rare occurrence, we can infer with considerable confidence that the black balls in the bowl do not exceed 10 per cent of the total, and on this basis accept the bowl of balls as meeting the minimum standard that we had set.

Complete Assurance Impossible With Sampling

Note, however, that the sample does not present absolute and conclusive evidence that not more than 10 per cent of the balls in the bowl are black, for we have already noted that we might find 2 black balls in a sample of 100 from a bowl in which as many as 12 per cent of the balls are black. Such lack of absolute assurance is an important aspect of any form of sampling, or stated in other terms, only by inspecting every item in a population can complete assurance be obtained as to the absolute proportion of items in the population. Stated in still another way, the economy of sampling as compared with 100 per cent inspection of a population can be gained only at some sacrifice in the assurance that a correct conclusion will be reached about the proportions existing within the population.

Because sampling always involves some risk of an incorrect decision, the advantage of using statistical techniques is that the risk of reaching an incorrect conclusion can be measured. In the preceding illustration, we noted that only rarely would a sample of 100 contain as few as 2 black balls if the population contained in excess of 10 per cent black balls, and reading from the table, the risk can be evaluated as 0.2 per cent or 2 times in 1,000. Risks are also present, of course, when samples are evaluated on a judgmental basis, but there is then no real indication of the amount of risk involved.

Auditing Applications of Acceptance Sampling

The auditor should find acceptance sampling techniques of considerable value in any situation in which errors may be present, such as in the client's inventory counts, inventory prices and extensions, accounts receivable aging, the recording of employees' hours worked in payroll calculations, or the classification of expenses in the voucher register. In these or other instances where an excessive amount of error would cast doubt on the acceptability of financial statement figures, the auditor may use tests of the records in order to satisfy himself that the final results are not materially misstated.

To facilitate the use of acceptance sampling in such situations, the author has developed a special table that makes it possible for the auditor to obtain simply and directly the information that he needs for a quantitative interpretation of the results of his test checks. The table is presented on page 693, and is based on the Poisson distribution, which is a close approximation of the binomial distribution used in constructing the table on page 690.

Acceptance Sampling of Accounts Receivable Aging

To demonstrate the use of the table, let us assume that the auditor is faced with the problem of determining the acceptability of the client's aging of some 10,000 charge accounts in a retail store. The accounts are in various amounts ranging up to $500, and the auditor concludes that he would be justified in accepting the client's aging provided that not more than 2 per cent of the accounts are incorrectly aged. (Accounts incorrectly aged would be the equivalent of black balls in the preceding illustration.) Furthermore, the auditor concludes that he wants 95 per cent confidence that he will be correct if he accepts the aging as containing no more than 2 per cent errors. (Conversely, the 95 per cent confidence level means that

[1]Implications of Accepting Data Based on the Number of Errors
Disclosed by the Auditor's Test Checks*

Number of Items Test-Checked	Number of Errors Dis-closed	Number of Times in 100 that the Auditor Will be Justified in Deciding that the Actual Error Rate is Less than :				
		0.5%	1%	2%	5%	10%
25	0	12	22	39	72	92
25	1	1	3	9	36	71
25	2	0	0	1	13	46
25	3			0	4	24
25	4				1	11
25	5				0	4
25	6					1
25	7					0
50	0	22	39	63	92	99
50	1	3	9	26	71	96
50	2	0	1	8	46	87
50	3		0	2	24	73
50	4			0	11	56
50	5				4	38
50	6				1	24
50	7				0	13
50	8					7
50	9					3
50	10					1

* This table is developed from Poisson's distribution as follows:

$\overline{X}$ = Average number of occurrences of a given event

T = Number of times in 1,000 that X or fewer occurrences can be expected in a sample under the conditions of $\overline{X}$

Thus, if a sample of 100 is drawn from a series of data that has an average of 2 per cent errors, $\overline{X}$ is 2, and the values for T are

0 = 135	5 = 983
1 = 406	6 = 995
2 = 677	7 = 999
3 = 857	8 = 1,000
4 = 947	

In turn, when an average error of 2 per cent is present, a sample of 100 will reveal one error or less 406 times in 1,000. The auditor may therefore conclude that the probability of finding more than one error is 594 (the complement of 406) and that, in accepting a sample of 100 showing one error as coming from a population that must have contained less than 2 per cent errors, the probability of being correct is 59.4 per cent.

The value indicated in the previous example is found on the line of this table showing sample size 100, one error; under the 2 per cent column, the figure 59 appears.

All probabilities less than $\frac{1}{2}$ are shown in the table as 0.

All probabilities greater than $99\frac{1}{2}$ are shown in the table as 100.

This table covers only the sample sizes and maximum allowable rates of error that are most likely to be needed. Values not shown can be derived readily by using a table of the Poisson distribution as described above.

[1] This table originally appeared as part of an article on statistical sampling by the author published in *The Journal of Accountancy, January,* 1954, and is reproduced here with permission.

Number of Items Test-checked	Number of Errors Disclosed	Number of Times in 100 That the Auditor Will Be Justified in Deciding That the Actual Error Rate is Less Than:				
		0.5%	1%	2%	5%	10%
100	0	39	63	86	99	100
100	1	9	26	59	96	100
100	2	1	8	32	87	100
100	3	0	2	14	73	99
100	4		0	5	56	97
100	5			2	38	93
100	6			0	24	87
100	7				13	78
100	8				7	67
100	9				3	54
100	10				1	42
150	0	53	78	95	100	100
150	1	17	44	80	100	100
150	2	4	19	58	98	100
150	3	1	7	35	94	100
150	4	0	2	18	87	100
150	5		0	8	76	100
150	6			3	62	99
150	7			1	48	98
150	8			0	34	96
150	9				22	93
150	10				14	88
200	0	63	86	98	100	100
200	1	26	59	91	100	100
200	2	8	32	76	100	100
200	3	2	14	57	99	100
200	4	0	5	37	97	100
200	5		2	21	93	100
200	6		0	11	87	100
200	7			5	78	100
200	8			2	67	100
200	9			1	54	99
200	10			0	42	99
300	0	78	95	100	100	100
300	1	44	80	98	100	100
300	2	19	58	94	100	100
300	3	7	35	85	100	100
300	4	2	18	71	100	100
300	5	0	8	55	100	100
300	6		3	39	99	100
300	7		1	26	98	100
300	8		0	15	96	100
300	9			8	93	100
300	10			4	88	100
300	11			2	81	100
300	12			1	73	100
300	13			0	64	100
300	14				53	100
300	15				43	100

Number of Items Test-Checked	Number of Errors Dis-closed	Number of Times in 100 That the Auditor Will Be Justified in Deciding That the Actual Error Rate is Less Than:				
		0.5%	1%	2%	5%	10%
400	0	86	98	100	100	100
400	1	59	91	100	100	100
400	2	32	76	99	100	100
400	3	14	57	96	100	100
400	4	5	37	90	100	100
400	5	2	21	81	100	100
400	6	0	11	69	100	100
400	7		5	55	100	100
400	8		2	41	100	100
400	9		1	28	99	100
400	10		0	18	99	100
400	11			11	98	100
400	12			6	96	100
400	13			3	93	100
400	14			2	89	100
400	15			1	84	100
400	16			0	78	100
400	17				70	100
400	18				62	100
400	19				53	100
400	20				44	100
500	0	92	99	100	100	100
500	1	71	96	100	100	100
500	2	46	87	100	100	100
500	3	24	73	99	100	100
500	4	11	56	97	100	100
500	5	4	38	93	100	100
500	6	1	24	87	100	100
500	7	0	13	78	100	100
500	8		7	67	100	100
500	9		3	54	100	100
500	10		1	42	100	100
500	11		0	30	100	100
500	12			21	100	100
500	13			14	99	100
500	14			8	99	100
500	15			5	98	100
500	16			3	96	100
500	17			1	94	100
500	18			1	91	100
500	19			0	87	100
500	20				81	100
500	21				75	100
500	22				68	100
500	23				61	100
500	24				53	100
500	25				45	100

the auditor is willing to take the risk of accepting the aging even though it contains more than 2 per cent errors, as many as 5 times in 100.)

The first step is to determine the minimum number of account agings that would have to be tested in order to justify accepting the client's aging, and this figure can be readily determined from the table. Because we have said that we seek 95 per cent confidence that the error rate does not exceed 2 per cent, the minimum number of agings to be tested can be determined by reference to the figures in the column headed 2%. For various sample sizes and number of errors found, the figures in the column show the confidence with which the population can be accepted as containing less than 2 per cent errors. Thus for a test of 25 items revealing no errors, we would have only 39 per cent confidence in accepting the population as containing less than 2 per cent errors. Glancing at other sample sizes, we see that if 150 agings are tested with no errors found, we would have the desired confidence of 95 per cent in accepting the client's aging as containing less than 2 per cent errors. Thus our minimum sample size is 150, and the "acceptance number" is zero; that is, the client's aging can be accepted if no errors are found in sampling the aging of 150 accounts.

Selecting the Account Agings to Be Tested

In taking samples from the bowl containing black and white balls, it was quite easy to obtain a random selection merely by replacing each ball selected and stirring the contents of the bowl before selecting another ball. Under this procedure, each ball had an equal chance of being selected each time a ball was drawn. The same conditions cannot be readily duplicated in the agings of accounts receivable, however, so an alternative approach must be used to assure randomness. A table of random numbers offers a possible solution to the problem, and many such tables are available. All have been carefully prepared and then tested for randomness. The following table of random numbers represents a portion of a table published by the Bureau of Transport Economics and Statistics of the Interstate Commerce Commission, under the title, *Table of 105,000 Random Decimal Digits.*

			Column			
Line	(1)	(2)	(3)	(4)	(5)	(6)
1	10480	15011	01536	02011	81647	91646
2	22368	46573	25595	85393	30995	89198
3	24130	48360	22527	97265	76393	64809
4	42167	93093	06243	61680	07856	16376
5	37570	39975	81837	16656	06121	91782
6	77921	06907	11008	42751	27756	53498
7	99562	72905	56420	69994	98872	31016
8	96301	91977	05463	07972	18876	20922
9	89579	14342	63661	10281	17453	18103
10	85475	36857	53342	53988	53060	59533

If we assume that the client's accounts receivable are numbered from 0000 to 9,999, we can select 150 accounts on a random basis by using numbers selected from any starting place on the above table. Thus, starting at Column 4, Line 1, we find the figure 02011, and using only the last four digits, the first account we selected would be the account numbered 2011, the next would be 5393, and so on.

As an alternative, assume that the accounts are not numbered, but that the aging was prepared on 200 sheets of analysis paper, with each sheet containing the aging of 50 accounts. The table can then be used in the following manner, commencing, say, with Column 3 and Line 1. The first three digits can be used to identify the sheet number, in this case 015, and the next two digits the line number on the sheet, which would be line 36. The next number, 25595, can merely be ignored because there is no sheet 255 and no line 95. Many other numbers would also have to be ignored on this basis, and to reduce the amount of skipping, the table can be read in a different manner. Starting with Line 1, the table can be read across all the columns, ignoring single digits that are too high. Thus the first page would be 104, but as there is no line 80, the 8 would be ignored, making the next pair of digits 01, which would be usable as a line number. Next, 501 is too high for a page number, so the 5 would be ignored, making the next group of three digits 011 for the page number, 01 the line number, and so on.

Still another approach to the selection process would be to use systematic, or interval, sampling. On this basis, with 150 accounts to be selected from 10,000, after making a random start within the first 65 accounts, every 65th account thereafter would be selected for aging. Such a sample would not be truly random, but would nevertheless be adequate for most purposes.

Many other approaches may also be used for the selection process, but the reader is referred to any standard statistics text for information about further variations in the selection process.

Interpreting the Sampling Results

If the client's employees have been accurate in the aging of the accounts, no errors should be detected in our test, and we would then have the specified 95 per cent confidence in accepting the client's aging analysis. But what if 2 errors are noted in the test? We would then have only 58 per cent confidence in accepting the client's aging as having less than 2 per cent errors, and this would be clearly unacceptable. On the other hand, there is insufficient basis for rejecting the client's aging as unsatisfactory, because there is only 42 per cent confidence (the complement of 58 per cent) that the error rate exceeds 2 per cent, the figure originally set as making the client's aging unsatisfactory.

There are three possible courses of action that can be followed under these circumstances. The first would be to reject the client's work, in spite of the limited basis for concluding that the errors exceed 2 per cent, and have the client's employees completely re-check the work that they have done. Then a new sample would have to be taken to establish the acceptability of the corrected aging. A major difficulty in following this approach is that the re-check of the aging by the client's employees may disclose less than 2 per cent errors, with the client then blaming the auditor for the additional work that was actually unnecessary.

A second course of action is equally risky, but for a different reason. The auditor may reconsider his standard of 2 per cent error as being too severe, and decide that even as much as 5 per cent error would not seriously misstate the final results. Under these circumstances, the sample of 150 with 2 errors would yield a comforting 98 per cent confidence that the error rate does not exceed 5 per cent. Alternatively, the auditor might also accept a lesser degree of confidence, as for instance if the sample had disclosed only a single error, which would give 80 per cent confidence in accepting the client's work as being within the 2 per cent allowable rate of error. The danger in modifying either the originally specified confidence or error rate is, of course, that such action may expose the auditor to a subsequent charge of negligence or lack of independence if the statements on which the auditor gave a favorable opinion should prove to be misleading.

The third possible course of action will usually be the most desirable to follow, although eventually the auditor may still be forced to follow one of the first two alternatives. There is always a possibility that the auditor's sample has fallen in the range of extreme probability and is not actually representative of the population. In other words, just as there is a chance of a sample that would lead to acceptance of a population that is actually unacceptable, there is also a chance of the opposite situation occurring. To test this possibility, the auditor has only to extend his sampling to include additional items.

For example, if the actual error rate in the aging were 1 per cent, in 19 cases out of 100, a sample of 150 from such a population would contain 2 or more errors. Under these circumstances, additional sampling would be unlikely to reveal errors at the same rate as the initial sample of 150 agings. In fact, an additional test of 150 items might reveal no errors, giving a combined sample of 300 with only 2 errors, which would give 94 per cent confidence in accepting the aging under the original standard of a maximum 2 per cent error rate. Interpolating from the table, a sample of 320 with only 2 errors would give approximately the 95 per cent confidence originally specified. Of course, if continued sampling revealed additional errors, the auditor would eventually be forced to follow one of the first two alternatives.

Precautions for Use of Acceptance Sampling Table

In using the table on page 693, there are two points that should be kept in mind. First, the values shown represent close approximations of the results that would be obtained in sampling from data that are infinite in number. The auditor, of course, works with a finite series of data; but, if the sample does not exceed 10 per cent of the number of items in the series being tested, the table may be used with adequate assurance that the error resulting from the violation of the basic assumption inherent in the figures will be negligible. Even when the 10 per cent limitation is not adhered to, the table can still be used, however. In such cases the probability value in the table will be an understatement of the assurance the auditor may have.

There are no other limitations in the use of the table if the sample is no larger than 10 per cent of the series of data to be tested. Such a statement implies in turn that, if this condition is not violated, the table may be used in evaluating the results of a test of, say, 100 items, regardless of whether the series of data from which the items were selected contained 1,000 items, 1,500 items, 5,000 items, or any other number of items in excess of 1,000. Thus the frequently used technique of defining sample size in terms of a percentage of the total number of items to be examined has little place in a statistical approach to test-checking. The factor of major importance is the size of the sample taken, not the proportion of items sampled.

The reason that the size of the sample need not bear a given relationship to the size of the complete series of data being tested may be developed through reference to the original situation of the bowl containing 1,000 black and 9,000 white balls. Each ball has an equal chance of being drawn each time, and thus, as the size of the sample increases, the tabulation of results of the sample will evidence a tendency of the figures to move closer and closer to the actual 90-10 relationship of balls in the bowl. As the basic reason for the tabulated results is the selection from a group of balls with a 90-10 relationship, whether the bowl contained 1,000 balls in this ratio or 10,000 balls in this ratio would be of no consequence if each ball were replaced after notation of its color.

Defining the Population

In sampling for independent audit purposes, generally speaking, the population to be tested will be the complete series of items, because the independent auditor is interested in over-all results. Thus, even though several different people aged the accounts receivable, the independent auditor would rely on random selection to bring some examples of each employee's work under his scrutiny, and would make his decision to accept or reject the aging on an over-all basis. The internal auditor, however, might well be interested in the accuracy of the work of each employee, and would therefore consider each employee's work a separate population. In view of the earlier comment that population size has relatively little effect on sample size, the approximate result of considering the aging to consist of four populations would be to quadruple the amount of testing that would be required.

Uniform Levels of Acceptable Error Rate and Confidence

We have seen that in acceptance sampling the auditor must set both the maximum rate of error that he is willing to tolerate, and the degree of confidence that he seeks in his decision if the results of his sample indicate a decision to accept the population he is testing. Both of these quantitative measures are determined by the auditor, and it is at this point that his professional judgment enters the process, indicating that he has not surrendered control over his testing to a table or a formula.

As both materiality and relative risk will have a bearing on the percentage of error that the auditor will be willing to tolerate in any given situation, each testing situation becomes a separate case requiring a separate decision on the maximum rate of error that the auditor feels he can accept. As to the matter of the level of confidence in the acceptance decision, it is quite possible that more widespread use of statistics by auditors and increased understanding of the risk inherent in every decision based on a sample may lead to the adoption of a uniform standard of confidence for all audit sampling decisions. The profession may thus decide what percentage of the time it wants to be right when questionable decisions must be made. Agreement on some figure, such as 95 per cent, does not mean, however, that practitioners will consistently be wrong 5 per cent of the time. These figures apply only to the situation where the probability involved is exactly 95 per cent. In many instances the sample may disclose so few errors that, when considered relative to the maximum allowable percentage of error, the auditor's decision to accept the data will be right more than 95 per cent of the time. Thus at times the probability of being right may actually be close to 100 per cent, and a 95 per cent standard will result in an over-all performance considerably better than 95 per cent.

Interrelationship of Other Audit Procedures and Sampling

In setting confidence levels and acceptable error rates, auditors must approach the problem somewhat differently from what is true for most other applications of acceptance sampling. The difference stems from the fact that in the usual situation the sampling decision is completely independent of other factors, whereas in auditing applications the sampling results are frequently only one of several factors that may enter into the auditor's ultimate decision that a figure on the financial statements is fairly stated. The testing of inventory extensions offers a good illustration of this point. In addition to the results of tests of the extensions, the auditor may have these further indications of whether the extensions may have caused a material misstatement of the inventory figure:

1. The client's internal control over the work in the form of two inde-

pendent calculations of all extensions, and tests of the accuracy of the work by internal auditors.

2. The client's internal control over the recording of entries to the general ledger inventory control account and the independent auditor's tests of the entries performed in conjunction with his review of internal control.

3. The reasonableness of the variation between the physical inventory total and the balance of the general ledger control account, and the relation of this year's amount to the amounts in previous years.

4. The reasonableness of the physical inventory figure based on the gross profit test.

5. The reasonableness of the final inventory figure in relation to previous years and known changes in purchasing and selling activities.

6. The results of "scanning" all or part of the extensions.

With the availability of such supplementary evidence of the reliability of the inventory figure, it is obvious that the auditor does not rely solely on the results of his tests of the extensions. There is no clear indication, however, of how much the presence of such additional evidence should properly influence the confidence level or allowable rate of error that the auditor sets in conducting his tests.

The Magic Number of "One"

Frequently the sample size used in audit tests of recorded transactions is so small that statistical interpretation of the sample would show uncomfortably low confidence, or, if a satisfactory confidence level is specified, the resulting maximum rate of error would have to be much too high. A statistician would argue that such samples should be increased in size to permit reasonable confidence levels relative to an acceptable maximum rate of error. But it has been argued* that independent auditors in testing transactions may, if proper controls over internal control are present, proceed in the opposite direction and reduce samples to include only one of each type of transaction processed through the segment of the system being tested.

One argument for moving in this direction in testing transactions is that there is no meaningful basis for setting the maximum tolerable error rate that is required when using statistical sampling in tests of transactions for compliance with internal control. For example, if the system covering procedures for the recording of liabilities resulting from purchase transactions is to be tested, what is the maximum rate of error that an independent auditor might tolerate for such transactions? Failure of an audit clerk to verify quantities or prices on a vendor's invoice before approving the invoice for payment would not be likely materially to affect the financial state-

* See "Some Observations on Statistical Sampling in Auditing," by Howard F. Stettler, *The Journal of Accountancy*, April, 1966, pp. 55–62.

ments. In the first place, most of the quantities and prices would probably agree with the related receiving reports and purchase orders even if no verification was made. For the rare cases where differences might exist, the principal result would be to distort the inventory variance or gross margin for the year, and then only in terms of what might have been if the differences had been detected and the correct amount paid. But as the accounts would indicate the amounts actually paid, they would not be in error and would merely reflect the results of management's failure to have invoices audited properly before they are paid.

In some instances, reducing sample sizes in tests of transactions to the irreducible minimum of one of each type of transaction can be justified by the existence of over-all controls to assure compliance with a prescribed basic internal control system. Considering again the recording of inventory purchases and accounts payable, there can be a variety of controls to give assurance that the basic system of internal control is operating effectively. Failure of the audit clerk to make the necessary verifications of purchase prices and quantities could be detected if invoices are subjected to a final review before payment to ascertain that the initials of the audit clerk have been inscribed to show that quantities and prices were verified. Other controls would be the development of differences between book and physical inventory figures, the tests performed by an internal audit staff, the existence of procedures manuals and written job descriptions, and personnel selection and review procedures to assure a competent work force.

The presence of such factors may then raise the question, why not do away with all testing of transactions? The absolute minimum sample of one should be retained to give the auditor assurance that the system described to him does actually exist and that he is not simply dealing with an imaginary empire existing only on paper. The sample of one amounts to what is sometimes referred to as a "walkthrough" of each kind of transaction. The transaction selected is traced through the system from beginning to end, to show that each prescribed step of the system is in effect and being followed. Employees involved in the system are questioned about their duties and how they handle exceptions that may be encountered. The questioning that takes place is in terms of the handling of the documents pertaining to the selected transaction and represents an approach similar to the "test deck" method of interrogating a computer system (discussed in an earlier chapter). One interpretation that has been suggested for both the walkthrough and the test deck is that these are not so much devices to test the operation of a system as they are a means of asking questions about the system. The use of specific transactions, documents, or computer input precludes misunderstandings about the questions being asked or the answers being given in return.

The final point to be discussed about the minimum sample of one is, what happens if the controls present in the system are too weak to justify the auditor's reliance on the results produced by the system? Auditing standards require "... proper study and evaluation of the existing internal control as a basis for reliance thereon and for the determination of the resultant extent of the tests to which auditing procedures are to be restricted."* The usual interpretation of this standard has been that weak internal control requires more extensive tests of transactions to ascertain compliance with the client's prescribed system and the accuracy of the results produced. By contrast, the proposition is here introduced that lack of reliability of system output should be compensated for not by more extensive tests of transactions, but by more extensive tests of the resulting account balances. In other words, the auditor should require higher confidence levels in his tests of balances to offset the reduced reliability of the output of the system, and sampling theory would accordingly dictate larger sample sizes in testing the account balances.

Discovery Sampling

Although discovery sampling is undertaken with a slightly different objective from that of acceptance sampling, the two plans are closely related in terms of the probabilities that are involved. Discovery samples are based on the desire to encounter at least one erroneous item if there are erroneous items in the population, and discovery sampling is therefore best suited to the attempt to discover the existence of fraud when fraud is suspected. The sampling plan is useful, however, only if erroneous or fraudulent items occur in the population with a frequency in excess of about 1 per cent, for no sampling plan can provide meaningful assurance of discovering a "rare" item in a population. The only solution to the detection of the rare item is 100 per cent inspection.

To illustrate discovery sampling, let us assume that it is suspected that someone other than the treasurer of a client has been signing the checks that have been drawn during the past year. To discover if someone else has signed some of the checks, and to ascertain the person's identity, we would want to see at least one check signed by that person. In devising a discovery sample for such a situation, it is necessary to set the confidence desired so that at least one check not signed by the treasurer will be disclosed in a sample if it is assumed that such checks exist in the population in some stated proportion. For instance, we might desire 95 per cent confidence that we will encounter as least one such check if at least 1 per cent of the checks have been signed by a person other than the treasurer. To determine the sample size that will fulfill these requirements, we can use the table on pages 693 to 695. Under sample size of 300, we see that if no errors are disclosed, there is 95 per cent confidence that the actual error rate in the

---

* *Auditing Standards and Procedures.*

population does not exceed 1 per cent. Turning these figures about slightly, they indicate that 95 per cent of the times, 1 error or more will be found in a sample of 300 selected from a population containing at least 1 per cent errors. These conditions then meet our original requirements, for we have 95 chances in 100 that our sample will disclose at least one irregular check if 1 per cent or more of the checks are irregular.

Estimation Sampling

Estimation sampling, or survey sampling, as it is sometimes called, is perhaps the most useful statistical sampling technique for independent audit purposes. One of the principal features of estimation sampling is that it can be used with variables, such as dollar amounts, whereas acceptance sampling is readily usable only when attributes (presence or absence of an error) are involved.

For example, if accounts receivable confirmation is conducted on a test basis, the number of differences disclosed by replies received gives little indication of how much the dollar total of accounts receivable may be affected by such differences. Estimation sampling can accommodate such a problem quite readily. Other possible applications for estimation sampling would include estimating total receivables or inventories from a sampling of accounts receivable balances or the dollar amounts of selected inventory items, and estimating the aging of accounts receivable on the basis of aging a sample selected from the full group of receivables.

Theory Underlying Estimation Sampling

The distribution of a population of individual values in relation to the arithmetic mean of the population constitutes the underlying basis for estimation sampling. It is known, for example, that 68.3 per cent of the items in a normally distributed population will occur within plus or minus one standard deviation from the mean, 95.4 per cent within plus or minus two standard deviations, and 99.7 per cent within plus or minus three standard deviations. (The reader should recall that the standard deviation is computed by determining the deviation of each item in the population from the mean, squaring these deviations, computing the sum of the squared deviations, dividing this sum by the number that is one less than the number of items in the population, and calculating the square root of the resulting quotient.)

A second important statistical concept involved in estimation sampling describes the results of taking a series of samples of a stated size and calculating the mean of the items in each sample. The means of the samples will tend to form a normal distribution, with the mean of the sample means equal to the mean of the population. The standard deviation of the sample means (the standard error, in statistical parlance) also is important, and particularly significant is the behavior of the standard deviation of the sample means in relation to the size of the samples. The larger the sample size from which the sample means are computed, the smaller will be the standard deviation of the sample means. To indicate the extremes, if the sample size is one, the standard deviation of the sample means will be approximately equal to the standard deviation of the population means. Conversely, if the sample size is equal to the population size, the standard deviation of the sample means will be zero, for the mean of each sample should be approximately the same, and should equal the mean of the population. This relationship of sample size and the standard deviation of the sample means may be pictured graphically as follows:

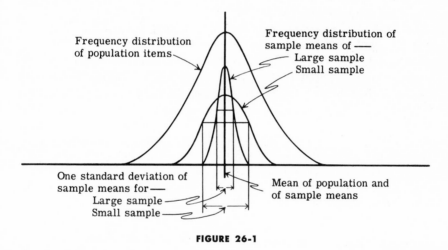

Frequency distribution of population items

Frequency distribution of sample means of ——
Large sample
Small sample

One standard deviation of sample means for ——
Large sample
Small sample

Mean of population and of sample means

FIGURE 26-1

The effect of sample size on the standard deviation of the sample means is also indicated by the following formula:

$$\text{Standard deviation of sample means} = \frac{\text{Standard deviation of population}}{\sqrt[2]{\text{Sample size}}}$$

This formula is based on an infinite population; the slight effect of the fact that the auditor works with finite populations is discussed at a later point.

Illustration of Estimation Sampling

Estimation sampling will be illustrated by showing how the total amount of accounts receivable can be estimated from a sample of the balances in an accounts receivable ledger. For instance, if we take a random sample of 100 accounts, total the accounts, and then determine the mean balance in the sample by dividing the total for the sample by 100, we might arrive at a mean of, say, $46.52 per account. Then, if by counting we determine that there are 1,400 accounts in the ledger, we would estimate the total accounts receivable to be $65,128.00. However, we also know that if we take a different random sample of 100 accounts, we will in all likelihood arrive at a different mean balance and estimate of the total receivables. How much the results of such samples of 100 might vary would depend on the variability of the population from which the samples are drawn, and of course, the variability of the sample results would represent an inverse relationship to the size of the sample.

Our immediate problem is to determine, for a given sample size from a stated population, how much the sample means might vary from the true mean of the population. It has been stated previously that the means of repeated samples of a given size from a stated population will tend to fall about the population mean in the pattern of a normal distribution. The dispersion of these sample means about the true mean has been expressed previously (page 705) as a function of the standard deviation of the population and the sample size. If for our population of accounts receivable balances we assume a standard deviation of $10.53, we can compute the standard deviation of the sample means to be $\dfrac{10.53}{\sqrt{100}}$ or $1.05. Given the behavior of a normally distributed population, we can graph the means of repeated samples of 100 in the following manner, if we assume for the moment that the true mean of the population is the $46.52 calculated from our sample of 100.

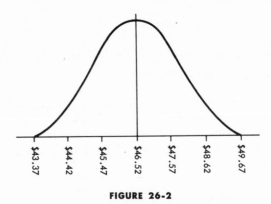

FIGURE 26-2

This graph can be interpreted as saying that given $46.52 to be the true mean of the population, 68 per cent of the means calculated from samples of 100 would fall between $45.47 and $ 47.57; 95 per cent of the sample means would fall between $44.42 and $48.62; and 99.7 per cent of the sample means would fall between $43.37 and $49.67. From the known information, we can be certain that the shape of the curve is as shown, but the placement of the curve on the horizontal line depends on where the true mean of the population falls. In estimation sampling, we attempt to find out something about the true mean of the population, but we cannot spot the mean precisely on the horizontal line; we can only estimate a range within which we would expect the true mean to lie, with some stated confidence for our estimate.

As stated above, if the true mean is $46.52, we would expect 95 per cent of the means of repeated samples of 100 to fall within two standard deviations, or a range from $44.42 to $48.62. But now let us drop the assumption that $46.52 is the true mean of the·population, and consider the usual situation where we have no information about the true mean. Our purpose in sampling is to estimate the mean of the population, but this estimate must of necessity be an interval estimate concerning a range of possible values. A point estimate of the true mean can be made only from a 100 per cent sample.

What can we conclude from our sample of 100 with a mean of $46.52? With 95 per cent confidence, we can say that it must have come from a population whose mean was no less than $44.42 and no greater than $48.62. This statement can be illustrated by the following graph:

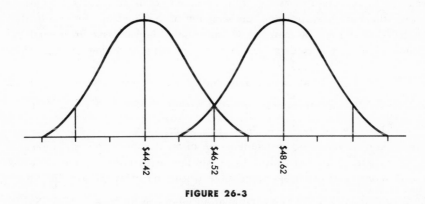

$44.42 $46.52 $48.62

FIGURE 26-3

Thus we can see that it is not likely that the population mean is greater than $48.62 nor less than $44.42, for there is only 2½ per cent risk that we would obtain a sample mean of $46.52 from a population with a mean greater than $48.62, and only 2½ per cent risk of obtaining a sample mean of $46.52 from a population with a mean less than $44.42. Combining these two statements, we can say with 95 per cent confidence (5 per cent risk of a sampling error) that the true mean of the population lies between $44.42

and $48.62, and thus we would estimate, with 95 per cent confidence, a total population of $65,128.00±$2,940 (1,400×$48.62 and 1,400×$44.42).

Determining Sample Size in Estimation Sampling

In the preceding illustration of estimation sampling, we utilized an arbitrarily assumed sample of 100, but one of the main purposes of using statistical sampling techniques is to determine what size sample must be taken. Two factors must be specified in estimation sampling to calculate sample size: confidence and precision. Confidence is an expression of desired assurance (or conversely, of the risk that a sampling error might occur), and precision relates to the range of the estimate. Auditors tend to work with confidence of 90 to 99 per cent, and we shall continue to use the 95 per cent figure of the previous illustration, which covers approximately two standard deviations of our sample means. The precision to be specified is a matter of materiality. To approach this problem, let us assume that the general ledger accounts receivable control account for our 1,400 accounts receivable shows a balance of $67,241.89. Also, we shall assume that a difference of ±$5,000 from this balance would not materially affect the client's financial statements. This decision of materiality would be based on the importance of the maximum difference to be tolerated of $5,000 relative to such figures as the total accounts receivable, the total current assets, the current ratio, and the amount of net income. By saying that ±$5,000 would not be material, we must be willing to issue an unqualified opinion even if the true receivable balance might be as low as $62,241.89 or as high as $72,241.89.

We also know that presumably the mean account balance is $48.03 $\left(\dfrac{\$67,241.89}{1,400}\right)$, and that the standard deviation of the population is $10.53.* Lastly, because we have specified precision of ±$5,000, we know that we are seeking a sampling distribution of means centered on the indicated mean of $48.03 and extending to points that with only $2\frac{1}{2}$ per cent risk could have come from a population whose mean is as low as $44.46 $\left(\dfrac{\$67,241.89 - \$5,000}{1,400}\right)$, or a population whose mean is as high as $51.60 $\left(\dfrac{\$67,241.89 + \$5,000}{1,400}\right)$. These requirements may be graphed as follows:

---

* The standard deviation can be estimated quite readily by randomly selecting 49 account balances, dividing the random listing of these 49 balances into seven groups of seven items, calculating the dollar range between the highest and lowest balance for each group, calculating the mean of these seven ranges, and dividing this mean by 2.704. (See Herbert Arkin, *Handbook of Sampling for Auditing and Accounting*, McGraw-Hill Book Company, Inc., 1963, p. 108.)

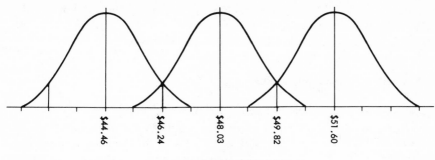

$44.46 $46.24 $48.03 $49.82 $51.60

FIGURE 26-4

This being the case, we are seeking a sample size in which the means of 95 per cent of the samples, if drawn from a population with a mean of $48.03, would fall between $46.24 and $49.82, or $48.03 ± $1.79. Under those circumstances, as the graph shows, we can be relatively certain (95 per cent confidence) that, even if we should draw a sample with a mean as low as $46.24, it did not come from a population with a mean less than $44.46; and if we should draw a sample with a mean as high as $49.82, that it did not come from a population with a mean greater than $51.60. We are thus saying that we desire a sampling distribution in which two standard deviations (which would include 95 per cent of the sample means) would be $1.79, and hence one standard deviation would be $0.90. At this point, sample size can be computed by inserting values into the formula given on page 705, which can be rearranged to show:

$$\text{Sample size} = \frac{(\text{Standard deviation of population})^2}{(\text{Standard deviation of sample means})^2}.$$

By inserting the values, we have:

$$\text{Sample size} = \frac{(10.53)^2}{(0.90)^2} = \frac{110.8809}{0.81} = 136.9 \text{ or } 137.$$

We may then proceed to randomly select the desired sample of 137 account balances, and if the mean of the sample is no less than $46.24 and no greater than $49.82, we would have 95 per cent confidence that the true value of the population is not less than $62,241.89, and not greater than $72,241.89. It may also be seen that if the true value of the population is $67,241.89, as indicated by the accounts receivable control, we would not be likely to obtain a sample mean of less than $46.24 or more than $49.82. Statistically speaking, the risk of a sampling error occurring, giving a mean outside of the specified range, would be 5 per cent.

It should be noted that the same approach can be used in confirming accounts receivable balances with customers. Use of estimation sampling in this manner does, however, obviate having to prove a trial balance of the accounts, because the confirmed balances would be used in ascertaining the range of possible total values of the receivables, thereby providing the same information normally acquired in testing a trial balance.

Additional Instructions and Precautions

The above example, based on 95 per cent confidence, involved 2 standard deviations in the permitted deviation of the sample means from the true mean, which necessitated dividing the permitted deviations of the sample means from the true mean by 2. More precisely, 95 per cent confidence encompasses only 1.96 standard deviations, and hence the $1.79 should have been divided by 1.96 rather than by 2. The divisors for other commonly specified confidence limits are

$$90\% \ldots\ldots\ldots 1.64$$
$$99\% \ldots\ldots\ldots 2.58$$

Use of 90 per cent confidence would, of course, permit a sample smaller than 137, and 99 per cent confidence would require a larger sample. Similarly, less precision (deviation from the true total of *more* than $5,000) would have permitted a smaller sample, whereas greater precision of the estimate would have required a larger sample.

As was true in the earlier discussion of acceptance sampling, for simplicity purposes, an infinite population has been assumed. This assumption will cause only minor distortion in either type of sampling, provided that the sample does not exceed about 10 per cent of the population size. The distortion that is produced is, however, on the side of safety to the auditor, and hence in the above illustration of estimation sampling the true confidence is slightly more than 95 per cent, or alternatively, the true precision is slightly greater than $5,000. Stated another way, had a correction factor for population size been used, the sample would have been slightly less than 137. For the interested reader, complete texts that discuss sampling for accountants and auditors contain formulas that involve such a correction factor.

Considerations in the Use of Statistical Sampling in Auditing

The preceding discussion of statistical sampling techniques, and the considerable amount of interest and curiosity being demonstrated by practitioners in the subject, suggest an important question: What are the implications of this highly specialized technique for auditing practice in general? The following summary indicates the situation as it appears at the present time:

1. Statistical sampling techniques are consistent with generally accepted auditing standards, which recognize the appropriateness of sampling.

2. In a given audit, statistical techniques may be deemed to be appropriate in one or more areas of the audit but not in others, and the use of such techniques in one area of an audit imposes no responsibility for using them in other areas where they are not appropriate.

3. If the techniques are used in one area of an audit, the auditor would be well advised to be prepared to defend the nonuse of statistical techniques in other areas of the audit where sampling is involved.

4. The use of any one statistical technique in an audit, as for example random selection, does not in itself require the use of other techniques, such as statistical determination of sample size or statistical evaluation of the sample results.

5. Statistical techniques appear to be most useful when the auditor is dealing with voluminous data and his tests of the data are not closely related to other areas of the audit. At the present time, known statistical techniques do not offer a satisfactory means of establishing a quantitative relationship between the results of a given audit test and other tests, or audit procedures that are closely related to it.

6. Improved control over audit procedures and more precise evaluation of sampling results are gained when objective statistical techniques are substituted for subjective judgmental selection and evaluation.

7. Knowledge of statistical techniques by auditors appears desirable so that the benefits of the techniques may be realized where the techniques are applicable, but the auditor should not have to become a trained statistician to obtain such knowledge.

8. If the auditor has only a general knowledge of statistics, he should seek the consultation and assistance of a trained statistician in resolving difficult applications of statistical techniques.

Statistical Sampling for Nonauditing Uses

Although the entire discussion of statistical sampling in this chapter has been in terms of auditing applications, the reader should recognize that the techniques discussed here, plus many others, are equally applicable to original accounting situations. Statistical sampling techniques have been successfully used in controlling the outgoing quality of the clerical work in invoicing customers, punching tabulating cards, auditing vendors' invoices for payment, estimating physical inventory amounts, and determining interline settlements for airlines and truck lines. Examples of all these applications have been reported in a variety of periodicals, and invariably the users have achieved substantial economies through the use of statistical sampling and evaluation techniques.

The independent auditor will be well advised to become familiar with the accounting applications of statistical techniques, for not only may he encounter them in his clients' operations, but more importantly, he is likely to observe many situations in which the use of the techniques would be valuable to his clients. The alert auditor will take every opportunity to recommend statistical techniques, when appropriate, as an excellent device to reduce clerical costs or improve internal control, thus providing still another form of "extra" services that can be so helpful to client relationships and the development of a successful practice.

REVIEW QUESTIONS

1. Do statistical sampling techniques supplant the auditor's judgment? Explain.
2. What are three principal types of statistical evaluation techniques that seem to be useful in auditing?
3. If a sample of 100 items reveals two errors, can the auditor reasonably conclude that roughly 2% of the items in the entire population are in error? Explain.
4. What must be sacrificed in order to obtain the economy of sampling as compared with 100% inspection of a population in arriving at a conclusion as to the proportion of errors or defectives in a population?
5. Since sampling always involves risk of a wrong conclusion, what is the advantage of using statistical sampling techniques?
6. What are the principal ways in which random samples can be obtained in auditing?
7. In acceptance sampling the auditor may reach either of three decisions about the population after completing his sample. Explain.
8. Since the acceptance sampling table in the text is based on an infinite population, what limitation should be kept in mind in using the table? Does the auditor assume added risk of improperly accepting an unacceptable population if the limitation is not observed?
9. Distinguish between sampling for attributes and sampling for variables in a test of inventory extensions.
10. Assume that a client utilizes three billing clerks, and the auditor is testing the accuracy of the billing work. Show how the auditor's definition of the population he is testing will affect the total amount of sampling that will be necessary.
11. What justification can be given for limiting tests of transactions to samples of one of each type of transaction under conditions of adequate internal control?
12. What modification in the auditor's examination should be made under the sample of one approach when there are deficiencies in the client's internal control?
13. Under what conditions would discovery sampling ordinarily be used?
14. In estimation sampling, what must be known (or calculated) about the population and what must be decided by the auditor in order to determine sample size and to estimate the value of the total population?
15. The auditor should be familiar with the intricacies of statistical sampling for other reasons, as well as in order to be able to use it in his auditing work. Explain.

QUESTIONS ON APPLICATION OF AUDITING STANDARDS

16. Your client is concerned that collusion may have occurred between his receiving department and some of the firm's major suppliers of materials. He fears that short shipments are received from time to time, and that the receiving department reports the quantity received as equal to the quantity ordered and invoiced, with a cash payment for half the difference then being made by the supplier to the receiving department head. The client proposes to make test recounts of materials when they are placed into stock, and asks how many such counts must be made. As a result of further discussion with you, the client concludes that he would like to be 98% certain that if the suspected manipulations are occurring, that not more than one in 100 shipments is involved. How many recounts should be made? Explain how you arrived at your answer.

17. Your client is a public utility that has approximately 10,000 unpaid customers' bills at the end of the year, with a single general ledger account controlling the entire amount of receivables. Explain how, as auditor, you might use sampling to ascertain the agreement of the detailed receivables with the control account.

18. The table in this chapter for acceptance sampling shows that a sample of 100 items revealing no errors provides 86% confidence in accepting a population as not containing in excess of 2% errors. The table shows that the same sample results provide only 63% confidence in accepting the population as containing not more than 1% errors. If you were testing payroll rates against personnel department records, would the two alternatives for evaluating the sample of 100 items be equally acceptable? Explain.

19. A sample of 100 disclosing one error affords only 59% confidence of accepting the population from which the sample was drawn as containing no more than 2% errors. Yet a sample of 400 containing exactly the same proportion of errors (4 errors, or 1%) affords 90% confidence in accepting the population as containing no more than 2% errors. How do you account for the difference in confidence when both samples contain the same proportion of errors?

20. Recent proposals would have auditors apply the principles of statistical sampling to auditing. Assuming that the claims made for the principles of statistical sampling as applied to auditing are valid, state the weaknesses of traditional auditing procedures which would be corrected and the improvements in auditing which would result from the application of such principles.

(Uniform C.P.A. Examination)

21. "Statistical sampling gives an audit partner more control over the conduct of the audit by the audit staff than does judgmental sampling." Justify this statement.

22. In statistical sampling terms, how are smaller samples in testing account balances justified under conditions of good internal control?

PROBLEMS

23. The Cowslip Milk Company's principal activity is buying milk from dairy farmers, processing the milk and delivering the milk to retail customers. You are engaged in auditing the retail accounts receivable of the Company and determine the following:

1. The Company has 50 retail routes; each route consists of 100 to 200 accounts, the number that can be serviced by a driver in a day.
2. The driver enters cash collections from the day's deliveries to each customer directly on a statement form in record books maintained for each route. Mail remittances are posted in the route record books by office personnel. At the end of the month the statements are priced, extended and footed. Photocopies of the statements are prepared and left in the customers' milk boxes with the next milk delivery.
3. The statements are reviewed by the office manager, who prepares a list for each route of accounts with 90-day balances or older. The list is used for intensive collection action.
4. The audit program used in prior audits for the selection of retail accounts receivable for confirmation stated: "Select two accounts from each route, one to be chosen by opening the route book at random and the other as the third item on each list of 90-day or older accounts."

Your review of the accounts receivable leads you to conclude that statistical sampling techniques may be applied to their examination.

Required:
   (a) Since statistical sampling techniques do not relieve the C.P.A. of his responsibilities in the exercise of his professional judgment, of what benefit are they to the C.P.A.? Discuss.
   (b) Give the reasons why the audit procedure previously used for selection of accounts receivable for confirmation (as given in #4 above) would not produce a valid statistical sample.
   (c) What are the audit objectives or purposes in selecting 90-day accounts for confirmation? Can the application of statistical sampling techniques help in attaining these objectives or purposes? Discuss.
   (d) Assume that the Company has 10,000 accounts receivable and that your statistical sampling disclosed 6 errors in a sample of 200 accounts. Is it reasonable to assume that 300 accounts in the entire population are in error? *Explain.* (Uniform C.P.A. Examination)

24. Increasing attention is being given by C.P.A.s to the application of statistical sampling techniques to audit testing.

Required:
   (a) List and explain the advantages of applying statistical sampling techniques to audit testing.
   (b) List and discuss the decisions involving professional judgment that must be made by the C.P.A. in applying statistical sampling techniques to audit testing.
   (c) You have applied probability sampling techniques to the client's pricing of the inventory and discovered from your sampling that the error rate exceeded your predetermined confidence level. Discuss the courses of action you can take. (Uniform C.P.A. Examination)

25. Your client's physical inventory totals $100,000 and is made up of approximately 10,000 items that are relatively homogeneous in value. You conclude that you can accept the inventory extensions if you can be 95% confident that the true inventory figure is within $5,000 of the stated figure of $100,000. In testing the accuracy of inventory extensions, what sample size should be used in order to accept the inventory, assuming that no errors are found in the sample? (Use an acceptance sampling approach based on a test of attributes.)

26. Give your calculations in using an estimation sampling approach to question 25. The standard deviation of the population is calculated to be $1.00.

27. Estimate the standard deviation of a population from the following sample drawn from the population:

175	49	143	114
52	63	124	71
98	135	88	142
92	76	117	51
68	131	132	93
105	165	156	44
73	104	80	78
121	57	91	141
148	115	145	65
81	45	65	82
118	82	127	115
55	97	77	127
			55

Internal control questionnaire*

Appendix A

[Each question must be answered "yes" or "no" or "N.A." (not applicable). If answer is qualified, key to a footnote.]

Name of client _____

Period covered by examination _____

CASH

ANSWER

Receipts

1. Are the duties or functions of all persons receiving or directly supervising the receiving of cash completely segregated from the following duties or functions?

    (a) Performing work on customers' sales invoices or credit memos as to:

_____   (1) Preparing

_____   (2) Checking

_____   (3) Recording

_____   (4) Summarizing

    (b) Performing work on customers' ledgers as to:

_____   (1) Recording

_____   (2) Balancing

_____   (c) Ageing accounts receivable

_____   (d) Following up delinquent receivables

_____   (e) Mailing or delivering statements to customers

_____   (f) Approving discounts or allowances

_____   (g) Preparing lists of bad accounts to be written off

_____   (h) Approving the write-off of bad accounts

* As given in *Case Studies in Internal Control Number 2,* "The Machine Manufacturing Company," published by the American Institute of Certified Public Accountants.

_____   (i) Reconciling bank accounts
_____   (j) Opening incoming mail
_____   (k) Preparing vouchers for payment
_____   (l) Approving vouchers for payment
_____   (m) Preparing general or payroll checks
_____   (n) Signing general or payroll checks (or countersigning)
_____   (o) Mailing or delivering general checks or payroll checks

       (p) Performing work on notes payable or any other evidences of indebtedness as to:

_____   (1) Preparing
_____   (2) Signing
_____   (q) Posting the general ledger
_____   (r) Recording entries in the purchase journal or invoice register

       (s) Custody (or access to):

_____   (1) Accounts receivable records
_____   (2) Securities
_____   (3) Notes receivable and/or negotiable collateral
_____   (4) Unclaimed wages and dividends
_____   (5) Petty cash funds

_____ 2. Are listings made of all mail receipts at the time the mail is opened?

_____ 3. Are the listings of mail receipts checked to records by someone other than the cashier?

_____ 4. Is a receipt issued to the payer for all cash collections other than mail receipts?

_____   (a) If the receipt is machine-made, is a separate copy of this receipt unavailable to the machine operator?

_____   (b) If hand-made, is a copy a part of a bound receipt book or is it prenumbered?

_____ 5. Is a copy of this receipt retained by the person receiving the cash?

_____ 6. Are these retained evidences of receipt checked against the record of cash received by someone other than the person receiving the cash or supervising the receipt of the cash?

_____ 7. Are all collections deposited intact with a minimum of delay?

_____ 8. Are branch collections deposited in an account subject only to withdrawal by the home office?

_____ 9. Does company policy prohibit the use of cash receipts to cash payroll or personal checks?

_____ 10. Are all bank accounts authorized by proper officials?

_____ 11. Is the person supervising the receipt of cash responsible for these receipts until they are deposited in the bank?

       12. Are duplicate deposit slips:

_____   (a) Prepared?
_____   (b) Stamped by the bank?

           (c) Checked against records of receipts?

_____   (1) Listings of mail receipts?
_____   (2) Cash book?

_____ 13. Are bank charge-backs checked out by someone other than the persons receiving or handling cash?

_____ 14. Are undeposited receipts satisfactorily controlled?

_____ 15. Are the persons receiving or handling funds properly bonded?

Disbursements

_____ 1. Are the duties and functions of all persons preparing checks or directly supervising the preparation of checks completely segregated from the following duties or functions:

_____ (a) Reconciling bank accounts?

_____ (b) Mailing or delivering general or payroll checks?

_____ (c) Preparation of payrolls?

_____ (d) Approving payrolls for payment?

_____ (e) Approving time records?

_____ (f) Approving discounts, allowances, or refunds?

_____ (g) Approving vouchers for payment?

_____ (h) Posting general ledger?

_____ (i) Recording entries in the purchase journal or invoice register?

(j) Custody (or access to):

_____ (1) General ledger?

_____ (2) Purchase journal or invoice register?

_____ (3) Accounts payable ledger?

_____ 2. Do only persons authorized to prepare or supervise the preparation of checks have access to blank checks?

_____ 3. Are all checks prenumbered?

_____ 4. Are all voided checks retained?

_____ 5. Are bank accounts reconciled regularly?

6. Do bank reconciliations include:

_____ (a) Inspection of checks for signatures?

_____ (b) Inspection of checks for endorsements?

_____ (c) Comparison of checks to check or payroll register for number, payee, date, and amount?

_____ (d) Accounting for all check numbers?

_____ 7. Are checks outstanding for a considerable time properly investigated?

8. Are invoices and supporting evidence:

_____ (a) Examined by the signer at the time of signing payment check?

_____ (b) Properly voided or marked to prevent re-use?

_____ 9. Are all vouchers approved for payment by someone other than the person requesting payment?

_____ 10. Are check protectors used?

_____ 11. Are mechanical check signers used?

If used,

_____ (a) Are keys and signature dies under control?

_____ (b) Does the person whose signature is mechanically signed approve vouchers passed for payment?

_____ (c) Are mechanical counting devices on the check signers?

_____ (d) Are totals of the mechanical counting devices regularly checked against the number of checks written?

_____ (e) Are persons operating the check signers denied access to blank checks?

_____ 12. Are all checks countersigned?

_____ 13. Are there limitations on the amounts of checks which require only one signature?

14. Does company policy prohibit:

_____ (a) The signing or countersigning of checks in advance?

_____ (b) The signing or countersigning of checks by petty cash custodians?

_____ (c) Checks drawn to "Cash"?

_____ 15. Are all employees paid by check?

_____ 16. If payrolls are paid by check, are the checks drawn on a separate bank account operated on an imprest system?

17. If payrolls are paid by cash or check:

_____ (a) Is a receipt signed by the employee? (An endorsed check is to be considered sufficient receipt.)

_____ (b) Is proper identification required before payment?

_____ (c) Is there an independent pay agent?

_____ (d) If there is no independent pay agent, are occasional pay-offs made by other than the regular employees?

18. Is the distribution of employees' pay made by persons other than:

_____ (a) Foremen to men under their supervision?

_____ (b) Persons reconciling bank accounts?

(c) Persons connected with the preparation of:

_____ (1) Payrolls?

_____ (2) Time records?

_____ (3) Checks?

_____ 19. Is there proper control over unclaimed wages and salaries?

_____ 20. Are all persons signing checks and those assisting in making disbursements properly bonded?

Disbursements—Petty Cash

_____ 1. Are all disbursements of currency made from an imprest petty cash fund?

_____ 2. Is each petty cash fund in the custody of one person only?

3. Are petty cash vouchers:

_____ (a) Prepared for each disbursement?

_____ (b) Prepared for some disbursements?

_____ (c) Supported?

_____ (d) In ink or typewriter?

_____ (e) Dated?

_____ (f) Fully descriptive of the item paid for?

_____ (g) Clearly marked to show the amount paid?

_____ (h) Checked and approved prior to payment by someone other than the petty cash custodian?

_____ (i) Receipted by the person receiving the cash?

_____ (j) Satisfactorily voided at the time of payment to prevent further use of the same voucher and its supporting evidences?

_____ 4. Do the reimbursing checks show the petty cash custodian as the payee?

_____ 5. Are the reimbursing checks endorsed by the petty cash custodian if the checks are drawn to "Cash"?

_____ 6. Are the petty cash funds occasionally checked by someone other than the petty cash custodians?

_____ 7. Are accounting records unavailable to the petty cash custodian?

_____ 8. Does the size of the fund appear to meet the normal requirements of the business and not to be in excess thereof?

_____ 9. Are the petty cash custodians properly bonded?

ACCOUNTS RECEIVABLE AND CUSTOMERS' DEPOSITS

ANSWER

1. Are the duties and functions of the accounts receivable bookkeepers or person supervising such bookkeepers completely segregated from the following duties or functions:

_____ (a) Handling any cash or performing any work on cash records?
_____ (b) Opening incoming mail?
_____ (c) Mailing or delivering statements to customers?
_____ (d) Ageing of accounts receivable?
_____ (e) Checking customers' statements to accounts receivable ledgers?
_____ (f) Investigation and follow-up of delinquent accounts receivable?
_____ (g) Settlement of accounts receivable items in question?
_____ (h) Approving the write-off of bad accounts?
        (i) Approving:
_____   (1) Discounts?
_____   (2) Allowances?
_____   (3) Refunds?
_____   (4) Other credits?
_____ 2. Are accounts receivable detail ledgers balanced with the control account each month?
_____ 3. Are accounts receivable ledgers balanced to the control account at frequent intervals by someone other than the accounts receivable bookkeeper?
_____ 4. Are the accounts aged regularly?
_____ 5. Are the aged accounts reviewed by an official?
_____ 6. Are detail ledger-keepers rotated occasionally?
_____ 7. Are monthly statements sent to all credit customers?
_____ 8. Is a check made to determine that no statements are mailed to the address of the accounts receivable bookkeepers other than statements of their own accounts?
_____ 9. Are detail balances occasionally confirmed by the customers directly
_____   to some employee not in the accounts receivable department?
_____ 10. Are bad debts controlled after their write-off?
        11. Is approval of an official obtained for:
_____   (a) Write-off of bad accounts?
_____   (b) Discounts in excess of regular rates?
_____   (c) Allowances or adjustments?
_____   (d) Refunds?
_____   (e) Other credits?
_____ 12. Are all credit memos prenumbered?
_____ 13. If credits are for returned goods, do routine procedures provide for a check of receivers?

NOTES RECEIVABLE

_____ 1. Is the acceptance of notes on sales and loans subject to approval by an official?
_____ 2. Are the notes occasionally confirmed directly with the makers?
_____ 3. Is a note register used?
_____ 4. Is the note register regularly balanced to the control account?
_____ 5. Are past-due notes promptly brought to the attention of an official?
_____ 6. Do extensions or renewals of notes require specific approval by an authorized person?
_____ 7. Are notes and collateral unaccessible to accounting department employees?

____ 8. Are part payments endorsed on the back of the notes?

____ 9. Are all persons having access to notes and collateral under proper bond?

____ 10. Are the safekeeping provisions indicated in the "Securities" section of this check-list maintained for notes?

INVENTORIES

____ 1. Are all incoming items cleared by a receiving department?

____ 2. Does the receiving department deliver or supervise the delivery of each item to the proper stores location?

3. Are materials held in stores:
____ (a) Unaccessible to anyone other than stores personnel?
____ (b) Stored in an orderly fashion?
____ (c) Issued only on properly approved requisitions?

4. Are perpetual stores records maintained on:
____ (a) Raw materials?
____ (b) Work in process?
____ (c) Finished goods?
____ (d) Supplies?

____ 5. Does the accounting department control the records of items owned by the company but which are in the hands of others; e.g., goods consigned out, materials being processed outside, goods in warehouses, etc.?

____ 6. Does the accounting department control the records of items owned by other persons but which are in the hands of the company; e.g., goods consigned in, materials being processed for others, etc.?

____ 7. Are functions so separated that employees keeping the stores records have no access to the stock held in stores?

____ 8. Are stores records periodically checked by physical inventories at least once a year?

9. In reference to the physical inventories:
   (a) Are employees taking the inventories properly:
____   (1) Instructed?
____   (2) Supervised?
____ (b) Are prenumbered tags used?
____ (c) Are all tags accounted for?
____ (d) Are accurate shipper and receiver cut-offs made?
____ (e) Do the employees taking the inventories have regular duties other than those of keeping stores or stores records?
____ (f) Are counts and descriptions as indicated by the tags checked?
____ (g) Are checks made to determine that all items were inventoried?
____ (h) Are obsolete items, scrap, customers' property, consigned goods, etc., so indicated?
____ (i) Are physical inventory units the same as the units used in pricing the inventory?
____   (1) If not, are checks made of the conversions from physical units to pricing units?
____ (j) Are detailed listings checked to original counts?
____ (k) Are prices, extensions, and footings of detailed listings checked?
____ (l) Are summaries of detailed listings checked?

_____ 10. Are discrepancies between stores records and physical inventories promptly investigated, particularly with regard to continued differences in the same items and/or differences of a material nature?

_____ 11. Do routine procedures provide for a frequent check of inventories for overstocked and slow items?

SECURITIES

ANSWER

_____ 1. Is a safekeeping agent employed?

_____ 2. Is a safe deposit vault used?

_____ 3. Are locked and fireproof containers used?

_____ 4. Are all securities physically safeguarded by means indicated in questions 1, 2, or 3 above?

_____ 5. Are procedures such that two or more persons are necessary to obtain access to the securities?

_____ 6. Do routine procedures provide for regular inspection of the securities or direct confirmation with the safekeeping agent?

_____ 7. Does the accounting department maintain records indicating complete descriptions of all securities including certificate numbers?

_____ 8. Are all securities in the name of the company if not in bearer form?

_____ 9. Is control maintained over securities which have been reduced to a book value of zero?

_____ 10. Are all persons who have access to securities properly bonded?

PROPERTY, PLANT AND EQUIPMENT

1. Do the proper officials:
_____ (a) Authorize the purchase of all property, plant and equipment?
_____ (b) Approve such purchases after purchase if not authorized prior to purchase?
_____ 2. Are actual costs checked against authorized costs?
_____ 3. Does a definite policy exist to aid the accounting department in distinguishing between capital items and repairs and maintenance, etc.?
4. Are plant ledgers, including records of accumulated depreciation:
_____ (a) Maintained?
_____ (b) Reviewed periodically?
_____ (c) Occasionally checked by actual physical inventories of the assets?
_____ (d) Balanced regularly to the control accounts?
_____ (e) Maintained for fully depreciated assets?
_____ 5. Are all pieces of equipment marked or tagged with an indentifying number of the company corresponding with the identifying number shown in the plant ledger?
_____ 6. Do sales of excess and scrapped equipment require specific authorization by proper officials?
7. Do routine procedures provide for prompt and accurate reporting to the accounting department of:
_____ (a) Sales of equipment?
_____ (b) All disposals and retirements of property, plant and equipment?

8. Are tools and small equipment:
   (a) Kept in special locations?
   (b) Accountable for by a few specific employees?

ACCOUNTS PAYABLE

1. Are monthly statements from vendors checked against balances shown by accounts payable detail?
2. Are any differences, noted in 1 above, promptly followed up?
3. Are adjustments resulting from differences approved by an official?
4. Is the accounts payable detail balanced each month to the control account?
5. Are debit balances brought to the attention of an official?

NOTES PAYABLE

1. Do the proper officials authorize all notes payable as to:
   (a) Amounts?
   (b) Purpose for which funds are borrowed?
   (c) Loaning institution?
2. Are note registers:
   (a) Maintained?
   (b) Balanced monthly to control accounts?
3. Are paid notes receipted by the payee upon settlement and retained in the maker's permanent files?

CAPITAL STOCK AND DIVIDENDS

1. Is there an independent:
   (a) Transfer agent?
   (b) Registrar?
2. Is proper control exercised over unissued stock certificates?
3. Are certificates received for transfer or cancellation properly voided?
4. Are evidences of payment of Federal issuance or transfer taxes properly affixed to the certificate stubs?
5. Are stockholders' ledgers:
   (a) Maintained?
   (b) Balanced frequently to control accounts?
6. If no ledgers are maintained, are certificate stubs frequently balanced to control accounts?
7. Is proper control exercised over dividend payments?
8. Are unclaimed dividends properly controlled?

SALES

1. Are orders approved by the credit department before they are accepted?
2. Is the credit function completely separated from other functions, particularly cash, sales, and accounting functions?

3. Are shippers:
_____ (a) Used?
_____ (b) Used on all items leaving plant?
_____ (c) Prenumbered?
_____ 4. Are shippers checked to customers' orders for quantity and descriptions to determine that items shipped are those ordered?
5. Are invoices:
_____ (a) Prepared on all sales?
_____ (b) Prenumbered?
_____ 6. Is a check made to determine that there are notices of shipment for all invoices and invoices for all notices of shipments?
_____ 7. Are invoices checked to notices of shipment for quantity and descriptions to determine that items shipped are being billed?
_____ 8. Is a check made to determine that all invoices are recorded and all invoice numbers accounted for?
9. Are invoices checked for:
_____ (a) Extensions?
_____ (b) Footings?
_____ (c) Terms?
_____ (d) Prices?
_____ 10. Are partial shipments subject to the same procedures as regular sales including relief of inventory for the cost thereof?
_____ 11. Do miscellaneous sales follow the same procedures as regular sales, e.g., sales of equipment, sales of scrap, and sales to employees, etc.?
_____ 12. Are sales summaries prepared, independent of the accounting department, which may be used as a check on recorded sales?

PURCHASES

_____ 1. Is there a separate and distinct purchasing department?
_____ 2. Is the purchasing function completely separated from other functions, particularly accounting and shipping and receiving functions?
_____ 3. Are purchase requisitions prepared?
_____ 4. If purchase requisitions are prepared are they approved by the department head?
_____ 5. If purchase requisitions are not prepared, are all purchases approved by someone other than the purchasing department?
6. Are purchase orders:
_____ (a) Used?
_____ (b) Used for all purchases?
_____ (c) Prenumbered?
_____ (d) Copy sent to the accounting department?
_____ 7. Are all purchase order numbers accounted for in routine procedures?
8. Are receivers:
_____ (a) Used?
_____ (b) Used for all items received in the plant?
_____ (c) Prenumbered?
_____ (d) Copy sent to the accounting department?
_____ 9. Are all receiver numbers accounted for in routine procedures?
_____ 10. Is a record made of all items rejected by the receiving department or items later returned to the vendors?

11. Are vendors' invoices checked:
_____   (a) Against purchase orders for terms, prices and quantities?
_____   (b) Against receivers for items and quantities received?
_____   (c) For extensions and footings?
_____ 12. Do the persons responsible for making the checks listed in question 11 above indicate in some manner on the invoices that the checks have been made?
_____ 13. Is a check made of freight charges?
_____ 14. Does the accounting department match purchase orders, receivers, and vendors' invoices before preparing the voucher for payment?
_____ 15. Are unmatched receivers, purchase orders, and vendors' invoices periodically investigated?
_____ 16. Is proper control and coordination exercised over purchase and sales invoices in cases where merchandise is purchased for direct shipment to company's customers?
_____ 17. Do employee accommodation purchases follow the same procedures as ordinary purchases?
_____ 18. Are all distributions reviewed or sufficiently tested by someone other than the person making original distribution?

PAYROLL

1. Are time cards:
_____   (a) Used?
_____   (b) Prepared by mechanical devices?
_____   (c) Initialed by an authorized person for changes?
_____   (d) Approved by foremen?
_____   (e) Approved by timekeeper?
_____   (f) Checked for computations of hours?
2. Are job time tickets:
_____   (a) Used?
_____   (b) Approved by foremen?
_____   (c) Reconciled with time cards?
3. Are checks made of:
_____   (a) Rates paid?
_____   (b) Extensions and footings?
_____   (c) Deductions?
4. Is written authorization required for all:
_____   (a) Initial wage and salary rates?
_____   (b) Changes in these initial rates?
_____   (c) Dismissals?
5. Is the payroll function separate from that of:
_____   (a) Timekeeping?
_____   (b) Bank reconciliation?
_____ 6. Are payroll duties frequently shifted among payroll personnel?
_____ 7. Are all payrolls and advances subject to the same routine procedures?
_____ 8. Are all payroll distributions reviewed or sufficiently tested by someone other than the person making the original distribution?
_____ 9. Is the accumulated time incurred on individual jobs checked to original estimates?

_____   (a) Are differences of a material nature promptly investigated?

_____   10. Are "floor-checks" of personnel made?

_____   11. Are adequate personnel records maintained including a specimen signature of each employee?

GENERAL

_____   1. Is there an internal audit department or auditor?

_____   2. Are reports and procedures of the internal audits reviewed by us?

          3. Are all books of account:

_____   (a) Appropriate and sufficient for the nature of the company's business?

_____   (b) Balanced monthly?

          4. Are all general journal entries:

_____   (a) Properly supported?

_____   (b) Approved by the chief accountant or comptroller prior to entry in the journal?

_____   5. Are income and expense accounts periodically reviewed by a responsible official?

_____   6. Do monthly statements adequately point up unusual situations?

_____   7. Does a current organization chart exist?

             (a) Do we have a copy of this chart?

_____   8. Are the duties and functions throughout the company governed by manuals of operating procedures?

_____   9. Do all officers and employees take vacations?

_____   10. During the vacations are the duties and functions of the officers and employees performed by other persons?

_____   11. Is the insurance coverage periodically reviewed?

Code of professional ethics

Appendix B

The reliance of the public and the business community on sound financial reporting and advice on business affairs imposes on the accounting profession an obligation to maintain high standards of technical competence, morality and integrity. To this end, a member or associate of the American Institute of Certified Public Accountants shall at all times maintain independence of thought and action, hold the affairs of his clients in strict confidence, strive continuously to improve his professional skills, observe generally accepted auditing standards, promote sound and informative financial reporting, uphold the dignity and honor of the accounting profession, and maintain high standards of personal conduct.

In further recognition of the public interest and his obligation to the profession, a member or associate agrees to comply with the following rules of ethical conduct, the enumeration of which should not be construed as a denial of the existence of other standards of conduct not specifically mentioned:

ARTICLE 1: Relations with Clients and Public

1.01 Neither a member or associate, nor a firm of which he is a partner, shall express an opinion on financial statements of any enterprise unless he and his firm are in fact independent with respect to such enterprise.

Independence is not susceptible of precise definition, but is an expression of the professional integrity of the individual. A member or associate, before expressing his opinon on financial statements, has the responsibility of assessing his relationships with an enterprise to determine whether, in the circumstances, he might expect his opinion to be considered independent, objective and unbiased by one who had knowledge of all the facts.

A member or associate will be considered not independent, for example, with respect to any enterprise if he, or one of his partners, (a) during the period of his professional engagement or at the time of expressing his opinion, had, or was committed to acquire, any direct financial interest or material indirect financial interest in the enterprise, or (b) during the period of his professional engagement, at the time of expressing his opinion or during the period covered by the financial statements, was connected with the enterprise as a promoter, underwriter, voting trustee, director, officer or key employee. In cases where a member or associate ceases to be the independent accountant for an enterprise and is subsequently called upon to re-express a previously expressed opinion on financial statements, the phrase "at the time of expressing his opinion" refers only to the time at which the member or associate first expressed his opinion on the financial statements in question. The word "director" is not intended to apply to a connection in such a capacity with a charitable, religious, civic or other similar type of nonprofit organization when the duties performed in such a capacity are such as to make it clear that the member or associate can express an independent opinion on the financial statements. The example cited in this paragraph, of circumstances under which a member or associate will be considered not independent, is not intended to be all-inclusive.

1.02   A member or associate shall not commit an act discreditable to the profession.

1.03   A member or associate shall not violate the confidential relationship between himself and his client.

1.04   Professional service shall not be rendered or offered for a fee which shall be contingent upon the findings or results of such service. This rule does not apply to cases involving federal, state, or other taxes, in which the findings are those of the tax authorities and not those of the accountant. Fees to be fixed by courts or other public authorities, which are therefore of an indeterminate amount at the time when an engagement is undertaken, are not regarded as contingent fees within the meaning of this rule.

ARTICLE 2:   Technical Standards

2.01   A member or associate shall not express his opinion on financial statements unless they have been examined by him, or by a member or employee of his firm, on a basis consistent with the requirements of Rule 2.02.

In obtaining sufficient information to warrant expression of an opinion he may utilize, in part, to the extent appropriate in the circumstances, the reports or other evidence of auditing work performed by another certified public accountant, or firm of public accountants, at least one of whom is a certified public accountant, who is authorized to practice in a state or territory of the United States or the District of Columbia, and whose independence and professional reputation he has ascertained to his satisfaction.

A member or associate may also utilize, in part, to the extent appropriate in the circumstances, the work of public accountants in other countries, but the member or associate so doing must satisfy himself that the person or firm is qualified and independent, that such work is performed in accordance with generally accepted auditing standards, as prevailing in the United States, and that financial statements are prepared in accordance with generally accepted accounting principles, as prevailing in the United States, or are accompanied by the information necessary to bring the statements into accord with such principles.

2.02   In expressing an opinion on representations in financial statements which he has examined, a member or associate may be held guilty of an act discreditable to the profession if

(a) he fails to disclose a material fact known to him which is not disclosed in the financial statements but disclosure of which is necessary to make the financial statements not misleading; or

(b) he fails to report any material misstatement known to him to appear in the financial statement; or

(c) he is materially negligent in the conduct of his examination or in making his report thereon; or

(d) he fails to acquire sufficient information to warrant expression of an opinion, or his exceptions are sufficiently material to negative the expression of an opinion; or

(e) he fails to direct attention to any material departure from generally accepted accounting principles or to disclose any material omission of generally accepted auditing procedure applicable in the circumstances.

2.03   A member or associate shall not permit his name to be associated with statements purporting to show financial position or results of operations in such a manner as to imply that he is acting as an independent public accountant unless he shall:

(a) express an unqualified opinion; or

(b) express a qualified opinion; or

(c) express an adverse opinion; or

(d) disclaim an opinion on the statements taken as a whole and indicate clearly his reasons therefor; or

(e) when unaudited financial statements are presented on his stationery without his comments, disclose prominently on each page of the financial statements that they were not audited.

2.04   A member or associate shall not permit his name to be used in conjunction with any forecast of the results of future transactions in a manner which may lead to the belief that the member or associate vouches for the accuracy of the forecast.

ARTICLE 3: Promotional Practices

3.01   A member or associate shall not advertise his professional attainments or services.

Publication in a newspaper, magazine or similar medium of an announcement or what is technically known as a card is prohibited.

A listing in a directory is restricted to the name, title, address and telephone number of the person or firm, and it shall not appear in a box, or other form of display or in a type or style which differentiates it from other listings in the same directory. Listing of the same name in more than one place in a classified directory is prohibited.

3.02   A member or associate shall not endeavor, directly or indirectly, to obtain clients by solicitation.

3.03   A member or associate shall not make a competitive bid for a professional engagement. Competitive bidding for public accounting services is not in the public interest, is a form of solicitation, and is unprofessional.

3.04   Commissions, brokerage, or other participation in the fees or profits of professional work shall not be allowed or paid directly or indirectly by a member or associate to any individual or firm not regularly engaged or employed in the practice of public accounting as a principal occupation.

Commissions, brokerage, or other participation in the fees, charges or profits of work recommended or turned over to any individual or firm not regularly engaged or employed in the practice of public accounting as a principal occupation, as incident to services for clients, shall not be accepted directly or indirectly by a member or associate.

ARTICLE 4 : Operating Practices

4.01 A firm or partnership, all the individual members of which are members of the Institute, may describe itself as "Members of the American Institute of Certified Public Accountants," but a firm or partnership, not all the individual members of which are members of the Institute, or an individual practicing under a style denoting a partnership when in fact there be no partner or partners, or a corporation, or an individual or individuals practicing under a style denoting a corporate organization shall not use the designation "Members of the American Institute of Certified Public Accountants."

4.02 A member or associate shall not practice in the name of another unless he is in partnership with him or in his employ, nor shall he allow any person to practice in his name who is not in partnership with him or in his employ.

This rule shall not prevent a partnership or its successors from continuing to practice under a firm name which consists of or includes the name or names of one or more former partners, nor shall it prevent the continuation of a partnership name for a reasonable period of time by the remaining partner practicing as a sole proprietor after the withdrawal or death of one or more partners.

4.03 A member or associate in his practice of public accounting shall not permit an employee to perform for the member's or associate's clients any services which the member or associate himself or his firm is not permitted to perform.

4.04. A member or associate shall not engage in any business or occupation conjointly with that of a public accountant, which is incompatible or inconsistent therewith.

4.05 A member or associate engaged in an occupation in which he renders services of a type performed by public accountants, or renders other professional services, must observe the by-laws and Code of Professional Ethics of the Institute in the conduct of that occupation.

4.06 A member or associate shall not be an officer, director, stockholder, representative, or agent of any corporation engaged in the practice of public accounting in any state or territory of the United States or the District of Columbia.

ARTICLE 5 : Relations with Fellow Members

5.01 A member or associate shall not encroach upon the practice of another public accountant. A member or associate may furnish service to those who request it.

5.02 A member or associate who receives an engagement for services by referral from another member or associate shall not discuss or accept an extension of his services beyond the specific engagement without first consulting with the referring member or associate.

5.03   Direct or indirect offer of employment shall not be made by a member or associate to an employee of another public accountant without first informing such accountant. This rule shall not be construed so as to inhibit negotiations with anyone who of his own initiative or in response to public advertisement shall apply to a member or associate for employment.

Index

American Institute of Certified Public Accountants (Cont.)
The Journal of Accountancy, 58, 390, 693, 701
Management Services, 583
Management Services Handbook, 668
publications, list of, 10
Standard Bank Confirmation Form, 372
Statements on Auditing Procedure, 600, 601, 602, 603, 633
Analytical auditing, 117-118
Arkin, Herbert, 708
Arthur Andersen Chronicle, 233
Attest function, 1
Audit block, 226
Audit trail, 26, 27
Auditing:
evolution of, 116-117
objectives and procedures (*see* Objectives and procedures)
standards:
defined and listed, 8-9
distinguished from procedures, 11
meaning of "generally accepted," 9-11
Auditors:
defined, 4
internal and independent distinguished, 79
opinion on financial statements (*see* Reports, short-form)
professional qualifications, 2-4
selection of, 88-89
Audits:
defined, 4
evolution of, 17-19
preliminaries to, 569
present status of auditors, 19
required by Federal government, 20
Authorization of transactions, 42

B

Balance-forward inventory records, 271
Balance sheet audit, 119
Bank proof machines, 34
Bank reconciliations (*see* Cash)
Batch billing, 272
Billing:
department, 159
machines, 33
punched-card, 160
Binomial distribution, 690
Blind:
cash count, 348
second count of inventories, 307
Board of directors:
minutes of meetings, 561
responsibilities, 537

Bond investments (*see* Investments)
Bonding of employees, 50, 57, 354
Bonds payable (*see* Liabilities)
Bookkeeping service, 680
Bookless records, 26
Bootleg records, 24
Budgets:
as aspect of internal control, 47
capital, 432
comparison with actual expenses, 244
operating expenses, 233
time estimates for audit control, 572
value for credit purposes, 640
Burroughs Corporation, 468
Business approach to auditing, 117-118

C

Canada, public accounting legislation, 3
Capital budgeting, 432
Capital stock (*see* Owners' equity)
Capitalization of plant expenditures, 445
Carey, John L., 85
Carman, Lewis A., 689
Cash:
accounting procedures, 341-353
audit objectives and procedures, 364-380
bank cut-off statement, 374
bank reconciliations:
audit, 373-379
preparation, 351-353
confirmation of bank balance, 372
count, 369-372
cut-off of receipts and disbursements, 366-368
deposit tickets, authentication of, 395, 397
detailed examination, 389-399
forecasts, 640
four-column bank reconciliation, 395
fraud:
defalcation methods, 390
detection, 395
interbank transfers, 393
internal audit, 355
internal control objectives, 341
kiting, 392
lapping, 394
ledger posting of receipts, 163
mailroom control, 344
management reports, 354
punched-card procedures, 353
rotation of bank accounts, 352, 378
sales, control of, 345
standards of statement presentation, 362
timing of examination, 379
window dressing, 368